A LIBRARY OF LITERARY CRITICISM

A LIBRARY

Volume II

H - P

Frederick Ungar Publishing Co., New York

OF LITERARY CRITICISM

Modern British Literature

Compiled and edited by

RUTH Z. TEMPLE

Professor of English
The City University of New York
(Brooklyn College)

MARTIN TUCKER

Assistant Professor of English
Long Island University

PERIODICALS USED

Listed below are their titles, their abbreviations, if any, place of publication, and, for the British journals, dates of publication. If no place is indicated, *London* is to be understood.

	The Academy and Literature. 1869-1916 (The Academy, 1869, absorbed Literature, 1902)
Adam	Adam International Review, 1932—
Adel	The Adelphi, 1923-55
Am. Hist. R.	The American Historical Review, New York
AmS	The American Scholar, Washington, D. C.
	The Anglo-Welsh Review, Wales, 1949—
AQ	The Arizona Quarterly, University of Arizona, Tucson, Arizona
Ath	The Athenæum, 1828-1921 (merged with The Nation)
At	The Atlantic Monthly, Boston, Mass.
BkmL	The Bookman, 1891-1934 (absorbed by The London Mercury)
Bkm	The Bookman, New York
Cal. Mod. Letters	The Calendar of Modern Letters, 1925-27
CJ	The Cambridge Journal, Cambridge, 1947-54
	The Central Literary Magazine, Birmingham, 1873—
	The Chicago Daily Tribune
CC	The Christian Century, Chicago, Ill.
	Colophon, The Monthly Magazine for Booklovers, 1950-51
The Colophon (N.Y.)	The Colophon, A Quarterly for Bookmen, New York (subtitle varies)
Cmty	Commentary, New York
Com	The Commonweal, New York
CR	The Contemporary Review, 1866—
	The Cornell University Library Readers' Report, Ithaca, N. Y.

Cnh	The Cornhill Magazine, 1860—
Crit	The Criterion, 1922-39 (title varies)
CQ	The Critical Quarterly, University of Hull, Hull, 1959—
	The Daily Telegraph
	The Dalhousie Review, Halifax, N. S., 1921—
	The Dial, Chicago, Ill., then New York
	Drama, 1919—
DM	The Dublin Magazine, Dublin, 1923—
DR	The Dublin Review, Dublin, 1936— (since 1961 The Wiseman Review, London)
Eg	The Egoist, 1914-19
	Encore, 1954—
Enc	Encounter, 1953—
Eng.	English, The Magazine of the English Association, 1936—
EJ	The English Journal, National Council of Teachers of English, Chicago, Ill., 1912— (title varies)
Eng.R.	The English Review, 1908-37 (merged with The National Review)
ES	English Studies, Amsterdam, Holland, 1919—
	Envoy, 1955—
EC	Essays in Criticism, Oxford, 1951—
Essays and Studies	Essays and Studies by Members of the English Association, Oxford, 1910— (annual)
	Ethics, Chicago, Ill., 1890—
FR	The Fortnightly Review, 1865-1934, The Fortnightly, 1934-54 (absorbed by The Contemporary Review)
	The Forum, Philadelphia, Penna., 1886-1950
	The Golden Blade, 1949—(annual)
	The Griffin, New York
G	The Guardian (see Manchester Guardian)
Hor	Horizon, 1940-50
HdR	The Hudson Review, New York
ILN	The Illustrated London News, 1842—
Irish Monthly	The Irish Monthly Magazine, Dublin, 1873—
JOL	John O'London's Weekly, 1919-54 (merged with Time and Tide)
KR	The Kenyon Review, Kenyon College, Gambier, Ohio
LL	Life and Letters, 1928-35, Life and Letters Today, 1935-50
List	The Listener, 1929— (now The Listener and BBC Television Review)
	The Living Age, Boston, Mass.

L	The London Magazine, 1954—
LM	The London Mercury, 1919-39 (merged with Life and Letters Today)
LQR	The London Quarterly Review, 1853-1931 (title changed: see next item)
LQHR	The London Quarterly and Holborn Review, 1932—
MG, G	The Manchester Guardian, Manchester, 1821— (title changed to The Guardian, 1959)
MGW	The Manchester Guardian Weekly, Manchester, 1919—
	The Mid-Century, New York
MFS	Modern Fiction Studies, Purdue University, Lafayette, Ind.
	The Month, 1863—(title varies)
NationL	The Nation, 1907-21 (merged with The Athenæum)
Nation	The Nation, New York
NA	The Nation and Athenæum, 1921-31 (merged with The New Statesman)
Nat. and Eng. R.	The National and English Review, 1937—
NR	The New Republic, Washington, D. C.
	New Saltire, Edinburgh, 1961—
NS	The New Statesman, 1913-February, 1931, June 1957—(see next item)
NSN	The New Statesman and Nation, February, 1931-June, 1957
NYEP	The New York Evening Post
NYHT	The New York Herald Tribune: Book Week, 1924— (title varies)
NYT	The New York Times Book Review
NYTts	The New York Times Theatre Section
TNY	The New Yorker
	Nimbus, 1951-58
	Nine, A Magazine of Literature and the Arts, 1950-52
NC	The Nineteenth Century, 1877-1901, then The Nineteenth Century and After, 1901-50, then see *TC*
Obs	The Observer, 1791—
OutL	The Outlook, a Weekly Review of Politics, Art, Literature and Finance, 1898-1928 (title varies)
Paris R.	The Paris Review, Paris, 1953—
PR	Partisan Review, New York
	Phoenix, Liverpool, 1960—
	Poetry, Chicago, Ill.

Poetry R.	The Poetry Review, 1912—
	The Proceedings of the British Academy, 1902— (annual)
	The Reflex, Chicago, Ill.
	The Review, 1962—
	Samhain, Dublin, 1901-8
SR	The Saturday Review of Politics, Literature, Science and Art, 1885-1938
Sat	The Saturday Review of Literature, then The Saturday Review, New York
Scy	Scrutiny, 1932-53
SwR	The Sewanee Review, University of the South, Sewanee, Tenn.
SoR	The Southern Review, Louisiana State University, Baton Rouge, La.
Spec	The Spectator, 1828—
Strand	The Strand Magazine, 1891-1950
TA	Theatre Arts, New York
TW	Theatre World, 1925—
	Thought, Fordham University, New York
TT	Time and Tide, 1920— (incorporated John O'London's Weekly, 1954)
TL	The Times, 1785—
TLS	The Times Literary Supplement, 1902—
	Transformation, 1943-47(?)
TC	The Twentieth Century, 1951— (continuation of The Nineteenth Century and After)
TCL	Twentieth Century Literature, Denver, Colo.
VQR	The Virginia Quarterly Review, University of Virginia, Charlottesville, Va.
WHR	The Western Humanities Review, University of Utah, Salt Lake City, Utah
	The Windmill, 1944—
	The World Today, 1923-32 (continuation of *The World's Work*, 1902-22)
YR	The Yale Review, Yale University, New Haven, Conn.
YWES	The Year's Work in English Studies (English Association), 1920— (annual)

NOTE: In citations of books throughout the text, the place of publication is to be understood as London if no other place is indicated.—The abbreviation BC/Longmans, Green means: published for the British Council by Longmans, Green.

HAGGARD, H. RIDER (1856-1925)

The People of the Mist was the first of many pot-boilers produced to feed the public created by his early successes, and the ever-popular Allan Quatermain figured in as many subsequent books as Conan Doyle devoted to Sherlock Holmes. When he wrote his autobiography in 1912, he was still writing of Allan in *Child of Storm*, the old hunter appeared as late as 1920 in *The Ancient Allan*, the story of *She* found repetition with almost identical characters under different guises in *Queen Sheba's Ring* of 1910, and the authentic sequel to *She, Ayesha, or the Return of She*, appeared in 1905. Whatever illusions he had cherished about his craft as an art were dispelled; he was disgusted when reviewers of *Eric Brighteyes* and *Nada the Lily* disregarded their quality as sagas, and treated them simply as tales of sanguinary adventure, moving Quiller-Couch to describe him as the novelist of Blood. Since the critics assured him that the public wanted more of *She* and *Allan Quatermain*, it should have them, and discarding further efforts at creative development, he mechanically manufactured imitations of his popular favourites as a profitable business. Once or twice he ventured again upon a modern subject, as in *Joan Haste* and *Doctor Therne*, though the latter was primarily propaganda against the anti-vaccinationist cranks, but whatever inclination to persevere with the modern analytical novel remaining after the disappointing reception of *Beatrice* was finally dispelled by attacks on the morality of that novel. Haggard showed himself ridiculously sensitive under this sort of criticism, the common sense of Lang and Longman with difficulty restraining him from withdrawing *Beatrice* from circulation, when he received anonymous letters from wives who alleged that their husbands—"one of them a middle-aged clergyman"—had made advances, after reading *Beatrice,* to ladies of that name, and he heard that another gentleman and lady had reconstructed the sleep-walking scene "with different results from those recorded in the book." . . .

His disinterested public work was fairly rewarded with a knighthood in 1912, the same year in which he was appointed one of the six English representatives to the Royal Commission of the Dominions, which took him on a world tour. During the war he visited the overseas dominions in 1916 on behalf of the Royal Colonial Institute with a view to the post-war settlement of ex-service men, and again in 1918 as a member of the Empire Settlement Committee, after which he received a K.B.E. in 1919. . . .

In its successfulness, its decisiveness, above all its direct simplicity, Haggard's life was unlike a literary man's. In his soul were none of the warring elements which play upon imaginative minds to create morbid obsessions amounting to misery, distraction, sometimes almost to madness, and make their victims great. Haggard's imagination was vivid and fertile, but detached, and he lacked the intellectual egotist's instinct, fatal to contentment but essential to creative genius, of introspection. He lived a life according to the conventions of his birth and breeding, dedicating himself diligently to endeavour, duty, and service, and when he died, it could be said with justice that there was a good man gone.

Greatness too rarely springs from goodness, and there is nothing of the first water in Haggard's literary legacy.

Malcolm Elwin. *Old Gods Falling* (N.Y., Macmillan, 1939), pp. 256–57, 260–61

Here we have an eager disciple of James Payn, of R. D. Blackmore, of Mrs. Henry Wood, who nevertheless, in a few books written at white heat (six weeks on the average) and full of slipshod, prejudice and nonsense, has succeeded in keeping afloat.

King Solomon's Mines, the first and best of the stories for "Big and Little Boys" (as the dedication has it), was admittedly written in imitation of *Treasure Island* and is still uncommonly readable. But *She,* that other most enduring product of Haggard's pen, is in a different category. Even his friends at the time were a little dubious about it. Henley called *She* "the heroic Barmaid—the Waitress in Apotheosis"; Marie Corelli was "dazzled to my very heart's core by the splendour of *She*"; and one of the kindest judgments was that of the *Pall Mall Budget,* which said: "It is as though a subject roughed out by Michelangelo had been executed with an eye to New Bond Street popularity by Gustave Doré."

Perhaps that hits the bull; for is it not Haggard's sedulous determination to repeat his early success that makes his later books so tiresome? He was a success, of course, in his lifetime; so was Edgar Rice Burroughs; so was Marie Corelli. Whatever has been a success at any time is of interest from the sociological point of view, and the fact that a number of these ill-written books are still in print and are still selling is no doubt an interesting sociological fact.

TLS. Sept. 30, 1960, p. 630

The many similar experiences the two men had in common, the resemblances in the external circumstances of their lives, and a strong inner affinity strengthened the ties between them. Neither had had a university education, and both had spent the impressionable years of their youth in one of the distant colonies of the Empire, Kipling in India, Haggard in South Africa, where they had gained experience and knowledge of imperial affairs. Each in turn suffered the pangs of unrequited love, but both had made suitable matches for themselves. Both men had small families with whom they lived on country estates, close to the land. Each had lost his first-born child, and with the loss of Kipling's son in the war, the men shared another grief, the loss of an only son. Though Haggard was by no means the artist Kipling was, this fact did not divide them and seems to have eluded them altogether. What is more, both insisted that they were essentially "un-literary," and it was easy for them to see the superficial similarities, if not the qualitative differences, of their literary output. Each had written of new places and new things, each had grown popular with a newly shaped reading public, and to each fame had come overnight. They also shared a deep feeling for the land, the land as a symbol of England, not England the island but England the Empire, the England of Allan Quatermain and Umslopogaas, of Tommy Atkins and Kim. . . .

Haggard, and even more Kipling, could not discuss his literary prompt-ings with many friends, and certainly neither Haggard nor Kipling ex-plored with anyone else outside his immediate family the shadowy recesses of what Haggard called his "second sight" and Kipling his "daemon." . . . Haggard fanned the psychic spark within himself, in-dulged it and let it influence his life in many ways; but it seemed that he saved most of his thoughts on the subject for Kipling. There is no ques-tion that the long afternoons they spent together in Kipling's study at Bateman's were full of talk about reincarnation, spiritualism, and fourth-dimensional psychic promptings they both felt, and that these afternoons invariably gave rise to much of the strange atmosphere of psychic mystery that infuses many of their stories.

Kipling and Haggard never published a book together. But although the two did not collaborate in the formal sense, they quite naturally con-sulted each other about their own work, often helped each other in plotting tales, and even wrote in each other's company.

Morton N. Cohen. *Dalhousie Review,* Fall, 1960,
pp. 306–7

His real life, Haggard would insist—half sincerely, half insincerely—was his public life: his championship of the cause of Empire and of British agriculture. His opinions on agriculture—on the need for smallholdings and for improved marketing and credit facilities—were indeed remark-ably sensible and his technical books on farming deserve high praise, but again with that curious perversity he advocated his opinions in ways that were from the first certain to make the advocacy ineffective, in order

—it is hard to resist the conclusion—to enjoy the luxury of complaining that he was a failure. . . .

He was obviously put on to futile committees because he was one of those rare beings who are willing to waste their time on futile committees. He was aware of this, but he preferred to serve and then to repay himself with self-pity. It is a strange and not a very attractive trait. . . . With Haggard, as with many other people, it is difficult to know where sincerity ended and insincerity began, but on the whole it must be said that he was an insincere man in his romantic writings. He knew a good deal about Africa. He did not really believe it at all probable that there was anything like King Solomon's Mines in the centre of Africa. He played about with notions of transmigration and of transcending death. He was not perhaps himself quite clear how far he believed these notions but on the whole he did not believe. The important thing about ideas of that sort with him was not whether they were true but whether they were marketable, and there is of course a natural public appetite for mystery.

Christopher Hollis. *L.* April, 1961, pp. 87–88

HALL, RADCLYFFE (1886?–1943)

It seems startling at first sight, but those who locked up copies of *Jane Eyre* were prompted by the same feelings as those who now have just banned *The Well of Loneliness*. They wished that *Jane Eyre* should not be read because it made people, especially young people, aware that women existed whose experience of love is passionate. . . . In the case of *The Well of Loneliness* the passion described is abnormal; it is the story of a woman who falls in love with another woman. That there is a very small percentage of human beings of both sexes whose love-life is centred on members of their own sex is a fact about human nature which is well known; why should it not be generally known? What harm can a book do which deals with the unfortunate complications which result from such aberrations? Here and there it might suddenly reveal a reader to herself. It might again suddenly explain to a reader of another kind the behaviour of some one else towards her. Why should this be bad for them? Is there not, on the contrary, a possibility that such a book may be of service, helping them to recognize traits in themselves and in others, and so know more surely where they are? . . . The fear that if such novels are not at once suppressed the book-market will be flooded with them, is empty. A curiosity sale is soon over. In my youth, when the tone of the times was stricter both in conversation and in print, *Moll Flanders* and translations of Maupassant and Flaubert were purchased and read furtively for the sake of the suggestions a few passages might carry to an eager curiosity. Now those books are read, as they ought to be, for their merits. The same thing would happen in the case of such books as *The Well of Loneliness*. History shows that only those communities have flourished in which men were allowed to pool their experience and comment freely on life, and that the suppression of freedom is a graver risk to civilization than the circulation of any particular book to morality.

Desmond MacCarthy. *LL*. Oct., 1928, pp. 340–41

The most ludicrous interference with an English book of recent years was the suppression of *The Well of Loneliness* by Radclyffe Hall, the theme of which was homosexuality among women. When the editor of a well-known Sunday newspaper had a screaming fit, and by his screams alarmed the Home Office, a prosecution was instituted, the result of which was that thousands of people, who had not been aware that there was such a thing as homosexuality among women and never would have been aware of it but for the advertisement it received at the hands of the Law, were not happy until they had managed to read *The Well of Loneliness* under the impression that they would find out the details of such odd behaviour. It is hardly necessary to add that many novels on the same subject have appeared since without interference and without making the public much wiser about homosexuality among women.

Compton Mackenzie. *Literature in My Time*
(Rich and Cowan, 1933), pp. 208–9

The work of Radclyffe Hall is serious, profound and beautiful work, in no way doctrinaire, yet thoroughly indoctrinated. Her emotion is still yet deep. She is like a quiet pool of great depth. She is ageless. It is work that might have come out of Greece. It is work that might have come from India. It seems to have nothing to do with the modern Western world and the flair of that world for the nonchalant, the bizarre and the funny. It has nothing to do with Victorian sentiment. It has nothing to do with Elizabethan delight in living; neither has it anything to do with eighteenth-century sophistication; nor yet anything to do with the romance that belongs to all centuries. She is preoccupied with the mysteries, as the priestesses were, and she pities the human race as it passes them by for things that can be added up and multiplied and subtracted and divided.

Margaret Lawrence. *The School of Femininity*
(N.Y., Frederick A. Stokes, 1936), pp. 329–30

HAMILTON, G. ROSTREVOR (1888–   )

Most of Mr. Hamilton's poems [*Apollyon*] deal with the war. The shorter ones display the author's admirable epigrammatic gift; the longer are somewhat disappointing. . . . The imagery is sometimes witty but has no depth. Mr. Hamilton never seems to have passed through the obscure stage and his poetry loses by it.

Edwin Muir. *NSN*. May 31, 1941, p. 558

Mr. Hamilton is clearly indebted to . . . I. A. Richards and William Empson, both English, both responsible for many of the refinements of verbal analysis which Mr. Hamilton . . . employs. But Mr. Hamilton is also responsive to another stream in English criticism, one less stylish just now, but having its own excellences. It can be described as "Arnoldian." . . . It is a criticism which at its best is commodious, ethical and legislative in temper; at its worst, pontifical and over-regulatory. In *The Tell-Tale Article* Mr. Hamilton displays the best and the worst features of this criticism.

Vivienne Koch. *NSN*. Oct. 1, 1949, p. 362

HANLEY, JAMES (1901–   )

Mr. James Hanley is, considered as a novelist, a fortunate man. His life —characteristics—circumstances have enabled him to grow and develop so to speak from the bottom layer upwards: broadening out from a basic realisation of the harshness and violence of existence to achieve a more spacious view of humanity; and this without losing his way or becoming less true to himself in the process. . . . He did not presumably start with the handicap of the old school tie; nor, beset by the pleasant beauties of cultured country houses or the dreaming spires of universities, has he trodden the primrose path to an everlasting dismay. . . . His surface is broad, level and simple, almost smooth; the roads and by-roads marked in plain outline; the completed world lies bare under a curiously uncoloured light: but life informs the whole of it. *The Secret Journey* is a continuation of Mr. Hanley's saga of the working classes. The first volume was called *The Furys*. . . . A tendency to diffuseness is Mr. Hanley's chief enemy; and there is something wrong with his dialogue. One cannot always recognize the individual voice speaking.

Rosamond Lehmann. *NSN*. Aug. 1, 1936, p. 163

James Hanley is that rarity, a writer born compassionate. As a schoolboy
I read his "Boy" and experienced uncomfortable growing pains of the
emotions. A stowaway dies a beastly death within hailing distance of
his thirteenth birthday. I feared the pessimism, misunderstood the merci-
less statement of our need for mercy. Mr. Hanley has remained an uncomfortable writer: he compels us to lay hand on heart. *Say Nothing* is
a Rillington Place of the soul, a stifled hope in every cupboard. A youth
lodges in a house of three people, Baines the stranded hulk, his cormorant
wife, and her demented sister Winifred. . . . "Say nothing," each urges
the lodger as they confide, but when he leaves, it is not the fetor he remembers. "They were alive," he says, and, whispering, yelling, or rolling
like tumbrils to their frowsty beds, they are. A strongbox of a book, from
which muffled cries still issue.

Christopher Wordsworth. MGW. May 10, 1962, p. 11

James Hanley, plugging away without much acclaim, is an English
Conrad-Camus who deserves more attention, especially for *Levine;* he
has come a long way from his working-class novels, *The Furys* and *The
Secret Journey,* which, however, the Gillian Freemans and the Sillitoes
would do well to study.

Paul West. The Modern Novel (Hutchinson, 1963),
p. 152

HARDY, THOMAS (1840–1928)

Mr. Hardy's volume [*Satires of Circumstance*] is full of poetry; and
yet it is also full of ugly and cumbrous expressions, clumsy metres, and
flat, prosaic turns of speech. . . . Even Mr. Hardy's grammar is not impeccable. . . . And his vocabulary, though in general it is rich and apt,
has occasional lapses. . . .

It is important to observe such characteristics, because, in Mr. Hardy's
case, they are not merely superficial and occasional blemishes; they are
in reality an essential ingredient in the very essence of his work. The
originality of his poetry lies in the fact that it bears everywhere upon it
the impress of a master of prose fiction. . . . Mr. Hardy has brought the
realism and sobriety of prose into the service of his poetry. The result
is a product of a kind very difficult to parallel in our literature. . . . what
gives Mr. Hardy's poems their unique flavor is precisely their utter lack
of romanticism, their common, undecorated presentments of things.
They are, in fact, modern as no other poems are. The author of *Jude the
Obscure* speaks in them, but with the concentration, the intensity, the

subtle disturbing force of poetry. And he speaks; he does not sing. Or rather, he talks—in the quiet voice of a modern man or woman, who finds it difficult, as modern men and women do, to put into words exactly what is in the mind. He is incorrect; but then how unreal and artificial a thing is correctness! He fumbles; but it is that very fumbling that brings him so near to ourselves. [1914]

Lytton Strachey. *Characters and Commentaries*
(N.Y., Harcourt, Brace, 1933), pp. 182–84

It is the history of the human race itself that holds him with a mesmeric spell, as century after century it unrolls its acts and scenes, under the indifferent stars. The continuity of life! The long, piteous "ascent of man," from those queer fossils in the Portland Quarries—to what we see today, so palpable, so real! And yet for all his tragic pity, Mr. Hardy is a sly and whimsical chronicler. He does not allow one point of the little jest the gods play on us—the little long-drawn-out jest—to lose its sting. With something of a goblin-like alertness he skips here and there, watching those strange scene shifters at their work. The dual stops of Mr. Hardy's country pipe are cut from the same reed. With the one he challenges the Immortals on behalf of humanity; with the other he plays such a shrewd Priapian tune that all the Satyrs dance.

I sometimes think that only those born and bred in the country can do justice to this great writer. That dual pipe of his is bewildering to city people. They over emphasize the "magnanimity" of his art, or they over emphasize its "miching-mallecho." They do not catch the secret of that mingled strain. The same type of cultured "foreigner" is puzzled by Mr. Hardy's self-possession. He ought to commit himself more completely, or he ought not to have committed himself at all! There is something that looks to them—so they are tempted to express it—like the cloven hoof of a most Satyrish cunning, about his attitude to certain things. That little caustic by-play, for instance, with which he girds at the established order, never denouncing it wholesale like Shelley, or accepting it wholesale like Wordsworth—and always with a tang, a dash of gall and wormwood, an impish malice.

The truth is, there are two spirits in Mr. Hardy, one infinitely sorrowful and tender, the other whimsical, elfish and malign.

The first spirit rises up in stern Promethean revolt against the decrees of Fate. The second spirit deliberately allies itself in wanton, bitter glee, with the humorous provocation of humanity, by the cruel Powers of the Air. The psychology of all this is not hard to unravel. The same abnormal sensitiveness that makes him pity the victims of destiny makes him also not unaware of what may be sweet to the palate of the gods in such "merry jests." These two tendencies seem to have grown upon him

as years went on and to have become more and more pronounced. . . .
But, after all, it is in the supreme passages of pure imaginative grandeur
that Mr. Hardy is greatest. Here he is "with Shakespeare," and we forget
both Titan and Goblin.

J. C. Powys. *Visions and Revisions*
(William Rider and Son, 1915), pp. 214–15, 217

In the matter of language at least, first Browning and then Mr. Hardy,
showed the way for the Imagiste group—Browning dragging in any
old word from an immense, and Mr. Hardy doing the same thing from
a rather limited, vocabulary. There is no one living with an affection
greater than mine for the poetry of Mr. Hardy: the *English Review* is
alive to this day to testify to it. So that I need not be taken as belittling
this great poet if I say that for me his vocabulary always seems to have
been taken from a country newspaper—from one of those good country
newspapers of the forties when the editors were scholars and gentlemen,
with here and there an article from Cobbett and with leaders ornamented
with quotations from Tully. But Browning, an immense and buoyant
personality, simply threw his immense ranges of syllogisms about as a
lusty child splashes in the water of his bath.

The value, however, of Browning and the very great value of Mr.
Hardy are not essentially vocabulary values—they are values of form.
For, in Verse, there is of course a Verse-form to be considered in addition to the architectonics of the novelist. . . . You ought at least to be able
to manage your "story" as well as a Paris feuilletonist or a far Western
raconteur. That Browning and still more Christina Rossetti conscientiously attempted, and that Mr. Hardy almost always triumphantly per-
forms. That, indeed, is why Mr. Hardy is so infinitely more important
as a verse-poet than as a prosateur. . . .

I am not, of course, claiming Mr. Hardy as an Imagiste, still further
am I from suggesting that he is unlearned or ignorant of formal verse,
accents, stresses, and what is called prosody. He has made his Imitations; his Sapphic fragments; his renderings of Catullus. Yet, as time
went on, and this great poet gave his attention less and less to story
telling and more and more to intimate self-expression, his versification
became, not so much more irregular, but more rough; until, if you read
the *Sunday Morning Tragedy,* it is much more the suggestiveness of
simple words grouped in twos and threes that matters than any smooth-
ness in the lines. In fact, you may say that Mr. Hardy's charm of
to-day—his power to excite—is that his writing is no longer a matter
of vowel-colouring and line-units—for he simply takes his lines by the
throat and squeezes them until they become as it were mutinously

obedient; it is a matter of mood-colouring and grouped-word units set anywhere in, or overlapping, the line.

Ford Madox Ford. *Thus To Revisit*
(N.Y., Dutton, 1925), pp. 153–55

When we say that the death of Thomas Hardy leaves English fiction without a leader, we mean that there is no other writer whose supremacy would be generally accepted, none to whom it seems so fitting and natural to pay homage. Nobody of course claimed it less. The unworldly and simple old man would have been painfully embarrassed by the rhetoric that flourishes on such occasions as this. Yet it is no less than the truth to say that while he lived there was one novelist at all events who made the art of fiction seem an honourable calling; while Hardy lived there was no excuse for thinking meanly of the art he practised. Nor was this solely the result of his peculiar genius. Something of it sprang from his character in its modesty and integrity, from his life, lived simply down in Dorsetshire without self-seeking or self-advertisement. For both reasons, because of his genius and because of the dignity with which his gift was used, it was impossible not to honour him as an artist and to feel respect and affection for the man. But it is of the work that we must speak, of the novels that were written so long ago that they seem as detached from the fiction of the moment as Hardy himself was remote from the stir of the present and its littleness. . . .

If we do not know his men and women in their relations to each other, we know them in their relations to time, death, and fate. If we do not see them in quick agitation against the lights and crowds of cities, we see them against the earth, the storm, and the seasons. We know their attitude towards some of the most tremendous problems that can confront mankind. They take on a more than mortal size in memory. We see them, not in detail but enlarged and dignified. We see Tess reading the baptismal service in her nightgown "with an impress of dignity that was almost regal." We see Marty South, "like a being who had rejected with indifference the attribute of sex for the loftier quality of abstract humanism," laying the flowers on Winterbourne's grave. Their speech has a Biblical dignity and poetry. They have a force in them which cannot be defined, a force of love or of hate, a force which in the men is the cause of rebellion against life, and in the women implies an illimitable capacity for suffering, and it is this which dominates the character and makes it unnecessary that we should see the finer features that lie hid. This is the tragic power. . . .

The Wessex Novels are not one book, but many. They cover an immense stretch; inevitably they are full of imperfections—some are failures, and others exhibit only the wrong side of their maker's genius. But undoubtedly, when we have submitted ourselves fully to them, when we come to take stock of our impression of the whole, the effect is commanding and satisfactory. We have been freed from the cramp and pettiness imposed by life. Our imaginations have been stretched and heightened; our humour has been made to laugh out; we have drunk deep of the beauty of the earth. Also we have been made to enter the shade of a sorrowful and brooding spirit which, even in its saddest mood, bore itself with a grave uprightness and never, even when most moved to anger, lost its deep compassion for the sufferings of men and women. Thus it is no mere transcript of life at a certain time and place that Hardy has given us. It is a vision of the world and of man's lot as they revealed themselves to a powerful imagination, a profound and poetic genius, a gentle and humane soul. [1928]

> Virginia Woolf. *The Common Reader* (Second Series)
> (Hogarth Pr., 1948), pp. 245, 253, 257

The popularity of which Thomas Hardy was the object at the time of his death is the most reassuring thing in the history of literature under democracy. There is nothing in his work to flatter the hopes and vanities of the great mass, as there is, we may say, in that of Mr. H. G. Wells; no escape into a fairyland such as is offered by Sir James Barrie; none of the abject sentimentalism which earns thousands of readers for authors who shall pass unnamed. Yet not certainly all at once, but after many years of labour, his austere presentation of life gained him, not only the highest honours, which after all were shared by so "exclusive" an author as Henry James, but the homage of the multitude of readers, who flocked in their crowds to his funeral in Westminster Abbey. As far as can be judged he is sure of a permanent place among those who are sustained not by adepts but by "broad rumour," though already, now and again, the voice of the incorrigible romantic is raised against him. . . .

Mr. Chesterton has suggested that Hardy's view of life was the distortion of the puritan spirit, wedded to pre-destination, baulked of its belief in hell. For Hardy, it can be seen, was not a Christian. Indeed it is difficult to see how a writer of tragedy can, at any rate while writing tragedy, be a Christian, since if there is redemption at the end, there can be no tragedy. For tragedy, at least since the Renaissance, is a vision not of divine justice, but of divine injustice, so far as the notion of justice is applicable to tragedy at all. It is a cry of protest. And in spite of his admirable, if bucolic comedy, it is as a writer of tragedy that Hardy is great, though it be domestic tragedy, that form it has taken nearly three hundred years to mature, which it has done, not in Hardy alone, but also in Ibsen. Thus it is by *Jude,* by *Tess,* by *The Return of the Native,* by *Far From the Madding Crowd,* and by *The Dynasts* that he will live, even if it be by *The Trumpet Major, The Woodlanders, Wessex Tales,* and *A Group of Noble Dames* that he has most charmed his readers.

None of this so far, we can see, makes for popularity, and the secret of his place in general favour resides possibly in the choice he has made of objects for his pity. And here we must slightly modify the statement that he does not flatter the vanity of the crowd. It is still true that he does not pander to the mob, but it is also true that his heroes do not differ in their circumstances from the average humbly placed man or woman. Any man might be Jude, any woman Tess, whereas few of us can start circumstanced like Lear or Lady Macbeth. Thus we can live ourselves into the characters, endow ourselves with the praiseworthy qualities they possess, attribute our failure not to our own weakness, but to the harshness of fate. This is a criticism which has to be made of his work; he seems a little to gratify the vanity of the weak, a sure road to popularity, one which Mr. Charlie Chaplin has trod with high success. It is a flaw in Hardy, but which he redeems, as Mr. Chaplin does not, by an aloofness, a sense of brooding, of detachment, foreign to the film actor. There is in the novelist a much higher complexity of art, a far profounder grasp of the way human beings work. The hopes which he touches so intimately are of the best; they have to do with endeavour, with longings for all things which are of good report; whereas the hopes which concern Mr. Chaplin are mostly superficial, and as often as not are no more than negative fears.

Bonamy Dobrée. *The Lamp and the Lute*
(Frank Cass, 1964 [c. 1929]), pp. 18, 24–25

Born in 1840, Hardy was confined from that very moment to the moment of his death nearly a century later by the boundaries of an age in which morality played a larger part in literature than ever before or since. The England that Hardy knew was supercharged with a consciousness of right and wrong; and Hardy, though the rights and wrongs of his characters were on a higher plane and were seen from his own refined and ennobled viewpoint, was supercharged with that consciousness too. He could hardly help it, but it made him and to my mind has kept him, in spite of his occasional greatness, a provincial writer. . . .

Hardy is the cart-horse, Conrad the race-horse, and appropriately Hardy's novels seem to me to resemble in form and progress and solidity those big, splendidly built but laborious wagons which must have been so common in his day, wagons heavily laden with goods and going on long journeys and made to resist the conflict of time and circumstance.

H. E. Bates in *The English Novelists*,
ed. Derek Verschoyle (Chatto and Windus,
1936), pp. 232–33

Undoubtedly, it would seem, the long years of personal unhappiness intensified his mood of revolt against a Power indifferent to man's misfortunes. He had always been inclined to collect instances of futile tragedy but the disposition grew so that the situations which Hardy devised for his characters seem often deliberately cruel as in *Tess* and deliberately squalid as in *Jude the Obscure*. He became an ingenious inventor of Life's Little Ironies. It was justifiably said by a reviewer of one of his last published collections of stories: "He just decoys his characters one by one into a circumstantial *cul de sac* and steadily blocks the entry."

One may be conscious of the weakness of Hardy's work and at the same time feel its greatness profoundly. His anger with God for not being there, as someone once described Hardy's attitude, has the effect of making his greatest figures, Eustacia and Clym in *The Return of the Native*, Henchard in *The Mayor of Casterbridge* and Tess, extraordinarily impressive, while his descriptions of nature and of country life are Victor Hugoesque in quality. There is the same deep poetic feeling for Nature as a whole in Hardy as in Victor Hugo, the same fine observation of detail. The massive reality and Biblical beauty of Hardy's pictures of rural occupations have surely never been surpassed. The vigil of the shepherd in lambing time, the sheep fair, the thunderstorm breaking up the fine harvest weather, the inside of the malthouse and its gossip, are scenes which Shakespeare or even Chaucer might have watched and Shakespeare himself might have created their attendant rustics.

Hardy wrote only one novel which profoundly stirred his readers to sympathy, *Tess of the D'Urbervilles*. He did not reach their emotions in his other books, though from the publication of *The Return of the Native*, in 1878, he had been regarded as in the forefront of British novelists. His designation of Tess as "a pure woman" roused enormous criticism, but mainly from people such as the mistress who found her maid reading it open at the chapter headed "Maiden No More" and confiscated the book. *Jude* was said to have been burnt by a Bishop, which amused Hardy, though other sounder criticism touched him so on the raw that he wrote no more novels and turned again to poetry.

Irene Cooper Willis. *NSN*. June 1, 1940, p. 698

Critics have disagreed and doubtless will continue to disagree about the order in which the great half dozen [novels] are to be ranked. *The*

Woodlanders, for instance, the novel least frequently referred to and, of the six, least widely known, is by some regarded as the best. We have Hardy's own word for it that "as a story" he liked it best of all. One hundred years from now, when the world is celebrating the second centenary of Hardy's birth, these are the six which are most certain to be remembered:

1. *Tess of the D'Urbervilles*
2. *The Return of the Native*
3. *The Mayor of Casterbridge*
4. *Far from the Madding Crowd*
5. *Jude the Obscure*
6. *The Woodlanders*

That is a list on which any novelist might be willing to risk his chance of survival. It is a list which tells why Hardy has been called the Shakespeare of the English novel.

His elevation to that rank is the more easily understood when it is noticed that five of the six books are tragedies. Hardy himself indicated that it is important to call them tragic rather than pessimistic. In the General Preface of 1911 he wrote his answer to all who had condemned his books as "pessimistic." "Differing natures," he pointed out, "find their tongue in the presence of differing spectacles. Some natures become vocal at tragedy, some are made vocal by comedy, and it seems to me that to whichever of these aspects of life a writer's instinct for expression the more readily responds, to that he should allow it to respond." Hardy made the English novel—as no other English novelist has done—a completely satisfactory medium for high tragedy. One thing at least was brought about by the completion of *The Dynasts* in 1908. In spite of some discriminating appreciation of his earlier books of poetry, most readers had been inclined to regard Hardy as a novelist who was trying rather ineffectively to learn to write verse. After all three parts of *The Dynasts* had appeared, Hardy the poet was given general recognition. Many who felt *The Dynasts* to be a failure still regarded it as a truly significant achievement, worth more than some successes. Hardy had himself observed that "the failure may be greater than the success. To have strength to roll a stone weighing a hundredweight to the top of the mount is a success, and to have the strength to roll a stone of ten hundredweight only half-way up that mount is a failure. But the latter is two or three times as strong a deed." *The Dynasts* did not reach the top of the mount, but it was a ten-hundredweight attempt and certainly carried Hardy more than half way up. The world was all the more ready to applaud because the heroic task had been attempted by a man of sixty-eight. The acclaim of the public was appropriately signalized on

July 19, 1910, when Hardy was invested by the King with the Order of Merit.

Carl J. Weber. *Hardy of Wessex*
(N.Y., Columbia Univ. Pr., 1940), pp. 182, 184, 204

Hardy takes a short cut to tragedy by reducing life to a formula. He gets rid beforehand of the main obstacle to tragedy, which is man's natural inclination to avoid it. His characters are passive, or at the best endlessly patient. He does not believe that character is fate; so that for him tragedy does not proceed from action, but resides with the power which determines all action. Misfortune is not brought about by men and women, but is arranged by this power which is indifferent to all arrangements and therefore to misfortune itself. Misfortune is a principle of the universe and falls upon the weak and the strong indiscriminately, neither averted by wisdom nor brought on by folly, striking inevitably and yet as if by chance. For it is the result of a mistake which man cannot correct, since he did not make it. It was made by the Maker of the universe. . . .

Hardy was partial to man; to be partial is to be involuntarily unjust; and in taking evil from man's shoulders he robbed man of one of his indispensable possessions. For in relieving man of evil he did not improve his situation, but made it worse, since he concentrated all evil against him. His characters, therefore, are curiously neutral; they gain colour only when passion or misfortune touches them, and are quite convincing only in their helplessness and instability. He draws women better than men. He sees woman and her response to love almost with a woman's eyes. He is on woman's side against man, just as he is on man's side against nature, and for the same reason; for woman is the final victim. He drew one man of strong and active character, Michael Henchard in *The Mayor of Casterbridge*. But most of his men are simple or priggish or effeminate. Their highest virtue is uncomplaining endurance of misfortune, a virtue which they share with women. In describing endurance Hardy is best, for by enduring man seems to rise above the malice of fate by a pure act of magnanimity comprehensible only to himself. The peasants who form a chorus to the novels are the final expression of this endurance, which has become so native to them that it has been transformed into a kind of humour. They are too low to fear a fall. They are in the position where the universe wants to have them; therefore beyond the reach of tragedy: the speakers of the epilogue to every action.

Edwin Muir. *Essays on Literature and Society*
(Hogarth Pr., 1949), pp. 110, 118-19

No poet more stubbornly resists selection. And this has not been to Hardy's advantage in the field where reputations are made. There is no core of pieces, no inner set of classic or perfect poems, which would prove his rank. Perhaps no poem of Hardy's is perfect; indeed, there is no great poet in whom imperfection is easier to find. Yet he is a great poet, and there are those who love him without limit even though they will admit his thousand failures and defects. With such persons it is the whole of him that registers and counts, one thing they would be reluctant to admit, namely, that out of his *Collected Poems* a *Selected Poems* might be put together which would contain everything pertaining to his essence. His essence, they would insist, is everywhere in the body of his work: in the capillaries, the tissues, no less than in the sinews and the heart. For them, in other words, the *Collected Poems* is neither too long nor too miscellaneous; its reputation with them depends upon the very richness that puts other readers off. They have made the effort the volume requires, and the reward of that effort is their knowledge of a poet who is great even when he is not writing well. He is great in himself, as one who thinks, feels, sees, and speaks; and he cannot lose their allegiance.

A poet's power to feel is best proved in the stories he tells, provided he can tell stories. Hardy could; that was where his genius lay; and so it may be that the heart of the *Collected Poems* beats in the narratives that throng it like so many persons, each one of them powerful in his or her own right. The final richness, perhaps, is here. Hardy is the envy of those who would be infinitely fertile in narrative ideas if only they could; it would seem to have been easy for him to be just that. Doubtless he worked harder than appears; there is evidence that he scoured newspapers for material, and took copious notes on stories he overheard in his native Wessex. The appearance, nevertheless, is of a fountain that cannot stop flowing; and its waters are strong waters that thrust forth from deep places. Hardy's stories are little melodramas, sensational, unrelenting, and if need be mournful beyond bearing, as the great ballads are.

Mark Van Doren in *Four Poets on Poetry*,
ed. Don Cameron Allen (Baltimore, Md.,
Johns Hopkins Univ. Pr., 1959), pp. 84–85, 97

In his lifetime, Thomas Hardy, though widely admired, had to suffer a good deal of abuse from critics whom he himself described as "manipulators . . . professed literary boxers who put on their convictions for the occasion." Yet these, in the long run, have been less damaging to him than that other minority which, professing urbanity, assumed that it could safely patronize him. "A little man with an earthy face," "clumsy," "autodidact": these and similar phrases have set the tone. George Eliot and Lawrence have also been called "autodidacts," which I think must be the critical equivalent of "peasant," since George Eliot was one of the best-educated women of her time, and both Hardy and Lawrence had quite good formal educations. The distinction really being offered is one of class, in its modern critical disguise of small urbanity. Hardy's open and strong feelings, in combination with his attachment to ordinarily inarticulate people, have continually exposed him to the worst that crude sophistication can manage. The defense is only just beginning to get established. . . .

Hardy wrote, not like one man, but like at least three, and the question of how good a writer he is cannot be settled by ordinary norms, but only by analysis of this fragmentation. There is a similar though much smaller division in George Eliot, and the case of whether Lawrence wrote well (it is common observation that he wrote both magnificently and very badly) is also relevant. With Hardy, the analysis is simpler than with either George Eliot or Lawrence: the fragmentation is much more on the surface, and the language of powerful description and dialogue, the language of firm statement, and the language of pretension and accommodation to fashionable academic and literary styles can be picked up almost as separate layers. The complexity of his social history as a writer can then be related to these variations.

Raymond Williams. *MGW*. May 4, 1961, p. 11

HARRIS, FRANK (1856–1931)

They are little jets of luminous spray [*Contemporary Portraits*]. As pen pictures, they could not be better done, for Harris is mellow; he has grown suave; he has obviously been at pains to paint as a work of love or art, and as an analyzer he certainly has no superior. . . . The best things are on other writers. Here Harris lets fly. Clearly his specialty is George Moore, whom he fails to appreciate. . . . This book is eminently enjoyable. It tingles. Harris has the supreme gift of lust of life and a dauntless self-assertion. Stung, he can sting back, yet always he is the searcher after truth, after his fashion. . . . His oratory and contradictoriness have been a perpetual source of trouble. Harris was a born actor who never acted, a made politician who never descended to the hustings; he might have been our "Billy Sunday," or the first lieutenant of the Salvation Army. When he recites his own stories audiences weep, and yet in conversation his tempest rouses all the conflicting winds, and silently his listeners slink away.

Lucifer. *Eng.R.* Feb., 1921, pp. 150–53

Never did such expense of realism produce effects so unrealistic. In execution the stories [*Undream'd of Shores*] are often extremely dexterous; but in almost every case the hollowness of the theme makes a mockery of its meticulously woven covering. . . . It is judgment and invention that fail him. . . . Many passages in the book would read more fittingly as memoirs, since they are connected with the names of real people, generally illustrious. The introduction of them dissipates illusion. . . . Unquestionably enormous in its extent, Mr. Harris's experiment stands like a vast engine, motionless; the power is absent that would make the wheels go round.

L. P. Hartley. *NA*. April 26, 1924, p. 120

I was always afraid of Mr. Frank Harris. I was conscious of being a just man but he affected me with a sense of the supernatural as if he could mysteriously work with hidden powers so that I committed crimes whilst I slept. I had known him with his high colour, his buffalo horn moustache and his voice of a town bull that was weeping over a sentimental novelette—had known him in the days when he had with infinite brilliance edited the *Saturday Review*. Later, whilst I was editing the *English Review*, he trepanned me into lunching with him at the Savoy. All through that meal he advanced arguments to me to force me to print a story of his so salacious that I thought that if I published it the front of the *English Review* office would become purple. In a case like that—it is the only one—I can be adamant. I *will* not print anything I do not want to print. Mr. Harris went on interminably with his persuasions and even threats. He pointed out that a touch of salaciousness would make the *Review* infinitely livelier. Moreover the ordinary man craved for salacious literature. His story would increase tenfold the circulation of the *Review*. But the great argument that his fruity and cavernous voice brought out again and again was that I was the only editor in the world who would have the courage to print his story.

Ford Madox Ford. *It Was the Nightingale*
(Lippincott, 1933), p. 316

Unless Harris's book [*The Life and Confessions of Oscar Wilde*] is definitely and effectively exposed as a worthless fabrication and his portrait of Wilde (from which the expressions recorded are derived by people who either did not know him at all, . . . or had only met him five or six times like Shaw) is shown to be an extremely false misrepresentation, physical, mental and moral, of this pre-eminent man, future students of English literature will be induced into grievous error and injustice and a high offence against the Republic of Letters allowed to become permanent in its malignant effect. . . .

I am dealing with what I consider a vile attack on a dead man for whom I had a great admiration and a sincere affection. . . . As long as Harris was alive, I allowed him to enjoy in peace to the last minute of his life the benefits in esteem and money that accrued to him from this evil act of his, all the more readily because I heard he was not very prosperous. That the man I remembered as bouyant, of radio-active vitality and an Ajax-like attitude towards the world, had come in his old age to no pleasant Latium, but "frail, feeble and given to somnolence," was fighting an up-hill battle for the existence (on lines of luxury certainly) of himself and the devoted wife whom he cherished.

But now that he is dead, this evil that he has done, this cruel traducement, under a mask of friendship, of a great and unhappy man, is not going to live after him if I can possibly help it.

> Robert Harborough Sherard. *Bernard Shaw, Frank Harris and Oscar Wilde* (T. Werner Laurie, 1937), pp. 31–32

Thirty years ago I was the Saturday Reviewer in the theatres. . . . The editor was Frank Harris, who had no quality of editorship except the supreme one of knowing good work from bad, and not being afraid of it. [1925]

> G. B. Shaw. *Shaw on Theatre*, ed. E. J. West (MacGibbon and Kee, 1958), p. 169

Such a legendary character as Frank Harris is not easily pinned down between the covers of a book. The stories that came so amusingly from the lips of friends, stories designed to show how outrageous or wicked or intrepid their hero was, look somehow cold in print. The amorous adventures, the scandals, the frauds, prompt always the question, never asked in conversation, whether what we are being told about them is true. . . .

Among the more interesting mysteries in Harris's career are those which involve his appointment, as a little-known journalist in his twenties, to the editorship of the *Evening News* (which increased in circulation from 7,000 to 70,000 under his hand), and his acquisition a few years later of the respectable *Fortnightly*. These were the vital steps in Harris's road to success, the key incidents of his life. . . . The last years had their pathos. The old man living at Nice, trying vainly to recreate the past, putting on his personality each morning with the painful care he used in assuming his dandyish clothes. . . . And he was no longer able to write. . . .   ,

The account of the writing of the book [*Bernard Shaw*] which carries Harris's name on the cover but was in fact almost wholly Scully's

[American journalist] work is the most richly farcical episode in the whole Harris saga; most nicely typical in that Harris did not live to enjoy the spoils. In America the book was a best-seller, in England it sold more than 20,000 copies on the day of publication. . . .

Beyond a certain easily imitable vigour, his style had no distinguishable characteristics at all. His work was marred by an extraordinary egotism, but that is not the same thing. He was a great talker—we are assured of it by those who heard much fine talk—yet it is not recorded that he ever said anything witty or profound. He was a brilliant editor, and he had an intuitive appreciation of genius in others; but it was surely as an ebullient character, rather than as a man of genius himself, that he was enjoyed by Wilde and Shaw. In the field of literature his greatest achievement was in blowing up this character to the size of a universal literary figure. That he should have been accepted at his own valuation by many who should have known better is certainly the best of the many jokes connected with Frank Harris.

TLS. Feb. 20, 1959, p. 91

HARTLEY, L. P. (1895–   )

I find Joyce Cary a less interesting writer than one who is more limited in his range, namely L. P. Hartley whose trilogy *The Shrimp and the Anemone, The Sixth Heaven,* and *Eustace and Hilda* is one of the most delightful of recent works. Hartley is a quieter writer and his work is more consciously literary in flavour, yet no situation or character in these three linked books has been accepted at second hand from another book. Every page is authentic and the vision, charmingly melancholy like a sunny day in late autumn, is shared by none of his contemporaries. Mr. Hartley gives us a study of a curious relationship between a brother, Eustace, and his sister, Hilda. . . . This first movement in the composition [*The Shrimp and the Anemone*]—it seems appropriate to talk in musical terms—is one of the best studies of childhood I have read. . . . The final volume is remarkable for the most beautiful evocation of Venice in the pages of a novel since Henry James; and, of course, for the culmination of the Eustace-Hilda relationship. It can scarcely be called tragic; the innocence of Eustace sweetens the pages and the novel is one of tenderness rather than pity or awe. But the reader must not mistake the quietness of this trilogy for any lack of creative vigour; nor must he be led astray by the felicities of style into thinking the subject-matter slight. *Eustace and Hilda* is creative writing of a very high order indeed. I can think of nothing else quite like it. Of all those writers established before 1945, L. P. Hartley is the only one who, in my view, has added substantially to his reputation by what he has published since that year.

P. H. Newby. *The Novel, 1945-1950* (BC/Longmans, 1951), pp. 35-36

The nearest thing to a great novel that I can discern in the post-war years is Hartley's *The Boat,* a rather neglected book which has the magnitude of conception, beauty of writing and construction and moral penetration which ought to add up to greatness, if anything does. If I have a reservation about it, and I am not sure that I have, it would be based on a certain daintiness or exclusiveness in Hartley's vision of his characters and their world, a kind of ultimate refusal to be serious that has affinities with Forster's refusal to be great. He seems to resist the tragic possibilities of his story, to fend them off or sterilize them, by too ready an exercise of his sense of the ridiculous. A reassuring decorum is preserved at the expense of a full recognition of the fact of evil. But his feeling for the absurd does contribute to the book's greatest triumph, the character, life and death of Mrs. Pirbright, to my mind the most moving human portrait in any modern novel.

Anthony Quinton. *L.* Nov., 1958, p. 14

When this book [*The Go-Between*] was published, it enjoyed great success as a serious work. From some of Mr. Hartley's other writings, a cosily tucked-in private joke might have been suspected, but, it seems, none was. Its literary derivation seems clear. The sire was *Lady Chatterley's Lover,* the dam *Cold Comfort Farm.* Grandma had seen "something horrid in the wood-shed." What had she seen? Mr. Hartley tells us. She had seen one of the love passages in *Lady Chatterley's Lover* being enacted. Mr. Hartley's mistake was to allow *his* Connie to be a virgin. He lacked Lawrence's social sense, to say the least. Lawrence had abandoned even *The Virgin and the Gypsy,* where the class thing was not a quarter so much involved.

TLS. Nov. 4, 1960, p. 708

Among our contemporary novelists Hartley is the master of sensibility. Of the sensibility, or susceptibility to impressions, of a man in whom the finer manifestations of civilised life meet with immediate response—in whom, indeed, they are to an unusual degree realised. Hartley was born more adult than most people; this, even if it seems a paradox, is why he has written so understandingly about children. But he has written with no less insight about grown-ups, and very sophisticated ones at that. His function as a writer, then, is not so much to be a moralist, and not at all to be a rebel. He is the transmitter of a civilised ethos. If we want a more civilised world we had better know all we can about what it is like to be civilised. And this is yet another reason why Hartley's novels are so well worth reading.

Paul Bloomfield. *L. P. Hartley*
(BC/Longmans, 1962), p. 22

These are very much novels of their time and class, reflecting a confused society and a highly educated writer. A lot of their cultural baggage is purely contingent. . . . Ideas are indeed present in the novels, though less as an active principle than as the sort of legacy that a novelist of Mr. Hartley's civilised kind can't easily avoid. . . . The effort and clarity that go into any advance of understanding in this field are outside Mr. Hartley's range, and the most we find in his novels, at the back of the elaborate surface treatment, are a few staid orthodoxies. As for human personality—he does indeed project the image of a certain social style, one that values the individual and is sensitive to his misuse; and the leisured-class settings emphasize this style. But in what exactly *are* his Eustace or Leo or Timothy valuable? They are very vulnerable and at the same time largely to blame for their failures, they have a marked inability to accept reality or even notice it, and they turn into pictures of frustration. Loss of nerve among the well-brought-up is Mr. Hartley's special subject, and he's sympathetic as well as acute. But anyone who cares about the value of the individual—at least as more than a fitful intimation of what might have been—must find these stories savagely pessimistic.

If in fact they don't disturb all that much I think it's because of the odd, rather numbing effect of Mr. Hartley's art. . . . His art is what makes Mr. Hartley worth discussing—it's of an exceptional kind, standing at an odd angle to life: though it has recently become fashionable and might be called the Oxford scholastic, after Iris Murdoch. It is the novel of manners heavily weighted with symbolism. Such novels are haunted by human failures, particularly those who cannot give themselves, and who like Prufrock have virtually turned into symbol. But there's also extraneous symbolism, and the feebler the character the more symbolism he carries. Mercury, the Zodiac and Robin Hood are used to tell us much of what we know of Leo in *The Go-Between*. It makes the novel of manners unwontedly stiff, and seems to me to rob moral issues of nearly all their force. But this sort of novel, half realistic and half mythological, observes conventions of its own—even verbally.

Robert Taubman. *NS*. June 21, 1963, pp. 936–37

HASSALL, CHRISTOPHER (1912–1963)

The "new" and the "traditional" work side by side; and at present there seem to exist three groups of writers. There are the "cerebralists," the followers of T. S. Eliot, William Empson and Ronald Bottrall; there are the disciples of Eliot and Pound, who are both individual writers and in close touch with the problems of their own time, headed by W. H. Auden and Day Lewis; and there is a small section in revolt against the merely witty, intellectual or academic group-poetry that has been so gallant an Aunt Sally of the critics. It is led by those of the Georgians whose work is still vital, and who have harked back for their inspiration to the pre-Romantics—to the age of Marvell or the decorous and unimpassioned contemporaries of Warton and Collins. They are for the most part escapists into worlds of fantasy, into a twilight of dream and childhood like Walter de la Mare, or into the idealized pastoralism of Edmund Blunden. To this group belongs the work of Mr. Christopher Hassall.

It is not easy to say how far, without writing *pastiche,* one can recapture what I can only call the "innocence" of the Eighteenth Century—the unconquerable integrity of Collins and Cowper, and that great line of novelists that ended with Jane Austen. Mr. Hassall has solved the problem in his own way, moving easily in a rich tradition and using the resources of the Eighteenth Century to express a contemporary mind. I am biassed a little, I suppose, in his favour, because I too turn reluctantly from Charles Cotton and Bishop King, from Collins and Cowper and Dyer, to the austere intellectualism of the present day. I find myself feeling for these *Poems of Two Years* something of that queer tenderness one has for the exquisite "second-ranker," for men like Lowes Dickinson and Dekker. They have not the bright emptiness of imitation, the unreality of a writer that turns back to a previous age defeated by his own. Nor are they the difficult strivings of a mind out of tune with its medium. Were these poems merely gracious and accomplished, they would scarcely be worth a second reading: but they are something more than gracious and accomplished. FitzGerald used to enjoy what he called the "half-meanings" of good verse ("just as the old women like sermons"), and by "half-meanings" he meant what we would call overtones—the emotional or intellectual stimulus of words. And indeed no poetry is worth sixpence that cannot set the mind adrift on stranger seas. For me at least, this evocative magic is continually present in Mr. Hassall's more characteristic work.

Ronald Fuller. Poetry R. May-June, 1936, pp. 186–87

Mr. Hassall . . . [*The Slow Night*] is as English as could be, and how stuffily so! I cannot understand how a poet with a high reputation for his mastery of traditional techniques can permit himself this mild Wordsworthian facetiousness, about a Demob Centre. . . . He is not in a trance. He is wide awake, and thinking, "What a good poem this will make!" And how wrong he is, at that! I have rarely read poems on the theme of war, even bad ones, that conveyed less of a feeling of tension. And the poems on other themes are just as flat.

G. S. Fraser. *NSN*. April 9, 1949, p. 362

In his review of Christopher Hassall's *The Slow Night,* Mr. G. S. Fraser refers to him as "a poet with a high reputation for mastery of the traditional techniques." He then dismisses all the poems as "flat and stuffy," finds their diction "slack and stilted," and accuses the author of insincere poetizing. As evidence, he quotes a few lines, carefully chosen to suit his plan of spiteful misrepresentation. It is impossible to believe that the critic, who discusses four other poets with sympathetic acuteness, has read *The Slow Night* with any attempt at fair-mindedness. Mr. Hassall does not conform to modernist fashions. Therefore he must be damned and insulted. I feel justified in protesting against this treatment of a volume which, in my opinion, contains so much beautiful and distinguished work. I do not propose to argue with your critic. I merely assert that there are at least six poems in the book which I should be proud to have written. And I could produce judgments more influential than mine to support me.

Siegfried Sassoon. *NSN*. April 23, 1949, p. 406

The libretto of Walton's opera *Troilus and Cressida* has stood up firmly to the test of performance at the Royal Opera House. . . . The construction is admirable, so that the dramatic action moves with extraordinary punctuality. Mr. Hassall's verse is quick enough for recitative, poetic enough for aria and ensemble. The great sextet in the third act is immensely telling in the theatre; when the text is read each character is seen to be precisely placed at the crisis of the action.

TLS. Jan. 14, 1955, p. 26

Of style it may at once be said that Mr. Hassall writes a vivid, easy English prose which, as befits a pupil of Sir Edward Marsh, is also scrupulously correct. . . . It is Mr. Christopher Hassall's own limpid and flexible style throughout this biography [*Edward Marsh*] which proves to us how much Sir Edward Marsh had to offer and to teach.

TLS. June 12, 1959, pp. 345–46

HEATH-STUBBS, JOHN (1918–   )

It is perhaps no accident that his images and rhythms are most convincingly alive when, as in "An Heroic Epistle," it is the elaboration of the poet's generic rhetorical quarrel with his age that is in question. . . . For the rest, for the modes of feeling he handles most habitually, Mr. Heath-Stubbs calls few interests into play. . . . There is an "intrinsically poetical" positive compounded of Mediterranean echoes, evoked through a lushness of epithet that offers much sensuous complexity and succeeds in realizing comparatively little. . . .

The Charity of the Stars is a selection from four previous books; but as there is no indication of chronology, it is impossible to say whether or not there is development. There are certainly isolated successes.

Hugh Kenner. *Poetry*. June, 1949, pp. 169–71

Generally, Mr. Heath-Stubbs [*The Triumph of the Muse*] needs to loosen up and shed his formality and inhibitions, for from time to time a goat-foot peeps out and there can be heard the beat of an honest heart under the scholar's musty gown. When he can face being himself, and speaks as person to person, all masks thrown aside, Mr. Heath-Stubbs can write simply and affectingly of love.

TLS. July 18, 1958, p. 410

John Heath-Stubbs has now adopted that "colloquial tone" which, in his last book, he "disdained" as inappropriate for the serious neo-classical poet and, as a result, his verse—though retaining much of its classical machinery (here in smart modern dress), its facetiousness, and its tendency to slip off into doggerel at the least opportunity—has become refreshingly readable and quite unpretentious. [*The Blue Fly in His Hand*]

Ian Hamilton. *L*. July, 1962, p. 77

HEPPENSTALL, RAYNER (1911–   )

Mr. Heppenstall's short poems—most of them on a religious theme—are arid, and without much rhythmical compulsion; and though in general his work is the product of a clever brain endeavouring to externalize its problems rather than of any great sensibility, the long mystical poem, *Sebastian,* has a certain power. The poet shows "what sensual orbit" brings him to the experience of the divine, the theme being explored in a manner that is sometimes illuminating, and sometimes extravagant, or merely pretentious. Free blank-verse is here employed in a subtly varied pattern; imagery, beaten out by an enflamed intellect, is daring at its best, but often relapsed into the "private," and obscure.

LM. May, 1937, p. 107

The absentees [*Four Absentees*], removed by death, are Eric Gill, J. Middleton Murry, George Orwell and Dylan Thomas. The book contains personal accounts of all four, and of the fifth man who links them, Mr. Heppenstall himself. He shared a flat with Orwell, had some hard drinking bouts with Thomas, stayed for some months at Murry's "community" near Colchester, often visited Gill.

It is not, though, the portraits themselves that one notices at first so much as the extraordinary fidelity of the setting. Those who ask: "What were the 1930s *really* like for artists?" (by which is meant, what sort of lives did they lead then?) may be referred to this book for part of the answer. . . .

Although he was a poet and, almost automatically, "left wing", Mr. Heppenstall did not at all notice the prevailing supremacy of the Three, Auden, Spender (whom he misquotes) and Day Lewis: he moved in another ambience altogether—and it is valuable to be reminded of its importance during the period—that of Adelphi summer schools, Roman Catholicism, the joy of making things, the simple life. . . .

At the end of this book, which evokes so finely what seems a very distant past, one is left with all sorts of questions and regrets: above all, the regret that Mr. Heppenstall, who writes so well, should have written, in serious terms, so little.

TLS. Sept. 2, 1960, p. 555

The novel has moved as far from the Henry James pattern as it could go; instead of stark situations artfully clothed in devious language we now have ambiguity and mystification lurking behind the utmost clarity of expression. James would no doubt delight in the fact that this complete reversal of the art of fiction as he comprehended it should be known as the "anti-novel," a field into which Mr. Heppenstall now confidently moves.

Though less austere than some examples of the French school to which Mr. Heppenstall has recently been turning the critical side of his mind, and though retaining a good deal of his own stylistic bite, this novel [*The Connecting Door*] confronts the reader with the characteristic anti-problems the chief of which seems to be the problem of cohesion. . . .

Action there is of a kind, but the characters buzz about sluggishly, like winter flies. It is this lack of dynamic of any recognizable sort that makes these products of the new school of fiction so difficult to read, and it is only fair in the consumer's interest to try to set the losses against the gains. . . . The final danger is not obscurity but paralysis. It may be the way, or one way, that writers have to go, but will they take their readers with them? At best, the will to read on is strained. At worst, the anti-novel may breed the anti-reader and turn itself into a form of literary suicide.

TLS. Feb. 2, 1962, p. 69

Philosophies and concepts are at home in Mr. Heppenstall's longest book of criticism, *The Fourfold Tradition* (1961). Some people were a little shy of this work when it first appeared. Readers are no longer accustomed to wayward "ideological" books by literary men, books with a sweeping background of intellectual information of the kind John Middleton Murry and Herbert Read used to write in the thirties. Moreover knowledge of French seems to have reached an all-time low with the younger generation. *The Fourfold Tradition* is in fact an Anglo-French book. The idea is that there are two traditions in England and two in France and that the separation between our two countries is a mere historical and geographical accident. . . . Mr. Heppenstall has always tended to rub sores and mention subjects about which people prefer to keep a gentlemanly silence. He does not mind being an irritant and in the smooth new orthodoxy that nearly everyone now accepts—left-liberal, interested in Africa rather than in Europe, anti-French—the Heppenstall brand of nonconformity is a cure for smugness.

Bernard Wall. *L.* March, 1963, pp. 63–64

HERBERT, A. P. (1890–)

Being a humourist, he is deadly serious. Sometimes he is so serious that his humour is lost and buried. He speaks a great deal in public, and makes his audiences laugh tumultuously; for he is a good speaker, and has that power of speech because he so well knows what he wants to say that he is never at a loss for eloquence or wit.

Now one advantage of having certain definite ideas about life is that you know where you are with yourself; and Herbert knows where he is. But one disadvantage is that you may be considered as a crank. . . . I am a great believer in variety of attack as a persuasive force; and as Herbert sometimes has the air of repeating himself I wonder whether he does not at times drive opponents into stubbornness. This is a point worth considering.

Furthermore, he might say as a lady once said to my mother: "I'm so *miscellaneous.*" The lady did not mean what she said (I think she meant "impulsive," or possibly "scatter-brained"); but if Herbert were to be asked what, as a writer and publicist, he called himself he could say what she said and mean it, and be accurate. I am not, indeed, sure how I ought to describe him, whether as a Reformer or a Conservative, a Humourist or a Bargee. He is all these things, a champion Skittles player, a believer in the working man's beer, a defender of the Middle Class, and a satirist of all that Intellectuals consider irreproachable. I am told by an expert that his light verse is not completely excellent in technique; and I am convinced that he suffers from what is for me the defect of moral indignation. But his novel, *The Secret Battle,* is the best account of the War on two Fronts that I have ever read, and *The Water Gypsies,* although it has defects of construction, is a very delectable panorama or peep-show of London life, which combines all Herbert's views of that life with his own delightful kind of nonsense.

Frank Swinnerton. *The Georgian Scene*
(N.Y., Farrar and Rinehart, 1934), p. 478

The present is the latest collection of Sir Alan Herbert's Misleading Cases. The previous volumes are acknowledged masterpieces of wisdom, wit and polite invective, and this one is of the same classic standard. The reason is not far to seek. There will always be so much wrong with a man-made system of justice that the reformer will always have an abundance of abuses and defects from which to choose. Usually when a popular series begins to fail in appeal it is for lack of material, not for lack of style. Sir Alan Herbert will never lack material and the present volume [*Codd's Last Case*] suggests no reason why his wit or outstanding powers of selection should fail. The great merit of these cases is that, although all of them delight and amuse and some of them are only designed for this purpose, many of them call attention in a most effective form to defects in law or legal procedure which ought to be rectified. Sometimes they suggest the remedy and sometimes the law is altered for the better. But much still remains to be done and it is hoped that A.P.H. will continue to tilt at some of the more glaring defects in the law until they, too, are altered.

TLS. Jan. 30, 1953, p. 68

Sir Alan Herbert (here [*Look Back and Laugh*] he carefully conceals his title) has laughed through much of his seventy years. His birthday book should be a good shock treatment for the mirthless—especially the mirthless young. Always, if he has seen a chip on a shoulder, A.P.H. has leveled at it. His aim, as we can see here, has been invariably true. . . .

It seems to us now that a dozen men must be synthesized under the initials "A.P.H." After reading what Sean O'Casey might call "a laughing look-over," it is enough to wish many happy returns to them all: poet, dramatist, politician, novelist, word-man, satirist, sailor, essayist, astronomer, and endeared man of letters.

TLS. Oct. 7, 1960, p. 649

HEWLETT, MAURICE (1861–1923)

Before the publication of *The Song of the Plow,* an event that we may regard as a turning point, Hewlett had proved himself, at least to all who used their eyes and did not blindly follow literary fashions, to be one of the cleverest, most versatile and delightful men-of-letters. Not only is *The Song of the Plow* his capital achievement, but it is also the best long poem (it has nearly five thousand lines) of our time, and perhaps it is the most neglected. The persons who are for ever crying out for sustained work from our poets, who ask for strong meat, something to get their teeth into, in short, the critics, are the very persons who are responsible for this sad neglect. Not all the critics were so blind, of course, for one or two of them strove hard to secure some recognition for the poem and did at least succeed in carrying it into its second edition, where it seems to have remained in a decent obscurity ever since. Many of us who were busy with other things in the autumn of 1916 probably glanced at the poem, noted, with approval, its robust masculine air, and quietly rejoiced in the fact that there was at least one poet who was not indulging in either patriotic rant, on the one hand, or egotistical whining, on the other; but having done this, we probably allowed both the poem and its author to fade out of our memory. To turn back to the poem now is to do more than recapture our first admiration for it; for high above the ruined contraptions of stucco, lath, and plaster it rises like a monument. A fine generous mood has been caught and fixed for ever.

But during the last ten years of his life, Hewlett was not only a poet, he was also what we may call, for want of a better word, a moralist. He had always a sharp eye for a man, a delight in character, but in his last years, he not only tried to understand, he judged; he was not content merely to explain a man, but always went on to pass sentence, not arbitrarily or harshly, on the one hand, nor with that irritating god-like detachment, on the other, but as a man who has lived his life, discovered for himself what there is of good and evil in it, and set up his standards accordingly; as a man, at once passionate and thoughtful, might speak of his neighbours. His biographical interests are easily discovered in his essays, and it is significant that he preferred to review biographies, memoirs, letters, and so on; in short, any books that showed him a fellow human being.

J. B. Priestley. *Figures in Modern Literature*
(John Lane, 1924), pp. 56, 63–64

Maurice Hewlett was a novelist who never enjoyed a just measure of popularity during his life and has yet to receive fair appreciation of his merits since his death in 1923. . . . An inveterate reader, he fell under the influence of Pater, and spent many of his holidays in Italy, saturating himself in the art and lore of the Renaissance. . . . Success came to him suddenly in 1898 when his mediaeval romance, *The Forest Lovers,* which he re-wrote four times in two years of work, was chosen by the *Academy* as the best book of the year. The most obvious criticism of *The Forest Lovers* applies equally to most of his subsequent books—the flowering of the wandering knight's romantic love affords a theme too frail to support the elaborate setting of the story. The criticism applies least forcibly to *The Life and Death of Richard Yea-and-Nay* (1900), a fine tapestry of Coeur de Lion and the Crusades, and *The Queen's Quair* (1904), one of the best romances ever written about Mary Queen of Scots, which was dedicated to Andrew Lang. Hewlett was a scholar and a poet much more than a story teller, and his invention rarely succeeded in creating plot and characters capable of sustaining the ornate tapestries of his backgrounds and the chiselled splendours of a polished style. He wrote carefully and the poetic imagery of his prose frequently falls into preciosity.

Malcolm Elwin. *Old Gods Falling*
(N.Y., Macmillan, 1939), pp. 269–70

Hewlett tried for twenty years or more to throw off the restrictions of the popular success that came to him with *The Forest Lovers* in 1898. That novel is among the best of its kind—and the kind need not be despised. But Hewlett disliked being labelled as a romantic medievalist. His interest, for a large part of his life, lay in other directions—in poetry, philosophy, and the study of agricultural conditions. In addition to several historical novels he wrote a trilogy about a gypsy-scholar, John Maxwell Senhouse, whose letters to Sanchia Percival express what may be accepted (at least in part) as Hewlett's own philosophy, based upon the maxim: "Now abide . . . Poverty, Temperance, Simplicity—these three. But the greatest of these is Poverty." Hewlett, without being tied to any religious denomination, was, by temperament, part Franciscan, part Quaker. For the last few years of his life he lived among Wiltshire villagers, and testified: "I who was once rich and now am poor, seriously declare that I had not the gleam of a notion what contentment was until I became as I am." His long poem, *The Song of the Plow* (1916) is a chronicle of the travail of the agricultural labourer through the centuries; and the cause of the English peasantry filled Maurice Hewlett's thoughts and guided his actions from the war-period onward. During those years he wrote his best work—a long sequence of essays gathered into four volumes. The English spirit—its placidity and depth, its sound common sense, its poetry and idealism—has seldom been better expressed.

A. C. Ward. *Twentieth-Century Literature*
(Methuen, 1940), pp. 217–18

HICHENS, ROBERT (1864–1950)

When a young man he came to London to become a student of the Royal College of Music; but by a happy inspiration he chose the moment when the aesthetic movement was at its height to publish a witty and spirited satire upon its extravagances. *The Green Carnation* was the book of the moment and a popular success. . . . Thenceforward Mr. Hichens was committed to the path of literature, and, diverging from his first direction, the writing of satiric extravaganza, he turned to more thoughtful and serious work, till with the most subtle and psychologically intricate of his books, *A Spirit in Prison,* he exhausted his powers, and his later volumes, despite the best efforts of the author, break down under the strain of trying to catch the former vigour and closeness of analysis. . . .

It was between the years 1904 and 1908 that Mr. Hichens reached his best in craftsmanship, insight and concentration with the three long novels, *The Garden of Allah, The Call of the Blood* and its sequel, *A Spirit in Prison.* . . . *The Garden of Allah* has a double thread running through its pages—the fascination of the vast silences of the sandy desert and the spell of the Roman Catholic faith. . . . If Mr. Hichens had not reasserted himself with *The Fruitful Vine* it would be natural to say that he had completely written himself out in 1908, the year of his greatest . . . novel, *A Spirit in Prison.* Among English novels written within this century this book, in its close analysis of character and motive, in the poetry of its background, and in the breadth with which Mr. Hichens outlines his moral drama, stands out as a noble and distinctive achievement.

Harold Williams. *Modern English Writers* (Sidgwick
and Jackson, 1918), pp. 395–96, 398

The Green Carnation was published anonymously in 1894 and with-drawn from circulation the year after. For two generations . . . it has been a legend only; and the Unicorn Press is much to be congratulated on having at last cajoled a new edition out of the author. For not only is it a wonderful period piece, but also a delightfully amusing skit in its own right.

It is very short and it has no plot. . . . The main characters are taken from life, and the movement of the book depends entirely on the glitter of its conversations. But since the talkers are mainly Wilde and Alfred Douglas—perfunctorily disguised as Esmé Amarinth and Lord Reggie Hastings—the glitter, agreeably pointed with malice, could hardly have been bettered by the real thing. . . .

Mr. Hichens, in 1894, firmly believed that Society was a going concern. . . . And it was this extravagant convention—like the equally extravagant convention of the Bright Young People thirty years later—which made it possible to write novels like *The Green Carnation*—or Firbank's *The Flower Beneath the Foot*. Nowadays, all the attention of writers is di-rected so forcibly to better things, while uninhibited frivolity is as rare (and suspect) as the high living on which it once depended, it may do us all good to catch at the guilty delight of putting the clock back to Mr. Hichens's perpetual summer time.

Arthur Pumphrey. NSN. April 30, 1949, p. 436

HILTON, JAMES (1900–1954)

Mr. James Hilton seems determined to leave no part of our little earth unexploited as setting for his fictional inventions. In *Contango* he girdled the globe, north and south with easy versatility, and *Knight Without Armour* led one into strange unexpected places in Eastern Europe and Northern Asia. The principal background in *Lost Horizon* is a particu-larly remote portion of Tibet, but minor episodes are staged in Berlin, China, India and elsewhere. In earlier books Mr. Hilton has proved amply his possession of the storyteller's gift of continuous new invention always adequately and often brilliantly clothed in the flesh-and-blood of convincing circumstance. For once, in the present case, he has perhaps exercised that gift too easily. He tells his story of the mysterious kidnap-ping of four passengers of—and in—an aeroplane on the Indian frontier with a sketchiness which the conditions indicated in the Prologue do not entirely excuse. Here he is nearer fantasy than perhaps anywhere in his earlier works; but he appears at times to forget that the fantastic above all demands the air of concrete realization if it is to pass muster, and to fit a lamastery in mid-Tibet with green porcelain baths from Akron, Ohio, and the works of George Moore, "and even Old Moore," is to make it rather more than less incredible. . . .

Certainly the book makes, if in its conception rather than its execution, the most of its opportunities. Mr. Hilton always writes with imagination; his characters are clearly drawn and revealed in constant dramatic movement; his dialogue is excellent. He does, however, having created a situation, rather get out of it than resolve it; and one is not entirely convinced by Conway's final return to action, nor is the rather abrupt ending really satisfactory.

TLS. Sept. 28, 1933, p. 648

[Here] . . . we have *Goodbye, Mr. Chips,* a little watercolor of the sentimental English school, and an excellent example of its type. No tears will flow over this story of a schoolmaster who gradually turned into a mythical salty character instead of a drone, but everyone will feel like crying, and that does us all good. The little tale gives us the soft English character in a hard nutshell. Mr. Chips is a mediocre classics master in a good but not-quite-first-rate public school. . . . This is a hard-boiled view of a harmless little story which Alexander Woollcott is quite within his rights in calling "tender and gentle," but let us not forget, ladies and gentleman, that we are in a picture gallery. The outside world is not so nicely framed.

T. S. Matthews. *NR.* July 18, 1934, p. 271

. . . "there was one thing in particular that cheered me about *Goodbye Mr. Chips,* which incidentally I think gave me more pleasure in the writing of it than any other book," continued Hilton. "And that was that for the first time in their lives—at least so I'm told—William Lyon Phelps and Alexander Woollcott shared the same critical opinion. I think you'll agree with me," he joked, "that that is something of an accomplishment."

Carroll Sibley. *Barrie and His Contemporaries*
(Webster Groves, Mo., International Mark
Twain Society, 1936), p. 40

James Hilton's new offering, *Random Harvest,* is likely to baffle any conscientious reviewer. The only important thing about it is its plot, and the plot is of such a nature that were I to tell it to you, I'd deserve drawing and quartering. I could say it's a pre-second-World-War story about an Englishman who was smashed up badly near Arras in '17 and whose life from that time until December, 1919, remained a complete blank in his memory, but that would merely give you a clue, not a summary. . . .

So I had better content myself with saying that Mr. Hilton has cranked out another deft piece of storytelling, combining the suspense of *Lost Horizon* with the mile-thick sentimentality of *Goodbye, Mr. Chips,* and that anyone who starts it will read it to the very end, impossible as that end is. . . .

Hilton the moralist (he *is* a moralist) interests me rather less than Hilton the plot-maker. There are certainly few writers as sheerly ingenious as he is, or as able to cut out and put together the complex jigsaw-puzzle kind of a story of which *Random Harvest* is so good an example. His storytelling capacity shows no sign of diminution and, for me, that's enough.

Clifton Fadiman. TNY. Jan. 25, 1941, p. 68

HODGSON, RALPH (1871–1962)

I found in Hodgson, devoted to dogs (of pure breed) as indeed he was, one of the most remarkable minds I had hitherto known. Here was a man; with a powerful head, held rather high, his face irregular and deeply lined, with wide, sensitive nostrils and an ample, rather loose mouth. (Walter Raleigh once declared a loose mouth to be a feature of an imaginative man.) And when he talked, he gave his whole mind, as it were, to creating wealth—wealth of observation, on man's past and present, on folk lore, history, psychology, art and literature; of this last he was an exacting critic. His contempt for the dishonesties and pretences of writers was withering; his passionate admiration for true poetry was expressed in terms so powerful and convincing, that one was fain to go, with a new zest and understanding, to Shelley, Blake and Coleridge.

Here, to my delight, was no doctrinaire critic, with theories to which writers must adjust themselves or be damned, but a man after my own heart, with no bias in favour of any form of art, who waited to be convinced by the ring of the voice to which he listened. . . . Hodgson's sensitive spirit would respond, like the needle of the compass to a magnetic field; a stream of ideas came rushing out, a spring fresh, clear and transparent, now descending in a cascade of foam, now passing through fields and villages and towns, reflecting sun and clouds, moon and stars, and the lovely and evil doings of men. I know only one other poet-talker who evokes so wide a view of life, James Stephens.

William Rothenstein. Men and Memories (N.Y.,
Coward McCann, 1932), p. 352

Unlike most poets, Mr. Ralph Hodgson has written too little; but almost all he has written is memorable, above all the rapturous "Song of

Honour" (modelled, too closely perhaps, on Smart's *Song to David*),
and the sculpturesque "The Bull."

> Herbert Grierson and J. C. Smith. *Critical
> History of English Poetry* (Chatto and
> Windus, 1950), p. 494

A new book of poems [*The Skylark and Other Poems*] by Mr. Ralph
Hodgson at the age of eighty-seven is an event which will probably take
a great many people by surprise. It is forty-five years since he published
Poems, the single slim work on which his reputation has entirely rested.
It is well over thirty years since he virtually became an expatriate; more
than twenty since he was last seen in this country. Indifferent to fame,
and positively shunning any kind of publicity, he has been living in Ohio,
remote from the literary world. Many may well have assumed that he
was no longer alive.

Regarded as a Georgian poet, he has seen (if he cared to notice it,
which is doubtful) his reputation among the critics follow a similar graph
to that of his fellow contributors: falling through the 1920's and 1930's
and lately rising again—a change happily marked by the award of the
Royal Gold Medal in 1954. We have now reached the point where those
who wish to go on sneering at the Georgians have first to make exceptions of the best of them, . . . de la Mare is one, the chief, and Mr. Ralph
Hodgson another. . . . There have always been those who regard "The
Song of Honour" as one of the best-sustained, and also noblest poems of
the century, and who find power and poignancy in one or two of the
shorter poems, "The Moor," for example. . . . No equal reputation of
our time has rested on so small a body of work. . . .

Between 1941 and 1951, unknown to the public, Mr. Hodgson was
issuing privately printed verse in very small quantities for the delectation
of his friends. . . . All this Mr. Colin Fenton has now collected. He has
added six short poems never printed before. And he has prefaced the
whole with a handful from the other end of the poet's career, poems
dating from before the First World War, yet excluded from the 1917
volume. . . .

The sources of inspiration are the same, whether early or late: Nature
and England—reverence for Nature, devotion to the English tradition;
love of animals and loathing of cruelty to them. But the style alters. The
early verse is more ornamented, consciously poetical, "highly-wrought."
. . . The later verse is robust, witty or sardonic, more compressed in
thought, close to spoken English and reflecting its rhythms. . . . In other
words, Mr. Hodgson . . . has been quietly making a journey familiar in
the verse of our century, and has achieved, in his own manner, a modern
style. . . .

Mr. Hodgson has no compulsive message but personality colours everything he writes. It is the most immediately noticeable thing about the book as a whole: a convincing voice.

TLS. Feb. 13, 1959, pp. 77–78

HOLLOWAY, JOHN (1920–   )

In a broadcast of September, 1956, Mr. Holloway suggested that the one-time revolutionary methods of "close reading, taking a poem to pieces," talk about imagery, ambiguities, associations, poetic textures, were degenerating into a ritual evasion of genuinely critical response. It was a valuable warning—critical traditions are as different and laborious to inherit as poetic ones—and for the same reason, so is *The Chartered Mirror*. Collecting various essays in support of his original and here amplified paper, Mr. Holloway now proposes that *"any guiding idea* with which the critic may equip himself . . . is likely to open up parts of his subject, *but certain parts only,"* so that in the case of any long work, poem, play or novel, to insist merely on "the words on the page" because "we must discuss *something* is wholly inadequate. . . ."

Mr. Holloway sets out to illustrate these and related contentions with three groups of essays: one each on poets, novelists, and critics. . . . The structure of the book, then, makes its main point: if it is necessary to have "guiding ideas," it is even more necessary to know precisely the scope and direction of your chosen assumptions. You come away from this final section with an admirably detailed recognition of how damaging lack of awareness can be, how thoroughly it mistranslates the keenest, most sensitive insight.

Graham Martin. *NS*. June 4, 1960, p. 831

The key to Dr. Holloway's impressive but difficult long poem [*The Land-fallers*] in terza-rima seems to be Dante. . . . Dr. Holloway has many advantages for writing a poem on this model. He is a philosopher and a student of modern society, with a wide knowledge of history and literature other than his own. Technically he has an immense vocabulary, important for the exacting need to sustain "triple rhyme" for 1800 lines.

Yet for all the skill and clarity of many of its parts, the whole poem remains obscure and vaguely unsatisfying, a narrative of shadows. . . . For one reader, at least, this poem remains a challenging technical achievement, but little more.

TLS. April 6, 1962, p. 234

HOLTBY, WINIFRED (1898–1935)

It is the merit, and it is a great merit, of *South Riding,* not that it is a picture of Local Government at work (all that should have been cut out) but that it has defined, in the most clear-minded way, the modern Fate. That Miss Holtby did not choose to be content with doing that, but wrote, also, a novel about social workers, and unsocial workers, in Yorkshire, so that one is so exhilarated by her enthusiasm that one wants, under the influence of that part of the book, to throw all his books out of the window and go and do things, is the measure of the greatness of her heart; and of her limitations as an artist. For it means that because of entirely subsidiary material we are distracted, as she was deflected, from the significance of the individual human tragedy. . . . She wrote in *South Riding* a book that is a grand picture of the life of our times, and created, incidentally, in Sarah Burton, a figure who must be one of the minor masterpieces of fiction. To have done that is to have accomplished a great deal.

Sean O'Faolain. *LM.* April, 1936, pp. 643–44

Winifred Holtby had one positive fault—the only one that the most exacting of her friends could find in her—and even that was a defect of the most conspicuous of her splendid qualities. She was so accessible to ideas, so generously eager to dash out and rescue them before they perished from contempt or indifference, to "try all notions for their gold" as her friend Hilda Reid has put it, that she was an erratic and unreliable critic. It was not that she praised, out of kindness, that which she did not believe to be good. The gay and gallant figure that stands out luminously in the mind from the confused and chilling background of the post-war scene, was utterly sincere, bone-honest. But she liked too much. She praised too often and too quickly. And then, life seeming (as it proved) so short, and there being so much to do, chiefly for other people, she hurried on to the next thing, seldom allowing herself time to reverse or confirm her judgments. It was on contemporary values that she went astray. She was as sound as the best on permanent literature. So that anyone editing, for instance, her letters [*Letters to a Friend*], does her no service by not editing them enough, or by giving her impulsive lightning views the solemn air of conclusions.

Violet Scott-James. *LM.* May, 1937, p. 82

The success of *South Riding* and its international fame make it a book which cannot be treated as merely one event amongst others in Winifred's complicated life. Her only novel that comes near to it in stature is

Mandoa, Mandoa! but except for those who know its hidden springs the earlier story belongs to a more intellectual and less broadly human category, and has therefore a less universal appeal. From the moment that *South Riding* appeared, critics and public alike acclaimed it as a masterpiece, a classic, a picture of England which, as the novelist Helen Simpson suggested in her broadcast review, may well stand as Winifred's monument. By the time that Winifred had finished this last and greatest novel, she knew her own work too well to be wholly unaware of her achievement. But her innate scepticism about her ability to capture a large public prevented her from counting upon even one of the many triumphs, won by the book, which came too late to reward her. *South Riding* was the choice of the English Book Society in the month of its publication, March 1936. Of the original 8/s English edition over forty thousand copies were sold; of the American between ten and twenty thousand. The following year Edinburgh University awarded the book its annual James Tait Black Memorial Prize for the best novel of 1936. Soon after its publication it was issued in the Albatross Continental edition, and has already been translated into Dutch, Danish, Swedish and Czech. . . .

South Riding was the work—and probably the first typical work—of Winifred's maturity. Amongst her writings it represents both an end and a beginning. It is an end in the sense that, when compared with her first novel, *Anderby Wold,* it gives an uncanny appearance of completion to her literary cycle. It is a beginning because it clearly indicates what she could and would have done had she survived for another decade. From its pages we can estimate the real measure of her quality.

For those who can read it, Winifred wrote her autobiography in *South Riding* as clearly as she had once written it in *Anderby Wold,* and far more profoundly. Her book is not only an achievement of the mind; it is a triumph of personality, a testament of its author's undaunted philosophy. Suffering and resolution, endurance beyond calculation, the brave gaiety of the unconquered spirit, held Winifred back from the grave and went to its making. Seed-time and harvest, love and birth, decay and resurrection are the immemorial stuff of which it has been created. In it lie both the intuitive and the conscious knowledge of imminent death. Its lovely country scenes go back to the earliest memories of the Yorkshire child who, only thirteen years before she died, had come as a brilliant Oxford graduate to London. Her unconcealed passion for the fields and wolds of her childhood suggests that she returned with relief to her beginning because she knew that, beyond the brave struggle for life and for time, the inevitable end was near.

Vera Brittain. *Testament of Friendship*
(Macmillan, 1944), pp. 408–10, 418–19

Winifred Holtby's *Mandoa, Mandoa!* is in intention a left-wing *Black Mischief,* written a year or two after Waugh's book came out; which fails not so much because she was less talented than he as because his sensibility and his form were incorruptibly one, and his sensibility was incorruptibly upper middle class. You can't put lower-class sympathies into that kind of work. And her *South Riding,* a respectable piece of work, built entirely on her "decent" values, with two categorically lower-middle-class heroines, a school-mistress and a woman alderman, is topped off with a romantic, reactionary, wounded, brooding, ineffectual, upper-middle-class hero. The hegemony was too much for her. For a hero she had to have a gentleman. Because *her* sensibility, *her* themes, had no contemporary forms.

> Martin Green. *A Mirror for Anglo-Saxons*
> (N.Y., Harper, 1950), p. 116

HOPE, ANTHONY (1863–1933)

Be good: be broad-shouldered: be unselfish: be comely and you will ultimately not only marry the heroine but get into Parliament, to double your bliss. Do not be a flirt, or the son of a squire, or an idle man of the town, or the reverse fate will overtake you. It only takes 569 pages [*Second String*] for Andy, the good but poor—we had almost said "apprentice," the tale runs on such traditional lines—the good but poor Andy to surpass the rich but frivolous Harry. Such an amiable moral disarms all criticism. The author plays his providential part in a style more pointed than is usual in fiction, and will deserve the applause he will undoubtedly receive.

> *Eng. R.* July, 1910, pp. 761–62

[In London] he settled down in chambers to wait patiently for briefs which were very slow to arrive. . . . He used to read law steadily every day till about five o'clock. But after tea he allowed himself to "scribble," took to writing novels with a perseverance quite undaunted by their small success. His first story, *A Man of Mark,* he published at his own expense. His second was almost still-born. His third, I think, *Mr. Witt's Widow,* received at last a notice by Mr. Andrew Lang in *The Times.* . . . It was not until he had been writing for six years that success suddenly came. Then, *The Prisoner of Zenda* took the world by storm, and the new *Westminster Gazette* began to publish *The Dolly Dialogues.* Within a short time their fortunate author found himself able to command the income of a judge. . . . He turned his back upon the Woolsack and dedicated his gifts to the amusement of mankind. He soon became a popular favorite. *The Dolly Dialogues* roused the admiration of George Meredith. But the Ruritanian romances won a larger public. . . . Anthony Hope possessed not only rich gifts of humour and imagination. He had gifts less often found in English authors, a scholar's sense of style, a philosopher's ironic observation, and wit both fine and rare. In one or two books, *The King's Mirror* and *Quisanté,* these gifts found almost adequate expression. In others they may seem to have been a little wasted on the subjects chosen for the tale.

Sir Charles Mallet. CR. Aug., 1933, p. 162–63

He was a thoroughly Balliol best-seller: a double first, a President of the Union, he took his popularity (£70,000 earned in the first ten years of writing) with admirable suavity. He was never really a professional writer: . . . he turned his novels off in a couple of months. Sometimes there were as many as three manuscripts awaiting publication. He managed in his delicate dealings with tragic or even blackguardly themes to retain the Union air of not being wholly serious. You could forgive his sentimentality because it struck so artificial an attitude. He was a Balliol man: he wasn't easily impressed by his great contemporaries. It seemed to him that Hardy was rather limited in his opinions, and when Henry James died, he wrote: "a dear old fellow, a great gentleman . . . The critics call him a 'great novelist': I can't think that." His own work was highly praised by Sir James Barrie and Sir Gilbert Parker, but he was not conceited. "Have you read my *Phroso?* I wrote it in seven weeks laughing, and now I have to be solemnly judged as though it were an effort of a life. It's really like explaining a kiss in the Divorce Court. . . ." An Isis Idol knows that next week he must inevitably be dethroned, and he was quite prepared to see himself superseded by another generation of popular writers who would appeal to a taste which was already beginning to reject the sentimental badinage of *The Dolly Dialogues.*

Graham Greene. The Lost Childhood (N.Y.,
Viking, 1951), pp. 102–3

A trivial best-seller may reveal more about social attitudes than a party manifesto, and our crudest myth-makers may tap our deepest impulses: these are lessons which critics have taken to heart perhaps too thoroughly, so that in 1960 every schoolboy knows that *The Prisoner of Zenda* is either an invaluable repository of monarcho-fascist attitudes or the product of a repressed homosexual conflict.

TLS. July 1, 1960, p. 418

HOPKINS, GERARD MANLEY (1844–1889)

My verse is less to be heard than read, as I have told you before; it is oratorical, that is the rhythm is so. I think if you will study what I have said you will be much more pleased with it and may I say? converted to it.

You ask may you call it "presumptious jugglery." No, but only for this reason, that presumptious is not English.

I cannot think of altering anything. Why shd. I? I do not write for the public. You are my public and I hope to convert you.

You say you wd. not for any money read my poem again [*The Wreck of the Deutschland*]. Nevertheless I beg you will. Besides money, you know, there is love. If it is obscure do not bother yourself with the meaning but pay attention to the best and most intelligible stanzas, as the two last of each part and the narrative of the wreck. If you had done this you wd. have liked it better and sent me some serviceable criticisms, but now your criticism is of no use, being only a protest memoralising me against my whole policy and proceedings. [1877]

Gerard Manley Hopkins. Letter xxxvii, in
*Letters of Gerard Manley Hopkins to
Robert Bridges,* ed. C. C. Abbott
(Oxford Univ. Pr., 1955), pp. 46–47

Gerard Hopkins may be described, without opposition, as the most obscure of English verse writers. Born in 1844, he became a Jesuit priest in 1868, a more probable fate for him then—he was at Oxford—than now. Before joining the Order he burnt what verses he had already written and "resolved to write no more, as not belonging to my profession, unless it were by the wish of my superiors." For seven years he wrote nothing. Then by good fortune this wish was expressed and Hopkins set to work. "I had long had haunting my ear the echo of a new rhythm which now I realized on paper. . . . However I had to mark the stresses . . . and a great many more oddnesses could not but dismay an editor's eye, so that when I offered it to our magazine . . . they dared not print it." Thenceforward he wrote a good deal, sending his poems in manuscript to Robert Bridges and to Canon Dixon. He died in 1899 leaving a bundle of papers among which were several of his best sonnets. In 1918 the Poet Laureate edited a volume of poems with an introduction and notes of great interest. From this volume comes all our knowledge of his work.

Possibly their obscurity may explain the fact that these poems are not yet widely known. But their originality and the audacity of their experimentation have much to do with the delay. Even their editor found himself compelled to apologize at length for what he termed "blemishes in the poet's style." "It is well to be clear that there is no pretence to reverse the condemnation of these faults, for which the poet has duly suffered. The extravagances are and will remain what they were . . . it may be assumed that they were not a part of his intention." But too many other experiments have been made recently, especially in the last eight years, for this lofty tone and confident assumption to be maintained. The more the poems are studied, the clearer it becomes that their oddities are always deliberate. They may be aberrations, they are not blemishes. It is easier to see this to-day since some of his most daring innovations have been, in part, attempted independently by later poets. . . .

If we compare those poems and passages of poems which were conceived definitely within the circle of Hopkins' theology with those which transcend it, we shall find difficulty in resisting the conclusion that the poet in him was often oppressed and stifled by the priest. In this case the conflict which seems to lie behind and prompt all Hopkins' better poems is temporarily resolved through a stoic acceptance of sacrifice. An asceticism which fails to reach ecstasy and accepts the failure. All Hopkins' poems are in this sense poems of defeat. . . .

His is a poetry of divided and equal passions—which very nearly makes a new thing out of a new fusion of them both. But Hopkins' intelligence, though its subtlety with details was extraordinary, failed to remould its materials sufficiently in attacking his central problem. He solved it emotionally, at a cost which amounted to martyrdom; intellectually he was too stiff, too "cogged and cumbered" with beliefs, those bundles of invested emotional capital, to escape except through appalling tension. The analysis of his poetry is hardly possible, however, without the use of technical language; the terms "intellectual" and "emotional" are too loose. His stature as a poet will not be recognized until the importance of the Belief problem from which his poetry sprang has been noticed. He did not need other beliefs than those he held. Like the rest of us, whatever our beliefs, he needed a change in belief, the mental attitude, itself.

I. A. Richards. *Dial*. Sept., 1926, pp. 195–96, 199, 203

A major objection to free verse as it has been written by . . . Hopkins, is this: that it tends to be a rapid run-over line, so that the poem, or in the case of a fairly long poem, the stanza or paragraph, is likely to be the most important rhythmic unit, the lines being secondary. Hopkins was aware of this tendency in his poems, but apparently not of its danger. In his own preface to his poems, he writes: "It is natural . . . for the lines to be *rove over,* that is, for the scanning of each line immediately to take up that of the one before, so that if the first has one or more syllables at its end the other must have as many the less at its beginning; and in fact the scanning runs on without break from the beginning, say, of a stanza to the end and all the stanza is one long strain, though written in lines asunder." The result is a kind of breathless rush, which may very well be exciting, but which tends to exclude or to falsify all save a certain kind of feeling, by enforcing what I have called, in my essay on Poetic Convention, a convention of heightened intensity.

Hopkins meets the difficulty by excluding from his poetry nearly all feeling that is not ecstatic. . . . But if a poem is written wholly in conventional language, it becomes, when the convention is of this type, merely melodramatic and violent, and, when the convention is of some other type, weak in some other and corresponding manner. . . . The extremely abnormal convention is seldom necessary, I believe, to the expression of powerful feeling. Shakespeare can be just as mad in a sonnet as can Hopkins, and he can be at the same time a great many other things which Hopkins cannot be. He has a more limber medium and is able to deal with more complex feelings. [1937]

Ivor Winters. In Defense of Reason ([Colorado]
Univ. of Denver, 1947), p. 125

He became a poet, but he might have been a musician—all his life, we are told, he was composing songs and melodies; and he might have been a painter—he had great aptitude in drawing and was advised to adopt painting as a profession. Finally, he had another kind of sensibility which is so often overlooked—I mean that sensibility for the quality and contour of ideas, on which the true metaphysician depends. He dreamed his way through childhood—bookish, pallid, desperately strong-willed and courageous; precocious, perhaps not a little pretentious. He wrote long elaborate prize-poems at school, poems too full of learning to have any suggestion of original genius. At Oxford he came under the influence of Jowett, and was, one of his friends tells us, "at first a little tinged with the liberalism prevalent among reading men." But only at first. . . .

In Hopkins's poetry, as perhaps in the work of other poets, we can distinguish (1) poetry which is the direct expression of religious beliefs, (2) poetry which has no direct or causal relation to any such beliefs at all, and (3) poetry which is not so much the expression of belief in any strict sense but more precisely of doubt. All Hopkins's poems of any importance can be grouped under these three categories. When this has been done, I think that there would be general agreement that in poetic value the second and third categories are immensely superior to the first. . . .

"The Windhover" is completely objective in its senseful catalogues: but Hopkins gets over his scruples by dedicating the poem "To Christ our Lord." But this is a patent deception. It does not alter the naked sensualism of the poem; and there is no asceticism in this poem; nor essentially in any of the other poems of this group. They are tributes to God's glory, as all poetry must be; but they are tributes of the senses; and a right conception of God and of religion is not hurt by such tributes.

In the third section, poems expressive not so much of belief as of doubt, I would place those final sonnets, Nos. 40, 41, 44, 45, 46, 47 and 50 in the published *Poems*. These all date from the last years of Hopkins's life—the first six from 1885, the other from 1889, the actual year of his death. But even earlier poems express at least despair: "Spring and Fall"—the blight man was born for; the "Sybil's Leaves"—the self-wrung rack where thoughts against thoughts grind. But the sonnets themselves are complete in their gloom, awful in their anguish. . . .

True originality is due to a conflict between sensibility and belief; both exist in the personality, but in counter-action. The evidence is clear to read in all genuine mysticism and poetry; and nowhere more clearly than in the poetry and mysticism of Gerard Hopkins.

Herbert Read. Collected Essays in Literary Criticism
(Faber, 1938), pp. 331–32, 334, 336–38

What the Society of Jesus did for Hopkins is clear: it did not make him happy—only Wales could do that—it prevented him from finishing even the little he did get written, but it turned an esthete, no better or worse than half a dozen bright young men of the sixties and seventies, into a serious and unique artist. . . . There are lines in his weaker poems like "The Bugler's First Communion," which show how constantly he had to struggle against that confusion of the religious with the erotic to which Whitman succumbed. Again, there was in Hopkins, as in most people whose senses are abnormally acute, an impulse towards their *dereglement*. To a skinny boy who, to compare his endurance with a shipwrecked sailor's can go without water for a week (some say three), the road that Masoch and Sade took is always open. It is precisely to such natures that Loyola's exercises are designed to give meaning and purpose, and "The Wreck of the Deutschland" is Hopkins' witness to their success. [1944]

W. H. Auden in Literary Opinion in America,
ed. Morton Dauwen Zabel (N.Y., Harper
Torchbooks, 1962 [repr. from NR]), pp. 254–55

That Hopkins has a permanent place among the English poets may now be taken as established beyond challenge: academic scholarship has canonized him, and the love of "a continuous literary decorum" has forgotten the terms in which it was apt to express itself only a decade ago. It is now timely to ask just what that place is. . . .

Hopkins was born—and died—in the age of Tennyson. This fact has an obvious bearing on the deliberateness with which Hopkins, starting with that peculiar genius, set himself to develop and exploit the modes and qualities of expression illustrated—the distinctive expressive resources of the English language ("English must be kept up"). The age in poetry *was* Tennyson's; and an age for which the ambition "to bring English as near the Italian as possible" seems a natural and essentially poetic one, is an age in which the genius conscious enough to form a contrary ambition is likely to be very conscious and very contrary. That he was consciously bent on bringing back into poetry the life and strength of the living, the spoken, language is explicit—the confirmation was pleasant to have, though hardly necessary—in the *Letters* (to Bridges, LXII): "it seems to me that the poetical language of the age shd. be the current language heightened, to any degree heightened and unlike it, but not (I mean normally: passing freaks and graces are another thing) an obsolete one." His praise of Dryden (CLV) held by Bridges to be no poet, is well-known: "His style and rhythms lay the strongest stress of all our literature on the naked thew and sinew of the English language." This preoccupation, pursued by a Victorian poet intensely given to technical experiment, would go far to explain the triumphs of invention, the extravagance and the oddities of Hopkins's verse.

But this is not the whole story. His bent for technical experiment can be seen to have been inseparable from a special kind of interest in pattern—his own term was "inscape." . . .

It is impossible to discuss for long the distinctive qualities of Hopkins's poetry without coming to his religion. . . .

Hopkins is the devotional poet of a dogmatic Christianity. For the literary critic there are consequent difficulties and delicacies. But there is something that can be seen, and said, at once: Hopkins's religious interests are bound up with the presence in his poetry of a vigour of mind that puts him in another poetic world from the other Victorians. It is a vitality of thought, a vigour of the thinking intelligence, that is at the same time a vitality of concreteness. The relation between this kind of poetic life and his religion manifests itself plainly in his addiction to Duns Scotus, whom, rather than St. Thomas, traditionally indicated for a Jesuit, he significantly embraced as his own philosopher. . . .

There is plainly a context of theological religion, and the devotional interest has plainly the kind of relation to the poetic qualities that has just been discussed. But the activities that go on within this context, even if they make Hopkins unlike Tennyson, Browning, Matthew Arnold, Rossetti, and Swinburne, don't do so by making him in any radical way like T. S. Eliot. It is a framework of the given, conditioning the system of tensions established within it, and these are those of a devotional poet.

F. R. Leavis. *The Common Pursuit* (Penguin, 1962 [c. Chatto and Windus, 1952]), pp. 44, 46–50

The Hopkins who pushed forward beyond Victorian taste in the direction of modern poetics also pushed backward beyond it in his love for the music of Purcell. The Hopkins who was isolated, who had "made writing so difficult," who had to endure being patronised and misunderstood by Patmore and Bridges, had in fact found a place for himself at the most sensitive point in the development of a new awareness.

This is nowhere more clearly seen than in his attitude towards language. The Hopkinsian idiom involves a continual effort to give words the solidity, the completeness of dimension, that one associates with physical things. (We might contrast him, in this respect, with a poet like Swinburne, whose words are always, and inescapably, merely *words.*) In his notebooks Hopkins often writes as if words were natural objects—which, in a sense, they are. If he heard a Lancashire gardener use an unfamiliar dialect word, he would treasure it up and, as often as not, use it in a poem. This explains why he could so consistently censure the literary archaism of Bridges, arguing for a poetry based on living speech, and yet stud his work with expressions likely to baffle the reader. If he heard a word on the lips of a living man, it was alive; if it were merely copied from book to book, it was "culture." All words, to him, were *objets trouvés*; he botanised among them and collected specimens for study. . . .

Hopkins's imagination is not only that of a painter and poet; it is performing one of the chief functions for which we now use the cinema and television—that of presenting an image which moves and takes form while it is focused. The eye grows as it sees: in other words, it magnifies, travels, takes on depth of focus. Nothing stands still in a Hopkins poem. Everything is captured within the one simultaneity of endlessly apprehended movement.

John Wain. *Essays on Literature and Ideas* (Macmillan, 1963), pp. 107–8

HOUSMAN, A. E. (1859–1936)

A Shropshire Lad appeared in 1896. It attracted little attention when it first came out, but it soon began to percolate underground, and after a few years it had become, what it still remains, a powerful influence over artists and the treasured companion of thousands of readers. It was a little book and a masterpiece. Its author, when he published it, was a young man. But he relapsed into silence. He became professor of Latin at Cambridge, he edited one of the obscurest classics he could find— expending enormous labour on it and great wit—and only once or twice in twenty-six years did he publish a poem which proved that his impulses and his powers were undiminished. Now, all new (I think) except the epigram on the Expeditionary Force, forty more poems appear in a vale-dictory volume [*Last Poems*]. . . . He has waited a quarter of a century, and the spirit which prompted the delay is very evident in the preface. At all events, he has made no mistake now. If there were some who thought that any successor to the *Shropshire Lad* must be an anti-climax, they may change their minds. . . .

It may be that when these poems are arranged in chronological order, those who study them will be able to trace some slight development in Mr. Housman's style; but they will record no change in his themes, none in his attitude towards the world. . . . He has an unquenchable desire and no hope. He is acutely sensitive both to the cruelty and the beauty of life, but even when most intensely aware of them he sees both under the shadow of obliterating death and against the background of a blind fea-tureless eternity about which he has no theories and with which he feels not even the slightest and most occasional mystical contact. . . .

So there he leaves us: with a hundred lyrics. It is a peculiar phenome-non in the history of poetry: a hundred lyrics, of which the majority are, humanly speaking, perfect; no failures, no padding, none of the crude attempts of youth, none of the merely habitual versifyings of senility, no effort to conquer any form but the one, none to write a "major work." No English poet has been so ruthless with himself as an artist; that alone would make him unique. . . . What is certain is that he is bound to be a considerable figure in our poetical history, and that his poems, unlike many great works, will continue to be widely read. . . . He is honest and courageous; he incites in the end to honesty and courage; he stimulates enjoyment even while he laments; and his music is so beautiful that what-ever he says must delight. . . . Whatever his limitations may be, he has written scarcely a line which is not perfectly musical, scarcely a word which is not accurate and necessary. He has disciplined himself to such a point that there is at least one poem in his new volume which does not contain a single adjective; he is always lucid, always truthful, and when he uses an epithet he uses it to some purpose. . . . Even hymn-writers could study him to advantage.

J. C. Squire. Essays on Poetry (N.Y., George H.
Doran [ca. 1923]), pp. 152–55, 158–59

In a certain volume that professes to review the poetry of the last thirty years, a volume that deals at some length with all manner of poets, from Lord de Tabley to Mr. Robert Nichols, there are but two references to *A Shropshire Lad,* and each time it is called the work of Mr. Laurence Housman. The mistake in the name we can afford to ignore, as it does at least keep the poems in the family, but surely it is very curious that such a book should be only referred to in passing and not discussed. *A Shropshire Lad* has been reprinted a dozen times, so that in such a detailed survey it could at least have been given some little notice, if only as popular verse—"the sort of thing the public likes." But the fact is, Mr. A. E. Housman's little volume has always been left to speak for itself, for critics have always tended to ignore it. Yet it is reprinted time after time; it has been widely read and, I fancy, widely discussed; its influence upon younger poets has been immense; and it has by this time passed lightly, easily, unopposed, into our great tradition of lyrical verse. Why, then, this silence?

J. B. Priestley. *Figures in Modern Literature*
(John Lane, 1924), pp. 78–79

It is true Housman neither looked nor talked like a poet. He prided himself on this, I think; he was grim and dry and seemed to disdain the artist in himself, to be contemptuous of temperament. But Housman and W. H. Hudson had an attractive quality in common; they were the only two men I knew whose opinions on any subject could never be gauged beforehand. Housman had few friends; but to those he admitted to intimacy he was very faithful. These he entertained usually at the Café Royal; the food and wine were carefully chosen; for Housman had a superfine palate. After dinner came a box at the play. Housman had formerly lived at Highgate, from whence he travelled daily by train to Gower Street. But the story goes that one day someone jumped into the carriage in which he was, and tried to get into conversation with him; upon which he moved to Pinner. . . .

William Rothenstein. *Men and Memories*
(N.Y., Coward-McCann, 1932), p. 39

It is the unanimous verdict of his admirers that Housman is essentially a classic poet. . . . This theory seems to have hoodwinked all his admirers; their awe of Housman as a scholar has blinded them to his imperfections as a poet. . . . The truth is that many of Housman's poems are of a triteness of technique equalled only by the banality of the thought; others are slovenly, and a quantity are derivative—not from the classics, but from Heine, or from popular trends—imperialism, place-nostalgia, games, beer—common to the poetry of his time. *A Shropshire Lad* includes some poems that are worthy of Kipling, others that are unworthy of Belloc, without the excuse of over-production through economic necessity which those writers might have urged. . . .

There are two themes in Housman: man's mortality, which intensifies for him the beauty of Nature, and man's rebellion against his lot. On his treatment of these themes subsists his reputation for classicism. But his presentation of both is hopelessly romantic and sentimental, the sentiment of his poems, in fact, is that of Omar Khayyám, which perhaps accounts for their popularity; . . . .

The fate which Housman's poems deserve, of course, is to be set to music by English composers and sung by English singers, and it has already overtaken them. He will live as long as the B.B.C. [1936]

Cyril Connolly. *The Condemned Playground*
(Routledge, 1945), pp. 47–49, 51

A popularity that would have exhilarated many other poets came to Housman unsought and, it sometimes appeared, against his wishes. Embarrassed by admiration and repelled by curiosity, he persistently averted himself from the consequences of becoming a successful author. Except for the demand that his books should be low-priced, and a fussy concern about the spelling and punctuation of each edition, he lived remote from the literary world and a recluse from his fame. There was almost the mark of anonymity about his work: a voice that could not easily be identified with the outward man. Small in volume and repetitive in theme, his poetry issued from a hidden source and was disciplined into a narrow channel. It had the intensity of a single experience long secreted, which at last forced its way, as if involuntarily, through all the bars of self-restraint. This belated trickle of inspiration, seeping out at the onset of middle age in defiance of the austere and reticent scholar which Housman had by then become, is the peculiar interest, the unravelled problem, of a life otherwise so firmly and methodically organized. He was a remarkable example, even in the Victorian age, of man's struggle to curb and adapt himself to his environment—a struggle, in Housman's case, discernible only in the bitter lyricism of his poetry. . . .

A prim and decorous personage who "appeared to be descended from a long succession of maiden aunts," as donnish gossip described him, Housman was outwardly indistinguishable from the stiffest model of propriety. With his old-fashioned clothes and meticulous habits, his unbending manner and glacial reserve, he reflected all the typical effects of a rigorous self-abnegation. . . .

As a poet of advancing years, who had virtually retired more than a decade ago, Housman was further embarrassed and exasperated by the steady increase of his popularity. Edition after edition of *A Shropshire Lad,* issued in pocket size and at ever-diminishing prices, had both enlarged its circle of readers and in their wake brought a constant solicitation from composers, anthologists or those who merely collect autographs. The ubiquitous little book which threatened to rival the success of *The Rubáiyát* or *Poems of Passion* became, for its author, not only an irksome responsibility but even more a baneful reminder that his poetic reputation was outdistancing his ability to sustain it. Capricious and erratic at best ("Poetry is either easy or impossible," he claimed in self-defence), the muse had lately all but deserted him, just when his audience at home and in America had begun to grow in sympathy as well as in numbers.

George I. Watson. *A. E. Housman: A Divided Life*
(Rupert Hart-Davis, 1957), pp. 9–10, 186

The collected poems of Housman contain one hundred and seventy-five poems, and three short translations of Greek Choruses. Of these, seventy poems were not published during the poet's lifetime, and Housman would certainly have wished the greater number of his posthumously published poems not to have appeared.

The publication of *More Poems* and *Additional Poems* disposes of any idea that the poems suppressed during his lifetime will deepen his reputation. The posthumous poems are interesting, but on the whole they do him a disservice. Although they contain beautiful lines, and even whole poems as good as many he wrote, they say in a cruder form (which sometimes amounts almost to parody) what he had said already, and they do what Housman made the greatest show of wishing to avoid—heighten the reader's curiosity about the biographical background to his poetry.

The number of Housman's poems in which he says what he alone would say, is few. Even in *A Shropshire Lad* and *Last Poems* many poems seem to be background scenery, stage properties, occasional pieces, and exercises which attempt something more successfully achieved in his other poems. Housman tends to unconscious self-parody, which means that he provides other poets, and the critics, with material to ridicule him. This is partly due to the meretricious aspects of his famous pessimism; . . .

There is—one feels—a personal tragedy concealed in this poetry. One's immediate impulse is to think that this is a love tragedy—until one reflects that what is lacking is, simply, love. The real tragedy is the repression which denies life every opportunity of satisfaction; and the theme of the tragedy is the negation of three-quarters of the mature experience of life.

All the same, we are left with a quarter—the experience of life which is called "adolescence." It is, of course, on account of its emotional adolescence that Housman's work is dismissed by most critics today. Certainly these critics are right if they maintain that immaturity prevents Housman from being a great poet. Yet it is not his stature which is in dispute. Housman's work is an Elgin marble presented to us proportioned with a justice that measures itself against other things; minor and immature in comparison with the great, but perfect in relation to that which is inferior.

It is in fact an admirable quality of his that he knows his range. He measures out his few miles of territory and peoples them with his youths and his statues.

It is possible—on the contrary—to argue that for a poet of limited aims, strong ideals, and a perfectionist technique, adolescence—according to Housman's way of interpreting it—is an admirable theme. If Housman's adolescence has a Greek quality, his pessimism is Victorian in a way that seems puzzling today. . . . Like Hardy, when he discovers that the world is not pure, just, beautiful, he is profoundly depressed by what seems to him a cosmic denial of, or indifference to, his ideals derived from Greek art.

The fallacy in this kind of pessimism seems to me a graver criticism of Housman than his protracted adolescence. . . . Housman's own poetry is a repudiation of his pessimism. His poems show, beyond doubt, that beauty and truth do exist, and hence they make the pessimism look silly. Housman would have been no poet if the poet in him had not repudiated his philosophy. And, as a poet, his world of immaturity, though limited, is certain, unconquerable despite his yearning for defeat.

Stephen Spender. The Making of a Poem (N.Y.,
Norton, 1962), pp. 159, 162–64

Alice in Wonderland as a mathematician and the Shropshire Lad as a classical scholar make a pretty pair of *non sequiturs*. The later contrast is perhaps the greater; Carroll stuffed his children's tales with argument, symbol and looking-glass logic, whereas Housman let his verses fall—infrequently—from heaven, reserving his entire intellect for scholarship. Not his intellect alone, though. Only the innocent could assume that the student of dead languages toppled off Wenlock Edge into an eyeless, passionless, folio-lined tomb and sat there poring on Manilius and Propertius, by the world forgot. Far from it. Housman was a critic and a fighter. Around him he saw the shapes of numerous fellow-editors, hostile and menacing as the hosts of Midian. To harry them, whether by species or example, was his moral and intellectual duty. In turn it provided a satiric delight. Much more of the aggressive, conscious Housman was involved in his pedantic battles than ever trickled into metrical lines. . . . Housman does not waste wisdom in these articles [Selected Prose]: he counters prejudice and offers some wilful perversities in the place of proofs. . . . The 1933 performance, under the title "The Name and Nature of Poetry," is his famous prose piece—an "incursion," as he chose to call it, "into the foreign territory of literary criticism." It is not remembered for his scathing judgments on Augustan verse, nor even for the terse pronouncement, "Meaning is of the intellect, poetry is not." That phrase, however, gives the clue. Housman was approaching Lawrence's solar plexus. He arrived at the pit of the stomach, which was bold enough.

What he proceeded to do, and why he caught the aspirants in thousands, was to produce a means test for the floundering critic, and a simple recipe for writing poems. Both were physical. Both have received more deference than their due.

TLS. Jan. 26, 1962, p. 58

HOUSMAN, LAURENCE (1865–1959)

The distinction of Mr. Laurence Housman's workmanship, the nimbleness of his fancy, and the sombre strength of his imagination, must be patent to all readers of Green Arras and Spikenard. No one is more authentically a poet than he; yet the forms of thought which almost exclusively pre-occupy him are to me so foreign, and, to be quite frank, so uninteresting, that I must own myself incapable of doing full justice even to his purely literary merits. He envisages the world from a point of view at which I cannot place myself, even in momentary make-believe. I lack all clue, in my own experience, to the processes of his mind. Consequently, I cannot but apologise in advance for the inadequate and perhaps utterly mistaken appreciation of his talent which is all I can offer. In the preface to his All Fellows, a book of prose legends "with insets of verse," Mr. Housman says, "Unfortunately there are to be found, to sit in judgment, minds of a literal persuasion, that take from the artist his own soul, to set it in the image that he has made." In what I have to say I may fall into this error. But a single attitude of mind is so consistently maintained throughout Mr. Housman's verse, that it is impossible to conceive it as a mere artistic pose.

On the contrary, it seems to me that sincerity is what distinguishes Mr. Housman from most of his school. His kinship with Rossetti, for example, is unmistakable; but what to Rossetti was mythology and decoration, is to Mr. Housman religion and tragic fact. His Catholicism is not like that of some other poets, a mere refuge from pantheism, a robe deliberately woven to clothe and confine an invisible, elusive deity. At the root of his thinking lies, I take it, a genuine Conviction of Sin. It is his instinct to prostrate and abase himself before the rulers of the universe, and to blame himself, not them, for whatever in himself he finds amiss. . . . It is his part rather to kiss the rod, and wreathe it in garlands of flowers; to groan in the fetters of flesh, while damascening their links. Life is to him a prison-house, and it does not occur to him to question the moral authority of the warrant that consigned him to it. The senses are tempters lurking in the darkness. He has not even the consolations of evangelical religion, the faith in another life and in personal salvation. He seems rather to conceive deity as the spirit of nothingness; to regard existence in itself as sin, and more especially the sense of beauty in existence; and to yearn for annihilation as the highest grace to which mankind, guilty of having been born, can possibly aspire. This spirit seems to me to inspire, not only his poems, but the designs which illustrate them: everywhere there is passionate depth of conception and great beauty of line; but everywhere there is a sense of oppression, of contortion, of grey gloom even in the sunshine, which not seldom results in a general effect of ugliness.

William Archer. Poets of the Younger Generation
(John Lane, 1901), pp. 196–97

In these tales [*Moonshine and Clover, A Doorway in Fairyland*] selected from four volumes published previously, the outstanding impression is that of moral sensibility; a heightened sense of the appropriateness of outward beauty to inward—as in the case of Mr. Housman's novel, *The Sheepfold*. But whereas the austerity and calm but torrential force in *The Sheepfold* make it unique, there is variableness in the symmetry and in the power of the telling of these later stories. The fairy-tale, like the question, bespeaks faith in the outcome of what is not yet evolved; and in their prime quality of illusory credibility, Mr. Housman's tales command belief. One reads eagerly until the end has been reached, infinitesimally disaffected by an occasional flaw. Although usually in the fairy-tale, good triumphs over evil and virtue is synonymous with beauty, an appearance of moral insouciance is essential; and in a number of these stories, one sees perhaps too plainly, the wish to bless. Also, evolving from an affection for the child mind and perhaps from a wish not to labour the matter, we have from time to time a kind of diminutive conversation as of an adult in the nursery, which is death to the illusion of make-believe. There is poetic security, however, in the statement, "he closed his eyes, and, with long silences between, spoke as one who prayed," and in the observation that Toonie's wife when her husband did not return, "became a kind of widow"; the pace is especially business-like in this story of Toonie. . . .

One must not monopolize; one need not avenge oneself; in improving the morals of the world, one should begin by improving one's own; these are the mordant preoccupations about which Mr. Housman's fancy plays.

Marianne Moore. *Dial.* Sept., 1923, p. 292

He is an illustrator, a poet, a novelist, a critic, a dramatist. To many readers he is known as the author of *An Englishwoman's Love Letters* (1900), one of the poorest and least characteristic of his writings. A number of his illustrations, chiefly of a grotesque and fanciful kind, appeared in the *Yellow Book*; he has also illustrated Christina Rossetti's *Goblin Market,* Meredith's *Jump to Glory Jane* and a number of his own books. As a poet he is to be counted with the inner circle of the mystics, for he often writes in hieroglyphs of no meaning to the esoteric mind. He has written volumes of verse haunted with a mystic consciousness and a spirit of morbid self-abasement before the thrones, dominions and powers of this universe, verse which places him at the opposite pole to his brother. The severe simplicity, the clear-eyed stoicism give place to cryptic involvements and a tangled spirituality. In wistfulness and melancholy the minds of the brothers meet, but while one faces life's complexities "abashless," . . . the younger brother is diffident and abashed to find himself alive. The note of morbid spiritual wistfulness makes the poems of *Green Arras* (1896), *Rue* (1899), and *Spikenard* (1898) almost un-readable save to the mind rightly attuned. The atmosphere of these poems is that of Medieval Catholicism, with its renunciation of the passions and its desire for virgin purity. *Spikenard* is a series of mystical rhapsodies following the cycle of the ecclesiastical year: *Rue* is the simplest and most intelligible of these volumes. Of the technical beauty of the verse there can be no question, though Mr. Laurence Housman does not rival his brother in mastery of the simplest form.

Harold Williams. *Modern English Writers*
(Sidgwick & Jackson, 1925), pp. 126–27

The Housman who has a Christian (and a very great saint's) name has been so brilliantly versatile that there is hardly a field of letters which he has left untried and unadorned. The overwhelming success of *Victoria* (on and off the stage) has lifted him as high as ambition can reasonably expect to climb. It leaves us speechless with admiration for the author's understanding of a life which he has never been compelled to share.

Dullness is not confined to courts. It is as universal as death. It gives lectures, it preaches sermons, it dines out, it sings comic operas. But it has never been so unerringly drawn as in Mr. Housman's two volumes on the Queen. The treadmill is riotously gay as compared to one of Victoria's dinners. . . .

Now to have made dullness entertaining is surely the triumph of a great artist. . . .

Laurence Housman takes the world of London lightly. It has been in a caressing mood, and he has submitted to, rather than courted, its caresses. Perhaps he recalls from time to time the short-lived enthusiasms of his own life, but we all expect to be remembered a little longer than we remember others. Perhaps he really knows how flawlessly he has done the work he assigned himself. Victoria's reign was a gold mine from which he extracted the pure metal. If the *Shropshire Lad* [by his brother, A. E. Housman] survives the Queen, it will be because of its medium, and because of its straight appeal to the human heart, which will be happy or unhappy for inadequate reasons until the final sun has set. Satire is bound to lose its point, and the mocking laugh be stilled; but nature which promises little and gives less will deceive men to the end.

Agnes Repplier. At. Jan., 1940, pp. 47, 49

HOWARD, ELIZABETH JANE (1923–   )

Bettina von Arnim, the subject of this biographical portrait, was a splendid specimen of the romantic temperament at its most engaging, and lucky enough to be thrown among kindred spirits in the age of sensibility, when romance was all the fashion. Born in 1785, a Brentano, of mixed German and Italian parentage, at the age of fifteen she read Goethe's *Wilhelm Meister* and forthwith decided that the character of Mignon was the one for her to impersonate. She accordingly climbed onto roofs and up apple trees, adopted wayward, unpredictable habits and occasionally dressed the part. . . .

About half this book [*Bettina*] consists of delightful excerpts from Bettina's writings and those of her friends. One wishes there were many more of these, for the authors' joint contribution [E. J. Howard and Arthur Helps] is often sadly at sea. In the course of providing the necessary biographical information they are exasperatingly discursive. Occasionally they introduce acute and well-timed comment, but too often they are tempted to air their views on the Teutonic mentality and road to Hitler. And what have Palmerston, *Punch,* Elinor Glyn, Home Chat and the Welfare State to do with their chosen subject? Moreover the index is ramshackle, and in the text it is difficult to tell where the misprints end and the mistranslations begin. Still, one must be duly grateful to them for bringing Bettina to England.

Ralph Partridge. NS. Sept. 21, 1957, p. 358

One of the trials of becoming an "important" novelist is that critics start to make hay with influences and trends. Miss Howard has already won a high reputation with her two earlier novels, and *The Sea Change* confirms her place among the important women novelists now writing. Though it would be a mistake to saddle her already with high-flown comparisons or influences—particularly since one is much aware of her potentialities and of the quiet confidence with which she is developing along her own lines—it may be worth quoting a remark of Henry James, who was similarly preoccupied with variations in technique. He says: "Really, universally, relations stop nowhere, and the exquisite problem of the artist is eternally but to draw, by a geometry of his own, the circle within which they shall happily *appear* to do so." This is Miss Howard's constant theme, the flux of relationships at a level of intimacy which demands the most delicate investigation if we are to discover truth, and the most intricate selection of situations that will appear both complete and natural.

The Sea Change is told through each of the four characters in turn, and this gives the reader the illusion of being at the centre of the circle of events, although it means the sacrifice of the surprise element and occasionally appears self-conscious because of the need to distinguish in style between the narrators.

TLS. Nov. 20, 1959, p. 673

HUDSON, STEPHEN (1868–1944)

Mr. Hudson's limitations are definite, but they are necessitated by his vision and his artistic purpose. They arise from the fact that being concerned with essentials, stating nakedly the motives of his characters, he has to a great extent to ignore that rich variety of manifestation which the motives create to be their disguise as much as their expression. Certain writers, perhaps the majority, have concerned themselves in detail with the disguises of the motives; have shown them tragically as illusion or in comedy as inconsistency, cant, deceit; but Mr. Hudson is so impatient of them that he takes us immediately to what underlies them, the particular object which by their means the ego wishes to secure. This limits his field of experience, but the limitation is organic, it is a concentration; so that even when the chief human passions are not exhaustively described they are as actually present in our minds as if they were. We feel them all the more strongly, perhaps, because they are assumed; for assumptions are more incontestable than statements; and the true value of economy in art is that, avoiding detailed description, it can convey intensely, and thus make it impossible for us to escape from, a solid mass of assumption. Mr. Hudson's work belongs to this rare and economical order.

Edwin Muir. *Transition* (N.Y., Viking,
1926), pp. 96–97

The only book I have written is an unfinished novel. The volumes which have been published are little more than the framework of it. I have for long been living that novel and am still living it.

I have never had any desire to write for the sake of writing and I am devoid of ambition. I have accumulated a quantity of vital experience which remains in a state of flux. Continuously passing in and out of my consciousness it demands to be sorted out and synthesised. When the chaos becomes unbearable I start writing and go on until the congestion is relieved. It does not follow that a book emerges as a result of this more or less painful parturition. . . .

Finally, the only one of my books which, in my opinion, survives close scrutiny, and, comparatively speaking, satisfies me, is *A True Story*. It is composed of the three volumes *Richard Kurt* (begun in 1911), *Elinor Colhouse* and *Prince Hempseed* and ends with the last episode of *Myrtle*. Thus condensed and closely revised it represents the best I have so far been able to accomplish.

Stephen Hudson in John Gawsworth,
Ten Contemporaries (Ernest Benn, 1932), pp. 99, 101

Stephen Hudson's is not a name commonly met with in assessments of contemporary fiction or in lists of "significant" novelists compiled by earnest critics. His novels were highly praised when they first appeared, but they were never poular, and they have been out of print for some years; the majority of readers likely to appreciate his work probably know him as the man who took over the translating of Proust on Scott-Moncrieff's death. Yet he was an artist in his own right; he added something to the English novel, and no account of our fiction during the past thirty years would be complete without reference to him.

A True Story, the life story of Richard Kurt, was first published in something like its present form in 1930. It consisted of three novels and part of a fourth, all of which had appeared separately under the different titles, which the present publisher might surely have given us. The new edition contains a fifth part, published by itself in 1937, with an epilogue hitherto unpublished. . . . A third novel, *Tony,* giving us Kurt through the eyes of his ne'er-do-well brother, has yet to appear. Hudson's theme throughout the books that make up *A True Story* is that of estrangement. . . . Viewed simply as a study of the Oedipus Complex working like a doom through a man's life, there is no parallel to *A True Story* in our fiction except *Sons and Lovers.* . . . *Sons and Lovers* is in the tradition of the chronicle-novel of Bennett; *A True Story,* as the first pages indicate, is post-Joyce; Hudson has learnt from *A Portrait of the Artist.* . . . Technically, Hudson's method remains interesting. He avoids the *longueurs* of the chronicle novel by taking up and dwelling upon his hero's life at certain points; and he writes always with great economy. . . .

If *A True Story* is judged as a single novel it cannot, I think, be considered a success. It would seem from the way Hudson published his work that his method of composition was one of accretion. The separate parts of the book are brilliantly written and designed, but strung out in sequence they do not form a whole. One is aware all the time of a lack of proportion between the parts. . . . One is saying, of course, that Hudson himself should have been a poet. Yet for all its structural faults, its failure in communication, *A True Story* remains one of the most impressive works of fiction of this century.

Walter Allen. *NSN.* May 21, 1949, pp. 535–36, 538

HUDSON, W. H. (1841–1922)

The Purple Land that England Lost belongs to that rare genus of narratives of adventurous wanderings of which Borrow's *Bible in Spain* and *Lavengro* are perhaps the most prominent examples, that rare genus which, through the subtle blending of fact and fiction, of observation and imagination, of wit, reflection, and insight, ranks less as travel books than as admirably unconventional works of art. . . . Mr. Hudson aims simply at interpreting for us the spirit of the old-fashioned Spanish American, of making us taste the wild free flavour of the *estancia* life. . . . But it is in the respect of quality, of original wit and philosophy of life that *The Purple Land* is a book among books; . . . apparently artless and casual, it is on a far higher plane than some of the carefully arranged and brilliant novels of Stevenson. . . .

Edward Garnett. *The Academy and Literature.*
June 21, 1902, pp. 632–33

For me, Mr. Hudson is the unapproached master of the English tongue. There are no doubt other English writers, though English as a language is woefully lacking in prose towards which one need not be kind—in unassailable prose. Still there are possibly other English writers. But there is no other English writer that you cannot say something about. . . .

Once, Mr. Conrad looked up from reading *Green Mansions* and said: "You can't tell how this fellow gets his effects!" And, a long time after I had agreed that I couldn't tell how Mr. Hudson got his effects, Mr. Conrad continued: "He writes as the grass grows. The Good God makes it be there. And that is all there is to it!"

And there is all there is to it. *Green Mansions* is the only English novel of passion; the *Purple Land* is the only English novel of Romance (and I don't except Mr. Conrad's and my own *Romance*), *Nature in Downland, Hampshire Days, Birds in a Village,* and the *Shepherd's Life* are the only English books about England. And you must remember that Mr. Hudson is an American of New England stock.

I suppose that the chief characteristic of great writers—of writers who are great by temperament as well as by industry or contrivance—is self-abandonment. You imagine Mr. Hudson watching a tiny being and his whole mind goes into the watching: then his whole mind goes into the rendering. Probably there is some delight in the watching and more austerity, more diligence, in the act of recording. That no doubt varies. Turgenev is such another as Mr. Hudson and I can recall no third.

Turgenev, I mean, watched humanity with much such another engrossment as Mr. Hudson devotes to kingfishers, sheep, or the grass of fields and rendered his results with the same tranquility. Probably, however, Turgenev had a greater self-consciousness in the act of writing: for of Mr. Hudson you might as well say that he never had read a book. The Good God makes his words be there.

And I daresay that is how Mr. Hudson, "gets his effects": gazing at his subject with the expressionless passion of a bird of prey: keeping as still as a tree; and then cutting down words to nothing.

Mr. Hudson was born in the Argentine, of New England stock, and when he came to England he was the first member of his family to set foot on these Islands for 250 years. So maybe he descends from the Navigator. At any rate from those facts which may or may not be facts— we may get certain glimpses of Mr. Hudson's secret. For Mr. Hudson is a secret and mysterious alchemist just as much as, or much more than, Dr. Dee.

Perhaps, owing to his Argentine birth and long racial absence from these Islands, Mr. Hudson has escaped the infection of the amateurish way we handle the language when we write: he has escaped the Authorised Version and the Morte d'Arthur and some one's Rabelais and some one else's Montaigne and Sir Thomas Browne's *Urn Burial,* and all the rest of it. . . . Then too, born in the Argentine in remote ages, Mr. Hudson had the advantage of seeing the light in a Latin country—at least I suppose nineteenth-century Argentina *was* a Latin country—and so he was among a population who used words for the expression of thoughts. For, among us Occidentals, it is only the Latin races who use words as clean tools, exactly, with decency and modesty. And just as he has escaped our exhausted use of the language so he has escaped our conventionally insular way of looking at a bill, a flower, a bird, an ivy leaf.

Ford Madox Ford. *Thus to Revisit* (N.Y., Dutton, 1925), pp. 69–70, 74–75

Hudson would walk in with his strange, rather crab-like walk; very tall he was, a little awkward as he sat himself down and disposed of his long limbs, folding his large, beautifully formed hands across his knees. He had haunting eyes, brown with yellow lights, eyes that scarcely moved in their orbits, but remained level, fixed on no particular point, held rather by memories of things past, than by what was before them. His cheek-bones were wide and prominent (once he said he had Indian blood in his veins), and his jaw seemed narrow by comparison, a narrowness emphasized by the shape of his beard. His fine, slightly narrowing brow was deeply furrowed, and his nose was that of a predatory bird. Yes, he put me in mind of those sad, caged eagles at the Zoo, whose motionless eyes look out beyond the bars of their cages, as they sit, desolate prisoners, their wings unused and drooping through the long dull days.

One could listen to Hudson for hours; he could describe, and make absorbingly interesting, things, people, animals; incidents he had observed, whether lately or long ago made no difference to the vividness of his account. The things he noticed were perhaps common things such as others pass by, though he would talk, too, of less usual adventures, especially when he spoke of his early days in the Pampas. . . .

Hudson never worried about his work; he usually spoke with contempt of his own writing and for the writer's craft. Yet no one cared for good literature or respected good writing more. It pleased Hudson to assume indifference, while he really loved to talk of books and writers. And he was fastidious about his own prose. But after a few months in London he longed for open spaces; and he would go off to Hampshire, Devonshire or Cornwall, or to the East Coast.

William Rothenstein. *Men and Memories* (N.Y., Coward-McCann, 1932), pp. 40, 160

Edward Garnett says it was the publication of *The Naturalist in La Plata* (1892) and *Idle Days in Patagonia* (1893) which made Hudson famous; but according to the *Manchester Guardian* not a single work of his had a circulation of a thousand copies up to 1910, when *A Shepherd's Life* just topped the thousand mark. A Civil Service pension of £150 was awarded to Hudson in 1901 "in recognition of the originality of his writings on natural history," and it was not till twenty years later—in the year before his death—that he was able to resign it on the ground that he needed it no longer, as his books brought him in enough to live on. In the twenty years intervening he had made two remarkable successes in *Green Mansions: A Romance of the Tropical Forest* (1904) and *Far Away and Long Ago: a History of my Early Life* (1918). But to the end he was a writer prized by the discerning few rather than by a large circle of readers.

> J. W. Cunliffe. *English Literature in the Twentieth Century* (N.Y., Macmillan, 1933), pp. 259–60

Of his work I continue to think *A Naturalist in La Plata* and *Idle Days in Patagonia* the best examples. The former is a collection of essays reprinted from magazines now of an obsolete type; the latter a narrative presumably based upon journals kept at the time. The material is authentic, and the manner plain, clear, and attractive. And although the English books are full of good observation, curious incidents, and excellent quiet writing, the freshness of his early first-hand acquaintance with nature is never quite recaptured.

> Frank Swinnerton. *The Georgian Scene* (N.Y., Farrar and Rinehart, 1934), pp. 142–43

HUGHES, RICHARD (1901–   )

The loss of this strange story would have been a real loss, and for one reader at least it has done much to bury the unsavoury memory of upwards of a hundred new works of fiction. . . . *A High Wind in Jamaica* is not only unsentimental, but brutal . . . in the simple and quiet fashion of the ancient Hebrews or of the Saga-writers. . . . Though not a satire, the story produces an effect like that of *Candide* in a less sophisticated way, and in the lucidness and impartiality of the narrative, it is not unlike Voltaire.

> Lyn Ll. Irvine. *NA.* Sept. 28, 1929, p. 830

Richard Hughes looks almost too good to be true. If he weren't a writer, one would suspect that he was an actor impersonating an author—a nineteenth-century author. He wears a beautifully trimmed pepper-and-salt beard and luxuriant moustache, the ends of which he twists and twirls absently as he talks, his eyes somehow simultaneously peering out from under thick gray brows at his companion and the middle distance. He smokes a solid pipe, of course, and does not wear an overcoat in December.

Except for the years during World War II, Hughes has always been a writer. "I always said I could never afford to hold a job," he laughed. . . . Hughes believes he may hold the unique distinction of receiving the worst degree ever awarded by Oxford—a double fourth in English and Classics. While still an undergraduate he had a play put on in London, and published stories, verse and criticism. He met and received help from Bennett, Yeats, Masefield and Robert Graves, "especially Graves, who was nearest my own age."

In Hazard, the second Hughes novel, was prompted by a real ship caught in a real storm. Hughes went to see the battered ship and the survivors and read the log. It was while he was working at the Admiralty during the war that he decided to undertake a long historical novel of modern times culminating in World War II, of which project *The Fox in the Attic* is the first volume. After the war, he put in a stint writing for the movies. He spent five years writing *The Fox in the Attic* in Wales and in cafes in Spain. Commenting upon his spareness of output in over forty years of writing, he says, "I am a very slow writer. Everyone tells me that. But a writer does not choose his subjects or his stories. He is compelled by them. I am compelled now to write this story. Of course, in an enterprise of this sort it is always a race between the publisher and the undertaker."

Robert Gutwillig. *NYT*. Feb. 4, 1962, pp. 1, 35

In 1929 Richard Hughes sprang into fame with *A High Wind in Jamaica,* which seems to me a work of genius. Since then he has written short stories, but only one other novel, *In Hazard*—and that was twenty-three years ago. Like E. M. Forster and Glenway Wescott, he seemed to have abandoned his wonderful gift for novel writing. Now, however, he comes back with a most ambitious and exciting enterprise.

If one has never read him before, the exceptional quality of his writing becomes evident upon the first page. We are then gripped throughout by qualities in which he is unsurpassd by any novelist alive—a concentrated, telling style that flows rapidly, a rich inventiveness in memorable characters and episodes, an intelligence always on the qui vive, a poet's large understanding of our tragic and comic human destiny.

Yet only a tentative, interim report on the book is possible. A critic could throw little light upon *Great Expectations* or *The Possessed* after reading only the first quarter of either masterpiece. I now find myself in a similar fix. *The Fox in the Attic* is not the first novel in a series but the opening section of a novel in three or four volumes. The author describes this as "a long historical novel of his own times culminating in the Second World War"; its title is *The Human Predicament,* and we are given no other hint about its character. . . .

Like Tolstoy in *War and Peace,* Mr. Hughes may not always succeed in fusing the background of historical facts and personages with the world created by himself. Yet if in the volumes still to come he can maintain the imaginative energy revealed here, the result must prove one of the major novels of our time.

Raymond Mortimer. NYT. Feb. 4, 1962, pp. 1, 35

Now Richard Hughes has published the first part of a three- or four-volume novel to be called *The Human Predicament,* assuming—and why not?—that a study of the English and German upper classes between the wars can add something to what we know of that subject. . . . His has been for years a name more honored than spoken. He has written two other novels, *A High Wind in Jamaica* and *In Hazard,* the first over thirty and the second over twenty years old. These books are very distinguished, the second and less celebrated being the more completely achieved—it is an extraordinary and almost successful attempt to over-go Conrad on the hurricane at sea, and combines a striking immediacy of effect with the accomplishment of profounder purposes. As it seemed that these books would have no successor, *The Fox in the Attic* is an unconvenanted boon to modern English fiction.

In his earlier work this very elaborate writer cultivated, when it suited him, a sort of ingenuousness, and let-me-tell-you-this-tale approach. There are reminiscences of this in *The Fox in the Attic,* though it is a sober, heavily-built piece, ambitious of permanence and grandeur. But if the scope is Tolstoyan, the manner is often more like Pasternak's, and there are carefully inlaid emblematic elements. These, however, do not prevent Hughes from speaking directly and at length to his thesis.

Frank Kermode. PR. Summer, 1962, pp. 466–67

HUGHES, TED (1930–   )

Complete communication is the target and the accomplishment of a new writer, Ted Hughes, whose book [*The Hawk in The Rain*] is the September choice of the Poetry Book Society. I am not surprised that he won an American First Publication award, judged by W. H. Auden, Stephen Spender and Marianne Moore. His verse is simple, sensuous and passionate, as direct as an arrow from a bow; and whether he is writing of a girl secretary, "all Day like a starling under the bellies of bulls She hurries among men, ducking, peeping," or of a famous poet wearing "the haggard stony exhaustion of a near-Finished variety artist," or of thought, like a fox, that "enters the dark hole of the head," Mr. Hughes compels instant attention. This is the most praiseworthy first collection that has come my way for years past; and it supplies a welcome pointer away from obscurity.

William Kean Seymour. *Poetry R*. Jan.-Mar., 1958, p. 43

Mr. Hughes's second volume [*Lupercal*] is startlingly better than his first. He is looking for the numinous, he is facing the terror of our contemporary world, and he finds, paradoxically, his central image of the numinous in the blind, instinctual thrust (in itself, in a way, an image of terror) of the animal and vegetable worlds. The most perfect short poem in this volume is one about a snowdrop, traditionally an image of pathetic and over-confident frailty. Mr. Hughes's emphasis is on the almost terrifying strength that pushes up the snowdrop's head through the harsh winter soil. The sympathy of the earlier volume with the brute creation has now become humorous and humanized. . . . It is a remarkable achievement of Mr. Hughes's to have made a narrow, vivid, rather obsessive range of images (images of blind but beautiful greed, terror, fierceness, lust for survival) seem so generally relevant to our contemporary world.

TLS. April 15, 1960, p. 238

Hughes's strength is that he can write about animals with a taut, respectful accuracy, not diluting nor prettying their experience but by force of resonant, mastered detail, investing it with a dramatic stature that makes it unignorable and often magnificent. He compels our attention to areas of sensation that are common to humans and animals, although in his best poems this is never felt to be a primary conditioning motive—it is simply what experiencing the poem involves. The message, if one wants one, occurs after the experience and it can take a variety of shapes such as can proliferate from significant real experience.

Unfortunately, this is not always the case; often Hughes seems to find that in order to effectively celebrate the animal he must correspondingly disfigure human experience into caricature situations of either Emotion or Intellect. "Thrushes" offers an instance of this—with the introduction of that leaden "With a man it is otherwise," the poem, which has opened excellently on to the "attent sleek thrushes on the lawn," tails off into spiritless generalization and cloying hosannas. It is in poems like this where, ironically enough, he seems consciously bent on extending his range, that Hughes's limitations are most glaringly to be perceived. Once he begins to recommend, in something approaching an earnest discursive idiom, that humans behave as animals (once, that is, there is no question that this is what he is recommending) then the terms on which he may be judged alter crucially; he ceases to be a finely alerted dramatist of personal situations and assumes the role of teacher and prophet.

On these terms, his celebration of the instinct can easily be made to seem eccentric, witlessly primitive and even dangerous (it becomes open to objective comparison with alternative, more intricately qualified prose recommendations, for instance).

Ian Hamilton. L. June, 1963, p. 63

HULME, T. E. (1883–1917)

He had a passion for general ideas, a remarkable gift for emphatic, vivid exposition, and much imagination. . . . Hulme is a decidedly "cindery" thinker. . . . His standpoint has some affinity with that of Mr. Santayana —"Truths of discourse" backed by "animal scepticism." The temperament which lies behind the applications he made of his philosophy is, however, utterly different. . . .

To follow a long train of abstract argument was not his *forte*. The natural form for him would have been a sort of *Zarathustric,* aphoristic, less excited, more analytical. Indeed such was the book he intended to write. . . . The peculiar flavour of it would have been derived from what was both disconcerting and stimulating in his personality—the clash between a self-assertive, sceptical temperament and an intellect which insisted upon discipline with the intransigence of a Pascal or a Loyola.

Speculations confirms what Hulme's friends felt when he was killed serving with the Royal Marines near Nieuport in September, 1917, that one of the most inquiring minds in the young generation had gone out.

Affable Hawk [Desmond MacCarthy]. NS. Jan. 12, 1924, p. 897

What appealed to me particularly in him was the vigour and sincerity of his thought. He was capable of kicking a theory as well as a man downstairs when the occasion demanded. . . . He was a man who had no regard for personal fame or notoriety, and he considered that his work lay entirely in the future. His whole life was a preparation for the task of interpretation which he had set himself. . . . His passion for truth was uncontrolled. . . . Like Plato and Socrates, he drew the intellectual youth of his time around him. [1924]

Jacob Epstein in T. E. Hulme, *Speculations*,
ed. Herbert Read (Routledge and Kegan
Paul, Sec. Ed., 1936), p. vii

If Hulme had one foe exposed before all others to his constant invective, it was obscurantism. He was not, by design, a systematic thinker. He was, in one sense at least, a poet; he preferred to see things in the emotional light of a metaphor rather than to reach reality through scientific analysis. His significance is none the less real; he knew very certainly that we were at the end of a way of thought that had prevailed for four hundred years; in this, and in his premonition of a more abstract philosophy of life, he had advanced the ideals of a new generation. [1924]

Herbert Read, Introduction to T. E. Hulme.
Speculations (Routledge and Kegan Paul,
Sec. Ed., 1936), p. xv

No layman put the case against Humanism more pungently than Thomas Ernest Hulme. Rousseau had proclaimed that man was naturally good and perfectible by his own efforts; on the contrary Hulme declared that man was by nature a poor, limited creature, who could be saved only by the grace of God. . . . Hulme denounced the Romantic poets, even the best of them, as "sloppy," always moaning or whining about something, always craving for the infinite, and wrapping up the truth in semireligious veils of "cosmic emotion." The poetry of the future would be cheerful, dry, and sophisticated, and exceedingly exact in its choice of words, since poetry—so he put it—"is no more nor less than a mosaic of words."

Herbert J. C. Grierson and J. C. Smith.
A Critical History of English Poetry
(Chatto and Windus, 1950), pp. 499–500

The second poets' club developed into the *Salon* of 1913-14 as Hulme's interest was turning to modern art, and the *salon* reflects this trend. The impression of contemporaries is that Hulme was more concerned with the visual arts than with poetry; his friends were principally painters and sculptors, and probably his closest friend was the sculptor Jacob Epstein. . . . He defended Epstein against the violent criticism occasioned by his work for the British Medical Association Building and for the Wilde Memorial in Paris, and with a brief series of *New Age* articles upheld the modern, geometrical, nonrepresentative art. . . . Hulme became known then, less through the poetry clubs and his poetic theory than through the Frith St. *Salon* and his theories on the new art; and it was not until 1914 that he found some demand for his lectures. . . . While he cannot be considered a prominent critic and theorist of the years 1908-17, neither can he be dismissed as a thinker of no significance for the artists of the period. . . . Imagism *could* have had its source in Hulme.

Stanley K. Coffman, Jr. *Imagism* (Norman, Okla.; Univ. Oklahoma Pr., 1951), pp. 49–50

An influence on Eliot probably second only to Pound was T. E. Hulme, who was killed in the war in 1917 at the age of thirty-four and whose work was not published until 1924, when Herbert Read edited a collection of his papers as *Speculations*. Hulme was a translator of Bergson and Sorel, a rationalist Catholic, classicist, militarist, and premature fascist. His notebooks circulated among friends in manuscript, and it is certain that Eliot, Pound, and a number of other critics were familiar with them long before their publication. From Hulme, Eliot to some extent derived his classical tradition, his concept of dogma as being the vital element in religion, for the sake of which it is possible to "swallow" sentiment and ritual, and his principal example of art and criticism in the service of religious orthodoxy and political reaction. . . . Hulme, in the quarter-century since his death, has acquired a reputation as the standard-bearer for traditional criticism. Besides Eliot, his influence is marked on Pound . . . , Allen Tate and others of the Southern school, the neo-humanists, T. Sturge Moore, and, in the other camp, [I. A.] Richards and Herbert Read.

Stanley Edgar Hyman. *The Armed Vision* (N.Y., Knopf, 1952), p. 98

During the years 1908-1912 he was the center of a shifting group of writers, painters, sculptors, architects, and philosophers over whom he exercised a considerable influence. He had the qualities of leadership. He was vigorous, aggressive, and original. He was also blessed with a sufficient income to allow him to devote all his time to study and controversy. . . .

. . . a group of five poems were printed with the exact if somewhat amusing title, "Complete Poetical Works of T. E. Hulme," as a supplement to Ezra Pound's *Ripostes*. . . . He was, in his own sense of the word, and likely in the truest sense, a poet. He may have written only five poems as such; that is, five compositions in the nature of lyrics; and these were done only as exercises, for purposes of illustration—but from the mass of his notes one may pick dozens of the most astonishing poetic statements, as concentrated as the finest *hokku* from Japan, as penetrating as the epigrams of Wilde, as fresh and startling in their imagery as the best efforts of his associates and followers, the professional imagists. The five lyrics are unpretentious, and this manner has been made familiar by hundreds of writers since, but if we think of Hulme as a philosopher, with a critical interest in poetry, writing in the days before the War, when the new poetic styles were really new, we will be able to appreciate their merit.

Glenn Hughes. *Imagism and the Imagists*
(Bowes and Bowes, 1960), pp. 10, 18

HUTCHINSON, R. C. (1907–   )

Shining Scabbard is, in effect, a French novel brilliantly translated at the moment of birth into English. The subject, as well as the manner, is French; the story, the foundations of which are laid in French provincial life, emerges out of a scaffolding of grand sentences which cross and recross with superb effect. . . . There are five hundred pages in this highly imaginative book and every one is good solid work.

Graham Bell. *NSN*. Sept. 26, 1936, p. 440

R. C. Hutchinson is an ambiguous figure on our literary horizon, gigantic, but blurred in outline and nebulous in substance. His admirers have made very high claims for him, and on at least two occasions, so the cover of this new book [*Elephant and Castle*] informs me, Mr. Day Lewis has singled him out for abiding fame. It is prophesied, in fact, that the wraith-like giant will solidify into a monolith, and that the English novel of our time may be represented for posterity by these colossal and far-flung narratives. Since no literary prophecy is safe, none can be safely contradicted. But we have the right to back our own fancies to the limit of our critical reputations, and I would happily lay odds of five hundred to one against the survival of Mr. Hutchinson. . . .

Can anyone seriously say that Mr. Hutchinson has contributed to our inheritance? My difficulty in writing about *Elephant and Castle* is that I cannot envisage the defence which I feel called upon to refute. . . . One thing must certainly be granted: Mr. Hutchinson's theme and intentions are high ones. He is in no sense a lightweight. . . . In fact, the texture of *Elephant and Castle* is quite peculiarly displeasing. Mr. Hutchinson writes with a lush flamboyance which cloys and sickens. . . .

It matters very little whether we are in sympathy with Mr. Hutchinson's view of life. What we require of him is that our own apprehension of life should be somehow deepened. . . . In *Elephant and Castle* the characters, the places and the situations are grossly *contrived;* any one of them could be dug out from the particular context of this book and rebedded without the loss of any "vital reality" in almost any pretentious popular novel of our time. Once again it is a case of life escaping, despite, or perhaps because of, the superficial gusto with which the task has been approached. *Elephant and Castle* has all the air of being a "great" novel. There are a lot of pages, a lot of people, a lot of events and a lot of purple. "Vital reality" is not a phrase which I would have chosen, but perhaps it may serve to describe what this novel utterly fails to exhibit.

Philip Toynbee. *NSN.* April 30, 1949, p. 446

Mr. R. C. Hutchinson has written *The Stepmother* with his usual craftsmanship, but I cannot feel that it will add greatly to his reputation. This tale . . . is conscientiously—some might say, temperately—written. It moves slowly with a kind of heavy, syrupy integrity to a climax that the reader has foreseen for more than a hundred pages. The Possessive Mum is one of the best-known skeletons in the English family cupboard and Mr. Hutchinson deceives himself if he imagines that he is springing any surprise on us by exhibiting her as a sinister novelty.

John Raymond. *NSN.* Sept. 17, 1955, p. 341

HUXLEY, ALDOUS (1894–1963)

Like Gide in the *Faux Monnayeurs,* among the other personages to whom he introduces us in his new long novel, Mr. Aldous Huxley includes a novelist, engaged upon one of the many parallel themes treated by Mr. Huxley himself. Like Gide's Oncle Edouard, Mr. Huxley's Philip Quarles keeps a note-book, pages of which are interpolated in the text; he, too, plays an individual part, but is also a convenient mouthpiece for the author's own personal interjections. Between the pair of novelists, the

real and the fictitious, there exists an inevitable sympathy, and even a
certain correspondence of outward traits. These superficial resemblances,
though aware of the danger he runs in thus confusing creature and
creator, a critic of Mr. Huxley's work would be inhuman did he not
exploit. "His books might be so much better," Mr. Huxley's imaginary
novelist exclaims, "if only he could resign himself to being less amusing."
Well, that is a suggestion which any of Mr. Huxley's admirers may have
ventured, during a perusal of his earlier work: much, much better! But
now Mr. Huxley has produced a book far less amusing than his wont,
indeed, hardly amusing at all, and the critic wonders whether, perhaps, he
has not made a mistake. It is a development, of course, bound sooner or
later to occur. Ever since the publication of *Crome Yellow,* a charming
little satire in the Romantic vein, agreeably pranked and diversified by
the promise of nobler things, Mr. Huxley would seem to have been
gradually and painfully struggling outside the narrow limits of his original
sentimental-satiric manner, a leg here, and arm there, as uncomfortable
as Alice in the White Rabbit's parlour, stretching an enormous hand
through the tiny window-frame and making determined snatches in the
void, listening for the resultant tinkle of broken glass. *Crome Yellow*
showed Mr. Huxley already grown rather large for his surroundings, but
still small enough to run up and down stairs, slam the doors, and make
"apple-pies" in the sheets of empty beds; *Antic Hay* and *These Barren
Leaves* represent progressive stages of his imprisonment. At last, he has
fairly prised the roof off, and is free to wander where he pleases. He
reaches the Mad Tea Party; *Point Counter Point* is a report of its proceedings. The March Hare and the Mad Hatter, figures vaguely recognizable as, say—I make the identification at random—Mr. D. H. Lawrence and Mr. Middleton Murry, are seated side by side amid a disarray
of unwashed plates and tea-cups (the condition of modern life as they
envisage it), and enjoy prolonged controversial exchanges, their general
tone often strangely reminiscent of the peculiar gloomy intensity of that
historic encounter. Meanwhile, they lean their elbows upon the shy re-
sentful Dormouse, or playfully thrust him head downwards into the pot.
He is the acutely self-conscious, morbidly incapable young man whom
Mr. Huxley loves to depict. Grimly introverted and mercifully aloof from
the noisy discussions of his friends, he broods the usual unsuccessful love-
affair. Poor young man! his fate, no doubt, was predestined; still, in his
new avatar Mr. Huxley, I think, might really have allowed him a different
object for his passion; it is cruel to have fobbed him off like this with a
palpable *réchauffé* of Myra Viveash!

Yes, the old tricks of characterization recur, though blurred and con-
siderably distorted like the tattooings on a fat man's skin. The familiar
personages, once endowed with an unpleasant yet vivid life of their own,

are more languid in their movements; their entities are less concrete. The relation of the characters to one another is less distinct than of old, and the entire novel, gaining in dignity and magnitude, has proportionately lost in shape.

LL. Nov., 1928, pp. 517–19

In any consideration of Mr. Huxley it is *Antic Hay* which must be taken into chief account. There the method is wholly justified, masque and anti-masque composed together, the formal attributes fused with the flesh beneath; the meditation on society which takes up so much time in other books reduced to action; repose as in Gumbril's *nuit blanche,* flight in his endless taxi-ride with Myra Viveash, or in the whirl of the starlings' flight round his father's house. In that portrait of an old architect, with his model of London as Wren would have built it, Mr. Huxley gives the best account of his most positive preoccupation, the love of order and splendour, wholly human, rational and lovely, the harmonious productions of man's spirit. . . .

The reason of this criticism is to ask why Mr. Huxley, identified within his limits as the Perfect Writer, should—save for an occasional idyll between girl and boy—lead his masque and its anti-masque so far, arrest it at a tragic point, and leave the dance unresolved. It does not occur in music or in painting, whatever the theme. And the answer seems to be that Mr. Huxley is the perfect mirror of our age, where misery and failure, idiocy and conclusions ludicrous or grotesque, have their perfect excuse and explanation; and where it seems impossible to account for human excellence or achievement any more. . . .

As a novelist Mr. Huxley gives no answer. Once only, at the end of his most brilliant *exposé* of human vanities, *Those Barren Leaves,* he admits the question and attempts an answer. . . . And Mr. Huxley . . . leaves his protagonist, a man he has drawn with interest and some love, alone with the moon and a cypress-tree, hastily and conventionally described, with no more than a pious hope that they will—in fact, that they must—lead him to some unique vision that will save the situation —mankind's and his own and Mr. Huxley's. And with that we are left with that.

Myra Butts in *Scrutinies,* Vol. II, coll. Edgell
Rickword (Wishart, 1931), pp. 81–82, 87–88

. . . the attitude towards life he has hitherto compelled us to share is one in which no one can remain contented for long together. It is detached, exacting—and inconclusive, and we find ourselves perpetually looking down on human nature; we never have the exhilaration of looking up.

To share his detachment is, for a while, flattering; for though we may often recognize our own failings and ignoble predicaments in his pages, these facts exist in our own lives, we know, in contexts which are omitted from his books and relieve them of much of their meanness. It is primarily, therefore, other people who appear to us to be mercilessly exposed. This is agreeable until we realize that, after all, it is as necessary to respect and like at least a few other people as it is to respect ourselves. And this Mr. Aldous Huxley seldom, or never, allows us to do. True, there is one character in *Point-Counter-Point* in whose behalf our admiration is claimed. . . . But what is Rampion? A point of view, a conduit-pipe of theories upon life.

It is not true, as has been said, that there are no amiable people in Mr. Huxley's stories; there are. But the aspects of them to which he attends are seldom admirable, and either chill or make us despise them. . . .

No one can deny the importance of his work to his contemporaries; and the interest which it has roused confirms it. He has succeeded in recording modes of feeling and thinking characteristic of his own generation which have never been described before. He has made his contemporaries more aware of their own responses, moral, amoral, æsthetic and intellectual; their indifference, impatience, obtusity, disappointment, sensibility. He has diagnosed subtly and mercilessly the diseases of modern self-consciousness, and described the ignobly comic falsifications of emotions which result from them. But this is not for the critic the central fact about him. His distinguishing mark is that he stands out as the most deeply and widely cultured of modern novelists. I am not sure that even in the past one can point to any other writer of fiction who has illumined his picture of life with cross lights drawn from an equal familiarity with contemporary knowledge and theory. George Eliot only comes near to him. . . .

The peculiarity of Mr. Huxley's work is that not only science in all its branches is frequently laid under contribution, but also the history of art, music, poetry, medicine, society and philosophy. What is disconcerting is the contrast between the extraordinary many-coloured richness of the light he pours upon his subjects, and that these subjects are taken from small and often stuffy corners of the big common world of experience. He is the most universal of novelists in his references and one of the most limited in focus. His constant theme is love and sex, and the result of his investigations is dissatisfaction, or more positively disgust. . . . This preoccupation he shares with his age, which is thinking as hard and confusedly about sex as the one preceding it thought about religion. Hence the peculiar interest of his fiction to his contemporaries. . . .

Clearly there is little that the critic can tell Mr. Aldous Huxley about his work that he does not already know himself. . . . Critics must accept him as a writer not "deep" but "wide." They must accept his novels and stories being disquisitions illustrated by characters, since his supreme merit lies in width of reference, and in putting facts in juxtaposition which his omnivorous reading and perpetual reflection have assembled. The deep pleasure in reading Mr. Huxley lies in following the movement of his mind. He is aware also of the irritation produced in some readers by his inevitably discursive methods.

Desmond MacCarthy. *Criticism* (Putnam, 1932),
pp. 236–39, 244

As we read Mr. Huxley for the first time, we are struck by the acuteness of his observations, impressed by the facility of his generalizations—by his knack of discovering an unexpected and witty analogy between two apparently quite unrelated aspects of life and art. But then a sort of weariness possesses our minds. . . . He is so blankly reasonable, so right. It is as if he had introduced us into a large well-furnished library, embellished with photographic reproductions of all the best pictures, stocked with copies of all the latest publications, had switched on a brilliant unshaded lamp, hurried us around the apartment, snatching down a learned volume here and there—and had left us, rather abruptly, on the threshold, interested yet a little out of breath. What next? But to this question Mr. Huxley does not pretend to propose an answer. The mind is its own place—neat, aseptic, somewhat comfortless. And, beyond the territories illuminated by an active academic intelligence, there is only limbo—the obscurity of pain, disease and death, and the dim half-fabulous regions—the imaginary Land of Cockayne—where we *might* enjoy ourselves, did the altitude of our brows, and the general bulkiness of our intellectual equipment, not make it extremely difficult to pass its gate.

Peter Quennell in *The English Novelists*, ed. Derek
Verschoyle (Chatto and Windus, 1936), p. 254

Mr. Huxley tells a story of Firbank meeting him in the Café Royal: "He gave his usual agonized wriggle of embarrassment and said, 'Aldous—always my *torture.*' " I think I feel the same way about him. At school I borrowed *Limbo* from one master only to have it confiscated by another, while the Frenchman who let me read Mallarmé's *L'Après-Midi d'un Faune* for extra studies had to turn repeatedly to Huxley's translation to find out what it meant. I bought *Crome Yellow* out of some prize money. After that his novels and stories continued to dominate my horizon, so enormously competent, so clever, sympathetic, and on the spot. During the twenties it was almost impossible for the average clever young man not to imitate him—just as he once had imitated Norman Douglas, Firbank, and Eliot. Now that I have been free for a few years I see *Crome Yellow* as his best book, backed up by *Limbo, Antic Hay,* and his short stories. His early work had a natural gaiety, his satire lacked the heavy hand of the moralist: Science, with its horrible plausibility, had not yet walked off with Art. The first forty years of Aldous Huxley's literary career have been marred by over-production, for which the present economic system is to blame. Conventionality of thought and diction, fatigue of style result—but his long silence since *Brave New World* is the most hopeful augury for the remaining threescore.

Cyril Connolly. *Enemies of Promise* (N.Y.,
Doubleday, 1960 [c. 1938]), pp. 293–94

Huxley's work as a whole has taken the form of a thinly disguised auto-biographical sequence. Its shape has been determined by the author's changing attitude to life, which has always found its corresponding intellectual expression (reviewers were wont, as a matter of course, to prostrate themselves before his overwhelming "intellect"). The problem for the critic therefore lies in the difficulty of keeping a just balance between Huxley's changing responses to life, the artistic productions which have arisen from and been shaped by those responses, and the resultant ideas which the novelist has abstracted, as it were, from the creative process, and which he now arrays formidably and somewhat menacingly before his public. . . . To-day there confronts us, not the sardonic portrayer of futility, but the prophet and the philosopher of Enlightenment, of Liberation, through a species of mystical contemplation. And this prophet, or teacher, quite overshadows, if he has not finally eliminated, the artist.

What in fact is the nature of the teaching which emerges? It is rather a simple doctrine. Man's final end, according to Huxley's most recent work, a compendium entitled *The Perennial Philosphy* (1946), is nothing less than "unitive love-knowledge of the Divine Ground," a knowledge which one must attain by "making oneself loving, pure in heart and poor in spirit," through "a discipline more arduous and unremitting than any imposed by ecclesiastical authority"—a discipline which involves, indeed, a "total dying to self."

That there is, in reality, more than a marked affinity between Huxley's earlier and his later work and ideas we shall discover if we scrutinize the underlying structure of the novelist's and the thinker's world. The fictional universe which he creates and populates possesses certain well-defined features which might be said to be explicable in the light of a fundamental *discontinuity*. If we say of Huxley's characters that they are static and isolated, that a certain impersonal detachment shows itself in their creator's attitude towards them, and that at the same time their existence presumes a context of pointlessness, we shall have sketched a readily recognizable picture of Huxley's constant frame of reference. For, by a curious irony, while Huxley himself would claim a radical discontinuity between the divergent attitudes to life—"Pyrrhonic hedonism" and contemplative mysticism—which in turn grow out of and condition his earlier and his later work, in fact the two originate in a common dislocation of being; the one exaggeration of attitude finds its balancing counterpart in the other; and the irony is pointed in the fact that discontinuity itself can even be said to be the only continuous factor in decisive operation throughout Huxley's artistic career.

D. S. Savage in *The Novelist as Thinker,* ed. B. Rajan
(Dennis Dobson, 1947), pp. 9–11

It would be too much to say that the metaphysical convulsions that seized Mr. Huxley under mescalin excessively try our patience. He is usually, in this [*The Doors of Perception*] as in all of his more supersonic flights, well worth attending. One might wish, however, considering the unusual nature of his spree, that he had given us a somewhat briefer review of his current intellectual preoccupations and a somewhat fuller account of exactly what happened, objectively and mechanistically, on that recent bright May morning.

Berton Roueché. *NYT.* Feb. 7, 1954, p. 6

Huxley has always shown a good deal of skill in giving us the illusion that he is quite detached or neutral. It is, however, almost entirely the illusion of one form of detachment, that which the intelligent writer may achieve—or seem to achieve—by the practice of intellectual discipline. Unfortunately for himself as a novelist he has practically nothing of that power—which Joyce, for instance, possessed in abundance, and which is essential to the truly effective novelist—whereby a writer associates himself sympathetically (or, if one prefers, empathically) with his characters in all their feelings, while skillfully concealing the fact from us. His intellect works too hard for that. His human sympathy is limited. . . .

These, then, are novels of ideas which are rationalizations of certain sentiments, instincts, dispositions of soul in a number of characters selected to convey the author's life view and to point his moral. But the general conclusion, or moral, or practical lesson, or general principle of the author's thought or life view does not in the end emerge with anything like the clarity one expects from a man of such apparently superlative intelligence. All one can do is to induce it confusedly and unsatisfactorily from the underlying spirit of invective, which one feels to be just as instinctive and emotional as in any congenital novelist. One is finally driven to conclude that all Huxley's intellectual paraphernalia conceals an intelligence at war with itself, or struggling vainly for a clear position from which to attack. And while in this essay I am interested directly only in the early novels, it would be unrealistic not to bear in mind also the constant gropings and changes of position in his later work.

The result has been that he has from the beginning attempted satire and achieved only what I have called invective. The absence of a firm standpoint made this inevitable, since of its nature satire implies a clear standpoint, or acceptable norm, from which to castigate. . . . The impression a rereading of these novels gives one today is of an arid and desiccated waste, bordering at many points on jungles of odorous despair, always blessedly watered by a constant dew of bitter wit and otherwise illuminated not by intelligence but by brilliant intellectual pyrotechnics.

Sean O'Faolain. The Vanishing Hero (N.Y., Grosset
and Dunlap, 1956), pp. 5, 8–9, 22

In his new book [*Brave New World Revisited*] Mr. Huxley surveys the technological advances and political trends of the last thirty years, and considers that, on the available evidence, the future is more likely to resemble his own Brave New World than the world of *1984.* . . . Refering to *1984,* he points out, with some justice, that "recent developments in Russia, and recent advances in science and technology, have robbed Orwell's books of some of its gruesome verisimilitude," and he considers that the further advance of totalitarian rule will be effected less by violence than by the increasing use of propaganda, brain-washing, subliminal persuasion and the various tranquillizing or stimulant drugs. The greater part of the book is taken up with a comparative analysis of these non-violent instruments of power, and the facts which Mr. Huxley has assembled are both fascinating and extremely frightening. He feels, as he says, a good deal less optimistic now than he did in 1932, when Hitler had not yet come to power and Stalinism had hardly got into its stride. . . .

This is a saddening book, not only because of its profound pessimism, but because it invites comparison with the novel to which it is a pendant. In *Brave New World* Mr. Huxley was still writing with much of his original brio, and one misses here, as in all his later work, the gaiety and wit which made his earlier books so enjoyable. Goodness knows, there is little enough nowadays to be gay about, but one notices an increasing tiredness in Mr. Huxley's writing, and a growing habit (always a danger with him) of dropping into literary clichés—e.g., Man's inhumanity to man, Beauty-is-truth-truth-beauty, Theirs not to reason why, etc, etc.

Mr. Huxley remains as wise, humane and inexhaustibly intelligent as ever; but he says little or nothing in this book which he has not said, more cogently and more eloquently, before.

Jocelyn Brooke. L. *June,* 1959, pp. 73–75

The novel [*Island*] becomes, in effect, a series of talks on industrialism, the family, flagellation, militarism, sexual technique, education, death, biology, the rarer drugs, affluence, true and false mysticism. The familiar coruscation of all his writing in this manner is here at its best. There is an interesting change from *Brave New World*: instead of the simple contrast of scientific modernity and naïve primitivism, there is a last desperate grasp towards integration. At a purely conceptual level, there is a consistency based on a genuine humanity.

At the actual level of the novel, it is less easy to assent. The breathtaking synthesis of biology, Sanskrit and political theory has to live with a flock of mynah birds trained to fly round the island singing (as spiritual reminders) "Attention" and "Here and now, boys." Tense intellectual argument is cut by extraordinary pseudo-poems and suddenly disastrous slang; the happy Palanese, more than once, are offered to us for our admiration as "full-blown human beings." . . . The theme is integration, and the identification of all the forces against it, but the experience (as so often in Mr. Huxley) is disintegration. The novel is new, but the critical problem (and, I would say, the decision) is what it has always been, since Mr. Huxley started writing.

Raymond Williams. *MGW.* April 5, 1962, p. 10

Like Bacon's jesting Pilate, from whom he borrowed a title, he asked and did not stay for an answer. He moved on. Nothing short of universal knowledge was his aim. No traveller through cultures, no connoisseur of human habits, no asker had lapped up so much. As a writer, he became a mellifluous but active, ever-extending, ever-dramatising encyclopedia and he had the gaiety and melancholy of mind to put it out in novels, essays, plays and works of speculation and criticism. Endlessly educable, he was, in the family tradition, a hybrid—the artist-educator; an extraordinary filler-in of the huge gaps in one's mind. To the very young in the Twenties, this was inestimable. One might clap a label on him ten years later but, in the meantime, the next decade had found him new. So it went on, until pretty well the present day. His range and his manner were irresistible to youth. The spell continued: to the latest appetites he offered the devils of Loudon; to the curious the merits of mescalin; to the pragmatic a therapy for blindness; to the terrified the possibility that man's survival was related to the non-human "otherness" he shared with

Nature. . . . One got from him a stereoscopic view of the world. One can call his method popularization; but really the attraction lay not only in the new facts, but in the opportunity for more speculation. . . .

His mind had, of course, the tricks of the man who knew too much and too well how to express it. He was one of the last of the Victorian liberals. He was totally pacifist. Logically he refused to be implicated. His manner had a lot of old Bloomsbury in it. "Significant. But significant of what?" "Possibly. But possibly not." . . . All the same these phrases were designed to drop us simple readers into a void where, defenceless, we were exposed to shock. Shock was one of the luxuries of the Twenties. But, for Huxley, perhaps the most accomplished educator of his generation, to shock was to ensure the course of intellectual freedom.

V. S. Pritchett. NS. Dec. 6, 1963, p. 834

ISHERWOOD, CHRISTOPHER (1904–   )

I have discussed the situation with Isherwood, whom I regard as a hope of English fiction and I have suggested how dangerous that fatal readability of his might become. The first person singular of the German stories, Herr Christoph, or Herr Issyvoo, is the most persuasive of literary salesmen—one moment's reading with him and one is tobogganing through the book, another second and one has bought it—but he is persuasive because he is so insinuatingly bland and anonymous, nothing rouses him, nothing shocks him. While secretly despising us he could not at the same time be more tolerant; his manners are charming and he is somehow on our side against the characters—confidential as, when playing with children, one child older or less animal than the rest, will suddenly attach itself to the grown-ups and discuss its former playmates.

Now for this a price has to be paid; Herr Issyvoo is not a dumb ox, for he is not condemned to the solidarity with his characters and with their background to which Hemingway is bound by his conception of art, but he is much less subtle, intelligent and articulate than he might be. [1938]

Cyril Connolly. *Enemies of Promise* (N.Y.,
Macmillan, 1948), p. 74

It is important to refrain from wondering why Mr. Isherwood thought it necessary to write it [*Lions and Shadows*]. Autobiographies are quite often written today by persons of equally modest age, but for reasons other than those which apparently have inspired Mr. Isherwood. He has not been driven into print, if one is to believe his explanatory note to the Reader, by personal vanity, by the wish to record the adolescent habits and sayings of those of his contemporaries who are now known to fame, or by the honest desire to make money . . . He has had the loftier intention of describing "the first stages in a lifelong education—the education of a novelist," and declares "that the young man happens to be myself is only of secondary importance."

Lions and Shadows in no way succeeds in what is declared to be its purpose. Nor does it satisfy overmuch in pursuing its secondary aim. Neither Mr. Isherwood's childhood nor his adolescence differed as much as he appears to suppose from the childhood and adolescence of the average person. For a distinguishing feature one can only point to the fact that he carried over into adolescence the fantasy worlds which are invariably built in childhood. Even at Cambridge he tried to retreat from the drabness of the University town into an intricate formal world of his own construction; this habit he describes at great length, and it is very boring. The parts by which Mr. Isherwood appears to set most store are in fact the parts of the book least worth reading. One must read it instead for its trivialities—its bright descriptions of unusual *milieux*, its anecdotes, its lively caricature—the things, in fact, for which one generally reads an autobiography.

Derek Verschoyle. *LM.* April, 1938, p. 660

One is not so much surprised that the novels of Isherwood should have been praised—for they are obviously the product of a considerable talent —as that they should have been praised in such extravagant terms. Isherwood "arrived" during the 'thirties and is still, if recent pronouncements are to be trusted, accepted more or less as a major figure. Mr. John Lehmann has spoken of expecting "a row of novels at once intensely English in spirit and European in sympathy" after *The Nowaks;* the undercurrent of disquiet over *Prater Violet* bore tribute to the expectations that the earlier works had aroused; and Mr. E. M. Forster has recently described him as "extremely intelligent." It is all this that makes a study of him of some importance, rather than the achievement of the novels themselves, interesting and amusing though they are. And so, bound up with the analysis of these novels must be sought an answer to the question; why should such a comparatively negligible figure—negligible that is to say, by any reasonable mature standards—have achieved the reputation he has? What characteristics have made Isherwood a representative—as indeed it must be admitted he was a representative—of a decade?

His largely autobiographical work, *Lions and Shadows (An Education in the Twenties)* affords something of an explanation of the particular quality of his novels and, as important, provides an insight into the nature of his appeal. An engagingly—almost naïvely—frank book, it reveals Isherwood's characteristic capacity for narrative. But more interesting is the information it affords about the peculiar fantasy life of its author and about his repeated inability to measure up to the life around him. The most striking feature revealed is perhaps the lack of what used to be known as character. This obviously rather charming, at bottom conventionally middle-class young man appears to have been easily influenced by his friends and to have accepted their fantasies as part of his own life; though, of course, to say that is to tell only half the story, for there must obviously have been a side to his nature that was ready to respond to their promptings. Part of the explanation of this he gives himself; he was afflicted, like so many of his generation, with the shame of not having taken part in the war of 1914-18, a war that was at once an adventure missed and a test unendured (especially perhaps, the latter, to one with Isherwood's nonconformist conscience). Hence the importance of what he calls the Test, the necessity, that is to say, of proving by some means his manhood, a sort of masochistic substitute for the trenches. It was an ordeal that he was always to avoid.

G. H. Bantock in *The Novelist as Thinker*,
ed. B. Rajan (Dennis Dobson, 1947), pp. 46-47

Do you write from notes? Letters? Diaries?

Diaries, yes. I've always kept diaries extensively, and they give me a great sense of security because I feel at least this part is factual. Having, however, built on these little islands of fact, I think one goes back and reconstructs everything and changes everything and interferes with everything. But I do find it a great reassurance—the only kind of reassurance one can have—to have had some notes of an actual experience or an actual scene or people or whatever.

I wonder if you have a potential reader in mind when you're writing fiction?

No, I don't think so. One's friends, of course, to some extent. Yet more and more I write for myself, I think. More and more, writing is appearing to me as a kind of self-analysis, a finding-out something about myself and about the past, and about what life is like, as far as I'm concerned; who I am; who these people are; what it's all about. And this comes from a subconscious level to some extent, so I really don't know what may spring out of the typewriter. . . .

You spoke of Forster earlier, and it's quite evident in *Lions and Shadows* that you thought a great deal of him at one time, that he had revolutionized the novel. Can you speak of any influence he had on your work? One of the characters in *All the Conspirators,* Victor Page, was said to be modelled on Charles Wilcox, for example.

Oh, really? Well, he might have been unconsciously modelled on him, that's perfectly true, because I suppose that certainly the whole thing was tremendously influenced by *Howards End,* or by all of Forster. Well, I think the great revelation about Forster (and Trilling has said all of this marvellously in his book) is that Forster is a comic writer, and that was our great slogan, Edward Upward's and mine, when we were young, that we were going to be essentially comic writers, since tragedy was no longer modern.

Tune down the pitch, play down the scenes, tea-table it.

Yes, but now, of course, I see that it's not by any means necessary to tune down the big scenes.

Yes, the violence of the first chapter of *The World in the Evening* is not at all Forsterean. . . .

Was moving to America a political gesture, a cutting off of national affiliation, or anything of that sort?

Oh, no, no, really not at all. People who think I moved to America as a symbolic gesture really aren't acquainted with my movements before that. I was eternally wandering about. I didn't live in England properly after I was twenty-four. So that I spent about ten years, first in Germany, then living in all kinds of countries in Europe, then going to China, and then going to America. I really like England a great deal more now. I mean not because I don't live there now, but because since the war I think it's a marvellous place, much better in every way.

Has living in America changed your attitude towards your work?

I really don't know the answer to that. You see, you have to realize that I've never lived, since I've been grown up, in any place nearly as long as I've lived in America. I'm so completely habituated to living in America that everything else seems very remote from me. Now I don't mean by this that I don't feel foreign here, because I do. But that I like. And I think it sort of heightens one's awareness of things to feel a little bit out of it.

Interview with Isherwood by Stanley Poss.
L. June, 1961, pp. 42, 55–56

The novels expose a great deal, but not believable people. Isherwood never quite emancipates himself from his fantasy world of Poshocracy, secret watchers, juvenile conspirators, glaciers, goat-tracks, departing trains, self-made misfits, the drama of ineffectuality and the hyperbolic interpretation of his own life as a Test whose worst trial is scruffy lodging-houses. . . . Philip in *All the Conspirators* never amounts to more than his feeble self; and the ending, which shows him winning second prize in a poetry competition, is not the final degradation of a sensitive soul but a tedious Q.E.D. Isherwood's main skill is in crisp narrative and cinematic reporting. As long as he can make one scene follow another, he is entertaining; but when he tries to go beyond, into moral significances, he achieves only an inflated pretentiousness. . . .

At his best, Isherwood is Issyvoo, the good listener, the affable unretiring jury; he has something in common with Somerset Maugham. Both compile a boyish, exotic, facilely worldly mythology of spiritual decay in foreign parts; both collect the facts, the fascinating copy, and hinge it all carefully into non-committal albums. Both have turned to oriental religions: Maugham in *Points of View* enthuses about the life of a Hindu saint; Isherwood edited a *Vedanta for the Western World* and in 1944 collaborated with Swami Nikhilananda on a translation of the *Bhagavad-Gita*. And Isherwood's *The World in the Evening* recommends charity and the Quaker way. It seems that only a thorough vision of the trivial, only a complete abdication from judging, pave the way for illumination.

Paul West. *The Modern Novel*
(Hutchinson, 1963), p. 78

Perhaps no novelist of the last thirty years seemed better equipped than Christopher Isherwood to catch the peculiar tone of his times; he had verbal facility, inventive ability, and a sense of form and movement. What he lacked in his early work was imaginative breadth, and this, the reader felt, would develop as his total powers grew. In *All the Conspirators,* Isherwood was obviously making his gesture of rebellion, and through his artist protagonist moving off to be his own man. The novel is reminiscent of a great many late-Victorian works, especially Butler's *The Way of all Flesh,* but nevertheless it is, despite its slightness (Isherwood was only 23), an honest statement of the conflict between an individual and his family.

Instead of maturing into a novelist, however, Isherwood demonstrated that his real skill lay with the short sketch, the vignette, the brief portrait, the episode. His verbal facility and grace of movement remained, but they were placed at the service of basically trivial characters. In *The Last of Mr. Norris* and *Goodbye to Berlin,* Isherwood was concerned with personal breakdown and corruption against the backdrop of pre-war Berlin. Perforce, his characters are trivial, for they bend with the times and corrupt easily. Nevertheless, his kind of corruption is slight: it is closer to seediness. . . . Perhaps Isherwood is suggesting that "modern" people . . . have been so conditioned by the times that they have no moral sense; for them to feel more would indicate that they are more substantial than we can rightfully expect. If this, however, is Isherwood's point, then he has failed to provide the necessary tensions for cosmic ennui; at most, he conveys petty boredom.

Frederick R. Karl. *A Reader's Guide to the
Contemporary English Novel* (Thames and
Hudson, 1963), pp. 290–92

JACOBS, W. W. (1863–1943)

Even when we have read one of these stories several times and could relate off-hand the whole train of events described in it, we can still read it again with pleasure simply because of the humour in the dialogue and the suggestive little flashes of description. I have seen it stated somewhere that Mr. Jacobs derives his humour from that of Smollett and Dickens; but this is a superficial criticism, and, like most superficial criticisms, it is unjust to everybody concerned in it. Smollett deals in externals; his humour is compact of horseplay and odd appearances; Dickens, carrying on from Smollett, began by describing horseplay and odd figures, but very quickly raised English humour to a height it had not reached since Shakespeare by the creation of richly comic characters who are themselves almost inexhaustible storehouses of absurdity. The humour of Mr. Jacobs, however, has neither the rude vigour of the first nor the imaginative richness of the second; it is limited, neat, finished; and, actually, it is a different kind of humour altogther, the humour of a witty dramatist, out to exploit a situation rather than a character, and achieving its end by verbal dexterity rather than by the absurdities of a poetic, extravagant, comic imagination.

J. B. Priestley. *Figures in Modern Literature*
(John Lane, 1924), p. 118

The talent of Jacobs is a small one, when he is compared with the masters, but like theirs, his types are not chosen until they are already dated; like theirs his humour is fantastic and artificial. No notions of realism or social purpose, as Mr. Henry Reed rightly says in an introduction to *Dialstone Lane,* cross his mind: he writes, so to say, from the ivory fo'c'sle. He recognises that in his nightwatchmen, his decisive widows, his sailormen, he is dealing with an advanced and sophisticated culture which has become firmly barnacled on the coarse surface of common life; and that the elegance, the speed, the riposte and the intricate plotting of something like Restoration comedy, can alone do justice to his highly-developed people. . . .

The plots in Jacobs are the breath of the fantasticating life of men. They are superior to the plots of a writer like O. Henry. They spring naturally from the wits of the characters as trickery comes naturally to cardsharpers; they seem to pour off the tongue.

The flavour and the skill of Jacobs are of course all in the handling of the talk. . . . There is no doubt that Jacobs is one of the supreme craftsmen of the short story.

V. S. Pritchett. *Books in General* (Chatto and Windus, 1953), pp. 237, 239–40

JAMES, HENRY (1843–1916)

Whatever his private views may be, we have no means of knowing them. He himself never appears, he never buttonholes us, he never moralises. He may be a Republican, he may be an Anglican; he may be a believer in autocracy. But he never, by the fifth of an inch, drags around his pictures of life so as to make it appear that, if the social state were what he desires it to be, all would be well with the world. We rise from extremely protracted readings of his works with the feeling that we have assisted at a great number of affairs, of having met a great number of people whom we should just recognize.

Eng. R. Dec., 1908, p. 160

All great writers have, of course, an atmosphere in which they seem most at their ease and at their best; a mood of the great general mind which they interpret and indeed almost discover, so that we come to read them rather for that than for any story or character or scene of separate excellence. For ourselves Henry James seems most entirely in his element, doing that is to say what everything favours his doing, when it is a question of recollection. The mellow light which swims over the past, the beauty which suffuses even the commonest little figures of that time, the shadow in which the detail of so many things can be discerned which the glare of day flattens out, the depth, the richness, the calm, the humour of the whole pageant—all this seems to have been his natural atmosphere and his most abiding mood. It is the atmosphere of all these stories in which aged Europe is the background for young America. It is the half light in which he sees most, and sees farthest. To Americans, indeed, to Henry James and to Hawthorne, we owe the best relish of the past in our literature—not the past of romance and chivalry, but the immediate past of vanished dignity and faded fashions. The novels teem with it; but wonderful as they are, we are tempted to say that the memories [*The Middle Years*] are yet more wonderful, in that they are more exactly Henry James, and give more precisely his tone and his gesture. In them his benignity is warmer, his humour richer, his solicitude more exquisite, his recognition of beauty, fineness, humanity more instant and direct. [1917]

Virginia Woolf. *The Death of the Moth* (Penguin Bks., 1961 [Hogarth Pr., 1942]), p. 116

No longer a figure that leans and looks out of a window, scanning a stretch of memory—that is not the image suggested by Henry James's book [*The Ambassadors*]. It is rather as though the reader himself were at the window, and as though the window opened straight into the depths of Strether's conscious existence. The energy of his perception and discrimination is there seen at work. His mind is the mirror of the scene beyond it, and the other people in the book exist only in relation to him; but his mind, his own thought of them, is there absolutely, its restless evolution is in full sight. I do not say that this is a complete account of the principle on which the book is constructed; for indeed the principle goes further. But for the moment let the book stand as the type of the novel in which a mind is dramatized—reflecting the life to which it is exposed, but itself performing its own peculiar and private life. This last, in the case of Strether, involves a gradual, long-drawn change, from the moment when he takes up the charge of rescuing his young friend from the siren of Paris, to the moment when he finds himself wishing that his young friend would refuse to be rescued. Such is the curve in the unexpected adventure of his imagination. It is given as nobody's view—not his own, as it would be if he told the story himself, and not the author's, as it would be if Henry James told the story. The author does not tell the story of Strether's mind; he makes it tell itself, he dramatizes it.

Percy Lubbock. *The Craft of Fiction* (N.Y.,
Peter Smith, 1947 [c. 1921]), pp. 146–47

I insist on his Americanism. I insist on it because of the very fact that he was in externals so Europeanised. For his Cosmopolitan surface was itself a product of a New England yearning towards a gentler and more glamourous Eastern Continent. That distinctively New England passion this great Master himself rendered in such stories as *The Four Meetings: A Passionate Pilgrim,* or *Europe.* These are tales of simple New England souls who desire to find a Europe of their Transatlantic dreams. And, either physically or figuratively these dreams are frustrated: either they never get to Europe or, getting there, they find, on the rich turf, under the shadows of the great elms and of the ancient spires a human society more mannered but in no shade more spiritualised than is to be found in Colorado. And that was the real tragedy of the Master's life—that he penetrated the Arcana of European mysteries to find only the universal human heart with its greeds, its materialisms and, in the end, its Armageddon of passionate disillusionment. . . .

I fancy that his mannerisms—his involutions, whether in speech or in writing, were due to a settled conviction that, neither in his public nor in his acquaintance, would he ever find any one who would not need talking down to. The desire of the Artist, of the creative writer, is that his words and his "scenes" shall suggest—of course with precision—far more than they actually express or project. But, having found that his limpidities, from *Daisy Miller* to the *Real Thing,* not only suggested less than he desired, but carried suggestions entirely unmeant, he gave up the attempt at Impressionism of that type—as if his audiences had tired him out. So he talked down to us, explaining and explaining, the ramifications of his mind. He was aiming at explicitness, never at obscurities—as if he were talking to children.

I will not say that loveableness was the predominating feature of the Old Man: he was too intent on his own particular aims to be lavishly sentimental over surrounding humanity. And his was not a character painted in the flat, in water-colour, like the caricatures of Rowlandson. For some protective reason or other, just as Shelley used to call himself the Atheist, he loved to appear in the character of a sort of Mr. Pickwick —with the rather superficial benevolences, and the mannerisms of which he was perfectly aware. But below that protective mask was undoubtedly a plane of nervous cruelty. I have heard him be—to simple and quite unpretentious people—more diabolically blighting than it was quite decent for a man to be—for he was always an artist in expression. And it needed a certain fortitude when, the studied benevolence and the chuckling, savouring, enjoyment of words, disappearing suddenly from his personality, his dark eyes rolled in their whites and he spoke very brutal and direct English. He chose in fact to appear as Henrietta Maria —but he could be atrocious to those who behaved as if they took him at that valuation.

And there was yet a third depth—a depth of religious, of mystical, benevolence such as you find just now and again in the stories he "wanted" to write—in the *Great Good Places.* His practical benevolences were innumerable, astonishing—and indefatigable.

Ford Madox Ford. Thus To Revisit (N.Y., Dutton,
1925), pp. 103, 117, 121

No writer has left a series of novels more of one moral piece. The differences between James's first works and his last are only differences of art as Conrad defined it. In his early works perhaps he rendered a little less than the highest kind of justice; the progress from *The American* to *The Golden Bowl* is a progress from a rather crude and inexperienced symbolization of truth to truth itself: a progress from evil represented rather obviously in terms of murder to evil *in propria persona,* walking down Bond Street, charming, cultured, sensitive—evil to be distinguished from good only in the complete egotism of its outlook. They are complete anarchists, these later Jamesian characters, they form the immoral background to that extraordinary period of haphazard violence which anticipated the war: the attempt on Greenwich Observatory, the siege of Sidney Street. . . .

. . . the last twist (it is always the friend, the intimate who betrays) is given to these studies of moral corruption. They represent an attitude which had been James's from very far back; they are not the slow painful fruit of experience. The attitude never varied from the time of *The American* onwards. Mme. de Bellegarde, who murdered her husband and sold her daughter, is only the first crude presentation of a woman gradually subtilized, by way of Madame Merle in *The Portrait of a Lady,* into the incomparable figures of evil Kate Croy and Charlotte Stant.

This point is of importance. James has been too often regarded as a novelist of superficial experience, as a painter of social types, who was cut off by exile from the deepest roots of experience (as if there were something superior in the Sussex or Shropshire of the localized talent to James's international scene). But James was not in that sense an exile; he could have dispensed with the international scene as easily as he dispensed with all the world of Wall Street finance. For the roots were not in Venice, Paris, London; they were in himself. Densher, the Prince, just as much as the redhaired valet Quint and the adulterous governess, were rooted in his own character. They were there when he wrote *The American* in 1876: all he needed afterwards to perfect his work to his own impeccable standard was technical subtlety and that other subtlety which comes from superficial observation, the ability to construct convincing masks for his own personality.

Graham Greene in *The English Novelists,* ed. Derek
Verschoyle (Chatto and Windus, 1936), pp. 216–17

To make ourselves familiar with the evolution of Henry James, from his early impersonal experiments in the 'sixties right through to the final magnificence of his later period, is to trace the historical development of the art of fiction at its intensest creative point. It is to be carried, as in some wonderful ship that somehow manages to keep pace with the sun, right from the world of *Adam Bede* to the world of *The Golden Bowl.* There are other craft in the water—we are in the wake of the rich and overladen argosy of Balzac; Meredith runs part of the course with us; and Turgenev is a rather remote sailing ship which we keep in sight all the way—but there is no doubt that the authentic craft, the only one to steer direct, is the very one we have boarded. . . .

There is a strict sense in which the novels of Henry James are a fund of practical advice. The novice, by the study of them, could learn a hundred useful precepts, and save himself years of unnecessary labour.

But the study must be severe, for the perfection is often so complete that we look in vain for any marks of the mould from which it was cast. . . .

He has sacrificed all that merely detached descriptive writing which constitutes, one might guess, at least a quarter of the bulk of English fiction. But nothing is now more evident than the fact that this drastic pruning was essential to any further growth; and no critic would now reject the rules worked out by Henry James on this subject. . . .

Henry James perceived, in a real sense which is distinctive of classical art, and in a sense which gives us the real meaning of the Greek conception of dramatic unity, that the problem of "presentation," of "projection," of the translation of action into verbal expression, was a problem of time. It is a question of creating an *illusion* of duration which shall correspond with an actual *sense* of duration. The illusion can only be effective if the strands of interest which we pick up at the beginning of a story are so woven that they duplicate our consciousness of real events. But consciousness, whether real or induced, is not a simple fact: it is rather a process or state which is only realized upon the completion of some definite rhythm or pattern. . . .

Now, in order to create personalities and set them in action (which is the object of fiction), it is necessary to repeat, on another plane, an analagous rhythm or pattern.

The discovery, or rediscovery and application to fiction, of this principle was the great technical advance made by Henry James. It is an advance of the very greatest importance: it is not too much to say that upon the making-good of this advance by future novelists the whole art of fiction depends.

> Herbert Read. *Collected Essays in Literary*
> *Criticism* (Faber, 1938), pp. 354–57

. . . the challenge, perhaps just because it was, for him, so particularly formidable, fascinated James from the first, and *The American Scene* is only the latest, most ambitious, and best of a series of topographical writings beginning in 1870 with sketches of Saratoga and Newport.

Immature as these early American pieces are, they seem to me more satisfactory than the subsequent descriptions of England and Europe, even the charming *A Little Tour of France* (1886). Confronted with the un-American scene, he seems prim and a little amateurish, as if he were a conscientious father writing letters to an intelligent daughter of fourteen: as guide books, the European travelogues are incomplete, and as personal impressions they are timid; the reader is conscious that the traveller must have seen and felt a great deal more than he says, and refrained either from a fear of shocking or from a lack of confidence in his own judgement; but even as a young man, James was unafraid of America as a subject: puzzled often, angry sometimes, yes, but quite certain of what he felt and of his right to say it.

W. H. Auden. *Hor.* Feb., 1947, p. 78

James was so incredibly productive over so long a period, and offers so many aspects for study, that nothing short of a book on him, and a book of formidable length, could pretend to adequacy. I have also in mind the way in which the cult of James of the last quarter of a century (a cult that, to judge by what has been written on them, doesn't seem to have involved intensive cultivation of the works admired) makes him pre-eminently the author of the later works. We are asked to admire *The Ambassadors* (1903); and *The Ambassadors* seems to me to be not only *not* one of his great books, but to be a bad one. If, as I was on the point of saying, it exhibits senility, then senility was more than setting in at the turn of the century in *The Sacred Fount.* It is as a matter of fact a more interesting disease than senility.

This is not to deny that there are achieved works in distinctively "late" styles. Critical admirers of *The Awkward Age* (1899), that astonishing work of genius (about which they will have reserves on some points), and of *What Maisie Knew* (which is perfect), will know of many fine short stories and *nouvelles.* But they will also be largely occupied, where this later work is concerned, with sifting, rejecting, qualifying and deploring; that is, they are faced inescapably with James's "case"—with the question of what went wrong in his later development; for something certainly did go wrong. The phase when his genius functioned with freest and fullest vitality is represented by *The Portrait of a Lady* (1881), together with *The Bostonians* (1885). . . .

The later development brings extraordinary subtleties of art—and poetic triumphs such as the method by which in *The Lesson of the Master* James dramatizes the complexities of his own attitude towards his career (about which he was clearly given to radical self-questioning) —but, for all the interest of the development, with its rich product of masterly tales, we can hardly follow it unregretting.

F. R. Leavis. *The Great Tradition*
(N.Y., Doubleday, 1954 [c. 1948]), pp. 155–56, 187

The last great exponents of the Mandarin style were Walter Pater and Henry James, who, although they wrote sentences which were able to express the subtlest inflexions of sensibility and meaning, at the worst grew prisoners of their style, committed to a tyranny of euphonious nothings. Such writers, the devotees of the long sentence, end by having to force everything into its framework, because habit has made it impossible for them to express themselves in any other way. They are like those birds that weave intricate nests in which they are as content to hatch out a pebble as an egg. But the case of Henry James is sadder still, for his best writing, that found in his later books, charged with all the wisdom and feeling of his long life, went unappreciated. As he reminded Gosse, he remained "insurmountably unsaleable," and of his collected edition of 1908 he could say, like Ozymandias, "Look on my *works* ye mortals and despair."

Cyril Connolly. *Enemies of Promise* (N.Y., Macmillan, 1948), p. 18

His prefaces—unique in English literature—constitute an art of the novel, but more than that they bring a subtle intelligence and a marvelous gift of expression to bear on the life of imagination in general. They are the story of a story—the thing caught in the act—told with delight, with absorption in the logic of intellectual events, with a luminous display of reasoning. The prefaces are a natural fruition, the expression of an interest in form dating from the beginning of James's career as a writer.

The lesson of Flaubert and of Maupassant is the lesson of form and style in a work of fiction. To James it seemed profoundly important, and its importance is of course illustrated in his own career as a novelist. This, he felt, is where the claims of imagination, the novelist's privilege as a poet, are most secure: in the need to compose freely, with a high hand, according to an idea and a method. The literal and the formless are much the same thing in a work of art. About the value of style James had no more doubt than Flaubert himself.

Morris Roberts in Henry James, *The Art of Fiction* (N.Y., Oxford Univ. Pr., 1948), pp. xvi–xvii

There is little doubt, I think, that the feminine streak in James himself was partly responsible for some of those features of his literary personality which critics of his work have found disturbing and equivocal: inquisitive detachment, vagueness about practical details, squeamishness, and an over-developed taste for the dubious virtues of renunciation. Without taking too much for granted, it may, I feel, be suggested that the theme of the prying outsider, which recurs so constantly in James's plots (e.g. in *The Sacred Fount, The Aspern Papers, Confidence, The Private Life*), is a fantasy of Destruction and would therefore tend to occur insistently to a man who was as careful as James to exclude anything resembling aggression from his personal relationships. The Renunciation theme is the obverse of the same, masculine medal. Renunciation may, of course, be a reasonable, as well as a strong-minded, act. But the evident alacrity with which James resorted to this method of solving the dilemmas of his heroes (from Christopher Newman to Guy Domville and the narrator of *The Sacred Fount*) suggests that his addiction to the idea of noble renunciation in fact concealed something less creditable—namely, lassitude, or a disinclination to face the indifference of others.

The excessive pains taken by his "nice" characters to avoid hurting each other's feelings—the kind of verbal fuss which becomes a mania in *The Awkward Age*—is probably traceable to the same source. . . . If, as I disengage, the supreme test of an artist's intelligence is his ability correctly to judge his own scope, then Henry James rarely betrayed the faculty for which, as a novelist, he is perhaps most justly famous.

Rarely, but not never. There is, after all, *The Princess Casamassima*. This embarrassing novel displays the author as a good and clever, but curiously naïve spinster who has rashly agreed to give a lantern lecture to a boys' club in a slum district. Her goodwill is not in question, but it is impossible not to titter. So entirely at sea did James find himself, when faced by the theme he had undertaken to illustrate, that his very first chapter recalls—unthinkably—the *Mystères de Paris* of Eugène Sue. Unthinkably, because in any context with which he was familiar James would not—at this date—have thought it desirable to employ the spotlight of crude melodrama. Like all James's large canvases, this one has well-realised passages, and the single character who bears signs of having been observed—Millicent Henning—is a distinct success, in spite of the conventional Cockney in which she is made to speak. The impression of objectivity is striking—until we realise that for once James was not in a position to be anything but objective. It might, however, be argued that he chose the right moment at which to write this book: we may safely assume that if he had attempted it earlier in his career, it would have been even worse than it is; later on, he would not have wanted to write it at all. We can, if we like, call the novel "a brave effort," so long as we remember that to write outside one's scope usually indicates a desire for approval from quarters that have hitherto withheld it.

James's excursion into the theatre was an error of judgment of a different kind. There is plenty of evidence in the novels that theatrical effect, even of quite a crude order, was not outside James's scope. It seems improbable that he realised how melodramatic his plots often were. To face this fact might have disconcerted him seriously: he preferred to complain, with some emphasis, that "I *may* be made for the Drama (God only knows!) but am not made for the theatre!" The result was that when he sat down to write for the stage his eye was only half on the ball. It seems almost too obvious to point out the futility of attempting a medium of which one feature—and that the most important—repels your taste; yet this is just what James did. The effort was not even brave.

Edward Sackville-West. Inclinations (Secker
and Warburg, 1949), pp. 44–46

In 1888, on the second day of January, which in any year is likely to be a sad day, Henry James wrote to his friend William Dean Howells that his reputation had been dreadfully injured by his last two novels. . . . And then, no doubt with the irony all writers use when they dare to speak of future recognition, but also, surely, with the necessary faith, he concludes the matter: "Very likely too, some day, all my buried prose will kick off its various tombstones at once." And so it happened. The "some day" has arrived and we have been hearing the clatter of marble as James's buried prose kicks off its monuments in a general resurrection. On all sides James is being given the serious and joyous interest he longed for in his lifetime.

One element of our interest must be the question of how some of James's prose ever came to be buried at all. It is not hard to understand why certain of James's books did not catch the contemporary fancy. But the two books on which James placed the blame for his diminishing popularity were *The Bostonians* and *The Princess Casamassima,* and of all James's novels these are the two which are most likely to make an immediate appeal to the reader of today. That they should not have delighted their contemporary public, but on the contrary should have turned it against James makes a lively problem in the history of taste.

In the masterpieces of his late years James became a difficult writer. This is the fact and nothing is gained for James by denying it. He himself knew that these late works were difficult: he wished them to be dealt with as if they were difficult. . . . But the hostility with which *The Bostonians* and *The Princess Casamassima* were received cannot be explained by any difficulty either of manner or intention, for in these books there is none. . . . In these novels James is at the point in his career at which society, in the largest and even the grossest sense, is offering itself to his mind with great force. . . . And more: his social observation is of a kind that we must find startlingly prescient when we consider that it was made some sixty years ago. It is just this prescience, of course, that explains the resistance of James's contemporaries. . . . Henry James in the eighties understood what we have painfully learned from our grim glossary of wars and concentration camps, after having seen the state and human nature laid open to our horrified inspection. "But I have the imagination of disaster—and see life as ferocious and sinister": James wrote this to A. C. Benson in 1896. . . . Nowadays we know that such an imagination is one of the keys to truth. It was, then, "the imagination of disaster" that cut James off from his contemporaries and it is what recommends him to us now.

Lionel Trilling. *The Liberal Imagination* (N.Y., Doubleday Anchor Books, 1950), pp. 55–57

When one considers these examples, one begins to feel certain that beneath the stylistic surface, the portentous snobbery, the golden display, of James's work, there lurk forms of violence and chaos. His technical mastery has the perfection of frightful balance and frightful tension: beneath the stretched out compositions there are abysses of despair and disbelief: *Ulysses* and *The Waste Land*.

What after all do these images of suffocation, of broken necks, of wailing, suggest but a collection of photographs of the dead and wounded during the Great War? We remember his phrase, made in 1915: "to have to take it all now for what the treacherous years were all the while really making for and *meaning,* is too tragic for any words."

Stephen Spender. *The Destructive Element* (Phila., Albert Saifer, 1953), p. 98

These letters [*Selected Letters of Henry James,* ed. Leon Edel] are not merely illustrative; most are interesting in their own right, to be read with pleasure as an artful account of a situation, a point of view, an incident, or as a skilful setting of a social tone, or as the distillation, as it were, of a relationship. . . . They are full of life and humour, and will interest even those who are not familiar with the novels. And those who do not know the novels may well be led to them by these letters. They should begin with the letter to Bernard Shaw of January 20, 1909, in which he justified his activity as an artist: "I do such things because I happen to be a man of imagination and taste, extremely interested in life, and because the imagination, thus, from the moment direction and motive play upon it from all sides, absolutely enjoys and insists on and incurably leads a life of its own, for which just this vivacity itself is its warrant." Vivacity is the keynote.

David Daiches. *MGW*. Feb. 16, 1956, p. 10

Most of the entries [*The Note-books of Henry James*] hinge on professional matters and reveal James's techniques in great detail, as he hammers out his material, catches an idea on the wing, elaborates an anecdote (there is a scenario for *The Ambassadors* which runs to some 20,000 words.) But though James is reticent about his innermost feelings to the last, and these are in no sense intimate journals, their chief interest is still what they show of the man himself. What they do show, most strikingly, is James's greed for experience, his ability to soak up the life around him, his avid curiosity: a promising piece of gossip he thinks of as "a morsel." This note, almost of gluttony, is characteristic of the great masters of fiction . . . , and the real reason why James, for all his fussiness and repressions, stands in their ranks.

John Gross. *MGW*. June 21, 1962, p. 11

Year by year, James's confidence and self-sufficiency, his command of his environment as of his art, become more and more firm: the long prepared strategy, of society and solitude duly balanced, is beginning to succeed. The suicide of Miss Woolson, and the failure to make money by writing plays, are the only reverses in these years.

It is again clear that James's philosophy was always closer to that of Balzac and Zola than to Flaubert and Pater. He had nothing in common with "the babyish decadents" of the Nineties, or with any French doctrine of art for art's sake. Vitality, and the exuberance of creativeness, were the qualities that he himself possessed and that he admired in others. Some of the stories written at this time are often vulgar, novelettish, facile; at their worst, they are fluently written, smart magazine pieces. In several of them, the author is too evidently pleased with himself, beaming and shining with the sense of his brilliance and worldly understanding. But the gross energy, the copiousness, never fail; and when he feels himself ready for a subject with a broad sweep, as in *The Bostonians* and *The Princess Casamassima,* the literary high spirits, the superb flow, carried him forward. There were no Flaubertian groans, or fears of sterility. James was not an exquisite, contrived, fastidious writer. Following his progress is like reading about the foundation of a great American manufacturing fortune: there is the same ruthless planning and egoism, the same pride in output. He was a professional, rather than a priest of art. He despised amateurs. . . .

He needed in London—the London of *The Princess Casamassima* and of a famous essay—the daily visible evidences of strong energies, the monuments to greed and rapacity in great houses, and the evidences also of their unavoidable cost in squalor and misery: he saw "the under side, the wrong side, of the London world". . . . Cruel energy and civilised achievement are inseparable: ruthless egoism succeeds and time gives it the patina of respectability and of culture. These are the world's values and James did not dispute them.

Stuart Hampshire. *NS*. April 26, 1963, p. 639

JAMESON, STORM (1897–   )

England has again an art-critic, and that phenomenon is a woman. . . . She is robustiously free from sex astigmatism, or type; indeed, there is no bias of sex in her judgements, unless it be found in a (perhaps feminine) weakness for Oscar Wilde and the author of *Peter Pan,* whereby she seems to betray the motherly instinct. . . . These are the two critical weaknesses in a book [*The Modern Drama in Europe*] which must be accounted a brilliantly sane estimate of the life forces which created the Modern Realist Drama wallowing in the commercial anarchy and art degradation of the present day. The author is epicenely stern. Her judgements are derived from right concepts. Her adjectives are few, and she is never deflected. She has the virility to see that Strindberg and Ibsen were the two dominant intellects of the age, and, on the whole, her instinct is sound. . . . Not only does she understand Nietzsche, she declines to misunderstand Bernard Shaw. . . . M. Storm Jameson is either a portent or an apparition, yet in any case a beacon. Her book reminds me of the first aeroplane over London. We look up.

S.O. *Eng. R.* Jan., 1921, pp. 57–58, 62

Miss Jameson's novel [*Love in Winter*] is far above the average, for to skill, variety of interest, and verisimilitude she can add the study of a rich emotional nature as familiar to us as an old friend, as true to life as a human instinct. Many widely acclaimed novels will seem crude after the simplicity of this careful portrait.

Osbert Burdett. *Eng. R.* May, 1935, p. 626

The Road from the Monument is a comfortable, well-padded novel set in the 1950s but written within the conventions of 50 years ago: . . . the characters are solid and subtly drawn, the story stuffed full of moral conundrums for them to solve. . . .

It's quite possible to find this compulsively readable and an artful fake, which of course it is. Miss Jameson pretends to a criticism of human vanities, but really offers complicity in a daydream. . . . and here we are back where Galsworthy left us, with a bunch of noble sentiments and a fast-weakening grasp of reality.

Robert Taubman. *NS.* Jan. 26, 1962, pp. 133–34

JENNINGS, ELIZABETH (1926–   )

Her great virtue is that of tone: in almost every page she has written she has preserved that gentle and modest tone in which she questions patiently her own powers of observation. Her subjects are admirably expressed by the titles of her last two books: *A Way of Looking* and *A Sense of the World.* . . . Not only her style is a questioning, but her subject-matter as well. But her poems (and I suppose her temperament) are such that she will not admit of the fixity of answers. . . . If she could get down to giving us a landscape, a particular one, she would surely have something new to say about it, and her questions might imply answers that are more precise.

Thom Gunn. *YR*. Summer, 1959, pp. 620–21

Robert Conquest's anthology, *New Lines,* in 1956 brought together the "Movement" (the label was not his, but the invention earlier of some journalist on the *Spectator*) rather as *New Signatures* had represented "the new movement" of the 1930s. This led to a great deal of publicity, little of which was critically useful. What in fact, *was* the Movement? The poets who appeared in Conquest's anthology—Conquest himself, Elizabeth Jennings, Kingsley Amis, John Holloway, Thom Gunn, Philip Larkin, John Wain, Donald Davie—did not obviously share a common set of beliefs about life or principles about what poetry should be. What they do seem to me, in retrospect, to have shared is a new attitude to their audience. They were no longer writing for a "poetry-loving" audience, or for a set of kindred spirits, or for the ideal reader, or for the Muse. They were not acting as spokesmen of beliefs or causes. Nor had they, though this is a more tricky question, a common "class" voice. Some were of working-class or *petit bourgeois* origin . . . but all of them had been to Oxford or Cambridge and represented a young, alert, professional middle-class attitude, not revolutionary, but certainly not reactionary, and on the whole rather indifferent to politics. A critic of their own generation, Alfred Alvarez, was to condemn them for being "genteel." Their poems have the tone of being addressed, with sometimes slightly conscious unaffectedness, to an ideal "plain reader.". . .

The Movement poets shared a common attitude, modest and craftsmanlike, to the craft of verse itself. Many of them thought, like the American critic Professor Yvor Winters, of the ideal poem as the expository poem: a situation is clearly presented, a judgement is made upon it, the reader is invited to agree with the poet's judgement. . . .

Yet these generalizations, though useful, have little to do with the poems of the Movement that one finds oneself remembering and still admiring: like the beautiful short early poem, "Winter Love," by Elizabeth Jennings. Only the rhyme "hurry" and "weary" and perhaps the tension of stresses which rhyme again forces on the word "snowflake" would enable a reader to date that as a modern poem. Its substance would be at home in the Greek anthology or in a volume of Elizabethan or Caroline short lyrics. . . . I think the best poems of the Movement, like that one, . . . are poems which, even if starting from the topical, explore perennial situations.

G. S. Fraser. *The Modern Writer and His World*
(Penguin Bks., rev. ed. 1964), pp. 346–50

JEROME, JEROME K. (1859–1927)

Far the best of these stories [*The Passing of the Third Floor Back*] is the first, which is touched so firmly, so lightly, with such admirable reticence and so much power of suggestion as to make us wish that Mr. Jerome's better, or real, literary self were more often with him. No amount of inspriration, it seems, can purify his style, or rid it of the parasitic scraps of smartness and the clichés without which it would no longer be easy; but the story can carry them all. . . . The book as a whole strikes strangely. It seems the work of a man of great cleverness, some fancy, and a shrewd humour; but one who has never tried his hardest to find out what is in him, and who speaks too often easily, from the surface, through ignorance or fear of what the depths may contain. We believe that the depths are there.

TLS. May 24, 1907, p. 166

This tenth-rate writer has been, for many years, prolific of his tenth-rate stuff. But I do not recall, in such stuff of his as I have happened to sample, anything quite so vilely stupid as *The Passing of the Third Floor Back*. . . . The most depressing aspect of the whole matter is that the play is so evidently a great success. . . . Twaddle and vulgarity will always have the upper hand. . . .

There is not a spark of verisimilitude in the whole dozen characters. . . . Mr. Jerome shows no sign of having observed a fellow-creature. His characters seem to be the result solely of a study of novelettes in the penny weekly papers, supplemented by a study of the works of Jerome K. Jerome. . . .

For a period of time that seemed like eternity, I had to sit knowing exactly what was about to happen, and how it was about to happen, and knowing that as soon as it happened it would happen again. . . . When the [supernatural] visitor passes out through the front door, a supernatural radiance bursts through the fan-light, flooding the stage; and then the curtain comes slowly down. Well, I suppose blasphemy pays. [1908]

Max Beerbohm. *Around Theatres* (Rupert Hart-Davis, 1953), pp. 516–19

He . . . was a clerk and an actor before becoming a journalist. *The Idle Thoughts of an Idle Fellow,* in 1889, gave him a popular vogue; *Three Men in a Boat,* in the same year, made him one of the most widely-read authors in the world. Its facetious humours, its jokes about house-maid's knee . . . and men making messes of their cooking, were of the period . . . ; the burlesque beautiful passages would have been good had a shade more trouble have been taken with them. The book would hardly get a start now, the atmosphere having changed. Of Jerome's later works the most successful was *The Passing of the Third Floor Back,* a sentimental religious play which the genius of Sir John Forbes Robertson made seem better than it was; but the best was *Paul Kelver,* a semi-autobiographical novel which never had the success it deserved. Jerome was at one time editor of *The Idler* (with Robert Barr), and then of *To-Day,* both lively though ephemeral publications with a Bohemian tone.

LM. July, 1927, p. 228

JOHNSON, PAMELA HANSFORD (1912–   )

Pamela Hansford Johnson is one of those several respected and respectable English novelists today whose position could almost be charted with a slide-rule, midway between literature and the insubstantial best-seller, high thinking in very plain words, the perturbing presence of saints and sinners encased reassuringly in a daily world that all of us in the *quasi-intelligentsia* can recognize, everything terrible made nonchalantly readable and nothing much resolved. Her new novel, *An Error of Judgment,* stretches the resources of this genre pretty far. . . . Miss Hansford Johnson was so talented when she confined herself to what might roughly be called conjugal problems. It is her new pre-occupation with the cosmic ones that does not become her.

Anne Duchene. *MGW.* July 26, 1962, p. 11

A petite and puckish Englishwoman, Pamela Hansford Johnson, like her husband C. P. Snow, has earned a considerable writer's reputation on both sides of the Atlantic. Her latest work [*Night and Silence—Who is Here?*], also petite and puckish, is an academic novel in which Lady Snow undertakes a merry lampoon of the donnish dilemmas and moral stratagems which have occupied Sir Charles in such famous fictions as *The Masters* and *The Affair.*

The basis of her story, as in so many of his, is the politics of academic preferment. But what a difference! . . . If the locale is American, the comedy itself is distinctly British, in the Dickensian tradition of broad caricature with interludes of farce. . . . These, one and all, are people whose predicaments can be enjoyed without our feeling the slightest compulsion to believe in their actuality. It is likely, nevertheless, that Lady Snow will be said to have written a *roman à clef.* She and her husband recently enjoyed a term as joint Visiting Fellows at Wesleyan University.

Carlos Baker. *NYT.* July 28, 1963, p. 4

The novels of Pamela Hansford Johnson are the basic material of the publisher looking for a well-made, intelligent novel that stands the chance of a book club selection and will go well with a public that wants its fiction neither light nor heavy. It is the kind of fiction that keeps the novel going in between the valleys and the peaks. It handles ideas in terms of the people involved; it rarely aims at abstractions, and the conflicts themselves are those one encounters in daily life. Emotions are of course played down; there are few powerful climaxes, few dramatic intensities that would weight the novel unduly. In brief, the novelist makes no attempt to exceed the tight, well-controlled world over which he or she is a master.

> Frederick R. Karl. *A Reader's Guide to the*
> *Contemporary English Novel* (Thames and
> Hudson, 1963), p. 275

JOHNSTON, DENIS (1901–   )

Denis Johnston's *The Moon in the Yellow River* was first produced at the Abbey Theatre, Dublin, in 1931. The Abbey, supported by the Irish government as a National Theatre, has not maintained that imaginative understanding of the Irish genius which characterized its early years: much of its production has been of a parochially realistic kind. But in Johnston it found for a time an author who was able to do for the modern Ireland, faced with the impact of science and invention upon its ancient way of life, what Yeats and Synge had done for the older Ireland. He wrote about Dublin herself in *The Old Lady Says No,* and about the coming of technology to the countryside in this play. Each is the product of a brilliant, subtle and essentially Irish mind; each of his characters has its own rich eccentricity, and no facile conclusion is sought for the complex conflicts both of personality and of ideas.

> E. Martin Browne. *Three Irish Plays*
> (Penguin Bks., 1959), p. 7

In 1918 a new theatrical grouping was established, the Dublin Drama League, with the intention of bringing to Ireland contemporary classics from the international stage. . . . In 1928 this group led to the founding of the Dublin Gate Theatre by Hilton Edwards and Michael LacLiammoir. Denis Johnston was at one time producer for this theatre, and though the subject-matter of his plays is still Irish, his treatment reflects the wider horizons of this company. *The Moon in the Yellow River,* which was welcomed in London and New York, as well as in Dublin, is a straight play within the Chehov-Ibsen tradition. It deals with the impact of material progress on a countryside still dominated by easy-going traditionalism and romantic nationalism. As in O'Casey, there is conflict between an advancing ideal and human nature, and as usual comedy and tragedy are juxtaposed. But unlike O'Casey, the conflict is presented with full intelligence instead of with despairing pity. It is seen as part of a wider context: the "message" of the play is to reflect a genuine perplexedness, which is as relevant to Russia or China (from which the title comes) as to Ireland.

Johnston's three most original plays, *The Old Lady Says 'No!'*, *A Bride For the Unicorn,* and *The Golden Cuckoo,* broke from conventional stagecraft and used a technique which was open and expressionist, similar to that of Toller and Brecht. Unfortunately, they depend for their full effect on a close acquaintance with Irish history and tradition and on the emotional undertones this involves. For this reason they have had little success abroad.

> P. N. Furbank in *The Modern Age* (*Pelican Guide
> to English Literature,* ed. Boris Ford)
> (Penguin Bks, 1961), pp. 203–4

JONES, DAVID (1895–   )

Am I dotty? For some fifteen years now Mr. David Jones has made me ask myself this question. When *In Parenthesis* came out in 1938, I thought it—I think so still—the greatest book about the First World War that I had read. But nobody seemed to notice or write about it. Having lived with *The Anathemata* for the last ten months, I feel as certain as one can feel of anything that it is one of the most important poems of our time. But where are the bells? Where are the cannon? I have given it to friends whose literary taste I have always found reliable (true, they are Americans), and they seem to be completely baffled by it. I cannot, therefore, write an evaluatory review, for that presupposes, or should presuppose, that the public are well acquainted with the text: I can only attempt to describe the sort of poem it is, the sort of thing I believe Mr. Jones is trying to do. . . .

Joyce certainly, and Dante probably, have had a hand in Mr. Jones' development, but his style is in no sense an imitation. Nor is this verse as "free" as at a superficial glance it looks. Mr. Jones is not a Welshman for nothing. Welsh poetry is famous for its use of internal rhyme and assonance, and a careful examination of the last quotation, for example, will disclose similar subtleties. Like Joyce, Mr. Jones uses a very wide vocabulary; like Joyce and Dante his poem is full of riddles which require considerable erudition to solve: unlike Joyce and Dante, however, he accompanies his text with his own commentary notes. . . .

The *Anathemata* is not an easy poem to describe. Imagine that, in the middle of the 20th century, in a world of atom-bombs, posters, and gossip-columnists, a man is attending Mass. This man is Adam, a European, a Welshman, a Londoner, a poet, himself. Some phrase or other from the rite catches his attention and his mind goes wool-gathering. And why not? Is not the rite he is attending itself a rite of anamnesis? The language sounding now in his physical ear is remote from the present age, formal, humourless, the creation of a vanished kind of society. . . .

Mr. Jones has set out to write a poem which should be at once epic, contemporary, and Christian. . . . I can only conclude by reiterating my profound admiration for this work and expressing the hope that many others will come to share it.

W. H. Auden. *Enc.* Feb. 1, 1954, pp. 67–68, 70–71

Mr. Jones's primitivism [*Anathemata*] is of the Romantic tradition; it would have seemed painfully odd neither to Joyce (whom Mr. Jones greatly admires) nor to Yeats, whose belief that art must be "constantly flooded with the passions and beliefs of ancient times" Mr. Jones would fully endorse. He is a Catholic, and obsessed with the *romanitas* of the Welsh tradition. These and other interests give Mr. Jones's writing a personal flavour; he is almost as mannered as Yeats, though much less skillful, and sometimes negligent in exposition and ugly in style. His most important essay, "Art and Sacrament," is however, blameless in these respects, and at his best Mr. Jones is a remarkably powerful writer. He is well read in an artist's way—his reading is assimilated into a growing body of ideas and convictions, not judged but ransacked. His major source is Maritain, but Maritain thought and felt and disagreed with (on the relation between "symbol" and "sacrament," for instance) . . . .

To argue for the absolute value of such systems, as some do, is manifestly absurd and harmful. They are not required to be valid in themselves, but to provide contexts for the anti-intellectualism that modern art, for historical reasons, requires; its character is such that it *must* be in conflict with a scientific world-view to survive at all.

This certainly creates problems for a peace-maker, and for anybody accustomed to thinking of problems as soluble and obscurities as undesirable. The artist's habit of conceiving life as a tragedy, his air of living in a fallen world, will strike a Rutherford as mere posing. To get a closer understanding between the two it would certainly be necessary to effect a major revolution in the arts; it is impossible, I think, to guess what the changes would be.

Anyone who calls this an extravagant statement should try to find scientists who could take Mr. Jones's book seriously, or artists willing to call it nonsense. [1959]

Frank Kermode. *Puzzles and Epiphanies* (Routledge and Kegan Paul, 1962), pp. 30, 34

In Parenthesis is the kind of book which can have no results, in that its form and style are so outrageously personal that no other writer could learn much from Jones's use of them. But it is indeed a remarkable work in that it succeeds in uniting the intentions of the Georgian war poets with the power of later prose narratives. . . . It may be the best book about World War I in English.

John Hollander. *PR*. Summer, 1962, p. 453

JONES, GLYN (1905–   )

I should advise students of modern fiction to look out for Mr. Glyn Jones's next production; but I am not sure that I should recommend them to try his present collection of short stories [*The Blue Bed*]. Mr. Jones is a Communist and a Welshman, and has a mystical tendency inherited from both sides. . . . Mr. Jones alternately illuminates his subject with some vivid straightforward pages and obscures it in a fog of angry rhetoric. . . . At present, he is too thorough a Communist to depend on art, but too good an artist to make a convincing political preacher.

Peter Quennell. *NSN*. Jan. 30, 1937, p. 164

The narrator [of *The Learning Lark*] is a reluctant school-master teaching reluctant young louts in a Secondary Modern school. . . . There are incidental humours and the author, without any direct preaching, shows himself decently shocked by the state of popular education on this lowest level; but it does not add up to much of a book.

TLS. Jan. 22, 1960, p. 45

JONES, GWYN (1907–   )

Mr. Gwyn Jones seems to be the best writer of short stories to have come out of Wales since Mr. Rhys Davies. *The Still Waters* is a very good collection indeed. The longest story in the collection, "The Green Island," is superb, challenging comparison with the best of Lawrence. . . . Not that Mr. Gwyn Jones owes any debt to Lawrence: he is a highly individual writer. But, like Lawrence, he has a poetic style which enables him to seize the living quality of landscape and that intuitive sense of symbolism which Mr. Forster in *Aspects of the Novel* calls prophetic. . . . At his finest, in "The Green Island" and "The Prisoners," he is at once magical and menacing.

Walter Allen. *NSN*. Jan. 1, 1949, p. 15

Professor Gwyn Jones has written stories in a variety of moods, and his eloquent prose has graced them all. Perhaps the role that suits him best is that of the impersonal judge; the form, that in which the story emerges singly; the subject, the relationship between man and beast. The grimness that marks his best stories about people becomes tenderness when he deals with animals.

TLS. June 1, 1956, p. 328

The immense value of the scholarly introduction apart, this new *Egil's Saga* demands praise for its treatment of the verse and the incomparably easy prose style of the narrative. This translator believes that . . . his translation must convey some measure of the sense and technical mastery of Egil's verse. He unquestionably succeeds in doing just this in the three long poems: his translation of "Sonatorrek" will stand comparison with Ezra Pound's version of the Old English poem, "The Seafarer." . . . In a similar fashion his prose strikes a happy balance between an accurate rendering of the original and the reader's just demand that he be carried along by the sheer power of the story. . . .

Professor Jones has been active and successful as a writer and translator for more than a quarter of a century. *Egil's Saga* is the best thing he has ever done.

TLS. Sept. 30, 1960, p. 628

JONES, HENRY ARTHUR (1851–1929)

The critics are ever eager to avenge themselves on a dramatist who gives them anything to think about; and Mr. Jones, therefore, even at his technically best, seldom gets a good word from the fraternity. The good word deserved by *The Lackey's Carnival* is . . . that here is the first effort made by a dramatist to penetrate the character of servants. . . . In projecting Thomas Tarboy Mr. Jones has brought upon the stage something that is (despite excrescences) as true essentially as it is new. What is painful in life is, if it be realized, delightful in art. Therefore I thank Mr.

Jones. But I hope that he will soon write a play in which *all* of the chief characters shall be servants. (Oct. 6, 1900)

Max Beerbohm. *Around Theatres* (Rupert
Hart-Davis, 1953), pp. 105, 108–9

Whatever else he may be, this author is a born playwright, an irrepressible practitioner of the dramatic form. . . . He has dramatic instinct in plenty; he has a certain sort of originality, and a certain sort of thought, of wit, of style; he has great fervor, if not clarity, of imagination; and he has often shown himself a master of the art of dramatic story-telling. His work has been throughout distinguished by an honorable ambition. Matthew Arnold applauded his first success, *The Silver King;* and this approbation . . . had a determining effect on Mr. Jones's development. He threw himself resolutely into the pursuit of culture. He read the *Nineteenth Century* and he wrote in it. He determined that his work should be a criticism of life, and especially of that British philistinism which his mentor despised, and which he himself, with his yeoman ancestry and his business antecedents, had studied at close quarters. The trouble was that his culture did not sit very lightly on him. It scarcely seemed made to his measure, and he wore it with a certain self-consciousness.

He had been cradled in melodrama and could never quite shake off its gestures and intonations. . . . To his works of a lighter order I have applied the term comedies of intrigue. Perhaps they might better have been called satiric comedies. Sometimes they flagellate Philistinism with a scourge remotely modelled on that of Matthew Arnold; sometimes, on the other hand, they scoff at idealism. . . .

But Mr. Jones's masterpiece in dramatic story-telling is undoubtedly *Mrs. Dane's Defence.* . . . As we listen to the dialogue, we canot but be conscious that we have got utterly away both from the convention of wit and the convention of rhetoric—"Flat and commonplace!" some people may say; but it is not flat and commonplace, for it is tingling with human emotion. . . .; and every speech, while perfectly natural in the situation, is placed, with the deftness of a mosaic artist, just where it is needed.

William Archer. *The Old Drama and the New*
(Heinemann, 1923), pp. 293, 298, 301–2

Ironically enough, his fight for a free theatre helped to open the door for Ibsen and the subsequent dramatic upheaval which was destined to render obsolete within a few years much of the work of Pinero, Chambers, Jones, and other leaders of the 'nineties.

Henry Arthur Jones is not a first-rate dramatist, partly because of artistic limitations, partly because of deliberate surrender to the unaesthetic gingerbread demands of the commercial theatre. His is a drama of compromise both because of his inherent conservatism and because of the combined pressure of manager, public, and censor. He frankly acknowledged that much of his work was modified by objective considerations. . . .

Jones exaggerates the value of his compromise. A study of his unacted plays reveals their inferiority to his successful comedies of manners, and in nearly every one of his commercial failures, the judgment of the public was sound. *The Divine Gift* which Jones wrote to please himself uncramped by demands of the theatre is a pseudo-literary, uncritical record of late Victorian prejudice and narrow-mindedness, and would bore a modern audience with its pompous homilies and primitive ideas of women and labor; whereas *Mary Goes First*, written for the London theatre of 1913, in years to come will bear revival along with *Love for Love, The School for Scandal, The Importance of Being Earnest*, and *The Liars*. Superficial and conventional as it is, *Mary Goes First* is genuinely humourous, the satire will continue to sting, and we shall see 1913 through Jones as we see 1775 through Sheridan.

Henry Arthur Jones found the contemporary English drama insignificant, puerile; he left it respected, flourishing, and mature. That he alone is responsible for the renascence is contrary to fact and reason; that to him belongs a generous share of the credit for restoring the drama in England to its rightful position as a civilized and civilizing art is indisputable.

Richard A. Cordell. *Henry Arthur Jones and the Modern Drama* (N.Y., Ray Long and Richard R. Smith, 1932), pp. 252–53

JOYCE, JAMES (1882–1941)

Let us not take it for granted that life exists more fully in what is commonly thought big than in what is commonly thought small. Any one who has read *The Portrait of the Artist as a Young Man* or, what promises to be a far more interesting work, *Ulysses*, now appearing in the *Little Review*, will have hazarded some theory of this nature as to Mr. Joyce's intention. On our part, with such a fragment before us, it is hazarded rather than affirmed; but whatever the intention of the whole, there can be no question but that it is of the utmost sincerity and that the result, difficult or unpleasant as we may judge it, is undeniably important. In contrast with those whom we have called materialists, Mr. Joyce is spiritual; he is concerned at all costs to reveal the flickerings of that innermost flame which flashes its messages through the brain, and in order to preserve it he disregards with complete courage whatever seems to him adventitious, whether it be probability, or coherence, or any other of these signposts which for generations have served to support the imagination of a reader when called upon to imagine what he can neither touch nor see. The scene in the cemetery, for instance, with its brilliancy, its sordidity, its incoherence, its sudden lightning flashes of significance, does undoubtedly come so close to the qiuck of the mind that, on a first reading at any rate, it is difficult not to acclaim a masterpiece. If we want life itself, here surely we have it. Indeed, we find ourselves fumbling rather awkwardly if we try to say what else we wish, and for what reason a work of such originality yet fails to compare, for we must take high examples, with *Youth* or *The Mayor of Casterbridge*. It fails because of the comparative poverty of the writer's mind, we might say simply and have done with it. But it is possible to press a little further and wonder whether we may not refer our sense of being in a bright yet narrow room, confined and shut in, rather than enlarged and set free, to some limitation imposed by the method as well as by the mind. Is it the method that inhibits the creative power? Is it due to the method that we feel neither jovial nor magnanimous, but centred in a self which, in spite of its tremor of susceptibility, never embraces or creates what is outside itself and beyond? Does the emphasis laid, perhaps didactically, upon indecency, contribute to the effect of something angular and isolated? Or is it merely that in any effort of such originality it is much easier, for contemporaries especially, to feel what it lacks than to name what it gives? . . . This method has the merit of bringing us closer to what we were prepared to call life itself; did not the reading of *Ulysses* suggest how much of life is excluded or ignored, and did it not come with a shock to open *Tristram Shandy* or even *Pendennis* and be by them convinced that there are not only other aspects of life, but more important ones into the bargain.

Virginia Woolf. *The Common Reader*
(Hogarth Pr., 1925), pp. 190–92

The new language of Joyce [in *Anna Livia Plurabelle*] is only a kind of piano-tuning, whereby he tightens up certain words by grafting fresher foreign equivalents on to them, approximates them to other words to strengthen their own vigour, above all puns with them freely, and gives words a synthetic meaning, with which either to express life, or simply to make a series of academic jokes. The experiment may be a failure, just as Esperanto or phonetic spelling may be a failure, but there is nothing that is contrary to reason in the idea itself. The chief defect of Mr. Joyce's new language is that, so far, it has swamped the lyrical quality of his other prose writings; he has not attempted purple patches in it so much as rhetorical imitations of them. [1929]

Cyril Connolly. *The Condemned Playground*
(Routledge, 1953), p. 9

This basic weakness, with all its compensatory self-deceptions, is seen flagrantly in the meagre harmonics of his verse, in which he seeks to put himself against the unadulterated twilight of local bards by a discreet admixture of Verlainish nuance and English sharper constructions. If *Chamber Music* were the work of a boy, it would not be fair to press the point of its etiolated emotional cadence; but Joyce published the book when he was past the middle twenties, and has sanctioned its reprint— even aggravated the offense with *Pomes Pennyeach*. It is recorded that he used to go about Dublin at the time of this versifying, claiming that he echoed the Elizabethan musicks—a vanity altogether without foundation. A much more bastard and feeble note sounds in these stanzas. . . .

We are forced back to Joyce's personal adolescence because Joyce has stayed there himself. The problems of adolescence remain unsolved in his work, though most cunningly hidden by (a) Flaubertian bitterness: *realism*; (b) infinite cubes of time: *Ulysses*; (c) infinite algebra of gossip: *Work in Progress*.

But it may be objected, this analysis is irrelevant—what do the personal limitations of Joyce matter if his work is technically exciting and adequate? I do not see how this plea can stand. If a technique is adequate, it is adequate to something. . . . If Joyce's difficult puberty stands in the way of his complete realisation of the characters he seeks to project, if it conditions the direction of his technique, it cannot be ignored. . . .

Not that Joyce can be dismissed by the demonstration of this schism at the heart of his experience and of his expression. Still, it does dispose of him as a first-class creator. On the second-rate level he remains a most interesting, ingenious, and suggestive writer, one of the greatest of comprehensive innovators. . . . His work is synthetic without being able to synthesise. . . .

Jack Lindsay in *Scrutinies*, Vol. II, coll. Edgell
Rickword (Wishart, 1931), pp. 101, 103, 107

The hubble-bubble of talk round Mr. Joyce's *Ulysses* has now subsided, but the book's influence is likely to be far-reaching. Although copies are destined to find their way into the libraries of those who collect books described in catalogues as "very curious," it is far from being pornographic. *Ulysses* is one of the most obscene books ever written, but not a lascivious one; it is, almost dismally indeed, the opposite of that. A nightmare-congregation of caricatures, parodies, obsessions, verbal clatter, noises, filth, terror and disgusts, it is at any rate a mass projected with tremendous force and hurled far from its author into the sphere of literature. . . .

Ulysses strikes me as less important as a work of art than as a symptom. For pages and pages it is nearly unreadable, making the reader ache with boredom; but it contains more artistic dynamite than any book published for years. That dynamite is placed under the modern novel. The author of *Ulysses* is a man of prodigious talents, and one by-product of his work is to show what is *not* worth doing in fiction, and he shows that by going one better than the modern novel in the directions in which it is moving. Is the object to put life under a magnifying glass and show its very texture, the stuff it is made of? Mr. Joyce employs a far stronger glass, and writes a vast book about twenty-four hours; one sees the carpet from the point of view of a beetle. Is Mr. X.'s object to catch the patter and interchange of talk? Mr. Joyce has invented a method of record which does it twice as well. Does Mr. Y. work the sex-interest for all it is worth? Mr. Joyce seems to say, "Oh, you rely on lust, do you, to interest people? You are very insipid; I'll give you the real thing." Does Mr. Z. aim at realism, priding himself on shirking nothing which is part of normal experience. Mr. Joyce soon has his hero firmly seated on the water-closet. But, above all, the up-to-date writer flatters himself that he conveys the drift of thoughts and feelings through the heads of his characters, and here Mr. Joyce undercuts him completely. I cannot conceive any modern novelist, who is capable of grasping the merits of this work and at the same time doubts its value, not being utterly discouraged.

Desmond MacCarthy. Criticism (Putnam,
1932), pp. 298–99, 304

Joyce is a man of violently original genius with a pedantic regard for tradition. Tradition binds him, he breaks its bonds, and proceeds to tie himself up again. For him it wears many guises, but, as with so many Irish writers, its most obstinate guise has been the Catholic Church. *Ulysses* is a great Catholic novel. Behind it, in direct line, even more inescapably than the *Odyssey* which has given it its form, and the French writers who suggested its technique, stand the Revelation of St. John, the early Fathers, the *Divina Commedia,* and the Inquisition. It is a classic of apostasy, the agonized attempt of the artist to bring all life within his scope, aware that the effort is essentially a religious effort, and agonized because, while his genius forces him to accept his own interpretation, he cannot forget the interpretations of others. Over the whole book, as over its predecessor, *A Portrait of the Artist as a Young Man,* broods the sense of sin, that terrific legacy which the Catholic Church irrevocably leaves her children. *"Introibo ad altare Dei"*—the words introducing the Martello tower are the text for that long June day, the hope of morning, the world's first innocence, the opening of the *Odyssey*, the banner that the day so quickly soils. *Ulysses,* although its chief character is no longer the artist but *l'homme moyen sensuel,* extended to his full capacity from ape to god, is the conflict between religion and experience, on a scale which most religious men are unable or unwilling to face: and the blasphemies which turn the short-sighted against it are the desperate gestures of a man doomed to accept, with his entrails if not with his intellect, certain Last Things. In all the analyses, examinations, glossaries and interpretations of Joyce's masterpiece, this, the central fact, has never been sufficiently stressed. *Ulysses* is a moral work, and Joyce, for all his detachment, a moralist: not a rational moralist like Shaw, but a superstitious moralist: a man with a sense of sin.

To say this is not for an instant to lose sight of his artistry. The staggering thing about *Ulysses* is the art which has controlled it, and the art which has been put into it. But Joyce is a Catholic artist. The Catholic artist is always aware, in theory, that none is better fitted to face and portray life in all its aspects, but he is hindered by the problems of expediency. Joyce, refusing to admit these problems, is uneasy in his mind over the refusal. He cannot but refuse: the originality of his genius gives him no choice: but he shares in the remorse, the Agenbite of Inwit, that remains among the ashes of Bloom's and Stephen's day.

L. A. G. Strong in *The English Novelists,* ed. Derek Verschoyle (Chatto and Windus, 1936), pp. 279–81

I have spoken of *Finnegans Wake* as a universe. We can now see that in describing the external universe through the veil of Earwicker's dream, it also describes the internal universe of the unconscious. The internal universe, too, captures the whole of time; it preserves, with that "prodigious conservatism" of which Jung spoke, the record of history. As Joyce says, "the world, mind, is, was and will be writing its wrunes for ever, man, on all matters that fall under the ban of our infrarational senses." Earwicker is all men: that is why he is called "Here Comes Everybody"; that is why he is "magnificently well worthy of any and all . . . universalization"; and that is why we discover in the dream of Earwicker a whole archeology of experience, "a jetsam litterage of convolvuli of times lost or strayed, of lands derelict and of tongues laggin too." Indeed, Earwicker descends below the human level of evolution. He is an animal, a fish, an insect, a compound known as H_2CE_3; he is an atom, in a nascent universe in which there is nothing but "atoms and ifs."

This opposition of the external and the internal universes leads us back to the life-and-death cycle which runs through *Finnegans Wake*. For in psychological terms the life-and-death cycle is the path of the mystic, the path back into the unconscious and the re-emergence of the mind with new vigor and new faith. A great many twentieth-century men of letters, having lost faith in rational thought, have become convinced that truth and goodness can be found in mysticism. Toynbee, to give one example, regards the mystic experience as the crucial one in human destiny.

Joyce too has his moments of mysticism. The rhythm of his book is the rhythm of his mind passing back and forth from the conscious and the civilized to the unconscious and the primitive. The mind of Earwicker rises and falls through the range of unconsciousness. The cries of his children, "Hide! Seek! Hide! Seek!" become "High! Sink! High! Sink! Highohigh! Sinkasink!" in time with the movements of his mind. This rhythm, embodied in the death-and-resurrection myths of all times and societies, is the main theme of *Finnegans Wake*.

It ought to be pointed out, however, that Joyce is not temperamentally a mystic; while one of the functions of *Finnegans Wake* is to record the apocalyptic mysticism and fertility worship of our time, another is to poke endless fun at them. . . .

There are, of course, various valid criticisms of Joyce's novel; each reader will find his own. What I have tried to suggest here is that the book cannot be put easily aside on the ground that it is irresponsibly unorthodox or of only special interest. If this is an oecumenical period of history, *Finnegans Wake* is our oecumenical novel. And far more striking than its exoticism is its appalling orthodoxy.

Richard Chase. *AmS*. Autumn, 1944, pp. 425–26

For curious words he ransacks Skeat's *Etymological Dictionary*, adds them to his treasure house, and taking them out, repeats them again and again. Although Stephen agrees that words are receptacles for thought, they acquire for him another value. Becoming intercessors, they stand between himself and reality. Through their agency alone he has "glimpses of the real world about him." Words do more than reveal that reality. They create it, and, as if God's compasses, draw significant form.

Like Rabelais, Joyce made grotesque catalogues of words. Like Nashe and Shakespeare, enamored of words in the age of discovery, he delighted in abundance. He called Shakespeare, whom he admired less as playwright than as poet, a "lord of language," richer than Dante and better to have on a desert island. Detesting "vague words for a vague emotion," he admired the precision of Flaubert. The Male Brutes who appear before unmanned Mr. Bloom in the brothel have only one thing to say. "Good!" they say. That is the *mot juste*. When the printers objected to the word "bloody" in the manuscript of *Dubliners*, Joyce replied that bloody is the one word in the language that can create the effect he wanted.

As he admired the words of other artists, so he exulted in his own command of what he considered the greatest of powers. To Eugene Jolas he announced: "I can do anything with language." His study of archaic language and his notes on living language in street or pub had made him master of all verbal effects from the divine speech of thunder to "low-quacity." The words "Sechseläuten" and "lebensquatsch," which occur throughout *Finnegans Wake,* are examples of both kinds. Sechseläuten is the spring festival of Zürich, and lebensquatsch or life's muddle is the interpretation by a Zürich waitress of Joyce's demand for lemon squash. He once told Frank Budgen that he had been working all day at two sentences of Ulysses: "Perfume of embraces all him assailed. With hungered flesh obscurely, he mutely craved to adore." When asked if he was seeking the *mot juste,* Joyce replied that he had the words already. What he wanted was a suitable order.

He composed a novel as great poets compose their poems. Under his hand all the resources of word, rhythm, and tone conspired to create intricate beauty. His novels are more like poems or symphonies or statues than like ordinary novels. Maybe they are not novels at all but works of their own kind like *Tristram Shandy* or *Gargantua,* which we call novels for want of a word for them. We must approach Joyce's greater works as we would a poem or a symphony. That reader who reads *Ulysses* as if it were a common thing would be disappointed.

W. Y. Tindall. *James Joyce* (Scribner's Sons, 1950), pp. 95–96

Yeats impressed Joyce with the importance of symbol in a story. But Joyce worked out his own technique and called it *epiphany.* . . . In essence, it may be put thus: radiance equals epiphany equals symbol. He sees epiphany as a device of expression that, perfect in its wholeness and harmony, will show forth in an instant of illumination a meaning and significance greater than the words in another combination would carry. Thus clay may be clay, but in Joyce's short story [in *Dubliners*] it becomes, through skillful arrangement of the total pattern, symbolically representative of impending death, and hence it lends meaning to the otherwise trivial narrative. . . .

The symbolic content of *Dubliners,* what it suggests and insinuates, is far more damaging to the object of his attack than the flippant reference to Edward VII in one story or the hint of perversion in another. The irony of the decade of delay in publishing the book is that it was caused by petty differences of opinion concerning what was proper. During all that time, nobody objected to the much more explosive symbolic content because nobody recognized its presence.

Marvin Magalaner, "Dubliners" in Magalaner and Richard Kain. *Joyce: The Man, The Work, The Reputation* (N.Y., N.Y. Univ. Pr., 1956), pp. 70–71, 57

On January 7 he wrote off in one day, and with scarcely any hesitation, an autobiographical story that mixed admiration for himself with irony. . . . He called it "A Portrait of the Artist," and sent it to the editors [of *Dana*]. This was the extraordinary beginning of Joyce's mature work. It was to be remolded into *Stephen Hero,* a very long work, and then shortened to a middle length to form *A Portrait of the Artist as a Young Man*. But this process took ten years.

In "A Portrait of the Artist," for the first time since writing *A Brilliant Career,* Joyce was willing to attempt an extended work, to give up the purity of lyrics and ephiphanies. He was resolved to gather the stages of his spiritual experience together in a connected pattern. It is difficult to say whether what he wrote was essay or story, for it has elements of both, the essay strained by apostrophe and dramatic exhortation, the narrative presented for the most part discursively. At the age of twenty-one, Joyce had found he could become an artist by writing about the process of becoming an artist, his life legitimizing his portrait by supplying the sitter, while the portrait indicated the sitter by its evident admiration for him. That admiration was already a little complicated by the attitude which, in the later book, *A Portrait of the Artist as a Young Man,* has led some readers to suppose that Joyce could not bear his own hero. But in both portraits, as well as in the intermediate *Stephen Hero,* there is no lack of sympathy on the author's part; he recognizes, however, that earlier stages of the hero's life were necessarily callow, and makes the callowness clear in order to establish the progress towards the mature man.

Richard Ellman. *James Joyce* (N.Y., Oxford Univ. Pr., 1959), pp. 149–50

A little while ago it was alleged that the task of "experiment" was accomplished and over; and the common cry was for a "consolidation of gains." Yet, although it is often reluctantly conceded that there is something wrong with the orthodox novel as a form, *Ulysses* is pointed to if at all as a still and rather brackish backwater. At the same time, by the law of ambiguity that surrounds these matters, it is alleged that its influence has been over-extensive. In fact it can be argued with more truth that it has been nil. By English criticism at any rate Joyce is still received with a mixture of awe, bemusement, indifference and even hostility. The awe is accorded to the relentlessness with which his conceptions were carried through, but is nearly always accompanied by the suggestion that these nocturnal peregrinations through blind alleys are enormous eccentricities in which serious people concerned with the political, scientific and philosophical preoccupations of the modern world—the sort of people who read C. P. Snow, for example—can scarcely be expected to take much interest.

In America, of course, the case is different. There Joyce has become an inexhausible hunting ground for hermeneutical exegesists to whom semeiology, both in the literary and in the medical-psychological sense, is a science beside which plain criticism offers no excitements and no advantages at all. . . . At least in America Joyce continues to be received as a great writer. That, however, will do little to alter the situation here, for piety is off-putting to all but the pious and simple affection is in the end the only doorway of perception where art is concerned.

TLS. Nov. 20, 1959, p. 669

The commonest charge against *Finnegans Wake* is that it is unreadable; and, if it is, exegesis will not help it very much, for although we may apprehend a book's quality and value long before we understand it, and need intelligent annotation to achieve understanding, there must be some initial apprehension and some original delight. You cannot prove a book's worth by axiom and though exegesis may increase a reader's excitement, it is unlikely to create it. . . .

But whatever else language such as that in the book is, it is also attractive and exciting, disturbing and enchanting in itself, nor is it impossible for the average reader to be affected by some at least of the associations—with Alice, both in wonderland and through the looking-glass, with Eden and with the Fall. . . .

Joyce paid very little attention to literary merit in his "subsuming," though he quotes from nearly all Shakespeare's plays and mentions them by name. He was, among other things, "psychoanaloosing" himself, and any writers, good, bad or indifferent, who had come into his life were used.

So also were any writers with whose life or work he could identify his themes. Swift, who stood in a quasi-sexual, quasi-parental attitude to two young women, could easily become H. C. Earwicker, for H.C.E. stands in such a relationship towards his own daughter Issy; and of course Stella and Vanessa could be made to illustrate the split personality theme in the treatment of the latter. Like any long poem, *Finnegans Wake* is tiring to read in long stretches and as with any poem it is hopeless to try to force the mind to it. But . . . its music, its comedy and its consolatory power must be apparent.

TLS. Feb. 5, 1960, p. 82

In a typical outburst of bitterness against his supporters and admirers in the United States James Joyce once complained that they "would bring out a collection of my selected pawn tickets," and, though this may have seemed to him the shrillest exaggeration, how right he was; any post-graduate student proffering such a collection to his professor today might well earn a distinguished Ph.D. But Joyce was the author of his own misfortune, if it was misfortune. Moriarty evokes Holmes; the more skillfully hidden the Pharoah, the more cunning the archeologist. If Sunny Jim Joyce of Dublin has become the Yams Yoyce of international letters he has only himself to blame, or thank. . . .

As a man he was in many ways despicable; he was dirty in youth and dandified in middle-age. He was cold and selfish and jealous—jealous of Synge, of Colum, of Proust, even of Picasso; he never retained a friend or forgot an enemy; every "slight" was exhibited in his black museum, every "disloyalty" was repaid with bitter contumely. He sponged on his brother, his friends, his acquaintances, from the days of Æ I.O.U. down to the thousands he received from Mrs. McCormick and Harriet Shaw Weaver. Of women he came to have a Tolstoyan hatred, saying "I don't see any (beautiful) women and I don't think there are any." Except with Frank Budgen he was a dull conversationalist; he was a compulsive drinker, an uncritical admirer of mediocrity; with no taste in art he was content to live in drab furnished rooms all over Europe, the sad satellites of his family revolving around him and the unfortunate Lucia ending at last in utter madness—she and her father, in Jung's phrase: like two people going to the bottom of a river, one falling and the other diving.

That is the dark, debit side of Joyce, the exterior life he lived in Trieste, in Zurich, in Paris. . . . But there was too the warmth, humour and the prodigious sense of fun, the fabulous concentration which he reserved for his work. Through the years when he was writing *Ulysses,* probably the funniest book of our time, he was continually in pain, in debt or in trouble. . . .

Joyce demanded that his readers should give their lives to reading his works, as he had given his to writing them. It is too much to ask, as it is too much to find the "ideal reader suffering from an ideal insomnia," but in a sense he has had his wish, and if there is no one reader willing to give his life to reading Joyce, there is a sufficiency of Joycemen through-

out the world to ensure that at any moment of any day someone is reading him somewhere.

Donagh MacDonagh. L. May, 1960, pp. 73–75

Until he had finished *Finnegans Wake,* there was little of the detail of his
life that Joyce did not use as a writer. He was fanatically, superstitiously
exhaustive. Because of the controversies about his work, the artist crys-
tallises too easily in our minds; in fact, artist and man are in mixed solution. . . . In a sense, Joyce is all on the surface, for despite his symbolism, his myth-making, and his odd vanity in thinking himself a prophet,
he has the clever laugh of one liable to say it is all Maskelyne and
Devant; he has the constantly spreading consciousnes of a man learning
one more language by ear, thinking of more words for the same things.
He had the brain of a first-class scholar, the temperament of a player,
the drastic courage of his genius; but does his emotional and imaginative
range really go deeper than the longing and the unspoiled sentiment, the
hail and farewell, that one meets in the lovely traditional Irish airs?

Joyce was the cool, proud, fanatical artist, who despite his scornful and
youthful desire to go for everything in life when he broke with Ireland,
in fact never left family life. Without invention as a writer, he plunged
into the known not the unknown, worked continually the same ground.
He was the artist of the lowest common domestic denominator which he
transposed so that it became myth. His imagination began with the word
and met the thing later and returned to the word again. In words he was
enclosed. He saw life as an illuminated pun. He was ready to believe at
the beginning of the last war, for example, that there was some mystic
connection between the resistance of Finland against Russia and the
apotheosis of Finn in *Finnegans Wake.* Such fantasies kept at bay the
boredom to which perhaps his isolation had exposed him; just as well
to make no distinction between language and life. One has seen the
same thing in other Irish writers—Beckett with his cries of "What te-
dium!"—whose gift of language knocks the intolerable minutes on the
head. But when Jung said that Joyce was a classic case of the schizo-
phrenic who successfully translated his obsessions into literature and
saved his reason, and added that, as a psycho-analyst, he had learned
a great deal from him, Joyce was pleased by the flattery, but laughed
at Jung for making such heavy weather out of comic writing. Psychoanalysis was blackmail, he said, on many occasions. There was not a
single serious line in *Ulysses!* What he meant was made clearer when he
spoke of the attempt of the psychiatrists to cure his daughter's madness.
What was the point of being cured when normality meant seeing the
"battered cabman's face" of the world? Better madness! Better words!

V.S. Pritchett. Enc. July, 1960, p. 80

Joyce's relations with the circle of Irish writers that emerged during his school days are most concisely put in the words with which he is said to have acknowledged an introduction to Yeats: "You are too old for me to help you." His own maturity did nothing to modify this brash condescension. In the opening scene of *Ulysses,* Irish art is dismissed as "the cracked lookingglass of a servant," and the old milkwoman representing Ireland mistakes Gaelic for French. Later, in the library episode, Joyce takes occasion to pay his sardonic respects to the chief personalities of the literary revival. It is hardly surprising that one of these personalities, W. K. Magee, the thoughtful Irish critic who writes under the name of John Eglinton, greeted *Ulysses* as "a violent interruption of what is known as the Irish literary renascence." A broader view of the situation, and a closer comprehension of Joyce's undeviating aims, prompted a continental critic, Valery Larbaud, to announce that Ireland had at last made "a sensational re-entry into high European literature." . . .

His best effort, and all his spare time, were devoted to his writing; but he worked slowly, and without encouragement. A small volume of poems, *Chamber Music,* was issued by a London publisher in 1907—Joyce's first book. Hardly anything he ever wrote was published without a struggle. If the editors accepted his manuscripts, the printers refused to set them up; if the publishers brought out his books, the censors destroyed them. If the charge was not obscenity, it was blasphemy; if not blasphemy, it was treason. When his writing was banned in Ireland, it was published in England; when banned in England, it was published in America; and at length it was banned in America. For years after he had become one of the acknowledged masters of English prose, it was illegal to read his books in any English-speaking country. Nor did every potential sponsor let him down so politely as the English printing firm which refused to handle the *Portrait of the Artist* because "we would not knowingly undertake any work of a doubtful character even though it may be a classic."

Harry Levin. *James Joyce* (Faber and
Faber, 1960), pp. 22, 26–27

KAYE-SMITH, SHEILA (1887–1956)

It is to Thomas Hardy and Maurice Hewlett that the English farmer is indebted for his high place in literature. . . . To the company of Hardy and Hewlett must be added Sheila Kaye-Smith. What they have done for the rural folk of Dorset, Devon and Wiltshire, she has done for the farming folk of Sussex. Her love for her country and its folk does not soar as does that of Hilaire Belloc: it goes deep down into the soil, and into the minds and hearts of the people. In the series of novels which began in 1908, and now includes thirteen volumes, Miss Kaye-Smith has portrayed the Sussex folk of the past and the present. . . . She is often brutally frank, in speech as in description, sparing no details of the dung and sweat of the farmyard. . . . Miss Kaye-Smith is as realistic in method as she is romantic in temperament.

Sussex Gorse was . . . hailed by the most competent critics as one of the most remarkable novels of the time. But it was with *Tamarisk Town* that Miss Kaye-Smith first achieved the large circle of readers which is called popularity. The publication of this novel in 1919 also differentiated her sharply from the other considerable women novelists of her time. It is again the story of a man told from a man's viewpoint and with a man's outlook. . . . *Green Apple Harvest* seems to have been somewhat of a respite precedent to the triumph of *Joanna Godden,* 1921. This is the life story of a woman, but a woman with a man's outlook and a man's occupation. She is, of course, a farmer. . . .

Miss Kaye-Smith's latest novels, *The End of the House of Alard,* and *The George and the Crown,* do not, unfortunately, sustain her previous triumph. *The End* is cramped and mechanical, with little of that vitality which gave such charm and power to even her very early work. . . . Its preoccupation with a thesis brings John Galsworthy to the mind of the reader rather than Sheila Kaye-Smith. It is the most popular of her books; it was one of the "best sellers" of its year, about fifty thousand copies being sold within a few months of publication.

Andrew E. Malone. FR. Aug., 1926, pp. 201–3, 206–8

Nothing is more characteristic of the modern novel in its abundance and variety than the existence of a book like this [*Susan Spray*], largely traditional in style and spirit, which is an excellent story and, if not quite "literature," is, at any rate what Mr. Priestley has called "a full-time job." Reviewers tend to accept writers like Miss Kaye-Smith and Mr.

Hergesheimer as novelists of genius, whereas seen in the perspective of literature they are, of course, nowhere. So far as genius goes, Sir Hall Caine has as much as either. They have the common habit of adopting a country or an island, of romanticising the common life, and exploring it through a series of books in extraordinary detail. It is like filling in the corners of a large canvas. There is no new canvas or fresh vision; the same picture becomes more and more complete. Miss Kaye-Smith is not interested in the modern world, not even to Mr. Chesterton's extent of exploding fireworks in it. She has chosen Sussex as a rambling ground because the life is old-flavoured and literary associations are strong.

FR. May, 1931, pp. 707–8

There is not much of accentuated femininity about Sheila Kaye-Smith. Her pages seldom rustle like the silk petticoats of once upon a time. Indeed, she seemed to enter the English novel in rather the same spirit as that in which land girls took up agriculture during the war, and she was one of the first women to assert her right to masculine objectivity without at the same time assuming the name George in order to do so.

Compton Mackenzie. Literature in My Time
(Rich and Cowan, 1933), p. 215

The early books were slight, a young girl's dreams of romance in dingles and upon the Downs; but the later ones, as the author's touch grew more sure, show an increase in confidence and power, as well as in bulk and solidity. *Little England* and *Joanna Godden,* the more ambitious *Tamarisk Town* and *The End of the House of Alard,* and their companions, have brought Sheila Kaye-Smith in the quarter-century of her literary activity to a high place among her male and female professional contemporaries; and in one respect she is, I believe, superior to all the other equally industrious traditional novelists of about her own age.

That respect is an important one in the craft of fiction, although it is often undervalued by amateurs. Sheila Kaye-Smith's novels, which at first took a rather conventionally unconventional view of love, grew steadily in that substance which comes of care in building. They told sober and progressive stories, into which one was slowly inducted and in which one never—the point is two-edged, and yet I must make it— wholly lost oneself. And above all they were models of construction, . . .

Frank Swinnerton. The Georgian Scene (N.Y.,
Farrar and Rinehart, 1934), p. 289

KENNEDY, MARGARET (1896–   )

Sometimes a very successful book proves a handicap to the writer. *The Constant Nymph* has made it hard for Miss Kennedy to get a hearing for her other books. . . . But she does deserve a fair hearing (without comparisons) for her other books. *A Long Time Ago* is not another *Constant Nymph*. Although it has a similar charm, it is another book altogether.

Helen Moran. *LM*. Dec., 1932, p. 171

[*The Constant Nymph*] did enjoy an epidemic success. I can testify from personal experience that in reading it I was not infected by the germ of American influenza. Naturally prejudiced against best-sellers I avoided reading it when it was first published; but when I did read it a few months later I fell a victim to it like everybody else. . . . *The Constant Nymph* appealed chiefly to men over forty and young women. During the epidemic it was read by everybody; but I heard much censoriousness about it from women of taste and experience.

Compton Mackenzie. *Literature in My Time*
(Rich and Cowan, 1933), p. 225

It is Miss Kennedy's tendency to put a little more into the popular novel than it will bear or a little less into the serious one than it requires. She is a perceptive writer who seems afraid to allow her perceptions full play. . . . In general, the novel [*The Oracles*] is agreeable light entertainment modified by the pathos of Miss Kennedy's always lifelike children and the resignation of a disappointed man.

TLS. June 24, 1955, p. 345

KER, W. P. (1855–1923)

The late Professor Ker, a list of whose academic and other distinctions would fill a third of the space at our disposal, . . . died, in his sixty-eighth year, while climbing at Macugnaga—a fitting end, some may think, to a long career which was certainly adventurous, even for a Scotsman. He was, indeed, a wanderer in two realms—the geographical and the intellectual. . . . It was Ker's mission in life to mitigate "the curse of Babel," which, though it does not affect the other arts, breaks up "the light of poetry" among the various languages. Much as he deplored the time thus expended, he acquired, in his journeyings, almost every European tongue, from that of Iceland to that of Spain; and it is his gift for comparing literatures, and for illuminating one through the light from another, that gives to these lectures and essays [*Collected Essays*] no small part of their interest and charm.

Like many men of vast learning, Ker was not a fundamentally original thinker. But, though an uncompromising Tory in politics, he was sturdily opposed to "labels" of every kind. . . . Ker does not work out his themes exhaustively and logically. He touches them here and there at unexpected, but revealing, angles. Curiosity, enthusiasm, observation, memory, and good humour: these are the prevailing qualities in his writing, which flows on like eager, spontaneous conversation, scholarly yet warm-blooded.

NA. Dec. 12, 1925, p. 410

He would come late to his classes, with a pile of books in his hand. . . . He would tiptoe down the theatre at University College with the same step he used on a mountain path, looking neither to left nor right, while a gentle stamping of students' feet showed him how popular he was. He told me that he disapproved of more than three-quarters of an hour for any lecture and came late on purpose. . . . He would say what he wanted in the shortest way and then open his books and read out of the authors themselves the things he wished you to remember. . . . He never insulted his classes by underestimating them: you could pick your treasures out from his three-quarters of an hour: but if you missed them it was your own affair—he never underlined them, and you had to do your thinking for yourself. . . . Once a month or so W. P. would be at home to all the students in the library of University College and we had tea out of a huge brown enamel tea-pot; I went, . . . suffocated with shyness . . . ; but he had this effect on a great many people, perhaps because of his slow speech, every word weighed and meant, and then a sudden look, shafted like a spear, from his blue eyes.

Freya Stark. *Traveller's Prelude* (Penguin Bks, 1962 [John Murray, 1950]), p. 127

For Ker . . . the teaching of English language and literature was something that could not be based, ultimately, on anything narrower than a grasp of the whole European literary tradition; . . . one should know Old Norse as well as Old English. . . . One should be able—in a phrase used by Professor B. Ifor Evans last year in the just published sixteenth W. P. Ker Memorial lecture—to "illuminate one author by reference to another, and often one of a different period and country." Thus Ker, in a passage which Dr. Ifor Evans quotes, relates Rabelais to Cervantes through their attitudes to the Middle Ages.

TLS. July 8, 1955, p. 381

KIPLING, RUDYARD (1865–1936)

Mr. Kipling is so far masculine that he has never displayed a knowledge of women as they are; but the unreality of his male creatures, with his worship of them, makes his name ring quaintly like a pseudonym. . . . Strange that these heroes, with their self-conscious blurtings of oaths and slang, their cheap cynicism about the female sex . . . were not, as they seem to have been, created out of the inner consciousness of a lady-novelist. Mr. Kipling is nothing—never was anything—if not unsqueamish. The ugly word, the ugly action, the ugly atmosphere—for all these he has an inevitable scent; and the uglier they be, the keener seems his relish of them. Strength, mere strength, is not enough to make a hero for him; his hero must also be a brute and a bounder. [1903]

> Max Beerbohm. *Around Theatres* (Rupert Hart-
> Davis, 1953), pp. 246–47

I can remember with what enormous enthusiasm I used to read the little shilling, paper-bound, bluish books which contain the first stories of Mr. Rudyard Kipling. Mr. Kipling himself is of an origin markedly Pre-Raphaelite. He is a nephew of Burne-Jones, and I suppose that the writings of poor "B. V." Thomson, the very Pre-Raphaelite author of *The City of Dreadful Night*—that these works more profoundly influenced the author of *The Man Who Would Be King* than any other pieces of contemporary literature. I do not know whether I knew this at the time, but I can very well remember coming up by a slow train from Hythe and attempting at one and the same time to read the volume of stories containing "Only a Subaltern" and to make a single pipe of shag last the whole of that long journey. And I can remember that when I came at almost the same moment to Charing Cross and the death of the subaltern I was crying so hard that a friendly ticket collector asked me if I was very ill, and saw me into a cab.

> Ford Madox Hueffer. *Memories and Impressions*
> (Harper, 1911), pp. 253–54

Plain Tales from the Hills appeared in 1887, but Kipling's vogue really began in 1891 with Henley's boosting and publication of *Barrack Room Ballads* in the *National Observer*. He was the topic of the hour, everybody was reading him, the circulating libraries needing the storing resources of a pelican, while Henry James sent him to Stevenson in Samoa. Kipling is lately dead, and the tendency to-day, evident successively with

Hardy, Bennett, Bridges, and even Galsworthy, is to forget after the funeral. But for thirty years there had been a gradually increasing inclination to reservations regarding the hasty acclamation of his genius in the 'nineties. It is to the credit of Henry James that, while subscribing to the general admiration in the early 'nineties, he was particular to underline the term *talent* as descriptive of Kipling's gift. Stevenson, too, felt wounded in "a kind of ambition we all have for our tongue and literature"; he felt that "if I had this man's fertility and courage, it seems to me I could heave a pyramid." Kipling never did heave a pyramid; he never did better than *Kim,* which, in spite of its impressive beginning, settles down to a tale of adventure for schoolboy reading. By 1897 Henry James had lost faith in him—at first he had thought that "he perhaps contained the seeds of an English Balzac," but he saw inevitable degeneration "in the light of one's increasingly observing how little of life he can make use of"—and in 1909 Arnold Bennett decided that "he was never great," though "the stories of twenty years ago are touching, if boyish." As a boys' author he may be reclaimed by the next generation, but it seems that his old reputation can never revive, for the scope of his material is only less limited than his capacity for characterisation, and he lacks Stevenson's saving grace of style—his notion of song was that of the baritone at a village cricket club dinner.

But in the 'nineties Kipling was a *furore,* a best-seller, a potent influence and an obvious pattern for imitation. Circumstances conspired to insure his success; he came with the wave of imperialism and pride of empire which followed Randolph Churchill's democratising of the Tory Party, with the popular reaction to romance from the new realism, which was marked as unrespectable by the banning of Zola and as highbrow on its adoption by young men like Crackanthorpe, with the craze of the suburban *bourgeoisie* to read about the picturesque and exciting as an antidote to the uneventful monotony of their own narrow lives. As Le Gallienne remarked, Kipling conveyed the feeling that "we peaceable stay-at-homes are poor milk-and-water creatures, and that there is nothing in the world worth doing save slicing and 'potting' your fellow-creatures." He also identified himself with India, the one sector of the empire not yet exploited by a novelist. . . .

Kipling was not original even in his glorification of "slicing and potting," for Rider Haggard was pre-eminently the novelist of "Blood," and *King Solomon's Mines* appeared a year before *Plain Tales from the Hills.* Haggard, in fact, paved the way for Kipling's reception, and the adulation of Kipling's "genius" by those who allow mere "talent" to Haggard offers an instance of the disciple stealing the prophet's thunder. Both Haggard and Kipling wrote tales of adventures for boys, both lacked skill in drawing character, both wrote more rapidly than was good for them, both possessed in an extraordinary degree the gift of narrative, and both had vivid imaginations, though Haggard's exceeded Kipling's in the ingenuity, variety, and daring of its range. Kipling enjoyed two advantages over Haggard—he specialised in the short story, which was just coming into fashion as an art, and he had a nose for publicity. His *Cleared!* published by Henley after the findings of the Parnell Commission in March 1890, witnessed his instinct for self-advertisement; while Haggard stuck simply to his job of story-telling and entered politics only as a serious advocate of the unpopular cause of agriculture, Kipling became the principal publicist of Henley's Jingoism, so that he, instead of Henley, soon appeared as its chief prophet. A shrewd commercial sense enabled him to gauge the gullibility of the public, and his greatest achievement was his hoaxing a public nourished on Gilbert and Sullivan, into mistaking for poetry of genius his talent for jingling doggerel.

Haggard and Kipling wrote books for boys, and boys proved better judges than their elders. In the first fourteen years of the twentieth century, Kipling hardly competed with Haggard as a schoolboy's favourite. To-day Kipling lies in Westminster Abbey, whither a certain Dr. Foxley Norris did not invite the ashes of John Galsworthy; there is a Kipling Society enabling the old boys of *Stalky and Co.* to dine together; there are many survivors of a passing generation who hope to see his continued cultivation as a "classic." Rider Haggard has been dead eleven years longer, and he is no longer the favourite with boys that he was before the war. But no humbug interferes with rational discussion of his merits, among the least of which appears the bare fact that he preceded Kipling in popularising the glories of bloody adventure.

Malcolm Elwin. *Old Gods Falling* (N.Y.,
Macmillan, 1939), pp. 218–20

Kipling, who anticipated Hitler in the use of the Swastika as an emblem for his work, had the same nostalgic admiration for the ruling caste of his country. In *Stalky and Company,* he pictured his old school as run on public school lines, with fags and the rest of the gear, as suffused, under the right-feeling headmaster, with imperialistic sentiment. But from a recent book of G. C. Beresford, who was a close friend of Kipling at school, it appears that there were no fags, that the boys were not interested in the Empire, and that the headmaster, an amiable man with aesthetic and socialistic leanings, was a friend of Burne-Jones, whom he once helped to organize a workmen's Neutrality Demonstration against the imperialistic Beaconsfield. Kipling, according to Beresford, was a podgy boy with spectacles, who hated games, as is plain in *Stalky and Company,* but was not, as in that book, a resourceful rebel against the masters and athletes. Almost as dark as a native of India, where he was born, Kipling was chiefly remarkable for his precocious knowledge of books and art. There was a tough set in the college, but Kipling avoided it, favoured by the unsystematized tone of the place. Yet even in an ordinary public school he would probably have got off lightly, for, as his cordial relations with the headmaster show, he soon developed that knack of being in with authority which was later to make him the spokesman of everything least congenial to his poetic side.

In all his work he accepted the collective instinct of the herd—"The law of the pack"—as infallible, and envied animals for obeying this law unquestioningly. "The poor brute man," he writes, "an imperfectly denatured animal intermittently subject to the unpredictable reactions of an unlocated Spiritual aura"—a sentence which reveals an attitude to religion similar to A. E. Housman's, another unharmonized poet who kindled more easily to Queen Victoria than to God.

With machines, as even more predictable than animals, Kipling always felt at ease, after he had invested them with enough personality to make them companionable, and not enough to make them capricious. Judging from one of his silliest and most famous poems, he would have enjoyed *Romeo and Juliet* more if Romeo had been a stoker and Juliet a turbine. . . . The cruelty in Kipling sprang from the envy of happier natures in which his deification of the machine, literally or metaphorically, was rooted. . . .

Kipling is always the observer, never the actor, in his imagined scenes of violence, finding a balm for his own self-contempt in picturing the humiliation and suffering of others. . . .

Though he valued knowledge in general, he preferred inside knowledge, which he communicated in what might be called an inside style, the tone of a man talking allusively with two or three friends as experienced as himself. A genteel public for whom the old English novelists were too coarse felt flattered at being allowed to overhear what Kipling was saying. . . .

Kipling's England was the England of the Athenaeum, Carlton and Beefsteak Clubs, of the country-house and the working population as it shows itself to the well-to-do; in the landscape of this England, as its best ornament, he placed Georgie, the Brushwood Boy, a strange bloom of that sentimentality of the upper classes which was one of the unexpected products of a democratic century. . . . As he shrank from understanding himself, he was unable to understand others. The characters in his stories are hardly more than puppets through whom Kipling ventriloquizes the sentiments he thinks proper to their place in the social hierarchy.

Hugh Kingsmill. *Hor.* Sept., 1940, pp. 129, 130, 133–34

Kipling's debt to Swinburne is considerable. . . . Why is the influence of Swinburne and Browning so different from what you would expect? It is due, I think, to a difference of motive: what they wrote they intended to be poetry; Kipling was not trying to write poetry at all. . . .

Kipling does write poetry, but that is not what he is setting out to do. It is this peculiarity of intention that I have in mind in calling Kipling a "ballad-writer". . . .

No writer has ever cared more for the craft of words than Kipling: a passion which gives him a prodigious respect for the artist of any art, and the craftsman of any craft and which is perhaps involved in his respect for Free Masonry. . . . It will not help us to decide the place of Kipling in poetry; we can only say that Kipling's craftsmanship is more reliable than that of some greater poets, and that there is hardly any poem, even in the collected works, in which he fails to do what he has set out to do. The great poet's craft may sometimes fail him: but at his greatest moments he is doing what Kipling is usually doing on a lower plane—writing transparently, so that our attention is directed to the object and not to the medium. . . .

An immense gift for using words, an amazing curiosity and power of observation with his mind and with all his senses, the mask of the entertainer, and beyond that a queer gift of second sight, of transmitting messages from elsewhere, a gift so disconcerting when we are made aware of it that thenceforth we are never sure when it is *not* present: all this makes Kipling a writer impossible wholly to understand and quite impossible to belittle.

T. S. Eliot. "Rudyard Kipling" in *A Choice of Kipling's Verse* (Faber, 1941), pp. 8, 9, 14, 22

Kipling belongs irrevocably to our past, and although the renewed critical attention he has lately been given by Edmund Wilson and T. S. Eliot is friendlier and more interesting than any he has received for a long time, it is less likely to make us revise our opinions than to revive our memories of him. But these memories, when revived, will be strong, for if Kipling belongs to our past, he belongs there very firmly, fixed deep in childhood feeling. . . .

In speaking of Kipling's politics, Mr. Eliot contents himself with denying that Kipling was a fascist; a tory, he says, is a very different thing, a tory considers fascism the last debasement of democracy. But this, I think, is not quite ingenuous of Mr. Eliot. A tory, to be sure, is not a fascist, and Kipling is not properly to be called a fascist, but neither is his political temperament to be adequately described merely by reference to a tradition which is honored by Dr. Johnson, Burke, and Walter Scott. Kipling is not like these men; he is not generous, and, although he makes much to-do about manliness, he is not manly; and he has none of the *mind* of the few great tories. His toryism often had in it a lower-middle-class snarl of defeated gentility, and it is this, rather than his love of authority and force, that might suggest an affinity with fascism. His imperialism is reprehensible not because it *is* imperialism but because it is a puny and mindless imperialism. In short, Kipling is unloved and unlovable not by reason of his beliefs but by reason of the temperament that gave them literary expression. . . .

We must make no mistake about it—Kipling was an honest man and he loved the national virtues. But I suppose no man ever did more harm to the national virtues than Kipling did. He mixed them up with a swagger and swank, with bullying, ruthlessness, and self-righteousness, and he set them up as necessarily antagonistic to intellect. He made them stink in the nostrils of youth.

Lionel Trilling. The Liberal Imagination (N.Y.,
Doubleday, 1950), pp. 114–16, 121–22

A reason why he appealed so strongly to respectable Victorians was that, however disreputable or disorderly some of his best-loved characters might be, they were faithful in the last resort to the same ideals of duty as their better-behaved superiors. Kipling's three soldiers and his three schoolboys were anarchists, but were not subversive anarchists. The soldiers, when not nefariously occupied, were models of law and order and their code did not differ from that of their officers. The schoolboys were rebels, but rebels whose ideals were oddly in accord with those of their headmaster. I fancy it was the mixture of the moralist and the anarchist in Kipling himself that gave him a hold over so vast and varied a public. In this respect at least he might be compared with Robert Burns.

That he conquered the critics as well as the general public was due to the religious zeal with which he applied himself to the art of writing. He was a writer who never betrayed his art through slackness or self-repetition. He passed from territory to territory in his triumphs—from soldiers and Anglo-Indians to the stuff of the *Jungle Books,* on to *Kim,* and thence to *Puck of Pook's Hill,* searching the world of men and animals, of time present and time past, with that intense vision of his that never grew dim. He was fond of psychic themes, and one feels at times that there is an element of the mediumistic in his vision, as though he were seeing wonderful things in a trance.

As for his style, I doubt whether Stevenson himself took the art of writing more seriously than Kipling. There are graces in Stevenson that were beyond Kipling's range, but with what mastery Kipling handles his own more workaday vocabulary. He may go wildly astray at times, as he

does with Mulvaney's picturesque brogue; but this does not prevent
him from being a prince of narrators even here. It is certainly worth
remembering that it was by pains and patience that the greatest body
of short stories ever written by an Englishman was produced.

On Kipling's stature in comparison with that of the other great writers
of short stories, such as Chekhov and Maupassant, it is hard—perhaps
foolish—to dogmatize. Chekhov, I think, had a profounder sympathy
with common life, its griefs and tendernesses. In his knowledge of life
Chekhov had the intimacy of a family doctor in contrast with Kipling
who was so much more the gadabout and casual visitor. Few of Kipling's
best stories are about people in their homes. I doubt again whether
Kipling ever wrote as great a short story as Maupassant's *Boule de Suif*
or as Conrad's *Typhoon*. These, however, are stories of a length halfway between that of a short story and a short novel.

Robert Lynd. *Books and Writers*
(Dent, 1952), pp. 92–93

Haggard's war diary, some of the letters that passed between the two
men, and a few quarto sheets of stationary with scribbled plot outlines
and other jottings which Haggard judiciously saved from extinction enable us to recapture the atmosphere of Kipling's study when both men
worked there together and something of their thoughts and feelings. On
May 22, 1918, after one of his visits to Bateman's, Haggard wrote in his
diary:

Most of the day I have spent with the Kiplings at Bateman's. Rudyard
is not well. . . . Seated together in his study in the old house at Bateman's we had a most interesting four hours together while he fiddled
about with fishing tackle with which he tries to catch trout in the
brook. . . . I happened to remark that I thought this world was one
of the hells. He replied he did not *think,* he was *certain* of it. . . . As
for the future he is inclined to let the matter drift. . . . His humility is
very striking. We were talking of our failings. I said that what grew
on me from day to day was a sense of my own utter insufficiency, of
complete humiliation both in the case of those things that I had done
and left undone. . . . I commented on the fact that he had wide fame
and was known as "the great Mr. Kipling," which should be a consolation to him. He thrust the idea aside with a gesture of disgust.
"What is it worth—what is it all worth?" he answered. Moreover he
went on to show that anything which any of us did *well* was no credit
to us: that it came from somewhere else: "We are only telephone
wires". As an example he instanced (I think) "Recessional" in his
own case and *She* in mine. "*You* didn't write *She* you know," he

said. "Something wrote it—through you!" or some such words.

. . . He opined in his amusing way, that if the present taxation, etc., goes much further, he and I should be seen on opposite sides of the Strand selling "Recessional" and *She* for our daily bread. . . . I believe honestly that outside of his own family, there is no one living to whom Rudyard opens his heart except to myself.

Morton N. Cohen. Dalhousie Review.
Fall, 1960, p. 308

No one has been more damaged in the mind of his immediate posterity than was Kipling by the great repute he suddenly enjoyed near the end of the last century, for work he had largely written before he came of age. Almost at once this high place was attacked by those whom he outraged on aesthetic grounds, as Edward Shanks described in his pioneer study of 1940, Max Beerbohm, especially, pursuing him with an almost vindictive hatred. . . .

Then, together with a growing popularity he incurred the wrath of the intellectual Left, partly because he made no disguise of his opinion that intellectuals approach human beings from the point of view of men who have no insides, and that "liberal 'principle' . . . ends not seldom in bloodshed"; partly from a total misunderstanding of his "Imperialism" (in his autobiographical sketch he always put this in the slightly ironical inverted commas.) He was accused, quite wrongly, of jingoism, especially at the time of the Boer War, it not being noticed that his two best poems on that subject were, one, a praise of "Piet," the other, homage to the enemy General Joubert.

Then later, since for him the only salvation for a man in this life was a devotion to his craft, or a selfless giving of himself to something greater than himself (which was afterwards stupidly confused with Fascism), he did not flourish during the literary phase where the personal relation was the only value to be cherished. He was, in short, in contradiction with the literary sentiment of his time.

As a consequence, the later collections embodying his riper intuitions passed hardly noticed. Readers expected the medicine as before, and did not bother to read at all closely the complex tales of his final period; they are, as the late G. M. Young phrased it, "the Kipling that nobody reads." It is in these that he explored in word and symbol his sense of the mystery of things, of the appalling gulf with which man is faced; he played variants on the theme of healing; and through all these stories there runs a thread of deep compassion. . . . Now that it is becoming possible to regard the heats and errors of fifty years ago as past history, he can be considered as a powerful and many-sided individual, and be

assessed for his qualities as an artist. The French have always been more
alert to this side of him than have been English writers.

TLS. Jan. 15, 1960, p. 25

He would first sell a poem or a story to a newspaper or periodical. He
would then sometimes have a very small separate edition printed, which
both protected his copyright (especially in the United States: there are
117 of these American pamphlets to fifteen English) and provided a
collector's item of genuine rarity. Finally, he would ensure, by including
a handful of unpublished or privately printed pieces, that the subsequent
volume of stories or verse was a must," not only for his faithful readers
but also for the collectors to whom it thus ranked as a first edition—if
only what the French call *édition en partie originale*.

Kipling was also quick to appreciate and to exploit the fad for signed
and limited editions. Furthermore, he perceived the advantages to a
popular writer of giving his works an easily recognizable identity; and in
his later books (and reprints) the bindings, the jackets, the pages, even
the watermarks in the paper, display the now familiar Kipling symbols.
(It was unfortunate that the most familiar of these was the swastika.)
He actually registered his literary trade-marks with the governments of
the United Kingdom and the United States. . . . The variety and the
ingenuity of the publishing procedures he adopted give a richness and
a complexity to his bibliography which remind us of Trollope.

TLS. Sept. 2, 1960, p. 568

KOESTLER, ARTHUR (1905–   )

Darkness at Noon is a grimly fascinating book, giving us as it does a
glimpse of the terrible, almost mad logic of the Russian revolutionary,
a logic which perverts because it forgets its premises (as applied logic
so often does), and sacrifices humanity to itself. Rubashov, the central
figure, was an old Leninist, who in his heart though not in his mind,
rebelled against Stalinism, and was in the end "physically liquidated."
It is a stern and pitiable story, profoundly interesting and superbly
done, with a mixture of cold terror, humour, and psychological insight
which is altogether convincing.

Bonamy Dobrée. *Spec.* Jan. 3, 1941, p. 20

As a political document [*Darkness at Noon*], the book is not particularly impressive. Mr. Koestler is repeating explanations that others have
already given, though he repeats them at greater length and with more

psychological subtlety and depth. He fails to consider a possibility for which there is at least circumstantial evidence, that an actual plot against Stalin came close to being successful. Moreover, he makes the worse mistake—from the novelist's point of view—of using statistical arguments. . . .

His novel is best when it is moral and personal rather than political. It is best when it tells the story, not of Russia as a collectivity, but of a Russian individual who was punished for crimes he never committed while admitting to himself that he was guilty of other crimes, and who in punishment found a sort of freedom or even salvation. From this point of view, *Darkness at Noon* bears a curious resemblance to *Native Son,* a book that sets out to express quite the opposite political opinions.

Malcolm Cowley. NR. June 2, 1941, p. 767

I feel unable to agree with those who call this book [*Darkness at Noon*] a good novel. It lacks in epic style, in poetry, in abundance of vision. I don't even like to accept the assumption of the author that he was writing a novel. This is just a psychological study of the strange Moscow trials. Only instead of the real characters who were victims to Stalin's propaganda condemnations, Koestler for reasons of simplification presents one fictitious figure, a typical old revolutionary, persecuted by Stalin and his GPU. This study is done with a clever mind, fond of sophistry and intellectual subtlety. In this respect it is a noteworthy commentary to the politics of our times and should not be neglected by future historians. The book is written in a nihilistic, gloomy mood. A materialistic and atheistic atmosphere is the hopeless *milieu* in which the story is set; future generations, no doubt, will wonder whether its cynic wretchedness can go further or is the high point of desolation among men who have lost the knowledge of God. People of a coming religious century who read such books of our times as Valtin's *Out of the Night* and its counterpart, Koestler's *Darkness at Noon,* will certainly be convinced we lived in hell.

Max Fischer. Com. June 13, 1941, pp. 186–87

Ignoring the neurotics and professional red-baiters, a score of observers from Sir Bernard Pares, Joseph Davies and Wendell Wilkie to John Scott and Maurice Hindus would regard Koestler's whole picture as a deliberate and irresponsible falsification. It is interesting to speculate on what would happen to him if he were confronted with the actual facts which he denies and distorts. If he could not wriggle out of them I expect his reason would snap like that of the young man in Chesterton's *Magic* when confronted with a fact which his philosophy made impossible. For of course we are dealing not with facts or reasons but with a neurosis and a rationalisation.

Koestler is the first to admit it. Both in *The Yogi and The Commissar* and in his novel *Arrival and Departure* he exalts the neurotic to the prophetic level.

Dividing mankind into the laughing multitude and the screaming few, Koestler finds in these frustrated and broken minds not a sickness to be healed but a special insight into truth that works by avoiding facts, by abandoning a firm grasp on reality. This overwhelming obsession which takes the place of reason is fundamentally a revelation of the essential horror of the world, its hopeless tragedy. This is his message and restlessly and stridently he utters it, certain only of the vanity of human efforts, the depravity of his fellow men, the uselessness of striving.

But his screaming defeatism attaches itself to one object in particular. It is what he calls "the collapse of the revolutionary movement." However much several hundred million people may be convinced that it is Nazism that has collapsed and the revolutionary movement that has defeated it, Koestler cannot allow this. The more the entire history of our times tell us that this is so, the more hysterically and frantically must Koestler deny it. This is his prophetic calling.

John Lewis and Reginald Bishop. *The Philosophy of Betrayal* (Russia Today Society, 1945), p. 2

This [*The Yogi and the Commissar*] is a disturbing book, as is to be expected, for the disillusion of an honest and very intelligent man "hath an art to make dust of all things." The book is a collection of essays, written at various times and for various places, but obviously during the last three years a compelling current of thought has been running consistently in Mr. Koestler's mind, and this gives an unity to his book, which is unusual when a writer harvests his journalism in "volume form." The title of his book points to the direction of his thought and disillusion. The Yogi is the saint and mystic who believes that nothing can be achieved by reason or action, and that, since the end is unpredictable, only the means count. . . . The Commissar is the revolutionary who believes only in reason and in "Change from Without." . . .

Mr. Koestler is a brilliant writer and often a profound thinker; he has the rare merit of being able to think important thoughts and to clothe them in words which reveal rather than conceal their importance. But he writes and thinks with a bitterness, sometimes a personal bitterness, which defeats his purpose, if it does not cloud his judgment. Fundamentally he remains on the side of the Commissar and there is no evidence in his books that he has any use for the way of the Yogi. But in the hard and fast line definition of his Commissar something essential is omitted. Even the most materialist and rigid of comrades has some standards of value, and it may perhaps be found with a little further exploration that where the Commissar goes wrong is not so much in his method as in the relation which he maintains between his method and standards of value. Mr. Koestler himself seems to catch a glimpse of the truth in his conclusion. . . .

Leonard Woolf. NSN. May 19, 1945, p. 324

Koestler's published work really centres about [sic] the Moscow trials. His main theme is the decadence of revolutions owing to the corrupting effects of power, but the special nature of the Stalin dictatorship has driven him back into a position not far removed from pessimistic conservatism. I do not know how many books he has written in all. He is a Hungarian whose earlier books were in German, and five books have been published in England: *Spanish Testament, The Gladiators, Darkness at Noon, Scum of the Earth,* and *Arrival and Departure.* The subject-matter of all of them is similar, and none of them ever escapes for more than a few pages from the atmosphere of nightmare. Of the five books, the action of three takes place entirely or almost entirely in prison.

In the opening months of the Spanish Civil War Koestler was the *News Chronicle's* correspondent in Spain and early in 1937 he was taken prisoner when the Fascists captured Malaga. He was nearly shot out of hand, then spent some months imprisoned in a fortress, listening every night to the roar of rifle-fire as batch after batch of Republicans was executed, and being most of the time in acute danger of execution himself. This was not a chance adventure which "might have happened to anybody," but was in accordance with Koestler's life style. A politically indifferent person would not have been in Spain at that date, a more cautious observer would have got out of Malaga before the Fascists arrived, and a British or American newspaperman would have been treated with more consideration. The book that Koestler wrote about this, *Spanish Testament,* has remarkable passages, but apart from the scrappiness that is usual in a book of reportage, it is definitely false in places. In the prison scenes Koestler successfully establishes the nightmare atmosphere which is, so to speak, his patent, but the rest of the book is too much coloured by the Popular Front orthodoxy of the time. One or two passages even look as though they had been doctored for the purposes of the Left Book Club. At that time Koestler still was, or recently had been, a member of the Communist Party, and the complex politics of the civil war made it impossible for any communist to write quite honestly about the internal struggle on the Government side. The sin of nearly all left-wingers from 1933 onwards is that they have wanted to be anti-fascist without being anti-totalitarian. In 1937 Koestler already knew this, but did not feel free to say so. He came much nearer to saying it—indeed, did say it, though he put on a mask to do so—in his next book, *The Gladiators,* which was published about a year before the war and for some reason attracted very little attention.

George Orwell. *Critical Essays* (Secker and Warburg, 1946), pp. 131–32

His latest novel, *Thieves in the Night,* is a passionately controversial account of the Zionist situation in Palestine between 1937 and 1939. Mr. Koestler has written nothing more gripping, and the subject allows him for the first time to make full use of his gift for sardonic comedy. Admittedly it is a novel only in form; and any criticism of it is bound to be concerned chiefly with estimating the accuracy and completeness of the picture it presents. Only an impartial expert upon Palestine could deal with it adequately; and even if such a phoenix could be found, his impartiality would be admitted by none of the contending parties. . . .

Passionate emotion, which in most people blunts the intelligence, serves to make Mr. Koestler's mind more vivacious. His direct experience of the sufferings of the Jews in Europe excites in him a burning enthusiasm for a Palestinian State as one answer to their difficulties. His Communist idealism, so cruelly disappointed by the U.S.S.R., finds in the Zionist communities a realization of his dreams. And also, perhaps, this stormy petrel finds just the material suited to his talents in the country which, now that the war is over, is most conspicuously racked with violence and terror. *Thieves in the Night* does not contain a dull page. It is a masterpiece of propaganda.

Raymond Mortimer. *At.* Nov., 1946, pp. 134–35

Arthur Koestler, the well-known author of *Darkness at Noon* and *The Yogi and the Commissar,* started his career as a student of science in Vienna, and was at one time science editor of a chain of newspapers in Germany. When he gave up political writing in 1954, he began work on this book, *The Sleepwalkers,* which is intended, he says, to contribute toward "the ending of the cold war between the humanities and the sciences." . . .

The Sleepwalkers is a substantial work of 624 pages, of which about 80 are devoted to notes, bibliography and index. A surprising feature is the high proportion of space given to the biographies of two or three leading astronomers: Copernicus gets a hundred pages, Kepler nearly two hundred, and we are even given a brief account of their ancestors and collaterals: so that we close the book with the feeling, on the whole, of having been engaged in a biographical rather than a philosophical or scientific voyage of discovery. Koestler has his reasons for this. He is interested, not only in the results, but in the psychological process of discovery. . . .

Moreover, the biographies are extremely well-done. One hardly knows whether more to admire the accumulation of industrious research which underlies them or the skill and lightness of touch with which the hoard is exploited.

Owen Barfield. *Golden Blade*. 1960, pp. 94–95

LANG, ANDREW (1844–1912)

A distracted generation seems to have forgotten the charm of Andrew Lang. I hope that the publication of a handsome body of his poetic works will revive the sense of what an enchanter he was. . . . I shall be still further delighted if it is followed by a revival of the best parts of his prose, since it must be admitted that Lang was only in the secondary degree a poet, while as a prose writer he was capable of effects unsurpassed by any one of his generation. . . .

His reiterated allusions to "the unpermitted bay" and to "the peaks forbidden" make it very pathetic for us to realize how clear-sighted he became. In his boyhood he nourished the ardent hope that he might rise to the topmost rank. . . . Lang achieved much in his laborious crowded life, but he did not quite become the leading poet of his age. . . .

Lang arrived from Oxford armed in a panoply of graces, and full of ambition to take his place in the forefront of the writers of his time. He had mastered, what few Englishmen fifty years ago knew or cared about, the romantic literature of France, and his earliest publication was in the main a paraphrase of selections from it. . . . His translations showed, if they showed nothing else, a sympathy interpreted by the most delicate skill. . . . His fame as a prose-writer of extraordinary delicacy and wit was founded on his articles, mainly anonymous; he revolutionized the "high-brow" section of a daily newspaper. . . .

Ballades in Blue China created a sensation which may be compared, . . . with the success of Théodore de Banville's *Odes funambulesques*. Most of Lang's ballades were playful and fantastic; occasionally in a serious mood, he proved what could be done in a higher strain. . . . The reason why Lang, with so great a devotion to the art of poetry, and so remarkable a skill in versification, did not achieve more uncontested success in the expression of it, may be sought in his temperament. Like Gray, it may be said of him that "he never spoke out." He shrank from a close examination of his life, and from passion as from a devouring flame. . . . In fine, I think that Lang should be regarded as a lyricist of artifice. . . . If we consider him too gravely, we lose him altogether.

Edmund Gosse. *Silhouettes* (Heinemann, 1925), pp. 163–64, 169–70

I daresay he meant to be kind. I have heard from people who knew him intimately that he was a really kind man. He may even have had the wish to please. But it was certain that one had to know him intimately before his wish could, in regard to oneself, be gratified. No man can easily be popular who has the Oxford manner in even a rudimentary degree: the perfection of that manner is a sovereign charm against popularity. It is no wonder that Lang was not beloved by people at large.

Especially was he not beloved by the eminent creative writers of his time. Indeed, very few critics get on well with creators. There is, no doubt, a point at which criticism does merge into creation, and it is always hard to say just where this point is—to determine whether this or that piece of fine criticism may or may not truly be called creative. But to this point, assuredly, Lang was never near. With all his gifts, he had of imagination not one spark. Fancy and wit he had in his earlier work; and grace he never lost; but for the rest he had only an immense quantity of that "cleverness'" which to the creative artist is of all qualities the most repellent. And this cleverness, which was always at the disposal of the classics, was never used in service of any great contemporary writer. He helped Stevenson, because Stevenson was a Scotsman imitating Scott (instead of following the true bent of his own fantastic genius, alas). For Browning and Meredith and Swinburne, for Henry James, for Bernard Shaw, for any spirit that was new or vital in current work, he had at best a chilly tolerance. Himself remote by nature, he could enjoy masterpieces only at a distance: their proximity jarred him. He loved "Mr. Thackery," but he loved Jane Austen more: she was further off. And Homer he loved most of all, because Homer was further off than any one. I think there was moreover in him (with all his Gipsy blood) a strain of pure mischievousness that impelled him to poke fun at any great man who was alive to be annoyed. And this I take to be the reason why he would write now and again a sudden rhapsody about some obviously third-rate new talent. I remember dear old Theodore Watts-Dunton thumping the table in his back-dining-room and saying in his most sonorous accents, "I never knew a man of genius who didn't loathe Lang." He himself was the perfect type of critic whom men of genius love. I am not a man of genius; but this did not prevent me from loving old Theodore. It did, however, prevent me from loathing Lang. I merely shared the common lot of men who met him for the first time: I did not like him.

Max Beerbohm. LL. June, 1928, pp. 4–5

Lang occupied an unique position in the literary world of his day, wielding a dominant influence beyond that of any individual critic before or since. Relating how an obscure shilling book on dining-out in London was made popular into a big success by a notice of Lang's in the *Daily News,* Mr. Grant Richards remarked in his *Memories of a Misspent*

Youth that, excepting Arnold Bennett's *Evening Standard* articles in the last years of his life, "no man alive, no newspaper, has all that power." Lang contributed largely to the making of Stevenson's reputation; he contributed equally to the making of Rider Haggard's; he started the sensational success of Anthony Hope's *Prisoner of Zenda,* the vogue of Stanley Weyman, and the selling of S. R. Crockett's novels. The secret of his power is far to seek in the constitution of a curious individuality. He commanded the respect of all classes by the profundity of his scholarship, the extent and variety of his reading; the barbs of his wit and sarcasm opponents were chary of challenging; he possessed an easy grace of style which won the envy of highbrows, and charmed the masses by its unpretentiousness, its familiarity, its lack of conscious superiority and condescension; he was not himself a popular writer, but he was a voluminous author in so many fields, with so much distinction, that he created the impression that he might do anything if he chose, and was therefore admirably qualified to assess the achievements of others. The humanity and variety of his interests captivated the general public; he was a bookman without the mustiness of the bookworm, for while he could argue with sedentary pundits the most abstruse difficulties of the classics, he expressed a preference for the swashbuckling in fiction, and while he was known to indulge in the pastime of poetry, the province of the longhaired, unwashed decadent, he loved nothing better than watching the cricket at Lord's or a day with the fly on the streams of his native Scotland. He was the Admirable Crichton of letters, the gallant cavalier of literary critics.

Malcolm Elwin. Old Gods Falling (N.Y.,
Macmillan, 1939), pp. 183–84

LARKIN, PHILIP (1922–   )

In *The Less Deceived* Mr. Larkin is writing well within his capabilities: the result is that almost every poem makes its point excellently and the collection as a whole is most readable and enjoyable. Particularly engaging are the poems—not exactly love poems—about the brief sexual clouds of glory trailed unwittingly by girls. . . .

. . . His trace of sentimentality . . . is a little disconcerting . . . and obviously Mr. Larkin must guard against it. The emotions he feels most sharply are pity and sympathy, and he is not always capable of finding satisfactory objects for them. "Myxomatosis," for instance, though subtle and not anthropomorphic, may be felt by some readers to be on the wrong side of the line between sensibility and sentimentality: on the other hand, in the poem (from which the book's title comes) on a rape in Mayhew's *London Labour and the London Poor,* the poet's comment has passed firmly over into objectivity and understanding without losing its poignancy. . . .

This is a book which relies heavily (and rightly so) on a youthful charm of tone and diction. Whether Mr. Larkin can find the intellectual interests, the emotional engagements, to take him further is a question the book begs, though in one or two places . . . there is a poetic density which is promising.

Roy Fuller. L. April, 1956, pp. 85–86

A Girl in Winter was first published in 1947 and got a deservedly good press. It is full of good dry-point vignettes of landscape. The strong suit of all poets' first novels and its narrative transitions are managed with skill and deliberation. I couldn't however raise much interest in the characters as characters, though the various settings and backgrounds remain quite vividly in my mind—the dusty library, the furnished room, the ice-bound park. . . . But the love story—if it can be called that—between Katherine the foreigner and Robin Fennel the Englishman seemed to me rather hollow and meaningless. And this is presumably the fulcrum of the book. Indeed there was something nightmarish about the lack of passion in their relations, the lack of the human ratio. Mr. Larkin has described the surfaces of his characters and their actions with a brilliant and microscopic fidelity which almost brings them to life: but not quite. What is missing is that insight into motive which lays bare the springs of human action and conveys significant depth to a given set of characters. Mr. Larkin's human beings are dry cell batteries unable to make contact with each other. They do not even try to signal across the dividing gulf.

The strength of the book is in its dry selective methods of description, its unerring sense of surfaces, and some unforgettable pictures of landscape; the people don't seem to matter much to the author.

Lawrence Durrell. L. April, 1957, pp. 67, 69

Philip Larkin is now thirty-six years old, and is librarian of a provincial university library. He has published two novels, *Jill* and *A Girl in Winter;* but his reputation was won by the volume of poetry, *The Less Deceived,* published in 1955. His work is characteristic of his generation, the young men who came to maturity during the 1939-45 war, and since then have succumbed to uncertainty or pessimism. *A Girl in Winter* is a very bleak book indeed, and there is little relief from gloom. But the poetry is quite different. It expresses uncertainty, but with a poignancy of feeling which makes Larkin one of the most important poets of the '50s.

Larkin's name is often linked with those of John Wain and Kingsley Amis, his contemporaries and friends at Oxford. Like them, he expresses that feeling of rootlessness so much discussed in recent years. . . . But Larkin's treatment of rootlessness is quite different from that of Wain or Amis. Separated from all the certainties provided by tradition, he turns in his poetry to an intimate questioning of his own personal experience. Wain and Amis seek for an answer to uncertainty in the ordinary daily routine of the working classes, or in the love of a woman; and occasionally they give up the struggle and become simply frivolous. But Larkin accepts uncertainty as a necessary condition of life. He writes repeatedly about time, showing that the continual flow of experience in the mind makes it impossible ever to be sure of the meaning of the present; "at once whatever happened starts receding," and we look upon our past selves in wonder and in doubt.

This uncertainty often brings a feeling of disillusion. In "Poetry of Departures," Larkin derides his own romantic longing to change his sober, industrious life for something more adventurous; wherever he might go, he would face the same problems. If he threw up his comfortable life, it would become merely what he would be striving for, the object of his more uncomfortable one. In "Next Please," he mocks our habit of seeing the experience of each moment in relation to an imaginary future. Illusion is interwoven with all our thinking, for we can never escape from the inadequacy of the present.

Larkin's irony is never cynical or bitter; he does not feel that he is the moral censor of his times, but includes himself in his own mockery. When he describes his own feelings, his tone is invariably self-depreciatory. He admits that "something sufficiently toad-like Squats in me, too"; he is "bored" and "uninformed," or threading his "pursed-up" way across the park. He does not rebel because failure seems to him one of the unchangeable facts of life. Many of his poems are written in a tone of resignation. In "Next, Please," he uses simple rhymes in a short concluding line—"every day *Till then* we say"—to make the statements appear truisms we must accept. We cannot alter these facts of our experience. . . .

Larkin's poetry, therefore, accepts experience as it is, and tries to do justice to its contradictions. At one moment he treats ironically even his own attempts to be a poet; at another, he links himself with all who suffer, and who do not understand. In his poem, "Myxomatosis," he looks at a stricken rabbit and feels glad that he cannot explain to it why it endures so much pain.

C. B. Cox. *CQ*. Spring, 1959, pp. 14–16

For the most part the poets of the 1950s, and particularly Philip Larkin, reject the traditions of their immediate past. Their poetry represents a revival of a tradition associated with Hardy and kept alive only through the vigour and persistence of poets like Robert Graves. Their distrust of political programmes or religious or philosophical ideas is profound; their hatred of the "old gang," whose faith in programmes and ideas led Europe into six years of slaughter, runs deep. In poetry they took pride in their craft, and in experience they felt themselves carefully forward taking nothing on trust. The poetry of Philip Larkin defines the mood of this post-war generation with great sensitivity. . . .

The strength of Philip Larkin's poetry lies in the sheer elegance of his craftsmanship, in the cool detachment of himself from his poetry, and in his tone. It is this sense of tone—in Larkin a delicate but precise irony continually undercutting the composure of the poem, largely self-directed but also used as a defensive intelligence through which to define the ambiguity of his attitude. Larkin is breaking new ground in English poetry; his poetry defines the attitudes of his time in his concern with the world of the individual unwilling to commit himself to ideas—philosophical, social, or even personal—and at the same time a world nonetheless concerned with these issues. He has managed to create a kind of poem in which he can set a space, a tension, between himself and poem and within this space manipulate, mainly through irony . . . a considerable range of attitudes that he clarifies with subtle intelligence and vigour. The ambiguity is removed from image and metaphor—where Empson detected it in the old Pound-Eliot-metaphysical tradition—and is clearly suggested through texture and tone. He refuses—even in personal relationships—to commit himself through word and gesture, to lose his freedom by binding himself to any statement or positive attitude, and his poetry reflects a world in which feeling and intelligence are actively engaged but in the manner of eighteenth-century scepticism. An intense sense of personal integrity. an urbane and sensitive intelligence, and a healthy, honest scepticism combining with a brilliantly polished control of poetic technique are the qualities admired and imitated by his contemporaries.

Alun R. Jones. WHR. Spring, 1962, pp. 145–46

What Mr. Larkin celebrates is love, and the celebration is ambiguous because of the context of that love. His main concern is with human lives in time. The time is a "Here" and a now which is the once only, in which, to borrow phrases from "No Road" in The Less Deceived, "all time's eroding agents" have been "turned loose." As Mr. Larkin writes in "The Importance of Elsewhere," "Here no elsewhere underwrites my existence." . . .

In Mr. Larkin's poetry two opposing images stand out. I see them as images of death and images of love: on the one hand, "The glare of that much-mentioned brilliance, love" of "Love Songs in Age"; on the other hand, the "cold sun" of "No Road" in *The Less Deceived*. The images in this new volume [*The Whitsun Weddings*] have an even greater immediacy because they are more localized. . . .

These images gain in richness and poignance from being linked by Larkin's recurrent concern with the death of love and the love of death. Some critics, disturbed by the ambivalence of this concern, by what they see as the poet's painful inability to unlink from his losses, cover their praise of his achievement (and their own confusion) with uneasy and vaguely formulated qualification. But it is precisely from what they would see as distressing negativism that Mr. Larkin's poetry derives its especial richness of poise. The ambivalence, far from being negative, willed intrusion, is the basic, forced premise from which the poetry arises. The poetry is written from the context of man's situation being one in which value and love were made possible by the same stroke as left Death the only absolute.

Harry Chambers. Phoenix. Spring, 1964, pp. 38–39

LASKI, MARGHANITA (1915–   )

Toasted English is an exhilarating story whose blandly devastating satire will especially regale those well versed in the mores of Miss Laski's natives. There is less sense of the fantastic here than in the early Waugh books—the inventions are clothed in an aura of normalcy; and the satire is innocent of Waugh's inhumanity. (Which is not to say that Miss Laski has Waugh's talent.). . . . Entirely by indirection, and with unfailing wit, Miss Laski has fashioned a scorching indictment of a hierarchical society.

Charles J. Rolo. At. May, 1949, p. 84

Marghanita Laski, in *The Victorian Chaise-Lounge,* brings off—or perhaps does not quite bring off—another imaginative *tour de force*. A light-hearted young wife of today, suffering from tuberculosis, falls asleep on the ugly, "amusing" Victorian piece she has whimsically bought for her charming Regency house and finds herself in the body of another girl dying on it in the last century. Whether or not we are really meant to believe that Melanie was Milly in a former life, the device enables Miss Laski to create an authentic sense of terror and frustration. Melanie's frantic efforts to force herself back to the present, her confused identity, the sharp physical reminders that what she is experiencing appears to be real, give one a genuine feeling of nightmare. Unfortunately, though the dream or experience are vividly conveyed, the characters in the Milly sequence are hardly more than conventional Victorian dummies.

Antonia White. *NSN*. Dec. 5, 1953, p. 738

Miss Laski has done her job [*Ecstasy*] with characteristic industry and intelligence. She has combed the literature, and not only the writings of the mystics and the poets, very thoroughly and subjected it to a content analysis. She has put carefully framed questionnaires to 63 persons and made a detailed statistical analysis of their replies.

Her book is a useful descriptive catalogue and it will deserve its place in the library together with, though not on the same shelf as, William James's *Varieties of Religious Experience* and Russell's *Mysticism and Logic*. . . . Miss Laski's conclusions are perhaps rather scanty, and in her anxiety to be strictly scientific she has adopted a style that reads as if a virgin contributor to *Nature* were making her debut.

Maurice Richardson. *NS*. Nov. 17, 1961, pp. 746, 748

Marghanita Laski's "study of some secular and religious experiences" bears all the outward status signs of a definitive work of scholarship. It has 533 pages exclusive of index, appendices from A to J, an average of at least one footnote per page, eighteen pages of tables and three of charts, analyses of seventy-four questionnaires, twenty-two religious and twenty-seven literary texts, and it costs fifty-five shillings [*Ecstasy*]. . . . Miss Laski has isolated and then enumerated some fascinating and unexpected ingredients of ecstasy. But by the end of the book, the reader is still not convinced that the patterns may not be accidental, or even illusory, because he cannot be certain that the minimum laboratory conditions for any kind of scientific study have been observed. . . . *Ecstasy* is a book which only the most tireless dedication could have produced. Unfortunately it requires almost equal dedication to read. And at the end, the reward to both author and reader is disappointingly small.

Alan Brien. *Spec*. Nov. 17, 1961, p. 717

LAVER, JAMES (1899–   )

. . . for entertainment plus a substantial slice of social history there is Mr. James Laver's compilation, *Edwardian Promenade*—which in fact carries its story right up to the end of the First World War.

NS. Dec. 20, 1958, p. 892

The rare bird who has never heard of Mr. James Laver might be misled by the title of his autobiography, *Museum Piece or The Education of an Iconographer,* into believing that he was a member of the British Museum, who spent his leisure hours sitting at the feet of the sages of the Warburg Institute. A quick glance at the photograph of the author on the frontispiece would bring the reader his first moment of doubt. Such casual sartorial elegance is surely quite out of the range of either institution. But perusing further (and who does not immediately look at the illustrations?) his doubts would turn to something like certainty when he found himself faced with a photograph of Mr. Douglas Fairbanks Jr., Miss Dolores Del Rio *and* Mr. James Laver. . . . The rare bird would declare that this does not fit his idea of the museum official or, to use the word in its modern sense, that specialized creature, the iconographer. And he would be right.

Mr. Laver is of course known for a variety of accomplishments outside his curatorial work in the Victoria and Albert Museum. In his time he has been poet, playwright, novelist, biographer and translator. (And what enjoyable novels he writes. He is one of the rare novelists to have pricked a few bubbles of the art-dealing world). He imbues all his work with a cosy good-humoured wit. He may not delve into the dark recesses of the mind, but he always writes stylishly and agreeably.

TLS. Dec. 5, 1963, p. 1007

LAWRENCE, D. H.   (1885—1930)

His novels produce always a double impression—of a breaking through, and of an imprisonment in the strange and beautiful, but subterranean realm to which he has broken through. From this subterranean place he sees a far richer world than others do who are content with the light of day. His trees and flowers he sees, as it were, from the inside; they have an interior glow and a violence of being which could only be rendered by one who by an unconditional act of imagination entered into their life. Mr. Lawrence's imagination has done this so completely that it has never entirely emerged again. There seems nothing which it cannot enter into, either in nature or in the instinctive life of men and women. It recoils solely before most of the things in which the imagination has till now found its inspiration: the conscious life of mankind, ordinary relations and problems, the tragedy and comedy of life as we know it. . . .

Nature he comprehends mainly through identification: mankind he comprehends almost as much through repulsion. What he understands in his characters is not the qualities which make up their personalities, but rather the thing which arouses this unconscious attraction or repulsion: their natural foundation, healthy or the reverse. He apprehends this exactly and subtly, with an unconscious knowledge which men in culti- vating their intellects have almost lost, and the remaining remnants of which they distrust. But Mr. Lawrence trusts this unconscious knowledge more than anything else. The responses of his instincts are not merely phenomena to him, to be judged by the mind; they are truths whose force is conclusive. What he tells us about his characters is simply what these responses tell him. . . .

Action arises in his novels when the instinctive field of one character impinges on that of another, producing something like an electric shock. Two vital principles are enraged, violated, or glorified by each other, while the mind looks on and knows its irrelevance. Thus Fate in Mr. Lawrence's novels is not woven by character, but by instincts which colour character, and sometimes seem independent of it. . . .

His problem as an artist was to present clearly this drama of the instincts. In reckoning up his success and failure one must take account not only of his achievement, but of the difficulties of his task. These were enormous. He had to translate into a conscious thing, language, states which are fluid and unconscious, and cannot be directly denoted.

He tried to do this by employing a peculiarly telepathic style, a style which does not render things so much as the feeling of things. Sometimes merely an unavailing struggle with language, a senselessly repeated as- sault which does not break through, this style has splendid moments when it sets the object before us in the full glow of its aura. His dialogue is a graph of the movements of the instincts: it does not depict character, nor define situation. . . .

Thus character in Mr. Lawrence's novels is always melting into in- stinct, and human nature into nature pure and simple. He does outline a struggle, vague and obsessed, between the humanly acquired attributes of his characters and instinct, but that struggle would be infinitely more moving if the two sides were more equally balanced. He was right in making the struggle vague, for it is vague; it has not the clarity which moralists and theologians have given it. But he was wrong in not stating more impressively the second, the conscious factor, as essential as the first. . . . He shows us one marvellous province of life, but not, like the great artists, life itself. . . . To this tremendous extent the tragedy in Mr. Lawrence's novels fails in significance. It is a tragedy almost purely of nature rather than of human nature; it might befall a lion caged or a tree mutilated as easily as a human being thwarted in his unconscious desires. It is new literature, it is sometimes very beautiful, but it has not the full significance of human tragedy. . . . His vision is not more lucid now than it was in *The Rainbow*; his philosophy is only more set and clear. That philosophy, in other words, has not been fused with his art; it has been arbitrarily imposed upon it. . . . So we have a novel like *Kangaroo*, which is mostly loose discussion, and a tale like "The Captain's Doll," which is falsified to point a moral. . . . Through an inner weakness, or that negligence which he dignifies into arrogance, Mr. Lawrence has not brought his art to its perfection; and he theorizes because there is something which he cannot see clearly enough to describe. . . .

He has not submitted himself to any discipline. But if he has not written any completely satisfying work, he has written in almost all his books more greatly than any other English writer of his time.

Edwin Muir. *Transition* (N.Y., Viking, 1926), pp. 50–63

He harangues us like Carlyle, whom he resembled in many aspects, the artist in him was doubled with the rhetorician. He too sprang from a poverty-cramped, sullen, illiterate fighting-stock; he too was the favored child of a mother who represented in those surroundings a superior and pious refinement; he too was born with a suspicion of any sort of agreement, and with a conviction, often agonized, that everybody must be wrong except himself; he was born too with a faculty for exquisite sympathy for individuals and an almost sadistic relish for the sufferings of people in general—"the mostly fools" of Carlyle being translatable in Lawrentian terms by "all corpses or swine"; he too was a humorist whose sense of fun sprang from a constantly tragic sense of life; he too was a prodigious egotist, yet in himself strangely lovable and fascinating, his egotism finding relief in minatory "uplift" diatribes, and showing itself in his intolerance of the smallest self-assertion on the part of others. For Lawrence the egotist, to whom the experience of "love" was the crucial test of individual excellence, egotism, legitimate or illegitimate, in that relation, was a central problem. He too was, in the sense in which that phrase has a meaning apart from accomplishment, "a great man," one whom to be near, whether through his writings, or directly, meant for others an enhancement of life; he too was an aesthete who constantly mistook himself for a moral teacher. (Not a fundamentally fatal mistake, since in individual life aesthetic and moral judgments are often indistinguishable, but fatal when the moralist pretends also to legislate for society at large. Thus the political philosophies of Carlyle and Lawrence are as weak as they are emphatic.) The prose of Lawrence was marred, too, by the same defect; like Carlyle he valued earnestness, a state of feeling in himself, more than truth. Both, as writers, were the victims of their own passionate garrulity. Both abounded in insight and in unforgettable phrases; but there was a certain headiness (how violently Lawrence himself would have repudiated that word!) in all they wrote. They have the same fault of letting their feelings run on without thinking of the reality of their object. Indeed, Lawrence's temper of mind was extraordinarily like Carlyle's, lending itself to histrionic gestures, to sweeping contempt, harsh laughter with aerial overtones, dramatic projections of his own emotions into things animate and inanimate, and a dangerous and lonely pride. Though his gospel that we ought to return to a more instinctive way of living is entirely different from Carlyle's, who was terrified of the body, Lawrence was just as dogmatic, just as sure that everyone round him was either sick or dead. In Carlyle this certainty often took the form of lofty commiseration—"poor" so-and-so was his favourite adjective; in Lawrence it took the form of indignation and terror of contamination.

Carlyle's rhetoric has become mere noise to this generation, intolerable because his "message" seems to concern nothing vital to them. It helps no one, yet it is delivered as though it were of the utmost moment. Most fatiguing. But that does not prevent the critic from recognizing Carlyle as a great English writer, or the historian from admitting his past influence. To many of his contemporaries his ideas were "seeds of creation lying burningly on the Divine Hand." They are cold now, while those of Lawrence are still glowing, and if I understand the times in which I live, they are likely to grow brighter in the years immediately ahead. Lawrence has something of vital importance to *us.* . . .

The discussion of sex fills to-day the place taken by religious controversy in the times of Mill, Carlyle, and Huxley. It needed then the same kind of courage to speak one's mind about Christianity, as it needs to-day to speak about sex; and the topic has the same kind of vital interest for all those who ask themselves the question: How ought I to live? . . . The young are interested in personal, not in social problems. Lawrence has therefore something to say on two questions crucial to them: how to preserve an inner integrity and hold themselves together in spite of rejecting all rules of thumb in conduct; and how to prevent sexual life degenerating into squalor, now that belief in prohibitions is going. The main drift of Lawrence's work, the strongest infection from it, is reverence for sex. Sex is the sun, which warms and animates his whole world. What, according to him, is wrong with civilization is that it does not recognize sex as the source of the natural warm flow of common sympathy between everybody as well as between man and woman.

There is the literature that lends the charm of imagination to reality (this is the kind I prefer myself at its best), and there is the literature which adds the force of reality to the imaginary. Lawrence's work on the whole belonged to the latter class. Neither his characters nor his stories owed much to observation. He was a seer rather than a fashioner. To read him is to be steeped in his personality, and his creations are projected, but never separated, from himself. He was one of those artists who do well to be absorbed in the salvation of their souls (so boring a preoccupation to others whose souls are different), because it was only in relation to that perpetual inner conflict that he could invent imaginary figures or be interested in imaginary events. His invention was entirely dependent upon that interest. He had, for example, a curious contempt for the eye and the reports of the eye. The eye apprehends from a distance, and the value of its reports depend on the mind. Lawrence yearned after closer contacts. The sense of touch, which can be so overwhelming, seemed to him to possess a mystic power of divination. But it was not through touch or sight, or any one sense alone, that he strove to apprehend the nature of things, but with his whole being at once. His peculiarity as a writer is that he succeeds so extraordinarily in responding with his whole body to what is before him. He interprets animals, plants, landscape, gestures, through his sex as well as his senses. Only of the judgments of the mind as to the nature of things was he distrustful, and he distrusted them because analytical observation and reason interrupted and destroyed that deep vascular response to them which he most valued. It is certainly a very serious limitation in one who set out to respond to life as a complete man that he should have omitted, as far as was consistent with sanity, to use the human reason. And he did his best not to use it.

Desmond MacCarthy. Criticism (Putnam,
1932), pp. 248–54

Lawrence's special and characteristic gift was an extraordinary sensitiveness to what Wordsworth called "unknown modes of being." He was always intensely aware of the mystery of the world, and the mystery was always for him a *numen,* divine. Lawrence could never forget, as most of us almost continuously forget, the dark presence of the otherness that lies beyond the boundaries of man's conscious mind. This special sensibility was accompanied by a prodigious power of rendering the immediately experienced otherness in terms of literary art.

Such was Lawrence's peculiar gift. His possession of it accounts for many things. It accounts, to begin with, for his attitude toward sex. His particular experiences as a son and as a lover may have intensified his preoccupation with the subject; but they certainly did not make it. Whatever his experiences, Lawrence *must* have been preoccupied with sex; his gift made it inevitable. For Lawrence, the significance of the sexual experience was this: that, in it, the immediate, non-mental knowledge of divine otherness is brought, so to speak, to a focus—a focus of darkness. Parodying Matthew Arnold's famous formula, we may say that sex is something not ourselves that makes for—not righteousness, for the essence of religion is not righteousness; there is a spiritual world, as Kierkegaard insists, beyond the ethical—rather, that makes for life, for divine-ness, for union with the mystery. Paradoxically, this something not our-selves is yet a something lodged within us; this quintessence of otherness is yet the quintessence of our proper being. "And God the Father, the Inscrutable, the Unknowable, we know in the flesh, in Woman. She is the door for our in-going and our out-coming. In her we go back to the Father; but like the witnesses of the transfiguration, blind and uncon-scious." Yes, blind and unconscious; otherwise it is a revelation, not of divine otherness, but of very human evil. . . . (About the time he was writing *Lady Chatterley's Lover* he read the memoirs of Casanova, and was profoundly shocked.) And how bitterly he loathed the Wilhelm-Meisterish view of love as an education, as a means to culture, a Sandow-exerciser for the soul! To *use* love in this way, consciously and deliber-ately, seemed to Lawrence wrong, almost a blasphemy. . . .

For someone with a gift for sensing the mystery of otherness, true love must necessarily be, in Lawrence's vocabulary, *nocturnal*. So must true knowledge. Nocturnal and tactual—a touching in the night. Man inhabits, for his own convenience, a home-made universe within the greater alien world of external matter and his own irrationality. Out of the illimitable blackness of that world the light of his customary thinking scoops, as it were, a little-illuminated cave—a tunnel of brightness, in which, from the birth of consciousness to its death, he lives, moves and has his being. For most of us this bright tunnel is the whole world. We ignore the outer darkness; or if we cannot ignore it, if it presses too insistently upon us, we disapprove, being afraid. Not so Lawrence. He had eyes that could see, beyond the walls of light, far into the darkness, sensitive fingers that kept him continually aware of the enveloping mystery. He could not be content with the homemade, human tunnel, could not conceive that anyone else should be content with it. Moreover—and in this he was unlike those others, to whom the world's mystery is continuously present, the great philosophers and men of science—he did not want to increase the illuminated area; he approved of the outer darkness, he felt at home in it. Most men live in a little puddle of light thrown by the gig-lamps of habit and their immediate interest; but there is also the pure and power-ful illumination of the disinterested scientific intellect. To Lawrence, both lights were suspect, both seemed to falsify what was, for him, the im-mediately apprehended reality—the darkness of mystery. "My great religion," he was already saying in 1912, "is a belief in the blood, the flesh, as being wiser than the intellect. We can go wrong in our minds. But what the blood feels, and believes, and says, is always true." Like Blake, who had prayed to be delivered from "single vision and Newton's sleep": like Keats, who had drunk destruction to Newton for having ex-plained the rainbow, Lawrence disapproved of too much knowledge, on the score that it diminished men's sense of wonder and blunted their sensitiveness to the great mystery. His dislike of science was passionate and expressed itself in the most fantastically unreasonable terms. "All scientists are liars," he would say, when I brought up some experimentally established fact, which he happened to dislike. "Liars, liars!" It was a most convenient theory. I remember in particular one long and violent argument on evolution, in the reality of which Lawrence always passionately disbelieved. "But look at the evidence, Lawrence," I insisted, "look at all the evidence." His answer was characteristic. "But I don't care about evidence. Evidence doesn't mean anything to me. I don't feel it *here*." And he pressed his two hands on his solar plexus. I abandoned the argument and thereafter never, if I could avoid it, mentioned the hated name of science in his presence. Lawrence could give so much, and what he gave was so valuable, that it was absurd and profitless to spend one's time with him disputing about a matter in which he absolutely refused to take a rational interest. Whatever the intellectual consequences, he remained through thick and thin unshakably loyal to his own genius. The *daimon* which possessed him was, he felt, a divine thing, which he would never deny or explain away, never even ask to accept a compromise. . . . It was not an incapacity to understand that made him reject those generalizations and abstractions by means of which the philosophers and the men of science try to open a path for the human spirit through the chaos of phenomena. Not incapacity, I repeat; for Lawrence had, over and above his peculiar gift, an extremely acute intelligence. He was a clever man as well as a man of genius. (In his boyhood and adolescence he had been a great passer of examinations.) He could have understood the aim and methods of science perfectly well if he had wanted to. Indeed, he did understand them perfectly well; and it was for that very reason that he rejected them. For the methods of science and critical philosophy were incompatible with the exercise of his gift— the immediate perception and artistic rendering of divine otherness. And their aim, which is to push back the frontier of the unknown, was not to be reconciled with his aim, which was to remain as intimately as possible in contact with the surrounding darkness.

Aldous Huxley. Introd. in *The Letters of
D. H. Lawrence* (N. Y. Viking, 1932), pp. xi-xv

I was horrified by *Women in Love,* and though it would be an exaggeration to say that I am horrified by it to-day, I reject it now just as vehemently as I did then. Its message seems to me false and deathly. Some years afterwards Lawrence, who read it when it appeared, talked to me about that review. He said that, even at the time, he bore me no grudge for it: I had taken him seriously, and nobody else had done that.

I was glad of that, but I told him I was just as opposed then (in 1924) to the underlying doctrine of *Women in Love* as I had been when I wrote the review. And there we left it.

But in fact, though I did not realize it, either in 1921 or in 1924, Lawrence himself had abandoned the ground he had taken in *Women in Love* even before the book was published. It is true that he never ceased to hanker after some sort of escape from consciousness; but he had quite ceased to believe in the possibility of such an escape as he put before himself in that novel. In 1921 he was trying to struggle out of his own deathly conclusions.

It was the irony of fate, therefore, that my most vehement attack upon him should have been made precisely in the year (1921) when he was writing what I regard as the two finest of his later books—*Fantasia of the Unconscious* and *Aaron's Rod*. No doubt it made it easier for him to take the attack lightly, for manifestly I seemed to be warring against a Lawrence whom he himself had discarded. But the confusion produced in my mind by the publication of *Women in Love* five years after it was actually written, was bewildering. If *The Lost Girl* had appeared after *Women in Love* as it should have done, instead of before it, I should have felt very differently about *The Lost Girl*. To add to my confusion, *Fantasia of the Unconscious* was published only in America. I knew nothing of it. Thus I was totally unprepared for *Aaron's Rod* when it came. It took me completely by surprise.

When *Aaron's Rod* appeared in 1922, I was perplexed and disconcerted—most joyfully perplexed and gladly disconcerted. The death-miasma that seemed to me then, and seems to me now, to hang over *Women in Love* was dissipated; and I welcomed the change with enthusiasm. Again, I would not now withdraw a word of what I wrote then. "*Aaron's Rod*," I said in the *Nation*, "is the most important thing that has happened to English literature since the war. Mr. Lawrence's new book ripples with the consciousness of victory; he is gay, he is careless, he is persuasive. To read *Aaron's Rod* is to drink of a fountain of life."

I read the *Fantasia* when it arrived; and I remember exactly the time and place where I read it—late into the spring night in a solitary cottage in Ashdown Forest. It was to me then, as it is to me now, a wonderful book. I had just emerged from an experience which had changed me radically. Lawrence's declaration of faith in the *Fantasia* was completely convincing to me in my new half-convalescent, half-confident condition. Here was something in which I did veritably believe with all my heart, and all my mind, and all my soul. What I had glimpsed in *Aaron's Rod*, I had now a full sight of. If this was what Lawrence believed and stood for, then I was his man; he should lead and I would follow. . . .

It did not occur to me that *Aaron's Rod* and *Fantasia* had been written nearly three years before, and that in those three years Lawrence must have changed. The book that had meant so much to me had become for him the expression of an aspiration, no longer of a conviction. The sense of doom had begun to triumph over the resolution to act. All the process which I have striven to demonstrate in the book I have written on Lawrence, a process so plain to me now, was concealed from me then. I did not understand that the revulsion he felt from the malevolence and cruelty of Mexico was also the fascination that held him there, as it held him in Cornwall during the war. He wanted to feed his sense of doom and death and corruption; to fulfil his own injunction that "we must disintegrate while we live." In the last issue, he could not make the effort towards a new and fuller life. Part of him wanted this, desired it as ardently as any man has ever desired it—that part of him that wanted to love and to forgive; but deeper still was his longing for hatred and revenge. The world, his own life, had deceived him; and he was not going to take it lying down. Mingled with all his passionate but partial professions of desire to make all things new was a thirst for destruction, a nostalgia for chaos.

> J. M. Murry. *Reminiscences of D. H. Lawrence*
> (Jonathan Cape, 1933), pp. 102–4, 108–9

I knew him before his marriage, in *White Peacock* days, and still hope that a certain photograph of him taken at that time may be reproduced somewhere. It was a charming likeness, with an ethereal expression in those youthful features. Then he came to see me with his newly-married wife; I cooked, in her honour, a German luncheon.

He sometimes turned up at the *English Review* office with stories like the "Prussian Officer" written in that impeccable hand-writing of his. They had to be cut down for magazine purposes; they were too redundant; and I was charged with the odious task of performing the operation. Would Lawrence never learn to be more succinct, and to hold himself in hand a little? No; he never would and he never did; diffuseness is a fault of much of his work. In *Women in Love,* for example, we find pages and pages of drivel. Those endless and pointless conversations! That dreary waste of words ! To give your reader a sample of the chatter of third-rate people is justifiable; ten consecutive pages of such stuff is realism gone crazy.

Lawrence never divined that conversations and dialogues are precious contrivances, to be built up *con amore;* that they should suggest a clue to character and carry forward the movement instead of retarding it; that they should be sparkling oases, not deserts of tiresome small-talk. Reading these flatulent passages, one wonders by what process his brain came to conceive them; one wonders, next, how, having written them, he could bear to see them in print. He must have known they were rubbish. His state of health, maybe, engendered an imperious need of unburdening himself of every idle thought which flitted through his head.

I suppose he was not much concerned with the form of his novels. They were explorations into himself. That is why, for us, they are explorations into Lawrence. There is *Kangaroo:* well, that intrusion of a Cornish element is an artistic outrage. Yet he could not help infecting Australian surroundings with this exotic taint; *c'était plus fort que lui;* and if it injures the story it certainly reveals some secrets of Lawrence's own psychology. The same applies to "The Trespasser"—the tale, a well-motivated one, of a husband entangled with another woman, who is harassed to such a point by his legitimate wife and family that, instead of pounding them all into a jelly, he hangs himself. Self-exploration! There was in Lawrence a masochistic strain, a strain of Christ, prophet and sufferer. Both of them were in disharmony with their environment; both took every opportunity of saying so, although in Jesus—if he ever existed—we find less hysteria than in Lawrence, whose Messianic utterances are delivered in shrill tones, and often in so paradoxical a language that he becomes a mere screamer, peevish and frothy. And even as Jesus performed the menial task of washing his disciples' feet, so Lawrence was never happier than when scrubbing floors or peeling potatoes: how frequently in his books are the men portrayed as doing the work of women or of servants!

Aaron's Rod lays bare another aspect of his character, namely, his love of scoring off people to whom he is under an obligation. The book teems with examples of this trait; I alone could give five of them, although not a quarter of the persons described are known to me. . . .

Lawrence was certainly one of the most envy-bitten mortals I have known. He was envious of other men's social rank, of their reputations and natural gifts, their health, and chiefly of their bank-balances; even the relative affluence of his own family was a grievance to him.

For the rest, the prevalent conception of Lawrence as a misanthrope is wrong. He was a man of naturally blithe disposition, full of childlike curiosity. The core of his mind was unsophisticated. He touched upon the common things of earth with tenderness and grace, like some butterfly poised over a flower—poised lightly, I mean, with fickle *insouciance* (for his books contain strange errors of observation). This, once more, was the direct reaction, the poet's reaction; the instantaneous record. No intervening medium, no mirage, hovered between Lawrence and what his eyes beheld. These things lay before him clear-cut, in their primordial candour, devoid of any veil of suggestion or association. It was his charm. There was something elemental in him, something of the *Erdgeist.*

His genius was pictorial and contemplative, impatient of causes save where the issue was plain to an infant's understanding, as in the matter of that pamphlet on Pornography and Obscenity—a noble pronouncement. Lawrence was no Bohemian; he was a provincial, an inspired provincial with marked puritan leanings. He had a shuddering horror of Casanova's Memoirs; he was furious with a friend for keeping two mistresses instead of one, and even with Florentine boys for showing an inch or so of bare flesh above the knee—"I don't like it! I don't like it! Why can't they wear trousers?"; my own improprieties of speech he ascribed to some perverse kink of nature, whereas they were merely an indication of good health. Had he been concerned for his own peace of mind he should have left the department of exact thinking to take care of itself and devoted his energies to that of feeling, for he insisted on discovering ever fresh riddles in the Universe, and these riddles annoyed him. He could flounder in philosophy as few have yet floundered; in his descriptive writings are phrases which none save Lawrence could have struck out. His life was restless, ever moving from place to place. His work moves restlessly from subject to subject, and sometimes, as in certain of his tales, with an enviable flair, an enviable freshness, and enviable mastery.

It is true that, being inwardly consumed and tormented, he never clarified his outlook. Lawrence had neither poise nor reserve. Nor had he a trace of humour. He had courage. He knew what would be the consequence if a notorious book of his should ever be published: a howl of execration. He went ahead. I think the writings of Lawrence have done good; his influence was needed by a large class of our fellow-creatures. He has done good negatively, as a warning to thinkers and on occasion to writers; positively, because his work is in the nature of a beneficent, tabu-shattering bomb. An American friend tells me that Lawrence's romances have been of incalculable service to genteel society out there. The same applies to genteel society in England. Scholars and men of the world will not find much inspiration in these novels. Lawrence opened a little window for the bourgeoisie. That is his life-work.

Norman Douglas. Looking Back (N.Y., Harcourt,
Brace, 1933), pp. 282–83, 286–87

The Man Who Died is Lawrence's swan-song—calm, lovely, painful as one of those Pietas in which Christ's body lies stretched across His mother's knees and passion has subsided into physical exhaustion. "I'm rather miserable," records the penultimate letter, printed in Mr. Huxley's volume. "I'm miserable" insists the very last; and an atmosphere of profound and haunting sadness seems to hang heavily over Lawrence's closing years, as he realized that the struggle was coming to an end. For

Lawrence had loved, while he hated, life. He had loved, though he hated, abused and spurned, his fellow human beings. Throughout his career, his greatest ambition was to form a society—an entirely new society—that should constitute a living nucleus in the dissolution of the old; and his chief disappointment was his repeated failure. . . .

For, paradoxically enough, Lawrence's contribution to modern literature may be summed up in the fact that he gave literature—as distinct from the art of living, in which, towards the end of his life, he knew that he had failed—a second place. Had he succeeded in life, it is probable that his literary work might have been more harmonious; but, having failed, he enriched literature by refusing to recognize that it was the main object, the natural termination, of a writer's existence. "I will live my life," he wrote, "and, if possible, be happy. . . ." It was not possible; and, casually, he continued to throw off tales, novels and essays that preserve an aesthetic value, even though the "message" that they attempt to enforce seems wrong-headed and absurd. Take, for instance, the long story entitled *St. Mawr*. Considered from one aspect, this account of the vicissitudes of a tiresome middle-class girl, out of patience with her husband and his immediate surroundings, and chimerically enamoured of a vicious horse, is the very height of perversity and affectation. But then the scene changes to New Mexico. Lawrence is writing of the mountain ranch in which he himself spent some time after the war; and every sentence almost has a felicity, vividness and suggestive power that few modern prose writers can claim to have equalled. . . .

Any of D. H. Lawrence's later novels is a lesson in how a work of literature should not be composed; yet they contain passages of which every line is an indication of the beauties that may still be extracted from the vocabulary of modern English.

Peter Quennell. "D. H. Lawrence and Aldous Huxley," in
The English Novelists, ed. Derek Verschoyle
(Chatto and Windus, 1936), pp. 250–52

Lawrence stood for life, and shows, in his criticism, tossed off as it was for the most part, in the most marginal way, an extraordinarily quick and sure sense for the difference between that which makes for life and that which makes against it. He exhibits a profound, and for those who come to the criticism knowing only the fiction, perhaps surprising, centrality.

F. R. Leavis. *The Common Pursuit* (Penguin, 1962
[c. Chatto and Windus, 1952]), p. 284

Lawrence's work is above all a revolt against the idea that the consciousness of civilized men is an *object* of the civilization in which they live, which, in turn, is an object of the present phase of history. He is forever proclaiming that before all else he is a man, with a physical body and an instinctive life, and that although his body and instincts exist *within* civilization they are not the products *of* its condition at our particular moment of history. His work is a grand refusal of an intellectual attitude which has become so universal that to reject it may appear to be a rejection of the intellect itself. What Lawrence protested against was not intellect but the kind of intellectualization whereby men create a shadow-world for themselves. Men develop, for example, a theory about the state of civilization, and then regard the flesh and blood, natural scenery, and stone buildings around them as ideas or symbols illustrating the conclusion they have come to. Long before cities are ruined, we have made metal ruins of them, and ghosts of ourselves.

Lawrence was essentially a dialectician, a preacher rather than a prophet, fighting his time with methods and arguments chosen to surprise and take his enemy (everyone!) off guard. Like all preachers he defended a position which was reasonable by appealing not to reason but to realities which most of the reasonable of his time chose to ignore. The religious preacher is concerned primarily with proving to his audience out of their own experience that they have souls which know God. Reasoning comes after he has widened the field of discussion to areas which the irreligious refuse to accept, and then it takes place on ground whose existence they have denied. Lawrence was also concerned with widening the field of discussion by appealing to our experience, in order to demonstrate that civilization is not just our idea of the contemporary condition of the West. It is also our lives, and our lives are not simply intellectual; still less are they mental concepts about ourselves. Our lives, besides being "The West in the twentieth century," are our physical bodies, the instinctual forces in us, and our relations with one another. . . .

Lawrence could not accept any current attitudes. He wanted to break through all the theories of art and society, the entire structure of individualism, and all the organizations of the Trades Unionists, the methods of the revolutionaries, and the plans of the planners. All were equally repellent to him because all treated individual man as a function within society. It has been pointed out that he had fascist tendencies. All this means, however, is that occasionally he was deluded into accepting the talk of fascists about blood, race, and instinct. So soon as he saw that the fascists, like everyone else, were bureaucratic organizers, he lost sympathy for them.

Perhaps Lawrence's greatest weakness was a kind of impatience which was the result of an absolute refusal to face necessary ugliness. There is very little ugliness in any but his early work, and whenever he is faced by it he reacts with disgust and horror. He hated the places of his child-hood and the life of the workers not just because he had grown away from them completely but because he could not endure the ugliness of the mining villages. And the hysteria in his work is not connected—as most critics think—with a sexual obsession but with a hatred which makes him want to run away from or destroy whatever ugliness he sees.

All the same, as a critic of contemporary life Lawrence is perhaps the greatest of this century, because he is the only one whose grasp of the values of living is never intellectualized or idealistic. It's always real. He tells us what we are not and what we could be. He reminds us that we live among other human beings and that in our relationships we could be much realer than we are. He warns us against the danger of using our gifts, or following those who use their gifts, to create mental worlds of "withinness" in the context of their fatalistic view of society. He has done more than any other writer to define the wholeness of individual existence, made up of body and instinct as well as intellect, and to show that this wholeness can be brought into relation with other people and the world outside.

Lawrence had social as well as individual passion, although he gave up as a bad job most of his attempts to save or to instruct society. But in one of his letters to Bertrand Russell written during the First World War he writes, referring to E. M. Forster: "His ultimate desire is for the continued action which has been called the social passion—the love for humanity—the desire to work for humanity. That is every man's ul-timate desire and need." And although Lawrence's attempts to get to-gether with Bertrand Russell and save the world were foredoomed and absurd, the social passion ultimately exists and is real in his writing. Lawrence's work holds out the feasible light of a kind of society where life is lived for the sake of the concrete realities of human separateness and human relations.

Stephen Spender. The Creative Element (Hamish
Hamilton, 1953), pp. 93, 105–7

The only native English poet of any importance to survive the First World War was D. H. Lawrence. Yet his verse is very little read. As a minor adjunct to the novels it has come in, on occasions, for a little offhand comment. More often it is used as a go-between, joining the prose to the biography. Anthologists have printed a few poems grudgingly, out of piety, and even the critic who introduced the best English selection, in the Penguin Poets, seemed to feel that the poems succeed despite themselves, because they were written by Lawrence.

I had better state my position straightaway: I think the poems very fine indeed, with a fineness of perception and development that was always Lawrence's, and an originality that makes them as important as any poetry of our time. For their excellence comes from something that is rare at best, and now, in the 1950's well-nigh lost: a complete truth to feeling. Lawrence is the foremost emotional realist of the century. He wrote too much verse, like Hardy and Whitman, the two poets who influenced him most. But even his badness is the badness of genius; and there are quite enough good poems to make up for it. . . . [The] intelligent honesty and pertinacity of Lawrence's verse has had very little attention. The poems which have come in for most notice, the Birds, Beasts and Flowers, are usually thought of as little more than vivid pieces of description. . . .

The theme of both the novels and the poems is fulfillment, the spiritual maturity achieved between man and woman. But in the novels the fulfillment is acted out; the forces, like the morality, are "passionate, implicit." By contrast, the poems present nakedly the inner flow that runs below the actions, the forces before they are externalized in drama. It is as though they presented not the body that acts but the blood itself, the lifeline of experience and feeling that feeds and supports the novels.

A. Alvarez. in *A D. H. Lawrence Miscellany,* ed.
Harry T. Moore (Carbondale, Ill.; Southern Illinois
Univ. Pr., 1959 [c. 1958]), pp. 342, 349, 351

Pondering over Lawrence's contradictions and perpetual self-contradictions one is inclined to say in despair that it is virtually impossible to generalize about him. Still, one aspect much in his favor seems beyond dispute. He was not mealy-mouthed, he was not a timeserver or a flatterer, and he was not a careerist. He lived and died poor, the more honor to him. If he had cringed and conformed, if he had climbed the social ladder prudently, if he had used others for his advancement and then dropped them when they ceased to be of service, there is no saying how high he might have risen in the magazine and high-royalties world. His awkward efforts "to cultivate the right people" always ended in mutual explosions of bad temper. There was no taming him. The Sun-God, Lord of Song, uses such devices to protect his few favorites from the contaminations of conformity, respectability, and success.

Richard Aldington, in *A D. H. Lawrence Miscellany,*
ed. Harry T. Moore (Carbondale, Southern Ill.
Univ. Pr., 1959), p. 153

Once Lawrence, forced by his opposition to the war, became a reformer, he never gave up the role. Give a man who has the need to dominate others the chance to lead the world out of its mess, and the need will never subside. It seeks satisfaction by any means at hand. Having tasted

that kind of intoxicating blood, our bengal is never satisfied with anything else. Art, pure art, is by comparison an insipid quarry. He tells
us somewhere that he used his novels as means of shedding his sickness.
This is true. But he also puts his novel to other uses. He will reform
mankind, just as he will tell Bertrand Russell what and how Russell
may think.

Because *Women in Love* had been conceived earlier than the brutal
trauma he underwent during the war (originally, as everybody knows,
this work and *The Rainbow* made up one single novel), the prophet did
not meddle with this book. But from *Aaron's Rod* on, this statement does
not hold. *Kangaroo* is hardly a novel. It is at best an effort, a futile effort, to solve a problem. After *Women in Love,* Lawrence is not able to
inform the matter of his experience with the success he had achieved
earlier. We find a continuous development in stylistic gifts. Some of the
short stories are quite successful, and in everything he writes are to be
found, in profusion, vignettes and even expository paragraphs that are
evidence of his mastery over the language. They are pure poetry. Several
chapters of *Morning In Mexico* are magnificent, although it would not
be astonishing to me if anthropological students of the Southwest found
his interpretations of the Indian dances offensive to their scientific con-
sciences and even utterly fantastic. As late as the posthumous *Apocalypse,*
we find whole paragraphs that constitute triumphant evidence of what a
gifted man can do with the English language. But on the whole the poet
has lost control. He is too deeply involved in a bitter struggle against
forces that he feels threaten him to handle them as he handled his experience up to and including *Women in Love.*

This passionate desire of Lawrence to do something about the world
was not subject matter that could be transformed into substance—or at
least that *he* could transform. It was, for him, too definitely addressed to
practical ends. What he could and did do was to handle with a messianic
fervor subjects he had formerly handled aesthetically. He changed settings. He took Aaron and Lilly to Florence, he took Lovat and his foreign wife to Australia, he went with Kate to "old Mexico." He added
to his interest in love a strong sociological and political interest that he
had not shown in his earlier work. The dances of the Indians of the
Southwest gave him a clearer grasp than he had previously achieved of
the insight that one of the profound needs of modern man is a religion
that will enable him to re-establish his broken connection with the
Cosmos. And thus, Lawrence managed to give himself and those of his
readers who do not grasp the distinction between quasi-art and art in
the most exacting sense, the impression that he was growing prodigiously
in an aesthetic sense. But the rate of growth, *exception faite* of his increasing mastery over language, was negligible.

A detailed examination of the work that Lawrence did after *Women in Love* will show that, whatever its many incidental aesthetic excellences and whatever its ideological value, on the whole it fails to come up to the purity exhibited in his two greatest works, *The Rainbow* and *Women in Love*.

Eliseo Vivas. *D. H. Lawrence* (Evanston, Ill.,
Northwestern Univ. Pr., 1960), pp. 16–17

Lawrence, we know, considered *Ulysses* dirty. Joyce thought *Lady Chatterley's Lover* lush and, in a letter to one of his patrons, further complained: ". . . the genuine article much more effectively done can be had in any back shop in Paris for one tenth of the money." That was written a few months after Lawrence's death, in 1930. . . .

That, in a general way, *Lady Chatterley's Lover* is not one of Lawrence's best books seems to be generally agreed. In the canon of Lawrence's work Dr. Leavis, for instance, places it decisively among the "minor" works. . . . We may regard *Lady Chatterley's Lover* as an extremely deliberated work, a work too deliberated for its writer, given all that we understand about him temperamentally, perhaps even physiologically. . . .

One should perhaps regard *Lady Chatterley's Lover* as, essentially, a "social" novel, perhaps the most perceptive since Disraeli. Its directly literary progeny has been strange. No doubt many readers have been led to compare it with Charles Morgan's *The Fountain,* inspired, one may feel, by pity for Chatterley, together with the notion that Mellors, though he had experienced the Army, had not experienced war. . . . A less-noticed comparison may be made with Mr. L. P. Hartley's *The Go-Between.* . . .

It is not easy to find a simple formula for *Lady Chatterley's Lover.* A failure by a dying man very much in his senses might be one attempt, it being understood that to be out of his senses had been one thing which helped to make D. H. Lawrence a great—as well as sometimes a very bad—writer. As for the passages which have been so much debated, the worst thing to be said about them is that they sometimes make one laugh. It is difficult to see how any young person could get a wrong idea from them. . . . Young persons of either sex are the last out of whose hands anybody should think of keeping this book. The worst it could do to them would be to make them a little over-solemn.

TLS. Nov. 4, 1960, p. 708

If *Lady Chatterley* is not a book about marriage or love (or, if about love, then about a rather odd and unsatisfactory sort of love), what then is it about? . . .

Certainly, the book is full of religious imagery and symbolism, and in the grave simplicity and majesty of its prose it is sometimes possible to catch more than an echo of the Authorised Version. Indeed, without any obvious defiance of the author's intentions the whole book can be read as an elaborate and blasphemous parody of the Gospels. . . .

This is what the book is really about: not love or marriage but the worship of the phallus. It is not a novel in the puritan tradition either as that tradition actually existed or as Mr. Hoggart somewhat naïvely defines it. (For surely it is naïve to interpret puritanism as a reliance upon one's own uninstructed conscience, without reference to God's teaching as revealed in the Holy Bible? Puritanism without the Book is not merely Hamlet without the prince; it is Hamlet without Shakespeare, without its creator. Without the Book, Jomo Kenyatta is a Puritan.)

No, *Lady Chatterley* is a novel in a far older and darker tradition, in a tradition which since the coming of Christianity has been half-submerged, emerging in the West only fitfully and surreptitiously in the guise of "the Old Religion." *Its tradition is the tradition of witchcraft*. The orgiastic rites it celebrates bear precisely the same relationship to the Holy Communion as the Black Mass does to the true Mass. Tam O'Shanter was at least drunk when, carried away by the young witch's ample charms, he suddenly roared out, "Weel done, Cutty-Sark!"

Nor is *Lady Chatterley* only a novel: it is a tract also. It does not merely depict: it preaches. And what it preaches is this: that mankind can only be regenerated by freeing itself from the tyranny of the intellect and the soul, from the tyranny of Jesus Christ, and by prostrating itself before its own phallus; in other words, by reducing itself almost to an animal level (almost, but not quite: for animals are mercifully incapable of the morbid cerebrations—"sex in the head"—which alone could generate such fantasies). If this is not a doctrine calculated to deprave and corrupt, I do not know what is.

"DEPRAVE AND CORRUPT"—was the jury's verdict confirmation of what many have long suspected, that these words have pretty well lost all meaning? Along with belief in original sin we seem to have discarded any belief in the original innocence which the verbs "to deprave and to corrupt" presuppose. And certainly it is slightly ridiculous to talk of a *book* corrupting a society in which, if present tendencies are maintained, it may soon be quite usual for a schoolgirl to have an abortion before she can read.

Nor is *Lady Chatterley* likely to deprave and corrupt *many people*. It is unlikely to corrupt anyone who reads it with as little attention and understanding as that displayed by most of those who spoke up on its behalf at the trial. Nor is it likely to corrupt those millions who are now going to read it for what are laughingly called "the wrong reasons," just skimming through looking for the dirty bits. There is nothing particularly depraving in the mere description of the sexual act, nor corrupting in a mere four-letter word, and the skimmers are unlikely to find much more in the book than that.

No, the people it is most likely to corrupt are those few who are going to read it "for the right reasons," the earnest ones who will read it carefully with sympathy and respect, and who have sufficient intelligence and knowledge to grasp the point. Heaven knows, it is difficult enough to keep one's sanity under the impact of Lawrence's torrential eloquence, his proud solemnity and poetic gifts. Was ever spring more tenderly or beautifully described than in this book? It is only too easy to surrender to his warlock spells and incantations, to his hallucinatory repetitions and variations, to his dithyrambic rhapsodising. Was ever book less boring? It is about as boring as the explosion of a moral H-bomb. To compel assent Lawrence has arts enough of his own. He hardly needed the full weight of clerical and academic approval to make him well-nigh irresistible.

A book which Christians *ought* to read? A book, rather, which Christians may read, or some Christians anyway—those, perhaps, with long spoons.

Colin Welch. *Enc.* Feb., 1961, pp. 77–79

Lady Chatterley's Lover is a response to a historical phenomenon; and it must be remembered, in judging the importance of that comment, that Lawrence is not one of those writers whose claim to greatness lies in their good sense. He is to be compared with Jean Jacques Rousseau, who was one of the silliest of men, but who managed to identify the issues concerning which men were going to be sensible or silly during the next few centuries with crucial effects on civilisation. Lawrence's opinions about men, women, and society were often foolish, but they referred to situations in which men, women, and society have in fact found themselves during our time. Of course Lawrence was talking nonsense when he expressed murderous intentions towards millions of Germans, said he could hardly wait for the deadly revolution, and cursed everybody who was doing any sort of job of work. But he was right in recognizing that there was something wrong in Germany, that there was going to be a deadly revolution, and that the makers of society had not been as successful as they had hoped. In *Lady Chatterley* he was dealing with another reality: a certain coldness of the flesh.

Rebecca West. *Enc.* March, 1961, p. 52

I began reading *Collected Letters* at random, and the curious thing was, turning the pages, that most of the letters might have been to anybody.

The majority are personal, though often with bits of business mixed up in them, yet they feel quite public. It is a very special gift that Lawrence had, though on an occasion like this a bit disconcerting. He had this style of extraordinarily direct address to the reader; you can feel, if you want to, that almost everything he wrote, of this kind, was written especially for you. But of course this is illusion, an illusion he probably went to some pains to cultivate. The apparent directness and intimacy are a kind of self-protection. Behind them is a remote and almost always lonely figure. It simply isn't possible to be direct and intimate so easily and with so many people, except as a form of address, a quick but fixed kind of relationship. Behind it in virtually every letter, is the guarded signature: D. H. Lawrence, or D.H.L., even to close friends, after many years. The personal quickness, ultimately, is a public literary style.

I don't know how these volumes can best be used. For students of Lawrence they will, of course, replace the Huxley edition of 1932; there are many more letters, and the texts are more complete, though still not final. Harry Moore's editing is excellent, and so many people have helped with this edition that it is really useful, academically.

But for more than this? Professor Moore suggests that they can be read as "one of the significant autobiographies of our time as well as a vital commentary on the time itself." At the simplest level, this is obviously true. Many of Lawrence's most decisive statements are in the letters, and the quickest way to get a real sense of the man is again to read the letters, particularly those of the middle years. At the same time, much of the autobiography is oblique. Lawrence appears, again and again, to be revealing himself with extraordinary candour, but I doubt this. Some of the decisive experiences, particularly of his later life, seem to me not to be here at all, they went their own way directly into his art. For this reason it's quite wrong to take Lawrence, as a personality, at his own valuation. There are many faults in the novels, wonderfully alive and moving as they are, but the letters belong, decidedly, to a much less important part of himself: the Lawrence who could all too easily present and dramatise himself, without the deep responsibilities and disciplines of real creation.

There's always been a danger of taking this Lawrence personality as central, and the novels as by-products; this has been the vice of so much of the criticism. I feel, after rereading the letters, in a much stronger position to reject the personality, though honouring the glimpses of the man behind it. And I find as I do this that the novels grow in stature, their remaining faults mainly the intrusion of this personality, which so many people, Lawrence among them, tried to warm their hands at. I move back, as I read the letters, to a different position, looking at the novelist and thinker this powerful and very vulnerable man struggled successfully to be.

Raymond Williams. *MGW*. March 29, 1962, p. 11

LAWRENCE, T. E. (1888–1935)

During his University career at Oxford he was noted for being a recluse. Frequently he would disappear most unexpectedly from the University for long tramps about Europe. He has always been eccentric in his habits. Although he finished the regular four years of academic work at Oxford in three, he never attended a single lecture during his college days, preferring to spend most of his time reading medieval literature. Much of the time he preferred to sleep during the day and work at night. He has never yet dined with anyone in the three Oxford colleges which he attended—Jesus, Magdalen, and All Souls.

Lawrence has always been a keen student of military writers. His favorite work, until he took part in the Arabian campaign, was Marshal Foch's *Principes de Guerre;* although he once told me in Arabia that his study of Caesar and Xenophon had been of more value to him in his desert campaign because in his irregular war against the Turks he had to adopt directly opposite tactics from those advocated by Marshal Foch. He has also been a keen student of medieval French literature, and is particularly fond of Gothic art.

Lowell Thomas. *Strand*. Jan., 1920, p. 44

Lawrence wrote his great history of the Arab Revolt, *Seven Pillars of Wisdom,* or seven out of ten books of it, between February and June, 1919, in Paris. He did the present beginning of the introduction in six hours in the Handley-Page aeroplane, on his way from Paris to collect his belongings in Cairo: the rhythm of it is affected, he says, by the slow "munch, munch, munch" of the great Rolls-Royce engines. In London he wrote an eighth book, but had all the eight stolen from him about Christmas, 1919 while changing trains at Reading. Only the introduction and the draft of two books remained.

He has never imagined a political motive for the theft, but his friends have. They even whisper darkly that one day the lost text may reappear in certain official archives. Lawrence himself hopes it will not: he had destroyed most of his war-time notes as he went along and when he began again the weary task of rewriting the quarter of a million words he could not quite trust his memory. However, Colonel Dawnay, who saw both texts, tells me that one chapter at least that he read more carefully than others in the original seems to be the same, word for word and almost comma for comma, in the second version. Lawrence still had two skeleton-diaries and some rough route-sheets, but little else.

This second writing was done in less than three months at the rate of some four to five thousand words a day. But Lawrence, immoderate as usual, did not keep to a daily ration. He did it in long sittings and probably set up a world's literary record by writing Book VI in twenty-four hours between sunrise and sunrise without a pause. Book VI was about 34,000 words in length! "Naturally the style was careless," he says. But it served as a basis for a careful literary rewriting; which is the *Seven Pillars* as it was finally published. He wrote it in London, Jiddah and Amman in 1921, again in London in 1922, in the Royal Tank Corps near Dorchester in 1923 and 1924, and in the Royal Air Force at Cranwell in 1925 and 1926. He checked the historical accuracy with the help of all available official documents and his British friends who had served with the Arab army.

Lawrence does nothing by halves and not only set about making the book a history of the Arab Revolt which the Arabs themselves would never write, but one that he would not be ashamed of as literature. For this last ambition he secured the advice of two of the best-known English writers and taught himself with their help to write professionally.

Seven Pillars of Wisdom is, beyond dispute, a great book; though there is such a thing as a book being too well-written, too much a part of literature. Lawrence himself realizes this and was once, indeed, on the point of throwing it into the Thames at Hammersmith. It should somehow, one feels, have been a little more casual, for the nervous strain of its ideal of faultlessness is oppressive. Lawrence charges himself with "literary priggishness," but that is unfair. His aim was, all the time, simplicity of style and statement and this he achieved in the most expert way. He has, somewhere, confessed to a general mistrust of experts and it may be that he should have carried it further, and dispensed with expert advice in literary matters too. (Possibly, though, in actual practice he did; he was always a difficult pupil.) On the whole I prefer the earliest surviving version, the so-called Oxford text, to the final printed book which was the version that I first read consecutively. This is a physical reaction. The earlier version is 330,000 words long instead of 280,000 and the greater looseness of the writing makes it easier to read. From a critical point of view no doubt the revised version is better. It is impossible that a man like Lawrence would spend four years on polishing the text without improving it, but the nervous rigor that the revised book gave me has seemingly dulled my critical judgment.

Robert Graves. *Lawrence and the Arabs*
(Jonathan Cape, 1927), pp. 406–8

His mind was too complex to permit of satisfaction for an achievement successfully carried out. He was too sensitive of his honour. . . . This attitude of mind has endured and may account for much which seems obscure to the outsider as regards Lawrence's life and outlook since the War: his self-immolation as an aircraftsman in the Air Force; his refusal of all rewards or honours; his refusal to touch one penny from his book *Revolt in the Desert,* all profit from which he has allotted to military charities. He carried on through the War for the sake of his country, but has steadfastly refused any advancement or profit resulting from his actions. Any breaking of faith, no matter how sound the political reasons might be, was abhorrent to him.

W. F. Stirling. *Cnh.* April, 1933, p. 507

About this time [1923] he remarked: "My own writing is only a dissatisfaction to me: so much disappointment and pain, without any faculty of pleasing myself or anyone else. For that reason I've tried translating, hoping to dodge thereby the creative effort: only to find myself as particular over the reproductive. Consequently I have given it up, and shall manufacture no more books. The trifle I tried to do lately for Garnett was only to pay a little of the debt I owe him for help and kindness . . . and even that stimulus didn't carry me to the achievement." [The "trifle" was an introduction which he wrote for Edward Garnett to go with a new edition of Richard Garnett's *Twilight of the Gods.*]

In 1926 I published a one-volume edition of Doughty's *Arabia Deserta,* a copy of which I sent him. "Congratulations on the one-volume edition," he wrote. "As regards my introduction, *Arabia Deserta,* as a work of art, is better without the discordance of a preface by a strange hand. Its value doesn't lie in its exactness to life in Arabia (on which I can pose as an authority), but in its goodness as writing."

About this time I was pressing him to write a memoir of Doughty. "I've thought of that 'life' idea, up and down: and I'm sorry that I can't touch it. I would not have delayed so in considering the life of anyone else: but for C.M.D. I had a very real regard. That *Seven Pillars* effort showed me my incompetence with a pen. Rule me 'off' in every respect."

Jonathan Cape in *T. E. Lawrence by His Friends,*
ed. A. W. Lawrence (Jonathan Cape, 1937), pp. 469–70

What halted Lawrence on the nearside of achievement so that instead of becoming the communist hero, which his gifts and his hatred for the evils of capitalism fitted him for, he became a bourgeois hero who miscarried? Lawrence's tragedy was partly due to his education. He was too intellectual. The hero should have plenty of native intelligence, but to be intellectual means that one's psychic-potentialities have been fully developed into the current forms. Lawrence was a man of high consciousness, but it was the consciousness of a culture now doomed. All the outworn symbols of the long noonday of bourgeois culture stiffened his prodigious memory, and made of his genius an elaborate osseous structure to tenacious for the instinctive movement of his soul. That is why thought, devised only to aid action, yet often seems to hamper action. Lawrence himself believed that his was the tragedy of the man of action who is also a thinker.

Christopher Caudwell. Studies in a Dying Culture
(John Lane, 1938), p. 39

There is hardly an originality in the articles, scraps, and diaries reprinted in this book [*Oriental Assembly*], and if the photographs had not been taken by the legendary Lawrence they would, technically, fall far short of publication standards. But we must pay the price for our hero-worship. And what a hero we have here! He certainly does not lack candour. In the only worthwhile section of the volume, we find the suppressed introductory to the *Seven Pillars*.

Mulk Raj. Anand. LL. Oct., 1939, p. 125

It may be as well to begin with an emphasis upon Lawrence's own view of himself as a craftsman: his love of the minute mechanics of writing and his aspiration towards major form—towards what he called, along with many, the architecture of his book. The emphasis cries for plain citation. Here are a few sentences and phrases isolated from the letters, of which the first set deal with words.

"That frenzied aching delight in a pattern of words that happen to run true. . . . My deepest satisfaction [is] in the collocation of words so ordinary and plain that they cannot mean anything to a book-jaded mind; and out of some such I can draw deep stuff. . . . Prose depends on a music in one's head which involuntarily chooses & balances the possible words to *keep tune* with the thought. The best passages in English prose all deal with death or the vanity of things, since that is a tune we all know, and the mind is set quite free to think while writing about it. . . . Only occasionally in things constantly dwelt upon, do you get an unconscious balance, & then you get a *spontaneous* and perfect arrangement of words to fit the idea, *as the tune*. Polishing is an attempt, by stages, to get what should be a single combined stride. . . . The worst of being a habitual translator is that one gets in the way of trying to squeeze every sponge dry—and so few authors ever really *intend* all the content of their sponges. Words get richer every time they are deliberately used . . . but only when deliberately used: and it is hard to be conscious of each single word, and yet not at the same time self-conscious. . . . What you say about the emphasis I get on simple words like Moon or chocolate bisquits, mayn't it be partly because I do try & feel every article and emotion that comes into the book? I tie myself into knots trying to re-act everything, as I write it out. It's like writing in front of a looking-glass, and never looking at the paper, but always at the imaginary scene. That, and a trick of arranging words, so that the one I care for most is either repeated, or syllable-echoed, or put in a startling position."

So much for the craft of words. The citations are emphatic, it seems to me, of the high degree in which Lawrence was a deliberate craftsman. It is not easy to make the emphasis as plain with regard to the more formal aspects of craft, because the citations seldom appear in compact phrases or sentences. Any reader of the Letters may find for himself instance after instance of Lawrence's effort to shape his books for sequence and balance and drama.

> Richard P. Blackmur. "The Everlasting Effort," in *The Expense of Greatness* (N.Y., Arrow Editions, 1940), pp. 3–4

T. E. Lawrence, whose experience of war had been in the Middle East, restored once again an element of romance and mystery, of adventure and glamour into what had been a dreary and sordid experience. Lawrence, it is true, suffered physically to an extreme degree, but he had a war of movement with the excitement of strange encounters. Above all, in the warfare which he had known, the individual was not overlaid by the mass, nor man by mechanism. Here was the picture of a hero riding again into Damascus, instead of civilized man degraded and befouled standing in endless horror in the water-logged trenches of France. Further, Lawrence could write, and could convert his unique experience in the war into one of the great books of Arabia, in the tradition of Doughty and Burton. It seems to complete the contrast when one discovers him saying in his letters of some of the poets of the Western front that they were not tough enough. Whatever he and his companions may have endured their experiences have no identity with the massed hordes waiting death in Western Europe, nor can Lawrence suppress an element of romance, however hard he may attempt to do so, for he carries us to his scenes: "the sweep of the open places, the taste of tide winds, the sunlight, and the hopes in which we worked. The morning freshness of the world-to-be intoxicated us. We were wrought up with ideas inexpressible and vaporous, but to be fought for."

The mystery which enshrouded Lawrence's contribution to the war continued into the record of his publication of his account of the campaign. In 1926 *The Seven Pillars of Wisdom* had been issued in an edition of little over a hundred subscription copies at a cost of some £13,000. To meet this outlay Lawrence found himself compelled to issue an abbreviated edition as *Revolt in the Desert* in 1927, and it was this volume which established his reputation with the wider public. In 1935 *The Seven Pillars of Wisdom* was itself issued in an ordinary edition and in 1938, after his death, Lawrence's remarkable collection of letters was published.

His reputation and influence increased because his popularity was not confined to those who admired his career in the war. The Left Wing writers and even the Communists found much in him that they could esteem. For them the appeal lay not so much for his share in the Arab campaign as for the later reputation gained from *The Mint,* his unpublished record of the life of an ordinary serviceman in the R.A.F. If Lawrence had pleased the romantics by his years of endurance in the Middle East, he had puzzled and delighted the proletarians by his twelve years' service in the ranks of the Air Force. A discriminating analysis, which is very largely a tribute, is to be found in the work of Ralph Fox, the Communist writer who was killed in Spain. He describes him as "certainly among the most remarkable figures of modern England," and he adds that "the important thing about Lawrence is that he is the only hero whom the English ruling classes have produced in our time, a hero who in his own lifetime gathered about him all the legendary atmosphere of the hero."

Apart altogether from his great talents as a writer T. E. Lawrence was one of the most remarkable men of his time.

> B. Ifor Evans. *English Literature Between the Wars*
> (Methuen and Co., 2nd ed., 1949), pp. 108–9

Lawrence, as he himself would have been the first to admit, was a made not a born writer, and the sustained effort required in the writing of *Seven Pillars* overtaxed his abilities, remarkable though these were. The best parts of that earlier book were the reflective passages and those directly inspired by agony or disgust; in *The Mint* such passages predominate, and show Lawrence's style at its best. It is a curious style— highly-wrought, angular, tautly concentrated, with something of the knotty, hand-carved awkwardness of Hardy; there are echoes, too, of a rather ninetyish preciosity ("the appellant moon") and here and there one is pulled up suddenly by an archaic or recondite word (e.g. "fescinnine"). In the scraps of dialogue, Lawrence shows an acute ear for talk— though in this unlimited edition one has to guess at most of it, for the barrack-room patois is heavily bowdlerized (and rather inconsistently at that—at least one word is printed in full in one passage and omitted in another). But perhaps the vividest pages are those which describe the squalid misery of fatigues—carting swill, washing-up greasy plates in cold water, etc., etc.; nobody who has served in the ranks will be able to read these without a reminiscent shudder.

Jocelyn Brooke. TT. Feb. 19, 1955, p. 237

Lawrence's reputation as a writer will, I believe, be immensely increased by the publication of <i>The Mint,</i> although had it been published earlier, it would have seemed more sensational than it does today; it is in reality the kind of "reportage," episodic detailed description of events, which became popular during the Second World War. It is not, as the author himself described it in one of his letters, an "iron, rectangular, abhorrent book"; nor, <i>pace</i> Mr. Richard Aldington, who cannot have realized that it was so soon to be made available for public circulation, is it "almost insane in its attack on the female sex," which is in point of fact hardly mentioned. . . .

There is extraordinary variety in the writing, particularly noticeable in the differences of pace in Part Three, which, compared with the jerky, almost angular writing of the first two parts, approaches near to a happy serenity. The literary mannerisms which I now feel mar so much of <i>The Seven Pillars</i> are still discernible, but they are much less in evidence than in the former book. <i>The Mint</i> is not, I think, a masterpiece of literature, it is too episodic for that, but no one can say after reading it that Lawrence was not a writer; as it is there are one or two descriptive passages of great beauty. . . .

The Mint does . . . suggest that Lawrence, had he lived, might have become a very considerable writer.

John Morris. Enc. April, 1955, pp. 79–80

LEAVIS, F. R. (1895–   )

Though F. R. Leavis is a first-rate critic, and he dominates this collection, it [<i>The Importance of Scrutiny</i>] is a rather dull book. So much of it is given over to an arid defense of the autonomy of literary criticism: it is not literary history, says Mr. Leavis in reply to F. W. Bateson; not philosophy, in reply to René Wellek and George Santayana; not a new science, in reply to I. A. Richards. "If I profess myself so freely to be no philosopher," Mr. Leavis says, "it is because I feel that I can afford my modesty; it is because I have pretensions—pretensions to being a literary critic." How priggish Mr. Leavis' declaration sounds when it is set off against what Eliot has said, who is also concerned to defend the autonomy of literary criticism. . . .

There is something of this priggishness about *Scrutiny* generally, and it prompts the editor of this book priggishly to praise it for refusing to follow the "fashion of the decade—Cynicism in the Twenties, Marxism in the Thirties, Existentialism and Crisis Theology in the Forties." *Scrutiny's* detachment has its value, but it springs as much from narrow insularity as from correct critical principles. The literary nominalism that Mr. Leavis so doggedly insists upon, with its pragmatical distrust of anything that goes beyond the hard particulars of the text and its horror of "abstractions," is peculiarly English and insular and excuses him from any acquaintance with the advanced thinking of the time. . . . His nominalist critical method, too, deprives his writings of form; for want of a strong controlling generalization they tend to resolve themselves into a series of points. They are not, for the most part, shaped from within, but mechanically borrow such order as they have from the texts they consider. . . .

But, having noted these things, one can go on to say that Mr. Leavis is a critic of genuine personal taste and independent conviction, though the evidence for this is less in these pages than in such a work as *The Great Tradition*. Judgment is paramount in all his writings; there is a refreshing absence of coyness in his constant committing of himself to an opinion about how good something is. Some of these opinions are egregiously wrongheaded—as for instance the denunciatory asides Mr. Leavis directs at Flaubert in *The Great Tradition;* but then, how pleasant to read a critic willing so plainly to mark out the limits of his sensibility. . . .

What you find in Mr. Leavis' writing, and what is so often missing elsewhere, is a genuine experiencing of the literary work. So much big critical talk, by people who may have a more sophisticated intelligence than he, conceals a poverty of response to literature, or the most timid conventional response; and they, I suppose, are quickest to call him "academic." Mr. Leavis is always sending you off to read, or back to re-read—off or back, that is, to the *experience* of a book, which is his only concern. For him, a piece of literature is in the last analysis more interesting than anything you can say about it. That is the essential modesty of the man, a modesty not incompatible with strong opinions.

Martin Greenberg. *PR.* Aug., 1949, pp. 856–58

In the anthology *Determinations,* and in *Scrutiny* itself (as well as in its predecessor *The Calendar of Modern Letters,* which ran from 1925 to 1927 and from which Leavis culled the anthology *Toward Standards of Criticism*), some of the sharpest close reading of our time is combined with a social emphasis of real value. F. R. Leavis, one of the editors of *Scrutiny* and more or less the leader of the group, has turned out a good deal of very usable criticism, at its best when technical and exegetical, particularly of the moderns in *New Bearings*; somewhat vitiated at other times by the characteristic flaws of sociological criticism: the tendency to beat writers with terms like "escape" and "evasion," a kind of Brooksian truncation of socially unsatisfactory writers like Yeats and Henry James, an eighteenth-century rationalism that uses "ritual" exclusively as a term of abuse, and an excessively pedagogic, proselytizing-for-poetry style. In *Revaluation*, which appeared serially in *Scrutiny* as a series of re-estimates, F. R. Leavis set out to revise the history of English poetry to emphasize metaphysical "wit" (what Burke would call "perspective by incongruity") as the tradition, an attempt in which Eliot had informally preceded him.

Stanley Edgar Hyman. *The Armed Vision*
(N.Y., Alfred Knopf, 1952), pp. 301–2

His eyes, under tufted eyebrows, have the glare of someone who has seen the truth, and keeps his gaze fixed on it, but also the used, chiseled, hammered look of infinite adjustments and double checking, often fierce and nerve-racked. As a whole, though marked with age, the fine-drawn, smallish features and limbs and body, as he lay slightly sprawling in his chair, his head back, talking, abounded in sanity and vigor and masculinity and Britishness. That was what I mostly heard.

He was intensely and integrally British. Not Europeanized, not of the intelligentsia, not of the upper classes, not of Bohemia, not of Bloomsbury, not of any group or set. Intensely private, as father and husband and critic and thinker, flesh and spirit bearing the marks of the same strenuous self-discipline, the same rejection of all "official" influence, he comes to us from generations of decency and conscience and reasonableness and separateness, of private houses hidden behind hedges, along the road from Matthew Arnold and John Stuart Mill, the road which took its most recent, still abortive, turning under the direction of D. H. Lawrence. Alone in all Cambridge his voice has echoes of the best things in my parents' England, makes connections between all the parts of my experience. . . .

Leavis is the plain man among the critics; to avoid so obvious a comparison as the American New Critics, put him even beside Reuben Brower, and surely he strikes us as not professional. He *is* professional, of course, but the intensity of his impact lifts him out of that classification. He is talking to us too urgently and personally, too *morally*, for that. His best criticism has the character of a sermon. Side by side with the New Critics he seems ignominiously unintellectual. He does not draw striking parallels between different arts and different disciplines. He does not reveal, however discreetly, recondite readings in philosophy and theology. He does not throw out hints of relationships between D. H. Lawrence and St. Augustine, or Crashaw and Polish Baroque, or whatever. He has nothing to say about the nature of knowledge or the language of poetry. All he talks about is English literature and which things in it are better and why. And his standards in judging those things have no metaphysical or theological basis. He judges things by whether they feel right to him. Instead of extending himself in systems and theories until everything can be held in his net and assigned a logical place, as nearly everyone else does, Leavis reduces himself to the residual essence of his experience, moral, social, sexual, intellectual, the single naked unprotected pulse, and records the reaction of that complex of nerves, so endlessly self-purging, to the play, poem, metaphor, opinion, etc.

Side by side with Lionel Trilling and Edmund Wilson, Leavis's personality is less that of the general thinker. He does not present himself as essentially a learned or a brilliant man. He does make you feel there is a lot to be *known* before you yourself can begin to criticize.

Martin Green. *A Mirror for Anglo-Saxons*
(N.Y., Harper, 1960), pp. 96, 101

In his youth, the man who was to become the twentieth century's most potent force in English literary criticism was considered by those who know these things to have all the makings of an Olympic cross-country runner. To-day, as Dr. Frank Raymond Leavis approaches his sixty-fifth birthday with undiminished vitality, it is worth recording that he always refused to join an established team. He ran as he has written and thought, on his own. . . .

Nor, for years, were his mental powers acknowledged. During most of his career, he was actively discouraged by many of his academic colleagues, and shunned by others who, although possibly sympathetic, were chary of his prickly manner and his repeated condemnations of the "academic ethos." Only recently was he made a Reader at his own university; he was well into his fifties before attaining a lectureship; and over 40 when he reached the lowest grade—part-time lecturer. Admittedly he had a post for a time in the 1920s but he lost it, some say partly because of shocked whispers about his daring to lecture on "that D. H. Lawrence." In fact, not so long ago he was convinced that his work still had formidable enemies, and he vehemently produced chapter and verse if anyone suggested he were "over sensitive."

The other day, I returned to his college, Downing, and listened in the Combination Room which overlooks the broad lawns and single magnolia bush as he talked about his 40 years of academic life. . . . Although small, he looks knobbly and hard, weather-beaten to an apparently time-less tan that extends from his chiselled features deep down to the V of his chest under the open-necked shirt. His voice is light and slightly nasal.

I had intended to discuss with Dr. Leavis what he thought of specific contemporary poets and novelists, a subject he has not really commented on since the thirties when he singled out Wiliam Empson and Ronald Bottrall as poets of promise. But he declined, remarking that he saw no point in criticising modern writers unless he had something good to say. Disparaging remarks about Iris Murdoch, for example, or Graham Greene, would serve no purpose; nor would his opinion of that "much over-valued poet," Dylan Thomas.

This reluctance to bring his critical values to play on present writing is disappointing. Yet, aided by the contributors to *Scrutiny*, he and his wife have brought about a major reversal of the values by which not only literature but education itself are judged. For years, he fought a rigorous and virtually lone crusade against the standards of gentlemanly "belles lettres" and dilettantism which dominated English studies, and to establish "intelligent discrimination" and "moral seriousness" in their place. Also with his early sociological criticism—"Culture and Environment" is now a classic—he tilled much of the ground worked by Richard Hoggart and Raymond Williams, and anticipated books like *The Hidden Persuaders* and *The Status Seekers*. His weaknesses are few. Perhaps the chief are his awkward prose, which is sometimes all knees and elbows, and his inability—particularly in the crowded classes after the war—to draw any but his better students into thinking independently. Conse-quently the mediocre have tended to become unquestioning disciples, taking his critical judgments as unalterable law and thus fostering an uncritical "Leavisite" dogmatism.

There have been—and still are—long and bitter skirmishes with what Dr. Leavis long ago called the literary "Establishment": but the wind of change is in the air. "Even the *New Statesman*—thirty years my enemy—is altering its mind," he said. "Yes, things have moved."

John Bourne. *MGW*. April 14, 1960, p. 13

Of F. R. Leavis it is only necessary to say in introduction that of all the critics in our period he has been the most actively and continuously con-cerned for the creation of a worthy and stimulating critical environment, as well as providing in his own work a body of criticism of the utmost consistency and distinction. It is impossible to separate a discussion of *Scrutiny* from that of his own contribution to it, for one cannot doubt that the review's incisiveness, centrality, and sense of relevance were the mark more than anything of his genius, and that without this its continuance for even half of its actual lifetime would have been out of the question.

"A sense of relevance" has not only led Leavis to see in a continuance of Arnold's spirit the critic's true business in the world, to see criticism as essentially practical and theory as subservient and secondary to practice, but also to find in values stemming from a fine sense of the whole breadth of life the standards by which literature must be judged. The truly relevant criteria—the futility, also, of ignoring them—come out admirably in a passage where he is discussing Jane Austen's position at the start of the great tradition of the English novel: " . . . It is in the same way true of the other great English novelists that . . . they are all distinguished by a vital capacity for experience, a kind of reverent openness before life, and a marked moral intensity." This grasp of criteria is what enabled Leavis to map out and define the significant tradition of the English novel from Jane Austen through George Eliot, James, and Conrad, to Lawrence—which, as Leavis himself says, "has become a fact of general acceptance . . . with the implication that it has always been so."

The appropriateness of these criteria in criticism of the novel would now perhaps be generally granted. But, as Leavis has shown in the course of practical analysis and revaluation of English poetry, they carry over into all literature, remain central to our judgment. In the sensitive and penetrating analysis of verse Leavis has certainly no master, but always his concern for "practical criticism," for close attention to "the words on the page," is a concern for something which far transcends the limits usually implied by these phrases: the accuracy arises out of a need to establish the relevance of a passage in the work as a whole and, by extension, the place which the work should take up in our cultural consciousness. Technique, in short, "can be studied and judged only in terms of the sensibility it expresses." The need to find and realize our contemporary sensibility should lie behind all discussions of technique, and justifies, in Leavis's case, the attention given to it.

> Andor Gomme in *The Modern Age* (*Pelican Guide
> to English Literature,* ed. Boris Ford)
> (Penguin Bks., 1961), pp. 363–64

As for Dr. Leavis, *The Common Pursuit* contains some of his finest, as well as some of his most irritating, work. The prickly quality, the gracelessness which seems, even to his admirers, to disfigure much of his writing, springs from a genuine and full-blooded concern with standards, with the whole truth as he sees it, which has had a profound if complex influence on most of the younger critics. Perhaps more than anyone else he has made the rewriting of recent literary history not only desirable but necessary.

TLS. Feb. 9, 1962, p. 90

. . . C. P. Snow's *The Two Cultures and the Scientific Revolution,* around which so curious a storm rages in England, was the Rede lecture of 1959. Sir Charles did not mention his great predecessor in the lecture-ship [Matthew Arnold], although his own discourse was exactly the opposite of Arnold's. And F. R. Leavis, whose admiration of Arnold is well known and whose position in respect to the relative importance of literature and of science in education is much the same as Arnold's, did not mention Arnold either, when, in his recent Richmond Lecture at Downing College, he launched an attack of unexampled ferocity upon the doctrine and the author of *The Two Cultures.* . . .

There can be no two opinions about the tone in which Dr. Leavis deals with Sir Charles. It is a bad tone, an impermissible tone. It is bad in a personal sense because it is cruel—it manifestly intends to wound. It is bad intellectually because by its use Dr. Leavis has diverted attention, his own included, from the matter he sought to illuminate. The doctrine of *The Two Cultures* is a momentous one and Dr. Leavis obscures its massive significance by bringing into consideration such matters as Sir Charles's abilities as a novelist, his club membership, his opinion of his own talents, his worldly success, and his relation to worldly power. Anger, scorn, and an excessive consciousness of persons have always been elements of Dr. Leavis's thought—of the very process of his thought, not merely his manner of expressing it. They were never exactly reassuring elements, but they could be set aside and made to seem of relatively small account in comparison with the remarkable cogency in criticism which Dr. Leavis so often achieved. But as they now appear in his valedictory address—for, in effect, that is what the Richmond Lecture was, since Dr. Leavis retires this year from his university post—they cannot be easily set aside, they stand in the way of what Dr. Leavis means to say.

And, indeed, our understanding of what he means to say is to be derived less from the passionate utterance of the lecture itself than from our knowledge of the whole direction of his career in criticism. That direction was from the first determined by Dr. Leavis's belief that the human faculty above all others to which literature addresses itself is the moral consciousness, which is also the source of all successful creation, the very root of poetic genius. The extent of his commitment to this idea results in what I believe to be a fault in his critical thought—he does not give anything like adequate recognition to those aspects of art which are gratuitous, which arise from high spirits and the impulse to play. One would suppose that the moral consciousness should, for its own purposes, take account of those aspects of art and life that do not fall within its dominion. But if the intensity of Dr. Leavis's commitment to the moral consciousness contrives to produce this deficiency of understanding, it is no less responsible for the accuracy and force which we recognize as the positive characteristics of his work. For Dr. Leavis, literature is what Matthew Arnold said it is, *the criticism of life*—he can understand it in no other way. Both in all its simplicity and in all its hidden complexity, he has made Arnold's saying his own, and from it he has drawn his strength.

Lionel Trilling. *Cmty*. June, 1962, pp. 461–64

Since Leavis and Connolly are generally supposed to represent the two opposite poles in contemporary English criticism it is just worth pointing out how much they have in common. Leavis's distrust of the modern world has led him into his well-known hardness to please; he would certainly agree that "the true function of a writer is to produce a masterpiece." Mr. Connolly, ultimately, is just as hard to please; he is always telling us that the game is up, that no good work can possibly be done any more. After ten years of editing *Horizon,* he wound it up with an editorial which declared, "It is closing time in the gardens of the West and from now on an artist will be judged only by the resonance of his solitude or the quality of his despair." The difference is that one says it with a tear, the other with a frown; Mr. Connolly genuinely regrets that the game is up and only wishes that the writers of his own time *could* rise to the true heights; whereas Dr. Leavis too often gives the impression of a man refusing, with tightened lips and cold eyes, to be taken in by a clumsy confidence trick; he seems to think that writers publish bad books simply to annoy *him*.

John Wain. *Essays on Literature and Ideas*
(Macmillan, 1963), p. 161

The impulses from Eliot and Richards were most effectively combined in England, at least, in the work of Frank Raymond Leavis and his disciples grouped around the magazine *Scrutiny*. Leavis is a man of strong convictions and harsh polemical manners. He has in recent years sharply underlined his disagreements with the later development of Eliot and Richards. But his starting point is there: in Eliot's taste and Richards's technique of analysis. He differs from them mainly by a strong Arnoldian concern for a moralistic humanism. Leavis practices close reading, a training of sensibility, which has little use for literary theory or history. But "sensibility" with Leavis means also a sense of tradition, a concern for local culture, the organic community of the old English countryside. He has criticized the commercialization of English literary life and has defended the need of a social code and order, "maturity," "sanity," and "discipline." But these terms are purely secular and include the ideals of D. H. Lawrence. Leavis's concern with the text is often deceptive: he quickly leaves the verbal surface in order to define the peculiar emotions which an author conveys. He becomes a social and moral critic who, however, insists on the continuity of language and ethics, on the morality of form.

René Wellek. *Concepts of Criticism*
(New Haven and London, Yale Univ. Pr., 1963), p. 358

The publication of the entire run of *Scrutiny* is a triumph of an extraordinary kind for those who produced the magazine; and especially for its chief editor and most famous contributor, Dr. Leavis. The occasion can be discussed in so many ways, and from so many viewpoints, that I should say at once that my own impulse is to use it to express the feeling of curiously personal gratitude which I have, and I know others have, to Dr. Leavis and his magazine. . . .

It was because of its concern to keep the past in vital relationship with the present that *Scrutiny* insisted it was necessary to have and to use in one's reading a map which would guide one through the immensities of available print; which would enable one to distinguish the few promontories from the many swamps. This may be said to be the central task which the magazine set itself; and in carrying it out it was ready—militantly ready—to overturn any authority which had been mistakenly institutionalized. I have used the word "respectable" previously: perhaps this is the place to mention that one of the great attractions of *Scrutiny* was that it was *not* respectable: it was embattled, fiercely "minority" in its views, quick to express scorn and derision. *Scrutiny,* in fact, was far from academic, and the artists it exalted were, as often as not, rebels, those who had broken the conventional codes of behaviour of the societies of their day—George Eliot and D. H. Lawrence, to name only two. Yet it wasn't just for the sake of rebellion that they were honoured; it was because in their lives and work they had obeyed and made manifest, in Dr. Leavis's words, "the precise and urgent command from within."

One could never doubt that that was the command he himself obeyed. It was he, I admit, who actually caught, held and continued to hold my attention, his voice was almost the only one I really listened to. . . . For a long time I thought of it as little more than his own platform. This I now feel to have been a misunderstanding on my own part: a misunderstanding even of the role the rest of the magazine played in the development of Dr. Leavis's own thought. It is undeniable that his own work gave the magazine its revolutionary force, and the range of his own contributions to it is incomparable—when people say that he is a "narrow" critic I am puzzled to know what they imagine a "broad" one would look like. But several other outstanding critical talents worked on it, as everybody is today ready to acknowledge, and the earlier issues, in particular, have a diversity and liveliness, as well as a seriousness of purpose, that no current critical journal can begin to match.

Dan Jacobson. NS. Oct. 25, 1963, p. 567

Dr. Leavis is not as original a critic as James Smith—or as Eliot, Empson, Wilson Knight or Donald Davie—but he has something of Dr. Johnson's genius for massing all the relevant critical considerations on a particular topic into a comprehensive judgement. At its best his criticism is "just." The reader has the feeling that justice has been done because the various qualities and defects, aspects and limitations, have not just been weighted against each but have been synthesized into a conclusion from which little or nothing has been excluded. The appeal is to common sense in the interest of common justice. And this fair-mindedness was the source of his great appeal to many of the younger intellectuals in the 1930s. . . .

F. W. Bateson. EC. Jan., 1964, p. 19

There seem to be two ways of regarding the <i>Scrutiny</i> movement. The first, which often has about it a wistful obituary air, sees Leavis as the great innovator of an established critical methodology, and the monuments most likely to be cited are <i>Revaluation</i> and <i>The Great Tradition;</i> occasionally if the tribute-bearer thinks he can walk warily enough, Lawrence will be mentioned, but rarely anything else and almost never <i>The Common Pursuit</i>. According to this view Leavis is a valuable if somewhat unvital and superannuated figure. To its counterpart he is the noisy tenant of modern criticism and <i>Scrutiny</i> is his disorderly house. . . . And unattractive, lacking in charm, has the world of Leavis and <i>Scrutiny</i> remained to most "common readers" without professional commitments or loyalties to a university milieu. . . .

It may be taken that the Universities (English, Commonwealth, Transatlantic in likely order of support) comprise the sector where <i>Scrutiny</i> is best known, esteemed, relied on, and that outside academe, repute and awareness vary between wet denigration and dry acceptance of what is widely regarded as a dead fact, a deed over. A movement with its strongholds of influence in universities was, of course, exactly what the founders of <i>Scrutiny</i> in 1932 hoped they were establishing.

Scrutiny, its readers were told at the outset, was concerned with fundamentals but not with their needless definition, their arid semantic anatomising. Examples of the stand are legion: "These 'standards of criticism' are assumed; nothing more is said about them. Nothing more needed to be said"; the maxim, that silver-thread of Leavis's critical manner. "This is so, it it not?"; the exchange with René Wellek; *How Many Children Had Lady Macbeth?* The ruthless pragmatism hallmarks the movement, and as a corrective to a half-century of "the Academic Mind" in its hydra forms, and as providing a fighting direction for that process of reassessment that used to be called modern criticism (early Eliot, Murry, Richards, Graves-Riding, etc.), is perhaps *Scrutiny's* most startling resisted success. But one need not be a trainee in what Q. D. Leavis pregnantly called "The Discipline of Letters" to feel that away from the great circle of unchallengeably superb critical exercises (e.g. Leavis on Keats, Pope and George Eliot, many of Mrs. Leavis's novel reviews, . . . nearly all of James Smith—the list has to stop, but to stop is unfair), the larger presuppositions on which the movement based its stance were in many ways ill-assimilated, complacently maintained, not often made subject to genuinely sceptical probing from within or without.

Kenneth Trodd. *EC*. Jan., 1964, pp. 21, 23–24, 30–31

LEE, LAURIE (1914–   )

Laurie Lee is an impressionist poet. His poems have no structure, no technique beyond the immediate requirements of producing a brilliant impression. He evidently concentrates his mind on some vivid sensation and then produces words with the aim of fixing this sensation. A too-marked metre, the necessity of searching for a rhyme, careful punctuation, would distract him from his aim, which is to create the sensation of an object by means of words, not to charm us with the delights of form and a sense of words. His poetry is also almost untouched by thought. . . .

The only powerful influence on Mr. Lee seems to be Lorca; a very bad influence on English poets . . . for English poets are attracted by what seems bizarre and unconnected in Lorca's dazzling imagery, and often they fail to see the hidden links of the Spanish tradition in his poetry. . . . Nevertheless, in many of . . . [his] poems, Laurie Lee succeeds in doing what he sets out to do; producing, that is to say, a sharp, sunlit impression.

Stephen Spender. *Hor*. Oct., 1944, p. 285

Poe refused to publish somebody's poems on the ground that the disparity between the good lines and the bad was so incredible that the good must have been stolen. By that criterion a fair amount of his own poetry would have been suspect. If Mr. Lee is certainly not open to the charge, nevertheless the mixture of the excellent and of the perfectly terrible in his verse is equally baffling; so thoroughly are they mingled that there is scarcely a poem in the book [*The Sun My Monument*] which can be dismissed altogether and scarcely one which succeeds as a whole or represents any kind of sustained achievement.

Both virtues and faults have their source in his employment of images. In this connection, readers should at least applaud his willingness to gamble for an idiom which is original, rich and strange, even at the risk of falling over into the absurd. . . . It is unfortunate, however, that he seems as yet unable to perform a simple labor of excision on lines and whole stanzas and so raise to a fairly impressive standard the poems they now ruin.

Fleming MacLeish. NYT. Dec. 21, 1947, p. 8

No one is more abundantly qualified than Laurie Lee to write about Spain, for his is the language of passions, hot suns and the thrilling high-frequency life of the senses. This tense and careful but never laborious chronicle of a winter's travel in Andalusia [*A Rose for Winter*], is constructed, sentence by sentence, as beautifully as music; and his prose has the effect of making the ear ever more sensitive to its melody and various rhythm. Every phrase is hand-picked for its bloom and freshness, and only once or twice does Mr. Lee's flair for voluptuous precision in his choice of words lead him to overreach his meaning. . . .

I am concentrating on the fineness, the pleasure and originality, with which Mr. Lee writes English because that is the first joy of his book. But apart from that, he observes the play of Spanish character with a sly shrewd humour which, though it is always concerned with the particular, implicitly raises questions of a general kind, involving universal topics and truths of which, as a subtle poet, he disdains to speak directly. In some curious way his thought is inextricably woven with the way he sees and smells and hears and touches. Very rarely does he make a generalization that might be debatable; often does he imply a truth that is unquestionable.

David Hughes. TT. June 11, 1955, pp. 722–23

Mr. Laurie Lee is a poet who sees and feels with instant and great intensity. He transmutes this intensity of physical sensation into poetry by making a disciplined intellectual effort to fix it as accurately as possible in words. In this mixture of deep sensuousness with forceful and elaborate use of image and metaphor he recalls certain sevententh-century poets. There is nothing slack or vague in his poetry; the more startling or fanciful the vision, the more firm and exact the words in which it is expresed. At his best he involves the reader with him completely in the intensity of the captured moment.

He is sensitive, in a highly original manner, to the resemblances in appearance or atmosphere between things at first sight totally unconnected. By imposing these unfamiliar or unexpected pictures on us, he makes the commonplace assume a new, enchanted life.

C. V. Wedgwood. *L.* June, 1955, p. 92

Mr. Lee's book [*Poems*], which was awarded the William Foyle poetry prize in England, contains only fifteen poems, none more than a page in length. . . . Mr. Lee's images are . . . vivid . . . but by no means violent or exotic. The beat is regular, firm, and controlled; the stanza forms show considerable variety in their patterns and rhyming. These are contemplative poems, a watching, not entirely without a saving trace of irony, the inner and outer day.

Rolfe Humphries. *NYHT.* July 28, 1957, p. 9

So many of Mr. Lee's reminiscences [*Cider with Rosie*] are of charm and interest that one feels he should have had more trust in their power to speak for themselves; instead, again and again, they are over-decorated and over-elaborated. One cannot help feeling, indeed, that Mr. Lee's book is a memorial of a kind different from the one he intended it to be: the fact that Mr. Lee, who grew up in a village as remote and isolated as the one he describes, and was educated in the village school, should yet write a prose so mannered, willed, and metropolitan—this fact is in itself a sign of how dead is the old order he has tried to evoke.

Dan Jacobson. *Spec.* Nov. 13, 1959, p. 678

LEE, VERNON (1856–1935)

I have always disliked—quite of course *pour le beau motif*—this author's writings. I have got out of their way whenever I could; they seem to offer me a sterilised atmosphere like that to be found in the work called *John Inglesant* or in the writings of the late Walter Pater. There is nothing that so much irritates and frightens me. This of course is no condemnation. . . . It simply means that this type of literature does not ring my poor old bell; or rather, that it evokes from that instrument of communication overtones that make my poor old head ache.

But I can perfectly well see the adroitness of the workmanship. I can also perfectly well see the culture of mind, the erudition of the historic still-life; I can perfectly realize that hours and hours must have been spent in meditation before such a novel as *Louis Norbert* could have been produced. To read it is like watching a player of another school playing a game that I do not like. I can admire the deft turn of wrist and the precise evolutions, but they seem to me—a hostile spectator— to be things that evoke no real warmth and an enthusiasm purely intellectual. . . . And it is all admirably done and almost too admirably engineered. There is so much restraint that it would appear as if Vernon Lee were incapable of passion. There are pictures here and there throughout the book—the picture of the English manor-house, the picture of the birth and smuggling away of the monarch's son; the picture of the Italian household, with the old marchese slumbering on a sofa, the young people poring over documents, the guests reading novels and illustrated papers. Yes, at precisely the right moment Vernon Lee turns on reflections; at precisely the right moment a description of a document, a remark about Mr. Cunninghame Graham, about Mr. Henry James, or about the *Roi Soleil*.

Ford Madox Hueffer. OutL. June 13, 1914, pp. 815–16

Dr. Vernon Lee has . . . produced some travel sketches [*The Golden Keys*]. They are very slight. . . . On the other hand it must be recorded that Dr. Lee has a tenderness uniquely her own, that her style is fluent and lucid as spring water, and that her culture, though a later age will find it *dates,* is amusingly presented. Dr. Lee talks pacifism, but she is really a reactionary. The Italy she loves is a picturesque ruin, and the Germany a medieval fairy tale. Her resentments are directed less against war, the estranger of nations, than against facts, those destroyers of dreams. It is no secret that she is no longer a young woman, but every reader of *The Golden Keys* will congratulate himself that its author survives to represent a calmer and—be it whispered—more inquisitive age than his own.

Milton Waldman. LM. Aug., 1925, p. 437

Most adults these days cannot read Poe; our world seems to us full of evil men and good and evil ideas, and we do not have the moral leisure to be titillated by those vague emotional outrages, all effects, all wrath, remorse and terror, and never a meaning. Poor Poe, ever the victim of responsibility (his own, of course) could not portray goodness and knew nothing about evil except the name of it. But the Englishwoman who called herself Vernon Lee knew a great deal about it. Beauty without goodness (which had fascinated Browning, upset Ruskin and spoiled Pater) made her both see and think. Brilliantly specific and frighteningly controlled are these tales [*The Snake Lady*] of ghosts and appetites, obsessions and revenge.

It is hard to imagine them coming from the straight little gray woman, the pro-German propagandist, with her powerful, orderly, suspicious intelligence, whom Frank Swinnerton met in 1916. It is hard to think of them being written by the scholarly girl who at fifteen began gathering material for a big historical treatise and published it at twenty-five. The author of a technical work on psychological esthetics; the metaphysician; the popular travel-book writer, the French-born, Italian-reared daughter of an eccentric British gentlewoman—each is an improbable author for these tales.

Yet all of them together were "Vernon Lee" who was really Violet Paget and who died at 79, totally forgotten in 1935. And all of them together produced these tales, which are the products, but not the by-products, of her studies of her esthetic sense acting on history. No other literary revival so interesting as this is likely to happen soon.

Donald Barr. NYT. March 21, 1954, p. 24

Violet Paget chose the pseudonym "Vernon Lee" because she believed that the public would scorn serious writing from a woman. Such reticence seemed uncharacteristic of a woman who never indicated the slightest hesitancy in pronouncing categorical judgments, who lectured H. G. Wells on his sexual irregularities, and who alienated good friends like Henry James by making them satirical butts in her novels. . . .

In her severe masculine garb, her habit of referring to men by their surnames, and her argumentative manner, no one better exemplified the "New Woman." Most of her life was spent in Italy, a situation which provided her with a defiantly independent attitude in her frequent forays on the English literary scene. Her cosmopolitanism was also responsible for her outspoken pacifism during the first world war.

Phyllis Grosskurth. London Daily Telegraph
July 23, 1964, p. 18

Ariadne in Mantua was perhaps the most widely known of Vernon Lee's works, with the exception of the *Genius Loci* essays. It went into three English editions; in America T. B. Mosher first published it in *The Bibelot* in January and February 1906, then in book form in the same year, and a second edition in 1912. Further, it was translated into the most important European languages. It does not appear that Vernon Lee wrote *Ariadne* for the stage. In April 1903, Edith Wharton, who had been asked her opinion of it, pointed out its dramatic defects. ". . . Certainly the idea is dramatic; but even for a play read in the closet it seems to me to lack movement and clash of emotions. . . . The whole romance lives in my memory like a more delicate, a paler, Pinturicchio. . . ." Sarah Orne Jewett was another of its warmest American admirers. In England it found favour especially in literary circles. Edmund Gosse thought it a "jewel"; Maurice Baring, Magdalen Ponsonby and Ethel Smyth (to whom it was dedicated, with a request for music) too, were full of its praises, and sought to have it produced on the stage. . . . Vernon Lee . . .[wrote] in a friendly letter to Mrs. Granville Barker: "I have never believed much in the possibility of performing *Ariadne* (I called it on the title-page not a play but a *romance in five acts*); and knowing that I would never consent to alter a word of it, I have never attempted to get it performed: it was intended for reading, not for the stage." However, it was later performed in England, and at a time when Vernon Lee was out of favour with the public, by reason of her pacifist views. In May 1916, the Countess Lytton produced *Ariadne* at the Gaiety Theatre, with Viola Tree as Diego-Magdalen. . . .

It was with her *Genius Loci* type of travel essay that Vernon Lee reached her widest public—in fact, later she rather resented that the public should have preferred what she considered was her minor work to her more serious contributions to aesthetics and sociology. These little essays on travel and places appeared, for the most part, weekly in the *Westminster Gazette*. In all, she published seven volumes of such notes, beginning with *Limbo* (1897). . . . Besides these, she published two further volumes of essays during this period: *Hortus Vitae* (1904) and *Laurus Nobilis* (1909). . . . these little personal essays on various subjects are in the tradition of Hazlitt and Charles Lamb. They are addressed to cultivated, travelled people with time on their hands: nothing separates us from this period so much as the realization that few of us today have the type of cultivated, discriminating taste which would allow us fully to catch their particular savour. . . .

She became in time a tireless observer, with a practised "eye" for texture, line movement, and with the subtlest discrimination of fleeting shades and tones, whether of landscape, water or buildings. And as an adjunct to this visual sensibility went her profound knowledge of European art, literature and history.

Maurice Baring has written how incomparably rich an experience it was to stroll with Vernon Lee through the streets of Rome or in the Italian countryside. . . .

The travel sketches are mostly of scenes in Italy, Switzerland, Germany and France—of a world, that is, which has almost completely passed away. For the true traveller, the "sentimental" one, in the old sense, these essays call up a poignant nostalgia; but, for the reason that there are few such travellers today, the essays are not likely now to be widely

read. Two wars have ravaged much of the countries and rendered callous
our spirit.

Peter Gunn. *Vernon Lee* (Oxford Univ.
Pr., 1964), pp. 179–83

LEHMANN, JOHN (1907–   )

These poems and short pieces [*The Noise of History*] follow "fairly
exactly," the author tells us, the order in which they were written, and
so trace "the course of a gradually developing point of view." The prose,
much of which was written in Berlin and Vienna, begins in 1933 at the
time of the Nazi rise to power, and ends shortly after the suppression of
the February insurrection in Vienna. . . .

As an example of literary craft the volume is unexciting. In the poems
Mr. Lehmann's thoughts and emotions are referred to rather than actively present in the texture and structure of his writing. . . . This looseness of apprehension is most noticeable where it is most important that
the reader's sympathy should be gained. . . .

Mr. Lehmann's prose pieces, closer to actual scenes and events, are
more successful than his poems. Suffering and fear are genuine pre-
sences in these sketches of oppressed and stricken cities.

LL. Oct., 1934, pp. 121–22

Mr. Lehmann . . . who could never remain passive where action seemed
required, feeling as time went on ever more drawn "towards the fire,"
acted in Vienna [in the 1930's] as a collecting and distributing centre
for information about underground activities. For him the miseries of
the world were miseries, and would not let him rest. So from there he
undertook, and brought into triumphant being, *New Writing,* which was
to give scope to the new ideas and the new literary forms bursting
through the crust of the old.

That is the really exciting part of the book [*The Whispering Gallery*],
the most intimately personal; for though one of Mr. Lehmann's objects
in writing his autobiography was to analyse and so understand himself,
being no Rousseau-like exhibitionist, he is reticent. All we are aware of,
and that somewhat objectively, is his continual dilemma: "Was I to go
to the left, to the poet's life, or to the right, to an editor's and publisher's
life?" The childhood part is a little lengthy and might have been confined to the particular ethos of the Lehmann home. . . . If we have
experienced that sort of life, much will be commonplace. . . . The accounts of Eton and Cambridge are more interesting if only because they

are more individual; but Mr. Lehmann really gets into his stride, holds us to the page, when he is taken into the Hogarth Press. There opens that part of the book which will gratify, as he suggests, "studious explorers of the byways of literary history."

Bonamy Dobrée. L. March, 1956, pp. 85–86

The first volume of Mr. John Lehmann's autobiography, *The Whispering Gallery,* brought his elaborately woven tapestry of recollection and evocative descriptive writing down to the outbreak of war: the second* ends with the peace of 1945. It must have been a much harder book to write, owing to the stern abnegation of Mr. Lehmann's approach to himself. We are shown only one aspect of him—that implied by a photograph entitled "The Editor at work in Carrington House." Mr. Lehmann, well dressed and carefully lit, is looking down on a crowded desk. A contemporary picture hangs on the wall behind him. He is reading, no doubt, a story by Mr. Jiri Mucha or a letter from some promising colleague in New Zealand. The war outside has been reduced to a tiresome clatter, while snipers from the offices of *Horizon* are given a more dangerous bill than any unliterary enemy dashing uselessly about in desert or steppe.

What his readers might wish is a far less reticent attitude. Wars—and this book is entirely set within the framework of a war—have an enlarging effect on personality. They make loves more intense and anguished, they underscore all experience with colours crude and thick, they tumble their victims into improbable situations and leave them recurrently in the plight of a drowning man the second time under. Mr. Lehmann can have been no exception to this, but he has chosen to move quietly between *New Writing* and the Hogarth Press as though that were the limit of his trajectory through the most vivid years of modern history.

TLS. Feb. 12, 1960, p. 91

Mr. Lehmann, in his second autobiographical volume, takes up *his* publishing story in 1939-40. Is it criticism to say that in *I Am My Brother* he does inadequate justice to himself as publisher, or to be precise, as editor? He had been associated with Leonard and Virginia Woolf in the Hogarth Press. His lasting achievement (as older readers know and younger ones should) was that through his firm, and then through *Penguin New Writing,* he worked throughout the war to maintain a forum for creative literature, and especially for the younger poets and prose writers of England and Europe. In this, as retrospect makes

---

* *I Am My Brother.*

all the clearer, Mr. Lehmann succeeded admirably. In this age of barren affluence it seems strange to think that, without journalistic concession, *Penguin New Writing* in wartime sold 80,000 copies a month and found its way to the lower-deck and other-ranks mass. . . .

. . . if *I Am My Brother* is taken as an essay in self-portraiture, the impression is that Mr. Lehmann is writing not enough as autobiographer and too much as publisher: he is too reticent, too polite, and the reader can therefore only feel that he is a more interesting person than he has made out. For instance, Mr. Lehmann started out in 1939 with strong Left-wing political views which he clearly no longer held in the same form in 1945; but we are not told nearly enough about this. He recalls how he moved with detachment between literary and high social circles, but permits himself only an occasional irony about the latter. Above all, Mr. Lehmann was friend and critic to a generation of contemporary writers: Auden, Spender, Connolly, Green, Isherwood, Orwell, Pritchett —Mr. Lehmann must have known their shortcomings as well as talents and one waits for his considered criticism and evaluation, but it never comes. One hopes that in his next volume he will not hold back so much.

T. R. Fyvel. *Enc.* July, 1960, p. 83

Haunted by change, by episodes and effects of war, he is by nature and background a traditionalist, instinctively a lover of the past, dutifully aware that the poet must follow the world's changes, though the revolutionary ardour of romantic poetry and modern communism in no way touches him. Mr. Lehmann does not pretend to acceptance, nor to faith and hope. [*Collected Poems*]

TLS. July 26, 1963, p. 556

John Lehmann's *Collected Poems* . . . show very little change over the years. The superficial attitudes have altered: he began languorous and rather ornamental, then went into mildly indignant social protest and now writes in a nostalgic man-of-the-world style, mostly about the Mediterranean. The verse is held together by an insistent mellifluousness, though this sounds less the result of skill than of half-heartedness. . . .

Lehmann's main weapons are charm and a pleasant ear, qualities I personally don't much go for in poetry. Considering his great editorial flair for the modern, and sympathy with it, it is odd that he himself should write so loosely and conventionally.

A. Alvarez. *Obs.* July 14, 1963, p. 25

LEHMANN, ROSAMOND (1903–   )

It is not surprising that *Dusty Answer* should be widely read and discussed. The novel is thought by the elderly to throw light on the young
generation; its merits appeared to me to lie not in being a picture of a
particular generation, but in giving a vivid account of youthful emotions.
The story has fervour; the author is sincerely interested in all she narrates
and describes, and without these elementary questions (it is extraordinary
how rare they are in fiction) no love story can hold the attention of a
reader worth having. . . .

   The author of *Dusty Answer* struck me as remembering passion well
and understanding it; and since the story she has to tell is, as the title
suggests, one of disillusionment, it is not unnatural that she should have
been driven to understand the nature of emotions which produced such
exaltation and withering pain. . . .

   The new frankness between the sexes does not prevent the old muddles,
for each continues to interpret the feelings of the other to meet their
own wishes. *Dusty Answer* is far above the average novel, but its merits
are not those which make one confident that the author will write a
better one.

Affable Hawk [Desmond MacCarthy]. NS. Aug. 6, 1927, p. 539

Miss Lehmann's widely heralded opus [*Dusty Answer*], dealing with
a group of young people in England, does not possess even . . . solidity.
Her style and outlook suffer from the same melancholy anemia which
is the keynote of her character. She is so sadly aware that her young
people are decadent and rotted at the core. Here we have a group of
young men and women in whom the subconscious acceptance of a failing
national destiny is so strong as to make them wearily impervious to all
experiences save one—romantic love. . . . They . . . are a refined end-
product, . . . the decayed remnant of an agricultural aristocracy whose
sentimental ethos is becoming more and more irrelevant to a mechanized
universe.

Clifton P. Fadiman. Nation. Nov. 23, 1927, p. 576

Miss Rosamond Lehmann's *Invitation to the Waltz* . . . is concerned with
Olivia's first dance, the preparations for it, and its aftermath. Miss Lehmann ruthlessly analyses the thoughts and reactions of the introspective
Olivia, but does not convince the reader either that this was worth doing
or that there was any real compulsion behind the doing of it; the result
is a mildly amusing but disappointing book.

Brian Roberts. LL. Dec., 1932, p. 480

The Ballad and the Source is a long book, written mainly in dialogue, full of subtle and often beautiful detail. Miss Lehmann's virtuosity is impressive; one is compelled to admire her fluency and her technical skill: and, apart from the interest of the actual narrative, this novel throws an intriguing sidelight on an odd aspect of the English character.

Mrs. Jardine, the heroine of the book, defines the word "convention" as another name for the habits of society. . . . Her admirers thrill in their sure and sanctified haven, vicariously enjoying her escapades. Individualism, even of the imitation variety, is to the tradition-worshipping Englishman the modern sin at which he peeps from afar in horrified fascination.

Miss Lehmann brings all this out very clearly in the composite picture of her heroine. But Mrs. Jardine is a sensation-seeker more than an individual; she is experimenting with life instead of living it fully: her experiences, being psychologically unexplained, appear uncoordinated, spasmodic, and lacking in natural rhythm. Some essential element has been omitted, without which the personality picture cannot be brought to life. The picture obstinately stays a picture right to the end. And because Mrs. Jardine never quite becomes a real person, her disjointed history is also without real emotional significance. In spite of the technical excellence of its construction, *The Ballad and the Source* fails, ultimately, to stimulate and engage the deeper attention.

Anna Kavan. *Hor.* Feb., 1945, p. 145

Some people besides writing prose fiction, or poetry, or narrative, or biography, also write magic. This has nothing to do with what they are writing about, neither their characters nor, in a larger sense, their theme. It is rather an ability to communicate emotion, to move the reader into a created world that is experienced with an immediacy, a totality of apprehension, similar to that with which one lives in one's own world. Rosamond Lehmann's books, particularly this new one [*The Echoing Grove*]—happen as completely and mysteriously as living happens. Twenty-five years ago *Dusty Answer,* her first novel, was felt by a whole generation of young people in England and America as a personal experience, and this has been true to some extent of all her books. What happens is less important than the vibration of emotion which accompanies it and is more truly the happening than the event itself,

Elizabeth Janeway. *NYT.* May 10, 1953, p. 1

Miss Lehmann's new novel [*The Echoing Grove*], her first since 1945, again proves what an exciting writer she is, not only because of what she writes and how, but on a third count as well: she has that infrequent and curious capacity which enables a writer to communicate to us at least a partial perception of what the creative act is. We finish her book with a sense of having been taken to the center of things. . . .

The people in Miss Lehmann's world are governed not by social dicta but by the laws of emotional supply and demand. For her the external milieu matters very little. The role that the war plays in *The Echoing Grove* is significant—it is simply one of the conditions of life, like the lack of money or the loss of health. It is not this, but the given moment of any given day, the moment when two people may be together or must be apart, that is momentous.

Adrienne Foulke. Com. May 22, 1953, pp. 183–84

LESLIE, SHANE (1885–   )

A poet who is not still a youngster and yet can only show the public a bare thirty pages, after many years, as his complete production in verse, might not seem worthy of serious attention, if it were not for the fine imaginative and epigrammatic qualities of that small output. Shane Leslie's chief virtue is that very restraint that gives him an advantage over many living poets. His religious poems have such a primitive freshness as seldom animates the religious poetry of civilization. An art so slim is better quoted than discussed.

Harold Monro. Some Contemporary Poets
(Leonard Parsons, 1920), p. 191

It is not . . . the merits, but the defects of *The Skull of Swift* which makes it significant as an example of modern biography. Ever since Mr. Lytton Strachey published *Eminent Victorians,* . . . biographers have resolved to arrest our attention by their opening sentence and to stuff every subsequent page with picturesque details. . . .

The manner of Macaulay was soon discredited by imitators who had no learning to support it; Mr. Lytton Strachey, too, has not been blessed in his literary descendants, the majority of whom ape his methods without understanding his discretion. . . . Now Mr. Shane Leslie, who attempts this form, has a strong imagination but lacks entirely literary tact. He is essentially a sensational writer and more careless than most of his kind. Undoubtedly he can write a good sentence, but he has no notion when he has written a preposterous one. . . . Mr. Leslie never stops to notice the implications of what he writes. He takes pot-shots at his ideas (I do not say he never hits the mark; he does so occasionally), and he nearly always prefers the heaviest missiles. . . . The narrative itself is violently emphatic without being clear. The reader sometimes does not know for pages together whether Swift is in Ireland or in England, only that he, the reader, is supposed to be in Swift's head.

A writer so careless in combining words would hardly be more scrupulous in arbitrarily combining facts. Mr. Leslie suggests, for instance, that Dryden's crushing comment on Swift's early poems . . . was spoken in The Rose coffee house . . . but there is no evidence that such a scene ever took place. This is typical of modern picturesque biographers—it *might* have happened, that is enough. Not all, of course, are quite as careless as Mr. Leslie, who, to make a phrase, will describe Swift's eyes as "glaring like sunken loadstones from their occiput," though a glance at Swift's portrait shows that they were unusually prominent; but in the matter of constructing scenes out of unrelated facts there is not much to choose between Mr. Leslie and many others.

Desmond MacCarthy. *LL.* July, 1928, pp. 137–39

For the ordinary reader this memoir [*Memoir of J. C. Bodley*] will be something of a disappointment. Mr. Shane Leslie has played a self-effacing part, editing diaries and fragments instead of summarising them in his own words, and this is a pity, for when he does intervene his comments are masterly. J. E. C. Bodley, author of the famous book on France, was not only a friend of many distinguished men, he was also that portentously rare creature, an Englishman who really understood and loved the French. As such, he would have been a good subject for analytical biography; whereas many of the diaries and letters reproduced here tell us nothing about Bodley himself, and are hardly better than gossip.

Adel. Feb., 1931, p. 446

After his book on George IV in 1926 and his *Dublin Review* article of October, 1925, on the Fitzherbert papers, it was almost inevitable that Mr. Shane Leslie would, in time, produce the standard Catholic life of Mrs. Fitzherbert [*Mrs. Fitzherbert*]. He has now done so, and, though epigrams are perhaps less in evidence, the writing is pleasant and clear, and the wealth of documentation is used with discretion. That his subject is not without its interest today is shown by the reappearance in Penguin format of Mr. Wilkins's two stout volumes of 1905, but where Wilkins was content, or perhaps compelled by circumstances, to say that the documents for this or that must be at Chatsworth or at Coutts' Bank or in Rome, Mr. Leslie has, in most cases, been able to produce the document or as much of it as is relevant, and he implies that a second volume is to follow which will presumably contain the full *dossier*.

J. H. C. *Month.* March, 1940, pp. 228–29

"Let the friends of Mrs. Fitzherbert observe strict silence," thundered *The Times* on the day before her funeral, April 5, 1837, and the injunction has met with a large measure of obedience for a century. Last year Mr. Shane Leslie broke silence so successfully with his volume on Mrs. Fitzherbert's life that a second volume, containing many of her letters along with other more formal documents, will be welcomed by all who are interested in the Regency scene. It is to be noticed that the character of Mrs. Fitzherbert emerges more clearly, with its blending of kindly good-nature with shrewdness, from these letters than it did from the pages of the Life which had perforce to give much attention to various special problems.

J. H. C. *Month* June, 1940, p 470

LESSING, DORIS (1919–   )

Miss Lessing's ten short stories [*This Was The Old Chief's Country*] are so essentially readable and entertaining that it is hard to realize that they are only her second published book. All of them have a vivid background of South African farm life, but Miss Lessing avoids monotony by focusing attention sometimes on the natives and sometimes on the Dutch and English settlers. She appreciates the dignity of the natives without overestimating their intelligence, and appears to prefer some Englishmen to most Afrikaners. Her descriptive writing is vivid and unforced and she is also very shrewd about social relationships. In the longest and best story, "Old John's Place," she gives a subtle portrait of a thirteen-year-old girl battling with uncertainties of adolescence in a world of well-meaning but not very edifying grown-ups. Miss Lessing, in short, appears to be a versatile and talented writer.

TLS. May 11, 1951, p. 289

Miss Lessing's little book [*Fourteen Poems*] is admirable. In lucid and restrained verses she engraves her compassionate observations and questions upon a tense listening silence that she herself has created. Her main theme is exile and she handles it with poignant objectivity and with an utterly convincing simplicity of manner. . . . She attacks the reader's conscience as well as his sensibility and her work is consistently mature and delicate.

Robin Skelton. *NS*. May 23, 1959, p. 733

Too often Miss Lessing's fiction is dissolved in a long sociological or journalistic insertion, like the accounts of communistic tactics and wrangles in *A Ripple from the Storm* or the long, dull, clinical study of discovering that one is pregnant which takes up about seventy pages of *A Proper Marriage*. Her politics are one-sided, her characters are limited in conception, and her world revolves in a simple pattern. . . .

Doris Lessing's intense feeling of political and social responsibility is carefully worked into specific historical situations. But the positive convictions can become heavy-handed, and the specific situations journalistic, while the strict allegiance to time and place can limit the range of perception about human beings. Miss Lessing's kind of intensity is simultaneously her greatest distinction and her principal defect. She produces an enormously lucid sociological journalism, honest and committed, but in much of her work she lacks a multiple awareness, a sense of comedy, a perception that parts of human experience cannot be categorized or precisely located, a human and intellectual depth. Intense commitment can cut off a whole dimension of human experience.

James Gindin. *Postwar British Fiction* (Berkeley,
Calif., Univ. of California Pr., 1962), pp. 85–86

What on earth are library-goers going to make of Doris Lessing's formidable multi-level novel? Without the author's note (printed on the jacket, but not in the book itself) Mrs. Lessing's purpose will be hard to discern. She says the book is about artist's block: "In describing the reasons for the block, I would also be making the criticisms I wanted to make about our society. I would be describing a disgust and self-division which afflicts people now, and not only artists." The novel is also "about what Marxists call alienation" and "an attempt to break a form; to break certain forms of consciousness and go beyond them." Quite a lot for one novel, in fact, even if it is 568 pages long.

A woman writer called Anna Wulf (*née* Freeman—and if that puts you in mind of the heroine of a play called *Play with a Tiger* I'd say you were right the first time) keeps four notebooks: a black one, which is an autobiographical novel about Anna's Northern Rhodesian Communist friends during the war; a red one, dealing with her experiences with the British Communist Party during the 1950s; her writer's journal (yellow) and her diary (blue). These are led off and interrupted by a story called "Free Women" about Anna and her friend Molly and Molly's son Tommy, who blinds himself trying to commit suicide. Near the end of the book comes "The Golden Notebook," about thirty pages describing a desperate affair between Anna and an American, and if *that* reminds you of a play called . . .

When a novelist writes a novel about a novelist writing what we know the real novelist has written, we have a right, I think, to object. Not having read all of Mrs. Lessing's work, I don't know how much of *The Golden Notebook* is self-parody, but I know some of it is. The self-division never for a moment disguises the self: each part of the book repeats the other parts without really adding to them. Using different kinds of type does not disguise this fact. The novel is a ponderous bore. Yet it shouldn't be: Mrs. Lessing has attempted something big and important, a portrait in depth of the loneliness of the "free" woman (liable to have that "free" misunderstood, needless to say) who has the courage to reject the bourgeois hypocrisies only to have her own self-deceptions and failures rejected by her child.

Julian Mitchell. Spec. April 20, 1962, p. 518

It is a particular distinction of *The Golden Notebook,* a long and ambitious novel by the gifted English writer Doris Lessing, that while dealing with some of the materials favored by novelists of sensibility, it escapes their constrictions of tone and outlook. Both Miss Lessing and her characters are deeply caught up with the cult of "personal relations," yet she is able to keep some critical distance from her material and to look upon it as merely the latest turn in the confusion of modern history. She yields her sympathies to those of her characters who fall back upon "personal relations" in order to get through their days, but she tries not to settle for the limitations of experience they must accept. She understands that the idea of "personal relations" has been shaped by the catastrophes of our time and, in the form we know it, is not to be taken as an absolute or uncontaminated value.

It is a further distinction of Miss Lessing's novel that its action is carried mainly by that rarity in modern fiction: a heroine, Anna Wulf, who is a mature intellectual woman. A writer with a sophisticated mind, sharp tongue and an abundance of emotional troubles, Anna Wulf is sufficiently representative of a certain kind of modern woman to persuade us that her troubles have a relevance beyond their immediate setting; she is also an intelligence keen enough to support the public combativeness and personal introspectiveness that Miss Lessing has given her. At the very least, Anna Wulf is someone who has measured the price for being what she chooses to be—"a free woman," she would say with pride and irony—and who is prepared, no matter how much she groans, to pay it.

Miss Lessing has a voice and a mind of her own. She is radically different from other women writers who have dealt with the problems of their sex, first in that she grasps the connection between Anna Wulf's neuroses and the public disorders of the day, and second in that she has no use either for the quaverings of the feminist writers or the aggressions of those female novelists whose every sentence leads a charge in the war of the sexes. The feminine element in *The Golden Notebook* does not become a self-contained universe of being, as in some of Virginia

Woolf's novels, nor is the narrative voice established through the minute gradations of the writer's sensibility, as in some of Elizabeth Bowen's. And Miss Lessing is far too serious for those displays of virtuoso bitchiness which are the blood and joy of certain American lady writers.

Irving Howe. *NR*. Dec. 15, 1962, p. 17

LEVERTOV, DENISE (1923–   )

In Denise Levertov we are in a less conventional mode, one more acceptable and pleasing to readers of modern poetry. She cannot think in rhyme but feels passionate, immediate realities, which are communicated in deft, loose forms.

Her poems [*Overland to the Islands*] have a feminine closeness to nature. She knows what she knows, immediately and deeply, and she tells it with richness, vigor and verve. Also with a certain looseness, a devil-may-care attitude expressing maturity. These are poems not from the top of the head but from the inner reaches of the psyche. Her psyche works when "The sink is full of dishes. Oh well." Events occur throughout the day in "The Dogwood," the irregular stanzas leading cunningly but naturally in "Oh well." The commonplace occasions her art.

Richard Eberhart. *NYT*. June 22, 1958, p. 4

Also emerging [in modern poetry] is an ultimately . . . serious body of nontraditional verse represented by the work of Charles Olson, Denise Levertov, Paul Blackburn, Robert Duncan, and Robert Creeley. Their poetry shows the same intransigence as that of [Allen] Ginsberg and [Lawrence] Ferlinghetti, the same fundamental assumption that the crack-up of values prophesied by an older generation has completed itself. Indeed, these qualities are at the heart of almost all the more impressive new work, traditional or not. . . . In the Olson group, a renewed emphasis on the feel of specific moments of awareness, as if they were totally detachable from the rest of life, is indispensable to the reordering of sensibility.

Denise Levertov . . . [is among] the most "open" and sensuous writers in this group. Miss Levertov may begin a poem ("The Flight") with a quite sophisticated proposition. . . . But that is just the bending of the bow. When the conception here stated in so cramped and paradoxical a way is embodied in an anecdote about a trapped bird, the poem flies as an arrow of insight into an important subjective reality. "The Hands" does the same sort of thing in reverse, beginning almost sensually. . . . The dreaming movement into ecstasy is then translated into abstract esthetic dimensions, a pattern of tensions like that set up by actors rehearsing "on a bare stage." In such pieces Miss Levertov gives us a world of awakened, contemplative self-awareness, in which sympathy with other selves may appear, but completely independent of social expectations. Even the poems which come closest to explicit statement of the toughened intransigence I have mentioned—poems like "The Dogwood" and "Something"—seem to regard the civilization against which they react as a sort of cobweb brushing the face, something alien and strangely cold, almost unreal.

M. L. Rosenthal. *The Modern Poets*
(N.Y., Oxford Univ. Pr., 1960), pp. 268–69

In San Francisco I heard Denise Levertov read her poems. A girl, poignantly lovely. The poem on the page is faithful to her voice. Anyone who assumes that he can read this poetry while running is self-deceived. She thinks with authority; from the buttons and bus-tickets of existence, she contrives significance; her eternities have timeliness. Like Perry she is unconcerned with "newsprint facts"; it is her excellence that she is intensely aware she is a "displaced" person—such perception Buddha had in his palace, the Christ in his fastings. Duncan said of her: "the care of the word . . . a guardian of inner orders". Rexroth wrote that she is superior to her former colleagues of the *Black Mountain Review,* "is securely civilized." Have her roots been fed by W. C. Williams or René Char? We might include the *Jataka Tales* or the *Lyra Graeca!* She uses devices, original or in new and disturbing ways. Warning: if you are sensitive only to traditional meanings, you will certainly miss the ideas that Denise Levertov fires at you. They will go by so fast you will not even know they were there Examine "The Artist": "The artist: disciple, abundant, multiple, restless./The true artist: capable, practicing, skillful;/maintains dialogue with his heart, meets things with his mind." There you have a paradigm presentation with the energy of talent—used in dynamic clusters (as in "The Gypsy's Window" in *Here & Now*), the power of the Cluster—like the primitive concept of God as a cluster of spirits. Each word adds a hot spark of *new* meaning. The reader has received an idea in the round—if he can receive. The "fact" is a physical energy, and in this open form poetry is observed with acuity.

Eve Triem. *Poetry.* Aug., 1960, p. 316

LEVY, BENN W. (1900–   )

This Woman Business would seem to demonstrate anew that a play may sustain itself even on a debate if the author does not take his thesis too seriously. . . . Mr. Levy, throughout his amusing and unpretentious spectacle, laughs at both sides of his own arguments and succeeds in entertaining his audience without giving them a chance of rebuttal. His five mysogynists explore all the familiar corners of the contrast between male and female, each taking his stand on some aspect of masculine superiority, but succumbing to the charm of the heroine in quite usual fashion even before she takes the opportunity of presenting the counter claims of her sex. The success of the play lies in the fact that the author conceives his characters from the very beginning to be funny, and keeps them so, no matter what they say or do. He declines to take his own arguments, or, in fact, any argument seriously and thus keeps his comedy firm on the best of planes, that of laughter.

Milton Waldman. LM. July, 1926, p. 301

Benn W. Levy's *The Devil Passes* (called *The Devil* in London where it fell under the ban of the official censor) has two virtues to commend it: Exceptionally well-written dialogue and an imaginative and provocative theme. Herein the Devil, assuming the pleasing shape of a youthful curate, passes through an English parish and assists in the readjustments of several lives by revealing to a group of dissatisfied humans their sounder virtues in place of stimulating their desire to capitalize their weaknesses. This is doing God's work as this Devil sees it, and makes for interesting discussion and the projection of varied philosophies.

Burns Mantle, ed. The Best Plays of 1931-32
(N.Y., Dodd, Mead, 1932), p. ix

Then there is Benn W. Levy who has spent so much time in America that he is often thought of as a native of our country. He began with an amusing comedy, *This Woman Business* (1925), turned to horror in the dramatization of Sir Hugh Walpole's story *The Man with Red Hair* (1928), and then to extreme sentimentality in *Mrs. Moonlight* (1929), which was a considerable success. *Art and Mrs. Bottle* (1929) was a shade less coy and commanded a respectable following. Certainly his best piece of comic writing has been *Springtime for Henry* (1931) which despite its farcical implications, was sound in its humour. This has proved his most popular play in America and has been widely performed. . . . His adaptation of Gaston Baty's *Madame Bovary* (1937) was only partially successful but revealed a sound dramatic technique.

George Freedley in A History of Modern Drama,
ed. Barrett H. Clarke and George Freedley (N.Y.,
Appleton-Century, 1947), p. 202

We must give Benn Levy credit for trying, in *The Rape of the Belt* . . . to break away from our domestic equations, even though he has not been successful. His plot puts Hercules and Theseus among the Amazons; his theme is that of Aristophanes, that war is a bad thing and that women, if they had the sense, could stop it—though in fact they do not have the sense. Mr. Levy's model here has been Giraudoux, but Ian Hay seems to have taken over as spirit guide.

J. W. Lambert. *Drama*. Spring, 1958, p. 20

LEWIS, ALUN (1915–1944)

At least two-thirds of the stories in Mr. Alun Lewis's book [*The Last Inspection*] are concerned with life in the Army, many of which read like scraps from a journal, and these at present are the best. Most of the work shows a very personal slant, which will I believe wear away as the author gets older and more mature. What is immediately apparent is his fine sensitive perception of life and character. He can write realistically without surrendering a delicacy of style, and his studies of army life are, with all their human brutishness, full of humour and colour. Of these stories, "They Came," is probably the best, where quite unconsciously its author puts his finger on one of the maladies of our time. The other stories are not so good, and in fact hardly matter, since what is best in *The Last Inspection* shows promise for the future.

James Hanley. *LL*. Aug., 1943, pp. 108–9

Most of the poets in uniform have . . . been writing either of what are by comparison the minor discomforts of service—separation, upheaval, routine—or else of the psychological unsettling caused by their development being rudely interrupted, by the loss of friends, by the uncertainty of the future. In consequence, a characteristic of their verse is a sense of loneliness. Alun Lewis may almost be said to have specialized in this aspect. . . .

Robert Herring. *LL*. Aug., 1943, p. 64

Lewis . . . was more conscious of his failures than of his successes, and it is probable that, had he survived, he would have changed his mind about many of his published poems. Since, however, he cannot review his work in retrospect someone should do it for him for his reputation is as yet unsubstantiated.

From the first few poems of *Raider's Dawn* it is clear that Lewis, possibly because of his life in the Army, was often unable to recognize the poetry and reject its by-products. Often the reader is almost overwhelmed by a smoky afflatus. . . .

Lewis had many obvious faults and his work could be pruned with advantage. Often he did not know when to stop and he marred many poems by tacking on trite endings; his rhythm sometimes stumbles or collapses into prose; sometimes he appeals to cheap sentiment. But he had little time to polish his work . . . [there are] sufficient reasons for believing that he had produced, in a short and harassed life, a not inconsiderable amount of good poetry.

Ralph Houston. *Adel.* Nov., 1951, pp. 403, 413

DAY LEWIS, C. (1904–   )

Mr. Day Lewis's unperformable play [*Noah and the Waters*] is good enough reading for a wet afternoon, but will leave his reputation where it was: high for the middlebrow public that can't read Auden and a long way below for those who understand Auden.

Hugh Gordon Porteus. *LL.* Summer, 1936, p. 36

Reviewing his *Collected Poems* 1929-1933, that insulting journal *New Verse* remarked: "If Spender's poems appeal chiefly to girls, it may be said that Day Lewis appeals chiefly to boys." And certainly his work is as full of trains, ships, aeroplanes, cricketers, bullies, spies, and explorers as *The Boy's Own Paper* itself. The trains, however, stand for Socialism and progress, and the mountain-climbers are those who break through glaciers and snowdrifts into the New Country. Lewis keeps his nose pretty close to the ground following Auden, but he has not yet picked up Auden's ability to write prosaically and still be a poet—not that Auden himself is always successful in this by any means. He is, however, a far more sophisticated writer than Lewis, and with him triviality and flatness is evidently a form of *faux naïveté* practised for the fun of the thing, though there are limits to one's enjoyment of this particular kind of fun. But Lewis has adopted the hearty scoutmaster manner in all seriousness. . . . Lewis is only at ease, indeed, he is only a poet—when he forgets the Marxist mountain, that has completely deranged his poetical compass, and allows his natural, and after all quite Georgian, lyrical talent free play.

Philip Henderson. *The Poet and Society*
(Secker and Warburg, 1939), pp. 216–17, 220

The New Hogarth Library selection of Mr. Day Lewis's verse is sensible, adequately representative, and justly gives most space to his personal and purely lyric work; for the near-communist adjurations, with their naïve optimism . . . were always jejune, and sound very faded now. In his own phrase, they were "a green illusion in the sky, born of our desert years."

The new volume, *Poems in Wartime,* adds little to his stature: "autres thèmes"—for the poet has joined the Home Guard—but not "autres cadences." Inland within a hollow vale he stands, and with the same kind of banal shapeless verse about this more orthodoxly patriotic activity, as he did when he bore from within, "working underground like a mole."

W.H.M. *Scy.* March, 1941, p. 377

Beside his social preoccupations, Lewis displays great intellectual abilities, so that two elements can be distinguished in his work: a constantly alert thought, and a desire to face the problems of his time. His poetry is an effort to unite these two tendencies, although he is not always successful in doing so because the first one predominates. . . .

His poetry does not always correspond to what he proclaims in his critical essays. When, for example, he rejects surrealism, he does so on the ground that the doctrine of André Breton is a form of escapism which deprives words of their social connotations, but what estranges him most from surrealism is the absence, in that school, of analytical thought. His reaction against the Dada Manifesto is shown in the following passage: "Every conscious human activity is to some extent a social activity and in consequence must be judged by social criteria." These criteria, however, could not be applied to the activities referred to, which are supposed to be unconscious. It would be more convenient to accuse the surrealists of working against the laws of the human mind, which are apparently not observed by a blind and indifferent society. Lewis's desire to be "contemporary," to address his readers directly, and his anxiety concerning the survival of poetry in a scientific era, are symptoms of a disintegration of society which compels him to serve two gods. It may be presumed that most poets, if they are anxious about the future, do not question the survival of poetry. The assimilation of modern knowledge, upon which Lewis insists so much, is not of vital importance to poetry. Fortunately Lewis, especially in his early poetry, is less expansive than he claims.

Raymond Tschumi. *Thought in Twentieth-Century English Poetry* (Routledge and Kegan Paul, 1951), pp. 196–97

The presence of the Audenesque is even more noticeable in the work that followed *From Feathers to Iron—The Magnetic Mountain* (1933). It must, however, be said here that in spite of the Auden influence in Day Lewis's work of this period, the work is still quite unmistakably

Day Lewis's own. The stimulus, and with it some of the diction, came from Auden, but the poetry that resulted acquired the quality of Day Lewis's personality, as a stream takes on the colour of the soil over which it flows. Although they were working in the same cultural environment, each produced work of different emotional texture from the other's: Auden's poetry, one feels, was written in clinics and classrooms, scribbled on envelopes and the fly-leaves of books on psycho-analysis and economics, whereas Day Lewis's was composed during walking tours in the southern counties of England, spoken hard into a wind blowing across the chalk downs or confided restfully to a companion in field or wood. Day Lewis's muse is hatless and sports-jacketed, Auden's wears horn-rim glasses and is a chain-smoker. The difference between them is at once noticeable in the way they make use of similar material.

Clifford Dyment. C. Day Lewis
(BC/Longmans, 1955), p. 26

The autobiography of the British poet Cecil Day Lewis [*The Buried Day*] is a quietly honest book largely taken up with his childhood and student days. Born in Ireland of Anglo-Irish stock on both sides, Day Lewis was the son of a Church of England curate, who settled in England when the future poet was barely three, and ended as a Church of England vicar in Nottinghamshire. The earliest Irish memories . . . are thus brief and fragmentary. So are the memories of the poet's mother, who died when he was four years old; it is in his scrupulous record of this event that Day Lewis's characteristic refusal to exaggerate first appears. . . .

Another thread is the author's search for his own identity. He seems to have been aware even more than most of us, and from a very early age, of the diverse aspects of his own nature and of his propensity to role-taking. . . .

This is less of a consciously literary biography than Stephen Spender's *World Within World*; it is also egotistic in tone as though the writer is standing back and observing himself.

David Daiches. NYT. Oct. 2, 1960, p. 6

A Welsh pirate called Nicholas the Black settled down on his plunder as a respectable wine-merchant in County Galway and changed his name to Blake; and so a young poet took the pseudonym Nicholas Blake when he started to write his brilliant detective stories, a poet who is rather arbitrarily grouped by critics with Auden, Spender and MacNeice.

In his autobiographical "self-portrait" [*The Buried Day*], Cecil Day Lewis does not tell us much about his days of fame, but a great deal about the enchanting hours of his childhood in the vicarages which his father occupied. . . .

Then he tells us about the birth of his own social conscience in a mining village, his first loves and his first marriage, when a friend sent as a wedding present an Oxford edition of Donne and a load of dung for the garden, his days as a schoolmaster, his friendship with William Plomer, who loved childish puns and captioned a Christmas card of an Egyptian princess dancing before a God with "Horus and his Horus Girls," his experience as a member of the Communist Party, his escape from Pedagogy as "Nicholas Blake," the war and the home guard, his second marriage, his children.

Finally, one is left with the picture of a poet with the sensitivity of a man who has always remained porous to Nature, of a live mind which has the self-honesty to say "What use is experience of life if you so hopelessly represent it?" and of a lover who refuses to believe that the only Paradise is Paradise Lost.

Oswell Blakeston. JOL. May 19, 1960, p. 592

Although he has an unfortunate tendency to write really appalling, keep-sake verses for public occasions such as Royal Birthdays—this seems a kind of nervous tick—Cecil Day Lewis . . . is usually an honest poet. He does not versify ideas or luxuriate in images for their own sake, since his gift seems dovetailed to his personal experience and he uses it to serve certain conceptions which are his poetic life.

To understand this truthfulness of Day Lewis one must take his work as a whole. The principal theme which runs through it is that of duality, the opposition between life and death, with which every human being is concerned. . . .

Day Lewis's response to mutability is not religious. Like some Elizabethan poets he feels that the shadow of death gives an extreme zest and meaning to the present moment. . . .

This is a tragic attitude. It is not a question of nostalgia for the past, or of longing for the future, but of the fulness of our response to the present moment which is doomed but quick with life.

Thomas Blackburn. The Price of an Eye
(Longmans, 1961), pp. 104–6

Cecil Day Lewis has said of his verse that "however much its style has altered from time to time by the demands of some new experience or ruling passion, there runs through it all an unbroken thread, the search for personal identity, the poet's restless compulsion to know himself." Looking over his work, it seems unfortunate that Day Lewis has felt no such "restless compulsion" to search out a personal *poetic* identity; too often the "new experience" has been a literary experience, the "ruling passion" for some idol poet, and the fresh beginning ("my verse seems to me a series of fresh beginnings") merely a surrender to yet another debilitating influence. There has been little or no attempt over the years to organize the materials of this literary experience into a frame that can be recognized as peculiarly of his own making.

"Transitional Poem"—a tepid conflict between the Georgian lyric and the "representative" long poem after the *Waste Land* example—can now be seen as an ominous beginning. The state of indecision which is said to be the poem's theme (the issues are kept scrupulously vague throughout) operates disastrously upon the language, where it becomes manifest as a style ranging from pastiche of Donne, Marvell, Yeats, to first steps in the Auden manner. It is this manner that is to transfix Day Lewis in an attitude of fascinated servility for some years after, until his ultimate release into slavery under Hardy and other eminent Victorians. The point is, though, that even in his early poem it is possible to see not so much Day Lewis's lack of a style as his lack of interest in creating one. Where the language is not frankly imitative, it is either turgid-prosaic or florid-romantic. And this has been a persistent characteristic of his verse. Where he has not stuck fairly rigorously to some master-idiom (where, that is to say, he has been more concerned to "know himself" than to pay his respects to an admired author) he has tended to relax into a comatose conventionality of theme and diction. His rambling, unpopulated, narrative poems, though "vigorous" enough, carry their fair share of cliché at those points where the language is required to take some emotional strain, and his lyrics are too often delivered in a kind of vulgar wrapping. . . .

Day Lewis's new collection offers a fresh supply of featureless lyrics, an execrable lump of rhetoric entitled "Requiem for the Living" and two dramatic monologues, after Browning. One of these, "The Disabused," is —for all its tedious stretches of rather obvious moralizing—a convincing statement of emotional importance. Where it goes wrong is that the speaker is too smugly aware of his "maimed condition" and tends to melodramatize it. Consequently, one has at times a souped up nervous excitement which dilutes one's interest more rapidly than those passages where the rhythm is less slickly energetic.

Ian Hamilton. L. July, 1962, pp. 75–76

LEWIS, C. S. (1898–1963)

The title [*The Allegory of Love*] is not a description of the book but of the excellent medieval works which it expounds and places in their long historical background; curious how one's heart sinks on supposing a modern specimen; what the romantics could read as wild and fascinating needs now to be praised as exact and important. The book is learned, witty, and sensible, and makes one ashamed of not having read its material; in the first flush of renewed admiration for the *Romance of the Rose* I tried to read the Chaucerian version. But it is intolerable. Far better to read Mr. Lewis and his admirable quotations, and recognise that these works were developing a method which is still normal and living, and frankly admit that there are great pleasures not our own. . . .

Such complaints as I can make are only an agreement about the interest of the topic. Mr. Lewis is excellent on the essential point of allegory, and on its growth in Silver Latin, as against the gods, because of a new consciousness of an inner world of moral struggle, so that it was the basis of psychology and gave St. Augustine tropes that no one has dared to call unreal. But the real use of the book for a general reader I think lies elsewhere; it gives an effective account of works whose beauty and reality for us we need to recognise, and yet which, in all willingness, nobody who simply likes a good book can read.

William Empson. Spec. Sept. 4, 1936, p. 389

Mr. Lewis's books follow each other with seasonal, almost quarterly, regularity. But they are little books (70 pages in this one), and they are to some extent by-products of other activities. This small volume [*Christian Behavior*] like its immediate predecessor, is the record of a series of radio talks. The author's special characteristics in thought and style are exhibited at their best in the discussion of ethical questions. Here, rather than in apologetics, is a field in which his sound, common sense, the freshness of his lay approach, and his confident though rather naive faith yield the most substantial results.

CC. Jan. 26, 1944, p. 114

Perelandra appears superficially to be . . . another adventure of Dr. Ransom in search of his unearthly utopia. But it is the natural, and arid, counterpart of *Christian Behaviour,* for it is a fantasy compensation for Mr. Lewis's deep dissatisfaction with mankind and the world he inhabits. It would make a magnificent analytic source-book, especially as the publishers obligingly preface it with Mr. Lewis's revealing notes on himself: "I was a younger son, and we lost my mother when I was a child. . . . My first stories were nearly all about mice, but mice usually in armor killing gigantic cats. . . . I loathed school. . . . I love rain. I love to hear it on the roof or gurgling down into the water butt." In *Perelandra,* which is Mr. Lewis's name for the more embarrassing planet Venus, Dr.

Ransom-Lewis swims in oceans of unsalted water ("It was drinkable"!),
rushes deliciously into gaping valleys, wins the battle of Temptation
against the spirit of evil . . . and—if it is not too bold a word—conceives
bliss in the scene of himself standing in an enchanted wood discussing
loneliness and death (he had travelled from earth in a coffin) with a
beautiful girl who is "totally naked" but sexless, because on Perelandra
they blessedly do not know about sex.

It is at this point that an earthly book-reviewer must uncross his gross
legs and tiptoe out, leaving Mr. Lewis to the absorbed serenity of his
dreams.

Alistair Cooke. *NR.* April 24, 1944, p. 580

The tremendous range which Mr. Lewis covers in this independent
sequel [*Perelandra*] to *Out of the Silent Planet* is evident in the fact that
the book can be ranked high in the fields of creative imagination, speculative theology and engrossing adventure. In the first, the author is superb
from many standpoints, writing whole passages of prose poetry that
inevitably suggest the sweep of Dante and Milton. As adventure, too,
Perelandra is . . . tense and thrilling. . . . When it comes to speculative
theology, however, the book is less successful although even here intensely
provocative. . . .

Definitely in the Wellsian vein, *Perelandra,* is, from all standpoints,
far superior to other tales of interplanetary adventures.

John Gilland Brunini. *Com.* May 12, 1944, pp. 90–91

Like an increasing number of modern works of art, *The Great Divorce*
revives the medieval literary device of the dream and, since Mr. Lewis
is a distinguished medieval scholar, revives it with unusual ease and
facility. . . .

I think it unlikely that if other books as generally entertaining as *The
Great Divorce* appear this year, they will be as generally instructive, and
vice versa, so that it seems ungracious to ask for more, but I cannot help
wishing that Mr. Lewis were a little less energetic or a little less patient.
He might then give us fewer books, which would be a pity, but our satisfaction in the books he did write might be more lasting and complete. . . .

. . . in a book which sets out to explain orthodox doctrine to the laity,
it is very important that there should be no possibilities of misunderstanding, and I think I have detected two. Dante or no Dante, it is theologically
not in order to present a historical character, in this case Napoleon, as a
lost soul; only fictional characters, like Othello, who have no life outside
our knowledge, can be so presented. We have no right to believe, far less
to hope, that even Hitler is in Hell. Secondly in his account of the conver-

sion of the young man, Mr. Lewis symbolizes the transformation of lust into sanctified desire by the transformation of a red lizard into a white stallion. Now a horse may be a more complex creature than a lizard, but it is not a better one, and a universe in which all lizards were horses would be a less valuable universe. Mr. Lewis may have a personal antipathy to reptiles, just as I have a nervous horror of insects, but such feelings are accidental and have certainly no theological validity.

But such reservations are minor indeed in comparison with all the positive merits of *The Great Divorce*.

W. H. Auden. *Sat*. April 13, 1946, pp. 22–23

The Screwtape Letters is the least creditable (and most successful) volume. *The Great Divorce* has fewer and less pronounced examples of . . . [his] vices; but the performance of this eschatological vision is just as unsatisfactory as that of the other books—which is to say that it fails, especially as propaganda, for the one necessity of this kind of creation is that it should give the *feeling* of completeness, of comprehending inclusiveness. The publisher says that *The Great Divorce* should be "disquieting"; I doubt whether anyone could find it *satisfying*. The satiric portraits of unredeemed personalities may provide some readers with a certain degree of satisfaction—but it is of a treacherous sort, just as any annoyance caused is of the wrong sort, to the wrong people; because, altogether, they are, morally, entirely *unrevealing*. . . .

I think, finally, that Mr. Lewis is not sufficiently self-conscious to be a good moralist. I have tried to show in several cases that there may be a submission of personal belief without subordination of his own interests, to doctrinal definition. Mr. Lewis's books bear no marks of ecclesiastical approbation, in spite of his reported popularity with the clergy of the Roman as well as the English Church; but *censores deputati* might well have his case in mind when they consider, as they do not always do, whether more than formal orthodoxy and primary intentions are involved in the effect of any book; whether any good possibly achieved by direct indoctrination may not often be outweighed and sometimes thwarted by the persistent nourishment of false attitudes; and if unscrutinized proselytizing interests and private motives aren't likely to vitiate the proper objects and intention of such writing, just as much as conspicuous adulteration and adaptation of fact and dogma. Ecclesiastical censorship will at least recognize its responsibility here; there is no acknowledgement, from those with responsible rank in the intellectual hierarchy, of the parallel, but more desperate problems of contemporary "social education."

E.K.T. Dock. *Scy*. Summer, 1946, pp. 57–58

Despite the incisiveness of his objective descriptions, it is with the inner experience that Dr. Lewis is mainly concerned; for *Surprised by Joy* is avowedly a "conversion story," written in response to readers' requests to trace the steps in his journey from atheism to Christianity. The key word in that pilgrimage is "Joy"; by which Dr. Lewis means that elusive and well-nigh incommunicable experience, coming unsought and unawares and never more surely chased away than by a "greedy impatience to snare it," which has the quality of "an unsatisfied desire which is itself more desirable than any other satisfaction." It was this hunger for an absolute, which no other attempted means—from the erotic to the occult—could ultimately satisfy, that led back at last to the Christian faith lost in youth. Dr. Lewis writes, as always, with a psychological penetration and perception of sophistry disconcertingly acute, and the aphoristic wit which makes the impact of spiritual truth so much more memorable. There is, in fact, a vigorous Chestertonian flavour to this wry, wise self-examination which is preoccupied less with the self as such than with the unpredictable and inescapable workings of God through the—often unwilling—human spirit.

Margaret Willy. Eng. Spring, 1956, pp. 27–28

Dr. C. S. Lewis has never lacked boldness; and in his new book [*The Four Loves*] he undertakes a task which none but the boldest would dare: he analyses Love into what he deems its four major parts; that is, Affection, Friendship, Eros and Charity, and then proceeds to subdivide again, so that most of the recognized (and particularly the Christian) aspects of Love are defined. By the very nature of its subject this book forms a challenge to the reader. One is alternately in complete accord and in violent disagreement with its author, depending on where one's own particular shades of definition in the subject happen to lie. . . .

. . . it is with the section on Charity that Dr. Lewis finds his surest touch. He is a Christian writing out of Christian conviction, and his praise of the selfless love that is Saint Paul's Charity opens the mind to what the highest expression of Love might be. Not Affection, Friendship or Eros merely—though all these may be a part of it—but a reaching out through these expressions of love, towards something purer, more complete and satisfying: a striving by the fraction towards reunion with the Whole which men call God.

An interesting, controversial book: a book to read, discuss and argue over. This, no doubt, is what its author intended when first he chose the subject. Though I am inclined to think that in this particular case the subject chose him.

Joan Forman. JOL. June 9, 1960, p. 690

Professor Lewis holds the Chair of Medieval and Renaissance English at Cambridge University and so naturally in his examination of word-roots [*Studies in Words*] he can go far back into our English vocabulary and can do so with the authority of great scholarship. He can also penetrate with no less right of learning into Latin and Greek origins. This is admirable for the specialist students of English Literature to whom he lectures. But to the amateur of words who finds semantics (or the study of meanings) a rewarding pastime, his methods may seem too thorough and too far-reaching among quotations from the ancient classics to make easy reading.

Ivor Brown. JOL. Sept. 8, 1960, p. 283

Dr. Lewis is distressed—as who is not?—by certain features of the contemporary critical scene. In the first place, he objects to the fashion followers: those whose literary judgments are based not upon a genuinely personal response to literature but on "the present view of the literary world." . . . Secondly, he is annoyed by those who, whilst they base their evaluations on inner conviction, nevertheless give the impression that their judgments are the product of some kind of mathematical certainty or statistical proof: as though they knew from external observation that all right thinking men agreed with them. And finally, he is disturbed by what he sees as a tendency, among those who emphasise the moral value of good literature, to be somewhat melodramatic about the unliterary: as though the man who does not appreciate a good poem is necessarily inhuman or sub-human.

Now if this were all there were to it, Dr. Lewis's book [*An Experiment in Criticism*] might have served a useful purpose. It would have been a reminder, especially to undergraduates perhaps, that true criticism is a record of the critic's own experience of literature (which does *not* mean, one would have to add, that anybody's opinion is as good as anybody else's). And to teachers of English Literature, intent on emphasising its importance in a technological age, it might have been a timely reminder that literature is not the only humanizing force; not the only thing that makes for life. Unfortunately, Dr. Lewis is not content to leave it there. So shocked is he by the illnesses to which criticism is liable, that he proposes a drastic experiment, the effect of which would be to cure the sickness by killing the patient.

Let us, he says, reverse the current procedure, which is, he tells us, to estimate the quality of a person's reading according to one's judgment of the books he reads. . . . Let no one pronounce a book bad who has not patiently investigated the kind—or kinds—of reading it elicits from a vast number of readers. . . . In other words, where Fielding, say, would remind us simply that the man of candour and true understanding is never hasty to condemn, Dr. Lewis goes to the absurd extreme of demanding that before we venture an adverse judgment of our own we should canvass all the readers of the book in question.

G. Ingli James. *Anglo-Welsh Review.*
Autumn, 1961, pp. 71–72

Regular readers of C. S. Lewis will be familiar with the more irritating aspects of his literary persona; the avuncular chattiness, the arch references to books that everyone has heard of but only Professor Lewis has read, the implication that not only is literature fun but that it should, ideally, be accompanied by the cracking of nuts and the imbibing of port wine, while the firelight flickers cosily upon the finely tooled backs of rows of well-loved volumes. This kind of thing is a nuisance, but it oughtn't to detract from the fact that Professor Lewis is one of the most intelligent and learned, if not one of the most invariably sensible, figures now operating in the Eng. Lit. field.

His new book [*An Experiment in Criticism*] is brief and polemical, though urbane; it is, in essentials, an all-out attack on the presuppositions and methods of the Leavisian critical establishment. The Doctor is nowhere mentioned, but his presence is everywhere felt. . . . One difficulty about his approach is that any book in the world, even the most apparently trashy, might get by on the "good" ticket if one could only produce a single truly dedicated reader. And the machinery of interrogation required before one could make any literary decisions with certainty would be impossibly elaborate. This theory has its attractive aspects, but it seems to me logically and practically difficult to establish. Professor Lewis's motive is admirable, since he would like all books to have a chance, and he is right to oppose the kind of criticism which regards a work with the air of a suspicious frontier guard examining the passport of an unfriendly alien. I am all for Professor Lewis's desire to introduce a greater degree of catholicity and generosity into contemporary criticism; but it is one thing to react against the excesses of certain kinds of evaluative criticism and another to reject evaluation altogether, as Professor Lewis seems, in places, inclined to do. A world where every book was potentially as good as every other book would present a singularly bizarre appearance.

Bernard Bergonzi. *Spec.* Nov. 17, 1961, p. 718

C. S. Lewis liked his friends to call him Jack. It was part of the apparatus of Anglo-Saxon joviality—like the connoisseur interest in beer, the comic logic-chopping, the inability to pronounce foreign languages, and the dark hints of heterosexual excess—with which he surrounded protectively a private Irish fire. The showmanship was what you noticed first; he had learnt it from G. K. Chesterton, and like Chesterton's it was often put to splendid polemic purpose. . . .

As a literary critic Lewis was in the first rank. Like Hazlitt and Saintsbury he is above all a reader's critic: occasionally perverse, sometimes the victim of a private enthusiasm, but always intelligent, lively, pertinent. Perhaps *The Allegory of Love* and the volume on the 16th century in the *Oxford History,* triumphs of wit over ignorance (recent scholarly discovery is simply by-passed), may not prove in the end to be more than *tours de force*. Like his grim Cambridge rival—whom he misunderstood as grossly as Dr. Leavis has misunderstood him—Lewis was happiest in the short critical essay, of which his output was enormous. . . . He was not a prophet—or an organization man. But the force of his example has helped to transform the academic study of English literature into a humaner discipline than it was a quarter of a century ago.

F. W. Bateson. *NS.* Dec. 6, 1963, pp. 835

To judge only by his writings, his affections and habits seem to be those of an earlier generation of dons than the one he actually belonged to; yet the very English turn-of-the-century cosiness is shot through with a deep imaginative understanding of the historical (not the Chestertonian or Morrisian) Middle Ages, and a perpetual need to use this understanding as a stick to beat the horrid period in which his later years were passed. His sympathy with his own time was small; but his understanding of it was probably greater than he pretended. The enormous success of his moral and theological writing would not have been possible if he had not spoken to something really present in the consciousness of his contemporaries. One may surmise that his knowledge of the graver kinds of suffering came to him late in life. His religion and his philosophy enabled him to outface it; and it deepened the tone of his later writing and edged him away from the current of robust complacency into which on earlier occasions he had sometimes strayed. . . .

His reading in modern literature was small, and was not sympathetic. He could use the past as a monitor to the present; but the need to relate the achievements of the past to the active imagination of his own time was one that he apparently never felt. He has some acute negative criticism of modern poetry and found it quite easy to blow up some of the cant of modern criticism; but he never discovered, and perhaps never tried to discover, what modern poetry and criticism were after. . . . It is in part this that accounts for the limitations and failures of his own creative work.

Lewis's verse is not without talent or dexterity and certainly not without feeling; but it is written in a variety of obsolescent modes. . . . And his rather worn range of reference is not improved by some crabbed and wilful metrical experiments. His real talent was not here—it was for narrative, in which he is always immensely skilful and happily at home. His children's books, his planetary romances, his theological allegories are all compellingly readable, whatever the reader thinks of their tendency or their message. In places, especially in the opening chapters of *That Hideous Strength,* there are signs of a regular novelist's power. But Lewis never cared to develop it. He preferred to keep to the byways, out of the main literary stream. He could best say what he had to say through genial fantasy or a childlike kind of romance. Here as in other respects the comparison with Chesterton is not far wrong.

TLS. Jan. 7, 1965, pp. 1–2

LEWIS, D. B. WYNDHAM (1894–   )

It seems a curious irony that such a tragic figure as Villon, an artist who was so very economical in his use of words, and one who was capable of such intensity of feeling, should always be written about by the best-fed and the most geniably voluble of writers.

Mr. D. B. Wyndham Lewis . . . is temperamentally in the tradition for Villon historians: but he is a conscientious and earnest scholar: he has a real knowledge of the Middle Ages, and above all he has a genuine feeling for Villon's poetry. These qualities counteract the misfortune of his too ebullient temperament and make this book [*François Villon*] well worth reading. Mr. Lewis has amassed in it almost everything that has been discovered about Villon's life. . . . But his amiability and his genuine desire to be at all costs entertaining lead him into many irritating tricks. His prose, none too solid at its best, is apt at any moment to trickle away into a thin stream of polite, emasculated Rabelaisianisms, which will immediately estrange him from any reader who has a decent respect for that master. . . . It would seem that Mr. Lewis not only makes no attempt to control his congenital gustiness, but that he deliberately exploits it. The result is that his style reminds us of the feverish and desperate quality with which we have become familiarized in the daily press by those cosmic journalists who, under the names of various kinds of touts and scavengers, actually rely for their living on being daily and consistently funny.

Roy Campbell. *NS.* March 24, 1928, p. 765

Mr. Lewis writes of Ronsard with genial enthusiasm [*Ronsard*], and has obviously made a deep study of the formidable complete works. Yet there is much quarrelsome irrelevance in the way we are baulked of the adventure into the poetry, on which we might have been ably and excitingly conducted, and are left in the end, as far as criticism goes, with a consideration of little more than the usual anthology pieces.

With regard to these, the way is clear enough. Mr. Lewis has only to praise, which he does with gusto. Yet here, too, his combativeness discovers a target. This time it is Walter Pater, who is soundly cudgelled for not being full-blooded enough in his own expression of appreciation.

T. W. Earp. *NSN.* Aug. 5, 1944, p. 92

In his introductory chapter [in *Molière: The Comic Mask*] Mr. Wyndham Lewis expresses relief at the thought that so few of the many books on Molière are essential reading. It is a mistake to begin a book by making disparaging remarks about the work of one's predecessors in the same field. A great deal of valuable work has been done on Molière in recent years, and if Mr. Lewis had treated it with more respect his own monograph might have been less disappointing. . . .

It is significant that Mr. Lewis commends a book by the dreary Faguet as "a useful corrective to over-adulation" of Molière. The trouble with his own chapters on the plays is not merely that they contain nothing new, but that his whole approach suffers from an evident lack of sympathy.

Martin Turnell. *Spec.* Oct. 9, 1959, p. 482

LEWIS, (PERCY) WYNDHAM (1886–1957)

. . . indeed Vorticism, Cubism, Imagism—and Blastism—may well sweep away anything for which I have stood or fought. That is the luck of the game; that is how we are laid to rest by inscrutable but august destiny. Let us however consider what chance Blastism has of becoming permanent. It has this chance. . . .

All great art has been produced by people interested in their own ages and their own climes. I do not mean to say that it was produced by men solely interested in their own day; but if they looked at the past they saw it in terms and represented it in the idiom of their own climes and nations. . . .

Well, in *Blast* you have Messrs. Aldington, Brzeska, Pound, Wadsworth, Lewis and others corporately blasting what in our time they dislike and blessing what appeals to them. And the blasting makes very amusing reading. You can laugh for an hour over their manifestoes. It is no good saying that *Blast* is vulgar and contains many misprints. That was said of Shakespeare and the Folios bristle with misprints too. It was said of Shakespeare with such effect that he went and hid himself in Stratford—as if Mr. Lewis should retire to Surbiton and pretend that he had made his fortune in the pork-trade. The parallels are quite exact —the British academic school of today hating to see their own times in terms of their own times just as did the upholders of the unities, and Gorboduc and Ferrex and Porrex, in the day when they frightened poor Shakespeare out of town. Of course Mr. Lewis is not yet Shakespeare; neither is Mr. [Ezra] Pound; I am only talking of the chances of permanence in the new movement.

And its chance of permanence consists in the fact that its method in attack is the obviously right one of being amusing and taking an interest in its own day. It is no good being not amusing, however earnest you may be. It is no good being serious if you cannot find hearers; it is no good avoiding sensationalism in an affair, like that of the arts, whose whole purpose is sensationalism and appeals to the emotions. It is no good being so careful to avoid misprints that you get nothing done. *Blast* is very amusing, very actual, very impressive now and then; it contains less dullness than any periodical now offered to this sad world. . . . Mr. Lewis presents you with a story that is to other stories what a piece of abstract music by Bach is to a piece of programme-music. I don't just figure out what it means, but I get from it ferociously odd sensations—but then I do not understand what Bach meant by the Fourth Fugue, and I don't want to. I get sensations enough from it.

Ford Madox Hueffer [Ford]. *OutL.* July 4, 1914,
pp. 14–15

For a long while the only advance it has seemed profitable to make in the elucidation of Shakespeare has been along the lines of textual criticism, but Mr. Lewis, though he does not ignore it, breaks new ground in this book [*The Lion and the Fox*] which has for sub-title: "The Rôle of the Hero in the Plays of Shakespeare." He has great resources at command, a sufficient knowledge of the literature of the period, of European history, and ethnology; and though perhaps in none of these subjects would he snatch academic honours, his use of them is so extraordinarily invigorating (even if it may be occasionally uncritical), he strikes so many sparks which throw light on possible approaches, that his use of them is fully justified. Everything is grist which comes to his mill and a miller he is rather than a baker. For he does not give you the loaf ready to swallow: it is not being spoon-fed to read one of his books. He expects active collaboration on the reader's part: he will not make it all too easy. This has for result that everything he says gains extraordinarily from the work one has oneself had to do with it; and the great value is that to the reader no subject is the same after he has read one of Mr. Lewis's books upon it, which in these days is a comparatively rare experience.

Bonamy Dobrée. Crit. June, 1927, p. 339

Space and Time, says Mr. Lewis [in The Childermass, Section I], are now one, as the body is one with the soul; we worship the God of Time and all our present emotional life proves us Time-children. This reminder of mortality makes us live for sensations, hence the flabby, oversexed, undeveloped, pessimistic new democracy. The drab industrial mills grind our workers, the threadbare barbaric hedonism engulfs our millionaires. Our only defence against this is to deny Time—to return to a belief in the extra-temporal nature of the human mind, to a classical life and not a romantic, an optimistic rational virility and not a credulous and effeminate indulgence in every kind of superstitious awe. Admirable as this gospel sounds, it is yet open to a good deal of criticism. To begin with, it is a retrograde and rather Fascist enterprise based on the co-operation of that dreary creature the "I-am-afraid-I-am-a-very-constructive-young-man." So far Mr. Lewis has paraded one disciple—and what has become of Mr. Henry John, the baby Chang, whose gawky mysticism formed the only outside contribution to The Enemy? Secondly, the Greeks, whom Mr. Lewis wishes us to return to, were more abjectly under the domination of Time than any of us, and said so in passages of exceptional beauty. Then the half-baked lava flow of Jewish-American civilisation that is now engulfing us, despite its stupidity, cruelty, blankness and sentimentality, is far the most vital force there is, and can only be combated by a principle of equal activity: we can find sanctuary in some half-timbered Utopia, but we cannot expect our sanctuary to turn out an arsenal. Besides, this obsession with the passage of Time that Mr. Lewis would remove is really the nearest approach to a unity of conception that we have. A common philosophic outlook is the basis of every great age, and to this belief in Time we owe Proust, Ulysses, and the novels of Mrs. Woolf, to mention a few of the most typical productions of to-day. Compared with these, neo-classicism, however admirable in intention, must certainly appear a sterile force. Also passion, that bugbear of Mr. Lewis, is not necessarily a stunting food. He has taken the shabbiest collection of gutless half-wits, made them adore passion, and argued that passion has made them what they are. Leaving out all the philosophical aspects of Mr. Lewis's theories, which it requires a philosopher to judge, one can at least say that Wuthering Heights is likely to inspire more good literature in the future than, for instance, Jane Austen or Candide. The Romantic revival has given us birth, and in the machine age we have our being. We are free to rebel against either, but we are not free to remove them. The Age of Reason is past, and neither the balance of Greece, nor the detachment of China, the Action Française, the neo-Thomists, nor even Mr. Lewis and his virile desperadoes will ever put Humpty-Dumpty together again.

The great feature of Mr. Lewis's brave stand against modernity is that he fights the age with its own weapons. No living writer has the same aggressive intellectual vitality, or the capacity to express it in such leathery, whip-cracking prose. Behind this lies a mind and a sensibility which are among the most interesting of our time, and, one suspects, a colossal egotism to give them force. His peculiar merit, as a stylist, is his painter's vision of human beings, the vorticist eye which enables him to see them half as monsters, half as ridiculous automatons, before he proceeds to a diagnosis of their vanity and their faults. In spite of the die-hard background of his thought, his interests and his arguments are all magnificently *dans le vrai*. It is this modern quality in his sensibility and his observation that makes one forget he is really a defender of the Faith. This book comes as a relief to those who pictured Mr. Lewis as a bullying pamphleteer, arriving late and heated at the queue of letters with no greater object than a desire ruthlessly to elbow his way to the top. All the same, one is tempted to suspect his passion for order. It is, after all, shared by Mussolini. The main point is that here is a superbly controversial section of a three-decker, ragged at first, but always alive, and deserving to be read by any intellectual follower of the social tendencies of to-day. The ring-craft, the "terrible punch" of Mr. Lewis have been already noted; add here his amazing chemical descriptions of scenery and human beings, his catchwords, his satire, and his superb vitality, and when irritated by his conceit or his dialectics, think of the majority of our living writers, whose only talent is the galvanic virtuosity by which they are enabled to walk and talk years after their heads have been cut off.

Cyril Connolly. NS. July 7, 1928, p. 426

This formidable volume of 625 pages measures 10 x 8 x 2½ inches, and weighs nearly 5½ pounds. The concentration required for reading is only equalled by the strain of holding it; and, quite frankly, neither is entirely worthwhile. For what Mr. Lewis essentially says in this book [*The Apes of God*] he has for the most part said better elsewhere. In *Time and Western Man,* in *Paleface,* there is admirable criticism of the postwar child-cult, and sense of inferiority, as well as of the effeminacy of our devitalized generation. In *The Wild Body* there is fine Swift-like satire on the ridiculous human frame. Large sections of *The Apes of God* are devoted to tremendous harangues (usually delivered at meals or during parties), in which disciples of "the god-like Pierpoint" (who can only, I am afraid, be Mr. Lewis himself) restate the familiar arguments less well—perhaps intentionally less well, since it is not the Master who speaks—and far more boringly.

Gladwyn Jebb. *Adel.* Oct., 1930, p. 74

In all Mr. Lewis's work it is possible to trace the presence of a conflict between two opposite principles. This conflict takes a variety of forms; or rather, the twin combatants fight again and again the same recurring battle, arrayed in a variety of disguises. The eternal protagonists are what Fichte . . . first termed the Self and the Not-Self. They tumble on the stage sometimes in the dual roles of Mind and Body, acting the drama of Contemplation and Action. Or they are the Philosopher, and the Artist together pitted against the sworn Enemy, "Life." It is to their antagonism that Mr. Lewis owes his creative impetus; and the tragedies they act are his art, they fall upon each other in mortal strife in order that their tragedies may be immortal. . . .

All Mr. Lewis's activities, as artist, as critic, as metaphysician, as sophist, as satirist, spring from this prime dilemma: either the Self engages with the Not-Self, or Self and Not-Self link themselves in league against common enemies.

Hugh Gordon Porteus. *Wyndham Lewis*
(Desmond Harmsworth, 1932), pp. 19–21

It is unfortunate that the first time one should be asked to write about Wyndham Lewis the occasion should be the publication of four books [*The Doom of Youth, Filibusters in Barbary, The Enemy of the Stars, Snooty Baronet*] so much below the highest level of his achievement as these; for it means that, while adverse criticism will have the emphasis of immediacy, admiration will be tempered by retrospection. The common faults of three of them at least—*The Enemy of the Stars* is a republication of one of his earliest works—are a slapdash carelessness in the writing, too great a reliance upon mere transcription of other people's views, and a proclivity to follow, at the expense of the central argument or narrative, any red herring that may cross his trail. In some measure these are present in much of Lewis's work, but in the best noticeable only as tendencies, to be passed over as the perhaps inevitable adjuncts of a uniquely vigorous style and a mind more than usually well-stored and enquiring. Here, however, since two of the books are expressly designed for a wider public than his others have enjoyed (see the Introduction to *Doom of Youth* and the dust-jacket of *Filibusters*), one suspects Lewis of that contempt for his readers which takes the form of refusal to exert himself.

Douglas Garman. *Scy.* Dec., 1932, pp. 279–80

About such a writer, a master of our time, pamphlets . . . should be unnecessary. However, Lewis has been, during the ten or twelve years, penalized (transiently, his admirers believe) both for his adherence to the mountain and for certain additional descents into the valley and additional incursions into the park where he has ventured, not always wisely, in the mountain's interest. Long ago Ezra Pound foretold of Lewis that a writer could not be intelligent in his way without becoming "prey to the furies"; and in some of these ventures he neglected to observe the supine civility of author to author, than which, in the shorter run, nothing is more dangerous. The penalty has been denigration, neglect and the disappearance of his books. . . . So to those who admired him so faithfully twenty-five years ago and have continued to admire and learn from him in the interval, the new editions [of his work] are gratifying. They believe much of Lewis's work is indestructible, much of it among the small amount of excellence bodied forth in the last four decades; and that much of it has the double nature—if you like, negative and positive—of being able to disinfect and being able to advance the intellectual and emotional health and the human dignity of its readers.

Geoffrey Grigson. A Master of Our Time
(Methuen, 1951), pp. 4–5

. . . if I were asked to nominate the man of the decade in fiction as American magazines nominate the man of the year, I think I would want to name . . . Wyndham Lewis. He has been writing now for fifty years, and the work he has produced before 1939 is among the high peaks of modern literature. Yet the creative energy he has shown during the past decade is as phenomenal as that of W. B. Yeats in poetry. Within the last five years, in addition to works of criticism, he has published a collection of stories, *Rotting Hill,* a most striking novel of tragic depth, *Self-Condemned,* and *The Human Age,* his long-awaited sequel to *The Childermass,* a work on the grand scale, terrifying and at times Swiftian in the vigour and sweep of its imaginative vision.

Walter Allen. The Novel Today
(BC/Longmans, 1955), p. 32

. . . we may find it useful to dwell briefly upon certain characteristics of Lewis's work which have tended to bewilder, if not alienate, certain readers. The first is his supposed *impersonality.* With this characteristic is associated a certain coldness and even inhumanity. To begin by reading his play *The Enemy of the Stars* and to follow it with a novel such as *The Apes of God* is to experience a sensation of having broken irrevocably with the "graces" of traditional drama and fiction. In such works the solaces or consolations of popular literature are absent. No warm "personality" meets the reader halfway with its bursting hold-all of humor, "whimsicality" and good fellowship. As *livres de cachet,* Lewis's books are hardly to be recommended. Taut and astringent, they may be prescribed in large doses for those who wish to read themselves awake. They are daylight creating. The curious paradox is this: although Lewis's books betray an apparent impersonality, the powerful personality of their author is everywhere present. On the purely verbal plane, each sentence is his and not somebody else's. There is a Lewis punch and *tournure* of phrase work which no one has come near to imitating. Whereas we can "identify" Dickens or Trollope because every few pages we light upon a typical Dickensian or Trollopean passage or scene, Lewis never thus erupts into his work. He exercises the true creative withdrawal. Pierpoint, the only "genuine" character in *The Apes of God* (i.e., Lewis himself), never puts in an appearance during the entire 625 pages. . . .

The question—what sort of writer is Lewis?—may therefore be answered, if only provisionally, as follows. He is a writer who has endeavoured to deploy in the service of his art all the forces of intellect, not merely the "sensitive" or the "aesthetic." Hence the importance of understanding *his* mind as a whole. That the human psyche can be divided into two spheres, the intellectual sphere and something vaguely called the "sensibility," he would energetically deny. Nothing whole or integrated can issue from a split-man; Part V of *The Apes of God* is devoted to the study of that phenomenon. Nor has Lewis entertained the view that the artist, being a specialist in the realm of feeling, is entrusted with the mission to compensate his fellows for the cold, abstract world of physical science. The artist is at the *centre.* He is neither an entertainer, nor an amateur psycho-analyst, nor a propagandist—all of whom are specialists in one side of man (including his inside), and all practitioners of some form of hypnosis. The artist's role, by contrast, is that of an eye-opener. . . .

E. W. F. Tomlin. *Wyndham Lewis*
(BC/Longmans, 1955), pp. 10–11, 13–14

In *Rude Assignment* Wyndham Lewis proclaims himself a persecuted hero and protests against the "malevolent suppression" of his work by "enemies." This may be true and it is not surprising that so belligerent a writer should arouse animosity. Nor should Lewis complain of unfair treatment when he can stoop from the iconclastic gaiety of the *Blast manifesto* to the perverse truculence of *Hitler,* parts of *Time and Western Man,* and, it must be added, *The Demon of Progress in the Arts.*

In this essay Wyndham Lewis is at his most exasperating. He puts forward the reasonable contention that abstraction in painting cannot be carried beyond a certain limit without becoming nonsense. But instead of discussing sensibly why this is so and where the limit should come he fixes it arbitrarily, though understandably, at the point to which he has taken his own painting. Experiment beyond this point is condemned *a priori*. There is no attempt to assess the qualities of the artists condemned; instead there are tendentious assertions and cheap jibes. Who would have expected vorticist Lewis to taunt artists with doing "their best to displease and startle the public instead of painting pictures which had a reasonable chance of selling"? Of course there are good things in the essay, such as the discussion of the varying degrees to which the different arts are dependent on their publics, for it is almost impossible for Lewis to be wholly bad. . . .

Wyndham Lewis "was better equipped than anyone else to write out of inner knowledge the tragedy of his time," says Mr. [Hugh] Kenner. This is perhaps true and the tragedy is that he has never quite achieved this in one wholly successful work. But one should not complain at the lack of such a masterpiece when he can produce sentences with . . . scorching vitality . . . stately, spectral rhythm . . . or wit. . . . Writing like this makes it reasonable to claim that in virtuosity of imagination and word-artistry Wyndham Lewis is unexcelled by any novelist since 1914, except Joyce.

Jocelyn Baines. L. April, 1955, pp. 82–84

Americans generally are not very familiar with Wyndham Lewis's art and polemics but the Tate Gallery Vorticist show [summer 1956] is belated recognition of his pre-World War I activities. Lewis, now 72 and blind, is still as for long a controversial figure. In an introduction to the catalogue he explains that Vorticism was largely what he did and thought at a certain time; visual Vorticism was militantly anti-realist; the aim was a visual language as abstract as music; mechanism was at least as real as nature's forms. . . .

The exhibition reveals Lewis as a diverse and powerful draftsman and Vorticism as an over-intellectualized abortive movement which never really got off the ground.

Howard Devree. NYT ts, July 29, 1956, p. 6X

In 1928 Lewis published *The Childermass,* a fictional satire announced as the first section of a trilogy whose second and third parts were shortly to follow. . . . It contains so many of Lewis' critical opinions as to make it fall almost between his satires and his "pamphlets"; he himself has called it an exception in his canon in *Rude Assignment.* "It is about Heaven," he tells us there, "the politics of which, although bitter in the extreme, have no relation to those of the earth."

Meanwhile, the two subsequent sections did not appear, and only came out as recently as 1955 in a volume called *The Human Age,* a title intended to subsume what has now turned into four parts—*The Childermass, Monstre Gai, Malign Fiesta,* and *The Trial of Man.* (A revised version of the first section, *The Childermass,* appeared in 1956.). . .

The whole work is difficult to the point of preciosity; Yeats, who called the first hundred pages of the first part "a masterpiece" in a letter to Olivia Shakespear, also said, "It is the most obscure piece of writing known to me." . . .

Originally entitled "Hoadipip," and then "Joint," Lewis' most complex and single mystagogical satire opens on the fringes of "Heaven." This celestial city, lying to "the heavenly north" of the plain where we begin, and whose battlemented shadow haunts this twentieth-century slaughter of the "Holy Innocents," turns out to be anything but a Dantesque paradise; what one character calls the "human age" at the end of *Malign Fiesta* seems to be a ghastly compromise between angel and animal, and in the city that is only glimpsed in *The Childermass* Lewis later dramatizes a sort of immortal folly, an existence of contemporary Struldbrugs. Blood-red clouds emerge from the city in the first volume and, sure enough, we learn in the sequels that state socialism prevails there. And we also have a hint in the first section that Third City, as it is later called, is peopled by children, or childish adults. . . .

In *The Childermass* we are mainly concerned with the attempts of two characters, Satterthwaite and Pullman, to reach this city, and with a Punch-like Bailiff (the "monstre gai" of the second part), the slaughters at whose court parallel the massacre of the children by Herod (Matthew 2:16) from which the book takes its name. . . .

The likeness to Flaubert's posthumous satiric masterpiece is suggestive but superficial. . . . Satters and Pulley we detest, and should detest, from the start. Flaubert's work is far more universal. It is the contemporary world that *The Childermass* deplores. . . . Satters, who above all characters in the work makes us think longingly of the title, continually "steins" and stutters, and is obviously meant to represent Gertrude Stein just as, on one level, Pulley stands for James Joyce. . . . The Bailiff . . . is everything Lewis dislikes. . . .

The Childermass is about "ignorance" in the form of "time-philosophy." The Bailiff explains "space-time," the element in which the purgatorial plain is cast, as precisely everything Lewis attacked in *Time and Western Man.* One can refer constantly from the Bailiff's speeches to the critical works Lewis wrote in the twenties and thirties, and vice versa. . . .

Not only does Lewis' critical position bind itself too closely to tradition to allow for the present at all, it also insists on continually assailing the present in a *parti pris* fashion. This insistence on particularities, on assailing our time and not all time, robs his satire of universality. Much of his work is contemporary in allusion, and some of it only contemporary. Is it just possible that Lewis' loss in powers of observation may be due to the "apriorist heresy," to his approaching reality subjectively (not to say, romantically), selecting from it data to confirm his theories? There are large areas of twentieth-century experience left untouched by Lewis' work, voluminous though it may be. One cannot say the same of Joyce. The recent satires show a serious loss of control of his material by Lewis, and if this decline continues, as one earnestly hopes it may not, we shall be faced with the spectacle of a potentially great satiric genius vitiated by prejudice.

> Geoffrey Wagner. *Wyndham Lewis: a Portrait of the Artist as the Enemy* (New Haven, Conn., Yale Univ. Pr., 1957), pp. 290–95, 298–300, 310–11

There aren't, unfortunately, many early letters [*The Letters of Wyndham Lewis*]. Those that survive are pretty consistent with Lewis's whole life-style. He began poor and went on being poor; as a student in Paris he scratched along on doles from his mother, and at 54—author of a long string of important books and one of the really important painters of his time—he justly complained that he had worked "twice as hard and . . . twice as well as the generality," without making enough money to have even short-term security. At 60 he was wandering about North America (the hell of New York, the limbo of Toronto) looking for a hack teaching job. He was over 70 and blind when the Tate retrospective won him general celebrity.

He began severe and went on being severe. The letters enact his quarrels; he is outrageously outspoken, a superb rejector of olive-branches. Among those for whom he goes baldheaded are Roger Fry, Clive Bell, Sickert, Paul Nash, Augustus John, the unhappy Ludovici (whom Hulme threatened with the abstract knuckleduster)—and his close associates Pound and Eliot. Geoffrey Wagner, who at the end of Lewis's life was writing his indispensable book about him, came under suspicion simply because of a family connection with Wadsworth. In his last days he would, but for illness, have gone for William Roberts over the "Vorticist" row that the Tate exhibition stirred up. From the earliest days he was fantastically vulnerable to affront, and so intensely suspicious and secretive. He concealed his telephone number, his address, his marital status; he told Naomi Mitchison that children should be taught to be suspicious. He defended himself at the slightest provocation "with a certain heat and precision."

> Frank Kermode. *MGW*. April 11, 1963, p. 10

LIDDELL, ROBERT (1908–   )

Mr. Liddell analyses a familiar situation with witty restraint and a nice discernment in shades of feeling [*The Almond Tree*]. The infatuation of the head master for Vera never devolves into mere scandal. The same theme is presented with highly amusing discrepancies from the point of view of the three people involved.

LM. Aug., 1938, p. 384

Mr. Liddell combines both faculties, being a novelist of distinction and the author of *A Treatise on the Novel,* which Desmond MacCarthy commended as likely to help novelists with their craft. . . . [In *Some Principles of Fiction*] Mr. Liddell . . . gathers quotations from other writers with a selective skill which demands . . . sensibility and acumen.

L. A. G. Strong. *Spec.* Sept. 14, 1953, p. 250

Mr. Robert Liddell . . . has already published some half-dozen or so novels and several books of criticism, but I am inclined to think that *Aegean Greece* is the best thing he has so far done; certainly it is no offshoot of his fiction, but a piece of creative writing in its own right, the fruit of many journeys and a lifetime of study and reflection.

John Morris. *Enc.* Nov., 1954, p. 77

There are informative handbooks, and one excellent recent French guide [on Istanbul]; and now here comes Mr. Robert Liddell, equipped with all the gifts for describing a city except tough nerves that can take ugliness and dirt—"vast quarters of insignificant ugliness"; filthy streets and foreshores, ugly faces, hideous modern architecture; these obviously too often got between Mr. Liddell and the magnificent beauties so aesthetically exciting to him yet never compelling his love, as Greece and her islands compel and keep it. Nevertheless he has (it scarcely needs saying) written a book [*Byzantium and Istanbul*] of great value, packed with a wealth of historical and descriptive information, vivid impressions, sensitive and nerve-ridden reactions both to splendours and squalors, good extracts from the descriptions of past travellers who saw and described things long since perished, so that the spectacular and lovely past rises for us like ghosts from the cinders and slums and modern hideousness that are now their tomb. Mr. Liddell runs competently over past history (and what history, what tremendousness, what turbulent and unceasing goings-on!). . . . He conducts us with careful discrimination and sensitive description through a byzanterie of churches, a turtledom of mosques, a whispering of the great ghosts of Rome, an encirclement of ancient, mighty and ruining walls, the whole spectacular city poised on the shores (filthy and squalid, says Mr. Liddell) of Marmara, the Bosphorus and the Golden Horn.

Rose Macaulay. TT. June 23, 1956, p. 749

Some Principles of Fiction (1953) and *A Treatise on the Novel* [are] two extraordinarily rich mines of useful and provocative thinking on fiction—not represented in [collections usually] only because of the difficulty of extracting a suitable passage from a closely interwoven and somewhat unsystematic text.

Robert Scholes. Approaches to the Novel
(San Francisco, Chandler, 1961), p. 314

LINKLATER, ERIC (1899–　　)

Mr. Linklater is a similarly tantalising novelist, though with more excuse, since this is his first attempt [*White Maa's Saga*]. It has innumerable faults. The material of which it is made up is heterogeneous in the extreme. Some of it is clever nonsense and some of it just nonsense. There is the girl who says to the man who has, not unprovoked, snatched a kiss from her, "You've spoilt everything." There is also another who says, "I'm one of the very few girls whose legs, above the knee, look nice from behind," and then in necessary explanation, "But please remember that I'm virtuous." There are also passages about the Orkneys, a couple of good fights and a number of credible persons, including one younger sister whose rare appearances are made all the more captivating by their rarity. I fancy that Mr. Linklater ought to write short stories rather than novels: he would then find less overwhelming the temptation to introduce irrelevant fragments. But in fiction of some sort or another he has a future.

Edward Shanks. LM. May, 1929, p. 89

Mr. Linklater's picaresque novel [*Juan in America*] goes with such a swing that one is almost tempted to forget its slightness. Event hurries upon event, and the book, though it has a ponderous beginning, has no end at all. . . . No character in this book has any reality, and Juan least of all, but the author is mildly knowing, and if the book will bore the intelligent reader it has just those qualities that will amuse the intelligentsia. Mr. Linklater may be dull, but, if pushed to it, can be rather naughty.

H. C. Harwood. SR. April 18, 1931, p. 572

The fact that this extravaganza of American life [*Juan in America*] was obviously written with a British audience in mind, far from diminishing our enjoyment, gives it an added fillip. For the author, with the gusto of a discoverer, describes in detail so much that we as Americans take for granted that we sometimes almost imagine we are reading about a foreign land. At the least, we see America through very unfamiliar eyes.

Mr. Linklater has turned loose upon our continent a young Englishman illegitimately descended from Byron's Don Juan, who possesses much of his ancestor's love of life. Juan Motley is never squeamish or shocked or timid about what he encounters: he is always glad to meet it half way. He encounters a great deal: after disgracing himself on the football field of an American college, he tries out bootlegging, singing head downward from a trapeze, soda-jerking, love-making on an island owned by a mighty racketeer, cross-country flying and gate-crashing in Hollywood. Mr. Linklater has taken pains not to neglect a single type of job, or class of society, or geographical district in America, and his book is superficially as cross-sectional as it is picaresque. . . .

This view of things is, of course, exceedingly naïve in itself but it is an excellent attitude for writing a successful extravaganza. It is a view which will undoubtedly mislead people into both overestimating and underestimating this book. There will be those who label it a penetrating satire, whereas it is neither satire nor penetrating. Mr. Linklater has simply seized on the most obvious and time worn of American fatuities: our go-getters, our hundred-percenters, our charlatans, our culture-fiends, treating them farcially and without a trace of genuine insight; and he has made our contemporary "bad men"—such as gangsters and bootleggers—the same romantic characters that a previous generation made of cowboys and desperados. To call such a performance satire is to overestimate it ridiculously. But there will also be people who, perceiving that it is not satire, will be so smugly concerned with allocating it critically that they will miss a lot of fun. These people are certain to underestimate the book.

Louis Kronenberger. Bkm. June, 1931, pp. 417—18

Mr. Eric Linklater's *Ripeness is All* is an amusing comedy of enforced philo-progenitiveness. An eccentric will lays on the competing relatives the necessity of raising large families in a short space of time: this joke is worked out ingeniously through a number of situations. Except for its air of sexual scandal, *Ripeness is All* maintains the conventions of *Punch,* and is entertaining though faintly old-fashioned.

G. W. Stonier. FR. May, 1935, p. 640

Twenty-five years ago the young Eric Linklater, through his *Juan in America,* stepped suddenly into the front rank of novelists writing in the English language. He did this by expressing one side of his nature, his rich curiosity about the modern world, his delight in life and his gusto in words. Resisting his publisher's understandable plea to "do it all over again and as quickly as possible" he discovered to his somewhat surprised readers in his next novel another and equally important quality in himself. In his almost icily austere historical novel based on the Icelandic sagas *The Men of Ness* he expressed his nostalgic passion for his native North, not merely the North of Scotland but the Ultimate Norse Islands where the grey storms rage, or where the infinite peace of tremendous midsummers streams over the endless horizon.

Eric Linklater has since, in many books, continued to display these two personal elements: his love of the rich tumultuous world of cities, men and the South on the one hand, and his longing for the North on the other. Never until the publication of this his latest novel *The Dark of Summer* has he so skillfully succeeded in bringing together these two parallel strands in his writing and intertwining them. This is Linklater at his best, both in his richest and most austere mood. His style is at times as luminous as his own North, at times as vigorous as in *Juan* or *Private Angelo.* A most readable book and an excellent tale. . . .

Here is indeed richness and diversity. It is a mark of Eric Linklater's maturity as well as his often acknowledged virtuosity that he manages to combine all these themes and subjects so successfully and so credibly in one novel. The book is full of characters as well as of character. If the love affair is perhaps not quite so convincing as some of the superficially less probable elements in the tale, does this matter?

Moray McLaren. *TT*. Sept. 22, 1956, p. 1128

One might not have thought that Edinburgh was a suitable place for a Saturnalia, but Eric Linklater has convincingly made that grave city the scene of an explosion of Dionysiac frenzy in a buoyant, witty and romantic story [*The Merry Muse*]. It would be pleasant and fitting if the City Fathers could co-operate by denouncing the book. . . . Mr. Linklater is back on his old ribald and revolutionary form, and very funny.

Frederick Laws. *JOL*. Oct. 15, 1959, p. 62

I do not suppose that *Roll of Honour* will do much to enhance Eric Linklater's reputation, but if it is not a book to enthuse about, it has as one would expect many marks of the master's skill. I do not think there are many novelists writing today who are more careful and more conscious of their craft—indeed at times in *Roll of Honour* consciousness slips over into self-consciousness. It is, therefore, always a pleasure to read Mr. Linklater's prose for its sound, its shape, its colour—if not always for its meaning. So it is with his new work.

W. G. Henderson. *New Saltire*. Spring, 1962, pp. 93–94

LOGUE, CHRISTOPHER (1926–   )

A reviewer plunged into a volume of verse by a new poet, evidently original, with an idiom of his own, is unavoidably in some difficulty, since he has to make what is virtually a snap judgement. . . .

But there is, it can be sensed at once, something compelling in Mr. Logue's poetry [*Wand and Quadrant*]. He is evidently trying to make language do something very complex, adding to all the virtuosities of imagery, symbolism, and a marked rhythm, the slight twisting of words to new meanings. It may even be said that here and there he does some violence to the language, forcing it occasionally, not beyond what is legitimate—everything is legitimate if it works—but beyond what is effective. . . .

Here is a young poet, we feel, with a distinctive attitude, still struggling for expression, still finding what it is he has to express. Thus the "objective correlative" of the state is often unconvincing, the instrumentation, one must think, sometimes clumsy. The former does not seem always to be intuitive, smells a little forced and *voulu*: and with respect to the latter there is often uncertainty, in spite of the strong rhythmic element, as to the value of line-endings and beginnings; even, in the freer verse-forms, of the length of the line, so that a destructive counter-rhythm, not a syncopation, is set up; or else there is a confusion of meaning-stress. But this is an impressive little volume, of accomplishment as well as of promise, symptomatic, possibly, of what is happening to poetry today. It is coming out into clearer realms; the burdensome cloak of "the age of anxiety" is being thrown off. There is a sense that life, after all, is to be lived, and that the fact of death can be absorbed into living.

Bonamy Dobrée. *Nimbus*. Autumn, 1954, pp. 66–67

Mr. Logue's small book of free adaptations* from Neruda's *20 Poemas de Amor* makes . . . [this] point insistently: "The element I have set out to put into English verse is the vigour and lack of restraint in the original" —qualities Mr. Logue implies, which are far to seek in the verse of today. Well, Mr. Logue may have set out to do this, but he has not

---

The Man Who Told His Love

arrived. In Neruda's own astonishing sequence there is certainly vigour: the vigour not only of eager and outspoken desire, but of shrewd observation, . . . of tenderness and comprehension. . . . Mr. Logue, however, has neither put into English verse Neruda's vigour and lack of restraint as these appear in his poems, nor recreated them in new form (as would have been entirely legitimate) through free adaptation. Over and over again, either by clever tricks or by mere feebleness, he has squandered these qualities. . . . Cases of being feeble or silly quite by oneself would matter less, though; for it is not to the credit of English letters that the work of a distinguished foreign writer should be played about with like this.

John Holloway. *L.* April, 1959, pp. 81, 83

LONSDALE, FREDERICK (1881–1954)

Fine feathers make fine birds, and fine birds make fine plays, or at least paying "propositions." Countless plays have proved beyond shadow of doubt the managerial contention that the number of playgoers in London alive and immediately curious about the intellectual theatre is at the most forty thousand, and may be very much less. But take forty thousand from seven millions and a considerable balance remains, to entertain which is a complicated business. The complications are lessened as soon as the playwright realises that the West End audience takes no interest in low life except on condition that it is above stairs. Mr. Lonsdale owes his success to his perfect realisation of this fact. There is no secret about successful playwriting. Avoidance of any kind of truth, wit which does not rise out of character but is an impartial distribution from the author's private storehouse, and, as to players, stars of whoppingest magnitude with no nonsense about team work—this cannot be wrong. The success of *The Last of Mrs. Cheyney* will, I imagine, be found to correspond exactly with the faithful carrying-out of this formula. It is not a good sort of play, but it is a very good play of its sort.

James Agate. *The Contemporary Theatre 1925*
(Chapman and Hall, 1926), pp. 144–45

The Last of Mrs. Cheyney ought to be acted in front of the Albert Memorial to an audience of Chelsea Pensioners. It is mostly decayed Wilde, though Mr. Shaw has unconsciously embellished it with an extraordinary butler, the depraved and unacknowledged brother of William in *You Never Can Tell*. The play has been made a popular success chiefly by that admirable comedienne Miss Ellis Jeffreys, who shows such mastery (over a part which has nothing to do with the plot) that she persuades the world it is listening to a witty play. There is one clever feature, the letter written by Lord Elton to Mrs. Cheyney in which he warns her of the vices afflicting all the other characters. For the rest, this is the hundredth exposition of the daring and touching theory that a woman may be so nice and true-hearted that though she will steal her hostess's pearls she will face prison rather than "immorality."

Gilbert Norwood. *LM*. July, 1926, p. 324

Frederick Lonsdale is back in form in this artless little comedy [*The Way Things Go*] in which a family of most attractive bankrupt English aristocrats is rescued by two equally attractive wealthy Americans.

There are no villains in the piece, though the relatives of the Duke of Bristol, save one, have little idea of working their passages in this present-day hard, devalued world.

F.S. *TW*. April, 1950, p. 10

Frederick Lonsdale had his first play produced in London in 1908 and his last in 1950, and between these two he wrote twenty-four plays or musical plays which were produced in London or New York. The years of his greatest success, however, were the nineteen-twenties and early-thirties. This was the period, too, to which he seemed to have belonged. At no other time could the world have worn for him so much the aspect of his own home ground; at no other time could it have been so receptive to his talents or so enchanted by his person. So that, although he lived until 1954, and lived in a charmed circle of appreciation and love, he always seemed in later years to be a figure from the nineteen-twenties.
. . .

It has been said that his plays, particularly the third act of *The Last of Mrs. Cheyney,* should be taken by all students of the dramatic art as a model of how to write dialogue which, though not lifelike, is apparently lifelike. Lately, however, some people have begun to decry him; to say that he was never a great playwright, merely a weaver of frivolous trifles, or, much more suprisingly, an Edwardian embroiderer of artificial plots with leisurely and rounded phrases. . . .

Few people, I suppose, remember exactly how successful he was during the years from 1923 until the early thirties. . . . In December 1930, after the productions of *On Approval, The High Road* and *Canaries Sometimes Sing,* it was possible for a writer in the *Daily Telegraph* to write as follows: "My reference yesterday to the loss the English theatre would suffer in the event of Mr. Lonsdale making good his threat to forsake it for the screen has inspired a statistically-minded colleague to research. The results are rather interesting. Mr. Lonsdale, he points out, is not merely the most popular playwright of the day; he is almost certainly the most popular who ever lived. Other men—Barrie, Maugham, Shaw, Pinero and Coward, for instance—have had successes, but is any of them quite immune to failure? Sir James Barrie comes nearest this blissful state. I believe that in his long and prolific career he has had only one full length play that failed to pass the 100 mark. . . .

Mr. Lonsdale has written seven or eight straight plays, and the book, or part of the book, of about half a dozen musical comedies. The shortest run he has ever had is the 110 nights of *Aren't We All?*—a total with which most authors would be satisfied. His record for straight and musical plays respectively are 514 nights for *The Last of Mrs. Cheyney* and 1,352 for *The Maid of the Mountains,* and his average run has been well over a year."

Frances Donaldson. *Freddy Lonsdale*
(Heinemann, 1957), pp. ix, xiii, 155–56

Frederick Lonsdale was so entirely of his age, and wrote so entirely for the moment, that immortality has been predicted for *Mrs. Cheyney*. He had almost no schooling and was ill-read, yet in his writing as in his life, there was style. He was what the Garrick Club used to call "authentic" —implying a kind of integrity that was not at all incompatible with his running-out on a Hollywood contract when he found that Hollywood conversation was not up to Garrick standards. He was the supposedly ne'er-do-well son of a Jersey tobacconist, and might have passed for an Old Etonian of the tougher sort; a spacious liver, if ever there was one, who turned out his first winners in lodgings, with his babies round him, and found it hard to write a line when he was more affluently circumstanced; an incurable idler with twenty-five works to his name: a harebrained spendthrift who provided handsomely for his dependents and died well out of the red; an affectionate but sometimes impossible father; a beloved but sometimes impossible friend; a cheerfully exacting egocentric who paid his money debts in cash and all the rest in the equally acceptable currency of charm. An unconscious moralist, he came to grief only when he tried to moralise; his one play with a message was his one failure. Astonishingly resourceful in his art, he had few resources in himself. He delighted the millions and was the prince of good companions; the party over, his mirror reflects an empty mask. Death came with merciful suddenness, when he was walking away from Claridge's with a friend.

W. Bridges-Adams. *Drama.* Autumn, 1957, p. 37

LOWRY, MALCOLM (1909-1957)

Under the Volcano, the scene of which is a small town in Mexico, is in effect a study of a dipsomaniac, a British consul, during little more than a day of his life with elucidating glances into the past, but the quality of the man's mind is such that what might have been merely pathological becomes truly tragic, and in following his confused thinking and speaking through nearly 400 closely printed pages you may be perplexed now and then but you are never bored.

Charles Marriott. *MG.* Sept. 12, 1947, p. 3

Mr. Lowry is concerned with the individual predicament; and the generally ambitious scope and complicated structure of his novel make his concentration upon so small a section of his characters' lives—the entire action takes place on one November day: the Day of the Dead—accordingly inadequate. . . . Mr. Lowry writes rather prolixly; a slight thread of incident carries too heavy a burden of reflections and perceptions. There is, too, some visual and emotive weakness in the book; the scenic descriptions are somewhat imprecise and do not successfully provide the "objective correlative" to the emotion which is struggling—or is it?—to get across. In spite of its many defects, however, I must testify that *Under the Volcano,* if not the most successful, is certainly the most interesting, the most perceptive, and the most promising novel it has fallen to my lot to review so far this year.

D. S. Savage. *Spec.* Oct. 10, 1947, p. 476

The book [*Under the Volcano*] has obviously been worked over and over with the most prolonged and loving care until every possibility of symbolism that situation and setting allow has been fully brought out. In the end, so much symbolism seems to come a little too pat; and, while it makes for an agonising concentration of the tragedy, together with the other factors of characterisation, style and method it makes also for an inescapable impression of pastiche. The total effect is much more than that of pastiche alone; but how much happier one would feel about this novel, impressive though it is, if one were not so conscious at every page of its literary sources.

Walter Allen. *NSN.* Dec. 6, 1947, pp. 455–56

One could have guessed that Lowry might find it difficult to carry on from his superb and consuming achievement [*Under the Volcano*]. He himself appears to have felt this and spent the last ten years of his brief life trying to finish a new novel or a group of novels of which *Under the Volcano* would have the center. Living on a lonely beach near Vancouver, he tried to reawaken in himself the stress of feeling which had made possible the incandescence of his early writing. There is no grimmer task for a writer than to meet his own standards. Lowry returned to England in 1957 and died suddenly, leaving only fragments.

They have now been gathered under Lowry's own, cumbersome title [*Hear Us O Lord From Heaven Thy Dwelling Place*]. These seven sketches do not form a coherent sequence. Several are loosely connected by the appearance in them of Sigbjorn Wilderness, Lowry's fictional persona. Some are independent narratives; others point to a larger design. They may best be understood as trials and assays from the workshop of a writer who was trying to escape from the confinement of his own success.

George Steiner. *Nation*. May 27, 1961, p. 465

Selected Poems is the first comprehensive collection of Lowry's poetry. . . . Made up of 71 poems, about one-fourth of those which Lowry completed, this little book has been divided into several groups, . . . and they reflect the chronology of his life and the development of his writing. . . .

Mr. Birney's [editor] words, in his introduction, are eloquently descriptive of Lowry and his poetry: "Neither *Under the Volcano* nor the success of it, nor all the growing company of readers and friends, could save him from his destructive element. He has dissolved into it now, leaving only the countenance, stricken yet curiously jovial, that haunts us from his writings. In the great novel, and in *Hear Us O Lord from Heaven Thy Dwelling Place,* and in those works still to be published we can see him through the naively translucent masks he put on. But here, in the poetry, we are confronted with the naked and doomed face of the man himself." Full of the distilled bitterness of Malcolm Lowry's life, these poems are alternately glowing and black in their reflection of the rich but agonized experiences of their creator.

J. M. Edelstein. *NR*. Nov. 17, 1962, pp. 22–23

Ultramarine remains, without doubt, an astonishing *tour de force*. Based on a journal kept by Malcolm Lowry, as an eighteen-year-old deck-hand and cabin boy, serving on a freighter out of Liverpool sailing East, the first version of the novel was finished when he was twenty. In the autumn of that year (1929) Lowry went up to St. Catharine's College, Cambridge, and he continued his work on the book—much of it at Rye, in the home of Mr. Conrad Aiken—for the next three years. In 1933, after some typical calamities of typescripts lost, reassembled, rewritten, the novel was published by Jonathan Cape. Malcolm Lowry was twenty-four. The book was a flop.

The same firm now deserves our thanks for restoring this early and neglected work to print after thirty years. For Lowry continued to annotate and revise the novel throughout his life, intending it to be the first volume of a series (*The Voyage That Never Ends*) of which only *Under the Volcano* and *Hear Us O Lord from Heaven Thy Dwelling Place* were ever completed. The style, the method, the verbal magic— the hallucinatory, drunken nightmare world which only Lowry could evoke—are all here. Only the content seems a trifle thin. The theme of a raw, inward youth among oafish sailors, of a boy winning the respect of his shipmates at the risk of losing his virginity, of manhood won at the expense of first, innocent love, was too easy, too obvious.

TLS. March 22, 1963, p. 197

LUBBOCK, PERCY (1879–   )

The problem of the novelist is to fix, reflect, transmit. He does not always solve it.

Dr. Lubbock has written the first book in which the problem is stated and a few solutions are examined. The only thing more important than a detailed criticism of the book is an indication of why the book is important. I can think of few contemporary writers and no critics who can afford to disregard *The Craft of Fiction,* and if there are readers who are still capable of taking esthetic pleasure in the novel, after all that has happened to debase that form of literature, I urge them, in the interest of "creative reading," to disregard the occasional obscurity of Dr. Lubbock's presentation and learn from him nearly all that can be learned, except from the novelists themselves, of the art.

Gilbert Seldes. *Dial.* March, 1922, p. 318

. . . if there are any who desire to be called critics without exercising a critical judgment, they should study Mr. Lubbock carefully. He will suggest many a formula which they may blindly apply. Suppose, for example, that a man is required to write about *The Pickwick Papers.* He is quite unable to judge whether the book is good or bad. He is ignorant of the author's intentions. Was Dickens trying to be funny? The illustrations *look funny.* It is no use measuring, because some of the editions may vary in size. He begins then: "When Dickens wrote he was still in solution; crystallisation was to come, but as yet his brushwork is niggling, his modulations are imperfectly fused, and the most salient characteristics of his later art are still entangled in the matrix of tenacious moralisation." This is good of its kind, but cannot go on much longer. He must look up *The Craft of Fiction*. . . .

It only remained to invent a jargon and turn literary criticism into studio gossip. Mr. Lubbock has done his best, but he is too frank and too modest to succeed. Still, there is hope yet. The time may yet come when even a Tolstoy will be superciliously challenged: "Are you crystallised?"

OutL. March 4, 1922, p. 177

Mr. Lubbock's new book [*Earlham*] is a delicate and lovely piece of work, the fruit, I imagine, of much leisurely writing, and certainly meant for leisurely reading. It is a picture of Earlham Hall, in Norfolk, where the author's childhood was passed with his grandparents. The principal personages we meet are his grandfather, a country clergyman of a fine old type, his grandmother, a country lady of an even finer type, and a number of relatives, for the most part of the Quaker family of Gurney. Using the beautiful old house as a connecting link, Mr. Lubbock does not hesitate to go beyond his own memories and introduce to us figures of the past, in particular, Elizabeth Fry and her family. But there is no discordance or break; all is of a piece; the house, the figures of its inmates, the little incidents of childhood, all are seen through the soft golden haze of memory. Given literary art, perhaps one man's memories are as good as another's. Neither the people nor the incidents here are of any great moment, yet by his beguiling manner and scrupulous style Mr. Lubbock can make everything as significant to us as it is, or was, to him. It is easy to recognise his masters, but nevertheless the book is his own, and a very individual piece of work. Those of us who read his fine *Craft of Fiction* and wondered at the style (which did not, I maintain, entirely suit the book), ought to have known what it was shaping for. Here it is where it should be; it flows on like wonderful talk, easy and often, seemingly half careless, yet in reality very scrupulous, very effective, and altogether the very instrument for such delicate hewing in the mine of reminiscence.

J. B. Priestley. LM. Feb., 1923, p. 436

It [his writing] possesses, to begin with, all the implications of what we today call a leisure-culture, the plain indice of its having been produced in an age more favourable to the graces than our own. This note of expansive and courteous procedure we may refer to, metaphorically, as Mr. Lubbock's Edwardian tone (metaphorically, since all his books came to be written after 1910). Apart from this suave urbanity of tone, which we may associate with the life of the English upper-classes before 1914, the subjects of his books have been taken very largely from the spheres of fashion and of leisure: Eton, the world of country-houses, of well-to-do socialites, and holidays abroad.

The second quality, comeliness of style, is in part related to the first, being, as it were, its appropriate speech. Like the subtle smoke of a long-extinct cigar, Mr. Lubbock's style preserves the illusion that things are with us which have since passed away. This magic is, no doubt, the more efficacious in that a social nostalgia, so often present when an author celebrates a lapsed way of life, is not discovered here. Nostalgia there is, as in his recollections of the summer-holiday house of his child-hood, but this is of a private order like Proust's remembrance of the madeleine, and is not infused with any conscious communal or historical pathos.

In seeming, then, to speak with the voice of the choicest connoisseurs of the Nineteen-hundreds, even when his subject exists in the Twenties, Mr. Lubbock's style becomes an exception: what was, we may fancy, the high shining norm of utterance in other decades and milieus is transformed in our own austere iron age, into a lonely rare phenomenon. . . . Suffice it to say that he can be described—to employ Mr. Cyril Connolly's distinction—as a "mandarin" author, a master of English in its literary rather than vernacular form.

Derek Stanford. Month. Dec., 1952, pp. 359–60

LUCAS, E. V. (1868–1938)

I called his output large. It is colossal. Nine times the space that meas-ures industry in writing-men, namely a page of the British Museum catalogue, he fills with his miscellanea. Nine pages!—with spaces (sig-nificant of popularity) for new editions and additions; and he is young enough, as literary years go, to fill other nine. The mere mass is remark-able; but what is really astonishing is its uniform excellence. Think, too, of its "infinite variety"—Verses, Essays, Novels (or "Entertainments," as he calls them), Topography, Biography, Editions of Lamb, Books for Children, Anthologies, Cricket, Satires, and Introductions innumer-able! Nor does this take into account the contributions to *Punch* and other papers, not yet included in any volume. Here, surely, is an illustra-tion of Hazlitt's remark: "I do not wonder at any quantity that an author is said to have written; for the more a man writes, the more he can write." He might have added, "the better he can write." Lucas and Hazlitt can both be called as evidence. . . .

[His] *Life of Lamb* contains one of Mr. Lucas's very finest essays. When I compile a "Best of Lucas" to match his own "Best of Lamb," the first thing I shall include will be Chap. XIV, entitled "George Dyer." So much for the *Lamb,* upon which I have dwelt with some formality because it is Mr. Lucas's *magnum opus,* the charm of all his other *opera* being that they are so delightfully not *magna.* The public, by the way, have identified Lucas and Lamb in a way highly complimentary to Mr. Lucas the editor, but probably infuriating to Mr. Lucas the author. The worst of doing one thing very thoroughly is that you are not allowed to do anything else. True, the public likes Mr. Lucas to write, as well as to edit; but its stupider members, who cannot get on without labels, insist on calling him a disciple of Lamb or even an imitator of Lamb, thereby proving that they can read neither Lucas nor Lamb, and probably cannot read anybody with intelligence. To find a likeness between the conversational simplicity of Lucas and the elaborated Gothic beauty of Lamb needs extraordinary obtuseness. The easy ripple of Lucas and the gyratory complexity of Lamb's digressions, progressions, retrogressions and circumgressions may be cited together for opposition, but for no other purpose. Moreover, there is such a thing as difference of scale, of plane, of intensity. Really, the comparison is too silly to discuss. The lunatics who call Lucas an imitator of Lamb are the kind of people who call Lamb "gentle."

George Sampson. BkmL. Feb., 1917, pp. 145–46

Mr. Lucas in *Rose and Rose* has written what may be called his first "straight" or, possibly, "legitimate" novel; and one may be permitted to doubt whether the effort which it must have cost him was worth the trouble. Mr. Lucas is nothing if he is not the prince of digressions; and for him deliberately to pass by opportunities for digressing, as he so obviously has done here, is merely to renounce the use of his chief gift.

Edward Shanks. LM. Nov., 1921, p. 97

The past year saw the production of some monumental biographies, the most remarkable being the finely illustrated monograph on Edwin Abbey, R.A., by Mr. E. V. Lucas. . . . Abbey, though an American, was the most archaeological and antiquarian of painters, and Henry James very truly said to him: "You would have invented Old England if it hadn't existed."

S. M. Ellis. FR. Jan., 1922, pp. 159–60

Mr. Lucas is novelist, essayist, biographer, poet, publisher, editor, and critic of *Arts & Letters.* For all of these things he has a keen and continuous interest. His travel books are filled with gayety and information. *Introducing London,* the most recent, is a gay and unconventional guide book. Last year he came to America to "Wander Among" our private and public art galleries. He travelled across the country and made innumerable friends. The notebook in his pocket, which I saw him take out occasionally, when something amused him, probably held many a tidbit for *Punch* when he returned, but if he was ever greatly amused by us [Americans], it was an amusement totally untinged by ill humor, and never in any sense, bitter.

He talked freely of his English and American writing friends, discussed their work with acumen, their personalities with extreme kindliness, and I heard him more than once put down a malicious piece of gossip with a witticism that was almost a rebuke. The biographer of Charles Lamb, he possesses an even gentler pen than gentle Elia. I like to think of him as I saw him once here, among old books and pictures, in a small company of those who enjoy excellent food and excellent stories, spinning yarns and listening to them. Here is a companionable man, who writes companionable books, a gay man who writes gay books, a studious man who writes studious books.

> John Farrar in *E. V. Lucas: Appreciations* (N.Y.,
> George H. Doran, 1925), pp. 1–2

These modern memoirs—voluminous, illustrated, epistolary; they are like lecture-rooms and concert-halls, the acoustics of which, one understands, it is impossible, with the best intentions in the world, to prophesy. Some that might have been guaranteed to resound turn out toneless, others are unexpectedly vibrant. One might have been forgiven for auguring not wholly sanguinely about this bulky handsome book [*The Colvins and Their Friends*]. Sidney Colvin was a conscientious, sensitive Cambridge professor somewhat lacking in humour. It soon appears as if Mr. Lucas had been content to leave most of his task to scissors and paste, and what he does say is largely precise, unadorned statement. But lo and behold! a complete success; here, for book-lovers particularly, are 350 delightful pages.

> *LL.* Feb., 1929, pp. 147–48

. . . Lucas is at his best in his wholly original work. For those who love the tradition of the familiar essay—its quiet humor, its polished urbanity, its mirroring of life's amenities—there is a store of delight in his volumes. "A writer who fain would quarrel with no one," he calls himself. Consequently it is—mostly—with the small things of life that he concerns himself. . . . In him there is an instinct for casual good things and he finds them wherever he looks. . . .

Though he discourses pleasantly on unpretentious subjects it is without descent to triviality in thought or manner. Not only is there charm in his writing: there is depth and breadth in his thinking; mingled seriousness and whimsical humor. He is always the patrician; always mild, humane, broadly tolerant, cheerful, healthy, well-bred, cultured, leisurely, allusive, widely-informed.

His understanding of character and human motive is made equally evident in the realm of fiction. It is a sweeping statement, but true, that few twentieth-century novels have given me equally great pleasure or as lasting profit as *Landmarks*.

Charles B. Shaw. *The Colphon* (N.Y.). March,
1935, not paginated

In other writers he admired robustness and power; he was quite ready to admire a type of writing which he himself scrupulously avoided. For instance, although no one can call William Faulkner a "bedroom" author, E. V. admired William Faulkner immensely. . . .

Above all, I believe that my father confined himself on paper to the urbane, the humorous and the delicate in order to protest against different aspects not of human nature only, but also of his own. By skimming life's surface, he could escape, particularly, from private depths. James Agate in his *Ego 3* says of E. V.: "I have an idea that the serenity of the writer was a mask hiding the torments of a man knowing as much about hell as any of Maupassant's characters, or even Maupassant himself."

Audrey Lucas. *E. V. Lucas* (Methuen,
1939), pp. 141–42

LUCAS, F. L. (1894–   )

Whilst never being hot-headed, Mr. Lucas is always whole-hearted; this may make some find his utterances pontifical, an impression heightened by his prose, in which the purple falls not so much into patches as vestments. But he follows no fashion and is rarely taken in. . . . He sees as well as reads, his essays draw upon life with a sure touch that picks out the attractive from the cheap, the durable from the artificially "everlasting." . . . The book [*Authors Dead and Living*], indeed, firmly expresses the spirit of the more intelligent side of the age; there is prose and there are sentences that make one glad of it beyond its avowed subject.

Robert Herring. *LM*. July, 1926, pp. 313–14

Authors, Dead and Living, by F. L. Lucas, lacks neither competence nor instruction. Mr. Lucas, we are informed, is a Fellow of King's College,

Cambridge, and that already is saying a good deal. It seems that he is responsible for the criticism of poetry in the *New Statesman*. . . . Mr. Lucas is a scholar; so far as I am able to judge, a liberal and accurate one. . . . If he does not know all literature, he clearly knows enough to establish himself as a critic who may be fallible but is at least not ignorant; even if he talks not too wisely, we know after reading a couple of pages of his book that he knows what he is talking about. If we want to pick a quarrel, here is a critic worth picking it with. . . . But Mr. Lucas is not only learned. His mind is attractive in its preferences as well as being well equipped. His opinions of individual authors, though it can never be said to be merely capricious, is as liable to accidents of personal taste as another's. . . .

Mr. Lucas has a bright, justly confident style. . . . He has the scholar's enthusiasm for old as well as new literature. . . . But above all, Mr. Lucas is right-minded. . . . He refuses to be duped by monstrosity, even though it may be fathered by genius.

Mr. Lucas's main contention is as follows. In its progress poetry has ever been becoming "more thoughtful, more full of association and analogy." . . . The fallacy that has ensnared Mr. Lucas is this: He writes under the not uncommon delusion that poetry makes a progressive movement that corresponds to the social and intellectual progression of mankind. . . . In this progress of civilization Mr. Lucas sees, and rightly, much to deplore. . . . But it is one thing to observe that the poets have always been acutely sensitive to the vicissitudes of their own times: it is quite another to contend that they have allowed these views to impair the quality and vigour of their poetry. . . . It is in failing to see this that Mr. Lucas's argument becomes abortive. . . . In conclusion, Mr. Lucas's analysis of poetry is not clearly realised thought, but a dialectical display. . . . Has Mr. Lucas troubled really to think out his important theme? Obviously he has not. He has been content to make a spectacular exhibition of a lovely and aristocratic art. . . . But he fails, and here is his most serious misdemeanor, to perceive that the poetry of our time does very splendidly uphold the integrity of which it is a part.

John Drinkwater. *FR*. Aug. 2, 1926,
pp. 151–53, 158, 160, 163

Mr. Lucas's whole lecture [*The Criticism of Poetry*] is a plea for a return to the sanity and balance, the proper appreciation of the relation between form and matter, feeling and its artistic expression, which inspired alike the poetry and the criticism of the Greeks. . . . He brings the same seriousness and discrimination, relieved by touches of a somewhat scathing wit, to bear upon the work of the wilder poets and critics of today as upon the work of their predecessors for whom he has a great admiration. His essay will delight those who welcome a breath of fresh air and sense in criticism, and may even convert some of those who prefer the stuffiness and nonsense which prevails today.

John Sparrow. LM. Oct., 1933, p. 566

Notable among the volumes of general criticism is F. L. Lucas's lively discussion of romanticism [*The Decline and Fall of the Romantic Ideal*]. He examines a number of the traditional distinctions between "classical" and "romantic," and finding them unsatisfactory he evolves one of his own, psychological in its foundation. . . . In some brilliantly composed chapters he analyzes [his] hypothesis in relation to literature from the classical period onwards. His style is pyrotechnical, never an easy light for steady vision, but his arguments are in the main well conducted, and despite the profusion of epigram he seldom sacrifices his argument for a phrase. Yet strangely enough he commends Aristotle's "dry way of writing." . . . The most debatable part of this work lies in his section on Coleridge.

B. Ifor Evans. YWES. 1936, pp. 8–9

As a whole, this book [*The Woman Clothed with the Sun*] produces the effect of being a collection of highly accomplished literary exercises coordinated by a hand skilled in the technique of prose expression under the guidance of an acute intelligence developed by much reflection and nourished by voluminous reading in many languages: the only thing wanting is that which gives life and impressive energy to creative art, call it inspiration, poetry or any other name you please. . . . This being said . . . one can readily pay a high tribute to the variety and accomplishment of this collection.

TLS. Aug. 19, 1937, p. 591

Mr. Lucas's attitude to literature one might call, broadly, an eighteenth century one. He admires clarity, brevity, good humour, simplicity. Over an important range of literature these tastes guide him soundly and surely; but there are a number of writers—Donne, Newman, D. H. Lawrence among them—to whom Mr. Lucas simply fails to do justice, because the eighteenth century standard of bluff common sense and man-of-the-world good manners by which he judges them are, quite frankly, irrelevent standards. . . . Yet it must be said also that Mr. Lucas's own directness and sincerity never leave the reader in any doubt about what his "imperfect sympathies" are: in that sense, he is a self-corrective critic. And young readers particularly should find his book

[*Style*] useful not only for what it has to say about style but for the supple and manly prose in which it is itself written.

TLS. Sept. 16, 1955, p. 541

Mr. Lucas is a Fowlerite. I do not mean that his book [*Style*] has been put together in the form of a dictionary (it is in fact an expansion of lectures). Nor it is much concerned with language points. The underlying conviction seems nevertheless to be that, when allowance has been made for the changes in "usage," rules may be deduced which, if liberally interpreted, will cover all cases. Probably there is no other point of view from which any but a purely historical book on style could be written. . . .

None of Mr. Lucas's views on style is surprising. None, so far as I can see, is wrong. . . . The book's most obvious merit lies in the quotations. There are almost as many in French as in English, and their range and aptness are remarkable. They stop conspicuously short of the present day. A piece of Virginia Woolf is subjected to rhythmical analysis, and there are passages from Synge and Hardy to show the virtues of popular speech. Belloc and Chesterton are convicted of hyperbole.

Mr. Lucas's references to the world of today consist in the main of commendations of Churchill and Montgomery, snarls at two living critics, references to a car Mr. Lucas evidently possesses, derisive quotations from the essays of students influenced by the New Criticism, and the expression of such blind untruths as "Aristocracy is now out of fashion." That is the book's least attractive side. (When Mr. Lucas himself aims at exemplifying good humour and gaiety, the result is not always what he may have intended. He quotes some excellent jokes made by other people. His own jokes are terrible.)

The most living thing in the book I found to be the portrait which emerges of Dr. Johnson. This is not a set-piece, but Mr. Lucas clearly feels a particular sympathy with Johnson, and one is led step by step to see him as the embodiment of almost everything which Mr. Lucas most properly admires: an impressive demonstration.

Rayner Heppenstall. *NSN*. Sept. 24, 1955, pp. 371–72

LYLE, ROB (1920–   )

Mr. Rob Lyle's *Guitar* is formal and controlled. . . . Infusing his own voice into traditional metres, he is perhaps representative of the newest romanticism, of a welcome return to the "single intention of creating beauty." . . . There is a strong classical-Mediterranean flavour about these poems; while in several of them one feels the influence of Roy Campbell to whom "Carrara," possibly the best poem, is dedicated.

Joseph Braddock. *FR*. April, 1952, p. 209

Among the younger poets writing today, Rob Lyle has already shown that he is both inspired and accomplished. His most recent book, *Poems from Limbo* should first be read at a single sitting for there is organic unity within its two long elegiac passages. These, called "Heroic Elegies" and "Orphic Elegies," are broken by an "Interval" of six lyrics which lighten but do not destroy their tragic mood.

The search for a solution to the human predicament has been pursued by all serious contemporary writers. Men of action and contemplatives are all haunted by the same spiritual anxiety: a need to find for Man a way out of his lonely position in a world which has lost its traditional beliefs and values. Sartre proposes a new humanism, without the "illusory" religious consolation; Mauriac offers the traditional Catholic answer, whilst Samuel Beckett implies that there is no solution, that the world is merely absurd. But Camus, in 1954, declared that we were at last emerging from a period of nihilism; and Rob Lyle is certainly among the writers and artists who are groping their way through dark reality to some pinpoint of light. That he does not find a new one is no denial of his poetic vision for he illuminates the search by the skill and dexterity with which he orders and concentrates, on a single point, a wide range of diverse orders of experience.

His poems are involved with the whole story of civilisation rather than with a particular age. He explores the cosmic process as a drama whose dominant moments, climaxes and culminations reveal the significance of the whole.

Betty Edwards. *CR*. Dec., 1960, p. 690

LYND, ROBERT (1879–1949)

The conspicuous quality of Mr. Lynd is what might be called a passionate commonsense. His essays are lay-sermons on The Working Man and His Sense of Duty, on The Importance of Forgetting History, on The Folly of Disappointment; but the reproach often so justly directed at the deliverers of lay-sermons, that they preach more unctuously and from a higher assumed level of rectitude than any cleric, is not one that he is likely to incur. He is reasonable, and, above all, he is tolerant; he knows too much about himself to be impatient with anyone else. This does not mean that he is complacently impartial before the follies and wickedness of mankind. He laughs at folly and accuses wickedness; but his attitude is that of a man who understands both because in some sort he is capable of both. This endows him with a natural wisdom which seems to flow from his pen without effort [*The Passion of Labour*].

Edward Shanks. *LM.* Dec., 1920, p. 226

All but one of these twenty-six essays appeared in the *New Statesman,* and they were well worth collecting into a book [*The Pleasures of Ignorance*]. They are of that type of literature which might be called writing for the sake of writing, for the writing is the thing that matters. The subject is immaterial. It is not what the writer says, but the special way he says it. Thus Mr. Lynd writes about "Virtue," "Cats," "Going to the Derby," "The Hum of Insects"; but he might equally well have written about Mustard Pots, Clapham Junction, and The Evolution of the Glad Eye. The advantage about this type of essay is that it is quite immaterial that the writer should know his subject. The essay called "Eggs: An Easter Homily," for instance, owes its existence precisely to the fact that Mr. Lynd knew nothing and could describe nothing about Easter Eggs. Ignorance, then, on these occasions is just as valuable an asset as knowledge. But to succeed in this sort of thing the writer must be a master of his instrument, and the point is, when all's said and done, that there is no one living who does it better than, or even as well as, Mr. Lynd. He has an alert and witty mind and a style to match it, so that one gets wit, buffoonery, observation, criticism, and poetry all mixed together in piquant concoction. . . . It is impossible here to give a just idea of the charm and variety of this small book. It reinforces our conviction that, whatever people may think of Mr. Lynd's virtues or shortcomings as a literary critic, there can be no doubt about his excellence as a writer of prose.

OutL. Jan. 14, 1922, p. 356

. . . it happens that Mr. Robert Lynd, one of the best miscellaneous prose writers of our generation, an essayist of rare charm, an acute, witty, yet tolerant critic, is a journalist. Moreover, he is a very good journalist, not of those men of letters who with a great show of disdain merely boil their pots in Fleet Street and can hardly bring themselves to endorse the cheques they receive from newspapers; but a real journalist and one so magnificently equipped that any editor, not a fool or a red-hot Tory, would welcome him with delight. In his time Mr. Lynd has probably done most things that can be done on either a newspaper or a weekly review, and it is certain that he can write any feature of the literary side of a paper, whether it is a piece of descriptive writing, a short article or a book review, better than almost anyone else. The mere fact of having to be topical, of being compelled to write about something merely because it happened yesterday, is in itself sufficient to dry up the source of wit and fancy in a great many literary men, but this necessity seems to stimulate Mr. Lynd. No matter where he is sent (if he is sent), he returns in triumph waving the brush. His descriptive writing, for example, is magnificent journalism, prompt to the occasion and ready to dance any reader's eye down to the bottom of a newspaper column; but even at its lightest it is also something more than journalism, for there is a quality in it that will withstand the lapse of a day or a month or a year. . . .

Mr. Lynd, then, instead of preening himself in a corner, has done what so many of our eighteenth-century writers did: he has marched into literature by way of journalism, the day's round, the common task. It is not everybody's way, but it is especially suitable for writers with well-stored, sane and masculine minds, men who can take hold of experience and translate it freely, who can ransack their own minds and plunder the outside world with an equal measure of success; and when once a man does enter literature by this road, there can be no doubt as to his capacity; he is worth hearing. While Mr. Lynd has been proving to all good judges that he is one of the ablest literary journalists of our time, he has also been creating for himself a singularly happy position in the literature of our time.

J. B. Priestley. LM. April, 1923, pp. 598–99

Of Mr. Lynd there is little fresh to be said. He is no prophet clothed with thunder, but he is on that account the better essayist. His new volume [*The Green Man*] exhibits in ample measure his now familiar geniality, tolerance, whimsicality and kindly humour. Once again he shows the same keen eye for the little oddities of life and character; the same delight in birds and animals; the same faculty for smiling gently at the foibles of humanity in general and at his own in particular. Since his book contains no essay called "The Green Man," we can only surmise that the title is intended to reflect upon the author's own greenness. . . . But his deftly sustained mask of ingenuousness hides, as his admirers know, a fund of sophistication and of solid wisdom. Mr. Lynd may be a laughing philosopher. But he is a philosopher none the less.

Gilbert Thomas. BkmL. Feb., 1929, p. 292

For an author of our own years to be included in the Everyman Library is high distinction. Robert Lynd has justly received this posthumous honor with the added tribute of an admirable introduction by Desmond MacCarthy. The selection properly includes the various phases of Lynd's affections and propensities, his devotion to Ireland, his connoisseurship of Dr. Johnson and his circle, his critical assessments of his contemporaries, and his mastery of the light, discursive essay [*Essays on Life and Literature*].

There was something of paradox about the faith and works of Robert Lynd. A Belfast Presbyterian by birth, he was a Dubliner at heart, a Nationalist whose friends and allegiances were certainly not in the Ulster camp. By profession and taste he was what is called "a bookman": yet in fifty years of writing he wrote very few books, the volumes under his name being mainly collections of essays and articles. . . .

In short, Lynd was the perfect essayist—he practised the craft for many years as "Y.Y." of the *New Statesman*—because he linked the style and vocabulary of the man in the study with the proclivities and sympathies of the man in the street. His range of comprehension was of the widest.

List. Jan. 25, 1951, p. 151

LYON, LILIAN BOWES (1895–1949)

With the death of Lilian Bowes Lyon in the summer of 1949, at the age of fifty-three, the world of contemporary letters lost a poet of rare integrity and maturity of vision. Quietly pursuing her own way, following no "school" or fashion, her voice might well have been lost amid more strident ones demanding notice during the inter-war years. Her work has, however, always enjoyed its small but appreciative following among discriminating readers of literary reviews such as *The Listener* and *The Wind and the Rain,* which published many of her poems. Her output was not considerable; but quantity is no criterion of worth. The five thin volumes of verse published at fairly regular intervals between 1934 and 1946, and brought together in her *Collected Poems* of 1948, contain sufficient poems of lasting value to ensure her a modest, but certain, place in twentieth-century English poetry. . . .

Few contemporary poets have succeeded in evoking more vividly than does Lilian Bowes Lyon the essence of a particular landscape: one engraved so deeply upon her imagination, so bound up with her individual way of seeing life, that its familiar features have become the natural and inevitable currency of her thought. In the use of the images of her native countryside she resembles, among contemporaries, the Cumberland poet, Norman Nicholson; and she, too, derives from an austere and rocky northern landscape—"Hill's edge, rock halt above a foundering pasture, sinewy ground." As powerfully as Emily Brontë, a century earlier, communicated through her poems the wild bleakness of the

Yorkshire moors, this poet gives us the stubborn character of the "ground-swell earth" of Northumberland: swept by the elements, a craggy upland of "tough and moorland grass" and "stone-bred stream," the mournful cry of curlew, plover and "silver lapwing" echoing over the "fanged and pirate fell." Her alert and appreciative response to the countryside is not, however, confined to these more austere aspects of her own county: delighting as she does in such serener sights as "mistily-burning sheaves That light some lean gold graveyard of the summer"; the "glint hush" and "clovery texture Of evening at pasture"; or plough-horses moving in a "cocoon of golden steam," flanks lacquered by early morning sunbeams, and Duchess, the great black mare, taking "the hill as a ship, figure-head noble."

But no more than Emily Brontë is she merely the sensitive observer and recorder of externals. Almost always this "too-memorable Earth" speaks to her in parables, illuminating, or revealing, some profound truth of the human spirit: her appreciation of temporal beauty is charged with the constant perception of a timeless and transcendent inner significance. An old oak, crumbling, stands symbolic of "centuries of patience"; the stony upland, where the green ends and the air grows thin, of that austere height ("the crag's adventure"), lonely and bare above the corn-filled valley, to which her spirit must climb. The example of the foxglove and the wild rose on the "foam-remembering fell" teaches a lesson of stillness; and she rebukes the turbulent discontent of ash-trees "weary of the flesh," as the epitome of those too apt, in restless straining after a remote and unattainable heaven, to miss that one lying close at hand. . . . Everywhere the belief is implicit that all life is one, the human drama played out in field and stream and wood: that the experience of heart and spirit has always its counterpart—or its pattern—in the forms of earth. It is for this reason that the earth is loved by Lilian Bowes Lyon, as it was by Gerard Manley Hopkins, on two planes: not only for itself, but as the visible bodying-forth of an invisible truth—"news from a foreign country."

Margaret Willy. *Essays and Studies.* 1952, pp. 52–53

Miss Lilian Bowes Lyon is a delicately sensitive artist who at times appears to be the vehicle of a larger spirit than she knows. But, usually instead of heightening experience into ecstasy, she congeals it into frozen patterns. *Tomorrow Is a Revealing,* with a few exceptions, is a collection of icicles.

Ranjee G. Shahani. *Poetry R.* Jan.-Feb., 1942, p. 32

MACAULAY, ROSE (1881–1958)

Rose Macaulay is of the very small band of writers in our day whose work counts. She is not for the great multitude who follow after the kingdom of this world and worship success. She lavishes all her art on the failure, the beloved vagabond who loses the world and saves his own soul: the poor in heart for whom is the kingdom of heaven. Unconsciously in writing of her books one finds oneself using scriptural or scriptural-sounding phrases. Nothing else fits her. Whether she will or not the moral of her books—if that is not too heavy and dull a word—is profoundly Christian. Her kingdom is not of this world.

She has written in all some eight books, and in every one there is the triumph of failure, most delicately, gaily and wittily rendered. Each one is a tragedy, but a tragedy presented with the gaiety of the Saints, or of the French widow who wrote of her bereavement "Je pleure mon Albert gaiement." There is that high lift of the human heart in sorrow which is surely a gift of the Holy Spirit. All of Miss Macaulay's heroes and heroines whom I know and love—Benjie in *Views and Vagabonds,* Peter in *The Lee Shore,* Eddy in *The Making of a Bigot,* and Alix in *Non-Combatants*—go out as failures from one point of view or another: prosperity is possibly the thing in human life which Miss Macaulay most abhors.

She has a rich and fruitful theory of life, or perhaps one should say, philosophy of life. She has an abundant and humane humour. She has an exquisite capacity for depicting natural beauty. She is a born lover of the Open Road. Her wit, lambent and tender, plays over the characters she creates. She makes an atmosphere reminding you now of Sterne, now of Stevenson, again of Borrow when he was not controversial. She creates a great number of characters and makes one realize each one. She is wise as well as witty. She has observed life with laughing and moist eyes, and her observations are scattered over the pages of her books. Altogether hers is a rich and manifold gift.

Katharine Tynan. BkmL. Nov., 1916, p. 37

There is one small volume of poems by Miss Macaulay, called *The Two Blind Countries.* It is curiously interesting, since it may be regarded as the testament of mysticism for the year of its appearance, 1914. That is, indeed, the most important fact about it, though no one need begin to fear that he is to be fobbed off with inferior poetry on that account.

For the truth is that the artistic value of this work is almost, if not quite, equal to the exceptional power of abstraction that it evinces. Poetry has really been achieved here, extremely individual in manner and in matter, and of a high order of beauty.

One is compelled, however, though one may a little regret the compulsion, to start from the fact of the poet's mystical tendency. Not that she would mind, presumably; the title of her book is an avowal, clear enough at a second glance, of its point of view. But the reader has an instinct, in which the mere interpreter but follows him, to accept a poem first as art rather than thought; and if he examines it at all, to begin with what may be called its concrete beauty. I will not say that the order is reversed in the case of Miss Macaulay's poetry, since that would be to accuse her of an artistic crime of which she is emphatically not guilty. But it is significant that the greater number of pieces in this book impress the mind with the idea they convey, simultaneously with the sounds in which it is expressed. And as the idea is generally adventurous, and sometimes fantastic, it is that which arrests the reader and on which he lingers, at any rate long enough to discover its originality.

Mary C. Sturgeon. Studies of Contemporary Poets
(George Harrap, 1919), pp. 181–82

She uses the novel for critical purposes; it is significant that *Told by an Idiot,* her last and best book, covers too many generations to allow of detailed characterisations, and will be remembered chiefly for its point-of-view. I do not mean that she cannot create character. She can, and does. But her main gift is for general judgment. Some critics, faced by this puzzle (since it is notorious that no woman can see a joke, keep a secret, or *think*), have hazarded the wide solution that Miss Macaulay does *not* make general judgments for the simple reason that she is a woman and can't. Miss Macaulay, unperturbed, has surpassed herself in a novel where the general judgments are more important than the characters. Of course, her generalisations are false—that goes without saying. All generalisations are false: but some of them are illuminating. Miss Macaulay is always—well, almost always—witty; I confess I did not find her so in *Mystery at Geneva,* but I am told that was a joke I did not see. Men have no sense of humour. In *Told by an Idiot* she fairly blazes with wit. There are, actually, enough good jokes in her first four pages to furnish a whole novel; and if she does not quite keep up that pitch, it is because nobody could. She has chosen a form which gives admirable scope to her *kind* of wit. She takes a whole family, parents, children, grand-children, through roughly half a century, touching off in each decade the absurdities and illusions which at each point have passed for wisdom, and insisting, in a refrain which gains by every repetition, that those absurdities and illusions belong to this year or that because they belong to all years—to the human heart itself. This panoramic method precludes the fond detailing of daily life; it calls for vivid pictures, and it gets them. All the same, Miss Macaulay gropes marvellously deep into some of her characters, especially Rome and Imogen; she has, as it were, packed twenty novels into one.

Gerald Gould. The English Novel of Today
(John Castle, 1924), pp. 71–73

Orphan Island is an ingenious comic story of a satirical nature which should have a wide popularity. It should appeal generally, and I venture to think only, to that mass of people to which reading means novel-reading. Particularly it should appeal to people brought up in the mid-Victorian era who are trying to throw off their Victorianism, to those for whom a delicate facetiousness stands for wit, and to those who admire skill in workmanship in preference to new ideas; there is, I believe, a large class of persons whose only joy in literature is to be able to say, *"How well that is put—that is what I have always thought (or observed, or deduced) myself."*

I. P. Fassett. Crit. April, 1925, p. 474

Miss Macaulay's genuine and deep-hearted sympathy is often ignored or unrecognized by those who fear her intellectual approach to emotional problems. She is here, to some of us, one of the most satisfactory of modern novelists in her firm conviction that nothing needs firm intellectual handling so much as that queer mess of superstition, allegory, sham science and herd-hysteria which so many people gravely call by such names as "psychological problems." Admirable as is the drawing of the Folyot [*Keeping Up Appearances*] household, with its passion for social work and science, its dislike of sloppiness, Miss Macaulay is perhaps even better in her account of the Arthurs in East Sheen. . . . Praise of this brilliant novel would not be complete without a word of admiration for the emotionally subtle portrait of Carey Folyot. . . .

R. E. Roberts. BkmL. May, 1928, p. 129

All these, all the great sites of classical Antiquity, many of the Orient and some in Yorkshire valleys or among Welsh hills go to build up this long, extremely pleasant book [*Pleasures of Ruins*]—a book in form by no means unlike some noble lapidary ruin: each stone an essay, each chapter a craggy, dry-jointed wall of indeterminate height, and one great big chapter, with Rome at its core, towering over the whole. The book ends with a brief "Note on New Ruins." Miss Macaulay does not think much of them. And in the last half-dozen lines she makes a confession which all but the hopelessly decadent and enervate must applaud. She prefers her buildings whole.

John Summerson. NSN. Dec. 12, 1953, p. 765

The Towers of Trebizond could have been written by no one but Rose Macaulay. Her many gifts are here fully expressed and the conflicting elements in her thought and manner are perfectly united.

The narrator of the story, young, intelligent, well-read, and enmeshed in an adulterous love affair, goes off to Turkey on a missionary venture with an aunt, a very High Church Canon and a camel. Miss Macaulay has evolved a style which exactly reflects Laurie's character—an easy, colloquial style, inconsequent but never incoherent, edged and witty, but flowering from time to time into ample passages of description, into dreamy musings, into religious argument. The book is a travel book about Turkey; it is an adventure story alive with high comedy, full of absurd but credible incidents on the shores of the Black Sea or the English countryside. It reads like a gay, learned, eventful, lyrical comedy, with never a dull patch. But it is not a comedy. . . .

Rose Macaulay alone of living writers could have achieved just this effect: this use of high comedy to convey a tragic meaning. She could not perhaps have done it earlier in her career, for in this book the different elements in her thought and feeling are for the first time wholly fused.

C. V. Wedgwood. TT. Sept. 8, 1956, p. 1073

. . . I have re-read Rose Macaulay's *They Were Defeated,* which is to be re-issued after long being out of print. It first appeared in 1932. I read it then and believed it to be by far her finest book. That is saying much, for Rose Macaulay is perhaps the most learned woman writer of distinction in our language. I should place her with George Eliot and Rebecca West, for intellectual capacity and for scholarship. Further, she was a literary artist, using words with full consciousness of their potentiality.

I remember telling her of my predilection for this historical romance, and saying that I thought it should be regarded in future as a companion book to Shorthouse's *John Inglesant,* doing for seventeenth-century Cambridge what the Victorian novel did for seventeenth-century Oxford. To my pleasure, she replied that it was her own favourite, and that she was disappointed because the public had not agreed, so far as the sales figures revealed. But there are some books which take many years to impress themselves. Both Somerset Maugham's *Of Human Bondage* and Arnold Bennett's *Old Wives' Tale* lacked immediate success. But now they are recognised as classics among the novels of the twentieth century.

So is *They were Defeated*. For me, it carries a vast scholarship as easily as does Santayana's *The Last Puritan*. It is a long tale, but I should not say it is told at leisure. It moves quickly, propelled by a passion that sweeps along like a prairie fire. But though the fire is wide it is, by a miracle such as only the human mind (being divine) can work, a cool, serene fire, and it throws a light into every corner of that period of English history; a period which Miss Veronica Wedgwood is exploring in her noble history of the Civil War.

Richard Church. *JOL*. Jan. 21, 1960, p. 57

Nobody should have known better than Rose Macaulay how dangerous a commodity words can be—especially today, especially the private words of a gifted and known personality. Did she expect these letters [*Letters to a Friend*] to be made public? They were written towards the end of her life to an Anglican priest, Father Hamilton Johnson of the Cowley Fathers' community in Boston, USA. He had known her very slightly through church attendances at the start of the First World War; but in 1916 he left for America and the connection ceased. In 1950 he read for the first time her early novel *They Were Defeated*, and wrote. Rose Macaulay cherished his letters yet thought it courteous to have them destroyed at her death. Her priestly correspondent did not do the same. He enlisted the editorial aid of a Macaulay cousin, Miss Babington Smith, and when he died in March 1961, at the age of 84, the book was already well in hand.

It should be said at once that the publicity which has vapoured up about these letters is quite misleading. Readers need not expect to find in them any intimate revelations—though to be sure, something of whatever may have been edited out of the text is set down in the editorial introduction, oddly recalling those censored Latin schoolroom books which Byron describes in *Don Juan*. But there is little to tell—only that Rose Macaulay had had a 20-year relationship with a married man who died in the early 1940s, and that the artificial compromise of those years seemed to her, in retrospect, vexing and sad.

Nor do the letters offer even the history of a dramatic religious conversion. Rose Macaulay, who came of long lines of clerical ancestors on both sides, had never really been out of the Church's sway. "I am Anglican profoundly," she wrote, "born and bred to it, the heir to it, and now well in it once more. . . . *What* a heritage we have . . ."

. . . It is on the whole a weakened R.M. who shows in these pages; this isn't the image that most of her readers would want to be left with finally. "One should," as she said herself, "consume one's own smoke"; and in the two years of passionate church-going, letter-writing, confessional-visiting, she certainly was not doing that. Happily the story need not end with this volume. For one thing, there is a hint that after 1952 (though a further collection is promised by the present editor Miss Babington Smith) letters to Father Hamilton became "less frequent". And then, in 1956, Rose Macaulay was to publish *The Towers of Trebizond*—surely the most brilliant and valuable novel of all her 50 years' writing. In this fantastic tragical-comedy she was able to look with her familiar sympathetic irony and a fresh tide of wit, and with something deeper too, at all the Macaulay obsessions—travel, the Church, family relationships, women and learning, the pains and the pleasures of love. Certainly there is more in this book on the themes of the letters than in all of the letters themselves. Her genius, after all, worked (as it had all her writing life) through the fictional transmutation, absorbing all problems and doubts, and not through the raw unordered thoughts of the airmail post. Her true smoke-consumer had always been here.

Naomi Lewis. *NS*. Nov. 3, 1961, p. 659

The Rose Macaulay we know through her witty, satirical books—from the early novel *Potterism* to the last and perhaps most winning of her works, *The Towers of Trebizond*—was as much at home in antiquity and in the seventeenth century, as in her own time; in Italy, Spain, Portugal and Turkey, as in England; in the literature of other lands and ages, as in that of her contemporaries. But from these letters emerges a Rose Macaulay who was certainly not heretofore fully understood. Now we see her in the round, three-dimensional in the range of her intellect, the quality of her opinion and the capacity of her heart. . . .

For an already elderly, established, distinguished woman to transcend not only worldly success and diminishing strength but the political, intellectual and moral chaos of the Nineteen Fifties and insist, with a wholly unsentimental, a beautifully precise, a consistently humble insistence upon living by the Reason and the Light she had come to see anew, was no minor victory. Those in England who have raised a hue and cry against the publication of Dame Rose Macaulay's letters to Father Johnson [*Letters to a Friend*] must have forgotten how much more heavily valor weighs on the human scales than mere discretion.

Virgilia Peterson. *NYT*. Feb. 25, 1962, p. 6

MACCAIG, NORMAN (1910–   )

. . . [His] quality of observation is very like Andrew Young's and, indeed, Mr. MacCaig occasionally writes a whole poem to the older poet's sharp formula, and successfully, too. But more frequently the conceit is merely incidental to a larger purpose, and in fact many of the more ambitious poems are extended conceits of considerable complexity. The validity of metaphysical verse such as this [*Riding Lights*] depends on how far the poet can convince the reader that his elaborations correspond to a state of affairs in reality and a real emotion in himself. By this test a fair number of Mr. MacCaig's poems fail to justify themselves. It is true that poems must tool themselves up to manufacture the article they propose to produce, but in Mr. MacCaig's case one is not sure that the article exists independently of the machinery. In other words, he makes not always a point but a pseudo-point, which cannot stand up to examination. . . .

I have dwelt on the faults of *Riding Lights* because it can resist criticism, because it reveals Mr. MacCaig as a poet who has already written some perfect poems ("Climbing Suilven," "Swimming Lizard," "Harpsichord Playing Bach," for instance), provided memorable bits in many more, and seems stuck in neither his Youngish nor Donnesque manner but capable of development in several ways—towards, say, the greater realism hinted at here in the poems with a specific background of Edinburgh. His intellectual approach is prompted by a true and subtle interest in nature, time, and personality, and can never harden into a trick while it remains invigorated by an observation working at the pressure of much of this volume.

Roy Fuller. *L.* July, 1955, pp. 82–83

Mr. MacCaig . . . is very much "Art" and very fond of words like "paradigm." He could be described as a Wallace Stevens Metaphysical with a Scotch tanginess to keep his metaphysics fresh, even if not warm. A good example [*A Common Grace*] is the poem "Ardmore," a completely successful metaphysical lyric. And yet it is amazing how poetry so professional in technique can remain so essentially amateur—the poet engages so little of his person that it remains "week-end poetry," however skilled.

Harry Fainlight. *Enc.* Nov., 1961, p. 72

. . . *A Round of Applause* is . . . disappointing. MacCaig is a poet who always has plenty of profound and original things to say, forcing a personal metaphysics out of that hard, impersonal Scottish landscape. And often he is accurate, incisive and intelligent. But equally often the thought and detail are packed so tight that the verse seems musclebound: awkward without being powerful.

The tension is in the minutiae not in the movement. It is all so concentrated that it seems, in the end, sluggish. I suppose this is because MacCaig is willing to take so little for granted. But he has reached the stage where the very quality which gives his work its distinction is debilitating it.

A. Alvarez. *Obs*. March 10, 1963, p. 24

MACCARTHY, DESMOND (1878–1952)

. . . [He pays] the penalty of the author who writes to please us; he occasionally forgets that there is no need, if he would give pleasure, to be too affable to the slighter modes and prejudices of today.

R. Ellis Roberts. *NSN*. Dec. 5, 1931, p. 720

In an excellent review recently contributed to *The Nation* Lionel Trilling remarked that no critic could possibly be very effective unless he wrote from some definite point of view. Even narrowness or wrong-headedness was, he maintained, preferable on the whole to mere detachment, because even the narrow and the wrong-headed stand for something, and because it is only by standing for something that one can exert can influence.

Undoubtedly there is much to be said for the contention, and undoubtedly the fact that Desmond MacCarthy does not, in this sense, "stand for anything" has something to do with the further fact that after many years of admirable critical writing he is mentioned far less often than other men who are certainly his superiors in nothing unless it be a more definite assertiveness. And yet, firmly as I believe what Mr. Trilling said, I cannot bring myself to reject Mr. MacCarthy's detachment as much as perhaps I should, or wish that he adhered less consistently to the famous formula: *"Je n'impose rien, je ne propose rien; j'expose."* There are, after all, so many activities in which one must be "effective" or fail, so few in which ineffectiveness is compatible with a kind of a success. . . . I confess that I find something infinitely refreshing in the work of a critic who is content to be merely sensitive, receptive, and intelligent. . . .

In any event, I must confess that I like Mr. MacCarthy's volume [*Portraits*] none the less for the fact that the thirty-four essays which it contains are so plainly in the tradition of Sainte-Beuve and Anatole France.

Joseph Wood Krutch. *Nation*. May 25, 1932, p. 603

Behind Desmond MacCarthy lie the uninterrupted centuries of tradition and culture. There is, as ever, an attraction for the new generation of readers in its grandparents, to balance its hardness towards the middle-aged. In a climate for the time unfavourable to [Aldous] Huxley, the trade winds should stand fair for MacCarthy, and it was a happy thought to reprint his *Portraits,* an anthology of thirty-four studies, ranging from Asquith, through Clough and Goethe, Horace and George Moore, Ruskin and Trollope, to Izaak Walton. They are the harvest of an urbane, mature, modest and receptive intellect, the work of a man whose critical faculties are ever tempered by tolerance, humility, understanding and courtesy. The unobtrusive translations of quotations in foreign languages tell us something about the writer.

In a cramped world of two and a quarter billion (American) [*sic*] people, it is increasingly rare and attractive to find a man who approaches a single human being as would a connoisseur some precious *objet d'art.* Himself now an elder statesman of the world of letters, Mr. MacCarthy is especially happy in his treatment of Asquith, with whom he was for many years acquainted, of Balfour and of Gladstone. The portrait of Asquith is a model exercise in the genre, intimate and self-effacing, compact of observation and understanding. What phrase could better indicate the quality of Asquith's mind than MacCarthy's "He drove a Roman road through every subject"?

His natural reverence for distinction extends equally to the writer, and there are valuable notes on Meredith and James. . . .

Henry de Villose. *Adel.* July-Sept., 1950, pp. 370–71

"Memory," he often said, "is an excellent composition." And in the midst of a group which included Lytton Strachey, Virginia Woolf, Maynard Keynes, he stood out in his command of the past, and in his power to rearrange it. I remember one paper of his in particular—if it can be called a paper. Perched away in a corner of Duncan Grant's studio, he had a suitcase open before him. The lid of the case, which he propped up, would be useful to rest his manuscript upon, he told us. On he read, delighting us as usual, with his brilliancy and humanity and wisdom, until—owing to a slight wave of his hand—the suitcase unfortunately fell over. Nothing was inside it. There was no paper, no manuscript. He had been improvising.

E. M. Forster. *Desmond MacCarthy*
(Stanford Dingley, Eng., Mill House Pr.,
1952), pp. 7–8

Desmond MacCarthy did not think much of his own work. In his later years, he would with smiling, rueful sadness compare the novels, biographies, dramas he had once dreamed of writing with what he had in fact achieved; a handful of short stories and reminiscences, a heap of reviews. The thought of this contrast did not sour him: he was too sensible and too unegotistic to allow it to do so. But remembering it cast a shadow over his spirit.

It need not have done so. Desmond MacCarthy's achievement was one to be proud of. Moreover, the form it took was in fact the form most suitable to his talent. The long single book was not the right unit for this to display itself, any more than it was for Addison or Hazlitt. Perhaps he had not the faculty for design on a big scale that was needed for it, and certainly it would not have given him the chance to exhibit the variety of his interests and sympathies. This was extraordinary. He is usually described as a literary critic. Indeed, he was one of the best that England ever produced. But the phrase does not portray him completely; for it implies one primarily interested in the art of literature, whereas Desmond MacCarthy, like Dr. Johnson, was first of all a student of human nature. Because he loved and appreciated good writing, he particularly enjoyed studying men as they revealed themselves through the medium of books. But he was just as ready to study them directly in actual persons and events and just as equipped to record his observations in the form of a memoir or a short story. This collection of tales and reviews and reminiscences by him is no heterogeneous hotch-potch, but a unity. For in it he employs different forms to achieve the same end, which was to express his own profound, acute, individual vision of human nature.

> David Cecil. Foreword, in Desmond MacCarthy,
> *Humanities* (MacGibbon and Kee, 1953), p. vi

When Desmond MacCarthy died, we lost the best of contemporary critics. If this judgment seems coloured by my gratitude and affection, let me ask what other writer in our time has responded to such a variety of work with an appreciation at once so discriminating and so infectious? His books take up only a small space on our shelves: except for a slight volume dealing with the Court Theatre, all his work was done for periodicals, and is now easily accessible only in the selections made by his friend Pearsall Smith, and later by Lady MacCarthy and Mr. James MacGibbon. If, however, an academic writer condemns it for this reason as journalism, he should similarly dismiss the greater part of Addison and Hazlitt.

> Raymond Mortimer. Foreword, in Desmond
> MacCarthy, *Memories* (MacGibbon and Kee,
> 1953), pp. 5–6

MACDIARMID, HUGH (1892–   )

It was not until C. M. Grieve, writing under the name of Hugh MacDiarmid, published *A Drunk Man Looks at a Thistle,* a long poem written in a synthetic Scots dug out from the whole treasure of the Scots language as far back as the Middle Ages, that a new spirit sprang to life in Scottish literature. The nearest approach in English to Grieve's experiment with words was that epic of C. M. Doughty's called *The Dawn in Britain,* though Doughty never strained his reader's philological erudition like Grieve. It is in reading a poem like *A Drunk Man Looks at a Thistle* that I am driven to face the possibility of poetry's becoming entirely hierophantic in the future, and able to appreciate that *The Waste Land* may burn with authentic fire, even if for myself it may present the appearance of wanton obscurity. The very nature of the medium of communication "Hugh MacDiarmid" has chosen forbids the possibility of any direct communication except to an infinitesimal minority, who, feeding on his poetry, must be the means of conveying it to the majority. I have no hesitation in calling C. M. Grieve the most powerful intellectually and emotionally fertilizing force Scotland has known since the death of Burns. Yet owing to the peculiar conditions of literature to-day few poets can have had such a small body of actual readers.

Compton Mackenzie. *Literature in My Time*
(Rich and Cowan, 1933), pp. 239–40

"Hugh MacDiarmid" is a baffling mixture. But it is not difficult to extract from these essays [*At the Sign of the Thistle*] a few principles for which Hugh MacDiarmid stands. The first essay, on "English Ascendancy in British Literature," presents his favourite thesis. The Scottish people have been forced to appreciate and to practise modes of expression essentially foreign to their native genius; and we must remedy this deplorable state of affairs. This is the cardinal point in Hugh MacDiarmid's programme. In "The Purpose of the Free Man" he gives his second point, which is concerned largely with the high spiritual as well as material value of the nationalist ideal and with the nature of individualism. In "Problems of Poetry Today" he presents his case for the "cerebration" of poetry, a process to be applied to the language as well as to the thought of the poet. In "The Case for Synthetic Scots" he defends his own practice in this connection by a series of questionable *a priori* assertions combined with a number of remotely relevant allusions. . . . There is also much general abuse of cultural "middle men" who spoil everything by talking down to the people, and endeavouring to explain things which should never be explained. . . .

There are many valuable things said in these essays. But the author is incapable of pursuing an argument with straightforward logic. Over and over again he is violently deflected from his course by some irrelevant bias.

His sense of proportion is woefully distorted; but everything he writes is a challenge to reconsider fundamentals, and that constitutes a sound claim to recognition.

LL. Aug., 1934, pp. 636–40

At a time when Scots poetry consisted of the sort of thing that might be imagined to appeal to the Glasgow Stock Exchange, and when research into Scots literature was of the type that collated all the passages in Burns that referred to birds, and classified them under Birds of Passage, Birds of Ill Omen, etc., C. M. Grieve did some necessary scavenging and cleared away a lot of literary scrap by debunking the St. Robert Burns of Burns's nights and reasserting the true claims of Burns to our attention as a poet. He himself employed Scots not nostalgically or sentimentally, but by putting it to adult, contemporary uses. He has been elaborately cold-shouldered by the Scottish press, criticised spitefully by Scottish public figures ("Yahoos," he calls them), and made the subject of a mean-minded "whispering campaign" for his pains. Almost alone he worked to rescue Scotland from provincialism, and in doing so tended to become a sort of second Admirable Crichton: he tried not only to be its critic and poet, but also its philosopher, archlinguist, Celtic folklorist, botanist, chemist, professor of semantics, orientalist and so on. To all comers he was also to prove a very good hand at the more virulent and envenomed sort of invective. The magnitude of his task was bound to sour the good nature of the most magnanimous of men and seriously corrode whatever critical acumen he started out with: and these 426 pages [*Lucky Poet*] bear ample evidence of the strain.

John Durkan. *Scy*. Winter, 1943, p. 72

His achievements as a poet are twofold. His earlier work established the Scots' language in its rightful place again amongst the tongues of the world. Into the lyrics in *Sangschaw* and *Penny Wheep* he put a vast amount of his observation and love of nature, at once erudite and sensuous. Thereafter he set about the task of intellectualizing Scottish poetry, and he achieved this purpose with a thoroughness that makes the intellectualization of English poetry by English poets of the twenties and thirties look childish. His work in this vein is vast in conception, vigorous in tone, and massive in execution.

Maurice Lindsay. *LL*. Dec., 1943, pp. 164–65

MacDiarmid is probably the least known of poets in our language who might conceivably be called "great." When I say "our language," I must correct myself at once. His finest work is in Scots, and to this fact is due his relative obscurity. He at first seems a very special kind of acquired taste, writing as he does in a half-foreign tongue that requires a sympathetic ear and, often, a glossary to be understood. . . .

MacDiarmid in this ("O wha's been here fore me, lass") does a quietly extraordinary thing. He has written a modern poem which re-possesses not only the diction and rhythm of the medieval folk-ballad, but also its implicit mentality—in this instance, its thrilled awe and ter-ror of the supernatural. It is difficult to think of more than two or three other "literary" ballads that approach this achievement. A poem like "The Rime of the Ancient Mariner" uses many folk-elements, but makes of them an elaborate embroidery with much sophisticated overlay. Mac-Diarmid's poem, it is true, is a sophistication also; without really violat-ing the native simplicity and "rudeness" of the form, he has buried intel-lectual sharpness and paradox within the demonic mystery and, as part of this effect, has given us a more suggestive imagery than we ordinarily find in the folk-ballad.

M. L. Rosenthal. The Modern Poets (N.Y.,
Oxford Univ. Pr., 1960), pp. 132–33

The inconsistencies and violences of his thought are bound up with his drive toward realizing his almost mystical vision of a people re-deemed from fakery and perpetual second-handedness. His poetry, which ranges from his wonderfully articulated early Scots lyrics, where reality is penetrated to its inexpressible core with an amazing combination of tenderness and violence, to his later long discursive pieces in English with their long Whitman-like catalogues covering the whole world of modern knowledge, defies classification.

There is nothing in English or Scottish poetry like those wonderful lyrics that make up the sequence "Au Clair de la Lune" from his vol-ume *Sangschaw,* or like the magnificently phrased mixture of natural ob-servation, grotesquerie, and mysticism in "Ex Vermibus," from the same volume. He can move from the cosmic to the intimate, from religious to domestic imagery, from eternity (a favorite word) to the kitchen sink or the farmyard dunghill or the slum streets of Glasgow. His poems seem to grow out of the language ("not an idea gradually shaping itself in words, but deriving entirely from words," he once explained) but yet at the same time to be the compelled utterance of an intense personal vision.

David Daiches. NYT. Feb. 25, 1962, p. 6

Hugh MacDiarmid's reputation south of the border is uncertain, and he probably likes it that way. Until this edition of *Collected Poems* his work has been almost impossible to obtain; his last book of verse was published in London in the mid-thirties. Much of the present volume is in a particularly *recherché* form of Scots: he seems literally to have reinvented the language from a mixture of Dunbar's poems, Ibrox Park chat and Jamieson's *Etymological Dictionary of the Scottish Language*. Without him Lallans would never have existed. Scarcely any critics have written on him; though the new *Festschrift* has useful essays by David Craig, Edwin Morgan, David Daiches and Walter Keir, no comment by outsiders is included.

With his virulent anti-Englishism, MacDiarmid clearly wouldn't give tuppence for what is thought of him here, anyway. Yet to celebrate his seventieth birthday the adulation, no doubt, will flow in. He is, after all, the most important Scottish poet since Burns, and the first English-speaking writer to make real poetry out of Communism.

MacDiarmid's *Collected Poems* represent a massive achievement. Massive in both senses: although a good many pieces have been dropped by the author, the volume still runs to almost 500 pages; and among them is poetry of the first importance.

But it is also an extraordinarily patchy achievement. Like Shelley, who was the last important English radical poet, or like Ezra Pound with whom, despite their politics, MacDiarmid has a good deal in common, he has written far too much. Even the first slight lyrics run on and on. He finds it hard to let a subject be, or to distinguish between what he once called "The Kind of Poetry I Want" and the kind of poetry he can write.

A. Alvarez. *Obs.* Aug. 12, 1962, p. 17

MACDOUGALL, ROGER (1910–   )

Roger MacDougall's second play [*The Gentle Gunman*] endorses and amplifies the promise held forth by his first, *Macadam and Eve*. . . . It is shapely, the dialogue is meaty, the characterisation convincing and the action exciting. We are made to feel that within a minute anything may happen. Whether anything does or not is of less importance in the theatre. All the gunmen in the play are comparatively gentle. Their bark is worse than their bite. Though their fingers are ever on the trigger, something always occurs to stay pressure and the only serious injury is the result of a road accident.

H. G. M. *TW*. Sept., 1950, p. 8

Roger MacDougall, a Scot born in 1910, became known only in the early nineteen-fifties when he had four plays produced in London within three years: none with any remote family resemblance. MacDougall has something of Ustinov's inventive faculty without the same exuberant, headlong wit. His humour, as in *Macadam and Eve,* can labour. This was his first play. In it he raises the Old Adam: an immortal who has been both the Wandering Jew and Shakespeare in his time, but who turns up (with a Scottish accent) in the damp resort of Tillyfruin, still remembering Eden and still tortured by Eve. There are fun and good sense in the play, but though it is probably the best fantasy we recall about Adam in Scotland, it babbles on too long in its fantastic-loquacious manner. I much preferred *The Gentle Gunman,* produced later in the year (1950), in which MacDougall united a charming gift for seeing both sides of an argument, with an equally agreeable delight in the kind of boys' adventure story that insists upon stick-'em-up raids and lethal weapons. Although technically an unsatisfying play, it is better in the theatre—and in the text—than some technically perfect, but stone-cold, pieces.

J. C. Trewin. *Dramatists of Today*
(Staples Pr., 1953), p. 200

MACHEN, ARTHUR (1863–1947)

Some thirty-odd years ago a young man of twenty-two, the son of a Welsh clergyman, fresh from school and with his head full of a curiously occult medievalism, privately acquired from yellowed palimpsests and dog-eared volumes of black letter, wrote a classic. More, he had it published. Only one review copy was sent out; that was to *Le Livre,* of Paris. It fell into the hands of Octave Uzanne, who instantly ordered Rabelais and Boccaccio to "shove over" on the immortal seats and make room by their side for the author. The Book was *The Chronicle of Clemendy;* the author, Arthur Machen.

Three years ago, about, not long after the great war first shook the world, a London evening newspaper published inconspicuously a purely fictional account of a supposed incident of the British retreat from Mons. It described the miraculous intervention of the English archers of Agincourt at a time when the British were sore pressed by the German hordes. Immediately, churchmen, spiritualists, and a host of others, seized upon it as an authentic record and the miracle as an omen. In the hysteria that followed, Arthur Machen, its author, found himself a talked-of man, because he wrote to the papers denying that the narrative was factual. Later, when his little volume, *The Bowmen and Other Legends of the War,* appeared in print, it met with an extraordinary and rather impertinent success. . . .

Of course, it is exactly because he does not write books of the ordinary kind that Arthur Machen's reputation as a writer was not made long ago. His apotheosis will begin after his death. . . .

More than Hawthorne or Tolstoy, Machen is a novelist of the soul. He writes of a strange borderland, lying somewhere between Dreams and Death, peopled with shades, beings, spirits, ghosts, men, women, souls—what shall we call them?—the very notion of whom stops vaguely just short of thought. He writes of the life Satyr-ic. For him Pan is not dead; his votaries still whirl through woodland windings to the mad pipe that was Syrinx, and carouse fiercely in unchanged forest grottoes (hidden somewhere, perhaps in the fourth dimension!). His meddling with the crucibles of science is appalling in its daring, its magnificence, and its horror. Even the greater works of fictional psychology—*Dr. Jekyll and Mr. Hyde,* if you like—shrink before his astounding inferences and suggestions.

Vincent Starrett. Arthur Machen (Chicago,
Walter M. Hill, 1918), pp. 9–12

The Hill of Dreams and his volume of tales "in the manner of the Renaissance" interested me in parts, but they did not make me a Machenite any more than reading James Branch Cabell makes me a Cabellite. Medievalism, introspection and borderland imaginations do not enthrall me, unless done by a Pater, a Shorthouse, or a Stevenson.

Hieroglyphics is a different matter. It was written between 1890 and 1900, but I did not read it until two years ago. I went frisking through it like a colt in a meadow, enjoying every page; then I went back to the beginning and read it all again carefully. If anything could make me a Machenite, it would be this *Hieroglyphics: a Note upon Ecstasy in Literature.* It is a monologue on literary valuations by a supposed "obscure literary hermit" (A. M. of course) done with sanity, insight, and humour, done at a gallop by this delightful hermit who is always "ready to defend the thesis that, all the arts being glorious, the literary art is the most glorious and wonderful of all."

C. Lewis Hind. More Authors and I (N.Y.,
Dodd, Mead, 1922), pp. 201–2

In *The Secret Glory* Mr. Machen attempts to describe the rebellion of a Celtic mystic against Anglicanism and the public school tradition. I say "attempts," because neither Anglicanism nor education interests him sufficiently to make him barb his satire. But the mysticism excites his dark and fantastic imagination, and there are bursts, in the latter half of the book, of successful paradox. . . . He incants Welsh names, and, as so often on lighter ground, he displays great power of giving a queer twist to the least uncanny events. Naturally, he fails to inform us what there was so remarkable in the Welsh Church which was ruined by "the Yellow Hag of Pestilence, the Red Hag of Rome, and the Black Hag of Geneva"; consequently, he fails to show why Ambrose [the hero] should have had all the spiritual experience desired in his own school chapel.

H. C. Harwood. *OutL*. March 11, 1922, p. 193

Mr. Arthur Machen gives a significantly playful subtitle to *The London Adventure: The Art of Wandering*. His long practice as a journalist gives him a certain privilege, and if this is a lazy book it is so because the author has earned the right to be lazy. The story—theme—argument— no, rather, the drift of the book is this, Mr. Machen has told some friend that he is to write a book about London, a really great book this time. *The London Adventure* wanders on and on, with little to keep it going or together, beyond the author's repeated returns to this book that he is going to begin tomorrow or next week. . . . In the course of writing he touches upon a great many interesting topics, but instead of letting us have the benefit of his ripe thoughts upon them he is so determined to wander that he nearly succeeds in making us angry. Once or twice he is very successful in recalling the feelings awakened by some little known part of London . . . and there are necessarily many pleasant personal touches and some few scraps of real autobiography. But of the *Art* of wandering, if such an art there is, Mr. Machen makes no exposition in this little book.

Frank Kendon. *LM*. March, 1925, pp. 547–48

The point on which attention may be focused is that while Machen is indubitably a mystic, in spite of (or because of) this fact, he is no longer an obscurity. His whole conception of literature is mystic, as any one may find out for himself by perusing *Hieroglyphics,* a volume which offers a test by which one may make the distinction between mere books and books which are works of art. Strangely enough—this correlation is almost unexampled in the world of letters—he has been consistent in creating his own works of fiction according to his own defined formula. One subject has always intrigued him, the rending of the veil, and the danger that awaits the adventurer who makes this dread experiment. Further, as he tells us in so many different ways in *Far Off Things,* his method has invariably been the same, to proceed from the external fact, a house, a mountain, a sunset, or a tree, to the internal, subconscious suggestion. With Hazlitt, he believes that all men of genius relate what they remember of what they knew before they were eighteen.

To the reader unskilled in such mysteries, *Far Off Things* will appear to be little more than a somewhat disconnected account of certain places, people, and incidents in the author's early life. Nevertheless, even such a reader will not find the book lacking in charm, for the prose is finely distinguished, simple, supple, and stamped with the writer's personality, and the incidents, places, and people described are far from uninteresting in themselves. But to one who comes to this book prepared, so to speak, by a reading of Mr. Machen's other work, every page, every line, in *Far Off Things* falls into its place as a symmetrical detail in a whole which is only concerned with a consideration of method in writing, the method of an adept.

Carl Van Vechten. *Excavations* (N.Y.,
Knopf, 1926), pp. 163–64

It is doubtful whether this collection of the best [*Tales of Horror and the Supernatural*]—so long out of print—of Arthur Machen's excursions into the horrible and the supernatural will revive any widespread interest in a fine but unsatisfying writer. The twenty-five years since the last of these tales was written have taken the edge off the particular sense of evil with which he was concerned. What one remembers after reading is what one remembers from long ago: the magnificent feeling for lonely and forbidding place, the scenes of ancient evil; the preoccupation with the sinister world which for Machen lay always under the daily surface; the dimness of characterization; and the long-drawn-out unclimactic climaxes of horror seen through a glass darkly. The failure here is that of most such tales: the atmosphere is always more convincing than anything that happens. The secret places visited by the bewitched child in "The White People" are unforgettable, and so are the Welsh countryside in "The Terror" and the mounting horror of "The Great God Pan," but one forgets what finally comes of all this. In purely rational writers such as Mrs. Radcliffe, also a master of atmosphere, these matters are likely to be better managed; there is the horrible and then there is a commonplace explanation. Although the art is impure, it has a kind of coherence. But Machen, abominating nineteenth-century science and twentieth-century psychoanalysis, believed in the Celtic occult, which in its very nature is not capable of rational explanation; so his dénouements are vague just where they should be clear. One wants to know about the evil which lies under the surface, and the atmosphere does not compensate for his failure to explain the inexplicable.

Ernest Jones. *Nation*. Aug. 14, 1948, p. 190

MACINNES, COLIN (1914—   )

As the presence in England of Africans and West Indians becomes increasingly noticeable, serious articles begin to appear in the press about whether or not this country is creating a "colour problem" for herself. From these, and from many private discussions of the subject, the human element is either absent altogether or else only present in the form of prejudice, and the understanding that comes from intimate first-hand knowledge is almost invariably lacking. Colin MacInnes's novel *City of Spades* imparts this knowledge more enjoyably and, I should have thought, more valuably than any statistical social survey. The city is London, the spades are the coloured immigrants and anyone not a spade is a jumble. To some people Mr. MacInnes's book may come as a slight shock. His attitude is far from the embarrassed, apologetic indignation of the liberal jumble as it is expressed by many intellectual spades; it may disconnect both races, but it is bound to stimulate them and should give offence to neither. And it will do no harm to those readers ignorant of the subject to learn that in many cases of miscegenation it is the spade who is felt by both parties to be conferring the greater favour.

Francis Wyndham. *Spec.* Sept. 13, 1957, p. 348

Until quite recently I believed (consequent upon reading his *City of Spades,* but not the blurb) that Mr. Colin MacInnes was a black man. Indeed, I not only believed it; I told other people as much, including a Cabinet Minister who wanted to know about him for some State purpose. For all I know, the belief may have rippled outwards from my ill-aimed pebble, so that there are now huge and growing files in various government offices, all containing references to the blackness of Mr. MacInnes, and hundreds, if not thousands, of people going about the country spreading the tale. Soon, perhaps, there will be nobody left to deny it, and Mr. MacInnes will be accused of imposture when he tries to sign in at hotels, or arrested when he applies for a new passport. It is a frightening load of responsibility for me to bear, and I am glad of the opportunity, in discussing his new book, to shed a little of it.

The trouble is that having read *England, Half English* I am rather more than half-inclined to believe that I was right all the time. At least, if Mr. MacInnes is not black, then he must be green. Or he has two heads, or three legs, or a Cyclops eye, or telepathic powers, or else he is one of the anthropophagi and men whose heads do grow beneath their shoulders. At any rate, he is different from us. To begin with, he is the first cousin, twice removed, of both Stanley Baldwin and Rudyard Kipling, the great-grandson of Burne-Jones, and the son of Angela Thirkell. (I am not making this up—though *he* may be.) Also, he was brought up in Australia. Also, he is a highly gifted writer of romantic novels (wrongly, and to his chagrin, called documentary) and of a recently published book about Sidney Nolan.

But all that could happen to anybody. What sets Mr. MacInnes quite apart is the fact that in him we have one of the most penetrating, sensible, balanced, yet deeply passionate observers of England to check in for centuries. Indeed, apart from Mr. Nirad Chaudhuri, whose electrifying book *A Passage to England* appeared a year or two ago, I can hardly think of any commentator on the ways of the English—not Voltaire, not Karel Capek, not G. J. Renier—who has seen this country so wisely and so well.

Bernard Levin. *Spec.* Sept. 1, 1963, p. 294

MACKAIL, J. W. (1859–1945)

In the bulk of his book [*Studies of English Poets*] he cultivates that unpromising field, the eighteenth century, which has been as unwisely adulated as decried. His critical attitude is admirably suited to his purpose. . . . No one has better dealt than he (though others have attempted it) with the textbook-propagated absurdity of Matthew Arnold that Pope is a classic of our prose. He does not merely argue that Pope is a poet; he makes us feel it. And with the much abused, little read Young he is even more effective, or perhaps only seems to be so because effective exposition was so much needed here. All these, under his hand, stand out like figures on the great roll, even if in the same volume he has printed rather superficial papers on Shakespeare and William Morris which have not the same value.

SR. Feb. 27, 1926, p. 262

By the death of J. W. Mackail on December 13, 1945, the [British] Academy lost a distinguished ex-President, a fine classical scholar with a wide knowledge of English and European literature. He wrote many volumes of criticism, chiefly on Greek and English poetry, which, while they bear witness to profound learning, are instinct with the love of literature and especially of poetry for its own sake. This love, based on an intimate understanding, it was his aim to stimulate in others, because he believed that poetry was not merely an enhancement of life, but an inspiration and a guide. . . .

The election of Mackail to the Professorship of Poetry at Oxford in 1906 gave him the opportunity of using his store of literary knowledge in a wider field than hitherto. He lectured more frequently than most holders of the Chair and his lectures were well attended and highly appreciated. He published them in three substantial volumes: the *Springs of Helicon,* 1909, *Lectures on Greek Poetry,* 1910, and *Lectures on Poetry,* 1911. Though the bulk of the poetry on which he commented as Professor is either Greek or English, he included in the last of the three volumes lectures given elsewhere on Virgil and on the *Divine Comedy*—Mackail was a great Dante scholar—and two of the Oxford lectures were on Arabic poetry, which he knew only in translations. The range is wide and the subjects might at first sight seem miscellaneous. But through them all run two threads which bind them together. These are enunciated in the "Definition of Poetry," which opens the third volume, and become more explicit in the concluding lecture on "The Progress of Poetry." The first is the conception of poetry as at once a function of life and therefore sharing life's quality of movement, the interpretation of life and therefore organic, and also a pattern of life, which, in words which Mackail quotes more than once from W. B. Yeats, "condenses out of the flying vapours of the world an image of human perfection." And the second thread is the belief in the continuous progress of poetry, at least in the western world. This he sees, as Gray did in the Ode, constantly referred to in these volumes, as passing from Greece to Rome and from them both to England, always moving, constantly changing, yet ever the same, like the movements of a flock of sheep, which, as Mackail quotes from Lucretius, seen from a distant hill looks like a still patch of white. He does not deny the occasional advent of other influences, such as that of Italian and even of Arabic poetry, which influenced the early French epics and through them Chaucer. It is perhaps not remarkable that there is no reference to German poetry, which might seem to lie outside the general current, but it is odd in one to whom the language and thought of the Bible meant so much that there is but little recognition of Hebrew poetry as a formative influence on the English poets.

Cyril Bailey. *Proceedings of British Academy,*
Vol. 33 (1947), pp. 1, 6–7

MACKENZIE, COMPTON (1883–   )

Those who found in Mr. Mackenzie's *Passionate Elopement*—which we noticed just a year ago—a mature humour, a ready love of humanity and Nature, and an extraordinary faculty of sympathy with its time that made it remarkable and enjoyable above most of the first novels of recent years, will turn with interest, perhaps with excitement, to see whether Mr. Mackenzie has been able to carry over these qualities into a second book treating, as *Carnival* does, of contemporary life. They will not be disappointed. *Carnival* is the story of a girl's life, told through from birth to its too early close with a wealth of loving detail, with a humanity and an unfailing humour which mark Mr. Mackenzie as a novelist with the ability to see life clearly and whole; not merely the selected life of his graceful earlier tale, but the very much more complicated life we are living today. It is of the best augury that, turning from a recreation of the England of Richardson and Fielding, he has shed the disquisitions and freedoms which those novelists allowed themselves, and which were quite proper to his earlier book, and has written a novel that for clearness and spareness can leave nothing to be desired.

OutL. Jan. 27, 1912, p. 137

Mr. Compton Mackenzie, for the moment, has eschewed serious achievement. Nevertheless he has achieved the most genuine personal success, not only of the season, but of the year. *Poor Relations* has been everybody's diversion, and it has been everybody's diversion because it has been Mr. Mackenzie's. There is plenty of time to take Michael Fane and his Sylvia through the rest of the war; in the meantime Mr. Mackenzie is out for a holiday. This very sound instinct of Mr. Mackenzie's has been so heartily endorsed by his public that it becomes permissible to doubt whether Michael Fane and his Sylvia ever will be taken through the rest of the war. But sufficient for a season are the novels thereof; and Mr. Mackenzie has achieved a success which may incline his extremely individual gifts, we feel, into any direction, even into that of the theatre. *Poor Relations* already has all the air of running an uncountable number of nights. . . .

P. P. Howe. *FR*. Jan., 1920, p. 66

Where gifts are eminent the failure is eminent: hence this preface to remarks upon the novels of Mr. Compton Mackenzie. Diligent, observant, experienced, inexhaustible, or at any rate unexhausted, he has made his opportunities and gained a hearing; indeed, as he reminded us in the second volume of *Sinister Street,* he has won the greater advantage of a hearing refused, the libraries having so ineffably rejected the first volume. Nevertheless, from him that hath not— What is it, in fact, that has deprived him of the purest fruit of the gifts which he has? I make no attempt to disguise the fact that Mr. Mackenzie appears to be a writer who is not an imaginative artist, yet who might have been an imaginative artist; a novelist who has not concerned himself with life at all save in its external and mechanic motions. He has not confined himself to a single manner: his first book, *The Passionate Elopement,* was an eighteenth-century story in a style familiarized by less capable and less versatile practitioners. . . . But Mr. Mackenzie's second novel, *Carnival,* disappointed expectation by being readable. Like some of its successors, it might be mistaken for realistic; while another, *Guy and Pauline,* might be termed idyllic by those who love the phrase. He . . . changes; he is a part of all that he has met; and you wonder at length what *he* is. For myself, I am reminded frequently of an ingenious character seen in provincial music-halls, who to the eyes of a happy audience swiftly and imperceptibly invests and divests himself of many costumes of marvellous hue—one growing plain as another is impetuously flung off, blue gloves giving place to pink, a crimson shirt to an emerald, a shooting-jacket to a dinner-jacket—until I laugh unrestrainably.

Mr. Mackenzie has not sought a fugitive and cloistered virtue; his characters . . . mingle in the great world without exemption from its follies and its vices. He loves their activities; he sets them going and follows their whirring motion with the ruthless gaiety of a child playing with toys, who stops them, breaks them, and sometimes sets them going again. He understands mechanics, and they must move; and when they are run down in one book he winds them up again for another. He hurries hither and thither, clutching at the skirts of perpetual motion like that other pageant master, time. His scene is the capitals of Europe or a railway train between them. He shares with his characters, of whatever age, their brilliant youth. He invents untiringly. He does not vex himself or his readers with description, but if he pauses to paint he paints with unmistakable bright colours. He writes clearly: there is seldom a slovenly sentence, never a memorable one. He has a cruelly accurate ear for slang, and presents vulgarity with fond verisimilitude. Femininity haunts him; his flowers, even, remind him of frills. Something of extreme youth clings to his books—its zestfulness, curiosity, indiscriminateness, and its unregretful volatility. But when, you may ask, remembering at once his gifts and his opportunities, his gifts and the world amid which they are exercised, when will he grow up? . . . When, amid all his brief preoccupations with men and women, will he touch life?

John Freeman. *LM.* Feb., 1920, pp. 448–50

Modern criticism has decided that, for all his outspoken revelations of the underworld, Mr. Compton Mackenzie is essentially romantic. He does not, in fact, see life as it is, but as he desires it to be; that is, as it will best illustrate the characters of his imagination, best occupy the light splendour and swift precision of his most opulent vocabulary. As he says of his own Michael, even his conception of irregularity is essentially romantic. He has invented London and peopled it with marionettes. Maybe the fact should not diminish our admiration as, certainly, it cannot decrease our enjoyment. The credit is all his own; he is quite irresistible. The keen vitality of his work, its sublime self-confidence, its youth, its colour and its movement, positively forbid reflection. We forgive the melodrama and condone the hysteria. The swift rush of ideas carry us captive; the brilliant pictures intoxicate; the narrative marches triumphant through a thousand fine threads—crossing each other again and again, darting hither and thither, yet never knotted or ravelled, ragged or in confusion, never broken in loose ends.

R. Brimley Johnson. *Some Contemporary Novelists*
(Leonard Parsons, 1922), p. 131

There is truer psychology in Mackenzie's novels than in the precious novels of most of our professed psychologists. He has done bigger work than theirs with a more modest conception of the novelist's function. "I confess that I like a book to be readable," he once wrote; "it seems to me that a capacity for entertaining a certain number of people is the chief justification for writing novels." He deprecates this as "a lowbrowed ambition," but it was high enough for the great novelists of the past, and the pseudo-medical methods of Freudism do not look like producing any that are greater.

Arthur St. John Adcock. *Gods of Modern Grub Street*
(Sampson Low, Marston, 1923), p. 190

Mr. Mackenzie's account [*Greek Memories*] of how he tried to establish an efficient branch of the Intelligence Service in Athens during the last War is now permitted publication. It is more pertinent today than it would have been when originally written, and it is still more important to read it than to spend time on the dozens of hastily manufactured books upon dictatorship in the Czech betrayal. *Greek Memories* is essential, not only for its picture of Greece and for its implication of what the official Secrets Act is able to do, but because it adds another piece to the puzzle which has fascinated for years; why do certain Englishmen continue to believe in England?

Bryher. *LL*. Sept., 1939, p. 494

All his life he has combined a detached professionalism with an intense and private passion that could spring only out of a religious faith that has been unwavering. Here is the secret of his individuality. It has set the tone of his work, dominating whatever theme might be under his hand, whether a novel, a chapter in history, a commissioned story of some industrial organization, or even a farce such as *Whiskey Galore.* The author of all these various excursions has been the individual Compton Mackenzie, a man of single faith, always defensive of that faith with the weapons of irony, ridicule, gusty laughter, and not infrequently the poignard of anger.

But there is the more positive side to the signature of that faith, manifesting itself in tenderness of mood, a fine, gentle relationship with his fellow creatures, based on respect for their personal isolation and integrity. It made itself known early, in *Sinister Street,* in that exquisite lyrical novel *Guy and Pauline,* and above all in *The Four Winds of Love.* This last major work of fiction has not yet been fully appreciated. It appeared in sequence just at the time when the Second World War started, and was thus overlaid by events.

Richard Church. JOL. Dec. 22, 1960, p. 792

MACNEICE, LOUIS (1907–1963)

Mr. MacNeice is not a great poet—in these days of superlatives, it is, perhaps, necessary to state this—but, to me, he is far more pleasing than many better-known contemporary poets. He has the great virtue of being entirely unaffected which, especially in view of the attitude he takes, is a definite achievement. He is what the unsympathetic might call a dilettante, and he is quite aware of this. He is also aware of the complicated social background of the time, and of the isolation which it imposes, of necessity, on a man who finds his greatest delight in what so many consider the surface things of life—not only those things which must remain the same whatever social upheaval may take place, but in the sensual impressions that are a direct result of contemporary conditions.

F. Chapman. Scy. Sept., 1935, pp. 300–1

Mr. MacNeice's publishers point out that his position "was incontestably established in 1935" by the publication of his *Poems.* Therefore the present collection [*The Earth Compels*] can hope to do little more than corroborate his position, and this it does. Although the rather liverish touch of penetration which distinguished his *Poems* has not yet evolved itself into a passion at all comparable with that of Swift, which is a metamorphosis we are not entitled to expect, nevertheless these poems have the two major virtues of being written by a conscientious poet, and of being completely true to their own causes. I mean that when Mr. Mac-Neice writes a poem about the Hebridean Islands, he writes a poem about the Hebridean Islands; and this is an extremely difficult thing for a poet to do. Matthew Arnold noticed it when he applauded the objectivity of the Greek genius.

George Barker. *LL*. Summer, 1938, p. 80

Now that the disturbance caused by the much-advertised impact of Auden, Spender, and Day Lewis has somewhat abated, it would appear that the most mature and in many ways the most interesting poet of this group is Louis MacNeice. As the publishers say of his last book, *The Earth Compels* (1938), now that he has arrived he needs no advertisement. MacNeice has quietly profited by the experiments of the other three without allowing himself to be taken in by any of their more facile enthusiasms. He is not concerned with their problems of growing-up because he is grown-up already. We may see in his example the much-talked-of ideal of the poet integrating himself with society. MacNeice is very much awake to everything going on around him, but he has sufficient strength and integrity to go his own way as well. His great value for us is that he is not ashamed to lead his own life, nor does he pretend to be something other than he is. He does not strike heroic attitudes or adopt a platform manner of address. He is not difficult or obscure, because he knows what he feels and thinks and is not afraid to say it out. You can feel at ease with him because he is not concerned with telling you what you ought to feel and think. These qualities are rare in modern poetry.

Philip Henderson. *The Poet and Society* (Secker and Warburg, 1939), pp. 226–27

Modern Poetry is a "plea for impure poetry," that is for poetry conditioned by the poet's life and the world around him. . . . Mr. MacNeice does three things; he sketches his own literary self-portrait, he attempts to establish himself and his friends as the poetic successors of Eliot and Yeats and he adds chapters on such topics as imagery and rhythm. The treatment given to these subjects is of a kind that one would ordinarily expect from someone who had read nothing more advanced than a school history of literature, though . . . the tone is one of deliberation and of authority. . . .

Since the *Times Literary Supplement* gave the book a lengthy review praising Mr. MacNeice's critical "detachment," in which he is compared to Coleridge writing on Wordsworth, and since it also made it the text for a first leader, I do not think that it is shouting "Wolf! Wolf!" to suggest that *Modern Poetry* is a sign of a concerted movement in the literary world. . . .

For all his newly-acquired Marxist sympathies Mr. MacNeice is here playing the well-known bourgeois game of passing off the mediocre and the watered down as the excellent, and he does it with all the pompousness, irresponsibility and tendentiousness which characterize the older generation of middlebrow propagandists, whom *Scrutiny* used to refer to as the literary racketeers.

Geoffrey Walton. *Scy*. March, 1939, pp. 437–39

In his *Modern Poetry* he takes in his stride the values of the metaphysical tradition, casually asserting where Mr. Brooks militantly asserts, for he is concerned with the freedom more than the purity of poetry. He remarks that we still do not know whether it is better to aim at Dr. Johnson's "wide effulgence" or to attempt Donne's "analytick" approach; he adds that judgment by hard-and-fast rules, whether Johnson's or Mr. Brooks', finds a greater distinction between one kind of poem and another than there is in fact; he is willing to allow the poet to express beliefs, make direct statements, even moralize. Mr. MacNeice's book is indeed somewhat disappointing. One might hope for more sensitive, illuminating observations on the craft of poetry, his own and that of his contemporaries; he is less acute here than the new critics. Also his catholicity and his social conscience seem a little self-conscious, as products of the recent rediscovery that the poet is "Man Functioning," just as his candor and unpretentiousness are a little studied. "I would have a poet able-bodied," he says, "fond of talking, a reader of newspapers, capable of pity and laughter, informed in economics, appreciative of women, involved in personal relationships, actively interested in politics, susceptible to physical impressions." This is fine and hearty; but it does not make for fine distinctions, and in his heartiness Mr. MacNeice may blur some important ones.

Yet he is more refreshing than most poets who talk shop, and an excellent antidote for puritanical habits of thought.

H. J. Muller. *SoR*. Spring, 1941, pp. 829–30

In many ways the member of this group [Auden, Spender, Day Lewis] who began most quietly but who has persisted in developing is Louis MacNeice. He has disclosed himself as a critic in *Modern Poetry: A Personal Estimate,* and here he allies himself with Auden and the others. But he has qualities which place him a little apart, including a wider range of culture, and a more profound knowledge of the classics. These help him a little in estimating the relative importance of the present as compared with the past.

B. Ifor Evans. *English Literature Between The Wars*
(Methuen, 2nd ed., 1949), p. 132

Like that of Day Lewis, the poetry of Louis MacNeice . . . derives its force from a realisation of the impermanence and yet intense significance of human life. He is not involved with Yeats's imperishable "Byzantium" or T. S. Eliot's "still point beyond the turning world" but with the ebb and flow of all the creatures of life between their polarities of birth and dying.

So, of course, are Yeats and Eliot, but with these poets there is always the struggle to apprehend some single state of being beyond the flux, a wholeness which resolves the duality of decaying flesh and imperishable spirit. For MacNeice the raw flux of existence is enough.

This does not mean, as has sometimes been suggested, that he is a shallow writer, a mere poetic journalist. "Journalist" gives the impression of someone who whisks up superficial information about events and people with whom he is not in the least involved. But MacNeice is always implicated in whatever he writes about. He is not the detached reporter commenting from a safe distance upon "the busy scene," but a poet who writes with open heart and mind, not about the "intersection of time with the timeless" but his own humanity as it opens to that of other men and women, and all the varieties of nature.

Thomas Blackburn. *The Price of an Eye*
(Longmans, 1961), p. 108

At the moment of writing, we are all oppressed by the unexpected death of Louis MacNeice. The vividness of his personality made him one of the best-known figures in literary London, and the distinction of his appearance was such that you would have picked him out in any crowd. He was that rare being, the poet who really looked a poet. But at the same time he looked a sporting man, a man you associated with horses and dogs and country pursuits. I notice that a writer in *The Guardian* (Manchester) says that he had "all the dangerous dark sly charm of an Irish groom." He was, in fact, a passionate lover of all games, of Rugby football, cricket and tennis particularly, and in his day he had been an enthusiastic player of them. Knowing this, I think you can sense the games-player's coordination of eye and muscle in the technique of his verse.

As a young poet, he had been a famous figure in the thirties, both in his own right and as the associate and collaborator of W. H. Auden. About 10 years ago, with changes in poetic taste, it seemed that his reputation had slumped. But this was temporary. Auden apart, he was probably the thirties poet most respected by the young. . . . He made some fine translations of Horace and was, I suppose, an Horatian; but he was very much a 20th century Horatian. If his poetry was minor poetry it was of a kind we can never have too much of and that was particularly rare in our time. MacNeice was the poet as journalist, or the journalist as poet. His poetry was a poetry of comment, and the whole of his life, and the life of his times, was his subject matter.

Walter Allen. *NYT*. Sept. 22, 1963, p. 38

In my opinion, Louis MacNeice's later poems, while continuing to exhibit the technical excellence and delicacy of ear which had always been his from the beginning, are both more moving and more original than his earlier. The last ones I read—in *The Observer,* I think—seem to me among his very best, and I look forward eagerly to the posthumous volume. It is a thousand pities, too, that when, with the assistance of Professor Ernest Stahl, he translated most of Goethe's *Faust,* he did not translate it all, for we are unlikely to see a better English version. . . .

We must certainly have met at Oxford though I have no clear recollection of doing so. I remember a tall dark languid undergraduate from Merton, rather foppishly dressed. Though the "aesthete" was soon to disappear, he always retained a dandy's interest in clothes which, in his case, was an authentic reflection of his fastidious artistic conscience. It is an interest which is impossible to my imagination, but it became him. When he won a First in Greats, gossip reported that his tutor was furious, having predicted he would only get a Third since he had done no work. The tutor's reaction does not surprise me. On anybody who did not know him well and had never witnessed his powers of concentration and the rapidity of his mind, the first impression must have been of a lazy, over-gregarious man who spent more time than he should pub-crawling. Even to me, it remains a mystery that he was able to produce work of the quantity and quality that he did: his constitution, physical and mental, was very tough indeed. . . .

"A man," says Thomas Fuller, "knows his companion in a long journey and a little inn." In Iceland our journeys were long, sometimes arduous, and our inn, more often than not, a tent for two which was not quite waterproof. Louis MacNeice turned out to be, so far as I was concerned, the ideal travelling companion, funny, observant, tolerant and good-tempered. I have rarely in my life enjoyed myself so much as I did during those weeks when we were constantly together.

W. H. Auden. *Enc*. Nov., 1963, pp. 48–49

MADGE, CHARLES (1912–   )

In *The Disappearing Castle* (1937), Mr. Madge was a poet of outstanding merit. His poems were constructed with tension and restraint—achieved by the use of assonance, half-rhyme, and punning, so that each line was linked to the next throughout the poem. Obscurity was a stumbling block, but it was occasional.

Here, in his second book, something has happened. There is far greater obscurity, and this is curious, since most poets tend to become less obscure as they develop. At the same time, he is fond of traditional forms of verse and sometimes these are successful. . . .

His rhymes are now often clumsy and discordant. . . . There is a long philosophic poem called "The Flight of the Margarine," which in certain parts is extremely impressive. In others, however, it is spoilt by the ridiculous contrast effects which occur so frequently throughout the book. . . .

We can only hope that the force and fluidity of his earlier promise will reassert itself, and that something better may come of the present jangling conflict.

Audrey Beecham. LL. Aug., 1941, pp. 69–70

Auden's friends were mostly Oxonians. At Cambridge a group grew up around William Empson, the author of *Seven Types of Ambiguity,* which included Charles Madge, Richard Eberhart and Kathleen Raine. There was something peculiarly American about them, something a little barbarous and Poe-esque. The Auden circle were very British, and seemed to believe that poetry could best be written from an attitude, a very British attitude exemplified by Byron's satires, Prior, Peacock, Clough, Lear, Benson, Calverly, Belloc, and the authors of the best dirty limericks. At utilitarian Cambridge, on the other hand, there is more than a suspicion that they believed that you could write poetry from a formula, and that, if you searched hard enough and with scientific methods learned from Ogden and Richards, you were sure to find the formula, what with all our modern advantages.

Kenneth Rexroth. Introd. in New British Poets,
ed. Kenneth Rexroth (N.Y., New Directions, 1949),
p. viii

The new critics [of America] are not so firmly entrenched here, but it does seem true that the Cambridge tradition does tend to have a constipating and intimidating effect on young poets or novelists who come most immediately under its influence. . . . This would be a fair criticism probably of some of the earlier work in verse of Mr. Bottrall, Mr. Empson, or Mr. Madge; is it necessary or natural to be so clever, oblique, and allusive as that, quite all the time?. . . .

G. S. Fraser. The Modern Writer and His World
(Derek Verschoyle, 1953), pp. 334–36

Those who remember Charles Madge as a poet, the co-founder of *Mass-Observation,* and a young journalist on the *Daily Mirror* may find it hard to believe that this book is by the same man. *Society in the Mind* is strong on sociological jargon, weak on readability; it deals in esoteric concepts like "residues," "collective representations," and "cathetic interests"; it is spattered with scholarly references to Saint-Simon and Pareto, Kant and Lévy-Bruhl. In short, it is addressed to the academic, rather than the general reader. This is perhaps not so surprising after all, for the author has changed; he has for some years been Professor Madge, the occupant of a Chair of Social Science at Birmingham University. . . .

The path that Professor Madge has tried to tread crosses a most treacherous terrain. It is therefore perhaps not surprising that he seems at times to be lost. His book lacks any real sense of direction and fails in the end to provide a convincing or sustained argument, a successful resolution of the important issues with which it tries to deal.

TLS. April 2, 1964, p. 271

MANNING, OLIVIA (? –   )

Miss Manning's husband Cartwright [*My Husband Cartwright*] has already endeared himself to readers of *Punch,* so I trust this collection of his misadventures will bring him many new friends—not acquaintances, for Cartwright is not a man who believes in acquaintances; he is a man who loves his fellow-men, even to the length of lending them money, which often they forget to return. . . . Miss Manning's picture of his likes and dislikes (for he dislikes ancient ruins, preferring to sit in a dark bar talking politics with a friend) is intensely human. It is warm, charming and alive—like Cartwright himself.

Fred Urquhart. *TT.* Dec. 22, 1956, p. 1591

The *Great Fortune* of Miss Manning's title is Life itself. Above all a humanitarian, her interest in people is not selective—idealists, eccentrics, self-assured prigs and the lonely and deprived are all subjected to her cool, unsentimental appraisal. This is an excellent recipe for a novelist.

Her new novel will consolidate Miss Manning's reputation as a very accomplished writer indeed. Its delicate balance, superb interplay between scene and character, and the general sense of control and economy mark it as the work of a true craftsman.

The book is particularly memorable for its brilliant evocation of

Bucharest in the period between the outbreak of war in 1939 and the fall of Paris.

John Barrows. JOL. Feb. 18, 1960, p. 186

The Great Fortune is a witty, charming, and civilized novel. The first volume of a trilogy, it is about the English colony in Bucharest during the winter and spring of 1939-40, and in particular about Guy Pringle, an English lecturer at the University, and his relationships with his wife Harriet and his friends. . . .

I think . . . Miss Manning shows an insight into English character which is deeper than may at first appear. The book is deceptively restrained and light: the local colour nicely done, the subsidiary characters funny. The writing is an object lesson in good manners. Miss Manning controls her narrative with the gentlest possible touch; one is never pushed or hurried, but has that rare and blessed sense of there being spaces between words: this is a matter of texture, and few writers have mastered it; but when you meet one who has, you notice it at once.

K. W. Gransden. Enc. May, 1960, p. 78

Perhaps the most eloquent fictional voices of our day will turn out to be the writers of the grave sort of comedy in which the laughter is as painful as it is rare, and tends to bleed inwardly. It is the way Evelyn Waugh has moved, and there are twinges of the same quality in *The Spoilt City,* Olivia Manning's latest novel—the second on the theme—about Bucharest in the shadow of war.

This book and its companion, *The Great Fortune,* deserve to win a place among the remembered novels of our time even though they have no technical interest beyond that of conventional craftsmanship. They are a swan-song for so many things; for the thirties, for the English amateur cosmopolitans like Guy Pringle, for the whole way of life such expatriates represented. Armed with his high, naïve intelligence, injected with good intentions, Pringle thinks he can protect the darkening world, but in the end can only protect himself, which is not what he wants at all. He is insulated from disaster and can never really believe, as a Rumanian puts it, "the things that happen to others."

Norman Shrapnel. MGW. May 17, 1962, p. 6

MANSFIELD, KATHERINE (1885–1923)

Some time ago I read Miss Katherine Mansfield's *Bliss.* I was good enough critic to see that she was an artist, in absolute command of her means, making her effects surely and (for the reader's eye) with ease, using words rightly, composing beautifully. But I was dissatisfied and in a way irritated. Always I wanted more. Always I asked for a definite outcome, for something final. The first piece in the book was called "Prelude," and as I finished it, admiring, I asked: Prelude to what? And almost everything was a prelude. What was the end of Mouse? Of the little Governess? What did Bertha do or not do that night when she knew that Harry was faithless? Miss Mansfield, I thought, was not doing her share, was leaving altogether too much to me (That subtle critic, the present reader, perceives that I was extremely stupid, but let him have patience). Then some time later, I read "The Daughters of the Late Colonel" in *The London Mercury*. I finished it in open-mouthed admiration for the genius which had told me so much, and this time I had no wish for more. That was not because I was uninterested in those pitiful women so delicately yet so completely presented to me, but because the presentment *was* complete, the phase of life fully rendered, the atmosphere given once for all. It was a final achievement. Further speculation would be vulgar, stupid. Being quite clear about "The Daughters of the Late Colonel," I had the sense to return to *Bliss,* recognizing that the expression of a phase of life, the conveying of an atmosphere, was the final purpose of this writer. There was no intention of telling a story or of asking the reader to tell one to himself. I read *Bliss* again completely satisfied. The artistic intention was achieved in every instance; there was no room for anything more.

G. S. Street. *LM*. Nov., 1921, p. 54

Miss Mansfield's collection, *Bliss,* boldly labelled "stories," is remarkable for not being tedious. It is far from tedious. She has so penetrating a mind and such a talent for expression that she would be interesting whatever form she were using and whatever subject she were writing about. It is not that she has a markedly personal view of things, a passionate or a philosophical attitude; she is restrained, and leaves her affections and her admirations too much to be guessed and deduced. It is not that she has a rich prose style; she checks the natural music in herself, and contents herself with a perpetual stream of exact statements as terse as she can make them. Every word counts to the intelligence and the eye, but none to the ear. But the fabric of her writing has no weak or dull places. She beats all the writers of dyspeptic "economical" "realistic" "studies" on their own ground. Every story is a tissue of accurate observations accurately expressed. Miss Mansfield has an extraordinary visual, and, if one may say so, olfactory, memory; her stories may vary in reality, but her material settings—in which one includes everything from vegetation to the human garment of flesh—never. Almost every page contains minor felicities which a man with the pencilling habit would be inclined to mark.

J. C. Squire. *Books Reviewed* (Hodder and
Stoughton, 1922), p. 10

By any standard, Miss Mansfield is a very great short story writer. In one particular she is the greatest of all. Her stories affect the reader not as transcriptions of life but as life itself. Other writers—Mr. Wells, Mr. Kipling, DeMaupassant—come back from hunting with a fine prey, but the prey is dead, even dressed and cooked. Miss Mansfield's spoil is still living. . . . In *The Garden Party* as in *Bliss,* Miss Mansfield gives the reader beyond his usual pleasures a pleasure which properly belongs to the artist, for, after selecting and arranging, she relinquishes the final stage, which might be called interpretation, to us. . . .

A . . . consequence of Miss Mansfield's abnegation is that she cannot afford to write lengthily. *The Garden Party* includes another instalment of the sensations of that family which we first met in "Prelude," and already, I think, the reader must be confused and tired of them. Superb as Miss Mansfield's art is, it is too impressionistic for a novel, and as "Prelude" swells beyond the normal size, as details grow richer, the field of observation, the eye of the reader is strained. Nothing is happening. The details are all significant—but of what? We begin to fail to adjust to them and relate to them, and Miss Mansfield, keeping silence, threatens to overwhelm us with facts that cannot be explained. It is a Frith picture, which can only be looked at in bits. . . .

To consider limitations upon the efficacy of Miss Mansfield's impressionism is not to censure Miss Mansfield. Her style, as her imitators will some day prove to us, is infertile, and its developments soon exhausted. But Miss Mansfield's own writings are immortal. *The Garden Party* ranks with *Bliss* as one of those rare volumes which are not only exceedingly good but are indisputably good. The gods of one generation are idols to the next. You can never tell—or hardly ever—what will last. Miss Mansfield's stories are the obvious exception.

H. C. Harwood. *OutL*. Feb. 25, 1922, p. 154

One asks involuntarily, is Miss Mansfield's new book [*The Garden Party*] as good as her last? It would need, of course, to be very much better to give one the same shock of delighted surprise; and there has hardly been an interval long enough for any great development in her genius. Therefore it is not unnatural that one's first judgment of it should be a trifle unenthusiastic. The more obvious qualities in that earlier book remain the same in this, and Miss Mansfield's more obvious qualities tend to be a trifle unsatisfying. Her themes lacked substance: not that there was an inherent lack of substance in her chosen characters and situations but rather in what she got out of them—though there can be no doubt that she got out of them precisely what she intended to. She is too fine and altogether too wise and severe an artist to do otherwise; it might be said, almost without exaggeration, that she never fails. But those earlier stories, unsatisfying as they were, had a conquering glitter and variety. Now, either these qualities have faded or I have grown used to them. Perhaps the second alternative is the true one. They are like drugs; if they are to have the same effect the dose must be increased.

Edward Shanks. *LM*. April, 1922, pp. 658–59

Ten years ago the name of Katherine Mansfield was hardly known in our literature. Since then, because of her short stories, it has been associated with Anton Tchekhov; and now that an abrupt end has come to her great brilliance and the promise of yet greater brilliance, she is, according to some, entitled to a place alongside Amiel and Bashkirtseff because of her private diaries. Doubtless the two volumes of letters [*Letters*] to her intimate friends which her husband, Mr. Middleton Murry, has selected with a devotion that remains unwearied, will cause her name to be linked in a third direction, with that of John Keats.

For Katherine Mansfield, like the author of "Endymion," wrote her last letters after her fatal illness had manifested itself and when her doom appeared inescapable. Keats was no more rebellious and alternately resigned than she, and exiled from active life and home and friends, they began to pour out their hearts on paper, honestly and earnestly, passionately and affectionately, and with a regularity that made each of them as a correspondent uncommonly prolific. But when every possible comparison has been offered, Katherine Mansfield still remains essentially a unique and solitary figure. A tragic figure, it need hardly be said. She had a precarious foothold on the border between two worlds, and while others in that state are often wholly high-spirited and gay, or utterly dismayed and dispirited, she was so seldom at one or the other extreme as to present a greater paradox than any individual to be found in a sphere—that of art—which is overcrowded with paradoxical people. . . .

Katherine Mansfield, with all her senses preternaturally acute because of her precarious position, saw life much more vividly than the most of us see it, but her ultimate desires were the ordinary man's or woman's. . . . And after all was she not already in her imagination a "child of the sun"? She loved light and the things of light—animals, birds and summer, Dickens, Tchekov, and birthdays. Her stories are themselves like sun-rays lighting up the little obvious and yet hitherto invisible things in the garden—the dusty particles that crowd the green air, the bits of sparkling grass or shell on the path. She distorted nothing. Thus, her letters, written in the nervous, staccato and yet liquid English that was in all her stories, and crowded with brilliant detail and vivid phrases, are an expression of the rare art that began with *Bliss and Other Stories, The Garden Party, The Doves' Nest* and *Something Childish,* and that the *Journal* illuminated technically; a finite perfect art, which reminds us in some ways of Jane Austen, and to which, alas, there are to be no further. contributions.

Thomas Moult. BkmL. Dec., 1928, pp. 183–84

"To be crystal clear," "to be 'simple' as one would be simple before God" —that was Katherine Mansfield's prayer; and before she prayed it was granted, for only single-mindedness could so pray. That quality by which we learned to know her in her stories is in these poems [*Poems*] so that, in spite of their uncommon kind, they seem familiar. They are more valuable for her personality in them than for themselves.

They are little poems, fancies rather than imaginings, with no fire that kindles us, but a cool clear glow that hushes us.

It is understandable that some of the poems could be written, evening after evening, on set themes, for they are not hot geysers issuing at some inscrutable timing of darkness; they come from cool wells, deeply kept; the sinking and lifting of a dipper finds them. Katherine Mansfield held all the beauty of the world that had crossed the threshold of eye and ear, and its meaning for her; she had a throng of words and images clamouring for use; she had inalienably her candid spirit; and so she had these poems. Utterance was necessary, but only a few of these poems were. Many of them are too cool and faultless, as if they knew too well what they aimed at and what they avoided. Faultier, they might have been greater.

Orgill Mackenzie. Adel. Oct., 1930, pp. 76–77

. . . in the delineation of children together Katherine Mansfield stands alone. Her life-long discipline in entering into the mind of her subject ("I have just finished a story with a canary for a hero, and almost feel I have lived in a cage and pecked a piece of chickweed myself") is no-where more essential than when the writer enters the mind of a child. . . . Katherine Mansfield portrays children as children, seen through their own eyes and the eyes of other children. Kezia and Lottie and Isabel Burnell and the Trout boys Pip and Rags (and their dog, a uniquely children's dog) in "Prelude" and "At the Bay," with the unforgettable Lil and Our Else in "The Doll's House" are creations that stand by themselves in English writing.

Ian A. Gordon. Katherine Mansfield
(BC/Longmans, 1954), p. 21

Katherine Mansfield is for me something unusual in the history of the short story. She is a woman of brilliance, perhaps of genius; she chose the short story as her own particular form and handled it with considerable skill, and yet for most of the time she wrote stories that I read and forget, read and forget. My experience of stories by real storytellers, even when the stories are not first-rate, is that they leave a deep impression on me. It may not be a total impression; it may not even be an accurate one, but it is usually deep and permanent. I remember it in the way in which I remember poetry. I do not remember Katherine Mansfield's stories in that way. She wrote a little group of stories about her native country, New Zealand, which are recognized as masterpieces and probably are masterpieces, but I find myself forgetting even these and rediscovering them as though they were the work of a new writer. . . .

Most of her work seems to me that of a clever, spoiled, malicious woman. Though I know nothing to suggest she had any homosexual experiences, the assertiveness, malice, and even destructiveness in her life and work makes me wonder whether she hadn't. It would be too much to exaggerate the significance of her occasionally sordid love affairs, of which we probably still have something to learn, but the idea of "experience" by which she justified them is a typical expedient of the woman with a homosexual streak who envies men and attributes their imaginary superiority to the greater freedom with which they are supposed to be able to satisfy their sexual appetite. . . .

There is one quality that is missing in almost everything that Katherine Mansfield wrote—even her New Zealand stories—and that is heart. Where heart should be we usually find sentimentality, the quality that seems to go with a brassy exterior, and nowhere more than with that of an "emancipated" woman. In literature sentimentality always means falsity, for whether or not one can perceive the lie, one is always aware of being in the presence of a lie.

Frank O'Connor. The Lonely Voice (N.Y.,
World, 1963), pp. 128, 130–31

MARRIOTT, CHARLES (1869–1957)

Mr. Marriott is clever, but too intentionally and consciously so in a violent and explosive way. He irritates, even when he convinces. In *The House on the Sands* he does not always convince.

SR. Sept. 19, 1903, p. 369

Fifteen years is a long time in the literary world, and Charles Marriott's *The Column*, which threw everybody into fever-heat somewhere about

1902, is, I suppose, forgotten. It was a "first" novel. Uncritical Ouida loved it; W. E. Henley unbent and wrote a Meredithian letter to its author; W. J. Courtney seized some of his short stories for *The Fortnightly Review*; and I suppose (though I don't really know this) *The Spectator* wrote five lines of disapproval. It was a brilliant book; fresh, original, provocative. It promised a lot: it promised too much; the author has since written many distinguished books, but none of them is as good as *The Column* said they would be.

Marriott was living at Lamorna, a tiny cove in Cornwall, when I first knew him. He was tall, lantern-jawed and spectacled. He was interested in everything, but it appeared to me even then that he was a little inhuman. He lacked vulgarity; rude things repelled him enormously, unnaturally; he had no literary delight—or else his delight was too literary: I don't know—in coarseness. Fastidious to the finger-tips, he would rather go without dinner than split an infinitive. Since those days Marriott has gone on refining himself until there is very little Marriott left. Even the longest and thickest pencil may be sharpened too frequently.

Many years after I met him at an exhibition of pictures in Bond Street. He is quite the last man to be a journalist; his art criticism is wonderfully fine, but a life standing on the polished floors of galleries between Bond Street and Leicester Square is soul-corroding and heart-breaking. Marriott's mind no longer darts and leaps. It moves gently, very gently.

Charles Frederick Kenyon. Set Down in Malice
(Grant Richards, 1919), pp. 134–35

Mr. Marriott has written a novel with a thesis [*The Grave Impertinence*]. To put it baldly, he believes that the happiness of England is threatened by the ascendancy of business over work, but that the fundamental England is resisting the threat and may succeed. . . . The idea is as subtle as it is attractive. It would be hard at the best to convey it, with the definiteness it deserves, by means of conversation and incident; and Mr. Marriott has invented for his purpose a group of people remarkably unsuited for it. They speculate on their own characters and motives and those of their friends, they hazard tentative formulas, they define situations and look for clues, until one suspects them of accumulating material for psychological novels of their own instead of getting on with Mr. Marriott's novel. Or, one feels that Mr. Marriott has made them all uniformly abnormal, has, as it were, given them all bismuth meals so as to get clearer results from the X-rays he turns on them.

Edward Shanks. LM. Oct., 1921, p. 659

How far the bewilderment in which *An Order to View* must leave the reader was necessary to Mr. Marriott's purpose I do not know. You are required by this author to find things out for yourself; to pass through the surprise, the suspicion, and the illumination of his hero. This time I must confess myself baffled.

H. C. Harwood. *OutL*. June 10, 1922, p. 463

MARSH, EDWARD (1872–1953)

The new collection of *Georgian Poetry* contains specimens of most of the work of nineteen poets, fourteen of whom have appeared in one or more of the series, while five are represented for the first time. The fourteen are Mr. Lascelles Abercrombie, Mr. Gordon Bottomley, Mr. W. H. Davies, Mr. Walter de la Mare, Mr. John Drinkwater, Mr. John Freeman, Mr. W. W. Gibson, Mr. Robert Graves, Mr. D. H. Lawrence, Mr. Harold Munro, Mr. Robert Nichols, Mr. Siegfried Sassoon, Mr. J. C. Squire, and Mr. W. J. Turner. The five are Mr. Francis Brett Young, Mr. Thomas Moult, Mr. J. D. C. Pellow, Mr. Edward Shanks, and Mrs. Fredegond Shove. . . .

"I hope," observes E. M. in his preface, "that [the present volume] may be thought to show that what for want of a better word is called Peace has not interfered with the writing of good poetry." Certainly many critics have supposed that war was the prime generator of what they admit to be a new movement in poetry. But the anthologist's hope is justified, on *a priori* grounds at least, by the fact that the movement began, however tentatively, before the late war. The first collection of Georgian Poetry appeared in 1912, when the title expressed an act of faith, based on an act of divination, which has since been confirmed. A comparison of the four members of the series suggests that what, for want of a better word, has received this name, is still in a state of slow development towards a certain community of spirit and attitude, which does not however connote any uniformity of style. In the third volume the nebula appeared to be taking shape, and in the fourth the process has advanced a stage. E. M. may be issuing the fourteenth before that shape can be accurately defined and described. The curve has not yet been drawn far enough for us to say what course it will trace; but there is already enough of it to look like a curve and not merely a wavy line.

That remote first volume, which was of course a symptom and a rallying-point of the new tendencies, not their origin, seems now to have been somewhat chaotic and lacking in direction. . . . At that time the most powerful tendency seemed to be leading towards the realism, sometimes informed with a conscious brutality, of Mr. Masefield, Mr. Gibson, and Mr. Abercrombie. In 1919 this sort is fully represented only by Mr. Abercrombie's "Witchcraft: New Style," a poem principally in dialogue which is realistic in method, if its conception has a fairy-tale brutality about it. . . .

At least this movement—we do not use the word in the sense of "organized movement" or "school"—has had the luck of early recognition and careful fostering. There are faults to be found with this as with the three earlier volumes of the series, but, in a world which has produced no faultless anthology, we ought not to expect the first to be a collection of contemporary verse. . . . But to E. M. we must assign the credit of having carried through an exceedingly difficult task with as few mistakes as could be thought possible. He has the extra distinction of having foreseen seven years ago the beginning of a "liveliness" which has justified him by enduring until at this moment it shows no signs of recession. He would be no doubt the last person to claim the invention, or even the discovery, of the "Georgian" movement. But he might reasonably claim, and if he does not, the honour must be thrust upon him, to have provided it with a means of growing naturally and without undue extravagance.

LM. Dec., 1919, pp. 201, 205

Mr. Marsh's idea [*Forty-two Fables of La Fontaine*] was delicious, and he has deliciously carried it out; nothing being wanted to complete his little book but a few engravings or cuts. La Fontaine is not read as he was; he has had little English influence since the Augustan age; and the fable is out of fashion. . . . His translator must know his world, must be capable of easy colloquialism and the classic poetic touch, he must have a large vocabulary and a precise sense of the meaning of words. . . . He must, in fact, have all the qualities which Mr. Marsh surprisingly (for one who has doubted that anybody could do the job so well) shows himself to possess. His elegance, ease, urbanity are admirable; and almost everywhere he may be read aloud with amusement, admiration and a complete absence of "that translation feeling," not his least achievement being the perpetration of elaborate rhymes that do not seem forced.

J. C. Squire. LM. Dec., 1924, p. 208

Edward Marsh was a scholar. He was also, and for many years, a great deal more, making active appearances where men of academic temperament do not normally feel at home—such as dancing his way through every ball of the London season, travelling on foot to the source of the Nile, playing mah-jong with the King of Portugal or bézique with the Aga Khan for sixpenny stakes. So it is advisable at the start to pinpoint the central being. He will only be imagined aright if seen as a scholar whose other qualities combined, sometimes for years at a stretch, to lead him away from his natural bent. He was, of course, an esthete of acute perception and an ornament of society with an inexhaustible fund of small talk; one, moreover, for whom no talk could be too small. Owing to these contrasts in personality his conversation was often an engaging blend of ambrosia and small beer. Concinnity of mind, perhaps the most striking element of his nature, while making a harmony of these differences, also made it impossible for him to be pedantic. His lightness of touch was so deceptively feather-light that it never seemed to carry the weight of authority.

. . . . His adventures were largely crises of the sensibility, but on occasion he was caught up in historical events and appeared a figure as it were suddenly dwarfed by his setting. . . . More in scale was the movement known as *Georgian Poetry,* which has taken its place in literary history. That history, or rather his own view of it from his editorial chair as it unfolded, is too important, and has been too often misunderstood, for it not to be allowed now and again to draw the reader's attention. . . .

Christopher V. Hassall. *Edward Marsh*
(Longmans, 1959), pp. ix–x

MASEFIELD, JOHN (1878–   )

Mr. Masefield, in the criticism his dramatic poems have got, has been a good deal a sufferer from the irrelevant objection. A line in them, he has been told, is not as good as another line by Keats or Arnold; what the young labourer said to his mates, or what the bo'sun said to the Dauber, is "not poetry." There is a kind of critic who has gone over the poems with an inch-rule, and objected to one of Mr. Masefield's feet. But the only question to ask of these poems is whether they have a good story to tell, and whether they tell it well—to greater effect in beauty and intensity, that is to say, than if it had been told in prose. The answer, with regard to *The Widow in the Bye-Street* certainly, could only be in the affirmative, as the politicians say. If the answer is less certain with regard to the new poem, that is not because its subject and manner unfit it for verse, but because there is, one thinks, a not quite equal mastery in the telling. Mr. Masefield, with the little work he has done for the contemporary theatre, has contributed already two to its small stock of true tragedies; and when he turned from the theatre to the larger audience which the dramatic poet may command (at present) through the printed page, he did not lose the secret. There is, in this story of the ship's Dauber whose attempts at beauty were cut to strings by the rabble of the inappreciative in the fo'c'sle, the same kind of pity as that which made moving the tragedy of Nan. If *Dauber* is not quite tragedy it is because, in reading it, we find a lack of unity, and are a little troubled also perhaps by a strain of self-consciousness that is hardly to be separated from a story in which a practising artist is the central figure.

OutL. June 21, 1913, p. 859

There is one sense at least in which Mr. Masefield is the most important figure amongst contemporary poets. For he has won the popular ear, he has cast the poetic spell further than any of his compeers, and it has been given to him to lure the multitudinous reader of magazines—that wary host which is usually stampeded by the sight of a page of verse.

Now I know there are cultured persons to whom this fact of uncritical appreciation is an offense, and to them a writer bent upon purely scientific criticism would be compelled to yield certain points. But they would be mainly on finicking questions, as an occasional lapse from fineness in thought or form, an incidental banality of word or phrase; or a lack of delicate effects of rhyme and metre. And the whole business would amount in the end to little more than a petulant complaint; an impertient grumble that Mr. Masefield happens to be himself and not, let us say, Mr. Robert Bridges; that his individual genius has carved its own channels and that, in effect, the music of the sea or the mountain torrent does not happen to be the same thing as the plash of a fountain in a valley.

But having no quarrel with this offending popularity: rejoicing in it rather, and the new army of poetry-readers which it has created; and believing it to be an authentic sign of the poetic spirit of our day, one is tempted to seek for the cause of it. Luckily, there is a poem called "Biography" which gives a clue and something more. It is a paean of zest for life, of the intense joy in actual living which seems to be the dynamic of Mr. Masefield's genius. There is, most conspicuous and significant, delight in beauty; a swift, keen, accurate response of sense to the external world, to sea and sky and hill, to field and flower. But there is fierce delight, too, in toil and danger, in strenuous action, in desperate struggle with wind and wave, in the supreme effort of physical power, in health and strength and skill and freedom and jollity; and above all, first, last and always, in ships. But there is delight no less in communion with humanity, in comradeship, in happy memories of kindred, in still happier mental kinships and intellectual affinities, in books, in "glittering moments" of spiritual perception, in the brooding sense of man's long history.

Mary C. Sturgeon. *Studies of Contemporary Poets*
(George Harrap, 1919), pp. 197–98

Overstrain is permanent with him. If we do not find it in his actual language (and, as we have said, he is ridding himself of the worst of his exaggerations), we are sure to find in the very vitals of his artistic effort. He is seeking always to be that which he is not, to lash himself into the illusion of a certainty which he knows he can never wholly possess. . . .

And here, perhaps, we have the secret of Mr. Masefield and of our sympathy with him. His work, for all its surface robustness and right-thinking, . . . is as deeply debilitated by reaction as any of our time. Its colour is hectic; its tempo feverish. He has sought the healing virtue where he believed it undefiled, in that miraculous English country whose magic (as Mr. Masefield so well knows) is in Shakespeare, and whose strong rhythm is in Hardy. But the virtue eludes all conscious inquisition. The man who seeks it feverishly sees riot where there is peace. And may it not be, in the long run, that Mr. Masefield would have done better not to delude himself into an identification he cannot feel, but rather to face his own disquiet where alone the artist can master it, in his consciousness? We will not presume to answer, mindful that Mr. Masefield may not recognize himself in our mirror, but we will content ourselves with recording our conviction that in spite of the almost heroic effort that has gone to its composition *Reynard the Fox* lacks all the qualities essential to durability.

John Middleton Murry. *Aspects of Literature*
(William Collins Sons, 1920), pp. 155–56

Nine years ago Mr. Masefield published *The Everlasting Mercy* in the *English Review*. Before he did so his name was known to a comparatively small number of persons who regarded him with some admiration and more curiosity; but afterwards he received fame instead of expectant attention. For some time he bulked large in two worlds. He made modern poetry popular before Rupert Brooke; and critical opinion, broadly speaking, agreed in owning the novelty and ambition of his work and the adequacy of his talents. In the theatre he seemed to be the inheritor of Synge, destined to make Synge's methods his own on a larger stage and before a wider audience. Mr. John Galsworthy, then at the zenith of a reputation which has followed a somewhat similar course, proclaimed him "the man of the hour, and the man of tomorrow, too, in poetry and the playwriting craft." . . . For a little while it really seemed to many that a new writer had emerged of the rare stature and originality which engage the interest both of the general public and of the sceptical and selective readers who attempt to anticipate the judgment of their descendants.

But I do not think that this is true any longer. Mr. Masefield's works were not found wanting in the qualities at first discerned in them. But radical defects, which had hitherto somehow escaped general notice, were revealed; and some of the very qualities turned out on cooler examination, not to have the value with which they had been credited. Worse still, the defects became apparent through, as it were, a sort of rash on the surface, an outcrop of awkwardness and ineptitudes which lent themselves quite charmingly to ridicule. The public continued to admire, possibly even more than ever; but first one voice was raised among the critics, then another and another.

In this swing of opinion there is some danger that Mr. Masefield's real achievements may be overlooked; and the danger continues so long as his demerits are not clearly stated. It is pretty certain that the general public, once he had been forced on its notice, liked him to a considerable extent for bad reasons. . . . But the fact remains that he actually has originality, enterprise, ambition, and some degree of force, that he is one of the most interesting figures in modern literature. Assuming that he has genius, that he did not capture opinion only by pretence, the mere range of his work must be considered and may be reckoned to his credit. He has experimented in many forms. He has written lyrics and sonnets and a series of narrative poems, plays, both in prose and in verse, which have stood the test of production, several novels and collections of stories, a book on Shakespeare, and books about the war. His sincerity as an artist may often be questioned . . . but his personal sincerity, in the broadest and most fundamental sense, is beyond doubt.

Edward Shanks. LM. Sept., 1920, pp. 578–79

His poems are, for the most part, as I have said, aflush with the joy of life. Is it possible that the flush is sometimes a trifle hectic, reminding one just a little of the consumptive who is feverishly eager, then and there, to cram all he can into life? Masefield's writings convey, perhaps are intended to convey, the impression of one who is robust alike in body and mind.

I do not question his physical health, but some of his poems seem to me to indicate a too self-conscious "nerviness," of which the violence which he mistakes for power, and the over-anxiety to emphasize seem to me to be signs. Not thus is power in poetry attained, any more than an ambitious pianist, too eager to seem Paderewski, can, by the keeping down of the loud pedal, achieve the effect which comes only of a born and trained musician's brilliancy of "touch."

Coulson Kernahan. Six Famous Living Poets
(Thornton Butterworth, 1922), p. 33

In the first line of the first poem of his <i>Collected Poems</i> Mr. Masefield announces that he is not concerned with "the princes and prelates with periwigged charioteers," and indeed the word "periwig" suggests at once all that is most opposite to his verse. Of all centuries Mr. Masefield seems to have least to do with the eighteenth, with that superb effort towards control and stability which was common to Pope and Johnson and Gibbon. . . .

The most fascinating thing about Mr. Masefield is . . . [the] appearance of an expansive romanticism. If there were nothing else, the modern poet's work would be almost a joke; but there is sufficient of something else to make us interested in the contrast. But that something is not what Mr. Masefield insisted upon in that "Consecration" of his first book, *Salt Water Ballads.* It was not when the book was published in 1902; it has certainly not been since. Ordinary men, working men, "the drowsy man at the wheel and the tired look-out," come in from time to time. But they come mostly, for all their modern properties, down those old Spenserian ways, those lengthy, twining roads, where even fights are drowsy, and crises are resolved into faery by the mere process of time.

Charles Williams. Poetry at Present (Oxford
Univ. Pr., 1930), pp. 114–15

The appearance of *The Everlasting Mercy* in 1911 caused a sensation analogous to that produced by *Childe Harold* in 1812, or—perhaps a better parallel—by *Poems* and *Ballads* in 1866. Like the latter book, it enjoyed a *succès de scandale.* It is among the ironies of literary history that two poets so different as Swinburne and Masefield should, in their respective generations, have kindled a similar furore: that Masefield, like Swinburne, should have been attacked not only for the novelty of his departures in art, but also in morals.

Swinburne, in 1866, was still in his phase of youthful rebellion and paganism. His intention was to shock the moral sense. If, in writing *The Everlasting Mercy,* Masefield thought consciously at all about shocking his readers, his aim was to shock them into a more vital morality. No two books were ever conceived in more antithetical moods than were *Poems and Ballads* and *The Everlasting Mercy.* The former, with naked abandon, deified the senses. The latter was passionately spiritual in inspiration. . . .

The Everlasting Mercy was the turning point in Masefield's career. It is, probably, his greatest—certainly his most characteristic—achievement. It is so well-known that few readers will need reminding that it is a study in conversion. The earlier part seeks, with the boldest possible realism, to depict Saul Kane, the blackguard of a small Herefordshire town, as he was before his redemption. The latter part presents the joy of salvation in sustained flights of lyrical ecstasy. There were, of course, clear-sighted reviewers who immediately appreciated Masefield's fine spirit and intention. Mr. Arthur Waugh, for example, hailed

The Everlasting Mercy as "a great poem, as true to the essentials of its ancient art as it is astoundingly modern in its method." "Its technical force," he added, "is on a level with its high, inspiring thought." But such was the world in 1911 that the poem presented an insoluble riddle to large numbers of critics and readers.

Gilbert Thomas. John Masefield (Thornton
Butterworth, 1932), pp. 109–10, 112–13

John Masefield is a copious writer, and one of the most uneven whom our time can show. His official position as Poet Laureate has stimulated him to produce, conscientiously and dutifully, a number of *morceaux,* the poetic equivalent of journalism, works of which the chief interest has been the occasion that evoked them. The volume of his collected poems is corpulent; he has written novels, and a number of other works in prose. The theatre knows him, and he has been, in memorable instances, a historian. . . .

The score, then, for John Masefield, his contribution to the life and literature of his time, is one supreme long narrative poem [*Reynard the Fox*], wholly English, which no one but he could have written: two or three other long poems, original in matter and manner, which brought violent gusts of energy to the polite, faintly countrified air of poetry in their day: a handful of short pieces which have passed into current thought: a just, spare, and impassioned commentary upon England's greatest writer: two chronicles of high achievement which match their theme: and other books, poems, and plays lit with flashes of intense but intermittent light. He has never written meanly, coldly or carelessly. He has sided always with the weak against the strong. The right things have moved him, whether to anger or joy. Sensitive, gentle and brave, he has found his mainspring in love of life and compassion for all that live it.

Besides this score, the debit side of his work does not matter. Call it the cost of an enthusiastic and vigorous craftsman, who never stopped work for fear of making a mistake, and was too humble to insist on appearing only on occasions of his own choice. Masefield has given to every task the best he could command; when all the bells of his talent chimed with the occasion, the result has been noble.

L. A. G. Strong. John Masefield (BC/Longmans,
1952), pp. 7, 17

The Poet Laureate has revised his brilliant and wayward book *William Shakespeare.* He has modified some of the more eccentric passages—about Prince Hal, for example. He no longer ranks *Measure for Measure* with the greater plays. He is still, perhaps, too apt to moralize Shakespeare's themes, and sometimes he throws more light on his own poetic aims than on Shakespeare's. It remains a stimulating book and one it is a pleasure to quarrel with.

Kenneth Muir. *L.* June, 1955, p. 108

MASON, A. E. W. (1865–1948)

Clementina is dedicated to Mr. Andrew Lang, and it should gratify that writer, to observe how much better a work was *Parson Kelly,* in which he lent a hand. For Mr. Charles Wogan of the former book is, as it were, the D'Artagnan of the present. He possesses three trusty comrades, gentlemen of Dillon's regiment, whereof one had never been limned had not Dumas created Porthos. In fact the book is a mosaic of literary parallels, though we are sure there is no actual plagiarism. Wogan's most usual predicaments are those which Mr. Stanley Weyman loves to portray, and he extricates himself very much in the methods of Mr. Hope's Rudolf Rassendyll. The Princess Clementina is wooed by a suitor of high rank, a twin brother, as it might be, of De Musset's Prince de Mantoue in *Fantasio*. But the most serious objection we have is that Mr. Mason, starting in the Dumas vein, degenerates into the Daudet manner. The treatment of Princess Clementina's emotions is at times horridly like Daudet's mishandling of the heroic queen in *Les Rois en Exil*. Probably Mr. Mason has read too much and has too good a memory. We do not suppose that any of the parallels suggested by us ever crossed his mind, but for all that he is not ploughing virgin soil, and his story has little freshness. The central episode, the escape of Clementina Sobieski to wed the Chevalier, is one of the most romantic in history, and the telling is spirited enough. *Clementina* is in fact an historic novel of some merit, and had Mr. Mason been courageous enough to bar what is termed psychology might have stood on its own feet as a good story. As it is, historical fact governs the event, while the writer's fancy plays defiantly with the might have been.

SR. Jan. 17, 1902, p. 84

The really important points about Mr. A. E. W. Mason's new play, *Running Water,* are that, in four acts, it enables Miss Edna Best to wear five different dresses . . . and that the *Running Water* music has been composed . . . by Mr. Norman O'Neill. . . .

Having disposed of the things that really matter, we will now turn to the play. It is adapted, so I am told, from a novel of the same title, which I have not read, and in this novel, for all I know, the title may have something to do with the story. In the play it and the occasional references made to it by the characters are of quite surprising irrelevance. . . .

I repeat that I have not read the novel on which the play is founded. But I have read other novels by Mr. Mason and have always found them ingenious and have never found them completely silly. This play strikes me as being almost completely silly; and I deduce, therefore, that something strange must have happened in the process of dramatisation. . . . I have made fun of Mr. Mason's play; but, believe me, dear reader, this is the laughter which seeks to conceal a breaking heart.

Edward Shanks. *OutL*. April 29, 1922, p. 341

The House of the Arrow was one of the best detective-novels of recent years. The play that has been made out of the novel is a poor affair in comparison. It is no better and no worse than all the other crook plays, whereas the book was right at the top of its profession. It is a commonplace to say that the adaptation for the stage of a successful novel can be at best merely a judicious selection of episodes and incidents. But the essential thing is that the selection should be really judicious. In this case, there was a novel crammed with movement as well as subtlety, with dramatic situations as well as dramatic characters, and the best that can be done with it is to produce a dull and commonplace play. It is hard luck on Mr. A. E. W. Mason.

A. G. Macdonell. *LM*. July, 1928, p. 309

MASTERS, JOHN (1914–   )

John Masters, O.B.E. and D.S.O., was born in Calcutta, spent fourteen years as a British officer in the Indian Army (the fifth successive generation of his family to serve in India), was a brigadier of Wingate's Chindits in 1944, and has just written a first novel called *Nightrunners of Bengal*. It is about the great Indian Mutiny of 1857. During the heyday of British dominion a novel on this subject by such an author would have been predictable in the extreme; perhaps today it is almost equally so though the point of view would be quite different. . . . Yesterday's fashion was confidence, today's is conscience.

So John Masters in *Nightrunners of Bengal* states the case of both sides fairly enough, not glossing over the cruelties of the mutineers, nor the equal cruelties of the suppressors. . . .

The best thing in the novel is the constant play of ideas and debate concerning the entire problem of India and imperial government—with the proviso again that this is not really a fictional merit. For Mr. Masters's entire story is permeated with hindsight: despite his overall picture of Bhowani society innocently unaware of what was to happen, his characters become clairvoyant too often and too eloquently.

All of which brings one to the preface with which *Nightrunners of Bengal* is somewhat unusually supplied and which it is to be hoped that the readers will not overlook. . . . The excellence of this, both in thought and wit, almost suggests that Mr. Masters should forget his steel-springed women and devote himself to the kind of straightforward comment for which he seems so admirably qualified.

James Hilton. *NYHT*. Jan. 21, 1951, p. 6

It is impossible to reach any understanding of the Raj without knowing a good deal about the Indian Army. The records of its final years—of splendid yet doomed vindication—are diffuse and dispersed. Sir Compton Mackenzie has begun, but not completed, his tremendous task of recounting its history in World War II. Individual narratives are to be found in regimental or divisional histories and in periodicals such as *Blackwoods*. Now Mr. John Masters (who has already written five vivid and memorable novels about India) comes forward with a lapidary account [*Bugles and a Tiger*]—autobiographical in form—of the Indian Army in its penultimate phase, that of the years immediately before World War II.

Mr. Masters is himself country-born (as Kipling was), and he comes —as Kipling did not—of a family with many generations of service in and to India to its record. Understanding of India is therefore in his bones and his bloodstream.

John Connell. *TT*. Feb. 4, 1956, p. 136

With seven of his proposed thirty-five Indian novels on the shelf, John Masters has changed course to a new publisher, style and setting. "I shall write again about India," he promises in his new novel, "but three years ago I knew that I must write about the people among whom I live and whose citizenship I have asked for and been given—the people of the United States."

This [*Fandango Rock*], then, is Mr. Masters's first attempt at an American novel, written from an American viewpoint in a distinctively American prose. This is not an easy task for a foreign-born writer who comes here in maturity. Georges Simenon, for example, was never able to write a truly "American" novel, despite his long sojourn here. Vladimir Nabokov and other European-born writers have been able to capture the matter but not the American manner. John Masters, however, comes reasonably close, but only because he has limited himself to covering merely part of his objective in this book.

Fandango Rock is, in fact, more a novel of Spain than of America, though half of its cast is American. Mr. Masters is intrigued by a problem that is still groping toward a solution in Spain, Morocco, Turkey, and wherever else our bombers are based on foreign soil. What happens when a self-contained, self-supporting, ultra-mechanized American military enclave imposes itself on a poor, proud, older civilization subsisting on its past? It is the answer to this question which the author seeks to work out. . . . Eventually Mr. Masters works it all out to a relatively happy ending for his characters, though the larger issues are left unresolved. As in his other books, the background is richly and expertly painted, and even the minor characters are fashioned with care. . . . In his use of American slang—the *bête noire* of foreign-born writers— he never puts a foot wrong. In his next book, I hope Mr. Masters will go all the way and give us a novel wholly in the American grain.

John Barkham. *NYT*. Feb. 23, 1959, pp. 5, 33

Perhaps the outstanding achievement of this second autobiographical volume [*The Road Past Mandalay*] is in making real and understandable the pride and appeal of soldierhood. One finishes it with the conviction that the soldier in combat, commanding other soldiers, meets demands upon character that no other category of human beings has to face, and that he comes closer to his fellow men, and mankind itself, than the rest of us—doctors, priests, politicians, humanitarians—can ever expect to. . . .

Masters is evidently a person of unusual vitality, with an unflagging gusto for experience and discovery, and with a gift for bringing effortlessly to life whatever he touches, be it a Himalayan sheep-dog, a C-47 snatching a glider from the ground, a Persian chambermaid or a battering-ram of a five-foot-two Welsh divisional commander. He is a writer to be read. . . .

The Road Past Mandalay begins in Iraq in 1942 and moves through Iran and India, but it is concerned most of all with Burma. . . . Those who were with Masters in combat must have felt that as an officer he was the right man in the right spot. Those who read him will have no doubt that as a writer he was; for he has to a very special degree both the human and the heroic view, both indispensable to telling what it was really like.

Charlton Ogburn, Jr. *NYT*. Aug. 20, 1961, p. 3

MAUGHAM, W. S. (1874–   )

In Mr. Maugham's story [*Mrs. Craddock*] a girl, young, well-born, imaginative, romantic and clever with "full red lips almost passionately sensual" marries a commonplace Philistine with broad shoulders and the heartiness and intolerant joviality of the prosperous farmer. . . . His strong body still appeals to her after she has learnt to hate his placid mind and pigmy soul. The idea is hackneyed enough and Mr. Maugham does not quite succeed in investing it with distinction. But there is a rugged strength about his work, a faithfulness to life, which makes us almost forgive a certain coarseness of conception and expression that seems inevitable with the modern realist. The inartistic finish and the crude trick by which the author kills off Mr. Craddock are quite out of keeping with the treatment of the earlier portions of the book.

SR. Jan. 10, 1903, Supplement p. i

Mr. Maugham has been inspired to write a strictly usual play [*The Land of Promise*] about Canada. He has evidently been there, but it is not so evident that he was tempted to stay. Mr. Maugham's Canadians say "Yeop" when they intend the answer to be in the affirmative, they speak of hiring out, and of half and quarter sections, and of the railway deepo; but when they become dithyrambic about the land of promise they carry, one fancies, less conviction. When Mr. Maugham's heroine plumps for staying in Canada, one does not find oneself forgetting that Mr. Maugham elected to come home. . . .

No, I do not think it is likely that Mr. Maugham's play will materially affect the emigration returns. Perhaps it was my fancy, but I thought it possible to detect a certain tenderness on the part of the dramatist towards the effete young Englishman, set over against the elemental Canadians for purposes of dramatic contrast, who announced himself as "fed up with God's own country."

P. P. Howe. *OutL*. March 7, 1914, pp. 307–8

His practice, through the many years since he emerged as a new author, has always squared with his precepts. Somebody writing of him a little while ago said he got his intimate knowledge of men and women, particularly of the London poor, while he was working as a doctor, but this is scarcely accurate. After completing his education at King's School, Canterbury, and Heidelberg University, he became a student at St. Thomas's Hospital, and in due course took his M.R.C.S. and L.R.C.P. degrees, but he never put up his brass plate and worked as a doctor. He had never seriously intended doing so. His family wished him to study medicine, and he yielded to that wish, but his own ambition from the first had been to write for the stage. He was convinced that stagecraft was a knack he could acquire if he made up his mind to it; but he had a saving leaven of common sense and had seen enough of things to know that it was infinitely harder to worry through all the difficulties between writing a play and getting it produced than to find a publisher for a novel, so he resolved to turn novelist as a means of earning bread and butter and winning a large enough reputation to move theatre managers to feel that it was at least worth their while to look at his dramas.

Arthur St. John Adcock. *Gods of Modern Grub Street*
(Sampson Low, Marston, 1923), p. 216

Before we complain that Mr. Maugham has not hit the bull's-eye, we must decide what target he was aiming at. In other words, what did Mr. Maugham set out to do? And did he do it? And in being disappointed were we, or more accurately was I, confusing the play [*Sheppey*] that Mr. Maugham had written with the play I would like him to have written? Or worse still, the play I would like Mr. Shaw to have written?

Mr. Maugham, then, must not be blamed for declining to be Shavian and insisting upon remaining Maughamesque. Whence it follows that we must ask what kind of delight we expected from the best Maughamesque treatment of this theme—the application of Christ's teaching to the modern world. Mr. Maugham, though never a deep thinker, was always a witty one. "It was the best butter," pleaded the March Hare, and from Mr. Maugham we are also entitled to the best wit, the best irony, and above all the best playcraft. Now, my first impression on Thursday was that the author had not devoted nearly enough time and trouble to what, given the subject, must be a major work. During the evening this clarified to the notion that Mr. Maugham had never quite decided what his subject was, and had been in three successive minds about it.

James Agate. *First Nights* (Ivor Nicholson and Watson,
1934), pp. 197–98

His first play was a one-act piece in German, entitled *Schiffbrüchig,* which was produced in Berlin in 1901 when its author was twenty-seven; but this was not to be his first work, for he began his career as a novelist, and not as a dramatist, and he had written four novels before his earliest play was performed. The first of them, *Liza of Lambeth,* was published in 1897, and immediately established him as a man writing with some authority. This is a remarkable novel for anyone to have written, but that it should have been written by a young medical student only just out of his teens is astonishing. It is a book that no one but a young doctor with a generous and indignant mind could have written, and it is the young and generous and socially indignant doctor in Mr. Maugham whose reappearance I still confidently await. It is not my business now to treat of Mr. Maugham's novels, of which he has written over a score except to say that they reveal the dramatist as effectively as do the plays. He tells a story in a terse and quick and vivid manner. He has views, but he subordinates them to his tale, and he can, when he chooses, indulge himself in a long, stylish piece of dialogue, but he prefers to tell a story without wasting time on opinions or extraneous decoration. He seldom diverges from the main avenue, nor is he distracted by side issues, however amusing they may be. No one who has studied his work can imagine him opening a play with a long irrelevant dialogue on ritualism, such as that with which Mr. Shaw opens *The Apple Cart,* nor can anyone imagine him digressing from his theme to discuss the state of the Irish people in the year A.D. 3000, as Mr. Shaw does so amusingly and at such length in the fourth part of *Back to Methuselah.* Mr. Shaw is, of course, the victim of his opinions and can easily be diverted from his intention by any idea that comes into his head, but Mr. Maugham is a more austerely disciplined man than Mr. Shaw—how can he be otherwise when he has so much law in his blood?—and will not allow himself to be distracted. His people are assembled and their purpose displayed without fuss or delay. The skill with which he deploys his forces makes one call him a great craftsman, and the fact that this skill has been apparent in all his plays and novels, from his first to his latest, entitles him to be called a born story-teller. His success has undoubtedly damaged him in the eyes of those critics who cannot believe that a writer has any merit if the sale of each of his novels exceeds 500 copies, or if his plays are seen by more than seventeen people. Earnest youths from Oxford and Cambridge and the Polytechnic, when they write assignments on modern literature, seldom deign to mention Mr. Maugham. But his place in our literature is secure and high. He is a better dramatist than Congreve, and his comedy, *The Circle,* is superior to *The Way of the World.* . . . Mr. Maugham's novels are better than his plays, but only because he takes them more seriously. He could, if he would, become the most important dramatist of his day.

St. John Ervine. *LL.* March, 1935, pp. 640–41

There was . . . a demand for comedy of a more sophisticated character and this need was met brilliantly in the 'twenties by Somerset Maugham. He had begun to write for the theatre as early as 1898, and between then and 1933 he had written some thirty plays. He first captured the

London theatre with *Lady Frederick* in 1907 and the play ran for a whole year. His success from that date had been continuous, and he entered the post-war period in 1919 with two successful pieces, *Caesar's Wife* and *Home and Beauty,* neither among the best of his plays. These were followed in 1921 with *The Circle,* which is probably the most skilful and finished of his comedies. It can claim a place with Sheridan and Wilde. A certain moral cynicism dwells in the action, but the whole theme is lightly touched. More precisely a portrait of the degenerate pleasures of the idle rich was *Our Betters* which appeared in 1923.

Had Maugham's success in the theatre come in a more sober period, he would probably have responded with a more profound type of drama for there is an ultimate seriousness in his nature. When in the passage from the 'twenties to the 'thirties the mood of the age changes, Maugham changes with it. *The Bread-winner* of 1930, though a comedy, has sardonic elements in its picture of a stockbroker who deserts his family because he is bored with their emptiness and their multifarious claims. In 1932 in *For Services Rendered* he writes a play, tragic in theme, of the cruel effects of the war on the lives of men and women, and with *Sheppey* (1933) he portrays a winner of a sweepstake ticket who tries, in a manner too literal for his family, to carry out the teaching of Jesus. Dramatically these more serious plays lacked the technical brilliance of the earlier comedies. It is in them that his greatest achievement as a dramatist lies. He exposes through a medium of comedy an expensive and cynical society, so that his plays sometimes have the appearance of being restoration comedy in modern dress. His characters have never the supreme self-confidence of Congreve's characters, for these modern figures lack much of the elegance and the wit of their restoration predecessors, and they are somehow conscious that the censorious eyes of democracy are upon them. Maugham is an undoubted artist with a great gift for the theatre, though probably with less affection for the drama than for fiction. One feels that his mind moves too narrowly upon the stage, as if he were excessively aware of the alleged and superficial needs of his audience.

B. Ifor Evans. *English Literature Between The Wars*
(Methuen, 2nd ed. 1949), pp. 118–19

Mr. Maugham is not so deft at catching life-rhythm in dialogue, and his wit is deliberate rather than quick. Consequently, when not first-rate, it disappoints. On the other hand he has a far firmer grip of what he is writing about, and the implications of his subject. He always knows where he is. He is adept in making his characters betray themselves in typical lines. Sometimes he abuses this power, and you think, "But if that person could *say* that, he or she would certainly know more about themselves than the dramatist intends them to know." But at others he puts into their mouths a line which illuminates character unconsciously, and the situation from top to bottom. He has a far firmer grasp of ultimate futilities about which Mr. [Noel] Coward tends to be sentimental.

Mr. Maugham's works can hardly be described as the harvest of an indulgent eye. His best jokes have grim implications; his best-drawn characters are exposures. His good people are apt to be conventional figures or hazy in outline; and he has evidently been much struck on his journey through the world by the impudent selfishness of certain types of women. In a sense he approves of selfishness. He sees it masquerading everywhere, and he has come to prefer it naked and unashamed. But really, we seem to hear him say, some women carry selfishness too far! They are such bilkers too, taking without giving, and without a notion of fair play.

Desmond MacCarthy. *Humanities*
(MacGibbon and Kee, 1953), p. 97

Somerset Maugham celebrates his eightieth birthday this month. There is scarcely anyone living who can remember a time when he was not one of the most prominent figures upon the literary scene. For over twenty years he has enjoyed a unique supremacy. Writers, he has said more than once, have their ups and downs, but for nearly half a century the current of his own success has been unchecked. An occasional play may have been taken off after a few weeks' run, but its withdrawal has usually coincided with the presence of a novel high in the best-seller list. Few writers have dominated their day to an equivalent extent. . . .

Right from the start he has been the object of curiosity and conjecture. His popularity in alternating terms of book-sales and box-office returns has been consistent, but his reputation in regard to critical opinion has known marked fluctuations. In 1918 W. L. George, who was very far from being a dilettante, published a book called *A Novelist on Novels*. In it, he posed the question, Who were the men who in 1940 would be occupying the positions at that moment filled by Wells, Bennett, Galsworthy, and Conrad? Maugham is not mentioned in the book although *Of Human Bondage* had been published only a few months before. It may well seem today astonishing that he was not, but his career in retrospect presents both in his life and work a fascinating sequence of surprises, anomalies, and contradictions. . . .

In *A Writer's Notebook* he expresses doubt as to whether so long a book can hope to survive the pressure of the future. But it is, it seems to me, on other grounds that *Of Human Bondage* is less likely to appeal to succeeding generations than many of his short stories. He has said himself that though a writer may set out to draw a picture of life, it can never be more than a partial one, but if he is fortunate he will succeed in doing something else, he will draw a complete picture of himself. And though Maugham has called *Of Human Bondage* an autobiographical novel, there is less of the essential Maugham there than in *Cakes and Ale* and in *The Moon and Sixpence*. Philip in *Of Human Bondage* may have shared many of Maugham's experiences, but he is not Maugham; he is an obscure doctor, not a successful doctor. A man with Maugham's temperament would never have remained obscure.

Alec Waugh. Enc. Jan. 1954, pp. 38, 43

The most impressive, most moving essay in *Points of View* (announced as his last book) is the story of a Hindu saint whom Maugham met. Yet, even here, the extroverted mind of the master falls short: he collects the facts, the fascinating "copy," and hinges it all carefully into his crisp album of curiosities. He does the same with Goethe, the Goncourts, Paul Léautaud, Henry James, Katherine Mansfield, and Chekhov. His portraits and summaries are entertaining, but he seems detached from them; his critical comments disappoint—a relaxing master's chit-chat for the Admass. He speaks movingly of the writer's vocation—"adding adornment to the grim business of living"—but he neither accepts or transcends. It is not that one asks him for a religious view, but simply that an evident faith deepens and stabilizes both books and people. . . . He offers no substitutes: religiousness is not the same as having a faith, and he knows it. Perhaps that is why he seems, in the end, . . . serenely literate in his lack of belief.

Paul West. Eng. Spring, 1959, pp. 148–49

As everybody knows, *Of Human Bondage* is based on Maugham's youth and early manhood, but it is a novel, not an autobiography, and therefore not always reliable as to the facts of Maugham's life, for a novelist made such changes as were necessary to translate fact into good fiction. There is, for example, no mention of the eight formative years in France. Philip Carey's early years are spent in England, and he is completely English. He is an only child; his mother dies after his father; he has a club foot. Whitstable becomes Blackstable in the novel; and Canterbury, where Willie went to school, becomes Tercanbury. . . .

Once, trying to separate fact from fiction in *Of Human Bondage*, I asked whether it was fair to say that the thoughts and emotions of Philip at a given time were his at that age, and he agreed that it was. He added that many of Philip's experiences were his; others happened to people he knew and he transferred them to Philip; some were imaginary.

Clearly, then, although many of the facts of Maugham's life are there, the novel is not the place to go for facts one can swear by.

Karl G. Pfeiffer. *W. Somerset Maugham* (N.Y.,
W. W. Norton, 1959), pp. 28–29

"If I had died twenty-four years ago when I was sixty," he said recently, "I think I would have been forgotten now. You see, a very strange thing has happened to me in the past ten years. During that time I have produced nothing of consequence—yet I have had more success than ever before. My collected stories have sold close to 300,000 copies in a year. You know how funny the English are about old age—once they take someone to their hearts, they are loyal to the last, whether it's a singer who has lost his voice, or an actor who forgets his lines. That seems to have happened to me!" Maugham's books have long had an excellent sale. By the middle of 1950, according to his American publishers, a total of 4,339,520 copies of the various editions of his novels, stories and plays had been sold. The best seller of them all was *The Razor's Edge,* published in 1944, which had sold 1,367,283 copies. *Of Human Bondage* has never sold fewer than 30,000 copies in any of its first thirty years. It is estimated that altogether his sales throughout the whole world have amounted to close on forty million copies.

Klaus W. Jonas. "The Gentleman from Cap Ferrat,"
in *The World of Somerset Maugham,* ed. Klaus W. Jonas
(N.Y., British Book Centre, 1959), pp. 32–33

It has often been suggested that this long novel [*Of Human Bondage*] could very well end with Philip's gaining his freedom from Mildred, for many readers feel that this sordid love story constitutes the novel's main concern. Actually the book's central theme is Philip's quest for a philosophy that will free him from intellectual and emotional bondage—that will enable him to meet life with equanimity, courage, and humor. The climax of the novel, one of the most moving scenes in modern fiction, in which Mildred plays a minor part, is the episode in the British Museum, when Philip finds the answer to his agonizing question as to the meaning of life. He rejoices in his new-found freedom from bondage to established beliefs that have offended his intelligence and to the bondage of his degrading passion for Mildred. His humiliating experience with her is only one of many experiences that have enabled him to know himself. . . .

He wrote *Of Human Bondage* after a long period of playwriting, the influence of which is discernible in the dialogue as well as in the general economy and precision. Here he follows more scrupulously his own advice, "Stick to the point," then he does in *The Moon and Sixpence* and *Cakes and Ale*. The dialogue is spare and stark like that in prewar plays by Barker, Hankin, and Galsworthy. The style of the novel is not exactly mannered but the attempt, like that of Hemingway a few years later, to make plain statements of fact with few adjectives results for occasional readers in monotony. They feel such a style cannot give proper expression to deeply felt emotions and lyrical feeling. They assert that Maugham in going so far to avoid richness and the jewelled phrase has not always escaped dryness and flatness. Some readers have wished that he would "let himself go." A reader of fiction interested in the disparate uses of the English language could profitably examine any page from a novel by Joseph Conrad or Thomas Wolfe and compare its style with that of *Of Human Bondage*. Maugham believed that the subject did not warrant the use of a relaxed and urbane colloquial style, which he was to handle with success later in *Cakes and Ale*. Most readers are certain that the novel often gains in strength and reality because of its severity and plainness; narrative passages such as those in the first four chapters are moving and powerful because they are stripped and bare.

Richard A. Cordell. *Somerset Maugham: A Biographical and Critical Study* (Bloomington, Indiana Univ. Pr., 1961), pp. 96–97, 98–99

The more outrageous the specimen confronting him, the greater Maugham's success. Then one finds him responding to the incalculability, the absurdity, of human behavior with a fascinated admiration—admiration in both the original and the current sense of the word—that is in no way lessened by the sardonic irony with which it is expressed. His response to absurdity, to the particularly gorgeous specimen, such as Alroy Kear in *Cakes and Ale,* has the effect not of diminishing but of enhancing the specimen. The response, indeed, is the response of the imagination Maugham denies he has. . . .

With Maugham, one comes back always to the point of view. It is not the most agreeable in the world, and its limitations are obvious; what it catches in its sights it often trivializes. Yet every now and then, in three or four novels, some short stories and three plays, it has provided a vision that is compelling and lingering. And in the end, one is forced to conclude that the man who could face up to and create the bleakly pessimistic world of *Of Human Bondage,* and also create the comic version of English literary life that is *Cakes and Ale,* is not a small writer—nor, for that matter, so very limited a one.

Walter Allen. *NYT*. Jan. 18, 1964, p. 24

MENEN, AUBREY (1912–   )

This [*The Prevalence of Witches*] is a lively and original first novel, a novel of ideas subscribing to the neo-Peacockian school of amusing, intelligent conversation and fantastic incident of *South Wind* and *Crome Yellow*. It is a school which loses pupils in wartime and fills up quickly during the frivolous aftermath. Not that Mr. Menen lacks high purpose in spite of his humour. His theme, indeed, is really religious belief; his setting, a remote part of India inhabited by aboriginals who have barely left the animistic stage. The chief English characters are the narrator and his cronies, a pair of immensely garrulous intellectuals named Catullus and Bay, and a surprisingly tolerant American missionary. . . .

Among his strong qualities is an insight into the primitive mind. He has real sympathy with his native characters and they come alive. He writes nicely, is seldom pompous, and makes a neat job of describing tropical scenery.

TLS. Dec. 6, 1947, p. 625

Aubrey Menen's *The Backward Bride* is a bright but disappointing satire on intellectual fashions of today. There is more in them than fashion, though. A charming Sicilian marries the priggish nephew of a comic-opera brigand, who escorts them on their honeymoon trip to England and France. Aquila, the husband, stuffed with learning, does not know how to manage his Anisetta, and she takes lessons, not from books, but from the types whom it is Mr. Menen's intention to guy. In life they are harder nuts than is insinuated here.

Paul Bloomfield. *MG*. Nov. 3, 1950, p. 4

Even in his novels Aubrey Menen is at his best when he is writing essays. My favorite scene in *The Prevalence of Witches,* for instance, is the one in which several of his characters decide (with relatively little motive except that they all love to talk) to make speeches to each other. This may sound like a flimsy excuse for Mr. Menen to amuse himself with a pleasant diversity of ideas, but the result is so entertaining and so provocative that one is quite happy to abandon the conventional novel form.

In *Dead Man in the Silver Market,* Mr. Menen has written his first book entirely of essays, and the result is everything that his admirers might have expected. The essays are not exactly sequential but are loosely connected by the general theme of nationalism—a subject about which Mr. Menen is singularly well-equipped to write because, with an

Indian father and Irish mother and an English upbringing, he has been exposed to three of the most virulent types in the world.

Santha Rama Rau. *NYT*. Aug. 23, 1953, p. 17

This [*Rama Retold*] is a diverting caper, based on the Ramayana, a 2,500-year-old epic by a poetic sage named Valmiki. It originally contained some sharp satire against the Brahmins, but its point became obscured by generations of toadies. Mr. Menen tells it straightforwardly with some interpolations of his own. These are mainly fables; one in particular about a fidelity test, a subject that is especially suitable to the Hindu approach with its passion for complication. They fit in well with the Rama story. . . .

Anyone who shys at the Indian penchant for interminability may be reassured. Mr. Menen manages to keep it within a couple of hundred pages.

Maurice Richardson. *NSN*. Aug. 7, 1954, p. 163

The chief virtue of Aubrey Menen's new novel [*The Abode of Love*] is that it is genuinely funny. Any author who chooses to write a comedy about a nineteenth-century harem at its center exposes himself to the danger of becoming coy or cute. Mr. Menen avoids this cloying possibility. His comedy rises naturally from his conception of character and from the dramatic, or at least conversational, situations in which he places his figures. . . .

Mr. Menen is a moralist, of course; the type is endemic among comic writers. He is not, however, satisfied that his story should directly or indirectly make comments on the conventional religion, morality, and economics of the nineteenth century. He must also insist that Prince [the hero] was basically at fault in his re-evaluation of right and wrong. For the most part his insistence is in character with the rest of the book. . . . In only one paragraph at the point where Prince is developing his new doctrine, does Mr. Menen step in to attempt to connect Prince's reversal of conventional right and wrong with more horrifying reversals of the twentieth century, the Nazis for instance. The paragraph is jarring, not because it is a sudden revelation of truth, but because it seems perverse in its forced comparison. It is impossible to take the *Abode of Love* seriously, to find a direct line from Henry James Prince's countryhouse harem to Belsen. Perhaps Menen's real intention is embedded in this revelatory paragraph, but the novel would have been better without it.

Gerald Weales. *Com*. June 8, 1956, pp. 256–57

MEW, CHARLOTTE, (1870–1928)

The Farmer's Bride is a book of forty pages containing seventeen poems. This at present is Charlotte Mew's only published work. The whole of Mrs. Browning's remains can hardly be compressed into five hundred pages of double column. Such poets would not, or could not, learn condensation or practise forbearance. They shirked weeding their own gardens which thus fell to seed, and the flowers are now lost in a tangle of forsaken undergrowth.

Charlotte Mew will not burden futurity with an "Essay on Mind" in two long books of rhymed couplets and with notes, nor with a "Battle of Marathon" in four cantos, nor an "Aurora Leigh" in nine books. Her poetry reveals plainly that she is too modest a person and too authentic an artist. Her imagination could not wander through hundreds of lines of blank verse, or, if it tried, discretion would certainly laugh it back homewards. . . .

She does not tire you with personality; but continually interests you in its strange reflections. There is a rumour through the whole book of Death (that favorite subject of all poetry), as of a fact in the background, not to be forgotten, yet not a reality. . . .

Charlotte Mew's poem "The Changeling" is one of the most original of its kind in modern poetry. It has nothing in common with Christina Rossetti, Stevenson, Walter de la Mare, or any other writer of fairy poetry. It is neither written down nor up: it is factful, not fanciful. It is not quaint or sweet, but hard and rather dreary. You do not smile; you shiver. This child has been born a changeling just as another may have had the misfortune to have been born an idiot, and it tries rather blunderingly, apologetically, and with a touch of bitterness to explain its inevitable fate. . . .

No words are wasted on describing its emotional effect. The method of this poem is to stir the reader to great apprehension and then abruptly leave his imagination to follow its natural course. . . .

No argument, or quotation, can prove that the poetry of Charlotte Mew is above the average of our day. She writes with the naturalness of one whom real passion has excited; her diction is free from artificial conceits, is inspired by the force of its subject, and creates its own direct intellectual contact with the reader. Her phraseology is hard and concentrated. To praise her poetry is to offer homage where it is due; and to recommend it is to desire for others the enjoyment one has oneself experienced.

Harold Monro. Some Contemporary Poets (Leonard
Parsons, 1920), pp. 75–82

Women have not often been great poets, but they often have had one or two special qualifications. If their poetry has been narrow, on the other hand, it has been seldom flat; and in that narrow space—feeling, moreover, no call to be vigorous—they can the more easily achieve a high degree of finish. Charlotte Mew's verse [*The Rambling Sailor*] is a distinguished example of this class: ladylike, intense, rather confined; with only here and there a spirited and lucky venture into the objective. Her style is sophisticated, but single; an instrument evidently valued for itself, contrived merely to render in each poem one vibration of sincere feeling, not very loud.

LL. Oct., 1929, p. 398

Looking back on Charlotte Mew's published work it is difficult to understand how it was that so gifted a woman should have produced so little in the sixty years given to her. Many writers give up in despair at failing to place their work, but such was not her case. From the very first she found a ready market for her stories—the poems were a later development of her talent. She wrote a one-act play in Cornish dialect, *The China Bowl,* which shows her sense of drama at its best; Violet Vanbrugh intended producing it, but almost at the time she made the decision circumstances prevented her from carrying it out and to Charlotte's intense disappointment no more was heard of it. I think from what she said this was one of the great disappointments of her life, and, characteristically, being disappointed she threw the MS. into a drawer and left it there. She herself attributed her small output to the difficulties of domestic life, doing the housekeeping and looking after "Ma," and the constant interruptions when she sat at her desk—Jane, the factotum, who was with her for years, knocking on the door to ask if she should "finish up" the rice pudding for her dinner? and should she run out for some kippers? or would Miss Lottie mind going herself?

I think myself that as she grew older she no longer had the power of concentration required to sit at a desk for hours at a time, that she lost interest in story writing which had been her main work till about 1916, after which she wrote no more prose at all and very little verse. The sustained prose work dwindled from the long stories printed in *Temple Bar* in the nineties, to short studies and occasional essays in the early 1900's and then to odd poems, and slowly work came to a standstill. Also, I think she was afflicted with a certain dilettante outlook, perhaps the result of her education, which was the limited one of the 1870's and 80's, and also was partly influenced by her mother's attitude to a daughter with a career. No one in the family except Anne took her work seriously.

She was almost 50 when her first book *The Farmer's Bride* (1916) appeared, and although she was greatly encouraged by its reception she wasn't capable by then of writing much more. Few of the poems which were published posthumously in *The Rambling Sailor* (1929) were written after 1916. She always spoke of stacks of MSS. salted away in trunks, but after her death very little was found. Perhaps there was some truth in the remark she once made casually to me one afternoon at tea in Gordon Street. She was sitting making spills, which she used to light her endless cigarettes, and which were also made for the parrot to chew and amuse himself with. Seeing some writing on some of these, I asked if she used up old letters that way, and she replied— "I'm burning up my work. I don't know what elso to do with it." Anne and I often wondered together whether she might be really destroying some original work, or whether it was just intended to whip us up. Who knows?

Only 500 copies of *The Farmer's Bride* were printed and they took five years to sell out, and yet out of that tiny edition came a great reputation. We published what was to us this big edition—many of the books that came from the Poetry Workshop had only 250 copies for their first edition—because we felt that in Charlotte Mew there was a poet whose work would justify our faith. Time has shown that we were right.

Alida Monro. *Adel.* Aug., 1953, pp. 286–88

Born in 1869, the poetess—tiny, bird-headed, iron-haired, bright-eyed, tweed-suited, velvet-collared, Oxford bow-ed and porkpie-hatted, just failing all her life long to keep up appearances—inhabited in extremely "reduced circumstances" the family house in Bloomsbury, together with a shrivelled and even tinier "Ma," a sister Anne who painted firescreens, and a ninety-year-old parrot with a festering claw. A third sister and only brother of this somewhat Brontë-ish household languished in insane asylums, and Charlotte and Anne had vowed themselves to chastity in order not to pass on the hereditary taint. . . . After the death of Anne in 1928, Charlotte's own reason became partly affected and she died by her own hand.

From this unhappy, enclosed, and haunted life, what poetry might be expected to come? Gentlewomanly landscapes, or ballads about cavaliers or fairies, or at best over-excited emotions brashly expressed? In timid, second-hand conventional techniques and forms, or perhaps in "free verse" with no form at all? Perhaps, if the gods were temporarily indulgent, a lucky-strike lyric and a little period charm? Nothing could be further from the actuality. Charlotte Mew is one of the most original and inventive of poets, her forms strong and entirely individual; her forte is the long semi-dramatic poem, in which she shows a control and sense of balance and effect that are quite astonishing; and her most successful subjects are such matters as "Madeleine in Church" (a prostitute's colloquy with the Virgin), or "The Fete"' (a boy's first sexual experience). A single poem by "queer lonely unhappy" Miss Mew tells us more about human beings and their relationships, one to another, more about this world we live in, more about "reality," than the whole corpus of Mr. [Wallace] Stevens' writings.

Hilary Corke. *Enc.* June, 1954, pp. 78, 80

MEYERSTEIN, E. H. W. (1889–1952)

"Surprise is the forerunner of success," says General Gammerlommer in . . . *Grobo,* and throughout the 95 chapters of this latter-day example of the Picaresque novel, the author does his utmost to live up to the General's dictum. As his hero he takes Grobo, a dream-a-day little son of a poor and rascally wine merchant . . . causes him to be adopted by the most unlikely person imaginable—Sir William Lockjaw, an animated ramrod, who brings him to England and in due course sends him to Harrow. . . .

Mr. Meyerstein's Oxford in wartime is, if possible, even more fantastic than his Harrow; but it must be confessed that the adventures there of his irresponsible Grobo . . . with dons, fairies, undergraduates, and others, become in the end, not a little wearying, for by that time the reader's capability of being surprised is utterly exhausted. Thus the author defeats his own imagination and humour, forgoes the success he might have attained.

TLS. April 23, 1925, p. 282

In his new volume Mr. Meyerstein [*Eclogues*] is at his best; interpreting, for the most part, personalities with whom his extensive reading has made him familiar, rather after the fashion of a Browning-in-little, although his manner owes nothing to that of the earlier poet. And still less is it akin to that of the modern contortionists. His is no private poetry: here is no introspective exhibitionism. Mr. Meyerstein is not concerned with the exploration of the abysmal confusion of subconscious obscurity, so beloved of those self-centered writers who seek to give expression to their own inconsequent personalities in an all too appropriate irruption of incoherent images; but draws his inspiration from a remarkable diversity of sources; while his verse has something of the precision and lucidity of that of the eighteenth-century poets. The characters of these

"Eclogues," some of them people of importance in their day, others of less consequence, are so various that I can only give an idea of the scope of Mr. Meyerstein's interests by enumerating their names. They are Clodia and Caelius; Meryon; Rimbaud; Clementi; Collins; Apollonius; Beddoes; Spinoza; Ducasse; Marryat; Karl, Beethoven's nephew; Sand, Kotzebue's assassin; Mendelssohn; Alexander; Pater and Wilde; Diomed and Cressid; and Chatterton; as well as several less well known or anonymous individuals.

Wilfrid Gibson. Eng. Spring, 1941, p. 194

This [*The Visionary*] is a series or cluster of short poems, each independent but linked together by similarity of mood, somewhat as the sections of *In Memoriam* are related to each other; the poems being all in one metre, *terza rima*. Mr. Meyerstein must be congratulated on his handling of this metre. Of the poets who have attempted the form in English, none, I think, has been more successful. Though the rhymes are occasionally a little forced, they are not weak or stale; and the true structure of the metre is observed and maintained. Perhaps the vein of mystic feeling in the poems has made Dante's metre a sympathetic medium for its expression, though there is no imitation of Dante in them.

Laurence Binyon. Eng. Summer, 1942, p. 62

Mr. Meyerstein's is a curious and eclectic talent. Fancy rather than imagination jogs his elbow, and is habitually projected in a style of urbane and impersonal gravity that leans by turns towards one or other of half-a-dozen eighteenth-century models, from Defoe to Horace Walpole. In *Tom Tallion* he assumes an innocence that is truly sinister; his modulations of fancy, for all their seeming sobriety, spill over into a flood of Gothic idiosyncrasy, which carries the story away on a tide of murder and sudden death. The book is, indeed, an odd mixture of the prosaic and the fantastic. It tells, in the first person, of a youth in his father's second-hand bookshop in Hampstead in the early years of the century who always kept the world at one remove from him and who became a spectacular and precocious artist. The bookshop atmosphere, which is thickened into a rich eccentricity by Tallion senior's moral teaching, his methods of salesmanship and the wanton humours of his customers, is amusingly done, and allows Mr. Meyerstein to show off his bibliophile's paces. What to make of Tom's absorption of his singular and bloody experiences, however, is another matter. It was very sensible of him, no doubt, to eat the pomegranate after he had experienced difficulty in drawing it and thus, symbolically speaking, to acquire the habit or artistic assimilation; but what logic of art or of fantasy is to be attached, for instance, to Mr. Glare, who made vestas and for whom Tom drew a terrific poster of the burning of the Alexandrian Library, or to the incandescent middle-aged passion he woke in the beautiful and aristocratic Mrs. Glare, who was a Pompquine? An inventive and ingenious book, but it prompts too many questions of the most literal sort.

R. D. Charques. *Spec.* Sept. 5, 1952, p. 310

The case I refer to was that of E. H. W. Meyerstein, whose acquaintance I made in my third term [at Oxford] and who was one of my closest companions for the rest of my undergraduate days. Meyerstein was such a fantastic figure that I doubt if I can make him credible to anyone who never met him: still, this being my story and he being one of the principal characters in it, I must see what I can do.

To begin with, let me fill in the public facts, so to speak, about Meyerstein. The son of a wealthy man (about whom I know nothing except that he seems to have been the caricaturist's ideal of the Edwardian Hampstead-Jewish Croesus) Edward Harry William, having got himself born and been equipped with three aggressively English Christian names, was launched into the pre-1914 world by way of Harrow and Magdalen. No expense was spared, and neither, if we are to believe the son's own posthumous narrative [*Of My Early Life*] was any ordeal or humiliation. Not only was "Eddie" expected to hold his own in the harsh world of the Edwardian public school, with its Spartan discipline and its frank, overt snobberies; he had also to justify his existence in the eyes of a large, interfering family who seemed to have achieved a rare blend of Jewish inquisitiveness with British arrogance. Dreamy, solitary, a passionate student, the boy was at home among books and music, awkward and troubled anywhere else; it is easy to imagine the ideal upbringing for such a child, one that would have brought out the latent sweetness of his character and developed his gifts, which were unquestionably very fine. What he actually got was an upbringing calculated to turn him into a raging neurotic by the time he was twenty-one, which it duly did.

Meyerstein was fifty-five when I first met him, and I don't want to waste time on speculation about things that happened twenty years before I was born; but this question of his upbringing really has some importance, since it accounts for a great many features of his behavior, tastes, and attitudes which I, as a youth of eighteen, found utterly baffling. What I could see—what anyone could see, at first glance—was that this man had spent his life in a long, desperately hard struggle to make some sort of a place for himself in literature. He had studied deeply, and had the Greek and Latin classics more or less by heart, as well as vast quantities of French and English literature; he had written hundreds of poems, publishing volume after volume at his own expense; he had translated the Elegies of Propertius, written a monumental life of Chatterton, contributed to scores of learned controversies in organs like the *Times Literary Supplement* and *Notes and Queries;* he had published immense novels, volumes of short stories, at least one play, and a mass of musical criticism in various papers. Day after day, year after year, he had guided his pen across paper, or hammered away at one or another of his beaten-up old typewriters. . . .

What I didn't realize at the time, of course, was that it had all come to nothing. All I could see was that Meyerstein was a wonderfully learned man who lived in a rich confusion of books and manuscripts and was always reading and writing. . . .

John Wain. Enc. Aug., 1962, pp. 29–30

MEYNELL, ALICE (1847–1922)

Alice Meynell published her first volume in 1875. She is an early example of the reticence that is now conspicuous in most branches of English poetry. . . .

Mrs. Meynell . . . and other poets . . . seem to have devoted themselves so exclusively to their art that they have not realized it as an outcome of the habit of Life that all poetry is intended to express.

Harold Monro. Some Contemporary Poets
(Leonard Parsons, 1920), pp. 41–42

Mrs. Meynell is a writer with an extraordinary power of raising the simple and the lowly to those lofty regions of the moral nature in which honour, dignity, and serenity—far from unimpassioned abstractions—sustain a triple sovereignty. If she touches grammatical questions you cannot for a moment think them mere grammatical questions. . . . Mrs. Meynell is one of our best critics, one of the subtlest, the austerest, the most constant in a regard for the obligations of the art of letters. Nothing slack or uneasy, nothing trivial or frivoulous, may endure her glance; and she does not mitigate it even when she confronts so especially admired a writer as Jane Austen. . . . Her essays on Coventry Patmore and George Meredith [*Second Person Singular*] are as independent in their praise as these others in blame; and all alike serve to remind us that a fine critic does not teach us what to believe or what to think or what to welcome, but how to judge for ourselves.

John Freeman. LM. Feb., 1922, p. 434

. . . Mrs. Meynell must place herself slightly at an oblique angle, and view the moments which possess her mind a little from one side. She shoots beside the mark rather than at it; and her arrows, like the bright glances of the robin, fly the straighter because they seem to spy their object from one side. This gave a bird-like quality to her writing, which is at once intense but detached.

We gain from her work, then, this: not, at first, an extension of our humanity but an added sharpness to our consciousness. But in so far as this consciousness is concerned with experiences not peculiar in themselves, but common to all men, it is enriching. The experience of Strephon in "St. Catharine of Siena" is an experience of mankind; Catharine herself is feminine humanity. Hackneyed or official themes are transformed by this insight. Shakespeare's Tercentenaries became two dates in Mrs. Meynell's own life, and the death of Edith Cavell is seen as perhaps Edith herself saw it: a nurse who watched at her own death-bed, a woman who quietly waited for the dawn. We penetrate beyond the heroine of the copy-book to the natural woman, and go with her to her execution. This is the quality which raises Mrs. Meynell's verse to the highest point possible to its own order. Each poem, too, is carefully reasoned, and the reader who does not follow the argument will miss the whole; for intellectually no less than emotionally the verse has point. This intellectual concentration is a dangerous quality. "Via et Veritas et Vita" is an epigram, but a good one. "Veni Creator" and "Why wilt Thou Chide?" seem, or seem near to, intellectual conceits. The latter poem apparently offers an impossibly subtle consolation. Renunciation, consolation—how the theme recurs!

Osbert Burdett. Critical Essays (Faber and Gwyer,
1925), pp. 132–33

Mrs. Meynell was never a professional writer, making daily recourse to a desk and producing books at regular intervals. She led an active and varied life. She bore and brought up a large family; she read and travelled; she entertained a large circle of friends; and Francis Thompson, whose noble poem "Her Portrait" was inspired by her, was only the most conspicuous of many writers, particularly young ones, who went to her for counsel and encouragement. She lived as well as wrote, and she would not have chosen to do otherwise. Yet there was no question with her of writing in spare moments. She wrote when she felt inclined; she spent great pains on preparation and revision; she had no desire to produce a great body of work. It is not easy to conceive any alteration of circumstances—even that economic pressure which she was happily spared—which would have led her to write more profusely or less carefully; and it may be assumed that what we have from her is all that she was born, or felt inclined, to give. By temperament and theory she was destined to do a few things as nearly perfectly as she could. Her philosophy was a kind of Christian stoicism, and she aimed at equanimity and self-control in her art as in her life.

There have been those whose careful and cunning artistry, tact and taste of expression, have arisen from a defect of passion. There was no defect of that in Alice Meynell; she had much to control, and control never froze the springs of emotion in her. In old age she retained the quick sensitiveness of youth, sweet and generous impulses, instant responsiveness to cruelty and injustice.

> J. C. Squire. *Essays on Poetry* (Hodder and Stoughton, 1925), pp. 98–99

Her poems were mostly the product of more leisured days, in youth and old age. The freakish taste of anthologists has made her best-known poem one with an almost disagreeable sentiment: ("She is so circumspect and right; she has her soul to keep.") The editors of the Centenary Volume have chosen the verse less surely than the prose. "Renouncement" (written at the enforced breaking of her youthful friendship with a priest) is popular, I think, because it treats of the widely felt grief of separation, also, perhaps, because it encloses a hidden resentment; but "Parted" is a much finer poem about the same experience. . . .

Hers is a craftsman's poetry, written with a fine tension on pensive and private subjects; such work will always give pleasure. But in prose she found greater scope.

Her writing shows curiously little fantasy. It contains portraits, but not a hint of fiction. It is not the literature of dreams but of ideas and observations, coming from an unusually sensitive and vigorous mind. Now that we are sufficiently far removed from Meredith's praise and Mr. Beerbohm's protest, we can discover for ourselves something of the stimulation that the contemporary reader found in her work.

> Naomi Lewis. *A Visit to Mrs. Wilcox* (The Cresset Press, 1957), pp. 209–11

MEYNELL, VIOLA (1886–1956)

Of the making of many books there is no end. But in all their thousands how few of them there are that in any striking fashion differentiate themselves from the rest. But the rarest of all pleasures that comes a critic's way—that of being able to assert with surety and conviction that he has found something with the stuff within it that makes for greatness—is the happy result of a perusal of *Modern Lovers*. With how much of it we cordially agree!. . . . The two books with which it makes an odd comparison are *Wuthering Heights* and, of all the stories in the world in this connection, Schnitzler's *The Road to the Open*. No two stories of course could be more dissimilar. But it is the curious intermixture of weirdness and strangeness and harshness that seemed built into the very stones of the grim house upon the heights in conjunction with Schnitzler's cynical modernity that makes this particular novel unlike any other novel we have ever lit upon.

OutL. Jan. 17, 1914, p. 84

She, like so many modern writers, rejects the realistic novel, the novel of ordinary manners; and, like them, in doing so she feels the need of some removed and, in the good sense, unreal setting for her stories. The classic examples of such settings are Mr. Conrad's ships at sea and his isolated and mysterious Asiatic lagoons. Here the novelist's characters are to be set free from the stream of everyday life and allowed to develop and act in an ideal manner. . . . Miss Meynell's attempt and partial failure here to remove and isolate her characters gives her book [Antonia] a bewildering and nightmare quality. The society in which the action takes place is cosmopolitan and bizarre in the extreme, but it remains attached to the world we know: not in any society, from whatever corners of the earth its members may have been brought, do people consistently behave as Miss Meynell makes them behave here, while simultaneously they are taking trains, shopping in Paris, and sending for doctors because the wife of the concierge has a touch of pleurisy. I shall not outline the story, the love passages of Antonia Borch with Oswald Brook, and her subsequent marriage to Prince Mitrany, because I do not pretend to understand it; least of all do I understand why the marriage should be so tragic a matter, though this is clearly the point of the book. But Miss Meynell's nightmare is vivid and, in its strange way, engrossing. In the intervals of doing the most common things her characters perform extraordinary gyrations of the spirit, which, incomprehensible as they are in themselves and in their further significance, have an undeniable interest. And Miss Meynell writes both eloquently and powerfully.

Edward Shanks. LM. Nov., 1921, p. 96

Miss Viola Meynell is distinguished by a gift for the broadly comic. Her girls who say: "Well, I don't know; I think people always like to do the things they're fond of doing," and "I put it down to the want of ignorance, don't you think so?" are adorable; and her elocution mistress might almost have come out of Martin Chuzzlewit. . . .

Women novelists have, on the whole, I think, succeeded better in the satiric delineation of men's foibles than in the direct delineation of their virtues (witness Jane Austen). I do not want to suggest any generalisation to the effect that this always must be so. But certainly, among the women writers of the day, and not least in Miss Meynell's work, I am troubled by a feeling that the male characters are too frequently relegated to a low moral level, a level of egoism and mere self-absorption. In *Columbine* the hero is amazingly self-centred: he sees everything as it affects his own personality, nothing objectively. In *Modern Lovers* the hero has faults to which one cannot help suspecting his creator was either blind or over-indulgent. It is not in the least that one wants didacticism, vice denounced, or virtue embarrassed with laudation: all one wants is the recognition, *felt* in the texture of the representation, revealed through it, that there is something abnormal, unrepresentative, unpleasant, in these egoistic excesses. *Narcissus* deals with two brothers, Victor and Jimmy. The relationship between them is one of the best things about them. Miss Meynell exercises upon it her rare gift of stressing sentimental values without ever becoming in the bad sense sentimental. She has a wonderful touch for the deep and recondite pleasure of simple things: the spiritual atmosphere of a living-room, the reading of a book.

Gerald Gould. The English Novel of Today
(John Castle, 1924), pp. 126–27

MILNE, A. A. (1882–1956)

Mr. Milne's . . . danger is that his dialogue flows with an ease so prodigious as at times almost to carry him beyond the scope of his subject. There must be tremendous temptations to one capable of spinning a glittering web of amusing nothings, until it ends like one of Edouard Strauss's waltzes that takes its title from this method—"Sans fin." Should he give way to this, he would soon come to out-Sacha Guitry, and would degenerate into an English stage boulevardier, with all the *longueurs* inflicted on us by that brilliant French actor when not himself on the scene to give life to his lines. But in Mr. Milne the sense of the play, as opposed to that of the theatre, is too strong for us to be in serious fear of such a fate overtaking him. Throughout his lightest badinage, and underlying his pleasantest epigrams, may be detected a healthy grip of the one thing that makes a play, and differentiates it from the hotch-potch of chatter that often passes for one—namely, the plot. It is precisely the fact that Mr. Milne, save for a few moments of diffuseness and redundancy, does not deviate from the necessarily narrow lines imposed by his subject, and strictly subordinates both characters and episodes to it, which allows the hope that he will give to England of our days, a comedy as perfectly typical of it, and as typically perfect, as were, in their centuries, *The Importance of Being Earnest, The School for Scandal,* and

Love for Love. In embroidery of his theme, in the construction of cunning little climaxes that advance its action, he is already an artist to whom few are superior.

John Pollock. *FR.* Aug., 1922, p. 340

Once in reviewing a volume of plays by Mr. A. A. Milne I said that I thought the best thing in the book was the Preface, and again I am tempted to make the same remark [*Three Plays*], although *The Dover Road,* which is printed in this volume, is an amusing light comedy.

W. J. Turner. *LM.* Aug., 1923, p. 429

I have asked the question whether success is not closing in on Mr. Milne. I think it is, in a way hardly superior to that in which it closed in on his hero [*Success*]. He began his career as a dramatist as a writer of high and artificial comedy, with talents for the genre not exceeded by anyone since Wilde save the late St. John Hankin. His *Belinda* was a work of great promise: his *Mr. Pim Passes By* was almost a fulfillment of that promise. But the first of these plays was nearly a failure: the second was a precarious success. Now Mr. Milne, who might have been one of the ornaments of the drama, prefers to dish up again the soft and easy modern doctrine of the importance of being a failure. This is nowadays one of the surest ways of becoming a success. But it appeals chiefly to persons who like to pity themselves . . . or to persons who, being successful, like to make the best of both worlds and flatter themselves that they can appreciate the virtues of the failures.

Edward Shanks. *OutL.* July 7, 1923, p. 14

Many thousands of people must have been waiting for this book [*When We Were Very Young*], which gives permanent form to the delightful nonsense rhymes which Mr. Milne has been contributing to *Punch* during the past year. It is difficult to review such a book, because it seems impossible to convey in any words, except their own, the odd sentimental charm of Mr. Milne's verses. . . . We certainly hope that Messrs. Milne and Shepard [illustrator] will continue their very successful collaboration and give us more of these verses and pictures which, if they are not better than any nursery rhymes that we possess, are at any rate comparable to the very best of them.

NS. Nov. 15, 1924, p. 178

The secret is, of course, that what the child enjoys is what it makes out of the book given it, and that is by no means necessarily the book as written. The pleasant absurdity of Mr. Milne's conceit [*Winnie The Pooh*] is just so much statement of fact to the child, to be found interesting or not as may happen. In this case it proves to be interesting. The child would find it fun to live in a forest under a name in gold letters and, besides, there is Mr. Shepard's convincingly realistic drawing of Winnie-the-Pooh doing so. And I think it is fair to say that the book would, among grown-ups, survive the loss of the illustrations, but not among children. For children they substantiate all the delightful facts mentioned in the text, the little houses, the parties, the balloons, Pooh's boats, and the rest of it. The comical subtleties of Mr. Shepard's draughtsmanship, so captivating to the grown-up, escape the child as completely as the verbal subtleties of Mr. Milne's style. And thus, be it remarked, the child enjoys books of which the authors never for a moment thought of being for his use. Children have been observed to like *Paradise Lost* and Young's *Night Thoughts.* They invariably like *Pilgrim's Progress* and the *Arabian Nights,* though neither was meant in the first place for use in the nursery.

Edward Shanks. *SR*. Oct. 30, 1926, p. 517

There is no writer of our time who has achieved success with more dignity, integrity and desert than has Mr. Milne. He belongs to that small but precious nucleus of high-principled, witty, solid Englishmen whose existence and efforts in all periods of English history have justified their country. This book [Am. ed. *Autobiography;* Eng. ed. *It's Too Late Now*] is worth reading, for it is a real book and an honest one. As essayist, humorist, playwright, its author has many admirers; his detective story *The Red House Mystery* ranks among the classics of that type of writing, and there is no need to stress the popularity of *Christopher Robin, Winnie the Pooh,* and his other books for children. . . .

When Mr. Milne turns to a discussion of his work, he permits himself no pose. He is professional, pragmatic, amused. He is satisfied if his peers and his public consider him a good workman who has given them the best he had. There is a very clever analysis of the play, *The Truth About Blayds,* given as a sample of his method of playwriting. He has many wise, down-to-earth observations to make on the subject of writing. There is little or no discussion of his contemporaries, no old scores paid off, and no exposés. Mr. Milne is artist enough to feel that this book is history, and not a cultural or social history of his time.

J. G. E. Hopkins. *Com.* Oct. 13, 1939, p. 568

It's Too Late Now is an accomplished, intimate and rather dandified account of the life of A. A. Milne. He reminds one of Noel Coward, a pre-war Noel Coward springing from the same unexpectedly lower middle-class stock, but moving with pre-war acceleration into a smooth heaven of light verse, cricketing weekend, good society, whimsical taste, and money, money, money. How fond A. A. Milne is of it: cheques and successes in all around he sees, and the more delightfully he writes, the more imminent is some financial climax: the sub-editorship of *Punch, Christopher Robin, When We Were Very Young,* or *Mr. Pim Passes By* This is a harmless and well-written book, but I found myself getting very angry with it—envy, possibly, of A. A. Milne's fat cut of the *douceur de vivre,* but irritation, certainly, at the gentlemanly good taste which veils both a shrewd eye on the main chance, and perhaps a fear of life. Such an impeccable *Times*-leading-article of a *petit-maître* existence, all success and whimsy, with never an unkind word for anyone else, and a deprecating smile for the humble recipient of so much honour—one wonders what Christopher Robin himself is like now, and what he would make of it.

Cyril Connolly. NSN. Nov. 11, 1939, p. 688

It has taken A. A. Milne a long time to live down the Christopher Robin episode. I think he makes final amends by the dedication of *Behind the Lines,* which is to Christopher Robin himself. These poems are mostly about the Dictators, at whom Milne *père* tilts with an almost fearless pen. The verses are neat but not gory, and a few chunks of the old wistful thinking are thrown in for good measure. But they do show that Mr. Milne can get hot, or at least fairly warm, under the collar on the right occasions.

Nicolas Bentley. Spec. Jan. 3, 1941, p. 20

The recent publication of *The Pooh Perplex* had the felicitous if unintended effect of sending many readers back to Pooh himself. In an age of parasitic criticism, [Frederic] Crew's book is bound to find favor, but Milne's was written to find favor in any age. Milne's animals and child-have kept the sense of miraculism alive; they attack the sense of certainty. How many pots of honey does Pooh have? He never really knows. Tigger has the problem of figuring out what he should eat for breakfast. Is there a part of the forest left out? Too many people would simply call it a hole and pass on. Milne teaches people how to wonder again.

David Ray. Cornell Univ. Library Readers'
Report, April, 1964, p. 6

MITCHISON, NAOMI (1897–   )

In writing a historical novel of Gaul in the time of Julius Caesar [*The Conquered*], Mrs. Mitchison has made a bold experiment that must be said, on the whole, to have succeeded. . . . There is in this story a fine objectivity, a close grip upon facts, not large historical facts, but the little facts that count for so much in romance, that carries conviction; and that and the writer's sound prose largely help to make it the surprising performance it is. Even its very faults as a story, a piece of drama . . . only help the author in her main purpose, for they leave us with the impression of long, dragging years of ineffectual heroism, divided loyalties and broken vows, the sudden sharp cruelties of fiery nationalists and jealous clans and the long heartbreaking cruelty of empires. This, I take it, is what Mrs. Mitchison intended when she put together so deftly this finely consistent prose narrative, and she may be said to have succeeded in doing something new that was really worth doing, for with this story she has occupied the space there is between the narrative poem (which may be in prose, if it is conceived as a poet conceives his work) and the historical novel. I hope she will contrive to stay there, for she has conquered the method, and the material, I imagine, is almost inexhaustible.

J. B. Priestley. LM. Sept., 1923, pp. 545–46

Black Sparta. . . . Twelve stories, with verses interspersed, of Greece in the fourth and fifth centuries. Mrs. Mitchison has put so much thought, work and feeling into them that I am sorry not to find the result more satisfactory. Transposition is, no doubt, the best device for making the ancient world alive, but Mrs. Mitchison transposes not into the key of modern life but into the key of a particular fiction—the kind in which the characters unroll their subconsciousness in a gurgling . . . [Greek], which reminds me more of Mrs. Pace in the *Weekly Dispatch* than of any Greek I have ever read. Now and then it comes off: the genesis of a Pindaric ode in "Lucky Thessaly" is well conceived and executed. But as a rule I have the feeling that Mrs. Mitchison has not apprehended her Greeks but compiled them out of elements which, apart from the conscientious homosexuality, are quite un-Hellenic. This would matter less if the stories were more interesting.

LL. Aug., 1928, pp. 230–31

Mrs. Mitchison does herself injustice when, in her foreword, she explains the neat little summaries which follow each section of her book by saying that "it is difficult to remember just what happened." The defect of *The Corn King and the Spring Queen* does not lie in any want of vividness. Her descriptive power never fails her. To a reader with even a moderate gift of visual memory there will remain at the end of his reading a complete and brightly coloured tapestry of great intricacy upon which, against backgrounds often of entrancing beauty, a number of queer figures, lively rather than life-like, appear in a vast variety of attitudes graceful or grotesque. One observes them with an admiring curiosity, but their cruelties excite one's horror as little as their loves engage one's emotions; their plots bring no catch to the breath; their fighting leaves the blood unstirred; even their obscenities do not shock. . . .

Yet, although the author's interest seems to have been devoted to archaeology rather than to the human aspect of her characters, and though a didactic tendency has led her to clog the narrative with redundancies, it is impossible not to admire the book. It is never for a moment dull.

Adel. Sept., 1931, pp. 549–50

Though not the best of . . . novels, *We Have Been Warned* is most interesting. Its theme is Left-wing politics in England, the activities and personal relationships of middle-class people feeling the draught of conscience and Communism, Oxford Socialist dons, the local Communist Party, strikes, Intourist trips to Russia, hunger marches to Hyde Park. Mrs. Mitchison knows her people. Some of the reporting is good, particularly the chapters about Russia. The different shades of Red opinion in this country and the changes of scene between Oxford, London, Scotland and Russia make the book varied and readable, and help also to disguise the muddled sentimentalism of the writing. But at times the Sunday-school atmosphere becomes overpowering.

G. W. Stonier. *FR.* June, 1935, p. 763

It is, at first, almost a relief to see that a new novel [*When We Become Men*] about African problems is by a name long familiar in our own literary circles, someone on whom one has at least some background information by which to measure not so much the treatment as the voice adopted. In fact, however, Mrs. Mitchison has deliberately invited attack from both political and literary sides of the African fence: she has become a member of the Batswana tribe in Bechuanaland, thus entitling herself to write not as an observer but through the eyes and hearts of the African; and she has chosen tribalism, in the "new and free" form which she believes may perhaps provide the ultimate answer to that unhappy continent's search for a just society, as the centre of a novel about pressures of old and new, democratic and feudal, which will very probably provoke all factions to denounce her picture of African life as unconvincing. . . .

Much of Mrs. Mitchison's argument is bound to sound not only facile but also unconvincing, stated self-consciously through the lips of young Africans. Indeed, until she is halfway into her novel one cannot help noticing both the extraordinary naivety of her style and the imaginative gaps the reader has to bridge for himself in accepting the tribal background. But the story moves fast and professionally, the characters do begin to live outside their utterances, and Mrs. Mitchison's experience as a writer for children is perhaps an asset in showing us, who may not know more than the newspapers tell us, a good deal of authentic detail about the way of life with which she has fallen in love.

TLS. Jan. 7, 1965, p. 5

MITFORD, NANCY (1904–)

Patience is needed . . . even with Miss Nancy Mitford's *The Pursuit of Love,* which is rewardingly funny in many places. This is the least, and indeed the most, one can say of it. It begins extremely well with a picture of the children of an artistocratic family called Radlett. Its early pages introduce, in Uncle Matthew and Captain Warbeck, two of the best comic figures in any modern novel. I cannot recall a funnier picture of the violent foreigner-hating patriarch than Uncle Matthew; his early morning foibles are beautifully recorded. . . . But, alas, though Uncle Matthew dodges in and out of the whole book, the later pages are given over to the affairs of one of his daughters, Linda. . . . The less successful episodes in her pursuit . . . are convincing enough; but at a moment of despair she is picked up by a French duke and installed as his mistress, and thenceforward the novel has the sentimental staginess of the late W. J. Locke.

Henry Reed. *NSN*. Feb. 2, 1946, p. 90

Nancy Mitford, having exhausted the comic possibilities of love in a cold climate, has moved on to less frigid shores. I am not sure the sea-change is beneficial. *The Blessing* is a curious little novel, French with an odd accent. It is as if Miss Mitford's characters, having crossed the channel, were determined to be as briskly gay about sex as they had always heard the French were; and a determined gaiety can grow wearing, particularly when it involves popping in and out of baroque bedrooms. *Love in a Cold Climate* had mockery and cruelty and wit, and it glittered like ice. *The Blessing* is only hard, and frivolous like rock candy.

However, even a confection can have its virtues, and this book has several, all satiric. . . . And there is all that grandeur which is the Mitford trademark.

Phyllis McGinley. *NYHT*. Oct. 14, 1951, p. 10

Now, into a fray involving a presumably beleaguered English aristocracy, has leaped the Honorable Mrs. Peter Rodd (Nancy Mitford) with results disquieting for the domestic tranquility of England (never say "Britain" without revealing that you are hopelessly middle class!). Miss Mitford, who regularly shocks and delights England and America with her perky novels, now sallies forth as editor of and major contributor to a lively volume of essays [*Noblesse Oblige*] about the mores and speech habits of what many others had passed off as a moribund English aristocracy.

The flurry began with the publication in an English philological journal of a study called "Linguistic Class-Indicators in Present-Day English," by Professor Alan Ross of Birmingham University. Miss Mitford gleefully took the main drift of the professor's study and applied it to her own observations of aristocracy ("upper middle class," she dubs it) with delightful comic effect. Her own essay, entitled "The English Aristocracy," was first published in *Encounter,* a magazine with distinctly upper middle-class appeal. Miss Mitford's major assertions are that in England there still exists a marked class structure; that the English aristocrat is "a wily old bird" who has lulled an unsuspecting world into believing that he is on his last legs politically and financially; that this clever aristocracy presumably is just biding its time until some happier day arrives; and that its sturdy survival is clearly manifest in certain linguistic habits. This upper middle-class speech and manner she designates as "U" and those of everyone else as "non-U." According to her neat distinctions, it is, for example, U to say "table-napkin" but unmistakably non-U to say "serviette." Only a non-U person would speak of a "teacher"; the U terms are "master," "mistress," or more specifically "maths-mistress." Professor Ross, whose study appears in a condensed version in this volume, informs us that one who spoofs at such U niceties by calling them "la-di-da" is most certainly non-U.

John R. Willingham. Nation. Sept. 15, 1956, p. 224

The book [*Voltaire in Love*], warns the author in a disarming note, is neither a biography nor a study of Voltaire's literary and philosophic achievements. . . . It concentrates instead upon Voltaire's love affair with the Marquise Emilie de Châtelet. . . .

Miss Mitford contributes much of her own. Her style is, as always, vivacious, the narrative headlong, the incidental humor often suitably wry, as in her quotations of Voltaire's letters. . . .

Miss Mitford is not concerned in her biographies with the inner motivations of her subjects. They enact their story upon her pages, they speak their lines, and they keep the reader absorbed and awake. In their way, because they are stamped in their creator's individuality, Miss Mitford's books are works of art.

Frances Winwar. *NYT*. Feb. 23, 1958, pp. 3, 38

Everyone should be told that this [*Don't Tell Alfred*] is one of Miss Mitford's very best. Not, perhaps, wholly as perfect as *The Blessing,* but definitely a runner-up. And many of the same enchanting characters appear as in *The Pursuit of Love* and *Love in a Cold Climate,* and their children are giggles from the same guffaw. Fanny, the heroine of *Don't Tell Alfred,* is the happily-married mother of four sons. Middle-aged, a trifle moth-eaten, she is in town for a day's shopping when Alfred, her husband, pastoral theologian at Oxford, is, quite unexpectedly made British Ambassador to Paris. . . .

All in all, this novel is crammed with vitamins, with wit, nostalgia, and trenchant comment. Miss Mitford understands the intricacies of French politics better than anyone else alive and explains them painlessly. Indeed, she provides sheer rollicking fun as well as a deep down tenderness for human foibles that she deftly conceals. She is perhaps the nearest our blurred, woolly and sadisto-sentimental age has gotten to the sane simplicity of Jane Austen. There is, in Miss Mitford, the same Chanel-like clarity of thought and line, the same deceptively unadorned style that is present almost by its absence. For she is, under it all, a serious writer, an artist who senses and sees the quirks and quiddities of the human condition.

Anne Fremantle. *Com*. June 30, 1961, pp. 357–58

MONKHOUSE, ALLAN (1858–1936)

War Plays, by Allan Monkhouse, ought to supersede the problem plays of our pre-war days, when people ran after the unholy, and the newest prophet was August Strindberg. Each little play has a strong dramatic situation: not a point is missed: the diction is good and pure, the moral for the hour in two of the plays at least. Perhaps the third play is rather distressing; but no one will deny that it is a very strong situation—not in the sense of the dramatist, novelist, or poet who is strong as putridity is strong. This last play has already been acted. The other two should be seen on the boards.

Katharine Tynan. *BkmL*. Jan., 1917, p. 136

Mr. Monkhouse is an author who drives a pen well under control. It is, we feel, a trained obedient pen, warranted neither to idle nor to run away, but to keep up a good round pace from the first moment of the journey until the last. While it has long since been broken of any inclination to shy at an occasional accidental object it is by no means wholly devoid of playfulness. This playfulness serves to illustrate how nice is the author's control in that he can afford not only to tolerate, but even to encourage it, while maintaining an easy equable measure. There is a moment when Geoffrey Arden, the hero [of *True Love*], dismissing the reasons for his confidence in the success of his new play, exclaims to his sister, "I'm a bit of a pro at this game, Mary." And that, with all respect to Mr. Monkhouse, is the abiding impression he leaves on us. He is a professional novelist, quietly confident, carefully ironical, and choosing always, at a crisis, to underrate the seriousness of the situation rather than to stress it unduly. Admirable as this temper undoubtedly is, it nevertheless leaves the reader a great deal cooler than he would wish. He is interested, stimulated, and even, towards the latter half of the book, moved, yet with what reservations! [1919]

Katherine Mansfield. *Novels and Novelists*
(Boston, Beacon Press, 1930), p. 114

Mr. Monkhouse has the rare power of respecting both his reader and his art, and succeeds in satisfying the one without betraying his standards in the other.

H. C. Harwood. *OutL*. April 29, 1922, p. 343

By his scrupulous desire to balance his picture and deal out justice to all, his artistic chiaroscuro becomes weakened. His handling shows a pleasing austerity of line, but his honesty to his brief not infrequently leads him to lose breadth of effect in niggling detail. We feel this in *True Love* (1919), a war novel of rare intellectual sincerity. . . . The same criticism may be made on *Dying Fires* (1912), the chronicle of an unhappy marriage, where the natural emotional force seems pent up and constrained in too rigidly intellectual a channel. In this last-named novel especially the author's imperative instinct for intellectualizing all features and aspects leads to a deficiency of visualization. It is as though the sensuous appeal of life and the sensuous instincts themselves became a little too rarefied in the author's thought so that the mental image loses colour. Thus while we know intimately the spirit, the character, the secret thoughts of his people, we rarely see their faces or hear their voices. In this element of irresponsiveness to sensuous nature, Mr. Monkhouse's art shows a puritanic strain, but in his alacrity in breaking down the barriers by which the Englishman fences off his moral from his sensuous being, and in his faculty for probing into this shifting double-mindedness and exposing to the dry light of the intellect all the strands of impulse and motive, Mr. Monkhouse excels nearly all his contemporaries. It is no doubt this keenly analytic habit of mind joined to an austere taste and a special mastery of irony that still keeps this author's work "caviare to the general." For Mr. Monkhouse is "out" to discover goodness and spiritual beauty and our interest in the moral issue is suddenly electrified by a current of ironical discernment and a dryly artistic appreciation of human frailty. His novel *My Daughter Helen* (1922), is a typical Monkhouse by the fact that while daily life grows sterner and more disconcerting for the characters, beauty persists, and the rarefied atmosphere of acceptance braces them to endure more.

Edward Garnett. *Adel.* May, 1924, pp. 1100–1

MONRO, HAROLD (1879–1932)

The poetry of Mr. Monro—that which counts most, the later work—is of fine texture and subtle perfume. It is, moreover, individual in its thought and form; and the unusual elements in it, which are yet not sufficiently bizarre to snatch attention, offer a new kind of charm to the poetry lover. But that person, as we know, still prefers to take his poetry in the traditional manner; and hence the audience for work like this, delicately sensitive and quietly thoughtful, is likely to be small. It will be fully appreciative, however, gladly exchanging stormy raptures for a quiet and satisfying beauty; and it will be of a temper which will delight to trace in this work, subdued almost to a murmur, the same influences which are urging some of his contemporaries to louder, more emphatic, and more copious expression.

A particular interest of this poetry is precisely the way in which those influences have been subdued. It is that which gives the individual stamp to its art; but, curiously, it is also that which marks its heredity, and defines its place in the succession of English poetry. There is independence here, but not isolation; nor is there violent conflict with an older poetic ideal. On the contrary, a reconciliation has been made; balance has been attained; and revolutionary principles, whether in the region of technique or ideas, have been harnessed and controlled. So that this work, while fairly representing the new poetry, is clearly related in a direct line to the old.

Mary C. Sturgeon. *Studies of Contemporary Poets*
(George Harrap, 1919), pp. 217–18

Mr. Monro's book [*Real Property*] is divided into two parts. . . . The poems in the second half are for the most part earlier than the others. The poet says of these that "they have no metaphysical background" and that "some of them are tainted with slight Georgian affectations which no amount of polishing could successfully remove." Presumably he is referring to the poem, which is not good, about the nightingale; the faults and the merits of the others are distinctly Mr. Monro's own. . . . Some of the poems may be described as attempts imaginatively to realise and present certain discoveries, and speculations, of science. . . . They are all interesting, and bear witness to their intense intellectual concentration; they make one very curious about their successors. But the task of depicting abstractions or mental processes in lucid and beautiful imagery is not easy, and in most of these poems Mr. Monro seems to be still groping—to have achieved only a partial success.

J. C. Squire. *LM*. May, 1922, p. 95

Monro was a curious and memorable figure. Giving his whole life and all his little fortune to the cause of modern poetry, he had the force which comes from such disinterested devotion, and his Bookshop and his [*Poetry*] *Review* won a considerable place in the intellectual life of London; but he was wanting in *le sentiment de la mesure,* and in that "concinnity of mind" which the Bishop found in Edmund Gosse; and partly from tormenting ill-health and partly from not giving himself time to think, he would be carried away to write foolish things. . . . But apart from these small embarrassments he was an admirable worker in the Vineyard, and I must always be grateful to him for his help in the matter of *Georgian Poetry,* which but for him could never have come into being.

Edward Marsh. *A Number of People*
(Heinemann, 1939), pp. 334–35

MONSARRAT, NICHOLAS (1910–   )

Mr. Monsarrat's novel [*The Story of Esther Costello*] in my view is a pointless and ugly piece of work. The heroine, a blind, dumb and deaf child, discovered in a foetid Irish rural slum by an American woman, grows into a beauty and is exploited by being put on public exhibition in the United States in aid of entirely bogus charities. . . . Doubtless what Mr. Monsarrat relates could occur, since in this world anything can happen at any time anywhere. But that does not justify a novel, and

The Story of Esther Costello, whatever its author's intention, doesn't amount to more than a bit of dingy sensationalism.

Walter Allen. *NSN.* Sept. 5, 1953, p. 266

Mr. Monsarrat's novel [*The Tribe That Lost Its Head*]—the scene of which is a fictional island off the southwest coast of Africa, and the issue it deals with the savage man's revolt against civilized man's rule—will doubtless be high on the bestseller list by the time these paragraphs see print. The book has everything to recommend it to such acclaim: an exotic background, a love story spiced with parked car and bedroom intimacies, a readable style, a sophisticated and authoritative tone, and scenes of orgy and torture that outrage, shock and grieve.

It is entirely possible that Mr. Monsarrat's satirical treatment of give-and-take in the House of Commons, and his wholesale caricaturing of the working press, will delight many readers, as will his malicious portrait of an easily-recognizable leader of the Opposition. Actually, the satire is tedious, the caricaturing is without wit or taste, and this reviewer was deeply disturbed by the author's attempt to cut the immense problem of colonial rule and native revolt—that problem which Richard Wright recently described as the "deep, psychological compulsion [which] drove the Europeans toward the native" and "the equally deep psychological compulsions" which brought about native subservience—down to bestseller size.

The size of Nicholas Monsarrat, as a man, seems more than adequate. He was a lieutenant commander in the Royal Navy during the war, with five years of Atlantic convoy service to his credit, and eight or nine published books, the best known of which is *The Cruel Sea.* After the war, he joined the Commonwealth Relations Office, and served a long stretch in South Africa, and then in Canada. But in *The Tribe That Lost Its Head* he must, as author, answer for a number of things that do not add up so handsomely. He must answer for a singularly unsavory cast of characters. . . .

Kay Boyle. *Nation.* Nov. 24, 1956, p. 462

The serious novelist's pennant has finally been struck and the Jolly Roger of unabashed hokum run to the masthead as Mr. Monsarrat embarks on a lavish historical adventure story [*The White Rajah*]. His hero, Richard Marriott, is a baronet's illegitimate son who finds that his only inheritance is a terrestial globe and a pair of silver-handled pistols. . . . The whole story is plastered thick with local colour and encrusted with choice cliches. If Mr. Monsarrat would write with greater care, his nonsense would be better fun.

TLS. Oct. 6, 1961, p. 669

MOORE, GEORGE (1852–1933)

Mr. George Moore, prancing uncinctured through a forest of mistakes, bruising himself and tumbling head over heels, groping and groaning his way further into darkness, emerges sooner or later, if only for an instant, into some brighter patch of sunlight than is to be found in the cool Academe where sits Mr. Archer, serene, amenable, scrupulously draped. . . . It is because men like Mr. Henley and Mr. Moore are so narrow, and therefore, almost invariably, wrong, that they are, now and again, so brilliantly right—and, always, so interesting. [1899]

Max Beerbohm. Around Theatres (Rupert
Hart-Davis, 1953), p. 42

Mr. George Moore may seem to many of us to-day to be only vulgarly frivolous in his attitude and method of expression, but it is scarcely possible for any writer to attain to such a position as he occupies unless his work is marked by some other qualities. For Mr. Moore enjoys not only popularity but prestige as a writer of English. That America thinks him a good writer is, unfortunately, of little account. American criticism might be to the literature of the future what the Platonic Academy at Florence was to the literature of the Renaissance, but so far it cannot be said to show much sense of its responsibility. And Anglo-Ireland, though its own prose from Berkeley to Yeats and from Swift to Shaw is almost invariably distinguished or vigorous, or both at once, obviously has other reasons as well as literary ones for reading Mr. Moore. But in England too he is read and taken seriously by most subscribers to the *Times Literary Supplement,* for instance; and he is spoken of with reverence by the critics of such reputable papers as the *Sunday Times,* the *Observer,* and the *New Statesman.*

Thomas McGreevy in Scrutinies, coll. Edgell Rickword
(Wishart, 1928), pp. 110–11

Mr. George Moore has a rare gift for confession. He has never been afraid of being silly, nor of being upset; he has never been afraid of exhibiting himself as selfish, complacent, limited. He does not mind giving himself away, he enjoys it; and if at the same time he gives away a few friends, he does so with a spontaneous serenity which should go far to placate their wrath. . . . There is no spite deeper than Puck's in Mr. Moore's detached presentment of his friends, and not a touch of that superiority of tone which almost always creeps into an author's account of other people, however little it may really correspond to his comparative estimate of himself. There is something ineradicably naïve in Mr. Moore which saves him from being patronising. He records and describes with astonished simplicity and joy. . . .

Mr. Moore never seems quite certain that he has succeeded, even when there is no doubt about it. No one will have the slightest difficulty in believing him when he confesses to being the most diffident of authors. Whistler once frightened Mr. Moore by suddenly saying: "You care about nothing except your writing." No wonder he was alarmed; it implies an inhuman degree of detachment. But many kinds of sanctity are inhuman, and Mr. Moore is a saint of the life of letters.

Desmond MacCarthy. Portraits (Putnam,
1931), pp. 198–99, 203

George Moore has succeeded in *The Brook Kerith* in transfixing the accent of Judea and procuratorial Rome, his Abélard is a miracle of insight into France of that strange period, and in *Aphrodite in Aulis* he has gone closer to the heart of the Athens of Pheidias than any scholar of them all. I do not feel that in *The Untilled Field* he has done as much for the Irish peasant and the Irish priest. . . . He had come to Ireland not for what he could give but for what he could get. The artist was triumphantly rewarded in his great trilogy [*Hail and Farewell*] but the man must have sorrowed a little . . . as he turned his back on his ten years' pilgrimage, . . . with the knowledge that he had lost something irretrievable. . . .

Though the Irish adventure is thus in a sense the tragic note in George Moore's life, unless he had had that experience he could never have written *The Brook Kerith* . . . the greatest single literary achievement of our time, and possibly the greatest prose book, except the Bible, in the English tongue.

Humbert Wolfe. George Moore (Thornton
Butterworth, 1933), pp. 62, 47–48, 78

The Communication [*A Communication to My Friends*] is, as usual, rather repetitious, but those who enjoy the "line of melody" in Moore's later prose do not much mind whether the theme be old or new which he sets to the familiar music. . . . Once again the mood of rippling reverie is the pleasure of Moore at his best. You either like Moore's prose or you dislike it, but it cannot be denied that he had consideration for our ears. That, and his impish humour of reminiscence, are the best of his titles to remembrance.

Osbert Burdett. LM. Sept., 1933, p. 467

While other writers of the eighties and early nineties were being "just literary," or witty at the expense of others (few can be witty, of course, at their own expense; but still fewer make the attempt), or romantic, or ingenious, Moore and Gissing alone, or almost alone, were trying in the published novel to tell the world something about life at first hand. And in Moore's case it was quite extraordinary how the choice of detail and the continuous succession of plain incidents produced both an effect of nature and a progressive interest. Where Gissing showed his personal grievance and rebelliousness, Moore recorded. He was detached. He did not explain or expound (as Gissing did), but refrained from all personal comment, leaving to his characters any reflections which had properly to be made upon such situations as seemed inevitably to arise in the course of the tale. To me these books miss a thousand shades; but that is their strength, for they are as firm as engravings. No wonder they impressed themselves, and still impress themselves, upon candid minds as very striking reproductions of reality. There is no question that they gave rise, towards the end of the nineties, to a new school of naturalistic writers, Edwin Pugh, Arthur Morrison, Somerset Maugham, and others. We know that a reading of *A Mummer's Wife* drew Arnold Bennett towards that re-creation of life in the Five Towns upon which his lasting fame depends. Merely to record the facts is to establish Moore's importance as an influence upon his age.

Frank Swinnerton. The Georgian Scene (N.Y., Farrar and Rinehart, 1934), p. 178

Mr. Moore is completely lacking in dramatic power. On the face of it, *Esther Waters* has all the appearance of a great novel; it has sincerity, shapeliness, style; it has surpassing seriousness and integrity; but because Mr. Moore has not the strength to project Esther from himself its virtues collapse and fall about it like a tent with a broken pole. There it lies, this novel without a heroine, and what remains of it is George Moore himself, a ruin of lovely language, and some exquisite descriptions of the Sussex downs. For the novelist who has no dramatic power, no fire of conviction within, leans upon nature for support; she lifts him up and enhances his mood without destroying it.

But the defects of a novelist may well be the glories of his brother the autobiographer, and we find, to our delight, that the very qualities which weaken Mr. Moore's novels are the making of his memoirs. . . . He has brought a new mind into the world; he has given us a new way of feeling and seeing; he has devised—very painfully, for he is above all things painstaking, eking out a delicate gift laboriously—a means of liquidating the capricious and volatile essence of himself and decanting it in these memoirs; and that, whatever the degree, is triumph, achievement, immortality.

Virginia Woolf. *The Death of The Moth* (Penguin
Bks., 1961 [Hogarth Pr., 1942]), pp. 136, 138

Moore himself speaks of having learned "the art of presentation" in Paris, and the word is significant. For what Moore did was to break away from the popular convention of telling a story by means of un-ravelling a series of artificial (moral, scientific, detective) dilemmas, and turn back to the presentation of common lives and to shaping his stories, as it were, out of natural common clay. The chance that nobody would take any notice is confirmed by the number of copies sold. Yet these stories of the Irish peasantry, the country priests, the exiles in America, have to-day a fresh exquisite realism that shows no sign, and I think will continue to show no sign, of the mildew that gathers so quickly even on the best of artificial products. Moreover, in an age still not free of the shackles of heavy prose tradition, these stories of Moore's are *short* stories: economical, pared down, light in structure, transparent. They have the natural poetry of earth and will remain, as Moore hoped they would remain, models for the future.

This is not quite true of Moore's later stories, which tended to grow longer and more exquisitely elaborate as Moore's love of his own voice became more and more a precious obsession. . . . I would not for a moment underestimate the beauties of Moore's later stories, but it is significant that it is on their exquisite surfaces that the dust begins to gather, and that the dew is still fresh on the natural earth of *The Untilled Field*.

H. E. Bates. *The Modern Short Story* (Thomas
Nelson and Sons, 1945), pp. 152–53

It was [at Mrs. Charles Hunter's Edwardian arcady at Hill in Essex] that I met George Moore, and I watched him delightedly, for, very often, he was out to shock; and when he had said something that he hoped would appal everyone in the house, or even in the garden, a seraphic smile would come over his face, and remain on it, imparting to it a kind of illumination of virtue, like that of a saint, for several minutes; the bland unself-conscious smile of a small boy—though at that time he must have been nearly sixty—saying to himself delightedly "I've smashed it!", and he would regard his audience attentively, with his eyes of a mild and rather misty blue, peering out of a plump, pear-shaped, pink-and-white face, surmounted by soft white hair. The lines of his drooping mouth seemed a little to contradict the spirit of enter-prise he showed. But his voice, fascinating though it was, had an almost aggressive distinctness about it, and its rhythm and stress seemed to proclaim that once he had formed an opinion, on however faulty grounds, he would be unwilling to alter it. . . . At first—or, at any rate, a year or two later—he took a great dislike to me, but in time that passed; it was based on the fact that I did not support with enthusiasm the idea of an indefinitely long war with Germany: but his own bellicose attitude gained greatly from his ignorance of geography, and his belief, for instance, that Baghdad was in Germany. In time, as I say, he grew friendly, and used to send for me to Ebury Street. His mind was not large, but its working was most original, and his sayings —and actions—were unexpected, even when he had no desire to shock. If his views were opposed, his voice would rise, as it did when he became angry; as it did, for example, I remember, some years later, when he took me up to the drawing-room in Ebury Street, and found the sun, unscreened by blinds, shining on the rosy and pale-blue splendours of his celebrated Aubusson carpet. . . . As I saw more of him, I began to find even greater pleasure in the personal idiom of his talk, to which the Irish run of his voice, and his startling accentuation of certain words, gave an added point: and those who read his prose can still, if they listen for it, hear his voice beneath its beautiful texture, like the echo of the living sea in a shell.

Osbert Sitwell. *Great Morning* (Macmillan,
1948), pp. 255–56

As a result of his having lived so long in Paris and of his natural incapacity to take in the rules of grammar, he had the utmost difficulty in writing English with even tolerable correctness. Every sentence had to be hammered out. He had a natural ear for language; he had a sense of rhythm; but he was like a dancer who had done the preliminary exercises and had not learned the steps. . . . If his ear told him that a sentence was wrong, he had no analytical means of detecting the error and correcting it. He had to dictate and re-dictate until the thing sounded right. This difficulty continued throughout his life. . . .

To produce, at forty-two, a great masterpiece—and *Esther Waters* is no less; to write before and after it a long series of books largely lamentable; and then, from your fiftieth year onward, to make yourself, still struggling, still revising, still exorcising the devil in you, into a master, is an extremely mysterious process. For make no mistake. Unto the end, the devil persisted. Every early draft that Moore dictated was full of him. Only by fourteen revisions and re-dictations could he be driven out. . . .

Moore had the genius to perceive that the modern English novel, even the naturalistic novel that he formerly practised, had become too

far removed from its origin in fables passed down by word of mouth.
. . . He set himself to apply the virtues of oral narrative to the rich
and complex language he had inherited from the past. His supreme
triumphs in this kind are the novels and stories of his later period,
particularly *The Brook Kerith* and *Héloïse and Abélard*. He justly
claimed that they were the only two prose epics in the English language.
. . . They are timeless books of rare lucidity and fabulous beauty. They
were written timelessly by the tragic artist whom sometimes in life the
comic mask disfigured. But if your eye should ever fall on a photograph of his death-mask—the face of a man of infinite grace, patience,
and refinement—then you will be looking at the inner man who wrote
those books.

Charles Morgan. List. Feb. 28, 1952, pp. 350–51

Successively and publicly he was: enthusiast, no less ardent than Swinburne, for *Marius the Epicurean* and *Mademoiselle de Maupin;* the
first thoroughgoing practitioner in England of naturalism; student, like
Huysmans, of the religious conflict of modern man; advocate in England of Nietzsche, of Wagner, of Dostoievski and Turgenev; experi-
menter after Dujardin and before Joyce with the interior monologue.
Thus he proclaimed a series of gods and gospels, and, in the course of
his education (pursued, as Oscar Wilde complained, in public), he was
the first to speak out in England for new French painters and writers
who have long since been accepted into the canon. For the enterprise
of discovery he was unusually well equipped, for he wrote without consideration of fear or favor and his unquenchable naïveté, so irritating
to his friends and comforting to his enemies, preserved him from the
enunciation of critical clichés. His reputation, now unduly depreciated,
will rest upon the informal discourse which is his invention—part
reminiscence, part imaginary narrative, part random observation.
Among the last there is a considerable volume of reference to French
literature; reference of high value, for, although it pretends to be no
more than a record of the impact of that literature on a temperament,
this temperament was for various reasons a singularly sensitive instrument. . . .

The story has often been told, repeatedly by Moore himself and first
in his *Confessions of a Young Man,* how after a meager formal education in Ireland he was enabled by the death of his father and his own
coming of age to realize a newly conceived ambition to study painting
in Paris. He presently found—like Gautier before him—that his talents
lay elsewhere, and he gave up experiments in painting for experiments
in literature. The technical initiation into art served its turn later when

Moore explained Degas and Manet to the English, pleading one of his unfashionable causes. The seven years in Paris (1873-80) gave him a command of spoken French probably not achieved even by the Francophile young Englishmen who in the nineties were said "to have fallen down on Boulogne pier and broken their English." And, besides a new language and the elements of literary and artistic taste, Moore's apprenticeship at the Café of the Nouvelle Athènes provided him with an unwavering devotion to his adopted country and a host of friends. It is one of the mysteries of literature how the young Irishman with no artistic achievement to his credit and presumably showing little promise of any, made his way into the circle of impressionist painters and symbolist poets who gathered at the Café. He must have had something of the charm and the persistence that helped Boswell to his interviews with Rousseau and Voltaire. . . . The theme of the Nouvelle Athènes runs through all his life and work.

> Ruth Zabriskie Temple. *The Critic's Alchemy* (New Haven, Conn., College and Univ. Pr., 1962 [N.Y., Twayne, 1953]), pp. 232–33, 241

Moore has always his own marked idiosyncrasy, and the criticism of our time, in its preoccupation with prevalent trends and successful revolutions rather than with individual quality, has been inclined to see it as a dead end. This is not, I think, true; and if it is necessary to jusitfy Moore to the trend-mongers one may do so by showing that he was leading, if not up the main road, into an area where the greatest prose experiment of our time has its beginning. We have seen Moore oscillating between aesthetic reveries and naturalism, and if we were to follow the development of his art we should find him in the end arriving at a style that was to harmonise the two. He manages in his best work to present in all their uncompromising contingency the actualities of common experience, and yet to preserve the inevitability of impression, the delicate rightness of diction and rhythm that he had learnt from the high priests of a scrupulous art. At the end of our period, when Moore was past the threshold of old age, another Irish writer brought out his youthful confessions; and in it he defined the function of the poet, the literary artist, as it appeared to his eyes. It is to be "the mediator between the world of reality and the world of dreams." No writer in the world has carried farther than James Joyce a dual allegiance to an exhaustive naturalism on the one hand and a complex aesthetic symbolism on the other; and I think it is likely that neither the title nor the content of Joyce's *Portrait of the Artist as a Young Man* would have been quite the same in 1916 if it had not been for the prior existence of Moore's *Confessions of a Young Man* in 1886. And there are other resemblances more strongly marked. Critics have often spoken about the absolute originality of Joyce's *Dubliners;* and that is a curious instance of how far George Moore's achievements have dropped out of sight—itself perhaps a curious instance of the general failure to recognise the importance of the *fin-de-siècle* as a formative power in modern literature. For *Dubliners* has an obvious ancestor in Moore's stories in *The Untilled Field*. . . . Moore said later that he began *The Untilled Field* "with the hope of furnishing the young Irish of the future with models"; and reading *Dubliners* beside the earlier book we can hardly doubt that for Joyce he achieved just that.

> Graham Hough. *Image and Experience* (Lincoln, Neb., Univ. of Nebraska Pr., 1960), pp. 197–98

MOORE, NICHOLAS (1918–   )

Mr. Moore seems torn between a kind of poetry which deals with personal relations by the use of bizarre symbolical imagery of which he is frequently not in control, and a kind that aims at speaking to the comrade workers in their own language [*A Wish in Season*]. His alternation between them is rather hectic. . . . And he is liable suddenly to drag into his world of myth an unassimilated image from the ordinary world we know. . . . Even the best of his poems are often marred by the introduction of proper names in the attempt to be topical. . . .

In these twenty-six poems there is a lack of unity, and I felt that many of his poems that I have seen, published and unpublished, could have been substituted for many that are in the book. . . . But this is probably a sign of promise that some day we may see a collection that will carry more weight to the people.

> Maurice James Craig. *LL.* Aug., 1941, p. 153

Nicholas Moore is a poet with a fund of gaiety and bright colour in his writing. He rarely writes with any close concentration and his work produces an impression of a light clear atmosphere in which he can develop ideas freely, rather than with any intensity.

> Stephen Spender. *Poetry Since 1939*
> (BC/Longmans, 1946), p. 58

Almost alone in the early forties, save for the thirties "age-group" school and a few belated Social Realists such as Hubert Nicholson and John Manifold, the figure of Nicholas Moore stands out as a poet writing chiefly in common speech. To some extent his work may be taken as moving towards a popular poetics; a far more inclusive mode of utterance than that prevailing this decade. . . .

In the refrains, the modernized fag-ends of folk-song, the lingo of the dance-lyric, the bouncing rhythm of the vaudeville number, and in the attempt to represent the simple lengths of spoken speech, there were items powerfully making for a popular poetics. But in the verbal farce and literary leg-pull, and in the self-consciously social conscious approach were elements productive of high-brow poetry; elements with minority appeal.

These two contrary factors have now been tuned down, and an equilibrium established in his work. This, it would seem, is as much as one can ask; for whatever may be the position in fiction the middle-brow poet is an all but unknown creature.

Derek Stanford. The Freedom of Poetry (Falcon
Press, 1947), pp. 137, 155–56

MOORE, T. STURGE (1870–1944)

There is an undying life, an eternal pliancy, in . . . [the] old world. But there is also the appearance of remoteness; to live, indeed, it must be taken out of time. Mr. Sturge Moore's recurrence to it may be one reason why he has not found a wider audience, but there is a more substantial reason in the nature of his art. He is less inclined than most of us to value an emotion or experience simply because it occurs. For him it must be not only remembered in tranquillity, but conceived through thought; and his loyalty to this ideal of conception, though stimulating to all who love poetry, is not a quality which makes a poet popular. It is more likely to do the opposite, among all who turn to poetry for an easy pleasure. . . .

Firmness and economy in design, joined to Mr. Sturge Moore's preference in subjects, seem the marks of a classical poet. He is individual enough, however, to prove the inadequacy of types. There is a classical temper in his Greek poems, but it means something more than a devotion to the beauty of order. If we could bring the old Greeks to life, we should probably find their passion and curiosity more obvious than their observance of the golden mean. And when Mr. Sturge Moore turns directly to their life, as he does in his *Sicilian Idyll,* he brings out this sharp accent of Greek realism, making it tell more pungently against the sunny calmness of the setting. The harmony of conception grows out of a divination of the facts. At other times, as we have seen, he changes this frank outline, giving it a new colour from romance or fantasy. . . .

The impression thus left by his poetry is that his outlook is singularly consistent with his method as an artist. There is its strength; motive and conception are of a piece and hang together. And there, also, is the possibility of weakness, if it makes us feel that imaginativeness is not a free indwelling spirit, but owes too much to thought.

Arthur McDowall. LM. April, 1922, pp. 607, 610, 616

It seems to me that the solid empirical character of Mr. Moore's poetry and his theories of art both spring from his primary occupation—that of a wood engraver. We have had painter poets and it is not hard to see the influence of their painting on their poetry. But wood-engraving is a very different thing from painting. It cannot be improvised; it has to make the best of a difficult medium; it must feel, in the doing, more the conscious work of one's own hands; and it requires greater self-control, technically, on the part of the artist.

Mr. Moore's thought, both his critical thought and his lyrical thought, always seems to me that of a man who has learned his world by touching first the things around him. . . .

I think I have said enough, however, to show that in T. Sturge Moore we have a man who deserves disciples. His aesthetic theories are his own and do justice to all the interests involved: to artist as well as to public and certainly to the moral issue in that aesthetic controversy which seems to go on and on. For our own times he is both a tonic and an anodyne: avoiding both the extremes of the men who put all their eggs into the one basket of social reform or Socialism or some form of political radicalism, and the less admirable extreme of the man who flees to an ivory tower—and indeed anyone who has read Mr. Moore's Danaë and seen how her brass tower was no protection, may well doubt whether an ivory tower would be any better. Yet we do need a refuge and Mr. Moore's mythical Greek uplands are as beautiful as and more bracing than the refuges of almost any other English poet. As countries of the mind they are more interesting than Morris's Earthly Paradise and less monotonous than Spenser's enchanted forests. Though remote they have a salty tang of real life in them.

Llewelyn Jones. First Impressions (N.Y., Knopf,
1925), pp. 168, 185–86

Mr. Sturge Moore has . . . resolutely explored the regions of myth and symbol, but he works his way through the ever-growing difficulties of the verse medium. He avoids the seven-league boots of imaginative opportunity. He is essentially a dramatic poet finding his own individuality in the symbolic mind of the past. Reading the second volume of his Collected Poems, we can observe how much he has concentrated upon

the imaginative drama of ancient Jewish life. Whether we are funda-
mentalists or not, we must realize the escape of the English mind for
centuries into that heroic or epic world. Uncountable numbers, by fireside or window-seat, have compounded their souls—following the kings,
warriors, and the dim angelophany of the Old Testament. . . . In bal-
ladry lines travel through many minds and are shaped mysteriously into
perfection. Mr. Sturge Moore's adaptations and revisions of Elizabethan
and other lyrics are a curious attempt to extend the range of the poetic
faculty. Modernists might well see in this a subtle snare—the last imprisonment of mind in tradition.

Austin Clarke. *LL*. June, 1932, pp. 232–33

Sturge Moore, like so many artists of his time, was deeply influenced by
the work and personality of Shannon and Ricketts when he first published his work in the early years of this century. His lengthy and diffuse
poetic drama, *Absalom,* his descriptive poem, *Danaë,* are embodiments
of the romantic conception of poetry as the close sister of painting,
portraying in words the sensuous elements in a scene which the descriptive painter also seeks to represent. His interest is in the static or
in the statuesque movement of the Spenserean world so that in *Absalom*
the narrative uncoils itself slowly and at length, while in the pictured
Danaë, revised in 1920, the effect aimed at is that of the creation of a
brilliantly lit, many-sided sparkling object, and therefore the movement of the poem is deliberately held up and returns upon itself.

In his critical work of 1929, *Armour for Aphrodite,* in which he considers the aesthetic basis for poetry, Sturge Moore speaks of his method
of writing. He says that the idea for a long poem arrives and that the
poet broods over it for weeks, for months and even for years, allowing
subsidiary notions to flock round the main one. While the poem is in
this state, "a wise poet will reject all suggestions of rhythm and phrasing."
He knows that they would "crystallize the fruit before it is ripe," before
the poet has lived long enough with his idea. This "holding-back"
process Sturge Moore regards as most important for the poet and says:
"Woe betide, if felicitous verses appear before the fundamental beauties
of his theme stand round him like mountains of necessity." This stage
of waiting, of meditation is a necessity, for "Every element must count
in the total effect of an organic whole, every implication; a great beauty
is always a highly organized whole."

Priscilla Thouless. *Modern Poetic Drama*
(Oxford, Basil Blackwell, 1934), pp. 186–87

MORGAN, CHARLES (1894–1958)

Mr. Morgan's *My Name Is Legion* is an amazing achievement, a work to whose excellence even the publisher's laudatory matter does less than justice. The mood is that of Dostoievsky, saintliness in conflict with lusts, seekings and remorse of gigantic abandon. The heroine, a young woman whose mother had borne her in an ecstasy of hate against the environment in which she lived and in which the daughter is destined to move, manifests early a queer power over those about her. . . . The scenic background is employed with certain effect, and the religious and mystic elements which are of the core of the book are reined in before they cross the danger line into hysteria.

Milton Waldman. LM. May, 1925, pp. 98–99

. . . [A] writer with whom the movement of his story is far less important than his own movement around it is Mr. Charles Morgan. On story-writing grounds he does not fight: probably a penny-in-the-slot machine on the pier could give him points in episode. All Mr. Morgan requires is a situation to which the workings of a fine mind can give the greatest degree of significance, letting every action have its full weight of moral importance. His stand, away from the threatened position of mere story-writing, and well into the security of literature, takes him into other recesses. . . . For *The Fountain,* a history of an officer interned in Holland during the War, and of the woman he loves and her husband, has brought into use no mere delightful exercise of observation, but philosophic and spiritual and contemplative powers of a rare quality and finely applied. The effect on the reader . . . is profound, for Mr. Morgan provides him with something permanent and far more than his mere pleasure.

Viola Meynell. LL. March, 1932, pp. 123–24

In many respects Charles Morgan's *Sparkenbroke* . . . belongs to an older tradition . . . and has certain characteristics in common with the works of George Meredith. The story, far from being infected by the rush and speed of the modern world, is unfolded in a leisurely fashion; there is a definite philosophical element in the book, the characters are approached from a psychological standpoint, while about Mr. Morgan's prose there is an impressiveness, a cadence and an artistry, a care for diction and expression that was more usual forty or fifty years ago than it is today. It is much more than a mere tale of human relationship or the interplay of character with character, personality with personality;

at bottom it is a study of the relation between the inner and the outer in the life of man; the growth and development of spiritual desires and spiritual consciousness and their expression through the reaction of the individual to the universe around him. As would be expected in such a work, there is a good deal of theorising and self-analysis on the part of the characters, and at times we come upon passages where the thought rises to heights of true sublimity.

Frederick T. Wood. *ES*. Aug., 1937, p. 137

Mr. Charles Morgan's three plays reveal his own deepening consciousness of a conflict of good and evil reflected within the changing pattern of contemporary events. His first play, *The Flashing Stream*, written in 1938, under the shadow of impending conflict, revealed a seriousness of purpose and an awareness of the trend of international events absent from his previous work: but his search was still, explicitly, for individual integrity, as in *Sparkenbroke* or *The Voyage*. By the time of *The River Line*, he passes on to an enquiry in *social* integrity, while in *The Burning Glass*, he extends his quest to probe into the springs of human responsibility in an atomic and de-personalised age, involving vast cosmic repercussions. Fundamentally, however, the question remains, implicitly, an individual one: *who is the just man?* whether the consequences of his actions prove private or universal. The answer, in the phase recurrent in his earlier work, is he who has achieved "singleness of mind," or, in the language of *The River Line*, who is "quiet and included." The modern threat to integration of personality comes from a number of sources, and their different origin, as conceived by Mr. Morgan, reflects his changing consciousness of the moral problem underlying outward events. Singleness of mind may be assailed on three planes; by sexual and social distractions, as in *The Flashing Stream*, by the violence of wartime conditions, in *The River Line*, or by the enticements of daemonic powers, in *The Burning Glass*. In each case, the development of the subsequent play is anticipated in its predecessor. As *The Flashing Stream* concerns experiments seeking to meet the threat to civilisation in a future war, so *The River Line*, which depicts that threat realised, foresees the growing abnormality of man's lust for power, leading to the totalitarian craving for control over both nature and the minds of other men, and involving a principle of evil which can be described only as "devilish," the theme of *The Burning Glass*.

Joan N. Harding. *CR*. Oct., 1955, pp. 244–45

Those who have sampled his earlier writing will know what I mean in saying that he has the distinction of being the worst prose stylist in our language—but one must be a stylist before graduating as a bad stylist.

Mr. Morgan's style is easily distinguishable—a combination of the a-logical flamboyance of the French metaphysicians with the more ghastly forms of English good taste. . . . If anything could excuse the more prosaic goings-on of the Movement, it would surely be that they were reacting against this kind of ornate grammatical pedantry, feathered with clichés as it is, and muscled with foam-rubber sentimentality. Nor is the construction of *Challenge to Venus* any less laboriously ugly than the verbal mahogany that went into the making of it. The plot, though a mere excuse for metaphysical prattle, succeeds in distorting the picture of Western civilisation as thoroughly as ten volumes of Marxist theorising; and this is the strange thing, distorting it in almost exactly the same way, although nobody could be less of a Marxist than Mr. Morgan. Tragic-opera Italian aristocrats masquerade as Italy while a gigantic bourgeois oaf impersonates Britain. Italian princess and English oaf get into bed together. Exit oaf, unaccompanied. He is off to Aden where, presumably, he will be "superior" to the "natives" and not just remain as one more National Insurance number in the Welfare State. And that's all, except for the "philosophy," and Mr. Morgan as philosopher is almost as distinguished as Mr. Morgan the stylist.

Burns Singer. Enc. June, 1957, pp. 82–83

Charles Morgan was over-rated by a devoted following both in this country and France; and as a result he was under-rated by most of our serious critics. In his non-fiction work he liked to pontificate and trade in abstractions—"Freedom and Liberty," "Ideas at War," and "Creative Imagination" are typical of the essays he wrote under the general title of *Reflections in a Mirror*. Translated into French and spoken from a platform, such essays no doubt had the oratorical *panache* which caused even the most critically-minded Frenchman to over-value their author, especially since Morgan frequently expressed his admiration for the Gallic tradition. . . .

Morgan himself did learn to write. Yet one sometimes feels that he doth protest too much, and that the self-conscious "fineness" of his style robs it of vigour and attack. At the same time he was right to think long and hard about the writer's craft, its possibilities and limitations. . . . Talent must make the most of its resources. As an eminently civilised writer of talent, Charles Morgan did just that.

Robert Graecen. JOL. Aug. 18, 1960, p. 204

MOTTRAM, R. H. (1883–   )

In this volume [*The Spanish Farm Trilogy*] Mr. Mottram has joined together *The Spanish Farm, Sixty-Four, Ninety-Four!* and *The Crime at Vanderlynden's*. . . . These three studies have been linked up by an extremely sympathetic analysis of French character entitled "D'Archeville," an almost equally revealing sketch of an elderly officer from Canada entitled "The Winner," while the whole is rounded off by an epilogue, at once poignant and disenchanted, entitled "The Stranger." The book, in its final form, is undoubtedly a noteworthy contribution not only to the history of the Great War but to literature. . . .

Centuries from now, perhaps, when the glamour of the flamboyant school of war literature has wholly faded, men and women who speak our language will still turn to *The Spanish Farm Trilogy* for a picture of reality all the more terrible because of the quietude of its tones and the sombre disillusion of its ultimate message.

J. A. T. Lloyd. FR. Oct., 1927, pp. 574–75

He is so marvellously reserved; he says so confoundedly little, and yet manages to get his meaning so brutally across, that he is the man for our English money every time. A bit more articulation on his pacifist philosophy, and we might get shy of him. But it is all there, mind you; all there, in overtones. Just as the overtones of the British Tommy's remark, "Blimey: This trench ain't safe! I'm goin 'ome," were really, "Well, here we are, and we've got to stick it; so I'll shoot me own bloomin' father if he tries to take this trench;" so does Mr. Mottram, with conscious art, raise all round his quiet, studiously underwritten sketches and essays the whole argument for the expulsion of militarism and war. Whether it is an aesthetic valuation or a human valuation, to say of a writer that he expresses a national temper, I am not quite sure; in Mr. Mottram's case I am inclined to think that it chances to pan out as the same thing. Anyhow most English critics, who were also soldiers, find themselves muttering as they read Mr. Mottram: "This is the proper way to tell it; this somehow is It, as we knew it; it's the Real Thing." In short, it's the stuff to give 'em.

Ernest Raymond. BkmL. Dec., 1928, pp. 144–45

Mr. Mottram is at his best in *Strawberry Time* and *The Banquet* [one volume]. He has returned here to those overtones which were noticeable in the poems he published many years ago; and it is a relief to discover that his absorption in plainer, more realistic work has not destroyed in him the power of the fantastic. It is true that, even here, he rarely lets himself go; and his excessive control has always seemed to spring not from strength but from an odd fear of some conjectural consequences; still these two stories show him once again as an author of genuine imagination.

LL. Jan., 1935, p. 480

Time to be Going is a careful study of a superannuated uncle who retires from his work overseas and comes home feeling deceptively young, falls in love with a college friend of his niece and then by dying saves his family the pain of disapproving him. The characters are quietly and effectively drawn and not dragooned into categories. Mr. Mottram makes skilful use of the switch-back in time. The book throughout is rather melancholy, as was perhaps inevitable in an honest treatment of such a theme. The standard novel is about one's own contemporaries and one's own locality; the danger in such is the danger of staleness and it is necessary to contrive a situation where one sees the scene afresh, sees the emphasis of light and shade instead of the skeleton outlines and labels of familiarity.

Louis MacNeice. *Spec.* March 19, 1957, p. 550

MUIR, EDWIN (1887–1959)

This new volume [*Journeys and Places*] by Edwin Muir contains the best poems he has written and some of the most serious, interesting, and individual poems of our time. It is necessary to emphasize this because superficial qualities of vocabulary and form in his poems may put off the reader familiar with a far looser "modern" idiom than his. The ballad form of his poems, the familiarity of the surface themes—Tristan and Iseult, the enchanted Knight, Troy, Judas, Merlin, etc.—the use of words like "helm" and "eld," the often romantic imagery, may give the reader a false idea of their real content. For in writing about the past Edwin Muir is not endeavouring to evade the present, he is illuminating problems of time, of death and of the relation of the past to the present.

In these poems, in which journeys are made through time so that the past may be expressed in terms of the present, his artistic aim is similar to that of Henry James, in *The Sense of the Past*. . . .

Edwin Muir is a poet who has certain very definite limitations, but in these new poems he has explored these limitations to their farthest extent. His great strength, which enables him to press the meaning of his poetry very deep, is a metaphysical way of thinking, and it is to the metaphysical poets, exploring set and limited forms, rather than to the romantics, that one has to look for poetry at all resembling his. His style is epigrammatic, his symbols, beautiful and living as they are, are not sufficient in themselves, they carry always the weight of their reference to an argument, which although it is contained within the poem, exists outside the poem. His poetry is not poetry for poetry's sake, it develops an argument about time, which, it strikes one, might have been developed in a prose thesis or in an imaginative fiction. Yet in his poetry Edwin Muir has discovered a language which expresses this argument in the most vivid and direct way possible by means of an imagery so precise that the prose meaning would seem a circuitous way of describing what can be held instantaneously by a single poetic image.

Stephen Spender. *LM*. Oct., 1937, pp. 579–80

The Story and the Fable is by far the most interesting book Edwin Muir has written. It is difficult to criticise a work which gives a single-minded impression of integrity. But I might say, perhaps not too fancifully, that Mr. Muir has lived his life in order to write this book; yes, perhaps that is the clue to the title and to the clarity of every page which gives a unity to the most diverse experiences and meetings.

All through his life, Edwin Muir has had a quite exceptional awareness of a pattern below the surface of his life—call it what you like, the subconscious or a purpose, or the Fable. He has never deviated from this— though the most anxious pages are where he almost Becomes Something which all the other jostling crowd of autobiographers so eagerly are. Mr. Muir is the son of an Orkney farmer who "went down" in the world, dragging his family with him. As a young man, he lived in conditions of dreadful and even macabre (when he got a job as a clerk in a bone factory) poverty. Now we all read his reviews in the *Listener* and know his name. A typical little Scotch life, subject of a hundred autobiographies by I.L.P. leaders, writers, business men, etc.! The difference is that one doesn't close his book feeling "Ah, he has done it. He has got somewhere. He has skilfully manoeuvred his past into our present of debates and literary weeklies, without making us uncomfortable." On the contrary, one feels that he still is what he always was. That he has lost nothing of his past and of his childhood, but added to them enormously.

Stephen Spender. *NSN*. June 22, 1940, p. 778

If I begin by speaking of myself in this brief memoir of Edwin Muir it is because I was always aware of a deep affinity of origins and experience, and this may be my best qualification for writing about such a man. We had both been born on remote farms, and though Orkney is a long way from North-East Yorkshire, they were both Viking or Scandinavian settlements and the place-names that echoed in our infant ears have a striking similarity: Wyre and Wass, Ness and Garth. In the farmyard our sensibilities had been assailed by the same elemental sights and smells, though I had no experience of the sea. The parallel does not end with childhood. At the age of fifteen we had both gone to large industrial cities to become clerks at the same salary of four shillings and twopence a week. But then after a few years our careers began to diverge. Muir's experience in Glasgow was grim, and lasted for eighteen years; mine in Leeds was genteeler and lasted for only three years. I was ambitious and resolved to better myself. Muir remained unambitious to the end of his life, and more reluctantly than anyone I have ever known had his greatness thrust upon him.

During our youth we had experienced the same intellectual excitements, acquiring our knowledge from public libraries and cheap books bought with the few pennies we managed to save. We were both swept away by Nietzsche, who became the guide to our further education. We both became interested in Guild Socialism, read *The New Age,* and eventually contributed to its pages. We both came under the influence of its editor, A. R. Orage—a man of great intelligence and intuitive understanding, who naturally attracted disciples, as Muir said of him. But there the parallel ends, for the First World War had meanwhile broken out and I was swept into it. Muir escaped because his physique was not equal to it. It plays little part in his *Autobiography,* whereas in my life it is the watershed that divides innocence from experience, faith from disillusion, hope from frustration. For this reason Muir could always attend and listen to a class of experiences to which the war had left me sardonically indifferent. He describes these experiences in his autobiography. . . .

The *Collected Poems* will have to be revised now, and brought to a sad conclusion. May we hope also for a volume of Collected Essays? This, too, would be impressive. Again of no school, grinding no academic axe, the criticism is yet firm and profound, and of remarkable range. There must be many scattered essays that have never been republished; I remember one that impressed me very much at the time of its publication on "Calvin and Marx." Muir was not politically-minded. I like to think that he was a fellow anarchist.

Herbert Read. *Enc.* April, 1959, pp. 71–72

Edwin Muir's heroism was not of the swash-buckling, his diction not of the world-rattling, kind. As a poet, as a critic, and as a man he was equally unassuming; and his utter lack of pretensions was due to a wholeness, an integrity—to repeat a much abused word—that has become so rare as to be incomprehensible to many. At a time when every activity was tending to become a technique, a discipline, an autotelic function not to be related to any other, he persisted in relating everything to everything, and subordinating every activity to one dominant concern. If Edwin Muir was incorruptible—and he has been described as saintlike—it was not because he shrank from corruption, but because he was whole; because his moral vision and his imaginative vision were not in conflict, and both were integral parts of his nature. . . .

As one would expect after the circumstances of his youth, Muir's first works are pervaded by a sense of duality. His utter estrangement from the false self imposed on him by society—from the clerk in the bone factory—induced a trance-like state in which he could project himself at will into dreams and visions of extraordinary vividness. These dreams and visions provided a store of archetypal images and actions on which he drew all his life; but the more urgent task was to reconcile dream with reality, the dreaming self with the waking self.

Tragic conflict and incompatibility are the theme of his short novel *The Marionette* (1927), an account of the relationship between an idiot child and his father, set in Austria (where Muir became interested in the educational theories of A. S. Neil). . . . This minute and claustrophobic narrative points to Muir's later affinities with Kafka, but it could only have been written while Muir himself suffered from a maladjustment less extreme than the boy's, but also basically due to a conflict between imagination and reality. . . .

In the early critical works, from *Latitudes* to *The Structure of the Novel,* Muir came to grips with "the problems of our time, which are so defacing, so unlike, in their search for unsightly things, the problems of more human eras" (*A Note on Ibsen*); in doing so he eliminated what was false in his own aims, and defined his own humanity. In exactly the same way, Muir's residence in Italy, Austria, Germany, and Czechoslovakia at the same period served to make him aware of his own roots; the exploration of foreign countries—*Latitudes* contains an essay on Prague—and the exploration of various literatures were what Hölderlin called "colonisation," a process which necessarily precedes the most difficult task of all, that of "going to the source" and "learning what is proper to oneself." . . .

With *Transition* and *The Structure of the Novel* Muir had arrived at criticism proper, less autobiographically revealing than the first book, because more certain of its own point of view. Perhaps it was an exaggeration to say that the neglect suffered by Muir did his work no harm, for the great majority of readers remember him only for the most ephemeral part of his critical work, his book-reviewing in later years. If it was this neglect that confined him to journalism even in his late maturity, the implications are distressing enough; but it certainly did not embitter Muir or prevent him from writing poetry right up to his last illness and death.

Michael Hamburger. *Enc.* Dec., 1960, pp. 46, 48–50

At the time of his death, early in 1959, Edwin Muir had achieved the writing of three works that are likely to endure. The first of these, written in collaboration with his wife, Willa Muir, was the classic translation into English of Franz Kafka's short stories and novels; the second, his *Autobiography*—one of the best autobiographies of the present century; and most important of all, his *Collected Poems* (1953). In retrospect, it is now clear that his singular, though unspectacular, dream-haunted imagination was of the first order. Among his contemporaries, he seemed to stand very much alone. He was almost shocking in his hypersensitive lack of showmanship. . . .

Muir's comments on Wordsworth show how clearly his own growth as a poet evolves from the Wordsworthian tradition. This does not mean that he imitated Wordsworth, or was unduly influenced by him, but rather that his poetry contains the values of Wordsworthian simplicities and the hidden strength of deeply felt emotional experience. . . . Archibald MacLeish in his Foreword speaks of him as "the only poet of his period in whom the crystal eye of poetry was also the limpid eye of innocence." This is fine rhetoric, and no doubt well-intended. Yet Muir's poems, "The Labyrinth," "Orpheus' Dream," "The Animals," "The Annunciation," "The Rider Victory," dream-like though they may be, were never seen through the "eye of innocence." . . . Muir's poems are filled with inspired pictures of transcendental figures. Whether they are of animal or human shape, or are recreated from Biblical or pagan sources, all are drawn with Giotto-like clarity. (Giotto's frescoes were among Muir's admirations.) Nor did Giotto view the world with an innocent eye.

Horace Gregory. *NYT*. March 11, 1962, p. 5

MUNRO, C. K. (1889–   )

Mr. C. K. Munro describes his play [*The Rumour*] as "a study in organisation" and as "a play in two parts." It is also divided into a prologue, four acts, fourteen scenes, and an epilogue, and contains about forty-six characters and a large number of supernumeraries. With this huge apparatus Mr. Munro has certainly succeeded in putting before us a plausible exposition of the way in which a war might originate between two countries neither of which wished to attack the other. . . .

But Mr. Munro is not content with showing us how the War happened. He goes on to show how Great Britain is drawn in. We get two deputations in the Prime Minister's room in Downing Street, the first deputation consisting of bankers and newspaper proprietors, who want Great Britain to help the Przimians because a great amount of British capital is sunk in Przimia. . . . The Labour deputation as drawn was a little bit out of date; this, no doubt, was done for comic effect.

It is at about this stage that Mr. Munro's play began to pall. It was too realistic: we were overburdened with detail: speech followed speech with all the long-windedness of Nature expressing herself through her oratorical wind-bags. By the time we arrived at the dock scene, where British soldiers are discovered boarding the troopship *en route* for the War, hurrahed by the assembled multitude, I had had as much as I could stand, and I left the theatre. Nevertheless this is an admirable play, and if Mr. Munro would ruthlessly cut it it might be a great success in the ordinary theatre. It is, in the best sense of the phrase, an educational tract; but it does not preach, it reveals, and it should bring the people who see it one step further on the great highway of disillusion. . . . It is Mr. Munro's asset that he has not gone far, for the mind of the "man in the street" can easily follow him. It is his justification for using the dramatic form for the presentation of his ideas that this play is theatrically effective and that it exposes the folly and credulity of mankind more vividly than would a hundred popular pamphlets or a million University essays.

W. J. Turner. *LM*. Feb., 1923, pp. 422–23

Mr. Munro attempts, in his most recent play [*The Mountain*], to test every conceivable theory of human government dramatically, and since such a process naturally involves an extensive use of dialectic, he brightens up the performance with his very strong gift of comedy. The net result is that one wishes that there had been more brightening and less substance. *The Mountain* was written with little regard for time and space; it requires sixteen scenes embracing seven different sets and four hours to produce, and long before the end its author is so intent on holding together the crumbling bits of his intellectual conception that he has little energy left for the humour by which he made it palatable at the beginning. It was an ambitious effort which at times suggested that it might rival in effect the better moments of Mr. Shaw's *Saint Joan,* but it defeated itself by its own effort to be comprehensive on a matter on which all human history has as yet failed to say the last word.

Milton Waldman. *LM*. July, 1926, p. 300

Mr. Munro's *Coronation Time at Mrs. Beam's* was all about Mrs. Beam's at coronation time. This farce would have been much more amusing if it had been shorter by, say, an hour.

James Agate. *The Amazing Theatre* (George G. Harrap, 1939), p. 153

MURDOCH, IRIS (1919–   )

Iris Murdoch had a late start, publishing her first novel in her middle-thirties, when she had already a reputation as a philosopher and literary critic. Her work is not in the least uneven, but has blossomed out most smoothly and steadily, with each new novel better than the one before. Her first, *Under The Net,* in which one can discern some affinity with the work of Raymond Queneau and of Joyce Cary, was received with more acclaim than understanding. It was even thought to have something to do with the cult of the Angry Young Men. It is certainly an enigmatic book. Miss Murdoch has never (so far as I know) made any statement about her intentions as a novelist, and it may be that it pleases her to fox her critics somewhat. One needs, I think, to look at each of her books in the light of the others. She has simplified her technique as she has gone forward, and improved it. Her last book *The Bell* is a triumph, and that very rare thing in literature, a work of compassionate satire.

Maurice Cranston. *L*. Nov., 1958, p. 26

Miss Murdoch's new novel [*A Severed Head*] is very strange indeed; both in itself and as coming from her. Like Mr. Angus Wilson in *The Middle Age of Mrs. Eliot,* she seems almost to have made a deliberate effort to pare away the characteristics by which she was becoming best known. . . .

Under the Net was in a sense a refusal to write a novel at all (as all picaresque novels are); the life shown in it is too fragmentary to be forced into the conventional novelist's pattern of turning-points and crises, problems and solutions, significant incidents and revelatory experiences; there is only a series of contingent adventures. . . .

In *The Flight from the Enchanter,* Miss Murdoch seemed to have come to terms with the novel far enough to permit herself a more elaborate plot, and to choose an impersonal narrative form which allowed her to generalize about her characters (Rainborough, for instance) in a series of epigrammatic asides which Hugo could hardly have sanctioned. . . . When *The Sandcastle* appeared, many people welcomed it as a sign that Miss Murdoch's writing had become more "realistic." It would be truer to say that it had become more conventional. The world of *The Sandcastle* is not necessarily more everyday than that of the earlier novels—the gipsy-like man who appears announcing disaster is quite as fantastic as anything in them—but it is more neatly and recognizably an artifact. It is the coherence as well as the plausibility of the plot that reassured critics that Miss Murdoch had, as it were, settled down to her trade. . . . The basic moral issue of *The Bell* is that of fundamentalist or interpretative ethics, as reflected in James's and Michael's sermons. It raises the infinitely difficult question of how far one can be guided by rules as opposed to experience, how far it can be good to renounce the world without knowing it, how far one must know one's own limits before setting oneself any moral objectives at all. . . . It is in every way an astonishing book, and one of its most impressive features is the extreme ease with which so tightly disciplined a conception is carried out. Even the style is supremely confident. . . .

In the light (if it is a light) of this, what can one make of *A Severed Head?* Obviously, Miss Murdoch has become more formal still—perhaps following as large a change of course as was marked by the publication of *The Sandcastle*. In her two previous novels the figures move to some extent in a pattern; in *A Severed Head* they go through an elaborate minuet worthy of Mr. Henry Green, in which six partners try out every possible heterosexual combination except one (Honor Klein and Alexander). Indeed the novel contains, in a sense, nothing but form. . . . The characters' backgrounds and occupations seem merely designed, as in the most crudely romantic novel, to give them the money and the leisure to pursue an intricate scheme of personal relations; and their personalities vanish in the midst of their own involvements. . . . The imperfections of *The Sandcastle* were a small and (if the suggestions of this article are true) a necessary price to pay for the smooth perfection of *The Bell;* the sequel to *A Severed Head* may be equally remarkable.

Francis Hope. L. August, 1961, pp. 84–87

To begin with, the surface of the novel [*An Unofficial Rose*] is of a grating "gracious living" vulgarity that is hard to bear. It is not so openly vulgar as the sort of expenses sheet pseudo-elegance of her last novel, *A Severed Head;* but it was still possible there to suppose that all the talk of vintage wines and Meissen birds was ironic in tone. In *An*

Unofficial Rose, although the statement of the novel is ambiguous, the tone is not ironic. . . . In civilised sensitiveness we are in the world of Virginia Woolf, although Miss Murdoch perhaps regards her characters with a slightly more aloof irony. What rings false, however, when her world is set down beside Mrs. Woolf's, is that none of her characters regards his or her way of living in its social, economic sense with any questioning whatever. Surely the unease of Mrs. Ramsay or even Mrs. Dalloway gives us a truth about this whole class that Miss Murdoch's world lacks. Indeed Miss Murdoch's characters approach such things as the Boulestin Restaurant or a château-bottled wine with an awe and an underlining which suggests that their creator is not entirely at ease in her chosen environment. The degree to which Miss Murdoch seems to have sold herself to this women's glossy paradise is betrayed by the distinction so harped upon between shrub roses and hybrid teas, a distinction embodied in the title of the book. There have been few more arrant snobberies since the war than the worship of the beauty of the shrub roses. . . .

To such a detective story I am inclined with my namesake Edmund Wilson to answer—who cares who murdered Roger Ackroyd? All I trust is that this review is sufficiently harsh, for in Miss Murdoch, the author of *The Bell,* we had the only English post-war novelist to set beside our other hope, Mr. William Golding, the author of *Lord of the Flies.*

Angus Wilson. MGW. June 14, 1962, p. 11

It seems to me that on the symbolic level Miss Murdoch fails dismally, because she has forgotten what a symbol is *for*—which is to make something clear that would otherwise not be. There is more symbolism in . . . Thurber's Unicorn at the bottom of the garden, than in the whole of *The Unicorn.* If you put a character into a symbolic robe instead of a simple little button-through, it must reveal something about the character; it cannot be a garment chosen equally at random from a celestial wardrobe. And these symbols fail in their own terms because they reveal no higher reality, make no final point: they are less than human, not more. She thinks she is creating archetypes when she is only producing arch types. . . .

What, then, is to be done with this maddening woman, in whose talent I still stubbornly insist on believing? I think what she badly needs is a change of medium—and quick, before she succumbs to the prevailing malaise and bores us all into the ground with a Trilogy. If she is going to be a fantasist with no feet on the ground and no sense of humour, it seems to me that she must tackle the one field where fantasy has a discipline: I think (quite seriously) that she should try science fiction.

She simply cannot go on doing this celestial knitting—not in a world where the crisp brilliance of Muriel Spark and the wit and insight of Mary McCarthy are there to put her to shame.

Katharine Whitehorn. *Enc.* Dec., 1963, p. 82

MURRAY, GILBERT (1866–1957)

It is easy to see why, with so much in Greek drama that awaits his re-covering hand, Professor Murray has turned next to a less-than-famous play, which is not even certainly Euripides'. The *Rhesus* is such a fascinating piece of territory to reclaim—however outlying. We think Professor Murray makes out a good case for the Euripidean authorship, but what affects us more intimately is that he has here a first-rate piece of work for the theatre which has persuaded him into doing his very best in the way of presentation; and how good that is everybody knows.

OutL. July 12, 1913, p. 57

We need someone—not a member of the Church of Rome, and perhaps preferably not a member of the Church of England—to explain how vital a matter it is, if Aristotle may be said to have been a moral pilot of Europe, whether we shall or shall not drop that pilot. And we need a number of educated poets who shall at least have opinions about Greek drama, and whether it is or is not of any use to us. And it must be said that Professor Gilbert Murray is not the man for this. Greek poetry will never have the slightest vitalizing effect upon English poetry if it can only appear masquerading as a vulgar debasement of the eminently personal idiom of Swinburne. These are strong words to use against the most popular Hellenist of his time; but we must witness of Professor Murray ere we die that these things are not otherwise but thus. . . .

It is to be hoped that we may be grateful to Professor Murray and his friends for what they have done, while we endeavor to neutralize Professor Murray's influence upon Greek literature and English language in his translations by making better translations. [1918]

T. S. Eliot. *Selected Essays 1917-1932* (N.Y., Harcourt,
Brace, 1932), pp. 47–48, 50

Naturally, the most personal chapters [of *Essays and Addresses*] are the most stimulating on a first reading, and hence the attraction of the opening chapter, in which Professor Murray expounds the religion of a man of letters—"letters" being defined as the record made by the human soul of those moments of life which it has valued most and most longs to preserve. He ignores esthetics for the sake of morals, and then his book falls wholly within the second of our crude classifications. Religion, he points out, is always seeking a way of escape from the terror to come, and a scholar finds it by keeping hold of the past, "so that in a present that may be angry or sordid he can call back memories of calm or of high passion. . . . He feels himself one of a long line of torchbearers." Professor Murray is among the torchbearers of our day, and every one of the chapters in his present volume is luminous.

John Freeman. LM. July, 1921, p. 435

Professor Murray is one of those sages in whom culture and scholarship are entirely free from pedantry. There is never any doubt that classical learning in him is merely an element in a liberal and well-furnished mind. Besides being Professor of Greek, he is a poet, a thinker, and a man of the world, and his active and mordant intellect and rich imagination view and exhibit ancient history and literature in a strongly human and modern light. All history, says Benedetto Croce, is contemporary; and to read Professor Murray's essays [*Essays and Addresses*] on "Aristophanes and the War Party," "*The Bacchae* of Euripides," "The Stoic Philosophy," is to realize the truth of Croce's seeming paradox. . . . All good criticism is creative; every good critic is an artist, and his criticism is something more than mere analysis and exposure of another—it should be, as Oscar Wilde said, a new independent work of art. This is always true of Professor Murray's essays. His article on the Stoic Philosophy is a fine study of human thought and the problems of human life.

OutL. April 29, 1922, p. 345

Mr. [T. S.] Eliot's condemnation of the popular Mr. Murray and his praise of the highbrow H. D. have of course been echoed by critics less qualified to judge of the merits of the case. Without disputing the general truth of Mr. Eliot's strictures, one may think that he is somewhat unkind to Mr. Murray and more than kind to H. D. The former had to frame a style which would serve for the rendering of whole plays, not merely "romantic crumbs"; the style he chose may be easily damned as vague, lush Swinburnese, but a whole play done in H. D.'s manner would be less readable and probably even less Greek. . . . Further, Mr. Murray was under obligation to translate all of his author's text, at least as much of it as any translator in verse can compass.

Douglas Bush. Mythology and the Romantic Tradition
in English Literature (Cambridge, Mass., Harvard
Univ. Pr., 1957), pp. 497–98

The Greeks have a saying, "A man must be either a politician or an idiot," and Gilbert Murray made this choice very early in life. He was always both a scholar and a politician—a man who sees the faults of the world, and who sets himself to improve them.

Gilbert Murray was a devoted scholar. He did not so much translate from the Greeks as relive their works, so that each word of his English versions of *The Trojan Women, Andromache* and *Hippolytus* sweeps us all back into Greek literature, not as onlookers, but as participants. We must wail for the women of Troy; we understand Phaedra's shame and heart-consuming love; we know that Andromache was a fit mate for Hector and love her like an elder sister of our own family. This was what the Greek world meant to Gilbert Murray, and this was exactly how he taught it to his scholars. He set them on fire with his own intensity. . . .

He was also a magnificent playwright and lecturer, so that he could open the doors of Greek thought to all the intelligent people of his day. Their house, too, was open to everyone who worked for human progress; and during the war years was always full of refugees.

Gilbert Murray's work as Vice-President of the League of Nations at Geneva, with Lord Robert Cecil his great friend, who was President, would have set the world forward into permanent peace had the Governments of the chief countries, who sent such men as Lord Cecil and Gilbert Murray as their exponents, had the least intention of carrying out what their emissaries tirelessly pursued.

Phyllis Bottome. *JOL*. April 21, 1960, p. 466

MURRY, JOHN MIDDLETON (1889–1957)

Mr. Middleton Murry's gentle and fantastic little play [*Cinnamon and Angelica*] is difficult to criticise: any instrument seems too blunt and coarse to probe it with. The kingdoms of Prince Cinnamon and Princess Angelica are at feud over a slice of land. There is war. Prince and Princess, each of them hating the bloodshed, meet, without knowing each other, on a dark hillside, and find in each other the incarnation of the dreaming of years; but an idyllic conclusion is shattered by a stray bullet, which kills the prince. The irritation caused at first by slightly stilted and archaic language passes automatically; it is all a little away from reality. . . . It is a story in porcelain, and it is all in tone, except the songs, which are slightly cumbrous.

J. C. Squire. *LM*. Dec., 1920, p. 221

The title of Mr. Murry's novel [*The Things We Are*] is as inconclusive as can be imagined: the novel itself is not so. Mr. Boston, the hero, is another young man who finds life fragile, unseizable, and bewildering. His sick thoughts turn to physical discomforts, or perhaps physical causes are at the root of his sick thoughts—I suspect that Mr. Murry himself does not know which of these alternatives states the precise truth. . . . Mr. Murry is not a stupid writer; he does not of course imagine that Boston in his outward particulars is Everyman. But he does imagine, I think, that in Boston something can be found which is of application to every man. It is not so. . . . He is a *part* of the character of a quite definite type of humanity: and the fact that only a part of the character is given, that this part is refined on till it assumes nightmare proportions, cuts off his connection with humanity, as does the peculiar muzzy atmosphere with which Mr. Murry surrounds him.

Edward Shanks. *LM.* May, 1922, p. 98

Mr. Middleton Murry's prose makes some little minds cross: and this is not to be wondered at, for they feel that in his wrestlings, sometimes truly painful, to express in prose what poetry alone can express, he is despising their placidity and assurance—that, like some mountaineer, looking down from a difficult crag and wondering how people can go on playing tennis, he is arrogant. They complain of his implied retort to their assertion that there are many kinds of truth: "Well, my kind is Shakespeare's." To that only Shakespeare could reply effectively. Indeed, Mr. Murry's style is not always happy: in it, occasionally, as in some of César Franck's music, there is a "seated one day at the organ" effect which repels, not because it is false, but because expression has been inadequate to feeling. The "grand Amen" is left rather menacingly in the air. But how foolish to be irritated by an imperfection, by a touch of nature, when there is so much to admire! Absolute sincerity, deep sensibility, passionate conviction, the love of what is best, and a profound loyalty to apprehended truth are things not so often found united in a modern writer. They are united in Mr. Middleton Murry, and no book of his has more completely proved them than this study of Keats as the type of great poet. The man who can read it without finding much new value added to his experience is, in a manner, to be envied, unless—as seems more likely—he is to be commiserated. When I reflect upon the applause that was lavished on M. André Maurois' *Ariel*—that shallow and facile caricature of Shelley—I find those critics truly unfortunate who have failed to see in *Keats and Shakespeare* an immeasurable superiority. The imaginative reconstruction of a great poet's inner development needs very different qualities to those of Colonel Bramble's creator: it needs an intensity like Mr. Murry's. To look deeply into a poet's soul, into the living and changing core from which the germs of his poetry sprang, a man must have looked deeply into his own soul.

Orlo Williams. *Crit.* Jan., 1926, p. 193

It is the peculiar merit of Mr. Middleton Murry's extraordinarily beautiful and impressive book [*The Life of Jesus*] that—working upon material which is familiar, and even over-familiar, to all of us—he has caught, and kept in the foreground, that note of strangeness, that heroic quality, which no sensitive reader of the Gospels can miss; yet which is commonly left behind by those who paraphrase or expand them. Written with great literary distinction and with a glowing realism, a restrained fervour, rare in works of this kind, his portrait of the historic Jesus is, to use Otto's already classic term, "numinous" in the highest degree. Though rejecting supernatural theories of Our Lord's person, and seeking only to present Him as "the Prince of Men," he yet, in doing this, succeeds in conveying Divine values to us; and this far more truly and strongly than do many more orthodox scholars. We have here in fact a remarkable demonstration of the cardinal importance of the personal factor in historical criticism.

Evelyn Underhill. *Spec.* Jan. 29, 1927, p. 155

Mr. Murry seems to me a perfect pupil of his master Bergson: just as at the end of *Evolution créatice* Bergson transforms every philosopher before his own time into a precursor and prophet of himself, so Mr. Murry transforms Shakespeare, Coleridge, Keats and Goethe into prophets of his own philosophy. One same historic myopia seems to make Bergson and Murry unable to distinguish the figures of Aristotle and Aquinas very clearly; for no manipulation could possibly give Aristotle or Aquinas any place in the Bergson or Murry scheme. . . . But there it is, there are still thinking human beings who are not quite convinced that psychology is the key to the universe.

T. S. Eliot. *Crit.* Oct., 1927, pp. 344–45

Mr. T. S. Eliot finds the language of his friendly philosophical antagonist, Mr. Murry, to be very gentle and odorous of sanctity—"modulated," he calls it, "to the old ladies' ears." But later on, in the same article, he speaks of Mr. Murry's taste for "summary evictions." The gentle, sanctimonious Mr. Murry has, it seems, rather shocked Mr. Eliot by his summary eviction of that hoary relic, old "Nobodaddy," from his philosophical premises. A few months earlier Mr. Eliot had been "given the creeps" by Mr. Murry's "brilliant" book on D. H. Lawrence.

Oh, Mr. Murry, you naughty, creepy, brilliant, sanctimonious, sum-

mary iconoclast! No wonder poor M. Gabriel Marcel finds himself embarrassed at having to review your *Son of Woman* in the *Nouvelle Revue
Française*. It is true that he considers your opinion of Lawrence "en
grande partie fondé"; in other words, he thinks you are right, but, really,
how *pénible* for a man of such exquisite taste as M. Marcel to have to
write about any book of yours. It is *such* bad taste on your part to write
books at all. Your pages are so "terriblement 'intelligentes' "—not
merely intelligent, but "intelligent." No wonder M. Marcel is terrified! . . .

Come now, Murry, have a heart! Don't go on writing these cold,
heartless, logical, intelligent, sanctimonious, sincere, emotional books.
Think of the pain you cause M. Marcel, even though you do please those
dear old ladies. (Bless their robust old hearts!) Take a leaf out of the
book of critic-philosophers like Catherine Carswell and Mabel Dodge
Sterne Luhan. The latter lady has a "live plangent force lying passive"
at the "core" of her being, and "by becoming entirely that" she "leaped
through space" to the "essential core" of Lawrence, to draw him to New
Mexico. That's the proper way to write. Why even that simple boyish
soul, Mr. Drage (or do I mean Mr. "Everyman," or was it the *editor* of
"Everyman"?) can understand that sort of talk, and he finds one passage
of Mrs. M. D. S. Luhan's book worth more than all you have ever
written about Lawrence. And as for your book on Communism, reeking
of Marx's bloodymindedness, he could not make head nor tail of it. He
had to mark time with a pun: "Middleton Murry Marx time." Was it
not clever of him?

Richard Rees. *Adel.* Aug., 1932, pp. 781–83

I do not think that Murry is congenitally without a sense of humour. In
fact I am sure he is not. But there is a certain evident distrust of wit and
humour as critical instruments—a distrust which a great deal of current
intellectual acrobatics more than justifies. In any case, Murry has recognized the characteristic, and the fundamentally humourless man hardly
does that. . . . This solemnity is there, in Murry's writing. It is the offence
of a sometimes excessive virtue. It is, intrinsically, a good quality. And it
is not unrelieved. But it does detract from the general effectiveness—the
immediate appeal—of critical work. It is not a valuable quality in controversy. And it does give scope to dilettante commentators on life and
letters who have nothing of their own to say. . . .

These general criticisms of Murry are external to the purpose of this
essay. I come to praise Murry, not to bury him. But since I do hold a far
higher estimate of his work than is considered proper in my generation,
since in fact I am going to be accused of uncritical adulation, I want to
discount some reactions by indicating, to begin with, that my view is

not due entirely to bad eyesight. I am, I must insist, aware of all that has been urged in condemnation of Murry's work, having spent more hours than I care to reckon in arguing to extinction or to a due placing one accusation after another—some of them made initially by myself. . . . The mainly significant fact, for me at least, is that Murry's thought represents the only contemporary intellectual atmosphere in which I find it possible to breathe at all deeply. This, and the feeling that, if I do any hard thinking myself during the next few years, Murry's is the thought with which I would most like my own to seem continuous.

Murry, in short, is one immeasurably antiseptic in his age.

> Rayner Heppenstall. *Middleton Murry: A Study in*
> *Excellent Normality* (Jonathan Cape,
> 1934), pp. 25–26

Murry's best book of criticism is *The Problem of Style* (1922), a set of six lectures delivered at Oxford. There is something paradoxical in the thought of a self-confessed Romantic critic busying himself with such a concern, proverbially the Classical critic's business. We take it that the latter figure occupies himself with the question of means, while his Romantic counterpart looks to origins and ends. Of critics set upon examining the roots of a work's creative growth, Sir Herbert Read stands representative, as of critics bent upon a work's conclusions, Andrew Bradley perhaps. Murry shared a number of traits with them both, yet differed as *The Problem of Style* makes clear. . . . Murry's approach and thought in *The Problem of Style* was personal. Style, he would have said, is personality; or, with Buffon, "Le style, c'est l'homme même." To seek, then, for a writer's personality through his style is only to examine that style in its essential depth.

> Derek Stanford. *EC*. Jan., 1958, p. 66

The portion of John Middleton Murry's work which is itself of the most literary value and is the most likely to appeal to posterity is his literary criticism. If, as I think, its importance has been somewhat underestimated during his life, it is because the prominence he attained as a literary personality was largely the result of his work in other and more widely controversial fields. As the editor of several periodical journals at sucessive periods of his life, he was involved in contemporary social and political argument; he wrote books about pacifism, communism, religion and theology. His autobiography, and the autobiographical element in other books that he wrote, drew attention to his personal life and moral strivings to an extent that is not expected of a literary critic, and, in his own day, alienated rather than attracted sympathy with his earnest, almost prophetic conception of his literary vocation. In his output and in the public reaction to it there was much that tended to divert attention from those works of his which will have the most enduring claim upon students of English letters.

Middleton Murry was a literary critic by propensity and by profession. Such was his own conception of his calling, and the destiny predicted for him by D. H. Lawrence in the early days of their intimacy. He was one of those writers, never very numerous, who are able to re-interpret the literary heritage and re-affirm its values, not in academic seclusion but in the dust and confusion of the journalistic arena, sensitive to the aspirations of the present and in conflict with its evils. They study the works of genius in order to make them relevant anew to the questions of current discourse, not only to vindicate criteria of literary expression.

Philip Moirer. *John Middleton Murry* (BC/Longmans, 1958), pp. 5, 32–33

It is perhaps necessary to make the reservation that Murry, although prolific, was certainly no original creative genius. He was sometimes inconsistent, and flirted unhappily with Communism, his own rather eccentric concepts of Christianity, and with Freudian criticism. There is room for doubt whether he ever achieved the inner unity which might have brought him greatness.

Murry's weakness was manifest in his relations with D. H. Lawrence, which were close and at times intense. Whenever, in Lawrence's lifetime, Murry partook of the heady wine of that genius, he quickly became intoxicated, but a hangover was never far behind. . . .

That Murry, in the main, personified his own high conception of the critic's function is established again and again in this selection [*Selected Criticism*]. In these 29 articles and extracts, he ranges over the whole continent of the writer's art, and in discussing artists as various as Dostoievsky and Lawrence, Keats and Proust, Stendhal and Whitman, Shakespeare and Rousseau, is always probing and worrying at the inner philosophy at their centre, finally to subject it to the scrutiny of his own idealism.

John Barrows. *JOL.* June 16, 1960, p. 719

The difficulty was that Murry the political thinker was also Murry the literary critic. In his political thinking he wanted to remain true to the great doctrines which he had learnt from Keats. He wanted to submit his mind to the whole of experience without making it a select party (the cultivation of "negative capability") and to prove all doctrines by "the beating of the pulses." It was a noble empiricism, but an unsteady basis for political action. Concerted activity demands agreement upon common principles: but the formulation of principles is only another way of making the mind a select party. Negative capability sorts ill with commitment.

It was a dilemma that Murry never faced. As his developing view of human experience led him to one apparent *volte-face* after another, he imagined that his followers and friends must also see the cogency of his latest arguments and turn about with him. The idea that there might be virtue in remaining loyal to a particular principle lay outside his philosophy. In the same way he would initiate experiments in community living which rested on the assumption that if men were brought together in a new experimental situation, they would immediately be able to live with each other face to face and man to man. As one might have expected, most of the people who responded to his appeals turned out to be either rugged individualists or lame dogs who had never grown up into full personality. In such a situation, it was not surprising if disasters ensued. The surprising thing was that his experiments worked as well as they did.

Perhaps his most glaring turn-about came at the end of the Second World War when, having edited *Peace News* (admittedly as a restrained pacifist) throughout the conflict, he finally came to feel that there had been a force which he had not admitted in the claim that war against a political tyranny could be just. The reason, as usual, was honesty: stories of atrocities in concentration camps which he had earlier discredited now turned out to be sickeningly true. It was not surprising, all the same, if his best friends displayed exasperation at times. Even Alex Wood was moved to say, in connection with one of Murry's favorite phrases, "the trouble with John is that he *will* 'think aloud' "—and his most affectionate supporters were sometimes heard to murmur as they turned to his weekly editorial, "I wonder if the wheel will have come full circle again this week."

J. B. Beer. CQ. Spring, 1961, p. 63

MYERS, L. H. (1881–1944)

The Orissers is a remarkable book, by a remarkable man. I know nothing of Mr. Myers save as the author of this one volume, but I am convinced that, if he had published only the casual aphorisms scattered— or rather heaped up—throughout his story, he would have established his reputation as a thinker of startling subtlety and originality. The book is like no other. It is so far removed from conventions that "original" sounds a mild word for it: it is extraordinary. If Mr. Myers reminds one of anybody in his theme, it is of the Brontës; but he reminds one of nobody in his technique. Where does he place his people? In the English countryside—but with what a difference! No soil overworked by serial crops will serve *his* purpose: he must have his own local colour: he must have his own locality. After a few preliminary glimpses at such comparatively familiar haunts as Egypt and Morocco, we are transported to Eamor, the family place of the Orissers: there is a large town, not far away, called Tornel, scarcely less sinister and remote, but it is actually at Eamor itself that the conflict rages. Conflict? Between what? It is hard to say, for everything moves, in these more than five hundred pages, under the surface: motive is chased and tortured through every by-way and subterranean recess of personality: and even when emotion and calculation break out into violent action, the action seems pale beside the reasons for it.

> Gerald Gould. *The English Novel of Today*
> (John Castle, 1924), pp. 158–59

There has been a good deal of a complimentary nature already written about Mr. Myers's recent book, *The Clio,* much of it, I think, because of the widespread praise which his earlier book, *The Orissers* . . . received at the time of its publication two or three years ago. The present volume, although obviously the work of an exceptionally deft craftsman, does not seem to me to live up to the expectations which the earlier work apparently aroused. It is a little too clever, too bright, too reminiscent of the attitudes of a smart set, to justify the author's rare knack of writing. . . .

Mr. Myers's special talents in this book are his ability to sketch character vividly and rapidly, to keep a story moving through a haze of complication and scenic description, and to render vividly the impression of strange, exotic, or repulsive scenery upon various types of human imagination. . . .

And yet the old question arises whether any striking ability is not largely wasted on the old theme of the sexual relations and obsessions of the *jeunesse dorée*. The scenes of the book are a little often reminiscent of *La Vie Parisienne* compositions in flesh and silk. Not a little of the suspense is obtained by the old method of setting the reader to wonder whether this or that couple will, or will not, spend the ensuing night together. . . . It is rather a pity that men like Mr. Myers and Mr. Aldous Huxley should set up shop in the neighbourhood of Mr. Noel Coward to attract some of the latter's trade away from him.

> Milton Waldman. *LM*. Jan., 1926, pp. 315–16

The frequency of abstract statement in Myers' work cannot . . . be considered in isolation. It is of course bound up with the wide sweep of the novels: the amount of personal history and the number of social contacts that he finds relevant to his themes as they come to expression in the characters; and the extent of the characters' contact (by means of the plots) with the still wider external world. Concreteness and specificity all the time would overwhelm the theme. But one notices, I think, an increase in concreteness towards the end of each novel when the necessary generalized preparations have been finished. . . .

Myers offers the curious combination of a devotion to the subtleties of social life that suggests Henry James, with the sort of plot that suggests a detective story. It might seem that the plot was merely added on as further entertainment for the reader, and we perhaps ought not to thrust it aside ungratefully on that account. It probably has, however, a good deal more significance than that. It serves first to make it evident that the conflicting scale of values and the independent moral judgment of Myers' characters have their material relevance and are not merely speculative constructions for private entertainment. . . .

The worth of Myers' work ought perhaps to be regarded as largely independent of one's opinion of the novels as works of art, where judgments may differ widely; essentially they are means of communicating, and they would still be of remarkable value if you concluded that they were scientific essays of an unusual kind. Their first value lies in the fact that they do succeed—by whatever means—in conveying extremely clear and sensitive insight into the conditions of adult and self-responsible lives in a civilized society.

D. W. Harding. Scy. June, 1934, pp. 56, 62–63

The Root and the Flower . . . is a book difficult to get into. . . . I can imagine that most people, picking it up on a library shelf and looking inside for a clue, would find it puzzling and move on to something else. It is, in fact, an exceedingly good book, which any sensitive reader will find absorbing. Two of the novels contained in it have already appeared; the third, *Rajah Amar,* is new. As the publishers say, "it is not an historical novel in the common sense, nor is it an attempt to portray specifically oriental modes of life and thought . . . the remoter scene is chosen with a view to obtaining certain fundamentals in human nature." It is, then, that rare thing a "philosophical" novel—but how admirably the beckground, true or fictitious, has been conveyed! . . .

I have given a very inadequate account of this book, which cannot in fact be reviewed in a brief space. Mr. Myers is as difficult to appraise as he is to place among contemporary novelists. Where does he stand? I don't know; but having read *The Root and the Flower,* I shall get hold of his earlier novels as soon as I can.

G. W. Stonier. FR. April, 1935, p. 509

At another extreme, both of intention and sensibility—and the art of the novel is prodigious in the number and quality of the extremes it provides

—there is L. H. Myers' trilogy, *The Root and the Flower*. Addressed avowedly to readers in the modern predicament, it states its theme of the moral sensibility on the spiritual plane, and the twin theme of character-discrimination on the social plane—in terms conscientiously removed as far as possible from the social, economic, political, and religious predicament of his audience. The action takes place in sixteenth-century India and its movement is governed by various intrigues concerning the succession to the throne of Akbar, the great emperor, with the intention that the significance of the work will be all the more clearly felt in the Western twentieth century because divorced from false issues and local spiritual vulgarity.

I do not think that the device works except against its purpose, and its use raises one of the great problems of the novel: the use of external action and the form it ought to take. It is in this case easier to recognize the nub of discussion because the action fails. The clear result of Mr. Myers' device is that his action counts chiefly as a frame. What happens, what is done, what eventuates, matters only as it helps us to envisage, to see as of concrete origin, what the characters think and feel and say apart from the action that may or may not have inspired them. I do not think Mr. Myers realizes the burden he has chosen for his prose to carry: which is the burden of making a great proportion of his words *tell* in and for themselves as separable, quotable, self-complete items of expression. Put the other way round, Mr. Myers is nowhere able to resort to the great advantages of plot, which are roundness in appearance, solidity of impact, the illusion of objectivity, and—here the greatest advantage—the releasing or precipitating force of psychological form. This last is emphatically the greatest advantage of plot in works like *The Root and the Flower* which mean to mirror or represent the ultimate conflicts of the spirit in relation both to God and the world; and the advantage consists in this, that the words released or precipitated by the crises of the plot will, however ordinary in themselves, gather from the plot an extraordinary or maximum force of meaning which will in turn suffuse and heighten qualities of meaning differently arrived at— *e.g.,* "The rest is silence." [1936]

R. P. Blackmur. The Expense of Greatness (N.Y.,
Arrow Editions, 1940), pp. 192–93

Not long ago, when I was talking to J. B. Priestley about various contemporaries, he warmed my heart by fervently praising Myers's masterpiece, *The Root and the Flower*. I said that I thought Myers the greatest English novelist of the century. While not prepared to go quite as far as this, Priestley said that he could well understand and sympathise with such a view. He had been reading the book again, and was enthralled by its depth and power.

The Root and the Flower, which appeared first of all in two separate volumes, was a sudden and staggering manifestation of maturity from a writer whose previous work gave no promise of anything so profound. I am not saying this to excuse my own lack of divination, but I very much doubt if anyone who met the author after his first novel had taken the town could have foreseen so swift and startling a development. *The Orissers* was by any standards a distinguished first novel. It caught brilliantly a certain limited section of the world of the early nineteen-twenties, and it showed that a fastidious and discerning intelligence had been contemplating, with faint distaste, the predicaments and perplexities which beset sensitive people who had money and intelligence and sufficient leisure to brood on their emotional difficulties. . . .

The Near and the Far, the first of the two volumes that went to make *The Root and the Flower,* was published in 1929. It lifted Myers at once to the level of the great novelists. To say that it reads as well today as it did then is no more than to prophesy that it will read just as well a hundred years hence, even though, as may well happen, it be forgotten in the interval and re-discovered by some curious reader then.

L. A. G. Strong. *Personal Remarks* (N.Y., Liveright, 1953), pp. 201–3

NEWBOLT, HENRY (1862–1938)

The very striking merit of Sir Henry Newbolt's *New Study of English Poetry* is that he faces the ultimate problem of poetry with courage, sincerity, and an obvious and passionate devotion to the highest spiritual activity of man. It has seldom been our good fortune to read a book of criticism in which we were so impressed by what we can only call a purity of intention; we feel throughout that the author's aim is single, to set before us the results of his own sincere thinking on a matter of infinite moment. Perhaps better, because subtler, books of literary criticism have appeared in England during the last ten years—if so, we have not read them; but there has been none more truly tolerant, more evidently free from malice, more certainly the product of a soul in which no lie remains. Whether it is that Sir Henry has like Plato's Cephalus lived his literary life blamelessly, we do not know, but certainly he produces upon us an effect akin to that of Cephalus's peaceful smile when he went on his way to sacrifice duly to the gods and left the younger men to the intricacies of their infinite debate.

Now it seems to us of importance that a writer like Sir Henry Newbolt should declare roundly that creative poetry and creative prose belong to the same kind. It is important not because there is anything very novel in the contention, but because it is opportune; and it is opportune because at the present moment we need to have emphasis laid on the vital element that is common both to creative poetry and creative prose.

John Middleton Murry. *Aspects of Literature*
(William Collins Sons, 1920), pp. 178–79

. . . Sir Henry Newbolt does not seem to me to possess, on a great scale, the gift or quality of high vision. I do not mean (to use homely imagery) that the maidservant, Invention, serves in the house of Poetry, where the queen and mistress, Imagination, should rule. Imagination Sir Henry Newbolt undoubtedly has (he were no poet without it), but he invests that which is, or was, within his own experience, or has come within his knowledge, with the glamour and the glow of his imagination; he rarely throws his imagination forward on that which is to be, that which is outside his own reading or experience—in a word, he is not primarily creative. There is always imagination in his poems, but his poems, for the most part, are not *greatly imagined*. They are chiefly memories, sometimes meditations, of culminating moments, of varying moods in the poet's own life; more often they are the crowning, the sacramental commemoration, even the immortalization of some superb deed, some supreme act of heroic self-sacrifice.

In the matter of technique—a false rhyme, an error in accent or the like—one remembers in this connection that Newbolt is an accomplished classical scholar—he gives no opening for criticism. And if it be true that the form in which he clothes his thought is generally as stately as it is perfect, it is equally true that the soul of poetry, which he has thus beautifully bodied, is fairer even than the form. Dignity, distinction, reticence, restraint, unerring judgment, and faultlessly exquisite taste, mark all his work. His military ballads make their own battle-march music; his songs of our unconquerable Navy, our incomparable Mercantile Marine, have the burst, the hurtle and the boom of great breakers. Some are shrill with the rage of the hurricane; others, hoarse with the roar of the central seas. His songs of Devon, of England, and of rural joys, ring alike with sincerity and with sweetness. One misses sometimes the sensuous beauty of which Keats was so consummate a master; and once or twice, a poem by Sir Henry Newbolt may soar, but to my ear fails to sing.

Coulson Kernahan. *Six Famous Living Poets*
(Thornton Butterworth, 1922), pp. 100–1

In simple and good English, in a vein of poetry, as we might expect, . . . [his prose] romances do not fail; but Sir Henry Newbolt is no story-teller, his plots are of the slightest, their development confused and uncertain, and his characters are thinly sketched. His range of thought is so limited, his treatment of his themes often so jejune, that, despite his reverence for style and his sense of literary responsibility, in prose he goes no further than in verse. He hardly writes even to kindle the imagination.

Harold Williams. *Modern English Writers*
(Sidgwick and Jackson, 1925), p. 420

This slender sheaf of gleanings [*A Perpetual Memory and Other Poems*] —thirty-three all told—will delight those lovers of poetry who know the work of Henry Newbolt well. They will recognize here, both in what is austerely fine and in what is pungently keen, the essence of a mind compact of those two qualities. The range of these brief poems, their sensitive craftsmanship, the deep compassion in some, the racy wit in others, may be a revelation to that body of readers which still believes that the good things which he gave us in his Blue Water days were all that he had to give.

In a recent broadcast there was much to puzzle Newbolt's friends, but there was a tincture of truth in the remark that to many people his name suggests nothing more than a retired Colonel with a knack of patriotic rhyme. *Drake's Drum* rattles in ears unacquainted with the very different music of his more tranquil verse—the music sometimes of the hautboy, sometimes of the oaten pipe. For, to vary the metaphor and borrow the heraldic terms he himself loved, *azur* and *or* gave place to *argent* as the years passed.

Among the *Other Poems* there are seven in unrhyming verse and three in lapidary prose. There is an epithalamium, a fable, a satire; there are Christmas carols, and epigrams in the Greek and Roman manner. Some are given in Latin as well as in English. The middle lines of "The Nightjar" read like a translation from a lost fragment of Virgil; and there are constant conscious reversions to Catullus, Martial, and the Greek Anthology. The "Letter to R. B." in his own "new narrative method" is a joyous piece of fooling, and it is sad that the late Laureate should have missed the point—as apparently he did.

Dorothy Margaret Stuart. Eng. Spring, 1940, pp. 38–39

NEWBY, P. H. (1918–   )

Mr. Newby is a new author. A thinker and an artist of force, he has the gift of being able—in the shortest of short, dry sentences—to strike at one and get one in the vital spot. He tells his story [*A Journey to the Interior*] with a sort of steely, muscular sureness and power. And he gets us, where he means to get us, fair and square (in his allegorical way) below the belt.

The story is about Love, or rather, the lack of it. . . . One hesitates to try to pin down baldly the meaning of this kind of book. And here particularly, where the significance is so closely married to the tune, perhaps one should not attempt—as Mr. Day Lewis puts it—to construe it with a key. . . . At any rate this book rouses many echoes, half heard in the tropical dusk; this fable of a once-loved person who is real no longer, but who nevertheless continues to steal the emotions of the living, and imprison them in her land of death.

Julia Strachey. Hor. May, 1946, p. 358

Mr. Newby—one of the most prolific of the younger English novelists—has often seemed a very gifted writer who somehow managed to produce dull books. But *The Retreat* is exciting. Indeed, it is the closest thing to *A Farewell to Arms* to come out of the Second World War. Like Hemingway's book, it begins with military disaster (the retreat from Dieppe and Dunkirk) and passes on to devote the main part of the narrative to the effort on the part of a young soldier caught up in that disaster to reconstruct some kind of personal life. The story comprises, in a phrase that occurs in the novel, "the movements of a ceremony for the composure of troubled spirits."

Paul Pickrel. *YR*. Summer, 1953, p. vi

An Egyptian police officer in *The Picnic at Sakkara* suspects for a moment that a young English lecturer at Cairo University might possibly be, of all things, sane. But he quickly changes his mind. "It is too much to believe," he says. "Sir, we are all mad here." And whether or not Mr. Newby means them to be, pretty well everyone in his *Picnic* is. . . .

I have the highest regard for Mr. Newby's talent but when his publishers assert that "this delicious comedy" is "wholly," I say shucks.

James Stern. *Enc*. May, 1955, p. 86

Ineptly titled, neatly written, intermittently entertaining, this serio-comic novel about the 1952 Neguid-Nasser Revolution shows the danger of mixing fictional genres. The theme is promising: an attractive English-woman journalist lands in Alexandria on the day of the officers' coup, producing confusions and bringing out the contrast between the British and Egyptian mentalities. But nothing is quite worked out; good comic characters are introduced (like Wyvell Spleen, the British journalist, and Waldo Grimbly, His Majesty's Acting Vice Consul) but are allowed to drift away unexploited. There are some very funny scenes and some fine comic inventions, but the effect is blurred because Mr. Newby seems undecided whether he is writing *Black Mischief* or *A Passage to India*. His main characters keep fluctuating between Waughian silhouettes and Forsterian portraits in depth. I think his talent is definitely for the former, and that his earlier, *The Picnic at Sakkara*, on the same theme of Anglo-Egyptian misunderstanding, was more successful because it was focused more on comedy [*Revolution and Roses*].

Dwight Macdonald. *Enc*. Sept., 1957, p. 77

In other company P. H. Newby's *Ten Miles From Anywhere* would be outstanding. He is a highly sensuous but economical writer; no words are wasted, yet sights, sounds and even smells are released for the reader without direct description. He is most himself when writing about the East—"Uncle Kevork," "The Beginning of Exile," "Khamseen" and "The China Tomato" are among the most successful stories in the book. When he chooses an English background he approaches it as if it were equally exotic; preciousness, the consciously poetic, is a danger

then, but it is nearly always avoided. Nothing is taken for granted, everything (even in the light, comic stories) is seen with a sense of wonder;
this is a rare quality in so sophisticated and versatile a writer. Essentially, his is a lyrical gift, but this strain is controlled by humour and a
certain robustness which operates, as it were, behind the scenes.

Francis Wyndham. *L.* Aug., 1958, p. 65

Part of the difficulty with Newby's comic novels is the fact that they
derive from Waugh and Powell and inevitably seem second hand. For
colonial satire, Waugh, Cary, and before them, Forster, hog the field;
for city comedy, Powell is there with his *Music of Time* series. As for
his serious fiction, Newby is intelligent, unpretentious, and in command
of an acute shaping talent; but he has set his sights so low and has so
minimized his characters that his novels lack vitality and intensity. He
writes about love and sex, but one rarely senses them as significant
forces; he is interested in eccentric and mysterious situations, but one
rarely feels that he is willing to explore them; he is drawn to characters
who have important problems, but one rarely finds that the characters
come alive beyond the settling of their problem. Their lives are circum-
scribed by the problem itself: how they react to it, how they will attempt
to solve it; as though they have achieved reality only through identification with a conflict. Often, there are forces in their background which
haunt them like furies and which must be exorcised, but these forces, like
the characters themselves, lack definition. . . .

So carefully has Newby tried to avoid the large scene and the large
character that he has curiously cut himself off from the very areas that
would have given life to his novel. All this is doubly curious, for Newby
has several of the gifts necessary for the effective novelist; but despite
his inventiveness, he has stayed too close to his source and failed to find
his own depth.

F. R. Karl. *The Contemporary English Novel* (N.Y.,
Farrar, Straus and Cudahy, 1962), pp. 272–73

NICHOLS, BEVERLEY (1899–   )

Mr. Beverley Nichols's book [*Prelude*] is another of the triumphs of
precocity—a novel describing the Public School system by a writer with
very recent experience of it. And, like other novels on this subject, it is
a novel with a thesis. Mr. Nichols is far from disapproving of the system.
He sets out, on the other hand, to show that it is capable of receiving
and making comfortable the most eccentric of boys if he will only make

the least effort of adjustment to his environment that can be reasonably expected of a human being in any circumstances. . . . The thesis of the book appears to be that the Public School system does not necessarily deprive those who come under it of their individuality, does not necessarily crush or torture those who depart from the normal. . . . As a piece of evidence, the book is interesting and useful. As a novel is it less remarkable than Mr. [Alec] Waugh's *Loom of Youth.* That book was not only a contribution to a dispute; it was also a work of fiction astonishingly well put together for its author's years and experience. Its characters and many of its incidents were well observed and drawn. Mr. Nichols fails as a writer of fiction. His characters are vague and unconvincing; they have no fundamental individuality. The construction of his novel is extremely loose and uneven; and the passages of reflection are introduced with a very clumsy hand. Whether he will succeed in correcting these faults it is impossible to predict; but he clearly has gifts which ought to come to something. Precocity in the things he lacks is not always a certain indication of success in maturity.

LM. March, 1920, pp. 599–600

. . . [A] second novel, *Patchwork,* by Mr. Beverley Nichols, well fulfils the promise of his first book, *Prelude.* It is a further contribution to the long list of books dealing with Oxford—this time of post-war Oxford; it reveals the disillusionments of a youth who had gone through the fires of war, and yet sought to recreate the old spirit of Oxford: "When I came back from France, for a time I just saturated myself in Oxford. I thought it was the most lovely place on earth. And then suddenly I realized it was all wrong—it was all lies. I'd been living in a dream, making up sonnets, and playing soft music, and wandering about in the moonlight. It wasn't real. All those beautiful curved domes and spires and things, all the old stone and the damnable picturesqueness of the place —why should they be so lovely when the world's what it is? . . . We ignored tragedy and we ignored death. And then suddenly they both came down on us, and we got nothing else." *Patchwork* is an able expression of the restlessness and malaise of the youth today—the inevitable result of the experiences of the last seven years.

S. M. Ellis. *FR.* Jan., 1922, p. 164

Mr. Beverley Nichols, whose earlier works were based upon his reminiscences of school and college, has now ventured upon an original romance [*Self*]; not, however, so original that it does not incur comparison with the adventures of Becky Sharp and *The Climber.* . . . Mr. Nichols writes of old women with an almost feminine malice, but his minx is a little dull, and his humour, too, often takes refuge in the grotesque. It would be unfortunate if the possession of a clear and coloured style tempted Mr. Nichols to ignore the importance of observation or of imagination. He can play very nicely with his dolls, but the game is an old one.

H. C. Harwood. *OutL*. May 27, 1922, p. 422

As a strategist in journalism Mr. Nichols has surely no superior. He has an extrordinary flair for determining the correct moment at which to muscle in on whatever racket popular feeling makes it most profitable to exploit. During the last few years he has been an infallible barometer of public taste in registering successively the thoughts of the unthinking about America, gardening, pacifism, God. In issuing at this moment in history this chatty and intimate demand for a stiffening of the national sinews [*News of England*] he will presumably have gone once more straight to the heart of the library subscriber. It is conceivable even that he has not overreached himself in representing Sir Oswald Mosley as the one man "who has in him the qualities of that hero for whom this country has waited so long." But I feel he has slipped up a little on his technique. He has not attempted to produce any arguments calculated to inspire confidence in Sir Oswald and his political intentions. . . . It is presumably on the "people who feel" rather than on those who "think" that Fascism has everywhere been built; and exactly what the arrival of Fascism in other countries has implied cannot be wholly unknown to even the most trustful of Mr. Nichols's readers.

Derek Verschoyle. *LM*. May, 1938, p. 79

Mr. Nichols, an experienced novelist and essayist, knows how to write. His last book [*Verdict on India*], the report of one year of contact with India, has a good chance of becoming a best seller. It is a breezy book, full of provocative thoughts and vivid images which will hold the reader's interest from cover to cover; and it offers an approach to the Indian problem rarely heard in the popular literature.

Mr. Nichols has come back from India highly critical of the Hindu position of Gandhi: he is deeply impressed by the leader of India's ninety million Mohammedans, Mohammed Ali Jinnah, and his demand for the creation of *Pakistan,* a Moslem state, in India. The Mohammedans in India have neither the money nor the intelligent agility for any expensive and active propaganda. Mr. Nichols fills the gap to a certain extent, but much remains yet to be said and done before the discussion of the Mohammedan position in India can be handled seriously and competently. . . .

Mr. Nichols wished to trace the workings of the Indian mind not only in politics but also in art, in literature, in medicine, in journalism, in the cinema and in religion. He has done it with sincerity, and there is no doubt that he has reported his impressions truthfully. But he has been so disappointed in the Hindis and their civilization that he has become uncharitable. His viewpoint lacks the deeper understanding which can only come from sympathy.

Hans Kohn. *NYT*. Dec. 17, 1944, p. 10

NICHOLS, ROBERT (1893–1944)

A war-poem in *The Times* in 1914 first brought the name of Robert Nichols before the public. At that moment the soldier-sonnets of Rupert Brooke were attracting wide-spread attention. General interest in the poets was much enlarged, and any verses of moderate quality expressing patriotic sentiments clearly and grammatically were granted large type in the Press. . . .

In 1917 appeared *Ardours and Endurances: also a Faun's Holiday and Poems and Phantasies, by Robert Nichols,* with its two hundred and seven pages, its numerous sub-titles and sub-sections and sub-titles to sub-sections, its notes on the manner, occasion, place and date of composition of most of its contents, and finally its frontispiece portrait, appropriately in uniform and dated 1915. Here we have the young war-poet standing forth, as it were, in full panoply before his potential public.

The war sections of the book are inflated with this idea. They are effective in a self-conscious way. We are told too often what sort of a man the poet is, and how he feels. . . .

The reader had been told by the Press that Robert Nichols was a brilliant young writer, a poet to be read. But the principal amusement to be derived from the greater part of the book is merely the pastime of puzzling how these verses have been put together, and trying constantly to recall from which particular passages of English poetry they happen to be derived. . . . Also, who is to be bothered now with all those classical allusions? We have new Gods.

The recently published twenty-seven *Sonnets to Aurelia* narrate the story of an unfortunate love-affair, but more unfortunate than the worst woes of any disappointed lover was Robert Nichols's choice of the Shakespearean sonnet form for its registration. . . .

Robert Nichols has made certain poems so promising that one may hope that he will outgrow his derivativeness and his megalomaniac poses. One of these better poems is "The Tower," a lyrical narrative of the betrayal of Jesus; another is "Danae: Mystery in Eight Poems."

Perhaps the professional critics may yet prove right in having wagered their reputations on this precocious young man, who, when he can cease being "young," may become a better and wiser poet.

Harold Monro. *Some Contemporary Poets*
(Leonard Parsons, 1920), pp. 167–72

If the whole of this book [*Aurelia and other Poems*] were on the level of the best things in it, it would be very remarkable. Nobody who read Mr. Nichols's *Ardours and Endurances* could fail to perceive that he had a natural gift for full-bodied pentatmeters, and the best of the blank verse in the new volume has an energy, an unforced originality very rare in modern blank verse. . . . Mr. Nichols can see; he can also feel and write. What is at present wrong with him is that all his powers are only intermittently exercised. Even in his worst poems the happy, the indubitably poetic phrase may come. But too many of them, as wholes, are disappointing. The metres are apt to grow slack; there is a frequent tendency to echo the sound, and even the sense, of some dead poet; and although Mr. Nichols's depth of feeling is sometimes evident . . . his feeling often can only be assumed to exist, for it is not communicated at all.

LM. July, 1920, p. 366

Mr. Robert Nichols has published his play *Guilty Souls* in book-form; and since there seems to be no immediate prospect of it being put on the stage, it is best to notice it here and now. It has many absurdities, but it is a sincere and often astonishing work. The preface is agreeably silly, Mr. Nichols's notions about religion and the human soul are really very much better expressed in the concrete shapes of his characters than in the vague meanderings of his spiritual autobiography. . . .

The last three acts are, with all their faults, splendid and encouraging work. The struggle between the two men and between each man and his conscience proceeds with a subtlety that never takes the edge off an acute psychological excitement. So far as I can judge, the dialogue by means of which this immense spiritual conflict is expressed would be, with very few alterations, entirely successful on the stage.

Edward Shanks. *OutL*. July 29, 1922, p. 92

The Assault was an ambitious attempt at presenting the sensations and emotions of an officer before and during an attack. Descriptive and impressionistic in method, crude in rhythm, it failed, like most others of its class, to suggest overpowering emotion.

Geoffrey Bullough. *The Trend of Modern Poetry*
(Oliver and Boyd, 1934), p. 96

NICHOLSON, NORMAN (1914–   )

Mr. Nicholson holds that style and choice of medium are as eloquent of an artist's faith as any explicit manifesto. On this basis, and never unaware of the dangers of pigeon-holing, he classifies modern conceptions of the human situation in three main groups: Liberal, Natural, and Imperfect. That his is a composite picture of man's striving through varying channels towards fulfilment, rather than evaluation of relative *literary* stature, explains such apparent disproportions as the allotment of the same space to Yeats and William Saroyan, and twice as much to William Faulkner as to T. S. Eliot [*Man and Literature*]. . . .

At times the treatment, notably of "The Satirists" and "The Younger Poets," is inadequate—perhaps inevitably where the whole field is so wide; and one questions the omission of Hopkins, as poetic exponent of Imperfect Man. These cavils apart, Mr. Nicholson's book is lit again and again by flashes of enlightened perception, expressed with that incisive colloquialism which gives his poetry such vividness. The reader receives the impact of widely divergent writers "direct on his own fingertips"—Mr. Nicholson's description of the reader of Lawrence—"like a blind man reading Braille." Although the author's faith is implicitly Christian, the width of his responsive sympathy makes him as sound a judge of literature as of life.

Margaret Willy. *Eng.* Spring, 1944, pp. 21–22

The most noticeable trait in Norman Nicholson's verse is its power of novelty; the freshness of its figures and diction. This is more truly remarkable in that so many of these poems deal with theological and Scriptural subjects and that all his work, broadly speaking, is religious. . . .

Writing as a religious poet Norman Nicholson has felt the need to enter the field of Christian polemics in the guise of a literary critic. . . . The sense of divinity, which finds its expression in the arts as well as in religion, is present as much in denial of duty as in the assertion of its existence. Much of the field of modern letters is for Norman Nicholson a negative field, but one whose negativity confutes itself. The implications that interest him most are naturally those that serve to prove the defects in the attitude of denial.

Derek Stanford. *The Freedom of Poetry*
(Falcon Press, 1947), pp. 158, 168–69

Mr. Nicholson is one of those regional writers who abide in their own country and write of it with knowledge and affection [*The Lakers*].

English writing seems to be less enriched now by the Localists, whether urban like Arnold Bennett (in his best work) or rural like Hardy in his Victorian Wessex and Eden Phillpotts in his Dartmoor days. John Moore, near Tewkesbury, is faithful to his Cotswold fringe and so is Mr. Nicholson to his Cumbrian coast and the finest of English mountain-scenery that lies so close to it. The fidelity bears fruit. As a reader and a lover of landscape I am always attracted by the artist who writes of where he is and of what he intimately understands.

Being a Laker Mr. Nicholson knows the waters below and the rocks above. He can rescue geology from the text-book and make the pre-history of the fells and tarns as vivid as any story of the people who live among them. Economics are no dismal science for him: he follows the dale-farmer down the centuries with the liveliest of journeys, from the "statesmen" who followed the Norsemen to the now mingled industry of minding the sheep and shepherding the tourists.

Being a poet himself, he is properly interested in the poets and the authors of topographical prose who either "stayed put" like Wordsworth or came in for longer or shorter periods like Southey, Coleridge and De Quincey. He is deeply interested also in the changing attitude of man to mountain and of the traveller to the landscape. The greater part of his book is devoted to the early tourists' discovery and enjoyment of the Lakes when the crags had ceased to be regarded as merely "horrid" and the Lake district, because of its exceptional beauty, was accepted as a paradise of the Picturesque Traveller or as a pulpit of Nature's ethical instruction.

Ivor Brown. *TT*. Jan. 22, 1955, p. 108

To be fair, Mr. Nicholson is a poet who justly commands admiration. *A Match for the Devil* is scrupulously and beautifully written, however mistaken one may think the manner. What happens, unfortunately, is that Mr. Nicholson falls into another of the traps of the poetic man-ner. . . . Mr. Nicholson's is Down Among the Church Mice.

A Match for the Devil . . . starts off with a good idea: a cuckolded husband who takes back his wife, allows his neighbours to joke about him, and turns their laughter into a "holy joke." Treated by Dostoievsky, this could achieve greatness; treated by Shaw it could have been mag-nificent and funny. Treated by Mr. Nicholson, it becomes sub-Fry. The Fry method is to subdue the action of characters to the charm and wit of verse. The temperature of human behaviour is lowered to the point where things like robbery, fornication and murder are made to appear merely verbal, and one soon ceases to care about them. This ruthless rhyme type facetiousness is then gathered up into the poetic sermon on

Sin, Grace, Boredom, etc. The general effect is as of beaded bubbles winking at the brim of a cup of cocoa.

Stephen Spender. *L*. Dec., 1955, pp. 79–80

NICOLSON, HAROLD (1886–   )

Mr. Harold Nicolson's monograph on Verlaine [*Paul Verlaine*] is not a very detailed study of a really not very eventful life. Verlaine had adventures, it is true. He moved from place to place, but only as a straw moves in an eddy; and it is not easy to make a very interesting account of a man whose greatest experiences came to him by pure accident, not by his own volition. The career of Rimbaud, in whose vagabondage there was some will and purpose, makes better material; and Mr. Nicolson's chapter on him is worth reading. But with Verlaine the biographer's task is to draw his character and temperament, to show how his poetry came out of these, and to decide which are his good poems, and precisely how good they are. Mr. Nicolson unfortunately does not make much of this task, though his remarks on Verlaine's rhythms are novel and interesting.

Edward Shanks. *LM*. May, 1921, p. 100

There is a great deal of work to be done in rescuing Tennyson's reputation from the undeserved flattery it had in his own day and the undeserved denigration it has had since. Very much of this work has been done by Mr. Nicolson at a blow [*Tennyson*]. . . .

For Mr. Nicolson has undoubtedly brought air into a very thick jungle of misapprehensions and prejudices; and he uses his pioneer's axe with careful but ruthless hand. To him Tennyson is not the Bard, ministered to by adoring wife and friends and by an adulatory monarch and people. Nor is Tennyson to him merely the humbug who assumed this ridiculously undeserved post. The subject of his portrait is a great, frustrated, unhappy, and profoundly interesting man. . . .

The turn of the tide is signalised by Mr. Nicolson's essay; but the tide has made a great amount of headway in its first moments. The book is a very vivid and readable study of a personality. It is also on the literary side a very discerning and acute analysis of a mass of poetry. Mr. Nicolson shirks part of the work he ought to have undertaken; but the literary criticism he does undertake is done very well indeed. It is high praise to say that his examination of Tennyson's literary method is often on a line with his examination of Tennyson's characters and ideas.

OutL. May 5, 1923, p. 372

No one who has seen any of Mr. Harold Nicolson's previous sketches of the major light in the firmament of his own too brief career will need to be assured that this more serious and sustained study of the late Lord Curzon [Curzon] possesses every merit. To be trite, but at the same time precise, Nicolson makes his Curzon live again for us. It is a cinematographic rather than a photographic portrait—or better still a "talkie," for Curzon's self indubitably stalks and talks on the pages of this brilliant monograph.

LL. July, 1934, p. 497

How fortunate we are . . . in having amongst us a writer as lucid and vivid as Sir Harold Nicolson, whose *The Age of Reason* gives us so clear a picture of its life through the main protagonists who occupied the stage of this tremendous century! The selection and assimilation of material necessary for this work are, in themselves, monumental feats of reading and learning.

Herbert Van Thal. *JOL*. Dec. 22, 1960, p. 789

Reading these "articles, lectures and addresses" [*The English Sense of Humour*] of Sir Harold Nicolson's is like being shown round some great house on a day when the owner himself is taking his turn among the guides. As the well-furnished apartments are perambulated and the courteous exposition proceeds we are made aware by a casual excursus, a sudden reach of allusion, a touch of authority at the apposite moment, that our *cicerone* was born amid these exhibits and commands them. But how pleasingly, how delicately he furthers the fond persuasion that all is ours too! No more than a glance, a tone is required, and we feel securely of our host's society for the brief half-hour. . . .

And certainly we have a varied tour. Sir Harold discourses agreeably on Bergson and Itma and the anthropological skill of Doctors Bruno and Van Millingen . . . on numerous Tennysons . . . on what Swinburne and Baudelaire had in common . . . on the intellectual curiosity of Alexander the Great. . . .

If we own any dissatisfaction at our entertainment it comes from a sense that it is over too soon.

J. I. M. Stewart. *L*. Sept., 1956, p. 62

NOYES, ALFRED (1880–1958)

It is at least plain fact, and no fancy, that certain of Alfred Noyes's poems float to us as lightly and as liltingly as the far chiming of vesper bells; as if the fairies danced for him when he wrote; as if the poem

came to him, wind-carried, butterfly-borne, or as softly a-sail as a rose
petal upon a stream's surface.

This is specially true of *The Forest of Wild Thyme*. Wherever that
forest may be, here on old earth or in fairyland, it is within sound of
a chime of bells, and a chime which rings strange, and many, changes.
First, it may be, we hear some home-reminding, home-remembering
strain familiar to our childhood; after that, the call to prayer of the
Angelus, followed by the slow tolling which tells that a soul is passing
or has passed to God. Then—is it from the belfry in the church tower,
or from the organ-loft within that the music comes?—for that surely is
the roll of a great hymn, gathering in volume of sound, as if swelled by
the voices of a congregation. Next we hear the volleying of wedding
bells, followed by such rippling merriment of bell-music, that every bell
a-swing in the tower seems to be shaking its sounding sides, and rock-
ing like a pendulum in one great chorus of glad bell-laughter.

But whether the music be sad and solemn, glad and gay; whether
the thought in the poet's mind be a quaintly-humorous thought, a beautiful thought, or, as it often is, a thought which opens up new worlds
of thought with the suddenness and vividness of the lightning flash—
thought and music alike go as it were together, hand in hand, like twin
children of one father whom each in some way strangely resembles. . . .

His sense of humour is so delightful that to read *The Forest of Wild
Thyme* is sheer joy. No one without a delicate sense of humour—which
means nearly always a sense of true reverence, as well as of perspective
—could have harmoniously interwoven the nursery rhymes of our childhood with an intensely symbolical, spiritual—one might even say "religious"—poem, and with never a shadow of offence.

Coulson Kernahan. *Six Famous Living Poets*
(Thornton Butterworth, 1922), pp. 168–69

No other poet of our time (not even the late Mrs. Wilcox, nor John
Oxenham) has won so spurious a reputation, or poured out ink in such
wanton disregard of the elements of true poetry.

His present printed works cover more than a thousand pages of
close type, and he is not yet middle-aged. There is hardly a theme that
he cannot handle with the same apparent facility, in the same careless
meretricious style. He is a master of the commonplace. It is plain that
it has not occurred to him to treasure his thought in order that it may
mature into significant beauty. Accurate observation, close inquiry, a
respect for detail; selection, condensation, rejection of the unnecessary;
choice of image, phrase or rhythm; æsthetic honesty, literary candour,
local truth, psychological accuracy; prudent management of rhyme,
economy of epithet, love of the true substantive, pleasure in the right

verb; imaginative curiosity, the joy of new philosophic discovery, the adventure of metaphysical speculation, the humility or courageous ardour of religious doubt, and finally toleration for these qualities or attributes when exemplified in his contemporaries—these apparently, one and all, are unknown to him.

His "epic" *Drake* is a pageant of all the faults of careless superficiality. The blank verse is without distinction. The images are ready-made. It is packed with the mannerisms of a counterfeit epic style. The fact should be noted that four of the twelve books begin with the word "Now," two others with "Meanwhile," and one is dignified with the opening line: "Dawn, everlasting and almighty Dawn." Effects are attempted by the mere piling up of colours. In thirteen consecutive lines no less than seven epithets of colour are used: gold, golden, purple, brown, silver, brown, green.

His declamatory lyrical pieces are written in the easiest metres to hand; they gallop along, according to their kind, in facile rhymed quatrains, lightly constructed stanzas, or lolloping pentameters, hexameters, or heptamerous hybrids, with frequent *italic* refrains. A few of them, such as the well-known "Highwayman," make exciting recitations and are much used by popular elocutionists. In America, and also by a certain type of English mind, he has been considered one of the leading British poets of the time. He has been universally praised by reviewers.

Harold Monro. *Some Contemporary Poets*
(Leonard Parsons, 1922), pp. 184–86

Early in his career, being rash as well as young, Alfred Noyes made the tactical mistake of writing poetry that became popular. He was crowned with eulogy by leading critics who, naturally, could not foresee that he would also win the applause of the multitude or, no doubt, they would have been more careful. Meredith helped to mislead them; he praised the beauty and finely restrained pathos of "Michael Oaktree," a narrative poem in Noyes's very first volume, *The Loom of Years*. But it was his third and fourth books, those exquisite fairy tales in verse, *The Flower of Old Japan* (1903) and *The Forest of Wild Thyme* (1905), that carried him right into the popularity which disillusioned those self-centred experts who cling to a narrow faith that poetry cannot be poetry if it makes a triumphant appeal to the large world that lives and works in outer darkness beyond the limits of their own select, small circle. . . .

Unprofessional lovers of poetry read Noyes not because it is the proper, high-brow thing to do, but solely because they enjoy reading him. It is an excellent reason; and for the same reason Tennyson and Browning are famous; so, in these times, are Masefield and Davies;

de la Mare and William Watson. Noyes differs from most of his contemporaries in being at once, like Chaucer, a born story-teller and, like
Swinburne, an amazing master of metre and rhyme. He is not alone in
being able more readily and adequately to express himself in metre and
rhyme than in prose, and it is ridiculous to assume that this ability
indicates any shallowness of thought; it indicates, rather, that he is
really efficient in an art he has taken pains to acquire.

Arthur St. John Adcock. Gods of Modern Grub Street
(Sampson Low, Marston, 1923), pp. 253–55

Coming to the work of Mr. Alfred Noyes after a certain interval, it has
been interesting to try to assess the permanence of the earlier impressions. I remember reading *Drake* when it first appeared, and how swiftly
that reading carried me from page to page; I remember being swept
away by the gusto of "Forty Singing Seamen" on the spring morning
when I first read that, too; and I remember the more closely knit pleasure
I had in reading "The Rock Pool." So when I took up this newly issued
volume entitled *Ballads and Poems,* which is in the nature of a selection
from all Mr. Noyes's work, I turned first to those three poems, of which
two are given completely but *Drake* only in excerpts, and read them
with a self-conscious curiosity as well as with the more serious intentness demanded of the critic. I may say that my first opinion still stands.
I thought then, and I still think, that Mr. Noyes has three gifts in prominence: the power of narration, the instinct for colour and tone in verse,
and the quality of spontaneity. . . .

Perhaps the least happy of his poems are his sonnets. None of the
examples in the sonnet form in this volume seem to me to have the
real sonnet touch. They are not constricted enough, nor is their music
sufficiently organ-toned or swelling to the climax. Again, there is a
curious lack of the dramatic sense. The last lines of Mr. Noyes's sonnets are nearly always weaker than the first.

But these few strictures made, there is a wealth of beauty and music
in the work of Mr. Noyes that is of a rare quality. He is almost alone
in the present time in having the feeling for a large design. He is no
"idle singer," but fills his verse with a noble seriousness that looks
back to the larger tradition. He is, above all, a narrative poet.

Wallace B. Nichols. *BkmL.* Jan., 1929, p. 226

. . . I have suggested that Alfred Noyes is a romantic poet. And I wrote
this because I feel that Noyes, unlike so many modern poets, is in a
limited sense merry. I suggest that he is romantic because some of his
best poetry has to do with *popular* romance. One of his most famous
poems is deservedly known as a fine romantic poem. And that is "The

Highwayman." There is true romance in this, getting back to the days when the roads were romantically dangerous because of highwaymen and not sordidly dangerous because of bad motor-drivers. There is even in his melancholy some keen degree of romance. For underlying all the poetry of Noyes we find a thrust after bravery, purity, hope. Life is for the poet worth living. He has none of the despair of Byron, the bitterness of some of the modern novelists, the hopeless paganism of so many of the writers of our own age. In this thrust after romance and the real truth that lies behind it we see the path which led Noyes eventually into the Catholic Church.

Patrick Braybrooke. *Some Victorian and Georgian Catholics* (Burns, Oates and Washbourne, 1932), pp. 174–75

Mr. Noyes is steeped in Horace: he writes with an enthusiasm and a mellow affection [*Portrait of Horace*] which will make many former classics take Horace down from the shelf again and look for Horatian echoes such as Mr. Noyes is quick to notice in Thackeray and Tennyson and R. L. Stevenson. But those who cannot check the accuracy of Mr. Noyes's *Portrait* by the original sources may be misled. The author sees his hero through romantic and highly imaginative spectacles. One would cavil less at this treatment of one poet by another were not Mr. Noyes himself so ready to criticise other interpreters, with their neglect of "historical accuracy" and their "modern fashion of attempting to bring the classics nearer by anglicising them."

J. T. Christie. *Spec.* Oct. 10, 1947, p. 471

In Alfred Noyes—poet, prose-writer, and lecturer, who died in his seventy-eighth year on 28 June in the Isle of Wight—there existed two strains of mind seldom discoverable together. The first was a vein of popular imagination, responsible for such justly famous lyrics as "The Barrel-Organ," "A Highwayman," "Dick Turpin's Ride," and "A Song of Sherwood," as well as for less fictitious but none the less rousing narrative compositions in the manner of *Drake* (1908) and *Tales of the Mermaid Tavern* (1912). The second strain was one of scientific curiosity, and led to the three-volume "epic *The Torchbearers* (1922-30), in which the poet celebrated the great figures of European science: Copernicus, Galileo, and others. It was also, in part, from this vein that he wrote, after entering the Roman Church, two works of unusual apologetic: *The Unknown God* (1934) and *Voltaire* (1936). Here, with a deal of originality, he tried to show that the scientific spirit had reached certain conclusions consonant with the Nicene Creed. Science, he suggested, was opposed to religion only in so far as it adopted a positivist temper foreign to its true workings. The agnosticism proper to the scientific spirit was essentially one of openness and wonder. . . .

In pin-pointing Noyes's strength as a poet, we are driven back to his use of rhythm as the means by which he secured his best effects. The changes and refrains of "The Barrel Organ" display this gift of his in its simplest and most undeniable performance. . . . Half of the attraction of Noyes's rhythm is allied to that of the music-hall in its palmy days before the Great War killed it. The rhythms of English poetry since 1918 have been esoteric. Their beat is that of a lonely pulse, of an occult school, not a vast community. And when (as in Eliot's *Sweeney Agonistes*) a poet employs the vulgar idiom to an emphatic rhythmic end, his intention is clearly ironic and reductive. He is not affirming, but criticizing, the current and swing of ordinary living. But Noyes, like Kipling, posits this un-self-censorious life and revels in it. And if he has not Kipling's artistry—his felicity of phrase and firm colloquial hold— his verse still retains a public inflection, an accent of the crowd and not the solitary person.

Derek Stanford. *Eng.* Autumn, 1958, pp. 86–87

O'CASEY, SEAN (1884–1964)

Mr. O'Casey's most recent play takes place immediately before and during the Easter Rebellion instead of during the post-war disturbances in which *Juno and the Paycock* was set. Nevertheless, it would seem to be increasingly obvious that Mr. O'Casey's dramatic inspiration comes almost entirely from the misfortunes of his countrymen during the last decade. Apparently he sees the sequence of revolutionary episodes as one vast drama, and from it selects for his own purposes dramatic episodes which he places against a shrewdly observed background of Irish proletarian life. This would seem to explain the very real lack of structure to be noticed in both these plays, since he conceives the frame of them to be outside of both of them, and many other plays which he has written and, it is to be hoped, will write. He himself sees so clearly a beginning, an end, and a middle in recent Irish history, that he conceives it unnecessary to stress these dramatic props in the segments of that history which he chooses to dramatise.

The Plough and the Stars is a better play than *Juno*, because there are not three distinct strings of plot to unravel—more poignant in the characters selected from Dublin's underworld as mediums for alternate passages of humour and terror. No one of the characters, perhaps, suggests the potential greatness of Captain Boyle, but none of them cheat their promise as did he. . . .

It is my guess that, although Mr. O'Casey will never *construct* a play so as to attain the maximum effect out of its rhythm and movement, he will in his succeeding plays increasingly eliminate such devices and other breaches of dramatic taste, with the result that we shall have greater power with no less of the entertainment which he undoubtedly affords.

Milton Waldman. LM. July, 1926, p. 299

When Mr. O'Casey's first play, *The Shadow of a Gunman,* was produced at the Abbey Theatre, Dublin, it was evident that he had everything that goes to the making of a fine dramatist except artistic integrity. The humanitarian red herring which has obtruded itself into all Protestant literature since Tolstoy with such persistence as to defeat its own ends was trailed across the stage almost as gratuitously as if Mr. O'Casey had been a Russian instead of an Irishman. He preached as maudlinly as Gorki (or Dostoievsky) if not quite as impertinently as Mr. Bernard Shaw. But apart from his excessive humanitarianism and one or two other slighter faults he indubitably had the root of the matter in him. He has at times a rich, occasionally an original, grotesque, poetry. At the Abbey he came, naturally, under the influence of Mr. Yeats whose *Player Queen* and *Plays for Dancers* will in time come to be recognized as turning points in the history of post-Renaissance drama. The result has been a steady and marked improvement in Mr. O'Casey's technique. *Juno and the Paycock* is written with a better sense of light and shade and is richer in content than *The Shadow of a Gunman* but it remains a play with a plot in the bad sense. There is no inevitability about the action. *The Plough and the Stars,* his latest play, marks a definite movement in this direction. It has bad faults. The doctrinaire humanitarianism has become doctrinaire irony, the love-making is so naïve as to make the spectator and even the reader embarrassed. But the progress of the action arises out of the characters and the situation to a much greater degree than in the earlier plays. Mr. O'Casey is learning not to spoil his effects, to handle his material like an artist.

L. St. S. *Crit.* May, 1927, p. 275

Do we imagine that in these victims of society we have at last fastened Mr. O'Casey down to something, if only a break in the evening hate? Never were playgoers more mistaken, for the play [*Within the Gates*] has a Dreamer, the ethereal offspring of Galsworthy and Mr. Drinkwater, who at the end of the play says roundly that the Down-and-Outs are scum and ought to be down-and-outed. After which he expresses the opinion that the street-walker is the best of the lot, since she has courage, if only of the despairing sort.

It is difficult to separate one's disagreement of opinion from the place of that opinion in a work of art. That we should impatiently ask what is biting Mr. O'Casey does not affect his right to be bitten, with, if he likes, unending objurgations; still, it would be a little boring if all Shakespeare's sonnets had been written on the theme of "Tired with all these, for restful death I cry." This play is obviously non-realistic, and therefore one must not put it to a naturalistic test. What a pity, then, that Mr. O'Casey should make it so difficult for us by making his characters both real and unreal, earthbound and fantastic, so that his play reads like *Alice in Wonderland* interleaved with Euclid!

But perhaps this is the new medium which the unusual rhythm of this play is said to usher in? If that is so, then there is one dramatic critic who will have to go out of business. I think I can understand park-keepers, prelates, and, at a pinch, prostitutes, and I try to grapple with symbols, sublimations, subfuscations and substantiations whereby an author shelves his characters to substitute himself. But I find it difficult to do these two things at the same time, and in my view the characters in every play should decide at the beginning whether they are going to be a metaphysical all-my-eye or a real Betty Martin. The trouble is that Mr. O'Casey is essentially an Irishman who, while labelling his characters English and dropping the accent, still retains the Irish idiom. Take the Old Woman, for example. Any drunken old lady who is Irish has that poetry in her which befits her for Kathleen-Ni-Houlihan, whereas the capacity to soar is not in the English Mrs. Gamp. If this play were translated back into the Irish in which it was conceived one might take a very different view of it.

James Agate. *First Nights* (Ivor Nicholson and
Watson, 1934), pp. 274–75

Mr. O'Casey tells his part of the story in *Inishfallen Fare Thee Well* and *Rose and Crown* (the fourth and fifth volumes of his autobiography). His three plays of the mid-twenties made enemies but they made powerful and numerous friends. They gave O'Casey an identity; and this proved precisely to be the problem when, a little later, he proceeded to write a little differently. . . .

Mr. O'Casey rightly implies that there is a sense in which even his early plays are not realistic. Conversely there is a sense in which it was the realism of the later plays that offended an influential section of the public. *The Silver Tassie* gave offence for not being *Journey's End*—that is, for exposing wounds instead of filming them over with gentility. *Within the Gates* gave offence for giving a close-up of a bishop instead of hiding him in a cloud of incense. *The Star Turns Red* gave offence for turning red—when the palette of a Cecil Beaton or an Oliver Messel had so many other colors to offer. It was opposed in England not for its brand of politics but for being political at all. The point of view is familiar to readers of Mr. O'Casey's arch-antagonist, James Agate, who, for example, complaining of J. B. Priestley, not that he wrote badly, but that he wrote politically, had clearly no means of distinguishing the Yorkshireman's defects from the Irishman's qualities.

One cannot study this man's career without convicting the world around him of jealous meanness. First, they shelved his early works as "classics"; second, they took a stand which explained and dismissed his later works before they appeared. Between these two phases, there was one crucial and receptive moment, a moment when the O'Casey story, as Hollywood would call it, could have been given another turn, and by a single man. This was the moment when W. B. Yeats was reading *The Silver Tassie* for the Abbey Theatre. Not understanding the crucial nature of this moment, we are likely to misread large portions of the autobiography as megalomania. Actually, we should be less surprised at Mr. O'Casey's continual return to the crisis of *The Silver Tassie* than at the fact that his attitude to Yeats even after it was one of filial love.

Eric Bentley. *Dramatic Event* (N.Y., Horizon
Press, 1954), pp. 43–44

. . . Mr. O'Casey buzzes forth on the stilly air of theatrical criticism. In the course of some two hundred pages of very readable discourse he tries to persuade the reader that he himself is wasp No. 1, and offers an array of stings to support the claim.

It is disappointing, this, because the stings are nothing like as deadly as the buzz would seem to threaten; and it is only Mr. [James] Agate who is stung.

The reader will be very tired of Mr. Agate by the end of the book. Barely a page is without some reference to him; line after line is taken up with the ridicule and exposure of his activities. Mr. O'Casey never lets up. . . .

The Flying Wasp is an unpretentious book of . . . essays but it is full of sincerity and hope for the English theatre. Here is one playwright at least who knows and cares for the written word of drama. He could well afford in future to overlook the activities of Mr. Agate.

John Pudney. *LL*. Summer, 1937, p. 180

It would be easier to write about Sean O'Casey's last play if the memory of *Within the Gates* did not stand in the way. Like that earlier work, *Red Roses for Me* is half mystic and half melodrama. Like the earlier play, it seems, from the printed page, not to be molded after any recognizable theatrical pattern. But when you remember the dramatic impact of *Within the Gates* as it was performed on the stage, you hesitate to say that *Red Roses for Me* is not an acting play. Yet that is how it seems in print. Moreover, it lacks the high poetic moments that were sprinkled lavishly over *Within the Gates,* moments in which the poetry had its own moving and dramatic effect. This lack emphasizes the inactive quality that hovers over a whole work that is filled with constant action and conflict. The play is a presentation of the poetic soul of Ireland, crossed by dogmatic and economic battles which fill Irish hearts with bitterness. It leaves no doubt of its noble intention but that is the only clear thing in it for a reader who does not know modern Ireland at first hand or understand fully the conflicts in modern Irish government and religion.

TA. April, 1944, p. 256

"Forget your theories and work on characterization," said Lady Gregory to Sean O'Casey when he came to her with his first play around 1919. O'Casey went back to his tenement room and soon fashioned from the stuff around him the immortal characters who came to life before an astounded audience when *Juno and the Paycock* was first put on the stage in 1924. A Dublin labourer had achieved the miracle of creation. James Agate called O'Casey's next play a "flaming masterpiece."

Another soon followed but it wasn't long before the theories were back again burrowing like termites in the butt-end of Sean's fertile brain. The stage is ill-used as a pulpit, and flag-waving with the intellectuals who gate-crashed the artistic world of the 'thirties had a morose effect on one who had composed with the same music in his ears as Yeats and Synge. Indeed Yeats wrote sadly of the decline of the Romantic movement, "that high horse riderless Though mounted in the saddle Homer rode," and it is certain now that he considered O'Casey among those unseated.

Those of us who hoped to see the playwright back in the saddle again in his play [*The Bishop's Bonfire*] on Monday night were sadly disappointed. It was preach, preach, preach from the start with little of the lightning flashes. None of the finer instruments were in use. The theme nagged its way across the footlights, with the monotonous whine of the barrel organ. "The Irish are never at their best when they're angry, only when they're smiling," says someone in the play. O'Casey's anger has changed him from a Colossus of the theatre to a jacked-up tub thumper.

Ulick O'Connor. TT. March 5, 1955, p. 296

I have an intense dislike of Mr. O'Casey's work. When, years ago, the poet Maurice Willows pressed a copy of *The Plough and the Stars* on me, assuring me that it was far greater than my *pet* admiration, Granville Barker's *Secret Life,* I began to read it on the bus on the way home, I was so anxious to read this new "great playwright." Ten pages finished me. Shallow theatrics, sentimental Irishisms. In Joyce's *Portrait of the Artist as a Young Man,* Stephen Dedalus looks at his father and his drinking comrades, and knows how disillusioned he feels in comparison; not theatrical disillusion, but the real sense of evacuation of the airless moon. . . . And a few years after Joyce's terrific restoration of the sense of reality, back comes Mr. O'Casey, with all the shallowness that Stephen saw in his father's drinking cronies.

Colin Wilson. Encore. June-July, 1957, p. 7

Sean O'Casey's *Cock-a-Doodle-Dandy,* which has reached London . . . ten years after he wrote it, is funny, passionate, and (though you'd never guess it from reading the press notices) intensely concerned with the world in which we live. It is a gay and savage assault on the forces of humbug and fear. Above all, it is explosively alive. . . .

O'Casey realises . . . [his] conflict with all the vitality of a man who really believes in popular theatre. Farce, pantomime, flights of wild, comic lyricism, outbursts of savage satire—he exploits them all with a zestful assurance. The struggle is both spiritual and physical.

Albert Hunt. Drama. Nov.-Dec., 1959, p. 39

O'Casey's world is chaotic and tragic but his vision of it is ironically comic. It is in this war-torn world of horrors and potential tragedy that he finds the rowdy humour which paradoxically satirizes and sustains his earthy characters: they are the victims of their foibles yet they revel in their voluble absurdities. And it is clear that O'Casey himself enjoys his people no less for their follies, as he intends his audience to enjoy them. There is a sharp tone of outrage in his Daumier-like portraits of life in the slums of a beleaguered city, and this tone becomes even stronger in his later plays, but he was not dramatizing case histories. His plays do not follow the documentary principles of Naturalism —of Hauptmann's *Weavers* or Galsworthy's *Strife*. Low comedy is not one of the handmaidens of Naturalism. Even when he is in a serious mood O'Casey is likely to be satiric not solemn, poignant not pathetic. And when the tragic events or consequences of war and poverty become most crucial he will open up the action and counterbalance the incipient tragedy with a music-hall turn or a randy ballad or a mock-battle. While everyone awaits a terrifying raid by the Black and Tans in *The Gunman* the well-oiled Dolphie Grigson parades into the house spouting songs and biblical rhetoric in drunken bravado. Just when Mrs. Tancred is on her way to bury her ambushed son in *Juno* the Boyles have launched their wild drinking and singing party. While the streets ring with patriotic speeches about heroic bloodshed in *The Plough* [*and the Stars*] the women of the tenements have a free-for-all fight about respectability in a Pub.

This pattern of ironic counterpoint is maintained as a tragicomic rhythm throughout the plays. For each tragic character there are comic foils who constantly bring the action round from the tragic to the comic mood. . . . It is this attitude which keeps his plays from becoming melancholy or pessimistic. His humour saves him and his characters from despair.

David Krause. Sean O'Casey (N.Y.,
Macmillan, 1960), pp. 71–72

Despite the richness of his conception [*The Drums of Father Ned*], there is some fault in the execution; like its immediate predecessors, *Cock-a-*

Doodle Dandy and *The Bishop's Bonfire,* the play is not quite satisfactory. The reason is not so much the overflow of gaudy rhetoric, for this is set off by passages of the greatest terseness, but the uneasy alliance of a poetic imagination with a prosaic stagecraft. O'Casey relies on too many corny "atmospheric" tricks like echoes, and shallow symbolic paraphernalia, quite below the level of his genius. He is trying to pour strong wine into some very old and fusty skins.

Brett Duffield. *JOL.* June 30, 1960, p. 795

What are the later plays? What are O'Casey's intentions? Briefly, his intentions would seem to be the destruction of dramatic realism. It is something of a paradox that the reigning convention of the modern theatre should be realism although the greatest modern dramatists in their greatest plays are not realists. Perhaps the subtle influence of the film is responsible, and perhaps it is easier to understand the Ibsen of *The Pillars of Society* than the Ibsen of *The Master Builder. . . .* Today's theatrical growth is from *Murder in the Cathedral* to *The Cocktail Party,* from poetry to prose. O'Casey, who has never attempted to come to terms with theatrical convention, has progressed from prose to poetry. . . .

O'Casey's work, however, has tended in the direction of freedom, of breaking down the forms and conventions of dramatic realism. He cries with Shaw that there are no rules, but this statement should be taken probably as one of narrow polemic against realism, rather than as a broad statement of dramatic theory. In his early plays O'Casey was thought to be a realist of erratic and primitive genius, a dramatist of great original talent who, if he learned to harness and control his structure, would produce quite overpowering plays. *The Silver Tassie* and the subsequent plays, however, indicated the dramatist was getting too big for his britches, was setting himself up as an intellectual and a member of the avant garde, was throwing discipline out the window, whimsically dissipating his meager power in the slough of Expressionism and perversely biting the pale and poetic hand that fed him from the door (back door probably) of the Abbey Theatre.

Actually the early plays, like the later ones of Chekhov, seemed slovenly in form and slipshod in structure only because they were not based on the four-point traditional structure of *Protasis, Epitasis, Catastasis,* and *Catastrophe* which, under various pseudonyms, have been chewed over by critics from Donatus to Scaliger to Dryden to the latest composer of a "How to Write a Play" textbook. The early plays are far from structureless, but have a structure akin to *Bartholomew Fair* and *The Alchemist.* From the beginning, then, O'Casey was straining against the confines of realism and by the poorly understood success of *The Plough and the Stars* reasserting the vitality of this second structure with its unique utilization of tragic irony and its broadness of scope that the conventional, four-point, single-action plays of his contemporaries denied.

Robert Hogan. *The Experiments of Sean O'Casey*
(N.Y., St. Martin's Press, 1960), pp. 10–11

O'CONNOR, FRANK (1903–   )

Guests of the Nation is a collection of short stories and sketches by a new writer. I say "and sketches," because if one were in search of something to find fault with one might perhaps complain of a certain inconclusiveness, a lack of shape. One or two of the stories do not so much end as fade out, and some have almost the air of being fragments of a larger work. Their vividness and power, however, make this criticism of small account. Mr. O'Connor has all the gifts of the storyteller: sympathy, humour, detachment, and a style so unobtrusively the servant of his purpose that one hardly pauses to admire it. He writes of what he knows, of what he has seen and heard, and if his work is in some degree personal reminiscence it is perhaps none the worse for that. Certainly it is impossible to tell where memory ends and invention begins, and there is never a hint of mere contrivance. Most of the stories concern the Irish civil war, but there are others, racy and unforgettable, in witness that this author is not a man of one theme. The title-piece, in which two English prisoners are shot (in reprisal) by their reluctant guard, is almost unbearable in its horror and poignancy. The last story in the book —of a boy and a night watchman and a prostitute—is a small perfect thing of another kind. Between these extremes are thirteen stories varying in length and mood and merit. The slightest are done with skill and spirit, and the best have a quality that suggests permanence.

Gerald Bullett. *NSN*. Oct. 17, 1931, p. 481

Bones of Contention . . . is an entertaining volume of short stories. You need not be very fond of the Irish, nor take very kindly to Irish *patois*, to enjoy tales as dextrous and good-humoured as "The English Soldier," which relates how the daughter of a devout Fenian is obliged to entertain a British private to tea, or the other eleven stories of this agreeable book. In fact, you may detest Irish humour. For Mr. O'Connor avoids its most irritating characteristics.

Peter Quennell. *NSN*. Feb. 22, 1936, p. 268

It is too bad that Frank O'Connor's books are not better known in this country [U.S.], because they illustrate qualities likely to be forgotten in a period like the present. It is not only their humor, or their peculiar variety of humor, but also the qualities of sympathy and detachment. . . . Mr. O'Connor is detached in the sense that he allows the observed experience to carry its own moral. And the moral is that anything less than a profound and all-inclusive charity is madness and death.

William Troy. *Nation*. April 29, 1936, p. 556

Frank O'Connor's *Dutch Interior* (his second novel) is a typical example of the better Irish novel, but it is not a very satisfactory novel. It contains all the types, the "Characters," of the spiritual crisis in question —the sceptic, the orthodox, the in-between, the Irish-American sentimentalist, and so on (I begin to think we shall soon have another kind of Stage Irishman, slightly better-class but not much of an improvement on the old one). He paints a very depressing and inconclusive picture of the modern Irish tension, that grappling of a vaguely-realized and elementary European culture with the rather provincial brand of Catholicism so firmly grounded in Ireland. For here the tension is only the tension of a corpse strung on the gallows. Everyone is frustrated: and it is that Tchehovian frustration which is the antithesis of tragedy— failure in ambitions that were never clearly apprehended, that indeed never existed except side by side with the sense of their failure. Here the "struggle" is a foregone conclusion; the quiet dream-like descriptions, rather reminiscent of Virginia Woolf, confirm this impression.

D. J. Enright. *Scy*. Spring, 1943, pp. 184–85

The extent of O'Connor's Irishness may be judged from the fact that he not only speaks Irish, but he has also won a prize for a study of Turgenev written in that language. It is the English peculiar to his world— to Cork and Kerry—not to Dublin and Joyce's world. A glance at any of the dialogue in *Dubliners* and then at that in *Crab Apple Jelly* will reveal immediately the difference. The dialogue of the former book is Dublinese. But so steeped is O'Connor in the ancient language that in the midst of a few words of conversation he will interrupt himself and in parenthesis, as though to remind both himself and the reader that he's writing in English, remark of his characters, "(in Irish they were speaking)". . . .

Their subjects of conversation, their interests, occupations (behind all of which, in both books, looms the inevitable church); their homes, their behavior, whether cautious and conspiratorial, under the influence of clinical eye, or wild, witty, rampageous and rhetorical, under that of liquor—in all these respects the two books and the people in them bear a remarkable resemblance. But the most remarkable similarity in both these writers' stories lies in that Irish quality of remoteness. Apart from the occasional mention by O'Connor of a ramshackle old car, *Crab Apple Jelly* might perfectly well have been written in 1904. In it there is no sound of an airplane, no mention of Hitler, Mussolini, or Marx; no reference to any world-shattering event that has taken place in the fifty-odd years since its author and *Dubliners* were born.

James Stern. *NYT*. Nov. 12, 1944, p. 3

Frank O'Connor is one of the few fine short-story writers of our time. It is this fact which lends initial interest to his study of the modern novel, for the judgments of a practitioner have a special interest and weight. His opinions and conclusions, even when they are least convincing, have a quality different from those reached by one who is primarily a critic, for, with the writer, the work seems to be examined from the inside out. And when the writer is Frank O'Connor, the initial interest is increased, for he has previously shown that he can maintain a considered opinion in happy independence of the general consensus. In *The Mirror in the Roadway,* Mr. O'Connor exceeds all just expectation.

James Finn. *Com*. Oct. 26, 1956, p. 108

What claim has a poet or writer of fiction to be listened to when he turns his hand to criticism? Despite a rather superstitious tradition of respect for his views the answer is obviously contingent on the criticism he proffers. Coleridge's was engrossing, Stephen Spender's and V. S. Pritchett's isn't. No doubt a critic without original literary experience of his own is at a disadvantage, working with his left hand only, but that experience will not by itself guarantee his criticism. The greatest dramatist to use our language was also an actor, but that doesn't mean that Frank Vosper and Emlyn Williams are great dramatists.

As a short-story writer Frank O'Connor enjoys a reputation for humanity, integrity, and humor that is thoroughly deserved. As a radio commentator, in the years when I used to hear him, he was crisp and engaging, a forceful enemy of cant. As a critic, so far as this book [*The Mirror in the Roadway*] reveals him, he is very uneven indeed—by turns precise, obscure, stimulating, almost pretentious, wise, and downright perverse. His one consistency lies in almost never being dull.

John Peter. *KR*. Winter, 1957, pp. 153–54

The Lonely Voice is a brilliant book on a subject about which little that is illuminating has been written. It carries, besides, the authority a critical work always possesses when its author is a distinguished practitioner of the art he is criticizing . . .

He has, of course, his defective sympathies. These make him less than fair, I think, to Hemingway, though his remarks on Hemingway's prose and its indebtedness to the Joyce of *Dubliners* are first-rate and, to my knowledge, new. More often, he turns even his defective sympathies to good account, for he is concerned to discover why they are defective and with what justification.

Walter Allen. *NYT*. May 5, 1963, p. 14

O'FAOLAIN, SEAN (1900–   )

Mr. O'Faolain knows his Ireland, and knows too how to recreate its varying atmosphere with a touch that is well-nigh magical [*An Irish Journey*]. And so we are conducted from Dublin round to Dublin— through frugal, self-preserving, close, idealistic Kilkenny, with its air of a lost city. . . . Mr. O'Faolain is pungent and provocative: he has a ready Irish Gascon about him. But this adds a piquancy to his rewards and, in any case, we freely forgive him for the sheer beauty of some of his passages and the haunting love of Ireland that pervades his pages. His is a remarkable travel book, and history, humour, and reminiscence are subtly blended with description.

D. L. K. *Month*. Oct., 1940, pp. 249–50

. . . Seán O'Faoláin's *Bird Alone* is, I think, a remarkably good novel. . . . The story of a young man's struggle against a Church that is too securely founded, his fight for freedom of thought and action—a freedom which costs him all he was living for and leaves him *"liber inter mortuos*—a freeman among the dead."* It is a kind of local *Crime and Punishment,* without the reconciliation that Raskolnikov is finally able to effect. O'Faoláin does not damn his hero *ipso facto,* nor does he damn the victorious Catholic-social conventions: he depicts without prejudice a straight, if hardly fair, fight, and though his hero's "individualism" culminates in something approaching murder (he is in love with a sincerely religious girl whose sense of sin drives her to suicide), he does not forfeit our sympathy and respect. This novel, too, might be charged with inconclusiveness, in that the hero's life is ruined beyond repair yet he does not in any way repent his actions. Had he made a success of his "freedom" or had he absolutely renounced it, the case would have been different: but he is simply an ordinary young man, unusual only in his smatterings of culture, and not intended to be a Prometheus or a Faust. But O'Faoláin has a clear grasp of the moral essentials of his story, and there is nothing stiff or sentimental about his attitude to tradition and the contemporary mentality. The same author's *A Nest of Simple Folk* is another tale of Troubles and troubles, sadly complicated, and nothing like as impressive as *Bird Alone*.

D. J. Enright. *Scy*. Spring, 1943, p. 185

What then of *The Vanishing Hero? I* must not say of so good an Irishman that Mr. O'Faolain's work seems to me to show all the English critical virtues. Yet it does so, and some special Irish ones for good measure. . . . I mean such things as reverence for the text; an open mind; enlightened empiricism—a sort of receptive teasing-out of the elusive essence rather than the bull-dozing formula; irony; the sense of the *pas trop sérieux* (if it must be one or the other, literature is another game, not another religion); above all, in the sore-headed context, urbane readability. Mr. O'Faolain considers Huxley, Waugh, Greene, Faulkner, Hemingway, Elizabeth Bowen, Virginia Woolf, Joyce—the representative novelists of the twenties. The tentative theme adumbrated in the title is more or less self-explanatory. The author regards the novelistic hero as essentially a social conformer. . . .

Mr. O'Faolain (who is incidentally one of the most sensible and reliable of contemporary novel-reviewers) develops this theme with liveliness and precision, seasoned with a welcome dash of Erse devilry whenever the laughing mood is on him. Which is usually.

Hilary Corke. *Enc*. Jan., 1957, p. 82

Sean O'Faolain is unique among writers. He is thoroughly Irish—neither expatriate nor estranged nor conformist and insular—but he writes within an American frame of reference which makes his stories particularly valid for us. Many Irish writers dealing with the simple poor folk of Ballycushnagorra describe what are often types from the past, fey or elemental or "racy-of-the-soil" or what have you; this sort of thing, although often deeply moving, is only good old local color at one remove.

What O'Faolain considers significant material is significant today, and even under the broader U. S. A. horizon. Nothing is merely national with him, although he can tap the nostalgic root as well as the next; nothing is merely disillusioned, though not a nuance of the present day Irish scene escapes him. His graduate years at Harvard and subsequent returns to the States, most recently as visiting professor at Princeton and Phi Beta Kappa lecturer at various colleges and universities, have almost binationalized him. His point of view is that of a very well-informed detached academic American, but he is no desiccated don—his vital, paradoxical Irish realism prevents it.

Anne O'Neill-Barna. *NYT*. Jan. 7, 1962, p. 4

On that rainy night [Jan. 1915] of Lennox Robinson's play [*Patriots*], that was what happened to me. My double doors opened on these same scraps of real life enlarged now by the powerful glass of dramatic emotion, heightened by the hovering presence of truth, shaped by and for the intelligence. My doorways thereby became, for the first time, doorways to that emotionalized reality which is the father of the truly creative imagination—life-based, life-transforming, what Berenson so often loved to call "life-enhancing." . . .

A year cannot have passed before I saw myself in print for the first time. It was a short story, in a weekly paper called the *Cork Outlook,* and it must have been one of the most remarkable stories to appear either in that or any other periodical before or since. I borrowed the opening from G. A. Henty, wrote the middle, very brief, myself, and leaned heavily for the conclusion on R. M. Ballantyne. This remarkable piece of collaboration was about a gallant young British cavalry officer sent with an urgent dispatch on the field of battle across enemy fire. As he galloped he waved his sword and his plume danced in the wind, and it goes without saying that he was shot through the heart and died as nobly as only George Alfred Henty, Robert Michael Ballantyne, and John Francis Whelan could do it between them. If Prometheus ever bothers with such small-fry activities, I fear he must have sighed many times as he read that week's edition of the *Cork Outlook* and decided that it was really going to take an awful lot of experience to awaken this minute mortal to the facts of life.

The old Fenian's cutaway coat hung in my wardrobe for years and years. The finery gradually fed the fatted moth. Yet when I published my first novel, twenty years later, called *A Nest of Simple Folk,* there was the old Fenian, and my father and my mother, and all my uncles and aunts among the fields, skies, and streams of the plain of Limerick.

Seán O'Faoláin. *At.* Jan., 1964, p. 100

O'FLAHERTY, LIAM (1896–   )

Over-emphasis, . . . is a fault of Mr. O'Flaherty's, but with him it is only one of the defects of his virtues. He tells the story [*The Black Soul*] of a neurotic, self-tormenting Irish ex-soldier and graduate who goes to Inverara, a wild western isle, to regain his health and peace of mind. He achieves both in the end through the agency of Nature and a peasant woman (herself not far removed from Nature in her bounty and simplicity); though it is difficult to believe that his peace of mind would last more than a fortnight. The tale is told in an excitable manner that successfully carries off all kinds of absurdities, and is actually a curious mixture of hard, close realism and rather high-falutin' rhetoric, which last at times even leads Mr. O'Flaherty to forget that he knows how to write very well indeed in that curiously monotonous, very Irish style of his. Here it is at its worst: "That spring at Booruck, when strong men live greedily every moment from the grey cold dawn to the mist-laden dusk! Life there is only to the strong and the ruthless. Oh, strong, beautiful sea! Hunger-inspiring! Life-giving! Oh, the icy clasp of the wind, like the stern command of a proud father." Oh, the wind—indeed. But Mr. O'Flaherty has that which will atone for a thousand faults in his manner; he has imagination, unifying his story and driving it forward, and the reader with it. He has the seeing eye; he believes in the narrative he has to tell, and, incredible as it may all appear after sober reflection, he makes us believe in it too. He is very Irish himself, and yet can stand aside sufficiently long to note, in his youthful compatriots, the sickening alternation between flagellation and the flesh-pots, a bitter and morbid asceticism and a gross, dreary sensuality. Not since the early work of Mr. Joyce has the temperament of a certain type of young Irishman been so securely caught and vividly displayed.

J. B. Priestley. *LM*. July, 1924, p. 212

Among the hundreds of novels which appear there are, each year, only two or three which rise so far above the normal as to become permanent literary achievements. The rest is current fiction. But on this lower level there are comparative heights, books which are not, indeed, events in the lifetime of those who read them, or books of destiny, but which in their own field have so much merit that they call for warm praise and serious attention. Such may be any kind, detective or adventure stories —like Masefield's *Sard Harker*—or tales of sentiment and character or new windows into a shadowed corner of life. Mr. O'Flaherty's *The Informer* is of the last type. Ireland has become a *terra incognita* to us of late, Dublin a town of mystery, and its inhabitants strangers. The Irish writers we know already wrote of a past era. And so Mr. O'Flaherty's story of the Dublin underworld to-day is, in all its grimness, so much of a revelation that for this alone it compels our interest. He never makes the common error, either, of falling into sentiment about Ireland or slipping out of the world of reality into that non-existent world of petulant, half-godlike and utterly fictitious Irishmen that other writers have created out of their false vision and saccharine fancy. *The Informer* is the terrible story of a revolutionary ex-policeman's betrayal of his bosom friend, a gunman wanted by the police.

Spec. Oct. 3, 1925, p. 560

Mr. Liam O'Flaherty, of course, has learnt from Tchekov [*The Tent and Other Stories*], and as in Ireland not alone the human beings but even the animals seem to have rather a Russian cast of mind, he could hardly have found any more suitable master. He has been praised and in some quarters over-praised, but he sees directly and puts down directly what he sees. His best pieces, such as "The Conger Eel," have the character of pictures, simple and moving because they mean no more than they say. He is perhaps at his best, because at his simplest, when he is dealing with animals.

Edward Shanks. *LM*. Aug., 1926, p. 432

What an amazing writer O'Flaherty is! There is not another writer living who could have got away with *The Martyr*. It is full to the neck of faults and absurdities. Its ending is wholly preposterous. It is at times so crude as to be almost laughable, and so brutal as to be disgusting. Yet, when you put it down and think it over, every single one of the four main characters remains in the memory with just the same vital effect as life itself. The story deals with the entry of the Free State forces into Sallytown in Kerry—I trust Sallytown will never recognize itself or it will cherish no warm feelings for Mr. O'Flaherty. There is here a slight variation from O'Flaherty's usual formula of a single character about whom the story swirls with such centrifugal force that one is swept out of incredulity by the excitement of feeling at the centre of a vortex. . . . Finally, one puts away the book in a fury with the author for such extravagant waste of genius, for there is no use pretending that the novel satisfies. When one recovers from the bludgeon effect of his method one realizes that he could, if he would only take pains, be one of the greatest writers living.

Seán O'Faoláin. *NSN*. Jan. 21, 1933, p. 76

Now and again . . . guts and taste are found in conjunction. They have seldom been found in happier conjunction than in *Famine*. Mr. O'Flaherty has long since made his name: this book ought to make it clear that he is one of the most distinguished writers of his generation. He has here a grand intention; his rare talents as a story-teller, his mastery of narrative and dialogue, have never been better employed; and he has this advantage over many of his shifting, shallow, urbanized contemporaries, that he is a man with roots and a background. His subject is the great Irish famine of the 'forties as it affected one small community and certain families and individuals in particular, but this book is very much more than a good historical novel. It is a magnificent assertion of sympathy with the perpetual struggle of the mass of humanity for bread, freedom and civilization. . . .

I can think of no greater compliment to pay this wholly unskippable book than to say that I believe Daumier would have read it with admiration, and with a just appreciation of its warmth and its grimness. . . .

William Plomer. *Spec.* Jan. 15, 1937, p. 98

. . . [His] world had much in common with Maupassant's, and O'Flaherty, as a novelist scrappy, sensational, and often cheap, had a keen and relentless eye for its colour, its drama, its contradictory forces of greed and religion, simplicity and craftiness, devotion and deception, and not least its primitively beautiful background of sea, earth, and sky. In consequence his stories give the effect of pictures dynamically conceived and flashed on a screen. The leisurely refined compassion of Joyce is missing; the precious musical periods of Moore are absent. Everything has in it a kind of impatient sting, a direct stabbing physical force, brutal, sensuous, and elemental.

The achievement of *Spring Sowing, The Tent, The Mountain Tavern* was notable—and was not continued. O'Flaherty, famous for a period as the author of *The Informer* and other novels, slipped out of the English literary scene for a life of international wandering. The loss was most notably the short story's: for if Joyce's stories had been revolutionary in a quiet way, O'Flaherty's were revolutionary in a way that could, like Maupassant's, have done much to popularize the short story. For O'Flaherty, like Maupassant, saw life in a strong light, dramatically, powerfully. Energy alone is not enough, but the sensuous poetic energy of O'Flaherty was like a flood; the reader was carried away by it and with it, slightly stunned and exalted by the experience. *The Dead,* unless I am mistaken about the future of the reading public and its taste, will always be read by the few; but O'Flaherty was the born popular writer.

H. E. Bates. *The Modern Short Story* (Thomas Nelson and Sons, 1945), pp. 158–59

Expertly put together, Liam O'Flaherty's *Insurrections* is a tale of the Easter Rising of 1916 in Dublin. It is a long short story drawn out, the padding is skillful but not altogether gripping—though one is interested in Madden, who is pushed into the fray by the indomitable Mrs. Colgan, because like him she comes from the West and means him to keep an eye on her Tommy. Well, Tommy is wet; a coward. Madden is nothing like that. The passion for "freedom" takes hold of him. I am not sure his state of mind is altogether convincingly analysed. However, the Irishness of it all, the lively incident, the pathos too, keep you going to the end.

Paul Bloomfield. *MG.* Nov. 3, 1950, p. 4

ONIONS, OLIVER (1873–   )

If strange things could happen anywhere, they might well be looked for in a remote Yorkshire dale at the close of the eighteenth century. And there Mr. Onions has found them. His book is full of weird superstitions, curious customs and lawless deeds. The atmosphere of these tales [*Tales of a Far Riding*] is one of sheer gloom, rarely relieved by touches of deep though hapless tenderness. Determined, seemingly, to be tragic at all costs, Mr. Onions too often sacrifices probability to his ideal. The further, too, he travels from probability, the more he decks out his theme with far-fetched phrases.

SR. Jan. 10, 1903. Supplement p. iii

It is difficult to realize that the author of *Widdershins,* with its depths of mystical philosophy and haunting lights of beauty, is also responsible for the present study of physical and moral ugliness. Not that Mr. Onions' hand has forgotten its cunning: *In Accordance with the Evidence* is unquestionably clever; its effects are bitten in as if with acid. But for the first time in his literary record he has lost touch with the essential sanity of life and concentrated his attention wholly on the evil, the weakness, the squalor of the world. The little group of men, and women, fellow-students at a "Business College," is admirably portrayed, and the struggles of poverty and ambition given with vivid realism. But not one touch of redeeming good is admitted; love, in these pages, is mere passion or vanity, friendship is only disguised rivalry. The narrative hints at vice and disease not to be openly named; the story's close seems, comparatively, a clean and decent action. It is to be hoped that the writer will be satisfied with his experiment in ignoble horror, and will return to his own line. Formerly, while never evading the tragic problem of sin, he had a keen eye for spiritual freshness; he was never meant to be one of those pseudo-realists who lose the significance of shadow by denying the existence of light.

OutL. May 4, 1912, p. 666

Those readers who appreciate Mr. Onions's hard, masculine bouts with the art of fiction, will probably be disappointed with *Peace in Our Time.* The book begins with a preface, unfortunate, I think, and unnecessary, in which the author tells how his book came to be written, and how he wished to air the question of "post-war conditions for the ex-service man." He shows a number of young ex-officers who did well in the war but have nothing to do in the peace; the fault is not entirely that of society; these young men do not seem "to fit in." . . . But the tale, which is very slight, is constantly held up by the author's remarks on all manner of topical subjects; and while a very useful book might have been written on the problem of the ex-officer, Mr. Onions has not done it because his young men are not typical specimens of the ex-officer in general, but only of a certain type to be found in West End bars.

J. B. Priestley. LM. Dec., 1923, p. 205

Onions, a Yorkshireman, was once for a period in control of an Art Department in the Amalgamated Press (publishers of many magazines and weekly periodicals founded by Alfred Harmsworth, Lord North-cliffe), and his first book was published at the beginning of the century. It was a collection of chats in the manner of *The Dolly Dialogues,* but it did not achieve the lightness of the original. He then wrote a number of short stories, many of them powerful and some of them dealing with uncanny themes, which he has collected into volume form as *Tales of a Far Riding, Widdershins,* and *Draw In Your Stool.* But his chief books were the two semi-autobiographical studies of ambitious young men, *Little Devil Doubt* and *Good Boy Seldom,* and the brief masterpiece of grimness, *In Accordance with the Evidence.* This last, which he injudiciously followed with sequels in *The Debit Account* and *The Story of Louie,* remains in its own genre unsurpassed.

It was begun as a short story; and it grew by the demands of its material to the length of a short novel. It arose from the notion that a young student of shorthand, bent upon murdering a rival, might obtain from that rival, under pretence of speed-exercise and subsequent transcription, a confession of suicide. He would thus clear his own path, and escape detection. The ruse succeeds; the tale, being told in the first person singular, is an exercise in that harsh vigour for which Onions's character yields all the stuff. *In Accordance with the Evidence* is not a pretty book; the manner of it is even common and gritty, as such a theme demands that it should be; but it is like no other book, and it bears re-reading after its dénouement has lost all surprise. It has, that is to say, a permanent quality.

The remaining works of Onions curiously lack momentum; one reads them with respect for their veracity, but one is conscious that the author is not a natural creator of illusion. He has no magic.

Frank Swinnerton. The Georgian Scene (N.Y.,
Farrar and Rinehart, 1934), pp. 293–94

ORWELL, GEORGE (1903–1950)

Mr. George Orwell set out on a difficult journey through snobbery, public school training, and dislike of smells to discover the working class. This book [*The Road to Wigan Pier*] is a sincere and vigorous, if sometimes bad-tempered and muddle-headed, account of his experiences and conclusions. Part I, which is accompanied by an admirable collection of illustrative photographs, he devotes to a vivid, shocking, and extremely salutary description of the working and living conditions in which thousands of our free citizens exist today. Part II is an attempt to answer the question, "What, then, must we do?"

Mr. Orwell believes in the necessity for Socialism—perhaps with too much facility—but contends that Socialism is failing to make progress owing to the snobbishness of the middle class, the dislike of the average man for the cranks whom he associates with Left-wing thought, the priggish didacticism of much Socialist propaganda, and the identification in the public mind of Socialism with mechanical progress.

V. M. L. Scott. *LM*. July, 1928, p. 643

Mr. George Orwell, who wrote a successful book called *Down and Out in Paris and London,* has a first-hand acquaintance with the kind of life led by Mr. Hanley's Furys, and with rigours worse than those. In *A Clergyman's Daughter* he turns some of his experiences to the account of fiction, and allows a rector's daughter to lose her memory, join the Kentish "hoppers," reach the depths of poverty represented by a bench in Trafalgar Square, and return thence by way of a job in an iniquitous private school to her old life in a country town. The style, for the most part, is chatty but overworked, though sometimes it achieves humour. The description of the hopfields is expert, and the conversation of the Trafalgar Square "down-and-outs" is vividly presented, but to lapse for the latter purpose into the form of stage-dialogue seems simply to shirk the technical difficulties of a novelist. Mr. Orwell was certainly better with fact than he shows himself with fiction.

Francis Watson. *FR*. April, 1935, p. 512

It is both agreeable and useful to have these essays of Mr. Orwell's [*Critical Essays*] under one cover, and most refreshing to read plain, sensible non-partisan writing about books and society without feeling queasily certain, as one finishes the first paragraph that one knows all too well what the last one will contain. . . . He is in the arena all right, and battling too probably; but he is putting up a one-man show, and not crawling round beneath a party-coloured shield. A special and nowadays unusual virtue in that he judges things according to what he thinks is right or wrong, not according to their particular ideological manner. . . .

To find out *why*—that is Mr. Orwell's main preoccupation. His equipment includes a varied first-hand experience of life at many social levels and the eye of a shrewd dispassionate anthropologist. . . . His main limitation—which can be seen by comparing his work with Edmund Wilson's best essays—is a certain bluntness of sensibility. . . . But when all reservations are made, this remains a book to read.

T. R. Barnes. *Scy*. Spring, 1946, pp. 320–21

For a number of years, every new book by George Orwell has raised the standards by which the next had to be judged. His technical powers —narrative ability and lucidity of expression, command of dialogue and skill in construction—have steadily increased, while his constant preoccupation with the social and political issues of the day has correspondingly enriched the substance of his work.

This old-Etonian ex-policeman, sometime soldier, and retired dishwasher, attained to the full expression of his gifts in *Animal Farm,* and so established his mastery as a satirist that I opened his latest novel with the keenest expectations.

The world of *Nineteen eighty-four* is divided into three chronically embattled super-states, Oceania, Eurasia, and Eastasia. The philosophies prevailing in them, though different in name, are actually "barely distinguishable at all. Everywhere there is the same pyramidal structure, the same worship of a divine leader, the same economy existing by and for continuous warfare." In Oceania, the pyramid consists of Big Brother (the numenous), the Inner Party (the head), the Outer Party (the hands), and the proles. . . .

In its structural conception, the novel is comparable to Sartre's *Crime Passionnel,* in which one whole comprises the exploration of a developing personality and the study of a complex ideology. But, while Sartre's play is a literary work, an emotional experience rather than an argument, to be judged according to its own imaginative laws, there is in *1984* a failure of the imagination which denies it the independence of an artistic work and lays it open to the application of non-artistic criteria.

To say that the failure exists is not to deny Mr. Orwell's inventiveness and ingenuity of a high order, but to draw attention to flaws of a more fundamental nature than these qualities.

Henry de Villose. *Adel.* July-Sept., 1949, pp. 327–28

George Orwell's *Homage to Catalonia* is one of the important documents of our time. It is a very modest book—it seems to say the least that can be said on a subject of great magnitude. But in saying the least it says the most. Its manifest subject is a period of the Spanish Civil War, in which, for some months, until he was almost mortally wounded, its author fought as a soldier in the trenches. Everyone knows that the Spanish war was a decisive event of our epoch, everyone said so when it was being fought, and everyone was right. But the Spanish War lies a decade and a half behind us, and nowadays our sense of history is being destroyed by the nature of our history—our memory is short and it grows shorter under the rapidity of the assault of events. What once occupied all our minds and filled the musty meeting halls with the awareness of heroism and destiny has now become chiefly a matter for the historical scholar. George Orwell's book would make only a limited claim upon our attention if it were nothing more than a record of personal experiences in the Spanish war. But it is much more than this. It is a testimony to the nature of modern political life. It is also a demonstration on the part of its author of one of the right ways of confronting that life. Its importance is therefore of the present moment and for years to come. . . .

Orwell's book, in one of its most significant aspects, is about disillusionment with Communism, but it is not a confession. I say this because it is one of the most important positive things to say about *Homage to Catalonia,* but my saying it does not imply that I share the *a priori* antagonistic feelings of many people toward those books which, on the basis of experience, expose and denounce the Communist party. . . . Nevertheless, human nature being what it is—and in the uneasy readers of such books as well as in the unhappy writers of them—it is a fact that public confession does often appear in an unfortunate light, that its moral tone is less simple and true than we might wish it to be. But the moral tone of Orwell's book is uniquely simple and true. Orwell's ascertaining of certain political facts was not the occasion for a change of heart, or for a crisis of the soul. What he learned from his experiences in Spain of course pained him very much, and it led him to change his course of conduct. But it did not destroy him; it did not, as people say, cut the ground from under him. It did not shatter his faith in what he had previously believed, nor weaken his political impulse, nor even change its direction. It produced not a moment of guilt or self-recrimination.

Perhaps this should not seem so very remarkable. Yet who can doubt that it constitutes in our time a genuine moral triumph? It suggests that Orwell was an unusual kind of man, that he had a temper of mind and heart which is now rare, although we still respond to it when we see it. [1952]

Lionel Trilling. *The Opposing Self*
(N.Y., Viking, 1955), pp. 151–53

Orwell was probably the most unwelcome guerrilla produced by this generation in England. He was always rounding on his own side on the eve of victory, calmly pointing out that the glorious advance was only another sort of retreat: a retreat, as he would put it, from the truth. He was about the first to perceive that the ideal of being a good anti-Fascist threatened to lapse into an *idée reçue,* fit for tub-thumpers but not for writers. Weapons of a kind had been continuously used by the Right against the Left since the intellectuals started fellow-travelling in the mid-1930s. But the weapon failed to strike home, because the Right failed to realize that Communism or near-Communism was a necessary experience for intellectuals then, even if later events proved the intellectuals misguided. Besides, the weapons were launched from a preposterous eminence.

. . . Reading this volume of essays [*England Your England*] today— some well-known as "Marrakech," "Inside the Whale," and a passage from *The Road to Wigan Pier,* others almost forgotten since they have been languishing in obscure periodicals and never reprinted—we are surprised to recall how revolutionary they seemed at their first appearance. For Orwell's opinions, largely owing to the fact that he expressed them and we have unconsciously absorbed them, now read as common sense, whereas at the time they read as thrilling heresies. His mistrust, for example, of Soviet "democracy," once thought perverse, is now orthodox; and his attack on the poets of the Thirties, not for having taken part in politics but for imagining that their literature was more *engagée* than in fact it was, no longer needs to be defended. This is no reason for ceasing to read him. For even if his views are now widely held, his qualities of mind—his glowing integrity, his search for the good and bad in everything solely for the sake of truth—remain rare. And we need his example to shake ourselves out of more recently acquired prejudices.

Benedict Nicolson. *NSN*. Dec. 19, 1953, pp. 800–1

Animal Farm is written on many levels. It is already a children's story in its own right. It is an attack on Stalinism—and it should be pointed out that it is an attack from the Left. Rightwing journalists tried to extract more comfort from it than was warranted. I have shown how Orwell believed that one of the difficulties Socialists had to contend with is the familiar belief that Soviet Russia is Socialist, and that therefore any criticism of Russia is a criticism of Socalism. *Animal Farm* is a Socialist's mockery at the expense of Soviet Russia. It contains very little real comfort for an English Conservative because it will make very few converts. Most Englishmen believed in *Animal Farm* before it was written, but they were delighted by the form in which their beliefs appeared. The book is also a lament for the fate of revolutions and the hopes contained in them. It is a moving comment on man's constant compromise with the truth. In a very short compass it contains most of Orwell's main ideas about men and politics.

In *Horizon* Cyril Connolly welcomed the book for three reasons. It broke down some of the artificial reserve with which Russia was always written about. Orwell would have put it more strongly, as he did in his reply to Obadiah Hornbooke and in many of his reviews. It restored the allegorical pamphlet to its rightful place as a literary force and it proved that Orwell had not been entirely seduced away by the opinion-airing attractions of weekly journalism from his true vocation, which was to write books. There is considerable substance in this last point. *Animal Farm* appeared in 1945 and was the first book of his since *The Lion and the Unicorn* (1941). Between these two publications appeared many of his London letters to *Partisan Review* and his reviews and "As I Please" column in the *Tribune,* writing which was nearly always spoilt by a too-clever-by-half attitude and an irritating brand of plausibility which often did anything but convince. *Animal Farm* proved that his literary powers remained undamaged.

John Atkins. *George Orwell* (N.Y.,
Frederick Ungar, 1954), p. 222

Misunderstanding is made easy because Orwell is accepted, by his middle-class readers, as an interpreter of the English working-class. Yet, in fact, such interpretations are merely the reports of the vagrant. He makes the characteristic mistake (which the occasional documentary accuracy only overlays) of conceiving the English working-class either in solely political terms, so that it is, to him, *merely* a political factor (and he is at once afraid of party bosses); or, in the "anthropological" strain —good anthropologists would reject it—by deduction from external cultural evidence. A good example of the latter is his belief that the contents of "a small newsagent's shop" are "the best available indication of what the mass of the English people really feels and thinks." What we notice here is, first, the exile-situation—an individual, *in his own society,* studying the "mass," a single, undifferentiated bloc that is beyond him; and, second, the familiar error of believing that what is read, by people largely untrained in reading, is an indication of what *they* (not the producers of this matter) "really feel and think." I do not know what a member of a primitive tribe might think of an anthropologist's report on his way of life; but I know that in this matter of the "English working-class" (a very varied body of people) Orwell's reports are indeed documents, but largely of himself.

Raymond Williams. *EC.* Jan., 1955, pp. 48–49

Whereas his previous books had never had more than small and struggling sales, *Animal Farm* at once caught the public fancy in almost every country of the world—particularly in the United States—was translated into every one of the leading languages, established him as one of the best-selling authors of the day and incidentally gave him for the first time in life a tolerable income.

Fortune favored him in the timing of the publication which it imposed upon him. *Animal Farm,* a short book of less than a hundred pages, was written between November 1943 and February 1944. It was, said Orwell, "the only one of my books I really sweated over." What would have been its fate had it immediately found a publisher and appeared in the winter of 1944, when Russia was still fighting and Western statesmen were full of optimism about the possibility of just arrangements with her, it is hard to say. Influences and the climate of opinion might well have prevented it from gaining any but a small and eccentric market. Happily for Orwell four publishers in succession rejected it on the ground that it would be against public policy at such a time to put on the market a book attacking our Russian ally. As a result it only appeared through Messrs. Secker and Warburg in the early summer of 1945, in the month of the German surrender, when fighting had come to an end, and its first circulation exactly coincided with the beginnings of popular disillusionment with Russian policy, as people in the West saw to their dismay the ugly methods by which the Russians were establishing themselves in the East. By chance it exactly struck the public mood and was the first book to strike it.

Christopher Hollis. *A Study of George Orwell*
(Chicago, Ill., Henry Regnery Co., 1956), pp. 139–40

How remarkable a book *1984* is, can be discovered only after a second reading. It offers true testimony, it speaks for our time. And because it derives from a perception of how our time may end, the book trembles with an eschatological fury that is certain to create among its readers, even those who sincerely believe they admire it, the most powerful kinds of resistance. It already has. Openly in England, more cautiously in America, there has arisen a desire among intellectuals to belittle Orwell's achievement, often in the guise of celebrating his humanity and his "goodness." They feel embarrassed before the apocalyptic desperation of the book, they begin to wonder whether it may not be just a little overdrawn and humorless, they even suspect it is tinged with the hysteria of the death-bed. Nor can it be denied that all of us would feel more comfortable if the book could be cast out. It is a remarkable book.

Irving Howe. *Politics and the Novel* (N.Y.,
Meridian/World, 1957), pp. 236–37

The basic idea for the story [*Animal Farm*] occurred to him one day in the country when he saw a little boy of about ten years old driving a huge horse along a narrow lane, whipping it whenever it tried to turn aside. "It struck me that if only such animals became conscious of their strength we should have no power over them; and that ordinary people exploit animals in much the same way as the rich exploit the proletariat."

A simple idea, which he developed into a short book of not much more than 30,000 words. . . .

The air of blitheness and buoyancy which fills *Animal Farm,* as it does *Homage to Catalonia,* in spite of the depressing theme, suggests that Orwell was still comparatively optimistic when he wrote it. But by comparing the working class to animals, even noble and attractive ones, he implies that they are at an irremediable disadvantage in the class struggle. The animals' difficulty in using tools is emphasized several times in the book; and it is only the clever but repulsive and odious pigs who are able to learn to use a pen, walk on two legs, and pass themselves off as human beings. One is reminded of Orwell's attitude many years earlier, when he returned from Burma at the age of twenty-four: "At that time failure seemed to me the only virtue. Every suspicion of self-advancement, even to 'succeed' in life to the extent of earning a few hundred a year, seemed to me spiritually ugly, a species of bullying."

It will be remembered that *Keep the Aspidistra Flying* was about a young man who held a sort of immature and self-centered version of the above doctrine; and although Orwell himself, having once found a political purpose for his writing, never relapsed into the mood of that early novel, it does appear in *Animal Farm,* and still more in *1984,* that he ceased to rely upon the generous, humane and unambitious instincts —the "crystal spirit"—of the common man as an effective political ally in the struggle against spiritual ugliness and bullying. And from a certain point of view *1984* can be seen as a restatement of the theme of *Keep the Aspidistra Flying* on a more comprehensive scale and with a deeper political and social awareness.

Richard Rees. *George Orwell: Fugitive from the Camp of Victory* (Carbondale, Ill., Southern Illinois Univ. Pr., 1962), pp. 83, 85–86

OSBORNE, JOHN (1929–   )

"They are scum" was Mr. Maugham's famous verdict on the class of State-aided university students to which Kingsley Amis's Lucky Jim belongs; and since Mr. Maugham seldom says anything controversial or uncertain of wide acceptance, his opinion must clearly be that of many. Those who share it had better stay well away from John Osborne's *Look Back in Anger,* which is all scum and a mile wide. . . .

Look Back in Anger presents post-war youth as it really is, with special emphasis on the non-U intelligentsia who live in bed-sitters and divide the Sunday papers into two groups, "posh" and "wet." To have done this at all would be a signal achievement; to have done it in a first play is a minor miracle. All the qualities are there, qualities one had despaired of ever seeing on the stage—the drift towards anarchy, the instinctive leftishness, the automatic rejection of "official" attitudes, the surrealist sense of humour (Jimmy describes a pansy friend as "a female Emily Brontë"), the casual promiscuity, the sense of lacking a crusade worth fighting for, and, underlying all these, the determination that no one who dies shall go unmourned. . . .

That the play needs changes I do not deny; it is twenty minutes too long. . . . I agree that *Look Back in Anger* is likely to remain a minority taste. What matters, however, is the size of the minority. I estimate it at roughly 6,733,000, which is the number of people in this country [England] between the ages of twenty and thirty. And this figure will doubtless be swelled by refugees from other age-groups who are curious to know precisely what the contemporary young pup is thinking and feeling. I doubt if I could love anyone who did not wish to see *Look Back in Anger.* It is the best young play of its decade. [1956]

Kenneth Tynan. *Curtains* (N.Y., Atheneum, 1961), pp. 130–31

There is no doubt that Mr. Osborne's play [*The Entertainer*] is an artistic failure. There is no doubt that he was trying to achieve something important. That such a gifted observer of modern people, with a highly tuned ear for idiomatic speech should so completely fail in his intentions is not merely disappointing, it demands a close examination of the author's methodology. . . .

The Entertainer is treated as a symbol: this is the major disappointment. He is a hero of defeat and resignation; a hero who, rather than start again, prefers imprisonment and even hints in a romantic way that he has always believed it to be his *destiny.* We are still in that zone of bourgeois creativity where the prison is the primary image. . . . No wonder Mr. Osborne is anti-Queen; Bastille-bound he can only hate the Monarch. He does not understand that it is not the symbol of power that is the enemy but rather the structures of power.

This is near the hub of the problem. It is the playwright's responsibility to present the conflict in terms of people, rather than statistically or ideologically. That there is conflict in society Mr. Osborne understands, that there is an inability to integrate one's own personal relationships, i.e. love and friendship, he feels deeply. The two are connected. But this must be shown. The social and the personal conflict must be revealed as warp and woof of the one cloth. . . .

It is salutary that Mr. Osborne wishes to be committed. . . . But he must conceive what engagement is at a deeper level. It is not just a matter of joining the Labour Party and reading *Tribune,* although both may be recommended. It is a matter of understanding how, in fact, you can effectively present the conflicts within late-capitalism here in Britain. Mr. Osborne has not a remarkable intellect and he cannot hold us with his polemics—compare the coarse generalities on one page of *Look Back in Anger* with any one page of Shaw where Shaw can specify both the social sin and its cure. He can, however, project exciting emotional conflicts and these can in themselves, on condition that he finds the right heroes, make for piercing social criticism. . . .

But if Mr. Osborne is on the side of the emergent human values and not, as he still appears to be, by reason of his unsureness, on the side of the bankrupt, then he must decide to affirm a new hero—not a shining Superman, for the tragic theatre is concerned with human sacrifice—but a victim who neither acquiesces in nor embraces his own destruction. We are looking for protestant men. It is good to be angry, but to be a writer you must protest.

Ian Dallas. Nimbus. Spring, 1957, pp. 3–5

I believe the play [*The Entertainer*] is an enormous contribution to the English Theatre—as was *Look Back in Anger.* In time, after a lot of thinking and a lot of imagination, when Osborne's plays are not even plays of an old man, they will form a great body of work full of strength and vision. John Osborne will then be a very important name in the theatre.

Michael Hastings. Encore. Nov.-Dec.,
1957, p. 35

Keats once observed that a man needed the fine point taken off his soul to be fit for this world. The same discovery was made by Jimmy Porter, hero of *Look Back In Anger* (and the original Angry Young Man); but he, unfortunately, was unable to accept the truth that life must always be uncomfortable, and frequently painful, for those who think at all or feel with any intensity. Young men at all times have raged and rebelled, but usually with some purpose and towards some end—from Coleridge's campaigning for his pantisocratic community to the attack of the 1930s poets upon social evils. Listening to the ceaseless, savage rant of Jimmy Porter's self-pity, we realize afresh that it is the purpose-less destructiveness of the now fashionable brand of anger that is so abortive. Directed against everything, it inevitably leads nowhere and achieves nothing. Not content to torment and consume itself, it lashes out with perverse and calculated malevolence at all within its range: punishing more especially the objects of its alleged love—as Jimmy Porter, here, felt impelled to humiliate his unfortunate wife for the crime of having enjoyed better material advantages than himself. The attitude of the Angry Young Man is essentially an immature one: the incapacity of egotistical adolescence to see beyond its own outraged responses, or acknowledge the possibility that suffering may be part of the human con-dition, to which others also are vulnerable. Raging, in his squalid attic, against the drabness, inequalities, and futility of living, Jimmy Porter is a horrifyingly authentic embodiment of a mood of the moment. John Osborne has put his finger unerringly on the malaise of the spiritually displaced of the mid-'50s.

Thespis. *Eng.* Spring, 1958, p. 16

Osborne's originality is not in any of his tentative technical experiments, which can be matched elsewhere, but in bringing back into our theatre the pungency and drab yet vital realism of a class of life too long ignored in the West End theatre, except as a basis for farce. Perhaps it is less original than that truth that needs to be reasserted every other genera-tion: creating the same kind of revolution as the famous "kitchen-sink" plays of the Irish and Manchester Repertory dramatists earlier this century.

Audrey Williamson. *Drama.* Summer, 1938, p. 35

John Osborne has written a strange, indignant, frightening dedication to *The World of Paul Slickey.* . . .

I have called this dedication frightening. I could have called it dis-gruntled, discourteous, derisive, disparaging, defensive or lacking in hu-mility, for it is all of these things.

But on finding that Mr. Osborne does not, cannot or will not see that a critic who has written a play should be all the better critic for the exercise it afforded him in the practice of theatre techniques (just as I do not doubt that Mr. Osborne is himself a better dramatist and Man of the Theatre for having acted in it) my overriding emotion is not fear for my integrity, which I cannot feel has been permanently undermined by the squalors and splendours of collaborating in my own plays: my concern here is solely for John Osborne, the writer with the chip on his shoulder.

My fear is that, having set a fashion in anger, the vogue for this brilliantly talented man of the theatre will tarnish like old tinsel once the rage becomes old hat. Even as I write, the cult of anger is no more a New Wave emotion. Spitting spleen was the passion of two winters ago.

Not to wreath my rod with roses, the Elizabethans could out-anger Osborne with half their invectives tied behind their backs. And the Restoration writers fashioned their wrath with a steely wit. *Paul Slickey,* on the other hand, which I sat through twice, was inept and boring. Since the play is neither inept nor boring in book form, John Osborne the dramatist can void his stale young anger upon John Osborne the producer, and let us have a rest from the word angry as a definition for young man 1957.

Caryl Brahms. JOL. Dec. 3, 1959, p. 292

Of John Osborne's two new plays* one is overtly and the other covertly about England. "The Blood of the Bambergs" is set in a nation which has a constitutional monarchy and a socialist government. Could be anywhere, could be Ruritania, but I do not think Mr. Osborne wants us to be in any doubt in our inner hearts. The other one, "Under Plain Cover," is placed four square in a suburb of Leicester.

The first is a satirical fantasy, impudent, rude, disrespectful, but not impertinent. The pertinence of some passages could cause pain to persons who thought it possible they were being represented on the stage —in particular a television commentator. To those who still attach a degree of divine right to Kings or Princesses the fantasy will seem distasteful, insulting and probably treasonable. To those who take a more relaxed view of royal symbololatry, it will seem more like a lighthearted crucifixion of excessive venerators.

There is a combination of cattiness and bitchiness, a blend of *The Prisoner of Zenda* with *The Applecart* which might almost make you think the play a product of collaboration rather than of a single mind. . . .

The play hangs together, hits its targets square, though not always fair, and provides a succession of laughs, some of them rather uncomfortable ones. It is one of Osborne's best works.

Gerard Fay. G. July 20, 1962, p. 7

Osborne shares with [Clifford] Odets the same nervous energy and the same keen ear for common speech—but also the same intellectual deficiencies, the same lack of control. All of these qualities are apparent in *Luther,* a work which is just as unfocussed as Osborne's previous efforts, and—despite its religious-historical setting—just as parochial. Osborne has finally abandoned lower-class England; still, the only consistent line

---

* [*Plays for England*]

in the play is its class line. After a soporific first act . . . Osborne proceeds to characterize the Protestant Reformation as the revolt of a peasant monk against an upper-class Church, followed by his subsequent betrayal of the class from which he sprang. . . . Luther emerges as an angry Midlands miner, determined to take the mickey out of his Papal Legate. . . .

Osborne understands that the Reformation had wider reference than this, and includes some extra-social material as well, but none of it is very coherent. . . . Thus a magnificent possibility dwindles into a sketchy, narrow, and inconsequential tintype, neither fully written nor fully thought through.

Robert Brustein. NR. Oct. 19, 1963, p. 30

The play [*Luther*] is ambivalent; its virtue and vice reside in a humility that is akin to arrogance. It is very well written, combining surface grossness with inner violence in a spate of splendid rhetoric. Its real social significance is that it describes so many of the young British today who are in the same state of confused but talented ferment as Osborne himself. Their "constipation" has provoked a movement—the consequences of which may be considered either noisome or purifying or both.

Harold Clurman. Nation. Oct. 19, 1963, p. 246

OWEN, WILFRED (1893–1918)

Wilfred Owen, who was killed just before the Armistice at the age of twenty-five, was unknown in his lifetime. Sometime after his death his "Strange Meeting" was published and immediately recognised as one of the most powerful of all the war poems and obviously the work of a man who, had he lived, would have been a very considerable writer: it was clearly not a mere solitary outburst born of a special streak but the product of an original mind which was habituated to the contemplation both of life and of the problems of the art. . . .

Every line [he wrote] betrays a passion for technical experiment and for every sort of detail which interests the most conscious kind of poet. But beyond doubt he (it is true of all good poets) knew that all that was merely a discovery of the best means to an end. What he really meant was that his prime object was not fame or the satisfaction of creating beautiful works of art, but the dedication of all his powers to the service of one ideal, the propagation of the truth about war, not in order that posterity might admire his powers of exact statement or his sensibility, but solely in order that they might quail from repeating such horrors.

He wrote out of overwhelming love. There is very little of satire in this book [*Poems*]: he faced and described what he saw—the agonies and exaltations which most men, in the field as at home, dared not brood on lest they should go mad.

J. C. Squire. *LM*. Jan., 1921, p. 334

Owen was a disciple of Keats who, in 1913, as a tutor in Bordeaux, became personally acquainted with Laurent Tailhade and was led to metrical experiment and a poetry of emotional suggestion. Mr. Blunden goes so far as to call him "at moments, an English Verlaine" [in "Memoir" in *The Poems of Wilfred Owen, 1931*]. His early sonnets show an excess of epithet and reiteration and a supremacy of verbal music over thought. Pieces such as "The Unreturning," "Music," "To Eros," betray the lingering echoes of the nineties. He came to feel the immaturity of such moods, and soon after his first experiences in France in 1917, and stimulated by his friendship with Mr. Sassoon, he wrote "efforts in Sassoon's manner" among which we may place "The Parable of the Old and Young," "The Dead Beat," "The Chances," "S.I.W. Disabled," and "Dulce et Decorum." Though he declared, "am I not myself a conscientious objector with a very seared conscience?" he was not so successful as his friend in poems of mordant bitterness. But he had to go through this phase in order to reach another. . . .

It was truth, and a harsh way of expressing it, which he found in Sassoon. In a few months he passed from "æsthetic" adolescence to a wise maturity. Because he never lost faith in men, his moods of disillusioned irony were less cruel than Mr. Sassoon's. His speculations struck deeper than the military or the social system ("Futility"). Nevertheless, he did not altogether lose his hope for man ("The Next War"), and he could rejoice in the exultation of battle as well as in the fellowship of comrades. . . .

Wilfred Owen's contribution to verse technique was considerable. From the first he experimented in a kind of half-rhyme. . . . Sometimes it is mere consonance with entirely dissimilar vowel-sounds, more usually it consists in impure rhyme, the studied difference of vowels having an effect of muted bells. Owen did not use *vers libre,* but for the most part the five-stressed line with an iambic basis freely patterned. Against the prevalent Georgian laxity in this form he set a cumulative use of balance and parallelism. . . . It was Owen's privilege to bring a new dignity to war-poetry and to familiar measures considered by many to be outworn.

Geoffrey Bullough. *The Trend of Modern Poetry*
(Oliver and Boyd, 1934), pp. 98–101

Wilfred Owen, though strongly influenced by Siegfried Sassoon, nevertheless went far beyond that poet in his efforts to comprehend war in all its various aspects and to grasp its real significance to the age in which he lived. It is for this reason, quite apart from his technical interest, that of all the poets who wrote of the First World War, Owen constitutes the strongest link between the poetry of the nineteenth century and that of today. . . .

Wilfred Owen was born in 1893 at Plas Wilmot, Oswestry. After matriculating at London University, he went to Bordeaux in 1913 as a tutor, and whilst he was living in France gained the friendship of the poet Laurent Tailhade. There is no evidence of any direct French influence upon his poetry, but it is not unlikely that Tailhade, himself an innovator, encouraged him in his technical experiments and that the two poets discussed Tailhade's pacifist ideas. Certainly Owen's study of French poetry strengthened his own writing, for until this period his major influence had been that of Keats, and the lushness of his earliest verse betrays the fact that it was Keats's appreciation of the sound-values of words rather than the depth of his imagination which appealed so strongly in the first instance to Wilfred Owen. Not that he ever renounced his earliest allegiance. His affinities with Keats are just as pronounced in his later work—particularly in "Strange Meeting," which many critics consider to be his finest poem—but they are revealed through the individual mastery of language combined with a fully developed outlook. . . .

It was, perhaps, his technique which made the greatest impression upon the poets of the next generation; but as the significance of his poetry in relation to ensuing events became apparent, Owen's reputation grew rapidly, and today he is generally acknowledged to be the most important of the poets of the First World War.

Howard Sergeant. *Eng.* Spring, 1954, pp. 9–12

If Brooke has played the war poet for those who are fascinated by the "idea" of poetry, Wilfred Owen is the war poet for those who desire the reality. . . .

While convalescing from his "neurasthenia," Owen met Sassoon, and the two became close friends. Sassoon's example confirmed Owen in his resolve to speak out against the War, in harsh, clear, and unpleasant words, unsoftened by any poetic or patriotic euphemisms. He entered his brief brilliant maturity. . . . The success of Sassoon's anti-war verse depends to a great extent upon the reader's personal attitude: you will only *agree* with what is said if you are already tending towards the same opinion. The power of Owen's poetry is greater. It can create an attitude, starting from nothing: it can impel agreement by the depth, the "density" of its expression. . . . Sassoon's most interesting poetry is composed of what have been called the "negative emotions"—horror, anger, disgust—and outside that field he inclines to become sentimental in a conventional way. . . . In Owen's work, the "positive emotions," of love, compassion, admiration, joy, are present as well, and their existence strengthens the poetry.

These comments should not be taken to suggest that Owen ever reverted to the simple-minded romanticism of Brooke or Julian Grenfell. . . . On the contrary, some of his poems are almost unbearably painful, in that they permit us no escape into cursing or self-righteousness or other satisfactions afforded by the squib or lampoon. The quiet accurate accounts of gas casualties, men who have gone mad, men who are technically alive although their bodies have been destroyed—these are in the end a more powerful indictment of war than Sassoon's fluent indignation. And they do not "date." . . .

When Owen was killed on 4 November, among his papers was found a draft preface to a future volume of poems. It is the best commentary on the work he left:

> This book is not about heroes. English poetry is not yet fit to speak of them.
>
> Nor is it about deeds, or lands, nor anything about glory, honour, might, majesty, dominion, or power, except War.
>
> Above all I am not concerned with Poetry.
>
> My subject is War, and the pity of War.
>
> The Poetry is in the pity.
>
> Yet these elegies are to this generation in no sense consolatory. They may be to the next. All a poet can do today is warn.
>
> That is why the true poets must be truthful.

D. J. Enright in The Modern Age (Pelican Guide to English Literature), ed. Boris Ford (Penguin Bks., 1963), pp. 161–63, 166–67

What, when its "abysmal follies" still remain to be revisited, has this volume [*Journal from Obscurity: Wilfred Owen, 1893-1918* by Harold Owen] told us for the first time concerning that gallant man and far-seeing poet Wilfred Owen? That he was a youth of the period, striving for a conventional career, seeking for a poetic triumph? . . . But probably of more importance than this is the suggestion of the inner life of Wilfred Owen in ordinary peace time, given in the account of his two years at Dunsden vicarage. Mrs. Owen had her opinion, that he should take Holy Orders; and he was willing, under the guidance of an admirable clergyman, to test this prospect thoroughly. The episode is one which his brother unfolds with fitting care and respect; and it helps to explain the high seriousness, even the details of Wilfred Owen's war poems and why he went back to the Western Front to die.

TLS. Aug. 16, 1963, p. 626

Wilfred Owen's 20 or so effective poems, all quite short, belong to a brief, abnormal moment in English history, and seem to refer to nothing specific outside it. That moment—the last two years of trench warfare in France, 1916-18—was so privately English (and perhaps German) and such a deeply shocking and formative experience for us that it is easy to see some of the reasons why Yeats dismissed Owen's verse (largely on principle), and why many discriminating American readers find it hard to account for his reputation, and why with the English his reputation is so high. . . .

The big thing behind these few short poems that makes them live—as for instance Sassoon's similarly indignant poems do not—is Owen's genius for immersing himself in and somehow absorbing that unprecedented experience of ghastliness, the reality of that huge mass of dumb, disillusioned, trapped, dying men. His every line is saturated with the vastness of it, a hallucinated telescope into the cluttered thick of it—and always, at bottom, the redeeming discovery.

His work is a version of old-style prophecy: apocalyptic scenes of woe and carnage mingled with fulminations against the Godless oppressors, and somewhere at the bottom of the carnage, the Messiah struggling to be born—"Christ is literally in no-man's land. There men often hear his voice," he wrote. It was the god of love and peace, of "passivity at any price." It was Owen who showed what that war really meant, to us, in immediate suffering and general implication, as nobody else did.

Ted Hughes. *NYT*. April 13, 1964, pp. 4, 18

When Yeats in 1936 excluded Wilfred Owen from the *Oxford Book of Modern Verse,* there was a storm of protest. Now when a professor from West Virginia [John H. Johnston, in *English Poetry of the First World War*] painstakingly and at length endorses Yeats's verdict, no one complains. I find this depressing. "The poetry is in the pity," said Owen. And Yeats was right: that is not the place for poetry to be, or not so exclusively. Owen was too categorical, and British poetry since has suffered for it. It has been, and it is still, too humanitarian to be altogether human. But failure on these terms is almost more honourable than success: it was certainly more honourable for Owen, writing as and when he did. . . .

Yeats's objection to Owen was quite bluntly that Owen wrote badly. He said that he considered him "unworthy of the poets' corner of a country newspaper." . . . Owen *does* write badly, he just is not skilful or resourceful enough to do justice to his own conceptions. . . .

But even if Yeats is thus proved right, what follows? That "Dead Man's Dump" [by Isaac Rosenberg] and Owen's "Greater Love" ought to be forgotten? They will not be. If we are moved when we read them, far more moved (this is certainly my own case) than by Yeats's "Irish Airman," ought we to be ashamed? . . . The truth is surely that for the British reader these pieces by Rosenberg and Owen are not poems at all, but something less than that and more; they are first-hand and faithful witnesses to a moment in the national destiny. Or, if that sounds chauvinistic, think of them as high-water marks in the national psychology.

Donald Davie. NS. Aug. 28, 1964, p. 282

PHILLIPS, STEPHEN (1868–1915)

Robert Montgomery had his day; he had a glory and a success almost as great, if not as substantial, as that enjoyed by Mr. Phillips: and to judge from Macaulay's essay, which conferred on him an immortality nothing else could ever have given him, by methods exactly similar to those whereby Mr. Phillips has risen to the surface. Macaulay's quotations from the publisher's announcements are, with a change in the name, almost word for word identical with the puffs of Mr. Phillips. Well, Robert Montgomery had his day, and we know his end. So that the Phillips boom—that is the *Times'* description of Mr. Phillips' career—is so far no new portent of this age and we might be content to leave it alone, looking to the end of these men. . . .

But the really sinister aspect of this boom is the part played by professed critics, some of whom are quite competent to judge of the truthfulness of their own criticism. That critics of the order of Mr. Le Gallienne should think Mr. Phillips a genius or, in Mr. Le Gallienne's words, "a real nightingale in love with a real rose," is no matter. The man who thinks himself competent to revise FitzGerald's version of Omar will naturally admire the audacity which undertakes to improve on Homer and Dante. But there are serious critics who have gone quite as far and made themselves quite as ridiculous. There is Mr. W. L. Courtney, saying in the language and style of a tubthumper's peroration, "We possess in Mr. Stephen Phillips one who redeems our age from its comparative barrenness in the higher realms of poetry." Conceive what would have happened if Mr. Courtney had talked such stuff to his pupils in the old days at Oxford! Then Mr. William Archer hears the "voice of Milton" in Mr. Phillips' lines; while Mr. James Douglas caps all with this rhapsody. *Ulysses* [much-enduring Ulysses!] "is a splendid shower of dazzling poetic jewels flung against gorgeous tapestries that are shaken by the wind of passion." We are willing to admit that some of these gentlemen, of whom we could have cited very many more and passages quite as brilliant, honestly believe what they say of Mr. Phillips because they do not know better, while others write drivel simply because they cannot write anything else. It is a pity this excuse cannot be pleaded for all; but it is not credible that so many able and cultivated men could lose their head at the same moment. The explanation is not want of ability.

Max Beerbohm. *SR*. Feb. 8, 1902, p. 171

For nine years Mr. Stephen Phillips's poetic drama entitled *Herod* has been familiar to readers in America. It seemed to us, when we read it first, not only interesting in itself but interesting even more as a harbinger of greater works to come; and there is a curious irony in the fact that its first presentation on the American stage should have been deferred until a time when the apparent high promise of the work has lost itself in a dreary decade of non-fulfilment. No longer can we pardon the defects of this play in favor of its illusory indications of high fulfilment in the future. We now know the melancholy sequel; and we are forced to consider *Herod* not as the first, but as the last, of its author's list of real achievements. Seen in the theatre, it shows itself to be a better play than *Paolo and Francesca*. At no point does it quite diffuse the pure poetic glow that emanated from the loveliest scenes of its predecessor on the board; but it is constructed with a firmer knowledge of the needs of the stage, and makes up in increase of sheer dramatic power what it suffers in decrease of lyric rapture. Concerning its successors in the theatre, it behooves us to maintain a charitable silence.

Clayton Hamilton. *Forum*. Dec., 1909, p. 578

For those who value the permanent elements in literature the enthusiastic welcome given to Mr. Stephen Phillips's poems and dramas is a great and much needed consolation at the present time. There is still, it would appear, an audience for a literature which is not all blood and drums, the literature of humanity as opposed to the truculent journalistic literature of inhumanity so fashionable during the last five years—a literature of beauty and imagination, of high meditation, of pity, of dignity. . . .

Mr. Phillips's success does not, indeed, provide the only sign of the return of a more clement literary regime. There are one or two poets, novelists, and essayists, whose continued appreciation by a considerable public during the dark period I have referred to shows that there are some still left among us who care to keep burning the lamps of humanistic art. But Mr. Phillips's success is the most significant, because of all of them he has done his work on the most severe and classical lines, with least concession to the fashions of contemporary pleasing. . . .

All of which is matter not only for Mr. Phillips's private congratulation, but for public rejoicing. Seldom has an Anglo-Saxon public done itself so much credit, so spontaneously acclaimed the good thing when they found it—or rather when they were shown it. For here, too, those much-abused people, the critics, deserve no small share in this general congratulation. With the exception of Mr. Kipling, I remember no young poet of our time who has been received with such a consensus of acceptance and encouragement by the most authoritative critics. . . .

Returning to that work of his which is at present interesting the public, some critics, I notice, while admirers of his poetry, have expressed surprise at his dramatic success. The surprise is that anyone can have read his poetry without feeling that its very essence is dramatic insight. Beautiful as his lines are, they are always muscular with reality. *Christ in Hades* was packed with the dramatic imagination from end to end. Its chief beauty was that of dramatic truth. Perhaps, as I have elsewhere said, it is rather the truth than the beauty of his poetry that first arrests one, or should one say that most of the beauty of his poetry comes of its truth, which is another way of saying that it is very real poetry indeed? At all events, I remember to have read nothing of Mr. Phillips's that was not essentially dramatic. That he should succeed in formal drama is to me, therefore, a secondary consideration; but that he has succeeded there can be no question, particularly in *Herod*. Perhaps, on the whole, the last act of *Herod* is the finest thing he has done.

Richard Le Gallienne. *Attitudes and Avowals.*
(John Lane, 1910), pp. 292–94, 304–5

The reading of *Lyrics and Dramas* must inevitably raise a general feeling of regret that the Laureateship has degenerated into a farcical appointment. For Mr. Stephen Phillips has assuredly deserved some public acknowledgment of the immense services he has rendered to poetry. Appearing at a time when poets and poetry alike were under a cloud—when Oscar Wilde, the high-priest of beauty, had destroyed its temple and lay buried under the ruins, he forced thinking people to realise that no denunciation by Philistines can mar the gold of song. Where we are most deeply indebted to Mr. Phillips is that by the public production of his plays he has brought home the beauty and the nobility of verse to many hundreds of thousands who before were seemingly ignorant of its existence as a factor in life as in literature.

There are many who consider, though they are now afraid to say it, that Mr. Phillips is the greatest English dramatic poet since Shakespeare. It is true beyond doubt that no poet since Shakespeare has had so extraordinary a sense of the theatre. This new volume furnishes additional proof.

OutL. Nov. 15, 1913, p. 679

News of the death of Mr. Stephen Phillips was received last month with wide-spread regret. . . . He died as the result of a chill, after ten weeks' illness. The public are often charged with being indifferent to poetry, but they gave instant and generous recognition to the fine work that is in his earlier books, *Christ in Hades, Marpessa,* and *Paolo and Francesca.* The latter, and *Herod,* were the best and most successful of the dozen plays of his that were put upon the stage. His last book, *Panama and other Poems,* was published . . . a few weeks ago. One would like to see the best of his work gathered into a single volume, for the best of his work will give him an assured place among the few true poets of our time.

BkmL. Jan., 1916, p. 109

When Stephen Phillips's drama *Herod* was originally produced in London in 1900, many believed that the dawn of the poetry-play had begun. "It will take oysters and champagne to recover from this," a hardened theatre-goer remarked between the acts. One of our best American critics, John Corbin, writing from London to *Harper's Weekly,* started off by saying, "To imagine that one has seen the dawning of a new and brighter day in art or in literature is easy—dangerously easy; but in witnessing the performance of Mr. Stephen Phillips's *Herod* it is perhaps more difficult to persuade oneself that one has not. I do not use the words lightly. A new day in the poetical drama of England means something that has not been witnessed since the decay of the School of Shakespeare. There have been plays in verse and to spare from Dryden to Sheridan Knowles—or let us say to Comyns Carr; but I do not know of any of them that has revealed a genuine poet of the stage."

Later in the year 1909, I witnessed in America a memorable performance of *Herod* by William Faversham and Julie Opp; the full beauty of the lines was rendered, and the whole production generously splendid. There were not a few dramatic moments. I should like to see it again. Yet we know now that Mr. Phillips was neither the morning-star nor the sunrise; it was another case of false dawn. And the reason? Simply because Stephen Phillips was more poet than dramatist.

William Lyon Phelps. The Twentieth-Century Theatre
(N.Y., Macmillan, 1918), pp. 91–92

PHILLPOTTS, EDEN (1862–1960)

Those who were enabled to see Mr. Phillpotts' play [*The Secret Woman*], by the public spirit of the twenty-four signatories to the letter to the *Times* and of Miss McCarthy and Mr. Granville Barker, found a play always interesting, frequently beautiful, and never, I think, objectionable. The folk of Mr. Phillpotts' "Dartymoor," as readers of the novels need not be told, live passionately and speak their minds. Accordingly, when Anthony Redvers, a strong farmer, loves away from his wife, and good husband and faithful father though he is, finds the mate one-half of his nature needs in an ardent young girl, daughter of old flockman Westaway, we hear plain words from the full-blooded man himself, and from his wife who is fierce as a bitter wind in her cold devotion: plain speech, it must surely be conceded, is the only speech in character. . . . My own only objection to the speech of Mr. Phill-potts' people is their fondness for dust and ashes, and similar com-modities of the literary man rather, one thinks, than of their personal thoughts; and a way they have of making rather long speeches in too conscious assistance of Mr. Phillpotts' private purposes. I find some ex-cessiveness too in Mr. Phillpotts' love of visible violence; the best dram-atists know better than to show too much fight, for it has a way of defeating its own ends. I do not think *The Secret Woman* is a master-piece. However, there is much fine work in the play. . . .

P. P. Howe. *OutL*. Feb. 24, 1912, p .283

. . . Mr. Phillpotts . . . was one of those young men of the nineties who took fast hold of a grand old tradition and refused to let it go. Instead of bothering about incidentals of form, as so many of his contemporaries did, he took up the tradition of the English novel as it was laid down by George Eliot and modified by Thomas Hardy, and, bringing to it a vision as individual as theirs, succeeded in achieving a beauty that is all his own. It has been Mr. Phillpotts' fate to find nearly every reviewer of each of his new books comparing him with Thomas Hardy. It must be rather irritating; and it is no more true than the assertion which is equally often repeated, that Thomas Hardy himself derives from George Eliot. . . .

The fact is, of course, that although Eliot, Hardy and Phillpotts each found the material for their art in the English countryside, and particu-larly in the psychology of the English peasant; though they each excel in showing men and women in intimate relation with their environment, and although they are alike too in their use of the smaller essentials of their craft—those devices of sub-plot and peasant chorus which give the atmosphere of their work—yet there is a fundamental difference which may be expressed quite simply in a very few words. George Eliot looked at life from the angle of the moralist; Hardy from the angle of the philosopher. But Eden Phillpotts is above all things else the humanist, and his interpretation of life, with just as great a justification as theirs, is marked by a greater sympathy, though not by a deeper comprehen-sion. . . .

The Mother is perhaps the most sympathetic of Mr. Phillpotts' novels. It came from the heart of a man to whom the maternal instinct has al-ways appealed as the most beautiful of the forces that sway humanity, and it makes its appeal direct to the heart. This book and *Demeter's Daughter,* which, rightly considered, is only another part of the same picture, show Mr. Phillpotts at his best in presenting noble types of womanhood. They have both faults of construction, and they are both a little diffuse, but this is more than atoned for by the depth of emotional power they display.

C. S. Evans. BkmL. Jan., 1916, pp. 115–17

The snare of descriptive writing in novels is as the snare of decorative passages in an imaginative painting; the descriptions may fail to combine, remain detached from the meaning and purpose of the novel, and finally the novelist may be tempted by his skill in such writing to indulge in it at the expense of his proper task. . . . Here are hundred of Mr. Phillpotts's best decorations [*One Hundred Pictures from Eden Phillpotts,* selected by L. H. Brewitt] full of observation, sensitive at times to another beauty than the merely observed, but rarely fused by that imaginative ardour which makes some of Mr. Hardy's and Mr. Conrad's descriptive passages an essential part of the novel. Sometimes, especially in his description of violence, Mr. Phillpotts's meaning is obscure. . . . He is more successful as a rule when he catches nature in softer moods, quick with spring or flushed with summer. . . . Mr. Phillpotts rarely drops into that snare of the writer of picturesque prose, the rhythm of blank verse; but his style is not always equal to the demands he makes upon it. It never has the sombre, heavy-hearted gravity of Hardy's, nor the gloomy colour and triumphant ecstasy of Ruskin's. This is indeed a photograph album rather than a book of pictures.

LM. March, 1920, p. 740

The crowding of his novels has led to an extraordinary result. Eden Phillpotts is a novelist whose name is well known to many thousands who would be unable to quote the title of one of his novels. He is much better known, of course, as the author of the phenomenally successful play *The Farmer's Wife,* which, when first produced in 1916, did not succeed, but with persistent and courageous help from Barry Jackson (later Sir Barry Jackson) in 1924 it ran for 1,329 performances at the Court Theatre. The Dartmoor novel which provided the incident on which the play was based, *Widecombe Fair,* is a much better novel than *The Farmer's Wife* is a play: the amusing courtship of the frustrated farmer is but one strand of the many that are woven into the fabric of the village in the one Dartmoor novel which is a comedy, the others being mostly tragic in form. *Widecombe Fair* is not unknown, but it richly deserves to be more widely appreciated. It is one of the Dartmoor novels that have been reprinted since the war: the new edition carries a perceptive introduction by L. A. G. Strong.

In nearly all the works of reference dealing with the fiction of this century Eden Phillpotts has been lucky if he has scored a mention: only occasionally has he attracted a detailed analysis of his best work. Whenever the regional novel is surveyed, his name, naturally, cannot be overlooked, but I often suspect that the writer has omitted to read his work. Many other authors, whose names are now forgotten, have, during their transit, been granted much greater respect. Among the comparatively few who read and re-read his major novels, it is accepted that Eden Phillpotts is a neglected and under-estimated novelist. If that is so, and I believe it is, it will be asked why, if his merits are considerable, his work should have been so slighted. The question is soon asked, but not so simply answered. There are several factors that have conspired against Eden Phillpotts's reputation.

One of these reasons has already been mentioned, his over-productivity in a number of literary fields. His first book was published in 1888. By 1900 he had written nearly twenty books. Since 1900 he has written at least two books a year, and often more. He has now written more than 250 books; they range from tragedy to farce, some have been written with a high purpose, others merely with the desire to entertain. He has, indeed, ventured into every literary field, with varying success, perhaps, but usually with success. Among such an enormous and varied output there is bound to be unevenness and occasionally repetition.

Waveny Girvan. Eden Phillpotts (Hutchinson, 1953), pp. 15–16

PINERO, ARTHUR WING (1855–1934)

If only Mr. Pinero would be simple! They say that he took two years to write *Letty*—three thousand hours or so, maybe, of solid labour. And not one too many. The modern form of dramaturgy is the most difficult of all the art-forms. Ibsen himself, even in his prime, was strictly biennial. Let Mr. Pinero be quinquennial, if so disposed. It is right for a work of art to be elaborate, in the literal sense of that word. But the elaboration of *Letty* is especially in the other sense. And to this difference I attribute the failure of *Letty* to evoke from me something beyond admiration for the author's amazing skill. An artist should labour to whittle away all that is superfluous to his main theme or idea. Even as an athlete is "trained" for the annihilation of every ounce of flesh that would impede the strong free play of his muscles, so must the work of art be "trained" till nothing is left but what is sharply essential to its effect. . . .

It may sound paradoxical, but it is not the less true that Mr. Pinero would write better plays if he were a less richly endowed playwright. . . .

If Mr. Pinero were less brilliant in his specific way, there would be more room in him for ideas. As it is, there is no room at all. Mr. Archer, rather touchingly, ventures to hope that this absence of ideas is but "a transient phase of Mr. Pinero's development." As Mr. Pinero never has harboured ideas, it is rather too much to expect that he will proceed to do so now. A horsedealer, commending the points of a pony, does not suggest that the pony is passing through "a transient phase of development" and will presently be a horse. Even so, Mr. Archer should not try to raise hopes that cannot be entertained—much less fulfilled. But, though the smooth and luscious fruit of Mr. Pinero's genius can no more prick us with underlying ideas than can thistles be gathered from grapes, there is in Mr. Pinero no lack of power for treating a human theme sincerely and fully. Mr. Pinero has a keen insight into human nature, more especially into the nature of women. And he might create really great pictures of life if he could but forget to show off his technical skill by bedevilling, as in *Letty* he bedevils, his main theme with a glittering congeries of inessential things. Let Mr. Archer concentrate his desires, not on making Mr. Pinero think, but on making him make us feel. A good quality cannot be implanted, but you can sometimes eliminate a bad one.

Max Beerbohm. SR. March 15, 1902, pp. 328–29

The third of the four great successes of the season, like *Dear Brutus,* is a revival. Our only surprise, and only regret, in seeing it is that the London stage is too stupidly organised to allow a play of such fame and acting power as *The Second Mrs. Tanqueray* a permanent place in our repertory. Such is the fate of English dramatists. The most celebrated work by the chief amongst them is thus now brought out of a drawer for, I think, the second time in a generation. It is necessary indeed to remind oneself that a generation, all but a year, has passed since *The Second Mrs. Tanqueray* took the town by storm, and made fortune and reputation for several persons. It is necessary, because the play seems in many respects so astoundingly fresh today that without constant reminder one is tempted to forget the explanation of certain points that now appear weaknesses in it—that the world has changed its angle of vision since the Eighteen Nineties. All plays, except the few greatest, have blemishes; nor is *Mrs. Tanqueray* an exception; but what play among moderns can one easily find that carries its years with equal ease, or has lost so little of its first vigour? *Mrs. Tanqueray* is not to my mind quite the finest of Sir Arthur Pinero's works. This is perhaps not the moment to discuss their relative merits, but however that may be, the vigour of this play is undeniable. Its solid construction, the deliberate pace with which its action marches from stage to stage like the march of destiny, the vivid, scintillating strokes in which the author depicts an atmosphere of social customs and individual habits: each of these, when we think of them separately, impresses us with a vigour not to be met with in many other plays, and receives further testimony from the vogue enjoyed by it from one end of Europe to the other.

John Pollock. *FR.* Aug., 1922, p. 345

The last of the four plays which definitely establish Pinero as a great dramatist is *The "Mind the Paint" Girl*; and here, too, we have a play in which coincidence is reduced to a minimum and the whole story springs from the characters and the opening situation. Its tale of a musical comedy actress who marries a lord is told with a skill which makes all later variations on the same theme look remarkably foolish; and the time is surely ripe for a revival of this clever and witty picture of theatrical life. Like *Mid-Channel,* it was not very successful at its first production; but although the playgoing public is not yet advanced enough for the acceptance of *Mid-Channel,* it may, in 1928, be sufficiently enlightened to appreciate *The "Mind the Paint" Girl* at its true value.

For Pinero's jubilee, then, let us take down these four plays—*His House in Order, The Thunderbolt, Mid-Channel* and *The "Mind the Paint" Girl*—from the bookshelves and let us carefully re-read them; and then let us ask ourselves how many later dramatists have written such brilliant and durable work. In his time Pinero has had some harsh treatment from the critics; but, as Archer has well said, "When history views things in their just proportions he will stand out as a great master of the essentials of drama." His plays, and particularly the later ones, are the work of a dignified and polished dramatist, who would not stoop to win popular favour by cheap and easy means. When, in deference to public opinion, he altered the ending of *The Big Drum,* he declared that he made the alteration "against my conscience and against my principles"; and anyone who surveys the great mass of his work to-day will find that it is the work of a man who was always guided by his conscience and his principles in the pursuit of his art. He stands before us, at his jubilee, as a great and honourable dramatist.

Edgar Holt. *FR.* March 1 ,1928, p. 330

. . . it is not so much for lofty and heroic inspiration that the Pinero drama is notable, as for the complete efficiency with which it has discharged its various yet unvarying purpose. We have seen this drama take its rise in the drama with a rural setting, and in the drama of "girls" and "boys." When the theatre wanted sweet lavender, an ample supply was conceded; when *Ghosts* and *Hedda Gabler* were heard of, it was

Sir Arthur Pinero who gave the theatre a profligate and a Paula Tanqueray; when England was in need of a Drama with which to front Europe, it was Sir Arthur Pinero who was found to have supplied it. This cumulative ability to give of the best that he knew is the essence of the achievement of Sir Arthur Pinero. Even in the comic plays that small boy in the early farce who set fire to the house with a firework only reaches his true apotheosis in the third act of *Mr. Panmure;* there is no scene in the Court Theatre farces which goes off with this stately precision of the set-piece. Perhaps it would not have been possible for Sir Arthur Pinero to have achieved the first act of *The Thunderbolt* if the third act of *The Voysey Inheritance* had not shown him the way. Certainly it would not have been possible for Sir Arthur Pinero to make *The Profligate* that determined essay in conjugal unhappiness he himself achieved in *Mid-Channel*. In the drama of Sir Arthur Pinero we may find in actual epitome the answers to a generation of anxious questionings, Is the Drama Advancing? No other hand could project characters so well fitted to the favourite actors of his generation, or cause them to tell so interesting a story through the medium of dialogue. No other hand could devise such skilful form and order as, within the limits of an ordinary theatrical representation, to give rise to so great an amount of that peculiar kind of emotional effect, the production of which was the one great function of his theatre. No other hand, in fact, could supply so efficiently the actual demand. When, in the fullness of time and honours, Sir Arthur Pinero has need of an epitaph, it may well be this: He kept the theatres open.

P. P. Howe. *Dramatic Portraits* (Martin
Secker, 1923), pp. 51–52

A hundred years since the birth of the creator of Paula Tanqueray! We have been so accustomed to thinking of him as a figure of just yesterday—if of a faded yesterday which it was impossible to recall or revive for a while without provoking the scoffers—that it is a jolt to find him a part of history, moving as it were among those shadowy figures surrounding his own Trelawney, to the sound of ghostly applause and hisses. Yet undoubtedly Arthur Wing Pinero, son of a London solicitor of Portuguese Jewish descent, made his first appearance on this mortal stage on May 24th, 1855. Now, more than twenty years after his death, the costumes, and even the manners of his heyday are being discovered to have a certain charm; and even the precise articulation of his plays, once despised, is now sometimes adduced in disparagement of more modern and less careful work. For so long—up to perhaps the beginning of the last War—he was customarily brought forward as a sort of playwriting puppet to be beaten, Punch fashion, to the greater glory of certain other playwrights, notably Bernard Shaw. It is not easy for those of us of a certain age to readjust our views of him and to realise that he occupies a not prominent but a distinctly honourable niche in the English dramatic pantheon.

Denzil England. *CR*. May, 1955, p. 313

PINTER, HAROLD (1930–   )

When the play [*The Birthday Party*] flared up briefly at the Lyric Opera House in May it provoked such anarchy of opinions, all very dogmatically held, that you have to look towards French government before finding a fit comparison. Nowadays there are two ways of saying you don't understand a play: the first is to bowl it out with that word "obscurity," once so popular in poetry reviews; the second way is to say that the seminal influence of Ionesco can be detected.

Mr. Pinter received the full treatment. As well as standing for *x* in the formulae outlined above, he was described as inferior N. F. Simpson, a lagging surrealist, and as the equal of Henry James. Remembering James's melancholy affair with the theatre this last one carries a nasty sting; and within a couple of days of receiving it, the *Birthday Party* was over.

The comparison with James is quite baffling. Far from being a cautious verbal artist struggling to "throw away cargo to save the ship," Mr. Pinter has no difficulty in putting theatrical requirements first. No matter what you may think of the contents, the ship is afloat. And it is his very instinct for what will work in the theatre that has prompted hostility. One character in *The Birthday Party,* for instance, is given to tearing up newspapers: we are not told why. But the spectacle of John Stratton . . . holding his breath while rapt in the task of tearing each strip of paper to the same width, took on a malevolent power perfectly in key with the play and requiring no explanation. The device is an extreme example of the playwright's habit of introducing an intrinsically theatrical idea and letting it find its own road back towards common sense. Mr. Pinter's way is the opposite of setting out deliberately to embody a theme in action.

All the same a theme does emerge, closely resembling that of *The Iceman Cometh:* the play demonstrates that a man who has withdrawn to protect his illusions is not going to be helped by being propelled into the outer world.

Irving Wardle. *Encore*. July, 1958, p. 39

For Pinter, there is no contradiction between the desire for realism and the basic absurdity of the situations that inspire him. Like Ionesco, he regards life in its absurdity as basically funny, funny up to a point. . . .

Pinter's clinically accurate ear for the absurdity of ordinary speech enables him to transcribe everyday conversation in all its repetitiveness, incoherence, and lack of logic or grammar. The dialogue of Pinter's plays is a casebook of the whole gamut of *non sequiturs* in small talk. . . . There are also the misunderstandings arising from inability to listen; incomprehension of polysyllabic words used for show by the more articulate characters; mishearings; and false anticipations. Instead of proceeding logically, Pinter's dialogue follows a line of associative think-ing in which sound regularly prevails over sense. Yet Pinter denies that he is trying to present a case for man's inability to communicate with his fellows. "I feel," he once said, "that instead of any inability to communicate there is a deliberate evasion of communication. Com-munication itself between people is so frightening that rather than do that there is continual cross-talk, a continual talking about other things, rather than what is at the root of their relationship."

> Martin Esslin. *The Theatre of the Absurd* (Eyre and
> Spottiswoode, 1961), pp. 211, 213

Mr. Harold Pinter is technically the most adroit and accomplished of the young playwrights. His work is never fumbling in the sense that both Osborne's and Wesker's often is. He knows exactly what effects he wants to get and exactly how to get them. But whereas in their different ways both Osborne and Wesker are very conscious of their audience—Osborne deliberately trying to shake them out of their complacency, Wesker try-ing to guide them towards his vision of the good society—Pinter is quite indifferent to the problem of communication. Indeed he himself asserts that it is not a problem for him, since he writes his plays entirely for himself and is surprised to find that anyone else is interested in them at all. And indeed it is, on the face of it, surprising—and particularly sur-prising that the television companies have opened their screens to him so freely—for he is far the most obscure of all the young writers.

What is baffling and unnerving about Pinter's plays is that he abso-lutely refuses to give us what we are accustomed to getting in most plays: a neat little explanation of the events that take place, an explicit motiva-tion for the characters together with some small potted history of their pasts. We come in on a play of his as we might come in on a street ac-cident or a street fight in which we are not involved. We stay to watch, fascinated by the event itself and the reactions of the participants. But we know nothing about them—where they came from, or how they came to be involved in these particular circumstances, or what happens to them afterwards. When the incident, whatever it is, is finished, we pass on. But what has happened has happened with a dazzling clarity and vividness.

The vividness and clarity come from two things. First, Pinter has an amazingly vivid apprehension of the insecurity that lurks behind the lives of most people today. If I had to define his theatre in a word, I'd call it the Theatre of Insecurity. Very often it is symbolized by characters who are the flotsam and jetsam of life, but it infects everyone around them. And this insecurity is caught remarkably exactly in his dialogue. The realism of his dialogue is often praised, but the exciting thing about it is that it is not just the documentary realism of the surface realists based on good observation. The dialogue, simple as it seems, very exactly catches the habits of mind behind it. He reveals to us that the inarticulate use speech not so much to communicate as to reassure themselves. Those reiterations and those platitudes and commonplaces they utter are a defense against others, a reassurance to themselves, a form almost of propitiation.

In description this may sound heavy going, but in fact it is primarily highly humorous. The most obvious surface experience of most of Pinter's plays is that they are very funny. *The Caretaker,* for instance, keeps its audience almost continually laughing. But it is laughter with a chill wind behind it. In Pinter's world we are always conscious that our hold on reality is very fragile; and in his characters who are desperately clinging on by only a toe and a finger, we recognize an image of the human condition in the world today.

T. C. Worsley. *TA*. Oct., 1961, p. 19

The thing hardly anybody seems to have noticed about the plays of Harold Pinter is that what is so effective about them is also the source of much that is unsatisfying. At his best, Pinter is a dramatist of high urgency, clear color and unimpeachable intentions. He has the right kind of dissatisfactions and impenitences, the accurate chimeras, the anxieties, hungers and vertigos proper to our time. And he has a high degree of freedom from the expectations of audiences, an aloofness from the theatre conceived of as a place of mutual congratulation, a toughness, or blessed innocence, to resist most of the pressures to make his plays serve other purposes than their own—to prevent them from "commenting" on our condition, or offering explanations or providing us with solace. . . .

Yet in Pinter the action is not in fact much more than an introduction, the beginning of recognition and affect and change. The shapes he creates are skeletal and unfinished, as though they have known what not to be but do not yet know what to become. Having stripped away much of what is exhausted in conventional drama, having made a psychology that confirms or explains yield to a metaphysics that invokes, and having made the logic of narrative continuity yield to the terrifying arbitrariness of the way we really experience the world, Pinter hovers still on the threshhold of the theatre of new events and new portrayals. Unlike Ionesco and Beckett, in whose light, especially the latter's, he has so clearly worked, he has been unable to do more than present the *reverse* side of existence, the underskin of emptiness that sheathes our habitual gestures and spent meanings.

Richard Gilman. *Com.* Dec. 28, 1962, p. 366

What needs opposing isn't Pinter, but Pinterism and the Pinterites. There's an obvious appeal to the small, closed milieu of the theatrical profession in a drama which exalts its special artifices and limitations into a philosophy. There's an even more obvious appeal to managers in the kind of play which puts three men in a bare room and simply sets them interacting. We have had a flood of them recently—they are easy to cast, easy to run, easy to sell to television, always on the lookout for small, inexpensive contemporary plays with no exposition to bore the casual viewer, and if possible no social setting to bring in the prickly assumptions of class.

Philosophy has always suffered from its literary importations—an image is so much more striking than a syllogism. The danger of Pinterism is that it tries to turn the image of three men in a room into a world-view which denies the validity of language and logic along with the notion of continuity and personality. . . . Pinter himself, in a limited way, is effective and entertaining. But while enjoying the theatricality of his impromptus, it seems worth bearing in mind that their only final importance may be this.

Ronald Bryden. *NS.* June 26, 1964, p. 1004

PITTER, RUTH (1897–)

In poetry, some of the best work has been done by Miss Ruth Pitter. A few poems are really first-rate. I recommend particularly "A Trophy of Arms" . . . and "The Spirit Watches." Here we have no jagged ends, no bleeding words; emotion and experience, like seed and soil, combine to produce new unities as natural as misted leaves and dewy flowers. But some inner reserve, some secret strength, perhaps saves Miss Pitter from the curse of finality. We always feel that the inward principle of growth is working in her. What she gives us is a dream, a vision, an apprehension woven round a chime of words. More is to come, she seems to be saying, while scattering jewels.

Ranjee G. Shahani. *Poetry R.* Jan.-Feb., 1942, pp. 27–28

There is a spinsterish book of verses called *The Rude Potato* by Miss Ruth Pitter: these things will out even in the best Anglo-Catholic circles; Miss Pitter conceived the thought of a tuber of irregular shape, and a book of irregular verses is the result. The readers of her more religious poems will be left, no doubt, piously hoping that she will now weave this erotic imagery into harmony with her devouter work, as other mystics before her have done.

Stephen Spender. *Hor.* Feb., 1942, p. 102

Miss Pitter rejoices some; those, I suspect, who need a chapel to go to, where they can examine the stained glass; no light, however, comes through the windows. The craftsmanship is there, that would ravish in a poem by Mr. Blunden or Mr. Andrew Young: no light, though. Not at any rate for me.

G. W. Stonier. *NSN.* April 28, 1945, p. 276

. . . she is "traditional" in the bad sense of the word, but her own sensibility and formal intelligence interrupt and occasionally transfigure her delicate, orthodox, and reasonably interesting exercises in what one might call Attic modes. What Miss Pitter is herself is sympathetic and valuable; but this no more than colors the aggregations of attitudes and techniques of which she is the unquestioning inheritor. She does not fully comprehend that these, like the linens in a tomb, vanish to the digger's "Ah!"—that the lives and possessions of the dead are inaccessible to us until we ourselves have lived and repossessed them. . . .

Randall Jarrell. *Nation.* May 25, 1946, p. 633

Ruth Pitter had scarcely emerged from her teens when she produced her *First Poems* (1920). A second volume, *First and Second Poems,* appeared in 1927. But it was *A Mad Lady's Garland* (1934) which convinced attentive critics that the writer was a lyrical poet deserving much more than a word of passing praise. The impression was confirmed by *A Trophy of Arms* (1936), *The Spirit Watches* (1939), *The Rude Potato* (1941, among the most gracious humorous poems known to me) and *The Bridge Poems* (1939-44). There is a beauty moving between the troubled and the serene in *The Spirit Watches*—the piece entitled "The Downward-Pointing Muse" would hold its own in any anthology. But some of *The Bridge Poems* showed further advance, not indeed in sensibility or percipience or metrical aptness, present in all her poetry, but in range and depth of vision.

She is not, in the sense in which the word has been used, a "modern" poet. She belongs to no clique. She follows no modern fashion. Some of her poems assume a form that was within the reach of poetry long ago, but of these many have a significance which differentiates them from poetry of the past. She is intensely alive in the contemporary world, and sees it through its own eyes. But she is not quite of it. She stands apart, inhabiting a region of her own; and if it has not been as extensively communicated to the reading public as it might have been, that is perhaps because she belongs to no recognizable school, has no trumpeter, and has not been at pains to assert herself.

She has written some lovely poetry, authentic, unmistakable, which in her later work is distilled in experience and projected in language fashioned with fine tact and metrical skill. It has substance, and form; hardness, and fragility; grit, with tenderness.

R. A. Scott-James. *Fifty Years of English Literature:*
1900-1950 (Longmans, 1951), p. 231

PLOMER, WILLIAM (1903–   )

Mr. Plomer's stories [*I Speak of Africa*] are not without literary merit: they have the energy and vividness which is [sic] common to much "literature" of to-day. But the "literature" to which they belong, and the criticism of which they are susceptible, have been forcibly described by Mr. Wyndham Lewis in No. 2 of *The Enemy*. The literary movement has its headquarters in Montparnasse, and the stories "Portraits in the Nude," "Ula Masondo," "Black Peril" and the rest are as typical of what Mr. Lewis calls the "Inferiority complex of the Romantic White" as an example that he quotes from Messrs. D. H. Lawrence and Sherwood Anderson. That there are farmers as bestial as the Van Ryn family in "Portraits in the Nude," or that a decent black man like Ula Masondo may become corrupted by association with bad whites in the mines, could not be denied: but the glorification of the black man, positively as in the phantasmagoria called "The Triumph of Justice," or by way of sentimental contrast as when a black man, cruelly beaten out of sheer lust, is named a "black Christ," show that Mr. Plomer's intelligence is thrall to certain fashionable fallacies of our day. The interest of his book is local, but its shortcomings are symptoms of a formidable and ubiquitous error.

Orlo Williams. *Crit.* Jan., 1928, p. 83

Mr. William Plomer . . . in his *Notes for Poems* ranges through a considerable number of techniques from the unabashed imagism of the early "Woman on a Balcony" (Mr. Plomer has very intelligently helped criticism by printing his poems chronologically) to the ballad epic style of his

African Poems, and the *Japonaiseries* of some of the later pieces. But Mr. Plomer has, with all this, very much of a note of his own, which he should develop. He is at heart a Rimbaud-intoxicated rebel against the shams of our civilization, and his rhythm, at its best, kicks and plunges like a mettlesome horse under its burden of satire.

J. G. Fletcher. *Scy*. June, 1929, pp. 133–34

Mr. William Plomer is a South African poet of some distinction, and *Paper Houses,* not strictly a novel, but a rather ramshackle collection of Japanese stories and impressions, reads as though he were uncertain whether prose or verse suited him best. His prose is vigorous, but often slatternly and down-at-heel. Again, it is chiefly his subject-matter, his sympathetic but severely unsentimental portrait of modern Japan, which makes his book worth reading.

LL. June, 1929, p. 481

Mr. Plomer's work [*The Child of Queen Victoria*] is . . . arranged in three groups, laid in Africa, Greece and France. He undoubtedly seems most at home in Africa where the title-story is laid. Writing boldly and clearly, he describes there the first contact of a good-natured young Englishman of public-school training with the life of the natives and the average run of white men who live among them as traders. The interest lies definitely in the matter, and in his thought upon it, and is very real, but the story lacks something as literature. Like Mr. [William] Faulkner, he is at best when his subject is an atmosphere, so that his manner and his matter are necessarily held together. But sometimes he is too conscious that manner is important. . . . There is no need for a naturally bold writer like Mr. Plomer to put himself to so much trouble.

LL. Feb., 1934, pp. 497–98

For him the beauty of life lies as much in comedy as in tragedy and human feelings are for him mysterious, peculiar and interesting at ordinary moments in ordinary surroundings. . . . For him the suburban bamboos whisper a comment on life, love and memory; a panther-heart may beat in the bosom of the cowman's daughter, dressed for the Gala Hop in her "apricot nylon dress and shoes from the Co-op". . . .

In his new collection of poems and ballads [*A Shot in the Park*] the streak of the macabre which marked *The Dorking Thigh* is less pronounced. His comedy has grown gayer and gentler. . . . Mr. Plomer has developed a style of narrative poem peculiar to himself, dependent on ingenious changes of rhythm and vocabulary, suitable to reading aloud preferably by more than one voice. Poems like "Anglo-Swiss," "A Shot in the Park," and "Bamboo" are really small dramas. "A Shot in the Park" has an almost cinematic technique. . . .

C. V. Wedgwood. *L.* June, 1955, p. 94

Mr. Plomer has, as all his writings have shown, the Poet's look-out: All he sees, everyone and everything that crosses his lens, is registered on the sensitive plate of his perceptions, and simultaneously transmuted into the stuff of poetry or of fantastic comic extravagance. . . . He admits that people are his main concern; personal relationships have been more to him than anything else, and have, he says, been a considerable distraction to his writing. They are, of course, the very stuff of his writing. They glint in and out of it, passing from his consciousness into ours with an added dimension, whether they are friends already familiar to us, or new. His portraits are witty, affectionate, and exact. Here [*At Home: Memoirs*] are Virginia Woolf, E. M. Forster, Christopher Isherwood, Anthony Butts, Stephen Spender, Joe Ackerly, Edith Smyth (a brilliant vignette), Lady Ottoline Morrell, and many more. . . .

Literary friends form only one of Mr. Plomer's several environments. He slips without effort from Bloomsbury to the extravagant comedy of Anthony Butts, the frowsy, crime-haunted drabness of Maida Vale or Bayswater, or the limpid ecstasy of Greek sun and sea and human beauty. In all these settings, he immerses himself in the sensory and visual sense, yet stands apart from it as a contemplator and correlator, viewing it and himself with civilized detachment. He is deeply committed to life, seldom to causes, except as each thing that presents itself commits him inevitably to sympathy or revolt. He is in this sense committed to civilization, to the arts, to the battle against the cheapening and levelling of life. He is committed also to the aspirations, if not all the achievements, of Christianity and more particularly in its Anglican expression.

Rose Macaulay. *Enc.* June, 1958, p. 82

POTTER, STEPHEN (1900–   )

It seems to be generally agreed that we have only recently begun to appreciate Coleridge's genius at its true value, and that in spite of the opium his positive achievement extends further than most people realize. There is unfortunately much less agreement as to where exactly the emphasis should fall, and no one has yet given an adequate account of the work in which his genius found its most fruitful field—his literary criticism. Mr. Potter has not attempted to supply this deficiency: his interests are biographical, psychological and philosophical, but only incidentally literary. *Coleridge and S.T.C.* is an account in Jekyll and Hyde terms: "S.T.C." stands for the fixed character with its failings and conventionalities, "Coleridge" for the ever-developing personality whose real depths were often obscured by the petty faults of "S.T.C." This division is ascribed to some failure on Coleridge's part to accept life after his unhappy marriage, and the rest of his life is seen not as decay, but rather as a continual extension of self-awareness in an effort—partially successful—to heal the breach. I am not sure how far this conception is valid, considered as more than a biographical convenience: it certainly involves a great deal of discussion of the less important aspects of Coleridge. Mr. Potter uses it as a kind of scale to evaluate Coleridge's various activities; thus he finds "esteceanism" in his personal relations, his poetry and criticism, his religion and philosophy, alongside of the genuine "Coleridge" elements.

It is to his estimate of these more important aspects that we naturally look for Mr. Potter's chief contribution to the subject, and it turns out to be woefully inadequate. He is aware of the subtlety and profundity of Coleridge's thought in general, but he shows no appreciation whatever of the fineness of his intelligence when it was directed upon poetry. Indeed, the chapter "Joint Authorship," dealing with the poetry and criticism, is probably the worst in the book.

R. G. Cox. *Scy*. Sept., 1935, p. 205

Stephen Potter has made an unmistakably determined effort to create the spirit, the ever changing but ever progressing purposiveness of this man [*Coleridge and S.T.C.*] of unstable purpose. Guided perhaps by his own discerning essay on D. H. Lawrence, the critic notes that Coleridge was not (like Lawrence) all of a piece. . . . Coleridge's personality was inhibited by his character; his self was held in check by his ego. Potter has set himself the task of examining this dualism which divided and nearly wrecked the poet's life, and of inquiring how far Coleridge freed himself from S.T.C. . . .

Thus literary scholarship is applied to clarify a moral and psychic problem of personal importance to every other reader of Coleridge. Compared with many critical essays, the inquiry almost constitutes a new departure . . . but, of course, the scheme bristles with difficulties, and Potter sometimes rather obscures the issue or at least complicates it. His effort at synthesis is occasionally above his powers. But at his worst he is stimulating, and at his best he cannot be read too carefully.

H. V. Routh. *YWES,* 1944, pp. 319–21

Let me first of all consider the great exponent of Lifemanship and the social ploy, the most adroit of gambiteers. A man less witty than

Mr. Potter might have worked his devices to death; it is far otherwise with the Master of Station Road, Yeovil. On he goes, continually scintillating, and rarely probing into his victim without a preliminary anaesthetic of good-humour. At first glance you might suppose that *One-Upmanship* is merely a playful and wittily benevolent exercise, written with kindly smiles to the accompaniment of tea and well-buttered muffins. On the contrary, it is a beautifully precise dissection of the ordinary man and even more ordinary woman, or at least of their more persistent weaknesses. Part of the reader's immense pleasure will doubtless be due to the complacent reflection, "Most amusing, almost pathetically so; and how unlike myself!" But is it? The mere readiness of denial implies a doubt.

How genial is Mr. Potter! Ah, yes: but how bewitchingly subtle and how daintily accurate! The 'ships, the crafts, the ploys and the gambits are subtly inverted parodies or paradoxes, ingenious abuse of technical or sporting jargon, all conveyed in the preposterous over-all satire of the correspondence college and the house-party. The Yeovil courses are stupefying in their lack of reticence and their unblushing thoroughness.

C. E. Vulliamy. *Spec.* Oct. 3, 1952, p. 438

I'm not a student of Gamesmanship or Lifemanship, so maybe I can't appreciate Mr. Potter's humour to the full. His impressions of America, which he visited twice recently for lecture tours and broadcasts [*Potter on America*], are interesting; but apart from a few strident and typical remarks from Lady Astor, who travelled on the same ship, the only story that made me laugh aloud is the one about the man who introduced him by saying: "I expect a lot of you think that the English have no sense of humour. But wait till you hear Mr. Potter."

Fred Urquhart. *TT*. Dec. 22, 1956, p. 1591

It is astonishing that Stephen Potter should have been able to sustain this joke so long. *Supermanship,* the fourth volume of the series that began with *Gamesmanship,* is in no respect inferior to the others. It begins with a report on the progress of the Lifemanship Correspondence College of One-Upness and Gameslifemastery.

I had supposed that the kind of covert dueling which Potter has been satirizing—though of course it goes on everywhere—was a phenomenon that, in this virulent form, was particularly characteristic of English life in the period since the last war—in which a fierce competition of pretenses has been stimulated by the recent lapsing of actual prestige and wealth. But a rereading of Thackeray's *Book of Snobs* has shown me that this habit is of very long standing. The fakery of Supercountry, as well as other themes of Potter's, appears here in more pompous and brutal terms. Of the pretenses that are satirized by Thackeray, wine-manship survives in Potter; but in Potter's more impoverished and less feudal world, there can hardly be any question of having the grocer brought in to play butler.

Edmund Wilson. *Nation.* Sept. 26, 1959, p. 174

POWELL, ANTHONY (1905–   )

The early novels like *Afternoon Men* and *Venusberg* and *From a View to a Death* shared a sharp, electric, almost lyrical, performance. One of the earliest writers to expose people, and even more their way of life, by the follies of their dialogues, Mr. Powell took a number of specimens of the Jazz Age and drily left little commentary. *Afternoon Men* gave one a stiff shot of party life; *Venusberg,* romantic yet lapidary, commemo-rated the love affair abroad; *From a View to a Death,* that social return-match: the undesirable artist among the speechless fox-hunters. Here Mr. Powell's Stendhalian dryness began to warm and a deadly moralist appeared. . . .

The characters in *From a View to a Death* are perennial in the clas-sical English comedy of country life and the national mixture is there, even to the mad cynicism of the cautionary tale. . . . But if the characters are the same, the observation is revised. They are done in new colours. Mr. Powell is, as we know, devoted to Aubrey's *Lives* and his comedy has behind it a stolid native melancholy that is terrifyingly full-blooded. He has wit, but it is not rapier-play: rather it leaves a skilful boxer's marks upon the body of the enemy. The characters retire bruised, not nicked, from the ring. And there an unusual dimension is added to his people: they are reconsidered. They are not only figures of fun and amusement; they have a serious relation to their own experience or to the author's, so that we are shown the comedy of social history.

V. S. Pritchett. *NSN.* June 28, 1952, p. 724

Mr. Powell is of the same generation as Evelyn Waugh, Cyril Connolly, Henry Green, Osbert Lancaster, and, indeed, Graham Greene. . . . All enjoyed the benefits, now so much debated, of the English public school system; all were at Oxford in the years following the first World War, were still young enough to play their parts, militarily or otherwise in the Second, and had fully entered upon creative life in the packed, tense decades lying between the two.

. . . . Alike at the outset, in circumstance, and amicably drawn together by some affinity, they are all the more strongly, as writers, detached from one another. Intellectually, they are fascinated by Society . . . but their reactions have been in each case different.

. . . . [Powell's] work as a novelist falls into two distinct parts, which it might not now seem pretentious to call periods—five novels published between 1931 and '39; then, after twelve years, two more. . . .

Between the two periods, Mr. Powell's silence, excellent as the reasons for it were—throughout the war he was in the Army, then he was editing and writing a study of John Aubrey—caused a sort of hedonistic depression. It is impossible to resign oneself to abstention on the part of a living writer capable of giving acute pleasure, and a nagging gap was felt in the fiction lists till, in 1951, Mr. Powell re-entered the field with *A Question of Upbringing*. Re-appearance, to which for the reading world so much importance attaches, is perhaps a still greater ordeal than first appearance. . . . He, however, not only fulfilled all expectation: he added an element of surprise—a change of angle, of manner, to an extent a change of subject, though never of temperament, declared itself. The light, apparently brittle, fortuitous-seeming continuity of the novels of the earlier group was gone. There was less impressionism and more reflection. Dialogue, instead of providing the main framework, was now introduced chiefly to add high-light. Characterization went deeper, and was at the same time deliberately more diffused. The aim was texture—almost a painted effect—and the underlying subject was continuity. Mr. Powell, in fact, has transposed himself from the mood of the '30s to the mood of the '50s. Instinctively—for such things cannot be calculated—he remains in time with the world.

Elizabeth Bowen. NYHT. Feb. 15, 1953, pp. 1, 8

If I were asked to recommend to a foreigner a book which would illuminate some of the baffling difficulties of English social life, I should choose above all Mr. Anthony Powell's projected sequence *The Music of Time* of which *The Acceptance World* is the third volume. At least, I would do so, provided the foreigner had a good grasp of our idiom, for Mr. Powell is a subtle writer, one who has to be approached slowly and read with a luxuriant pleasure in the sharp taste of a phrase. The segment of English life which he dissects with a sort of wry and affectionate relish is, it is true, a very narrow one indeed; the existence of anyone below the thousand-a-year level is barely recognised for anything but such banausically practical purposes as driving its taxis for it or serving it with expensive food and frequent drinks. But that itself is as typically English of the time as it could possibly be. Mr. Powell's characters live on the frontiers of the upper classes and, like most frontier peoples, combine the worst characteristics of those on each side of the border they inhabit. For to one side their territory slopes up to the country houses, the assured incomes, the coronets on the napkins; on the other it slopes down through picture galleries and publishing houses into the higher Bohemia, and from below there whiffs even of Fitzrovia drift up. These in-betweeners have the instability of the second group without the justification or the zest, and the complacence of the first without the sense of responsibility or values. . . . Theirs is a mean and passionless existence, devoid alike of faith and principle and even of a sense of direction, much less of achievement. They engage themselves a certain amount with the arts and with "love." But art for them is some sort of inverted snobbery game where the trump cards are the worst pictures, while "love" is a barren and unrelated state which serves periodically to isolate its victims in a temporary state of ruttish anxiety. This is for all its brilliance and funniness a sad book, so it strikes me. There is no pleasure anywhere, no enjoyment, no enthusiasm. The most active observable emotion is malice, a sly pleasure at the news of a couple's parting or a friend's failure to get on. They are a doomed lot wriggling in a closed circle from which they do not even want to get out.

Mr. Powell evokes the scene brilliantly, and my only doubt about his book is whether he is aware that the world he describes is as nasty as it is. . . . Apart from his ironic twist of phrase and observation, he has a tolerant forbearance and a marked absence of point of view.

Richard Lister. *NSN*. May 28, 1955, p. 754

On the first page of the first novel In the *Music of Time* sequence, *A Question of Upbringing,* we have the whole aesthetic of the work laid bare.

It is dominated by the image of human beings as participants in a dance, a dance over which they have no control because its movements and their steps in it are governed by the music of time. . . .

But they dance, Powell's characters, "facing outward," as in Poussin's painting [A Dance to the Music of Time]. . . . not to the reader directly, but to Jenkins [the narrator]. . . . What happens happens with relation to Jenkins. He mediates between us and the action; he interprets it for us. . . . [Powell's] interest is in the analysis of human behaviour and the motives that prompt it. The main motive appears to be the will to power. . . . The converse of the will to power is the envy of failure. . . . [Jenkins] is constantly being reminded either of one or of the other, a narrowness of interpretation that makes for a certain monotony in the work . . . he shows absolutely no interest in the events of contemporary history or in the ideas that shape men's minds at a given period; except in so far as they can be used and exploited by men with a will to power.

The effect of this is not to increase but to diminish the stature of the characters Jenkins observes. It is to make them puppets of time; and the dance performed to the music of time appears to be uncommonly like the dance of death. . . . What we are all awaiting now is the great generalisation one hopes will come at the end, Mr. Powell's *Le Temps Retrouvé,* which may well cause us to revise radically all the judgements we made while the work was in progress.

Walter Allen. *List.* April 3, 1958, p. 584

Anthony Powell is, deservedly, among the most highly-praised of contemporary novelists, and one of the very few about whose merits the critics seem almost unanimously agreed. Evelyn Waugh, for instance, is one of his most fervent admirers, but so, rather surprisingly, is Kingsley Amis. However, it seems to me that the majority of his critics have been content to praise Mr. Powell unreservedly without any attempt to analyse his methods, and to describe his books in terms which are often wildly misleading. Even the terms in which his work is so fulsomely praised produce a false impression: he is apt to be described as brilliant, witty, satirical, a master of style, a comic writer of the highest order, etc., etc.; all of which is, broadly speaking, perfectly true, but such labels entirely fail to convey the peculiar quality which makes him so different from any other novelist now writing. To the reader wholly unacquainted with his work, such descriptions of it would suggest a writer akin, perhaps, to Evelyn Waugh or the early Huxley; yet nothing could be further from the truth. Equally misleading is the label applied to him by a French critic: "un Proust anglais." Mr. Powell surely deserves better than this.

It may be as well to dispose, in the first place, of the Proustian parallel. Mr. Powell is engaged upon a long continuous novel, whose title admittedly carries a Proustian echo, and which deals, for the most part, with the higher ranks of society; but there the resemblance ends. One might just as profitably compare Proust with Galsworthy. . . .

How, then, would one describe Anthony Powell's novels to somebody who had never read them? . . . . His first book, *Afternoon Men* (1931), was a kind of wry epitaph upon the twenties: there had been a fashion for what used to be called "party" novels (in the convivial rather than the political sense of the word), dealing with smart Bohemia and the Bright Young People: *Afternoon Men* blew the gaff on the false glamour attributed to this kind of society. Mr. Powell made the night-clubs, the wild parties, etc., seem not glamourous at all, but just deadly dull. This he achieved by a sort of tape-recorder-cum-photo-montage technique which at times seems to carry echoes of Hemingway or even of Gertrude Stein. Curt, laconic, related mostly in dialogue, *Afternoon Men* is deliberately boring; nothing is emphasized, there are no climaxes to speak of; the book has something of the cosmic squalor of *Sweeney Agonistes; . . . .* Though writing about roughly the same sort of people as Evelyn Waugh (*Decline and Fall, Vile Bodies*), Mr. Powell played them down, whereas Mr. Waugh had played them up; one could say —though the distinction is a facile one—that Powell is a classicist and Waugh, by comparison, a romantic. . . .

A Question of Upbringing was in sharp contrast with its predecessors: the style had become more complex, with longer sentences and a more ponderously ironic note, yet many of the old qualities remained. The early novels, one felt, had been so many experiments, tentative rehearsals for a mature and far more ambitious work.

What, then, are these essential qualities which, adumbrated in the pre-war novels, link *Afternoon Men* with *The Music of Time . . . ?* The most important, I think, is Mr. Powell's attitude of almost complete detachment towards his characters; then, too, there is the intentional lack of emphasis, the monochrome flatness of the scenes and persons he describes. One might say of him that he is what used to be called a "black-and-white man" . . . his originality lies not so much in what he does, as in what he manages to avoid doing. . . . His virtues, in fact, are largely negative, which is what, I think, makes the critic's task difficult.

Jocelyn Brooke. L. Sept., 1960, pp. 60–64

The great thing about writing a novel is to have the right conditions for putting your material on paper after you have digested it. For example, I could not have written a line of a novel during the war, but later I found the war had been a good time for literary digestion.

In dealing with any situation—humorous or otherwise—one writer will pick a certain aspect, another, quite a different way of approach. That explains why most—indeed, it would be true to say *all*—writers, even the greatest, work within a comparatively limited range. They are all preoccupied with certain basic material, and any given writer will turn out on examination to be concerned almost always with certain given situations, with certain characters, and not with certain others.

When readers talk to a writer about his books, they sometimes suggest that someone would be a good character—especially a funny character—to be put in a novel. The persons thus suggested are usually the last in the world one would use for models. If one did use them, it would probably be to write about a side of them not in the least obvious —perhaps not revealed at all—to the person who made the suggestion. People who are funny in real life are not at all the people who can be funny in a book, and vice versa.

I do not myself set out to be a humourous writer, so much as one who tries to show things in my own way—perhaps to describe old things in a new way. You are bound to go on dealing with the same situations, because human beings go on doing the same things—adultery, murder, marriage—so you simply have to find a fresh way of expressing them on paper.

One approach, for example, that may lead to humorous results is the examination of the behaviour of people who regard themselves as having a keen sense of the ridiculous. This is especially true, I should say at the moment, among persons who would describe themselves as "anti-Establishment." Such people often turn out to have amusing pomposities that far outstrip anything against which they are themselves up in arms. A recent good example of humour of perhaps a rather terrifying kind was the American play called *The Connection,* about dope addicts. It seemed to me both frightening and funny, but the critics could not take it all. Even the supposedly progressive ones were inclined to sit on the fence. The fact is that people are even more afraid of laughter than they are of tears, and where you get laughter and horror, unrelieved by any small touch of sentimentality, very few British critics can stand up to it.

Life in England is, of course, full of material for a novelist. The stratification of our society sometimes makes it more difficult to make direct points in a way that can be done in, say America, but I think the emphasis people make on the question of class here, and absence of class in America, seems to me exaggerated—or at least treated as if the final results were quite different from what they are. It is always assumed nowadays that it is a bad thing to be stratified, but one of the aspects that is often left out when the matter is discussed is that if Snooks looks down on Brown, Brown looks down equally on Snooks. It may be silly, but that is how we live in this country, and it is impossible to find an income bracket too low for this not to be felt within itself. I think it has some basis in English diffidence, and is perhaps a support against pure power-worship or pure money-worship.

After the war, when I came out of the Army and returned to the writing of novels, I decided that the thing to do was to produce a really large work about all the things I was interested in—the whole of one's life, in fact—for I have no talent for inventing plots of a dramatic kind in a comparatively small space—80,000 words. Such a scheme has great advantages, but you pay a price in the large number of characters you have to stick to. You have an overall picture of how they live and must limit yourself in what you deal with. You cannot write about everybody. What you do must be thoroughly done, so that inevitably certain groups of characters and their friends and relations get, as it were, preferential treatment. If one lived a thousand years, one might bring everything in, but then you would have to cope with a thousand years of experience rather than the normal span.

Anthony Powell. *TC*. July, 1961, pp. 52–53

Parallel with the changes in Jenkins's world, there seems to be a certain change in Mr. Powell's attitude to his characters. Is he, improbably, becoming a moralist? Previously his attitude could be summed up by the title of an earlier volume—*The Acceptance World*—a wry, amused tolerance of even the most boring or odious figures, and a steadfast refusal to pass judgments. Now, however, I feel that characters such as General Conyers, and perhaps Ted Jeavons and his brother Stanley, are seen as embodying positives, while Widmerpool, appearing as an obstructive Army officer, has become disagreeable beyond even the point of his creator's copious toleration.

The Kindly Ones shows that *The Music of Time* is continuing to develop, to reveal fresh aspects. It leaves me more than ever convinced that Mr. Powell is writing a comic masterpiece, and the major achievement in post-war English fiction.

Bernard Bergonzi. *MGW*. July 5, 1962, p. 11

POWYS, JOHN COWPER (1872–1963)

No one will urge that Mr. Powys's *Ducdame* is too short. It is a stout volume running to about 130,000 words, I should estimate, nearly twice as many as the average novel to which we are accustomed. This alone is not, of course, a blemish; many of us have a weakness for the leisurely, discursive fiction which spun itself out in the nineteenth century, and the present theme might easily have lent itself to such treatment. It concerns the fortunes of one family, the Ashovers, a county stock which has more or less run to seed. . . .

Here is the chief reason for the sense of excessive length of the novel —Mr. Powys is continually forced to explain, *ex post facto,* the factors in a character's, usually his hero's, psychology, which impelled him to do such or such a bizarre thing. Mr. Powys, also following Mr. Lawrence, devotes long passages to finding sexual meanings in landscape or other associations; certain days are women days; in others men more easily triumph. . . . Yet he has an undeniable feeling for landscape, even though his interpretations of its moods may be rather fantastic and unconvincing. He has, furthermore, a very real power of conception and a large scale, a faculty of seeing logically down long corridors of time and viewing in proportion the pettiness of temporarily absorbing events in relation to their ultimate significance. *Ducdame* is a far better book than the only other novel of its author's that I have read, *Wood and*

Stone, and if the next one shows the same growth it will be, beyond doubt, a masterpiece.

Milton Waldman. LM. Sept., 1925, pp. 543–44

Mr. Powys has ingeniously made a novel of nearly 1,200 pages [*A Glastonbury Romance*] out of material sufficient for a long short story. He has achieved this by writing a "masterpiece" of a kind that was more fashionable in Germany than in England until recently. . . . Thinly disguised, he has written a novel for those who thirst for a new Hall Caine or Marie Corelli. A fake philosophy of primal motivations of good and evil is introduced in "This Amazing Universe" language, his characters hover on the borderland of Wessex, a will is read out to a family gathering, there is a sprinkling of old ladies and of yokels who talk the most delightful dialect: there are lots of conversations about the universe, and the whole is thinly strung on a cord of lichenous, duckweedy rural description. The opening passage of the novel is pure Corelli, the love scenes decline to Dell, but for the benefit of critics the keynote of the whole is Hardy; it is safe to assume that the majority of critics think that supposing a Hardy were born today he would assiduously write poor cribs of his own work, so the moment the Wessex note is struck all these critics echo "a second Hardy, a second Hardy."

Unfortunately, there are moments in this novel when Mr. Powys seems to be sincere. For instance, he seems sincerely interested in vice, and a tedious and petty latitude of mind is impressed on the reader by the repeated insistence on nastiness. Of course, Mr. Powys knows that nastiness is naughty, but he also seems to think it is very important and the prime interest of the prime movers of good and evil. . . . The second defect in Mr. Powys which seems genuinely sincere, is that he attaches enormous importance to every stray, wispy thought that happens to attract him or one of his characters. . . .

LL. Sept., 1933, pp. 376–377

The chief antagonism I myself feel to Mr. Powys's pleasures [*The Pleasures of Literature*] is that they seem a little to undervalue the energy of a certain kind of lucidity. He is almost peevish about the Fourth Gospel and the "abstract remoteness to earth-life" of its beginning; and he says of Dante that unless we are passionate students of theological symbolism "it is hard to retain our concentration of vision as fixedly on the Purgatorio and Paradiso as upon the Inferno." He limits what he calls "the philosophy of Shakespeare" to "Courage, Magnanimity, and an Open Mind." . . . But this is only to say that where Mr. Powys talks of "agnosticism" I should talk of "ambiguity." He feels that "the exact tone upon religious matters" taken by Cervantes and Shakespeare is "a tone too profoundly agnostic ever to approach irony." It may be; or it may be that its trick is assertion and denial at once, and that what we have over is the kind of assertion that arises in a new form through the denial. It will remain one of my own "Pleasures of Literature" to consider this, and many other matters, in the light of Mr. Powys's monstrous, thrilling and engaging volume.

Charles Williams. *LM*. Jan., 1939, pp. 362–63

Mr. Powys's study of Dostoievsky [*Dostoievsky*] is not a critical one in the usual sense of the word; rather it is interpretative in a highly individual way. "The temperamental peculiarities of an honest critic," he says, "are the tools of his trade. . . . The secret essence and innermost virtue of an author can only be wrung out of him by hate or love." It need hardly be said which of these two is the means Mr. Powys uses to wring the last significance out of Dostoievsky. His natural sympathies with his subject are powerful ones, and there is no doubt that this very distinguished novelist is excellently equipped for the understanding of the Russian writer's temperament and for the discussion of the psychological foundations of his work. . . .

Mr. Powys discusses at length, at various junctures in the book, his very suggestive contention that Dostoievsky was a "nervous" writer who harped upon the chord of race, religion and sex; under these heads he has some of his most important things to say. But, indeed, his admirers are unlikely to be disappointed with any aspect of this study; it is, I think, the richest example so far of his very personal, highly impressive and wickedly irritating style—the quintessential Powys, achieved not so much by distilling out the inessential as by some magical process of putting absolutely everything in. (There are even new ingredients—one does not remember to have been so delighted by Mr. Powys's wry humour before.) The finest passages, whole pages of splendid writing, are only what we should expect; but I hope I do not seem ungenerous if I say that there are others less worthy of Mr. Powys or his subject. Whether he will quite succeed in conveying to his readers the depth of his insight into Dostoievsky is perhaps in doubt. . . . But there will be few whom this book will not send back to Dostoievsky's novels, either to find out if Mr. Powys is really talking the nonsense they think he is, or to see in the novels themselves the new meanings he seems to be lending them.

R. H. Ward. *Adel*. July-Sept., 1947, pp. 236–37

John Cowper Powys is one of those writers about whom it is exceedingly difficult to be wholly detached and impersonal: either you like him or you don't, and too many critics of his work have tended either to hail him, unreservedly, as a great genius, or to dismiss him as a pretentious charlatan unworthy of serious consideration. I am inclined, myself, to think that the truth lies somewhere about midway between these two extremes, and that Mr. Powys—like Johnny Geard in *A Glastonbury Romance*—is part genius, part charlatan: a magician who is half-sceptical of his own magic, a sceptic with an innate capacity for self-delusion.

I first read *A Glastonbury Romance* in the year of its publication (1933), and have recently spent the best part of three weeks in a careful re-reading of what is probably the longest and certainly the most extraordinary novel to have appeared in England since *Ulysses*. That first reading, nearly a quarter of a century ago, made a vivid rather than a deep impression upon me; I had read *Wolf Solent* (which I thought then and still do think a better novel), and *Glastonbury*, by comparison, struck me as pretentious, overwritten, and, generally speaking, rather bogus.

Yet it was *Glastonbury* which, in retrospect, haunted my imagination, becoming—though I hardly realized it—a part of what Powys himself would call my private "mythology." Of the narrative or of the individual characters I remembered little: it was the mood of the book which remained—the unforgettable atmosphere, the unique "taste" of it. This essential "Powys-ishness" is a quality hard to pin down, but I think that Powys's most characteristic effects are achieved by an imaginative identification of character with landscape and *vice versa*. A Powys novel is really a "landscape with figures" in which the characters seem as rooted and autochthonous, as much a part of the natural scene, as the flowers, the mossy tree-stumps, the funguses and rank water-weeds by which Mr. Powys is so passionately obsessed. The "Wessex" about which he writes is recognizably the English countryside; yet is is so deeply infused with his own eccentric and highly personal "mythology" that one sees it from a wholly new and unfamiliar aspect. Above all, he has a marvellous faculty for conveying the "inscape" of natural objects— stones and gates, and paving slabs, and patches of moss, and fragments of old walls, and carved mouldings and dead tree stumps and ploughed-up furrows, and wayside puddles and gutters. He will describe, for instance, a muddy river-bank or a back garden in a country town with an intensity which suggests, more than anything else, a displaced and "fetichistic" erotic excitement; his whole work, indeed, is pervaded by a profound and all-embracing sensuality, and it is, I think precisely this pan-erotic aspect of the Powys "myth" which gives its unique flavour to his writing (one is reminded, at times, of a more cerebral and more sexually sophisticated D. H. Lawrence).

Jocelyn Brooke. *L.* April, 1956, pp. 44–45

With scarcely a single earthly acknowledgment, *All or Nothing* transcends the world of appearances and offers a key to other space-time continuums with their different qualities and experiences. It can be regarded as a metaphysical discourse, a mockery of rationalism, metafiction or space poetry. . . .

Abandoning any connecting thread, Mr. Powys relies on boisterous imagination to carry along the jumble of erratic incidents, symbolism and blind-alleys. The diffusion detracts from the book's obvious merit as a great energetic outburst, for there is much that seems to belong to the worst sort of fairy story, wilful and childish. At moments when the imagery becomes poetic deliberate silliness is liable to intrude, and the use of cerebral whimsy as a means of exposing the dullness of the human race occasionally degenerates into petulance. It is too often as if Beowulf was overlaid by Peter Pan.

TLS. June 17, 1960, p. 381

The literary market now shows a slight upturn in the stock of John Cowper Powys (pronounced "Cooper Poois"), but the man himself is far from such worldly considerations. Even at the peak of his powers, he seemed more other worldly: a poet, novelist, and essayist—one of the old "men of letters"—steeped in fantasy rather than realism. . . .

In a present day city, in an England poorer in originals, he would seem like an unexploded bomb ready to go off at any moment among the organisation men. And, like most writers, he seems the sum of all his books rather than being truly represented by any one of them. If you take even one of his more typical novels, like *A Glastonbury Romance,* a majestic imaginative passage can suddenly slump into too flighty fantasy; but in the sum of his work the Powys character stands out. His work is really a reflection, a continuing autobiography, a heroic "tale" (a favourite word). He rarely writes about the real world, but when he does he is not only strict in his frankness—he does a Freudian job on himself in the autobiography—but piercing about society with no holds barred.

W. J. Weatherby. *MGW.* July 27, 1961, p. 12

Powys' general world-view concentrates heavily, though not exclusively, on the powers coming from below in man and on the inanimate and the lower life-forms in nature, with a kind of mystical sensuality blending Wordsworth, Joyce and Lawrence. Now in the story of *A Glastonbury Romance* Sam, after an experience of passionate love, moves beyond the sexual to a state of saintliness and service, and while on a river coal-barge has a vision of the Holy Grail after a physical invasion by some transcendental power. . . . Powys' prose unfurls with an unhurried and unperturbed ease that goes far to witness its authority; and on the strength of his revelatory passages the tormenting obsessions of Swift, the tragic lives of Byron and Wilde, the sex-agonies of Lawrence and obscenities of Joyce, may all receive, in retrospect, a new sympathy and justification.

G. Wilson Knight. *EC*. Oct., 1961, pp. 415, 417

John Cowper Powys, who died last Monday at the age of 90, was the most original English writer of our century. His originality can best be defined by negatives: he was untouched by Jamesian concern for craft; he cared little or nothing for the English puritan tradition; he saw society as the least important of all man's concerns in the universe; and, in his constant metaphysical absorption, he remained always both intensely reverent and vigilantly sceptical and quite separate from Christian or any other orthodoxies. Beside his extraordinary combination of sensuality and serenity, D. H. Lawrence, a writer of comparable unorthodoxy, seems rancourous, destructive and power-infatuated. . . .

Powys's novels have been compared to Tolstoy, but his masters in the craft are Dostoevsky, Scott and Hardy (a strange trio). To them he has added his wonderful self-knowledge and honesty as shown in his *Autobiography* (a tribute to Rousseau, whom he revered), his passionate belief in the goodness of all sexuality that is not purely cerebral and his hatred of all cruelty (a hatred that came from his victory in middle age against his own deep sadistic instincts).

Angus Wilson. *Obs*. June 23, 1963, p. 23

In *Weymouth Sands* Powys cannot make his people wrestle with life, so he merely *tells* us that they do so. Worse still: on the evidence of this book at least, he had an uninteresting and commonplace mind. And so this novel is above all a bore: long before the reader has managed to escape from the tenuous seaweed of thoughts and impressions, he has entirely lost interest in finding out what "happens" to such an insignificant lot of nonentities.

TLS. Dec. 19, 1963, p. 1045

POWYS, T. F. (1875–1953)

Mr. Powys appears to be allowing his resentment at the conventional falsification of rustic life in fiction to distort his work. A result of his honourable, though inartistic, impulse to be true to facts instead of being content to be true to his imaginative comprehension of them, is the introduction of much material alien to his idiom. . . .

Mr. Powys belongs to the rare class of novelists whose work has poetic value, though it must be admitted that, even when the disturbing elements mentioned are absent, his imagination is not consistently capable of assimilating and transforming into art the heterogeneous materials necessary to the scheme of his book. . . .

Much of his failure is due to the crude naivety of his sybmolism, which has a sentimental origin in a desire to emphasise the universal significance of his persons. . . . Possibly Mr. Powys' proper medium is the short story.

C. H. Rickword. *Cal. Mod. Letters.* Nov., 1925, p. 213

In 1923 Mr. T. F. Powys hit on the amusing idea of writing a piece of fiction that should have at once the sharp visual appeal of a woodcut and the rhythmic appeal of a simple fugue-pattern. He achieved both effects, almost at one stroke, by means of a ruthless and often irritating simplication of character. His people existed in only one dimension, and each of them possessed only one quality, or, to put it another way, each of them was hagridden by some one desire which, having no root in emotion, was both arbitrary and idiotic. This desire removed, the character at once fell down, dead as mutton. This means—since sanity consists in a balance of qualities—that all the characters were lunatics. There was (in *The Left Leg*) Tom Button, admittedly mad, but no worse than the rest, who spent his time chasing unreluctant village drabs and chattering to inanimate objects. There was old Ann Patch, who hated all young children and whose one joy in life, as we were told a hundred times, was killing blackbeetles with her boot. . . . *The Left Leg* introduced us to a place, naively called Wessex, that bore no relation at all to any county trodden by the foot of man, a nightmare region of the mind populated by devils, goblins, and halfwits. It was a kind of obscene fairy-tale, a grim joke; and I for one laughed as heartily as the next man, finding Mr. Powys's gall at least preferable to the milk-and-water of those more amiable writers who delight to idealise rural life and character. But when a second book appeared that was built on exactly the same formula, I began to yawn. When the second was followed by a third and a fourth, I protested that the joke was wearing thin. And with the publication of *Mockery Gap* I was forced to the conclusion that Mr. Powys is determined to go on producing book after book (already we have had five in two years) depicting all rustics as dolts and rascals, bestially lustful and cruel, and all sophisticated characters as nervous wrecks and ineffectual sentimentalists. . . .

Three parts of his time Mr. Powys is not a novelist at all: he is the proprietor of a menagerie. His work presents the converse of the world depicted by Mr. Kipling in *The Jungle Book*. Mr. Kipling shows us animals with human psychology; Mr. Powys shows us men and women moved by purely animal (and therefore uninteresting) impulses. Mr. Powys's anger is demonstrably absurd. . . . Mr. Powys cannot have it both ways. It cannot be too often repeated that mere appetite, whether sexual or otherwise, is a dull theme, and that preoccupation with it has already been the artistic ruin of many a clever novel.

Gerald Bullett. *Modern English Fiction*
(Herbert Jenkins, 1926), pp. 102–6

I have a quite separate and special kind of admiration for this author's work, though it is comprehensible to me that there are persons who are unable to enjoy it.

Powys creates a world of his own. His books are not different novels, they are part of a whole, each illuminating a different aspect or section of his world. . . . Somehow, Powys manages to write pure fantasy and at the same time create living people and atmospheres.

LL. Aug., 1930, pp. 139–40

The case of Powys, were it known as widely, would be hardly less instructive than that of Lawrence in the matter of right appreciation and public attitudes. He is, of course, a challenge to facile and illusory thinking; he questions (though for the most part implicitly) the assumptions and sanctions which underlie and govern our civilisation. But this alone would hardly account for lack of recognition. Nor, in the twentieth century, would his frankness and sometimes violence when he is dealing with sex. Some readers may find his insistence on the fact of death unpleasant; some find his treatment of "God" blasphemous; some may consider him too moralistic. But while these may be adequate reasons for a lack of wide popularity they do not explain the comparative meagreness of recognition by advanced opinion. Perhaps the two main causes are these: a failure to see that his "narrow" rural world is a perfectly adequate basis for the expression of a whole attitude to life, and the consequent or allied failure to appreciate the nature of his conventions. Simply, Powys is a great and an extraordinary writer. He has, to adapt T. S. Eliot's words about Blake, "the terrifying honesty of genius." Much of our task lies in coming to see that what may at first seem "terrifying" is in reality healthy and nourishing.

H. Coombes. *T. F. Powys* (Barrie
and Rockliffe, 1960), p. 19

. . . Theodore Powys was doubly significant since, also, he was probably the first of our definitely non-representational writers of fiction; those who dominate the scene today not by holding the mirror up to life but by emphasising life's essence through arresting symbols and distortions. Thus he was a pioneer and something more.

Yet, though one of the best of our novelists of the second rank, he seems to make less impression than several who are only of the third. Many readers are repelled by his strangeness and a certain monotony; and some by the persistent and inescapable, though quite uncharacteristic, suggestion of a snigger. There is an impression abroad that he is a cult, even if a cult of the worthier sort.

Yet, if narrower, he is no less original and individual than the few rivals with whom he can be decently compared: richer than Bennett, a surer artist than Lawrence, more integral than Conrad, more at the heart of things than Forster. It is sometimes contended . . . that he is not a novelist at all but a fabulist or a writer of the *conte* with a uniquely strong centre of gravity. But it proves quite impossible to account for his achievement within such a concept: his is the novelist's whole vision of life. Fabulists, from Aesop to Bunyan and La Fontaine, *reveal* a moral order, while the significant novelist alternately creates and challenges it. Theodore Powys' short stories turn out rather surprisingly (as do, so differently, Henry James') to be really novels in miniature: this is a wholly different art from Maupassant's or Chekhov's or Kipling's. *The Only Penitent* must surely take its smaller place beside *Mr. Weston's Good Wine* as the purest expression of Theodore Powys; and in nature the two are exactly the same. What ultimately marks the author's boundaries is his social withdrawal (cause or effect?): his psychology is generalised, he is not really strong in individual character-drawing. His humans have their being in poetry—though definitely prose-poetry rather than in society. . . .

If we may invert Madame de Staël's famous phrase, Powys is an artist in whom fixedness of disposition imperils imaginative scope. But though the *idée fixe* rarely relaxes, and the perverse and the macabre recur to a wearisome degree in his pages, he never loses his imaginative sincerity. "I am without a belief," he wrote, "belief is too easy a road to God." His crisis is essentially a religious crisis, and he never flinches from it. But, being to some extent a bigot by inversion, he never accepts life fully. Morally he is less Hardy than Housman, spiritually less Milton than Bunyan. He could be both too charitable and too uncharitable. He conceived of God as a far from good man; yet the good man is a failure in these stories, an unreal figure, unless he is also God. Again, though the evil characters are (as Lord Shaftesbury might have put it) vomited from the jaws of Hell, Powys had—in common with Hardy himself—a curious innocence of how horrible the ordinary respectable citizen is.

H. P. Collins. *EC*. Oct., 1961, p. 463

PRIESTLEY, J. B. (1894–   )

Mr. Priestley's tales [*Brief Diversions*] are charming, but he will improve on them; some of his parodies could not be better. He does not go over the old ground; his subjects are all moderns, and include Mr. James Stephens, AE, and the author of *Trivia,* none of whom, so far as I know, has been parodied before. The "AE" is a masterpiece, and nothing could be better than the pomp and ceremony on Sir W. Watson's lines on receiving an *edition de luxe* of the late Mrs. Wilcox. . . .

Other successes are the travesties of the verse of Mr. Yeats and Mr. Noyes, and the prose of Professors Saintsbury and Quiller-Couch. But perhaps Mr. Priestley's jolliest idea is a "Biographical Drama, *Bubb Dodington,* not yet written by Mr. John Drinkwater." He supplies the introduction by two Chronicles. The volume ends with some good epigrams, and, as a whole, is evidently the work of a first-rate critical mind.

John C. Squire. *LM*. Sept., 1922, pp. 544–45

Mr. Priestley's modesty, carried over from his title [*Papers from Lilliput*] to several of his papers, might lead us to fancy him a Lilliputian merely; but he is more than amusing, more considerable than he pretends, and writes much better than most of the Lilliputians of the press. There are some wholly admirable things. . . . There are, too, light broomstickeries here, often ingenious, always alert. . . . Well, Mr. Priestley contrives to give us the sense that we are meeting him on every page, without thinking the worse of his book.

John Freeman. *LM*. June, 1923, p. 212

There is no end of good things in his pages [*English Humour*]. . . . The truth is, Mr. Priestley undertook an impossible task. One cannot dissect humour any more than one can find from whence the rainbow springs. . . . But Mr. Priestley has to pontificate about humour; he says many things that are just. . . . But there it is, a writer can neither be serious with humour, nor humourous with humour. All we can say is that no one could have fulfilled his task better than Mr. Priestley; his book is worth reading, and has a goodly store of fine quotations.

LL. Jan., 1930, p. 85

J. B. Priestley made his name as a novelist with *The Good Companions*. He has never written anything else quite so good as that, but his latest novel, *They Walk in the City,* comes near to it. In many respects Mr. Priestley is the Dickens of the modern age. He epitomises the spirit of the average Englishman of the twentieth century as Dickens did of the nineteenth; his stories, too, have the same air of free, hearty humour, the same spontaneity and inconsequentiality. One feels that there is no particular reason that they should end where they do, for they have no plot in the Aristotelian sense—no beginning, middle and end. Then too, as is so often the case with Dickens, the central figure is frequently but a name; those who really live are the minor characters who only enter and re-enter for odd moments, but remain clearly imprinted on the memory. Most of these characteristics are to be found in *They Walk in the City*. As the title of the book suggests, the story is concerned with no exceptional type of person and no unusual situation; it has no thesis to expound and attempts to solve no problem. Rather Mr. Priestley's aim is to present to us the life of the average man or woman in a large city or an industrial town; and by "life," of course, he means not merely the outward, but also the inner existence; not merely what people do and say, but also what they feel and think. He writes with an understanding and a sympathy that speaks a depth of experience and a wide contact with humanity. There is both tragedy and comedy in this book; the two are blended together as they so often are in actual life; the author can rejoice with those who rejoice and weep with those who weep, and the result is a mixture of joviality, wistfulness and tenderness such as one is accustomed to associate with the writings of Charles Lamb.

Frederick T. Wood. ES. Aug., 1937, p. 136

Authors approaching middle age are often exercised about death; it is sometimes the only exercise they get. This play [*Johnson over Jordan*] shows that Mr. Priestley has been thinking a great deal about his and everybody else's approaching dissolution. Unfortunately he has not been thinking very freshly, for though I listened hard on Wednesday evening, I could gather no hint of any new thought on the subject. . . .

Mr. Priestley's peppering of the play with the Burial Service—it happened at the beginning of every act—was piling up agony for agony's sake, except that the second *reprise* made for titters rathen than jitters. Then why harp upon physical corruption, of which no man is conscious? Even death itself ceases to exist once he who is to suffer it realises that, as the old writer said, "either it has happened, or it is not yet." . . .

Come, come, my dear Jack! If I were your schoolmaster I should make you write out Browning's "Prospice" ten times. As I am only your greatest admirer when you are at your best, the limit of my severity is to permit myself . . . [an] Epigram on a Dramatist Aiming High but Wide. . . . But this, after all, is the theatre. And, it may be argued, if you are not going to think about your theme in a striking way, how about making the audience sit up in the matter of presentation? In this, the most old-fashioned piece he has yet contrived, our author has gone back to the Expressionism of the nineteen-twenties as practised by Messrs. Toller, Kaiser, Molnar, and Elmer Rice, and dead almost before it was alive. You know the kind of thing.

James Agate. The Amazing Theatre (George G.
Harrap, 1939), pp. 231–32

In 1932 J. B. Priestley entered the London theatre successfully with *Dangerous Corner,* after a version of his novel *The Good Companions* had been dramatized in 1931. Critics were at first uncertain whether Priestley had succeeded by fortunate accident, or whether he possessed some enduring dramatic talent. The years which followed were generous in their proofs: *Laburnum Grove* in 1933 was followed by *Eden End* (1934), and in 1937 by both *I Have Been Here Before* and *Time and the Conways.* Priestley's range as a dramatist was unusual. He had a very sure skill in the portrayal of dramatic types, and a very happy command of dialogue. Comedy he had too, sometimes a little obvious, but generous and lively. To all this was added in a number of the plays a rare, imaginative overtone. It was as if amid all the boldly drawn characters and the Yorkshire fun a sensitive and metaphysical mind was operating. This appeared notably in the plays which explored dramatically the concept of time, as in *Time and the Conways.* Priestley showed here and in a number of other plays a considerable command of the theatre as a technical instrument. He wrote rapidly, some would say, possibly in envy, too rapidly. At times he allowed himself to produce mere dramatic entertainments as in *When We Are Married* (1938). But it is clear from *Johnson Over Jordan* (1938) that his mind was also contemplating the use of the theatre for more ambitious and imaginative purposes. In that play, which makes use of an expressionist technique, he explores Everyman in modern life in his hopes and perplexities. He carried here as elsewhere a theme of hope and encouragement which had a valiant quality within it. The play could not be described as wholly successful, and yet it showed a mind at work which had something fresh to bring to the theatre.

B. Ifor Evans. English Literature Between the Wars
(Methuen, 2nd ed. 1949), pp. 123–24

For every ten people who admire, or dislike, Mr. J. B. Priestley the novelist and Mr. J. B. Priestley the playwright, there are only two or three who are aware of a third Mr. J. B. Priestley, Mr. Priestley the essayist and the critic, who has used the medium of the essay to write some of the best critical appreciations that have appeared in this century. . . .

But although Mr. Priestley, the essayist, is not now read as much as he should be—and, after all, until the publication of *Delight* in 1949, Mr. Priestley had, from the late 'twenties onwards, been busy with other forms of expression—it is nevertheless his likeness, the impression that he himself, through his essays, has given us, which springs to the mind whenever his name or his work is mentioned. That is the broad figure with the pipe and the survival of the Bruddersford accent, inconspicuously dressed—"I am the kind of man who can make any suit of clothes look shabby and undistinguished after about a fortnight's wear"—a man with no nonsense about him, avuncular in a way that alternates between the whimsical and the severe, tolerant of the follies of mankind and yet possessed of the reformer's itch to do something about them, one who speaks his own mind and who, like the bluff, representative Englishman this all so misleadingly seems to add up to, enjoys a good grumble.

Dudley Carew. *TT*. May 22, 1956, p. 625

Sir Ifor Evans has pointed out that Priestley belongs to the long tradition in English letters which has created literature out of its genuine detestation of poverty; but it was only indirectly as a social reformer that Priestley wrote *Angel Pavement*. The apprehensive years after the depression, the moods of fear, the hanging on to an existence hardly worth keeping, are captured in the book. They are not, however, turned into an opportunity for proposing changes and castigating the responsible. Priestley has not yet taken to preaching, for he is much more engaged in the difficulties of living, the inner tangles that an individual can only sort out for himself, than in the problems of society which require a political solution. *Angel Pavement* may be regarded as the imaginative companion-piece to *English Journey,* which is a factual survey of this country during the early thirties; the mood of the two books strikes the same chord, in a minor key, disturbingly. But the novel is about isolated people living in a city, and the problems which occupy their suffering hours will never be quietened by social reform. . . .

In *Angel Pavement,* Priestley's descriptions not only satisfy curiosity by pouncing on details and exposing them but also rise to flights of language which pull the reader irresistibly into the thick of the atmosphere.

David Hughes. *J. B. Priestley* (Rupert Hart-Davis, 1958), pp. 110–11

And yet the highbrows are right, I think; Priestley, despite his scope and wide range of reference, his energy and the size of his production, *is* lightweight. The organic concern for craft, the deep moral passion and above all, the genuinely candid eye of the truly important novelist are too seldom there.

A. Thwaite. *L*. April, 1959, p. 91

. . . Mr. Priestley has written a conspectus in the grand manner [*Literature and Western Man*]. It is written by the *real* Priestley, not the one who has presented to the world what he himself calls a *persona,* or mask, a champion grumbler, something of a curmudgeon with chips on both shoulders, a professional grouser treading in the angry spoor of Carlyle. Behind that *persona* lives and works the Priestley whom I will dare to call the poet, the word-master (thus contradicting many critics who either ignore or deny the artist in Priestley)*.* This is the man whose writing I have always followed with interest and usually with pleasure. He is a master in the art of the essay. As a dramatist he has ranged widely, and always with an authoritative touch. His play *Johnson Over Jordan* shows the courage and power of his imagination (always a *moral* imagination since it is concerned with human responsibility). . . . As a novelist he needs no bush (I think of *Angel Pavement* as the most mature). As a journalist I put him with E. M. Forster. Here are two writers always crystal clear, concise, and possessing that exciting quality, *readability*. And both are always on the side of the angels, fighting for justice, with fire in their bellies.

There is yet another side to Mr. Priestley. He is a sound literary critic. He has no use for fashion, cliques and literary snobbery. He bases his judgment on his wide reading, as a conscious estimate, and on a native fairness and compassionate common-sense, as an unconscious estimate. This aspect of him showed early in his career, when he wrote two volumes in *The English Men of Letters Series,* on Meredith and T. L. Peacock (Meredith's father-in-law, friend of Shelley, and what Meredith would have called a *comedic* novelist). Those two books have stood the test of thirty years. A year is a long time in the modern world of supersonic speed.

The critic Priestley has written this new book. . . . It shows throughout the best in the whole man. It is warm with compassionate understanding. When Priestley took off his coat to this task, he threw the chips from his shoulders. He has enjoyed himself, because he has been writing about that ringing, musical overtone, the literature of Europe produced since the introduction of the printing press. . . .

Now I am at a loss how to compress the excitement rekindled from another look at my notes, made during the week spent with this book. The fact is that Priestley has written at white-heat, in spite of the length and variety. Something has got hold of him in the autumn of his professional career, a kind of re-birth to enthusiasm. It is as though the

young man, enraptured and even ecstatic at a first meeting with the
wonders of literature, avid and insatiable, has been recalled from the
past of forty or more years ago, and introduced by the professional
author of long experience, many disillusionments and betrayals, gradual
eliminations of false enthusiasms and disproportionate claims. But the
youth has won. He has emerged with his passionate delight undiminished, his valuable naïvety (that sure sign of creative spirit as distinct
from a literary or other fashion-monger) still enabling him to penetrate
to the core of character and to the few simple bed-rock values in this
strange activity of the handling of words. Be assured, then, that this is a
book which will not bore you with academic catalogue and pedantry.
It is on fire. It is a festival. Readers who sit down to it hungry will come
away satisfied, yet eager for more.

Richard Church. *JOL*. Feb. 18, 1960, p. 179

PRINCE, F. T. (1912–   )

One poet stands out with Vernon Watkins as of importance. This is
F. T. Prince, who is one of the finest young poets now writing in English. F. T. Prince published a first volume, *Poems,* before the war. Since
the war he has written only a few poems, one of which, "Soldiers Bathing," is magnificent. . . .

Stephen Spender. *Poetry Since 1939*
(BC/Longmans, 1946), p. 52

Mr. Prince's merits as a poet have won him the recognition of other
poets and of that small public which both reads and discriminates among
contemporary writers of verse. He has been drawn upon by anthologists,
and reviewers of varying weight, advancing their claims as talent-scouts
or literary tipsters, have praised him. It is to be hoped that the publication of this volume [*Soldiers Bathing*], his second, will extend a reputation already established.

In a sense all Mr. Prince's poems are love poems. A group of them
here are classified as such: in their strict forms, their imagery, their
intricate thought and emotion, they have a seventeenth-century air and
yet a newness, and they tend to reverberate in the mind's ear.

William Plomer. *L*. August, 1954, pp. 93–94

The present volume, *The Doors of Stone,* which contains all that Mr.
Prince wishes to preserve from previous collections plus a number of
new poems, may surprise many who know only his anthology piece
["Soldiers Bathing"]. He is for one thing one of the best love poets of
the age, a lyricist of great charm and tenderness of emotion, counter-

balanced by a subtlety of thought and metaphor which often remind one
of Donne, and he frequently succeeds in creating at least glimpses of the
relationship of human love to the divine. Like most good love poems in
English from Donne onwards these poems are constructed to reveal their
meaning epigrammatically and through prolonged metaphor and analogy.

TLS. July 26, 1963, p. 557

PRITCHETT, V. S. (1900–   )

The second volume of Mr. Lehmann's magazine-anthology [*New Writing II*]—it is difficult to know just what to call it—contains one excellent contribution, a short story by V. S. Pritchett. It is the sort of story Lawrence might have written, . . . a Lawrence story with elements of "darkness" which he would only too eagerly have brought out. Three or four years ago, perhaps, Mr. Pritchett might have seen the story in the same way, and told it, more jerkily, in the Lawrence manner. How much he has learnt since then! "Sense of Humour"—as this story is called—is individual to Mr. Pritchett; style, characters, dialogue are all his. I do not know of any other novelist writing to-day who could have constructed this story as he has, on wiry dialogue which is trivial and commonplace and yet now and then gives out a note as pure as a tuning-fork's. . . . The whole thing is a triumph in that kind of writing, *sans commentaire,* which I particularly admire and which so few of our novelists to-day have the talent to bring off. Mr. Pritchett's last novel was good; his next should be an event.

G. W. Stonier. *NSN*. Dec. 12, 1936, p. 99

Mr. Pritchett's talent is specifically that of a novelist; that is to say, his perceptions, interpreted by an acute intelligence, clothe themselves in characters, in human situations, in stories. He never makes the impression, as Mr. Huxley does, of having deliberately clothed his ideas in human form. Nor does he suffer from that poverty of invention which makes many cultured novels consist of a thin sprinkling of events, like the events of any middle-class life, floating on a thin wash of such musings and reasonings as are common to cultivated, introspective persons. . . . I found his last novel, *Nothing Like Leather,* dull; but I suspect that this was not so much that tanning is a bore as that he required of the reader more intellectual and intuitive co-operation than I was willing to give. Not that he is a difficult or prolix writer; his style is terse, precise and lively, individual without being in the least precious. But his subject-matter and his approach are so much his own that they require alertness and a total absence of preconceived ideas.

His characters are seldom, if ever, sympathetic; he is not interested in agreeable people, liking them gritty, high-flavoured, subtle and eccentric. He has a special line in girls: there was one of them in *Shirley Sanz,* and Lucy in *Dead Man Leading* belongs to the same order—I am not implying that Mr. Pritchett repeats himself, only that his attention has been engaged by, and has not yet exhausted, an unexploited type of bold, sensual thickset young woman, an intriguing and convincing mixture of feminine yieldingness and of masculine enterprise. . . .

The feat achieved by *Dead Man Leading* lies in the similarity established, but only once, I think, stated, between the jungle, huge, uncharted and charged with terrific vitality, and the nature, the unconscious, the life-principle in man.

Dead Man Leading is a rich, a deeply-assimilated, original and satisfying book.

E. B. C. Jones. *Spec.* April 9, 1937, p. 676

One would say that he regards mankind as participants in a bizarre adventure. This does not mean that he seeks out oddities. They don't have to be sought out. Every artist knows that even the "normal" is so rare that it too is an oddity.

Two great things about Mr. Pritchett are his gusto and cheerfulness. . . . By paying close attention to the surface of things, Mr. Pritchett gets at the roots, just as a portrait painter gets the sitter's character from the circles under his eyes, the dimple in his chin, and his tell-tale thumbs. . . . If to shun whimsy is to be a realist then Mr. Pritchett is a realist, but if to be a realist is to see only what the unobservant see then he is nothing of the kind, for his observations are touched with life-giving poetry. A man is "nervous and private as a silvery fish"; rain "lashed on the windows like gravel"; a woman "looked rat-like, with that peculiar busyness, inquisitiveness, intelligence and even charm of rats." . . . He is a specialist in the physical presence, and so one may say that he is in the tradition of D. H. Lawrence.

Two stories here are ambitious discoveries of complicated human relationships. Each has more colour and more knowledge of life in it than many a novel. [*You Make Your Own Life*]

William Plomer. *LM.* March, 1938, pp. 549–50

For readers not acquainted with the novels and stories of Mr. V. S. Pritchett the air of his new book, *Mr. Beluncle,* will have about it a familiar and yet perhaps at first unidentifiable smell. . . . Mr. Beluncle, in fact, speaks much the same language and breathes much the same atmosphere as a character in one of the early books of H. G. Wells. That is what seems familiar in him: what seems strange is that Mr.

Beluncle, with this Wellsian odour of suburban optimism and vulgar gentility clinging to him, has been created by a man whose view of life and characters is so manifestly un-Wellsian. For Mr. Pritchett the amiable self-deception of the Wellsian little man, which was a necessary part of his human dignity, has become an ugly growth of deceit and egotism; and for the Beluncle of Mr. Pritchett's conception, enmeshed in the toils of a dissenting religious sect called Mrs. Parkinson's Group, Wells would have had little understanding and less sympathy. . . . This book about him, indeed, gives the impression of being a series of episodes strung loosely together over a long period; and in fact *Mr. Beluncle* has been ten years or more in the writing. . . .

Nothing Like Leather is in some ways the most satisfactory of Mr. Pritchett's novels. The first three books have the same defect as *Mr. Beluncle;* they seem to have been begun with some purpose, abandoned or forgotten long before their end. There is much to admire, however, in *Nothing Like Leather.* The scene is finely observed, the atmosphere surrounding a small business in the early years of this century—a time still of business expansion—is beautifully caught; and Burkle is a kind of minor Beluncle, less wholly lost in a fantasy world but equally obsessed by sin and righteousness.

TLS. Oct. 19, 1951, p. 660

V. S. Pritchett has revealed in this discouraging landscape a teeming profusion of saints, eccentrics, cozeners, windbags, heroes, wits, madmen, and harpies, worthy of Dickens, Smollett, Gorki, Raymond Queneau or H. G. Wells.

His, indeed, is the shirtsleeve world, where middle-aged ladies sip mid-morning port in the local; where Sid and Bert perch, heads down, bottoms up, on their racing roadsters; where uncles induct their nephews into uncertain family businesses; where seedy revivalists tout for converts in small provincial streets. As reportage, Mr. Pritchett's stories succeed magnificently: their dialogue is clipped and lively—their atmosphere is utterly authentic—their mood is genial, compassionate, subtly robust. But to label them as a mere chronicle of their beer-and-cola society would be inadequate and unfair: not all of them, even, belong to that world. Without Graham Greene's self-pity or melodrama, without William Sansom's quizzical whimsicality, Mr. Pritchett delineates with great skill and affection the strangeness of "ordinary people," the paradox of human solitude and solidarity, the moments when alien loneliness is touched by shafts of perception. His secret, perhaps, is the fine precision of his writing, inducing a careful and minute attention to the currents and small landmarks by which our lives are steered. His style, a little mannered, is purposeful and very exact; but his grave intentness can convey wild comedy as well as its own mood. . . . I can only repeat what this volume [*Collected Stories*] makes abundantly evident—that Mr. Pritchett is one of the four or five British masters of his delicate and incisive art.

Richard Mayne. *TT*. May 19, 1956, p. 594

Lower middle class in origin, he never attended the university, moving on from an early career in business (he was, among other things, a traveling salesman) to journalism. And he has remained a professional writer, producing his novels, travel books, critical essays, and short stories while working as a foreign correspondent, broadcaster, and literary editor of *The New Statesman and Nation*. . . . In style, however, in *air,* he has adapted to the prevailing upper-class modes; he has "passed."

It is this refusal to reject good manners which will, I suspect, isolate Pritchett, for all his excellence, from the newer generation of British writers, the Wains and the Amises. . . . It is as a critic that Pritchett's force is chiefly felt; and the essays in *The Living Novel* are, many of them at least, full of genuine insight and revelation rendered with grace and wit; but the whole is so unremittingly amateurish and off-hand, so resolutely relaxed as to be finally a little annoying. . . . The point is never (and here Mr. Pritchett has taken on the central pose of the early twentieth century British upper middle class) to appear too much in earnest lest one appear underbred. . . .

Some of the stories in the present collection [*The Sailor, Sense of Humour, and Other Stories*] were written in the 30's, others just before and during the Second World War; some appear to be quite recent, but all look backward for setting and in manner as well as in scope and ambition; so that . . . the whole body of his work is in effect nostalgic. . . .

I find his stories (to him "the only kind of writing that has given me great pleasure") the most impressive part of his work. His novel *Dead Man Leading* remains in my memory as an especially successful and moving attempt to explore the kind of mind that itself likes to explore unmapped territories; but I do not have a sense of Mr. Pritchett as a real novelist. He seems most at home to me in longish fictions.

Leslie A. Fiedler. *Cmty*. March, 1957, p. 294

PUDNEY, JOHN (1909–   )

This first collection of short stories [*And Lastly the Fireworks*] by a well-known young poet is one of the most interesting that has appeared for some time. It is interesting, firstly, because many of the tales are courageous experiments in technique and secondly because the stories are essentially of today, without being imitations of Mr. Ernest Hemingway—the literary Godfather of too many young men. Indeed, Mr. Pudney's stories are markedly free from superficial influences and he seems straight away to have forged an idiom of his own. . . .

While most of his stories happen to be entertaining, it is obvious that Mr. Pudney is trying to do much more than merely entertain. Life is not one easily apprehended design; rather is it a complexity of many designs for which an artist has to sort out one of his own. Mr. Pudney, at the moment, seems bewildered by the multiplicity of designs with which life surrounds him, and consequently his stories become dissertations upon, rather than resolutions of, his problems. This book, therefore, is somewhat like a collection of questions which have, as yet, no answers. They are, though, vital questions, and it is to be hoped that Mr. Pudney will be able to find the proper answers.

Clifford Dyment. *LL*. Dec., 1935, p. 205

The collection [*Jacobson's Ladder*] of strange, trogloditic creatures chosen by John Pudney to inhabit the street markets and byways of Soho become almost human when described by him. They become, therefore, objects of pity, hate and even some affection and one cannot help following their careers with considerable interest, forgiving in the journey, their crudity and strangeness. . . . There are flashes of dream worlds which give refreshing colour, though the suicide of a rather unkempt character jolts the imagination into a reality which is not carried through and does nothing to improve the whole.

M. D. Cole. *LL*. Nov., 1938, pp. 102–3

John Pudney is an English airman whose verse has a tendency to fall off a cloudbank every time he lets loose of *Leaves of Grass*. . . . An inspirational poet and a derivative one, to whom pity is sufficient and hope is easy, he has no new word for a new world; though he does, occasionally, strike off a sound and poignant line. . . . To this poet [*Flight Above Cloud*], a man of action writing within the sound of aircraft motors, gunfire alone is real: ". . . and the brief handclasps which must tear/The lonely from the lonely." He rewards the reader with nothing stronger, for the volume's conclusion, than the assurance that: "We will fly away one day with no need to kill—which we all knew all along anyhow."

Nelson Algren. *Poetry*. Oct., 1944, pp. 51–52

BIBLIOGRAPHY

GENRE ABBREVIATIONS

a	autobiography	p	poetry
b	biography	pd	poetic drama
c	criticism	r	reminiscence
d	drama	rd	radio drama
e	essay	s	short stories
h	history	sk	sketches
m	memoir	t	travel or topography
misc	miscellany	tr	translation
n	novel		

For explanatory note on Bibliography see page 510.

H. RIDER HAGGARD
1856-1925

Cetywayo and His White Neighbors, 1882 (e); Dawn, 1884 (n); The Witch's Head, 1884 (n); King Solomon's Mines, 1885 (n); She, 1887 (n); Jess, 1887 (n); Allan Quatermain, 1887 (n); A Tale of Three Lions, 1887 (n); Mr. Meeson's Will, 1888 (n); Maiwa's Revenge, 1888 (n); My Fellow Laborer and the Wreck of the "Copeland," 1888 (n); Colonel Quaritch, 1888 (n); Cleopatra, 1889 (n); Allan's Wife, 1889 (s); Beatrice, 1890 (n); (with Andrew Lang) The World's Desire, 1890 (n); Eric Brighteyes, 1891 (n); Nada the Lily, 1892 (n); Montezuma's Daughter, 1893 (n); The People of the Mist, 1894 (n); Church and State, 1895 (e); Joan Haste, 1895 (n); Heart of the World, 1896 (n); The Wizard, 1896 (n); Doctor Therne, 1898 (n); The Last Boer War, 1899 (Am. ed. A History of the Transvaal) (h); Swallow, 1899 (n); The Spring of a Lion, 1899 (n); A Farmer's Year, 1899 (e); Black Heart and White Heart, 1900 (s); The New South Africa, 1900 (e); Lysbeth, 1901 (n); A Winter Pilgrimage, 1901 (t); Rural England, 1902 (e); Pearl Maiden, 1903 (n); Stella Fregelius, 1904 (n); The Brethern, 1904 (n); A Gardener's Year, 1905 (e); The Poor and the Land, Being a Report on Salvation Army Colonies, 1905 (e); Ayesha: The Return of She, 1905 (n); The Way of the Spirit, 1906 (n); Benita, 1906 (Am. ed. The Spirit of Bambatse) (n); Fair Margaret, 1907 (Am. ed. Margaret) (n); The Ghost Kings, 1908 (Am. ed. The Lady of the Heavens) (n); The Yellow God, 1909 (n); The Lady of Blossholme, 1909 (n); Morning Star, 1910 (n); Queen Sheba's Ring, 1910 (n); Regeneration, 1910 (e); Rural Denmark and its Lessons, 1911 (e); Red Eve, 1911 (n); The Mahatma and the Hare, 1911 (n); Marie, 1912 (n); Child of Storm, 1913 (n); The Wanderer's Necklace, 1914 (n); A Call to Arms, 1914 (e); The Holy Flower, 1915 (Am. ed. Allan and the Holy Flower) (n); The Ivory Child, 1916 (n); Finished, 1917 (n); Love Eternal, 1918 (n); Moon of Israel, 1918 (n); When the World Shook, 1919 (n); The Ancient Allan, 1920 (n); The Missionary and the Witch-Doctor, 1920 (n); Smith and the Pharaohs, 1920 (s); She and Allan, 1922 (n); The Virgin of the Sun, 1922 (n); Wisdom's Daughter, 1923 (n); Heu-Heu, 1924 (n); Queen of the Dawn, 1925 (n); Treasure of the Lake, 1926 (n); The Days of My Life, 1926 (a); Allan and the Ice Gods, 1927 (n); Mary of Marion Isle, 1929 (n)

George L. MacKay, *A Bibliography of the Writings of Sir Rider Haggard*, 1930 (rev. 1939, 1947)

RADCLYFFE HALL
188?-1943

Twixt Earth and Stars, 1906 (p); *A Sheaf of Verses*, 1908 (p); *Poems of the Past and Present*, 1910 (p); *Songs of Three Counties*, 1913 (p); *The Forgotten Island*, 1915 (p); *The Forge*, 1924 (n); *The Unlit Lamp*, 1924 (n); *A Saturday Life*, 1925 (n); *Adam's Breed*, 1926 (n); *The Well of Loneliness*, 1928 (n); *The Master of the House*, 1932 (n); *Miss Ogilvy Finds Herself*, 1934 (s); *The Sixth Beatitude*, 1936 (n)

G. ROSTREVOR HAMILTON
1888-

The Search for Loveliness, 1910 (p); *The Making*, 1926 (p); *Epigrams*, 1928 (p); *Light in 6 Moods*, 1930 (p); *John Lord, Satirist: a Satire*, 1934 (p); *Unknown Lovers*, 1935 (p); *Poetry and Contemplation*, 1937 (c); *Memoir, 1887-1937*, 1938 (p); *The World to Come*, 1939 (e); *The Sober War*, 1940 (p); *The Trumpeter of St. George*, 1941 (p); *Apollyon*, 1941 (p); *Death in April*, 1944 (p); *Hero or Fool? A Study of Milton's Satan*, 1944 (c); *Selected Poems and Epigrams*, 1945 (p); *Crazy Gaunt and Other Dramatic Sketches*, 1946 (d); *The Inner Room*, 1947 (p); *The Tell-tale Article*, 1949 (c); *The Carved Stone*, 1952 (p); *The Russian Sister*, 1955 (p); *Guides and Marshals*, 1956 (c); *Collected Poems and Epigrams*, 1958; *Walter Savage Landor*, 1960 (c)

JAMES HANLEY
1901-

Drift, 1930 n; *Boy*, 1931 (n); *The Last Voyage*, 1931 (n); *Men in Darkness*, 1931 (s); *Aria and Finale*, 1932 (s); *Ebb and Flood*, 1932 (n); *Stoker Haslett*, 1932 (n); *Captain Bottell*, 1933 (n); *Quartermaster Clausen*, 1934 (n); *The Furys*, 1935 (n); *Stoker Bush*, 1935 (n); *At Bay*, 1935 (s); *The Secret Journey* (seq. to *The Furys*), 1936 (n); *Broken Water: An Autobiographical Excursion*, 1937 (a); *Grey Children*, 1937 (e); *Half-an-Eye*, 1937 (s); *Hollow Sea*, 1938 (n); *People Are Curious*, 1938 (s); *Between the Tides*, 1939 (1949 ed. *Towards Horizons*) (e); *Our Time is Gone* (seq. to *The Secret Journey*), 1940 (n); *The Ocean*, 1941 (repr. 1954) (n); *No Directions*, 1943 (n); *Sailor's Song*, 1943 (n); *Crilley*, 1945 (s); *What Farrar Saw*, 1946 (n); *Selected Stories*, 1947 (n); *Emily* 1948 (n); *A Walk in the Wilderness*, 1950 (n); *Winter Song* (seq. to *Our Time is Gone*), 1950 (n); *The Closed Harbour*, 1952 (n); *Collected Stories*, 1953; *Don Quixote Drowned*, 1953 (s); *The Welsh Sonata: Variations with a Theme*, 1954 (n); *Levine*, 1956 (n); *An End and a Beginning* (seq. to *Winter Song*), 1958 (n); *Say Nothing*, 1962 (n)

THOMAS HARDY
1840-1928

Desperate Remedies, 1871 (n); *Under the Greenwood Tree*, 1872 (n); *A Pair of Blue Eyes*, 1873 (repr. 1886) (n); *Far from the Madding Crowd*, 1874 (n); *The Return of the Native*, 1878 (n); *A Laodicean*, 1881 (n); *Two on a Tower*, 1882 (n); *The Mayor of Casterbridge*, 1886 (n); *The Trumpet Major*, 1888 (n); *Tess of the d'Urbervilles*, 1891 (n); *A Group of Noble Dames*, 1891 (s); *Life's Little Ironies*, 1894 (s); *Jude the Obscure*, 1896 (n); *The Well-Beloved*, 1897 (n); *Wessex Poems*, 1898 (p); *Poems of the Past and Present*, 1902 (p); *The Dynasts*, 3 pts., 1903, 1906, 1908 (pd); *Time's Laughingstocks*, 1909 (p); *A Changed Man*, 1913 (s); *Satires of Circumstance*, 1914 (p); *Moments of Vision*, 1917 (p); *Collected Poems*, 1919; *The Works* (Mellstock ed.), 37 vols., 1919-1920; *Late Lyrics and Earlier*, 1922 (p); *Human Shows*, 1925 (p); *Life and Art: Essays, Notes and Letters*, coll. Ernest Brennecke, 1925; *Winter Words*, 1928 (p); *The Short Stories*, 1928 (s); *Collected Poems*, 1930; *Selected Poems*, ed. G. M. Young, 1940 (p); *Letters*, ed. Carl J. Weber, 1954; *Thomas Hardy's Notebooks and Some Letters from Julia Augusta Martin*, ed. Evelyn Hardy, 1955; *Love Poems*, ed. Carl J. Weber, 1963 (p)

Richard Little Purdy, *Thomas Hardy, a Bibliographical Study*, 1954

FRANK HARRIS
1856-1931

Elder Conklin, 1894 (s); *Montes the Matador*, 1900 (s); *Mr. and Mrs. Daventry*, 1900 (d); *The Road to Ridgeby's*, 1901 (s); *The Bomb*, 1908 (n); *The Man Shakespeare and his Tragic Life Story*, 1909 (b); *Shakespeare and his Love*, 1910 (d); *The Women of Shakespeare*, 1911 (c); *Great Days*, 1913 (n); *Unpath'd Waters*, 1913 (n); *The Yellow Ticket*, 1914 (s); *Contemporary Portraits*, 1915 (c); *The Veils of Isis*, 1915 (s); *Oscar Wilde: His Life and Confessions*, 1916, 1918, enlgd. ed. 1932 (Am.) (b); *Love in Youth*, 1916 (n); *Stories of Jesus the Christ*, 1919 (s); *Contemporary Portraits*, second series, 1919 (c); *Contemportary Portraits*, third series, 1920 (c); *A Mad Love*, 1920 (n); **My Life and Loves*, 1923-27 (a); *Contemporary Portraits*, fourth series, 1919, (c); *Undream'd of Shores*, 1924 (s); *Joan La Romée*, 1926 (d); *Latest Contemporary Portraits*, 1921 (c); *On the Trail, My Reminiscences as a Cowboy*, 1930 (r); *Confessional*, 1930 (a); *Frank Harris on Bernard Shaw: An Unauthorised Biography*, 1931 (b); *Oscar Wilde* (with preface by Bernard Shaw) 1938 (b) **ed. John F. Gallagher, 1964

Vincent Brome, *Frank Harris*, 1959

L. P. HARTLEY
1895-

Night Fears, 1924 (s); *Simonetta Perkins*, 1925 (n); *The Killing Bottle*, 1932 (s); *The Shrimp and the Anemone* (Am. ed. *The West Window*), 1944 (n); *The Sixth Heaven*, 1946 (n); *Eustace and Hilda*, 1947 (n); *The Boat*, 1949 (n); *The Travelling Grave*, 1951 (s); *My Fellow Devils*, 1951 (n); *The Go-Between*, 1953 (n); *The White Wand*, 1954 (s); *A Perfect Woman*, 1955 (n); *The Hireling*, 1957 (n); *Eustace and Hilda* (a trilogy composed of *The Shrimp and the Anemone, The Sixth Heaven,* and *Eustace and Hilda*) 1958 (3n); *Facial Justice*, 1960 (n); *Two for the River*, 1961 (s); *The Brickfield*, 1964 (n)

Peter Bien, *L. P. Hartley*, 1963 and *Adam International Review* XXIX (1961), nos. 294-6

CHRISTOPHER HASSALL
1912-1963

Poems of Two Years, 1935 (p); *Devil's Dyke*, 1936 (p); *Christ's Comet*, 1937 (d); *Penthesperon*, 1938 (p); *Crisis*, 1939 (p); *Ivor Novello, Glamourous Night*, 1939 (lyrics by C.H.); *S.O.S.—Ludlow*, 1940 (p); *The Timeless Quest: Stephen Haggard*, 1946 (b); *Notes on the Verse Drama*, 1948 (c); *The Slow Night, Poems, 1940-1948*, 1949 (p); *Words by Request*, 1952 (misc.); *Out of the Whirlwind*, 1953 (d); *The Player King*, 1953 (d); W. Walton, *Troilus and Cressida* [opera libretto], 1954; *Ivor Novello, King's Rhapsody* (lyrics by C.H.), 1955; *The Red Leaf*, 1957 (p); *Edward Marsh, Patron of the Arts*, 1959 (Am. ed. *Biography of Edward Marsh*) (b); *Bell Harry*, 1963 (p); *Rupert Brooke*, 1964 (b)

JOHN HEATH-STUBBS
1918-

Wounded Thammuz, 1942 (p); *Beauty and the Beast*, 1943 (p); *The Divided Ways*, 1946 (p); *The Charity of the Stars*, 1949 (p); *The Darkling Plain*, 1950 (c); *The Swarming of the Bees*, 1950 (p); *A Charm against the Toothache*, 1954 (p); *Charles Williams*, 1955 (c); *The Triumph of the Muse*, 1958 (p); *Helen in Egypt*, 1959 (d); *The Blue-Fly in his Head*, 1962 (p)

RAYNER HEPPENSTALL
1911-

Patins, 1932 (p); *Middleton Murry: A Study in Excellent Normality*, 1934 (c); *First Poems*, 1935 (p); *Apology for Dancing*, 1936 (e); *Sebastian*, 1937 (p); *The Blaze of Noon*, 1939 (n); *Blind Men's Flowers Are Green*, 1940 (p); *Saturnine*, 1943 (n); *Poems, 1933-45*, 1946 (p); *The Double Image*, 1947 (c); (with Michael Innes) *Three Tales of Hamlet*, 1950 (s); *Léon Bloy*, 1953 (c); *The Lesser Infortune*, 1953 (n); *My Bit of Dylan Thomas*, 1957 (c); *The Greater Infortune*, 1960 (n); *Four Absentees* [Gill, Orwell, Dylan Thomas, Middleton Murry], 1960 (r); *The Fourfold Tradition: Notes on the French and English Literatures*, 1961 (c); *The Woodshed*, 1962 (n); *The Connecting Door*, 1962 (n); *The Intellectual Part*, 1963 (a)

A. P. HERBERT
1890-

Poor Poems and Rotton Rhymes, 1910
(p); *Play Hours with Pegasus,* 1912 (p);
Half-Hours at Helles, 1916 (p); *The
Bomber Gipsy,* 1918 (p); *The Secret
Battle,* 1919 (n); *The House by the
River,* 1920 (n); *The Wherefore and the
Why,* 1921 (p); *Light Articles Only,*
1921 (Am. ed. *Little Rays of Moon-
shine*) (n); *"Tinker, Tailor . . . ,"* 1922
(p); *The Man About Town,* 1923 (e);
Four One-Act Plays, 1923 (Am. ed.
*Double Demon and Other One-Act
Plays*) (4d); *The Old Flame,* 1925 (n);
Laughing Ann, 1925 (p); *She-Shanties,*
1926 (p); *Double Demon: An Absurdity
in One Act,* 1926 (d); (with Nigel Play-
fair) *Riverside Nights: An Entertain-
ment,* 1926 (d); *Plain Jane,* 1927 (p);
Fat King Melon and Princess Caraway,
1927 (d); *The Red Pen,* 1927 (d); *Two
Gentlemen of Soho,* 1927 (d); *Mislead-
ing Cases in the Common Law,* 1927;
The Trials of Topsy, 1928 (n); *Honey-
bubble and Company,* 1928 (n); *Topsy,
M.P.,* 1929 (n); (with A. Davies-Adams)
La Vie Parisienne: A Comic Opera . . . ,
1929 (d); *The Water Gipsies,* 1930 (n);
Ballads for Broadbrows, 1930 (p);
Wisdom for the Wise, 1930 (p); *More
Misleading Cases,* 1930; *A Book of
Ballads, Being the Collected Light
Verse of A. P. Herbert,* 1931 (Am.
ed. *Ballads for Broadbrows and Others*)
(p); *Derby Day: A Comic Opera,* 1931
(d); *Tantivy Towers: A Light Opera,*
1931 (d); *Helen: A Comic Opera,* adap-
tation of *La Belle Hélène* by Henri
Meilhac and Ludovic Halévy, 1932 (d);
No Boats on the River, 1932 (e); *A. P.
Herbert,* 1933 (anthol. of humor); *Still
More Misleading Cases,* 1933; *Holy
Deadlock,* 1934 (n); *Mr. Pewter,* 1934
(e); *The Old Flame,* 1935 (n); *Uncommon Law* (rev. enlgd. 1935, 1952; ed.
of coll. *Misleading Cases*) 1935 (e);
What a Word!, 1935 (e); *Mild and
Bitter,* 1936 (n); *The Secret Battle,* 1936
(n); *Sip! Swallow!,* 1937 (e); *The Ayes
Have It: The Story of the Marriage Bill,*
1937 (e); *General Cargo,* 1939 (e);
Siren Song, 1940 (e); *Let Us Be Gay,*
1941, (p); *Let Us Be Glum,* 1941 (p);
Well, Anyhow . . . , or, Little Talks,
1942 (e); *Bring Back the Bells,* 1943
(p); *A.T.1,* 1944 (p); *A Better Sky, or,*

Name This Star, 1944 (p); *"Less
Nonsense!",* 1944 (p); *Light the Lights,*
1945 (p); *Big Ben,* 1946 (d); *Point of
Parliament,* 1946 (e); *Leave My Old
Morale Alone,* (e); *Mr. Gay's London,*
1948 (e); *Bless the Bride,* 1948 (d); *The
Topsy Omnibus (The Trials of Topsy,
Topsy M.P., Topsy Turvey),* 1949 (n);
The English Laugh, 1950 (e); *Indepen-
dent Member* (announced with title
University Member), 1950 (a); *Number
Nine, or, The Mind Sweepers,* 1951 (n);
(with Reginald Arkell) *Come to the
Ball* (adaptation of *Die Fledermaus*),
1951 (d); *Codd's Last Case,* 1952 (e);
Full Enjoyment and Other Verses, 1952
(p); *Pool's Pilot, or, Why Not You?,*
1953 (e); *Why Waterloo?,* 1953 (n); *The
Right to Marry,* (e); *No Fine on
Fun,* 1957 (e); *Made for Man,* 1958 (n);
Look Back and Laugh, 1960 (e); *Anything But Action?,* 1960 (e); (with
others) *Radical Reaction,* ed. Ralph
Harris, 1961 (e); *The Secret Battle,* 1963
(e)

Gilbert H. Fabes, *The First Editions
of A. E. Coppard, A. P. Herbert, and
Charles Morgan,* 1933

MAURICE HEWLETT
1861-1923

The Wreath, 1894-1914 (misc.); *A
Masque of Dead Florentines,* 1895 (p);
Earthwork Out of Tuscany, 1895 (e,tr);
Songs and Meditations, 1896 (p); *The
Forest Lovers,* 1898 (n); *Pan and the
Young Shepherd,* 1898 (d); *The Judge-
ment of Borso,* 1899 (s); *Little Novels of
Italy,* 1899 (s); *Madonna of the Peach-
Tree,* 1899 (s); *The Paduan Pastoral,*
1899 (s); *The Life and Death of Richard
Yea-and-Nay,* 1900 (n); *Saint Ger-
vase of Plessy,* 1900 (e); *New Canterbury
Tales,* 1901 (repr. 1921) (s); *The Queen's
Quair, or, The Six Years' Tragedy,*
1904 (n); *The Road in Tuscany,* 1904
(t); *The Fool Errant,* 1905 (n); *Fond
Adventures, Tales of the Youth of the
World,* 1905 (s); *The Stooping Lady,*
1907 (n); *Halfway House* (trilogy, Vol.
I); 1908 (n); *The Spanish Jade,* 1908
(n); *Open Country* (trilogy, Vol. II),
1909 (n); *Artemision, Idylls and Songs,*
1909 (p); *The Ruinous Face,* 1909 (n);
Rest Harrow, (trilogy, Vol. III), 1910
(n); *Brazenhead the Great,* 1911 (n);

The Song of Renny, 1911 (n); The Birth of Roland, 1911 (s); The Agonists, A Trilogy of God and Man (Minos, King of Crete; Ariadne in Naxos; The Death of Hippolytus), 1911 (d); Mrs. Lancelot, 1912 (n); Bendish, A Study in Prodigality, 1913 (n); Helen Redeemed and Other Poems, 1913 (p); Lore of Proserpine, 1913, (n); A Ballad of "The Gloster" and "The Goeben", 1914 (p); Singsongs of the War, 1914 (p); The Little Illiad, 1915 (n); A Lover's Tale, 1915 (n); Frey and His Wife, 1916 (n); Love and Lucy, 1916 (n); Gai Saber, Tales and Songs, 1916 (p); The Song of the Plow, Being the English Chronicle, 1916 (p); Thorgils of Treadholt, 1917 (n); The Loving History of Peridore and Paravail, 1917 (p); Gudrid the Fair, 1918 (n); The Village Wife's Lament, 1918 (p); The Outlaw, 1919 (n); The Light Heart, 1920 (n); Mainwaring, 1920 (n); Flowers in the Grass, 1920 (p); In a Green Shade, A Country Commentary, 1920 (e); Wiltshire Essays, 1921 (e); Extemporary Essays, 1922 (e); Last Essays of Maurice Hewlett, 1924 (e); The Letters of Maurice Hewlett, to which is Added a Diary in Greece, ed. Lawrence Binyon, 1926; Maurice Hewlett [Selected Poems], 1926 (p)

Percy H. Muir, A Bibliography of the First Editions of Books by Maurice Henry Hewlett, 1927

ROBERT HICHENS
1864-1950

The Coastguard's Secret, 1886 (n); The Green Carnation, 1894 (n); An Imaginative Man, 1895 (n); The Folly of Eustace, 1896 (s); Flames, 1897 (n); Byeways, 1897 (s); The Londoners, 1898 (n); (with Wilson Barrett) The Daughters of Babylon, 1899 (n); The Slave, 1899 (n); Tongues of Conscience, 1900 (n); The Prophet of Berkeley Square, 1901 (s); Felix, 1902 (n); The Woman With the Fan, 1904 (n); The Garden of Allah, 1904 (n); The Black Spaniel, 1905 (s); The Call of the Blood, 1906 (n); Egypt and Its Monuments, 1908 (repr. as The Spell of Egypt, 1910) (t); A Spirit in Prison, 1908 (n); Barbary Sheep, 1909 (n); Bella Donna, 1909 (n); The Knock on the Door, 1909 (n); The Holy Land, 1910 (t); The Dweller on

the Threshold, 1911 (n); The Fruitful Vine, 1911 (n); The Near East, 1913 (t); The Way of Ambition, 1913 (n); In the Wilderness, 1917 (n); Mrs. Marsden, 1919 (n); Snake-Bite, 1919 (s); The Spirit of the Time, 1921 (n); December Love, 1922 (n)

JAMES HILTON
1900-1954

Catherine Herself, 1920 (n); Storm Passage, 1922 (n); The Passionate Year, 1923 (n); The Dawn of Reckoning, 1925 (n); The Meadows of the Moon, 1926 (n); Terry, 1927 (n); The Silver Flame, 1928 (n); And Now Goodbye, 1931 (n); (Glen Trevor, pseud.) Murder at School, 1931 (Am. ed. James Hilton, Was It Murder?) (n); Contango, 1932 (n); Knight Without Armour, 1933 (n); Lost Horizon, 1933 (n); Goodbye, Mr. Chips, 1934 (n); We Are Not Alone, 1937 (n); (with B. Burnham), dramatization of Goodbye, Mr. Chips, 1938; To You, Mr. Chips, [one chapt. of autobiog. included], 1938 (s,a); Random Harvest, 1941 (n); The Story of Dr. Wassell, 1944 (b); So Well Remembered, 1947 (n); Nothing So Strange, 1948 (n); Morning Journey, 1951 (n); Time and Time Again, 1953 (n); The Duke of Edinburgh, 1954 (b)

RALPH HODGSON
1871-1962

The Last Blackbird, 1907 (p); The Bull, 1913 (p); Eve, 1913 (p); The Mystery, 1913 (repr. 1956) (p); The Song of Honour, 1913 (p); Poems, 1917 (p); Hymn to Moloch, 1921 (p); Silver Wedding, 1941 (p); The Muse and The Mastiff, Part 1, 1942 (p); Skylark, 1959 (p); Collected Poems, 1961; In addition, Hodgson published seven undated broadsides: The Beggar, The Bird Catcher, February, The Gypsy Girl, The Late Last Rook, Playmates, and A Song.

JOHN HOLLOWAY
1920-

Language and Intelligence, 1951 (e); Victorian Sage: Studies in Argument, 1953 (c); Poems, 1954 (p); The Minute and Longer Poems, 1956 (p); Charted

Mirror: Literary and Critical Essays, 1960 (c); *The Fugue, and Shorter Pieces,* 1960 (p); *The Story of the Night, Studies in Shakespeare's Major Tragedies,* 1961 (c); *The Landfallers,* 1962 (p); *The Colours of Clarity,* 1964 (c); *The Lion Hunt: A Pursuit of Poetry and Reality,* 1964 (e)

WINIFRED HOLTBY
1898-1935

Anderby Wold, 1923 (n); *The Crowded Street,* 1924 (n); *Eutychus,* 1928 (e); *The Land of Green Ginger,* 1928 (n); *A New Voter's Guide to Party Programmes: Political Dialogues,* 1929 (e); *Poor Caroline,* 1931 (n); *Virginia Woolf,* 1932 (c); *The Astonishing Island,* 1933 (n); *Mandoa, Mandoa!,* 1933 (n); *Women and a Changing Civilisation,* 1934 (e); *Truth is Not Sober,* 1934 (s); *The Frozen Earth,* 1935 (p); *South Riding,* 1936 (n); *Letters to a Friend,* ed. Alice Holtby and Jean McWilliam, 1937

Geoffrey H. Taylor, *Winifred Holtby: A Bibliography Together with Some Letters,* 1955

ANTHONY HOPE
1863-1933

A Man of Mark, 1890 (n); *Father Strafford,* 1891 (n); *Mr. Witt's Widow,* 1892 (n); *Sport Royal,* 1893 (s); *Half a Hero,* 1893 (n); *A Change of Air,* 1893 (n); *The God in the Car,* 1894 (n); *Dolly Dialogues,* 1894 (s); *The Prisoner of Zenda,* 1894 (n); *The Indiscretion of the Duchess,* 1894 (n); *The Chronicles of Count Antonio,* 1895 (n); *The Heart of Princess Osra,* 1896 (n); *Comedies of Courtship,* 1896 (s); *Phroso,* 1897 (n); *Rupert of Hentzau,* 1898 (n); *The King's Mirror,* 1899 (n); *Quisanté,* 1900 (n); *Tristram of Blent,* 1901 (n); *The Intrusions of Peggy,* 1902 (n); *Double Harness,* 1903 (n); *Servant of the Public,* 1905 (n); *Sophy of Kravonia,* 1906 (n); *The Duke's Allotment,* 1906 (n); *Tales of Two People,* 1907 (s); *The Great Miss Driver,* 1908 (n); *Simon Dale,* 1908 (n); *Second String,* 1910 (n); *Mrs. Maxon Protests,* 1911 (n); *Young Man's Year,* 1915 (n); *Captain Dieppe,* 1918 (n); *Beaumaroy Home from the Wars,* 1919 (n); *Lucinda,* 1920 (n); *Pilkerton's Peerage,* 1921 (d); *The Adventure of Lady Ursula,* 1921 (d); *Little Tiger,* 1925

(n); *Memories and Notes,* 1927 (r); *The Philosopher in the Apple Orchard,* 1936 (d)

GERARD MANLEY HOPKINS
1844-1889

The Poems of Gerard Manley Hopkins, ed. Robert Bridges, 1918 (enlgd. 1944, enlgd. ed. W. H. Gardner, 1948); *The Letters of Gerard Manley Hopkins to Robert Bridges,* ed. Claude C. Abbott, 1935 (Vol. II, *The Correspondence of Gerard Manley Hopkins and Richard Watson Dixon,* rev. 1955); *Further Letters,* ed. Claude C. Abbott, 1938 (rev. enlgd. 1956); *The Notebooks and Papers,* ed. Humphry House, 1937 (rev., including next item, as *Journals and Papers,* completed Graham Storey, 1959); *The Sermons and Devotional Writings,* ed. Christopher Devlin, 1959

W. H. Gardner, *Gerard Manley Hopkins,* 2 vols., 1948

A. E. HOUSMAN
1859-1936

A Shropshire Lad, 1896 (p); *Last Poems,* 1922 (p); *The Name and Nature of Poetry,* 1933 (c); *More Poems,* ed. Lawrence Housman, 1936 (p); *Collected Poems,* 1939, 1953, 1956; *Manuscript Poems,* ed. Tom B. Haber, 1955; *Thirty Housman Letters to Witter Bynner,* 1957; *Complete Poems,* 1960; *Selected Prose,* ed. John Carter, 1961 (e)

John Carter and John Sparrow, *Housman: an Annotated Hand-List,* 1952; George L. Watson, *A. E. Housman, a Divided Life,* 1957

LAURENCE HOUSMAN
1865-1959

All-Fellows, Seven Legends of Lower Redemption with Insets in Verse, 1896 (repr. 1923) (s); *Green Arras,* 1896 (p); *Gods and Their Makers,* 1897 (repr. 1920) (s); *Spikenard,* 1898 (p); *The Little Land, with Songs from its Four Rivers,* 1899 (p); *Rue,* 1899 (p); [Anon.] *An Englishwoman's Love-Letters,* 1900 (n); [Anon.] *A Modern Antaeus,* 1901 (n); [Anon.] *The Missing Answers to "An Englishwoman's Love-Letters",* 1901; *Of Aucassin and Nicolette* (with *Amabel and Amoris*), 1902 (repr. 1925) (tr); *Bethlehem, a Nativity Play,* and *The Pageant of Our Lady,* 1902

(*Bethlehem*, repr. 1955) (d,p); *Sabrina Warham*, 1904 (n); *The Blue Moon*, 1904 (s); *The Cloak of Friendship*, 1905 (s); (with Harley Granville Barker) *Prunella*, 1906 (repr. 1930) (d); *Mendicant Rhymes*, 1906 (p); *The Vicar of Wakefield* (opera based on Oliver Goldsmith's novel), 1906 (lyrics); *A Chinese Lantern*, 1908 (d); *Selected Poems*, 1908 (p); *Alice in Ganderland*, 1911 (d); Aristophanes, *Lysistrata*, 1911 (tr); *Pains and Penalties, the Defence of Queen Caroline*, 1911 (d); *John of Jingalo*, 1912 (n); *The Royal Runaway and Jingalo in Revolution* (seq. to *John of Jingalo*), 1914 (n); *As Good as Gold*, 1916 (d); *Bird in Hand*, 1916 (d); *A Likely Story*, 1916 (d); *The Lord of the Harvest*, 1916 (d); *Nazareth*, 1916 (d); *The Return of Alcestis*, 1916 (d); *The Snow Man*, 1916 (d); *The Sheepfold*, 1918 (n); *The Heart of Peace*, 1918 (p); *Ploughshare and Pruninghook*, 1919 (lectures); *The Wheel*, 1919 (pd); *Gods and Their Makers*, 1920 (s); *Angels and Ministers*, 1921 (3d); *The Death of Orpheus*, 1921 (pd); *Possession, a Peep-Show in Paradise*, 1921 (d); *Selected Poems*, 1921 (p); *A Doorway in Fairyland* (sel. child's stories), also pub. as *Moonshine and Clover*, 1922; *Dethronements, Imaginary Portraits of Political Characters*, 1922 (3d); *False Premises*, 1922 (5d); *Little Plays of St. Francis*, 1922 (18d); *Followers of St. Francis*, 1923 (4d); *Echo de Paris, a Study from Life* [Oscar Wilde etc.], 1923 (d); *All-Fellows and the Cloak of Friendship*, 1923 (s); *Trimblerigg*, 1924 (n); *Odd Pairs*, 1925 (s); *The Death of Socrates*, 1925 (d); *Ironical Tales*, 1926 (s); *The Comments of Juniper*, 1926 (6d); *Uncle Tom Pudd*, 1927 (n); *The "Little Plays" Handbook*, 1927 (c); *The Life of H.R.H. the Duke of Flamborough, by Benjamin Bunny*, 1928 (n); *The Love Concealed*, 1928 (p); *Ways and Means*, 1928 (5d); *Cornered Poets*, 1929 (7d); *Turn Again Tales*, 1930 (s); *The New Hangman*, 1930 (d); *Palace Plays*, 1930 (repr. 1951) (d); *Little Plays of St. Francis, Second Series*, 1931 (18d); *The Queen's Progress, Palace Plays, Second Series*, 1932 (9d); *Ye Fearful Saints!*, 1932 (9d); *Nunc Dimittis, An Epilogue to "Little Plays of St. Francis"*, 1933 (d); *Victoria and Albert, Palace Plays, Third Series*, 1933 (13d); *Four Plays of St. Clare*, 1934 (4d); *Victoria Regina, a Dramatic Biography* [Plays from *Angels and Ministers, Palace Plays, The Queen's Progress,* and *Victoria and Albert*], 1934 (d); *Little Plays of St. Francis, Complete Series in Three Volumes*, 1935 (45d); *The Golden Sovereign* (coll. plays), 1937 (d); *The Unexpected Years*, 1937 (a); *Palace Scenes: More Plays of Queen Victoria*, 1937 (d); *Collected Poems*, 1937; *What Next*, 1937 (s); *A.E.H.*, 1938 (Am. ed. *My Brother, A. E. Housman*) (b); *Gracious Majesty*, 1941 (12d); *The Preparation of Peace*, 1941 (e); *Palestine Plays*, 1942 (4d); *Samuel, the King-Maker*, 1944 (d); *Back Words and Fore Words*, 1945 (misc.); *Strange Ends and Discoveries*, 1948 (s); *Happy and Glorious, Forty-Seven Plays Selected from Victoria Regina, The Golden Sovereign,* and *Gracious Majesty*, 1949 (47d); *The Family Honour*, 1950 (d); *Old Testament Plays*, 1950 (5d); *The Kind and the Foolish*, 1952 (s)

ELIZABETH JANE HOWARD
1923-

The Beautiful Visit, 1950 (n); (with Robert Aickman) *We Are For the Dark*, 1951 (s); *The Long View*, 1956 (n); (with Arthur Helps) *Bettina* [Bettina (Brentano) von Arnim], 1957 (b); *The Sea Change*, 1959 (n)

STEPHEN HUDSON
1868-1944

War-Time Silhouettes, 1916 (s); *Richard Kurt*, 1919 (n); *Elinor Colhouse*, 1921 (n); *Prince Hempseed*, 1923 (n); *Tony*, 1924 (n); *Richard, Myrtle and I*, 1926 (n); *A True Story*, 1930 (n); *Celeste*, 1930 (s); *The Other Side*, 1937 (n)

Richard, Myrtle and I (ed. Violet Schiff, with a biographical note and critical essay by Theophilus E. M. Boll), 1962; *See also* John Gawsworth, *Ten Contemporaries*, 1932

W. H. HUDSON
1841-1922

The Purple Land That England Lost, 1885 (n); *A Crystal Age*, 1887 (n); *Osprey, or, Egrets and Aigrettes*, 1891 (e); *The Naturalist in La Plata*, 1892 (e); (pseud. Henry Harford) *Fan*, 1892 (n); *Birds in a Village*, 1893 (e); *Bird-Catching*, 1893 (e); *Feathered Women*, 1893 (e); *Idle Days in Patagonia*, 1893 (tr); *Lost British Birds*, 1894 (e); *Letter to Clergymen, Ministers and Others*, 1895 (e); *British Birds*, 1895 (e); *Pipits*, 1897 (e); *The Trade in Birds' Feathers*, 1898 (e); *Birds in London*, 1898 (e); *Nature in Downland*, 1900 (e); *Birds and Man*, 1901 (e); *El Ombú*, 1902 (repr. 1909 as *South American Sketches*; Am. ed. *Tales of the Pampas*) (s); *Hampshire Days*, 1903 (t); *A Linnet for Sixpence!*, 1904 (e); *Green Mansions. A Romance of the Tropical Forest*, 1904 (n); *A Little Boy Lost*, 1905 (n); *The Land's End*, 1908 (t); *Afoot in England*, 1909 (t); *A Shepherd's Life: Impressions of the South Wiltshire Downs*, 1910 (t); *A Thrush That Never Lived*, 1911 (e); *Adventures Among Birds*, 1913 (e); *On Liberating Caged Birds*, 1914 (e); *Roff and a Linnet, Chain and Cage*, 1918 (e); *Far Away and Long Ago*, 1918 (a); *Birds in Town and Village* (rev. ed. *Birds in A Village*), 1919 (e); *The Book of a Naturalist*, 1919 (e); *Birds of La Plata*, 1920 (e); *Dead Man's Plack and An Old Thorn*, 1920 (s); *A Tired Traveller*, 1921 (repr. from *Adventures Among the Birds*) (e); *A Traveller in Little Things*, 1921 (t); *Seagulls in London*, 1922 (e); *A Hind in Richmond Park*, 1922 (e); *Ralph Herne*, 1923 (n); *Rare, Vanishing and Lost British Birds* (compiled from notes by Hudson by Linda Gardiner), 1923 (enlgd. ed. of *Lost British Birds*) (e); *153 Letters from W. H. Hudson*, ed. Edward Garnett, 1923 (Am. ed. *Letters from W. H. Hudson 1901-1922*; also pub. as *Letters from W. H. Hudson to Edward Garnett*, 1925); *Men, Books, and Birds*, 1925 (e); *Mary's Little Lamb*, 1929 (e); *W. H. Hudson's Letters to R. B. Cunninghame Graham*, 1941; *Letters on the Ornithology of Buenos Ayres*, 1951

George F. Wilson, *A Bibliography of the Writings of W. H. Hudson*, 1922

RICHARD HUGHES
1901-

Gipsy-Night, 1922 (p); *The Sisters' Tragedy*, 1922 (d); *The Sisters' Tragedy and Three Other Plays*, 1924 (Am. ed. *A Rabbit and A Leg, Collected Plays*) (d); *Confessio Juvenis, Collected Poems*, 1926; *A Moment of Time*, 1926 (s); *The Innocent Voyage*, 1929 (Am. ed. *A High Wind in Jamaica*) (n); *The Spider's Palace*, 1931 (s); *Richard Hughes, An Omnibus* (with an autobiographical introduction), 1931; *In Hazard*, 1938 (n); *The Fox in the Attic*, 1961 (Vol. I of *The Human Predicament*) (n)

TED HUGHES
1930-

The Hawk in the Rain, 1957 (p); *Lupercal*, 1960 (p); *Meet My Folks!*, 1961 (s); (with Thom Gunn) *Selected Poems*, 1962; *The Earth-Owl*, 1963 (s)

T. E. HULME
1883-1917

The Complete Poetical Works of Hulme, appended to Ezra Pound, *Ripostes*, 1912 (repr. in *Speculations*, 1924); Henri Bergson, *An Introduction to Metaphysics*, 1913 (tr); Georges Sorel, *Réflections sur la Violence*, 1916 (tr); *Speculations*, ed. Herbert Read, 1924 (repr. 1960) (e); *Notes on Language and Style*, ed. Herbert Read, 1929 (e)

Alun Richard Jones, *The Life and Opinions of T. E. Hulme*, 1960

R. C. HUTCHINSON
1907-

Thou Hast a Devil, 1930 (n); *The Answering Glory*, 1932 (n); *The Unforgotten Prisoner* 1933 (n); *One Light Burning*, 1935 (n); *Shining Scabbard*, 1936 (n); *Testament*, 1938 (n); *The Fire and the Wood*, 1940 (n); *Interim*, 1945 (r); *Elephant and Castle*, 1949 (n); *Recollection of a Journey*, 1949 (Am. ed. *Journey with Strangers*) (n); *The Stepmother*, 1955 (n); *March the Ninth*, 1957 (n); *Image of My Father*, 1961 (Am. ed. *The Inheritor*) (n); *A Child Possessed*, 1964 (n)

ALDOUS HUXLEY
1894-1963

The Burning Wheel, 1916, (p); *The Defeat of Youth*, 1918 (p); *Leda*, 1920 (p); *Limbo*, 1920 (s); (with T. S. Eliot,

F. S. Flint) *Chapbook*, 1920 (c); *Crome Yellow*, 1921 (n); *Mortal Coils*, 1922 (s); *Antic Hay*, 1923 (n); *On the Margin: Notes and Essays*, 1923 (e); *Little Mexican*, 1924 (Am. ed. *Young Archimedes*) (s); *Those Barren Leaves*, 1925 (n); *Selected Poems*, 1925 (p); *Along the Road: Notes and Essays of a Tourist*, 1925 (t); *Two or Three Graces*, 1926 (s); *Essays, New and Old*, 1926 (e); *Jesting Pilate*, 1926 (e); *Proper Studies*, 1927 (e); *Point Counter Point*, 1928 (n); *Arabia Infelix*, 1929 (p); *Holy Face*, 1929 (e); *Do What You Will*, 1929 (e); *Brief Candles*, 1930 (one Am. ed. *After the Fireworks*) (s); *Vulgarity in Literature: Disgressions from a Theme*, 1930 (e); *The Cicadas*, 1931 (p); *Music at Night*, 1931 (e); *The World of Light*, 1931 (d); *Brave New World*, 1932 (n); *T. H. Huxley as a Man of Letters*, 1932 (e); *Texts and Pretexts: An Anthology with Commentaries*, 1932 (e); *Rotunda: A Selection from the Works of Aldous Huxley*, 1932; *Retrospect: An Omnibus of Aldous Huxley's Books*, 1933; *Beyond the Mexique Bay*, 1934 (s); *Eyeless in Gaza*, 1936 (n); *The Olive Tree*, 1936 (e); *What Are You Going to do About It? The Case for Constructive Peace*, 1936 (e); *Stories, Essays and Poems*, 1937; *Ends and Means*, 1937 (e); *The Gioconda Smile*, 1938 (s); *After Many a Summer*, 1939 (Am. ed. *After Many a Summer Dies the Swan*), (n); *Grey Eminence: A Study in Religion and Politics*, 1941 (e); *The Art of Seeing*, 1942 (e); *Time Must Have a Stop*, 1944 (n); *The Perennial Philosophy*, 1945 (e); *Verses and A Comedy*, 1946 (p,d); *Science, Liberty, and Peace*, 1946 (e); *The World of Aldous Huxley: An Omnibus of his Fiction and Non-Fiction over Three Decades*, ed. Charles Rolo, 1947; *The Gioconda Smile*, 1948 (d); *Ape and Essence*, 1948 (e); *Themes and Variations*, 1950 (e); *The Devils of Loudon*, 1952 (e); (with Stuart Gilbert) *Joyce, The Artificer; Two Studies of Joyce's Method*, 1952 (c); *The Doors of Perception*, 1954 (e); *The Genius and the Goddess*, 1955 (n); *Adonis and the Alphabet*, 1956 (Am. ed. *Tomorrow and Tomorrow and Tomorrow*) (e); *Heaven and Hell*, 1956 (e); *Collected Short Stories*, 1957; *Brave New World Revisited*, 1958 (n); *Collected Essays*, 1959; *On Art and Artists*, 1960 (e); *Island*, 1962 (n); *Literature and Science*, 1963 (e)

Claire John Eschelbach and Joyce Lee Shober, *Aldous Huxley: A Bibliography 1916-1959*, 1961

CHRISTOPHER ISHERWOOD 1904-

All the Conspirators, 1928 (n); *Intimate Journals of Baudelaire*, 1930 (tr); *The Memorial*, 1932 (n); *Mr. Norris Changes Trains* (Am. ed. *The Last of Mr. Norris*), 1935 (n); (with W. H. Auden) *The Dog Beneath the Skin*, 1935 (d); (with W. H. Auden) *The Ascent of F6*, 1936 (d); (with Desmond I. Vesey) *A Penny for the Poor*, by Berthold Brecht, 1937 (Am. ed. *The Threepenny Novel*, 1958) (tr); *Sally Bowles*, 1937 (n); *Lions and Shadows*, 1938 (a); (with W. H. Auden) *On the Frontier*, 1938 (d); (with W. H. Auden) *Journey to a War*, 1939 (t); *Goodbye to Berlin*, 1939 (n); (with Swami Prabhavananda) *Bhagavad-Gita, Song of God*, 1944 (tr); *Prater Violet*, 1945 (n); *The Memorial*, 1946 (n); (with Swami Prabhavananda) Shankara's *The Crest-Jewel of Discrimination*, 1946 (tr); *The Condor and the Cows* [S. America], 1949 (t); *Vedanta for Modern Man*, 1951 (e); *The World in the Evening*, 1952 (n); *Down There on a Visit*, 1962 (n); *A Single Man*, 1964 (n)

W. W. JACOBS 1863-1943

Many Cargoes, 1896 (repr. 1936) (s); *The Skipper's Wooing and The Brown Man's Servant*, 1897 (s); *Sea Urchins*, 1898 (s); *A Master of Craft*, 1900 (n); *Light Freights*, 1901 (s); *At Sunwich Port*, 1902 (s); *The Lady of the Barge*, 1902 (repr. 1943) (s); *Odd Craft*, 1903 (repr. 1936) (s); *Dialstone Lane*, 1904 (n); *Captains All*, 1905 (s); *Short Cruises*, 1907 (s); (with Herbert C. Sargent) *The Boatswain's Mate*, 1907 (d); *Salthaven*, 1908 (n); (with H. C. Sargent) *The Changeling*, 1908 (d); (with Charles Rock) *The Ghost of Jerry Bundler*, 1908 (d); (with Charles Rock) *The Grey Parrot*, 1908 (d); *Sailors' Knots*, 1909 (s); (with Horace Mills) *Admiral Peters*, 1909 (d); (with Louis

N. Parker) *Beauty and the Barge,* 1910 (d); (with Louis N. Parker) *The Monkey's Paw,* 1910 (d); *Ship's Company,* 1911 (s); (with H. C. Sargent) *In the Library,* 1913 (d); (with P. E. Hubbard) *A Love Passage,* 1913 (d); *Night Watches,* 1914 (s); *The Castaways,* 1916 (n); *Deep Waters,* 1919 (n); *Keeping Up Appearances,* 1919 (d); (with Herbert C. Sargent) *The Castaway,* 1924 (d); *Establishing Relations,* 1925 (d); *Sea Whispers,* 1926 (n); *The Warming Pan,* 1929 (d); *A Distant Relative,* 1930 (d); *Master Mariners,* 1930 (d); *Matrimonial Openings,* 1931 (d); *Snug Harbour, Collected Stories,* 1931 (s); *Dixon's Return,* 1932 (d); *The Nightwatchman and Other Longshoremen: 57 Stories,* 1932 (s); *Cruises and Cargoes: Omnibus,* 1934 (s)

HENRY JAMES
1843-1916

Note: The numerous recent reprints not noted.

A Passionate Pilgrim, 1875 (s); *Transatlantic Sketches,* 1875 (t); *Roderick Hudson,* 1876 (n); *The American,* 1877 (n); *French Poets and Novelists,* 1878 (c); *The Europeans,* 1878 (n); *Daisy Miller,* 1879 (n); *Hawthorne,* 1879 (c); *Washington Square,* 1880 (n); *The Portrait of a Lady,* 1881 (n); *Portraits of Places,* 1883 (t); *The Bostonians,* 1886 (n); *The Princess Casamassima,* 1886 (n); *Partial Portraits,* 1888 (c); *The Reverberator,* 1888 (n); *The Tragic Muse,* 1890 (n); *The Other House,* 1896 (n); *The Spoils of Poynton,* 1897 (n); *What Maisie Knew,* 1897 (n); *In the Cage,* 1898 (n); *The Turn of the Screw,* 1898 (n); *The Awkward Age,* 1899 (n); *The Sacred Fount,* 1901 (n); *The Wings of the Dove,* 1902 (n); *The Ambassadors,* 1903 (n); *William Wetmore Story and his Friends,* 1903 (n); *The Golden Bowl,* 1904 (n); *The American Scene,* 1907 (t); *The Novels and Tales,* "New York Edition," 26 vols., 1907-1917; *Views and Reviews,* 1908 (c); *The Outcry,* 1911 (n); *A Small Boy and Others,* 1913 (a); *Notes of a Son and Brother,* 1914 (a); *Notes on Novelists,* 1914 (c); *The Ivory Tower,* 1917 (n); *The Sense of the Past,* 1917 (n); *The Middle Years,* 1917 (a); *The*

Letters, ed. Percy Lubbock, 2 vols., 1920; *The Art of the Novel,* ed. Richard P. Blackmur, 1934 (c); *The Notebooks,* ed. F. O. Mathiessen and Kenneth B. Murdock, 1947; *The Scenic Art,* ed. Allan Wade, 1948 (c); *The Complete Plays,* ed. Leon Edel, 1949; *The Painter's Eye: Notes and Essays on the Pictorial Arts,* sel. and ed. John L. Sweeney, 1956 (c); *Henry James: An Autobiography (A Small Boy, Notes of a Son and Brother, The Middle Years),* ed. Frederick W. Dupee, 1956; *The Complete Tales,* ed. Leon Edel, 1962ff (6 vols. to 1963)

Leon Edel and Dan H. Laurence, *A Bibliography of Henry James,* 1957 (rev. 1961)

STORM JAMESON
1897-

The Pot Boils, 1919 (n); *The Happy Highways,* 1920 (n); *Modern Drama in Europe,* 1920 (c); *The Clash,* 1922 (n); *Lady Susan and Life, An Indiscretion,* 1923 (n); *The Pitiful Wife,* 1923 (n); *Three Kingdoms,* 1926 (n); *The Lovely Ship* (Part I of trilogy), 1927 (n); *Farewell to Youth,* 1928 (n); *Full Circle,* 1928 (d); *The Georgian Novel and Mr. Robinson,* 1929 (c); *The Voyage Home* (Part II of trilogy), 1930 (n); *The Decline of Merry England,* 1930 (e); *A Richer Dust* (Part III of trilogy), 1931 (n); *The Single Heart,* 1932 (n); *That Was Yesterday,* 1932 (n); *The Triumph of Time,* Trilogy, 1932 (3n); *A Day Off,* 1933 (n); *Women Against Men,* 1933 (3n); *No Time Like the Present,* 1933 (a); *Company Parade,* 1934 (n); *Love in Winter,* 1935 (n); *The Soul of Man in the Age of Leisure,* 1935 (e); *In the Second Year,* 1936 (n); *None Turn Back,* 1936 (n); *Delicate Monster,* 1937 (n); *The Moon Is Making,* 1937 (n); *The Novel in Contemporary Life,* 1938 (c); *Civil Journey,* 1939 (e); *Farewell, Night; Welcome, Day* (Am. ed. *Captain's Wife*), 1939 (n); *Here Comes A Candle,* 1939 (n); *Cousin Honore,* 1940 (n); *Europe To Let,* 1940 (n); *The Fort,* 1941 (n); *The End of this War,* 1941 (e); *Then We Shall Hear Singing,* 1942 (n); *Cloudless May,* 1943 (n); *The Journal of Mary Hervey Russell,* 1945 (n); *The Other Side,* 1946 (n); *Before the Crossing*, 1947 (n); *The Black Laurel*, 1948 (n); *The Moment of Truth*, 1949 (n); *The Writer's Situation*, 1950 (e); (with others) *Hidden Streams: Essays on Writing*, 1951 (e); *The Green Man*, 1952 (n); *The Hidden River*, 1955 (n); *Intruder*, 1956 (n); *A Cup of Tea for Mr. Thorgill*, 1957 (n); *A Ulysses Too Many* (Am. ed. *One Ulysses Too Many*), 1958 (n); *A Day Off*, 1959 (s); *Last Score, or, The Private Life of Sir Richard Ormston*, 1961 (n); *Morley Roberts: The Last Eminent Victorian*, 1961 (b); *The Road From the Monument*, 1962 (n); *A Month Soon Goes*, 1962 (n); *The Aristide Case*, 1964 (n)

ELIZABETH JENNINGS
1926-

A Way of Looking, 1955 (p); *A Sense of the World*, 1958 (p); *Let's Have Some Poetry*, 1960 (e); *Every Changing Hope*, 1961 (c); *Poetry Today*, 1961 (c); *Song for a Birth or a Death*, 1961 (p); *The Sonnets of Michel Angelo Buonarroti*, 1961 (tr); *Recoveries*, 1964 (p)

JEROME K. JEROME
1859-1927

On the Stage—and Off, 1885 (r); *The Idle Thoughts of an Idle Fellow*, 1886 (repr. 1928, 1938) (e); *Barbara*, 1886 (d); *Sunset* (founded on second Tennyson poem of "The Sisters"), 1888 (d); *Stage-Land*, 1889 (reissued as *Twelfth Thousand*) (e); *Three Men in a Boat*, 1889 (repr. 1929 etc.) (n); *Diary of a Pilgrimage*, 1891 (e); *Told After Supper*, 1891 (s); *John Ingerfield*, 1894 (s); (with Eden Phillpotts) *The Prude's Progress*, 1895 (d); *Sketches in Lavender, Blue and Green*, 1897 (s); *The Second Thoughts of an Idle Fellow*, 1898 (e); *Three Men on the Bummel*, 1900 (repr. 1929) (n); *The Observations of Henry*, 1901 (s); *"Miss Hobbs"*, 1902 (d); *Paul Kelver*, 1902 (n); *Tea-Table Talk*, 1903 (c); *American Wives and Others*, 1904 (e,s); *Tommy and Co.*, 1904 (s); *Idle Ideas*, 1905 (e); *The Passing of the Third Floor Back*, 1907 (s); *The Angel and the Author—and Others*, 1908 (e,s); *Fanny and the Servant Problem*, 1909 (d); *They and I*, 1909 (n); *The Passing of the Third Floor Back*, 1910 (d); *The Master*

of Mrs. Chilvers, 1911 (d); *Robina in Search of a Husband*, 1914 (d); *Malvina of Brittany*, 1916 (n); *All Roads Lead to Calvary*, 1919 (n); *Woodbarrow Farm*, 1921 (d); *Anthony John: a Biography*, 1923 (n); *The Celebrity*, 1926 (d); *My Life and Times*, 1926 (a); *The Soul of Nicholas Snyders*, 1927 (d)

Alfred Moss, *Jerome K. Jerome: His Life and Work*, 1929 [no bibliog.]

PAMELA HANSFORD JOHNSON
1912-

Symphony for Full Orchestra, 1934 (p); *This Bed Thy Centre*, 1935 (n); *Blessed Above Women*, 1936 (n); *Here Today*, 1937 (n); *World's End*, 1937 (n); *The Monument*, 1938 (n); *Girdle of Venus*, 1939 (n); *Too Dear for my Possessing*, 1940 (n); (with Neil Stewart) (pseud. Nap Lombard) *Tidy Death*, 1940 (n); *The Family Pattern*, 1942 (n); *Winter Quarters*, 1943 (n); (with Neil Stewart) (pseud. Nap Lombard) *Murder's a Swine* (Am. ed. *Grinning Pig*), 1943 (n); *The Trojan Brothers*, 1944 (n); *An Avenue of Stone*, 1947 (n); *Thomas Wolfe* (Am. ed. *Hungry Gulliver*), 1947 (c); *A Summer to Decide*, 1948 (n); *The Philistines*, 1949 (n); *Ivy Compton-Burnett*, 1951 (c); *Catherine Carter*, 1952 (n); *Corinth House*, 1954 (d); *An Impossible Marriage*, 1954 (n); *The Last Resort* (Am. ed. *The Sea and the Wedding*), 1956 (n); *Six Proust Reconstructions* (Am. ed. *Proust Recaptured*), 1958; *The Humbler Creation*, 1959 (n); *The Unspeakable Skipton*, 1959 (n); *An Error of Judgement*, 1962 (n); (with Kitty Black) Jean Anouilh, *The Rehearsal*, 1926 (tr); *Night and Silence! Who is Here?*, 1963 (n)

DENIS JOHNSTON
1901-

The Moon in the Yellow River, and *The Old Lady Says No!*, 1932 (2d); *Storm Song* and *A Bride for the Unicorn*, 1935 (2d); (with Ernst Toller) *Blind Man's Buff*, 1938 (d); *The Golden Cuckoo*, 1954 (d); *Nine Rivers from Jordan*, 1955 (r); *In Search of Swift*, 1959 (c); *Collected Plays*, 1960 (Am. ed. *The Old Lady Says No! and Other Plays*) (d)

DAVID JONES
1895-

In Parenthesis, 1937 (n); The Anathemata: Fragments of an Attempted
Writing, 1952 (p); Epoch and Artist:
Selected Writings, ed. Harman Grise-
wood, 1959

GLYN JONES
1905-

The Blue Bed, 1937 (s); Poems, 1939
(p); The Water Music, 1944 (s); The
Dream of Jake Hopkins, 1954 (p); (with
Dr. T. J. Morgan, reconstruction) The
Saga of Llywarch the Old, 1955; The
Valley, the City, the Village, 1956 (n);
The Learning Lark, 1960 (n)

GWYN JONES
1907-

Richard Savage, 1935 (b); Times Like
These, 1936 (n); The Nine-Days
Wonder, 1937 (n); Garland of Bays,
1938 (n); The Buttercup Field, 1946 (s);
The Green Island, 1946 (n); The Still
Waters, 1948 (s); The Walk Home: A
Prospect of Wales, 1948 (t); The
Flowers Beneath the Scythe, 1952 (n);
Shepherd's Hey, 1953 (s); Welsh
Legends and Folk Tales (Retold), 1955
(s); Scandinavian Legends and Folk
Tales (Retold), 1956 (s); The First Forty
Years, 1957 (a); Egil's Saga, 1960 (tr);
The Norse Atlantic Saga, 1964 (h)

HENRY ARTHUR JONES
1851-1929

Note: The numerous plays before
1900 omitted except the very
famous one, The Liars.

The Renascence of the English
Drama, 1895 (misc.); The Liars, 1897
(d); The Lackey's Carnival, 1900 (d);
Mrs. Dane's Defence, 1900 (d); Chance,
The Idol, 1902 (d); The Princess's Nose,
1902 (d); Whitewashing Julia, 1903 (d);
A Clerical Error, 1904 (d); Joseph En-
tangled, 1904 (d); The Heroic Stubbs,
1906 (d); The Hypocrites, 1906 (d);
The Corner Stones of Modern Drama,
1906 (c); On Reading Modern Plays,
1906 (c); The Dancing Girl, 1907 (d);
The Galilean's Victory, 1907 (d); The
Middleman, 1907 (d); Literature
and The Modern Drama, 1907 (c);
Dolly Reforming Herself, 1908 (d);
The Knife, 1909 (d); The Censorship
Muddle and A Way Out Of It, 1909
(e); Fall In, Rookies!, 1910 (d); We
Can't Be As Bad As All That!, 1910
(d); The Divine Gift, 1913 (d); Mary
Goes First, 1913 (d); The Foundations
of a National Drama, 1913 (misc.); The
Lie, 1915 (d); The Theatre of Ideas, A
Burlesque Allegory and Three One-Act
Plays, 1915 (e,d); The Pacifists, A
Parable in a Farce in Three Acts, 1917
(d); Representative Plays, ed. Clayton
Hamilton, 4 vols., 1925

Doris Arthur Jones, The Life and Letters
of Henry Arthur Jones, 1930; Richard A.
Cordell, Henry Arthur Jones and the
Modern Drama, 1932

JAMES JOYCE
1882-1941

Chamber Music, 1907 (ed. William York
Tindall, 1954) (p); Gas from a Burner,
1912 (p); Dubliners, 1914 (s); A Portrait of the Artist as a Young Man,
1916 (n); Exiles, 1918 (d); Ulysses, 1922
(n); Pomes Penyeach, 1927 (p); Anna
Livia Plurabelle [fragment from *Work
in Progress], 1928; Tales Told of Shem
and Shaun [three fragments from Work
in Progress], 1929; Haveth Childers
Everywhere [fragment from Work in
Progress], 1928; Tales Told of Shem
and Shaun [fragments from Work in
Progress], 1932; The Mime of Mick,
Nick and the Maggies [fragment from
Work in Progress], 1934; Collected
Poems, 1936; Storiello as She is Syung
[fragment from Work in Progress],
1937; Finnegans Wake, 1939 (corrected
edition, N.Y., 1945) (n); Stephen Hero
(ed. from ms. by Theodore Spencer),
1944 (rev. enlgd. ed. J. J. Slocum and
Herbert Cahoon, 1955) (n); Letters of
James Joyce, ed. Stuart Gilbert, 1957;
The Critical Writings of James Joyce, ed.
Ellsworth Mason and Richard Ellman,
1959 (c); Scribbledehobble: The Ur-
Workbook for Finnegan's Wake, ed.
Thomas E. Connolly, 1961; A First
Draft Version of Finnegan's Wake, ed.

David Hayman, 1963 (n); *Work in Progress* became *Finnegan's Wake*

John J. Slocum and Herbert Cahoon, *A Bibliography of Joyce,* 1953; Richard Ellmann, *James Joyce,* 1959

SHEILA KAYE-SMITH
1887-1956

The Tramping Methodist, 1908 (n); Starbrace, 1909 (n); Spell Land, 1910 (n); Isle of Thorns, 1913 (n); Three Against the World, 1914 (Am. ed. The Three Furlongers) (n); Willow's Forge, 1914 (p); Sussex Gorse, 1916 (n); John Galsworthy, 1916 (c); The Challenge to Sirius, 1917 (n); Little England, 1918 (Am. ed. The Four Roads) (n); Tamarisk Town, 1919 (n); Green Apple Harvest, 1920 (n); Joanna Godden, 1921 (n); The End of the House of Alard, 1923 (n); Saints in Sussex, 1923 (p); The George and the Crown, 1925 (n); Anglo-Catholicism, 1925 (e); The Mirror of the Months, 1925 (e); Joanna Godden Married 1926 (s); Iron and Smoke, 1928 (n); A Wedding Morn, 1928 (n); The Village Doctor, 1929 (n); Sin, 1929 (e); (with John Hampden) Mrs. Adis, and The Mock-Beggar, 1929 (d); Shepherds in Sackcloth, 1930 (n); The History of Susan Spray, The Female Preacher, 1931 (Am. ed. Susan Spray) (n); Songs Late and Early, 1931 (p); The Children's Summer, 1932 (Am. ed. Summer Holiday) (n); The Ploughman's Progress, 1933 (Am. ed. Gipsy Waggon) (n); Gallybird, 1934 (n); Superstition Corner, 1934 (n); Selina Is Older, 1935 (Am. ed. Selina) (n); Rose Deeprose, 1936 (n); Three Ways Home, 1937 (a); Faithful Stranger, 1938 (s); The Valiant Woman, 1938 (n); Ember Lane, 1940 (n); The Hidden Son, 1941 (Am. ed. Secret Son) (n); Tambourine, Trumpet, and Drum, 1943 (ñ); (with G. B. Stern) Talking of Jane Austen, 1943 (Am. ed. Speaking of Jane Austen) (c); Kitchen Fugue, 1945 (e); The Lardners and The Laurelwoods, 1947 (n); (with G. B. Stern) More Talk of Jane Austen, 1950 (Am. ed. More About Jane Austen) (c); The Treasures of the Snow, 1950 (Am. ed. The Happy Tree) (n); Mrs. Gailey, 1951 (n); Quartet in Heaven, 1952 (b); The Weald of Kent and Sussex, 1953 (t); The View from the Parsonage, 1954 (n); All the Books of My Life, 1956 (a)

MARGARET KENNEDY
1896-

A Century of Revolution, 1789-1920, 1922 (h); The Ladies of Lyndon, 1923 (n); The Constant Nymph, 1924 (n); (with Basil Dean) The Constant Nymph, 1926 (d); A Long Week-End, 1927 (n); Red Sky at Morning, 1927 (n); Dewdrops, 1928 (s); The Game and The Candle, 1928 (s); (with Basil Dean) Come With Me, 1928 (d); The Fool of the Family (seq. to The Constant Nymph), 1930 (n); Return I Dare Not, 1931 (n); A Long Time Ago, 1932 (n); Escape Me Never!, 1934 (d); Together and Apart, 1936 (n); The Midas Touch, 1938 (n); (with Gregory Ratoff) Autumn, 1940 (d); Where Stands a Winged Sentry, 1941 (a); The Mechanized Muse, 1942 (c); Who Will Remember?, 1946 (d); The Feast, 1950 (n); Jane Austen, 1950 (c); Lucy Carmichael, 1951 (n); Troy Chimneys, 1951 (n); The Oracles, 1955 (Am. ed. Act of God) (n); The Heroes of Clone, 1957 (s); Wild Swan, 1957 (s); The Outlaws on Parnassus, 1958 (c); A Night in Cold Harbour, 1960 (n); The Forgotten Smile, 1961 (n); The Twins and the Move, 1962 (n); Not in the Calendar, 1964 (n)

W. P. KER
1855-1923

The Philosophy of Art, 1883 (e); Epic and Romance, 1897 (c); Oration on Founders and Benefactors of University College, 1899 (e); Boccaccio, 1900 (c); The Dark Ages, 1904 (h); Essays on Medieval Literature, 1905 (c); Sturla the Historian, 1906 (e); Romance, 1907 (c); The Eighteenth Century, 1907 (c); Tennyson, 1909 (e); On the Philosophy of History, 1909 (e); Browning, 1910 (c); On the History of the Ballads, 1100-1500, 1910 (h); Thomas Warton, 1911 (c); The Literary Influence of the Middle Ages, 1913 (c); Jacob Grimm, 1915 (e); Two Essays, 1918 (c); The Humanist Ideal, 1920 (e); Joseph Ritson, 1922 (e); Hazlitt, 1922 (c); The Art of Poetry: Seven Lectures, 1923 (c); English Literature: Medieval, 1924 (c); Collected Essays, ed. Charles Whibley, 1925; Form and Style in Poetry, ed. R. W. Chambers, 1928 (c)

J. H. P. Pafford, *W. P. Ker, 1855-1923: a Bibliography*, 1950

RUDYARD KIPLING
1865-1936

(Selective Bibliography)

Note: Only the best known of R.K's very numerous works are included. His lectures are omitted.

Departmental Ditties 1886 (p); *Plain Tales from the Hills*, 1888 (s); *Soldiers Three*, 1888 (s); *The Phantom 'Rickshaw*, 1888 (s); *The Light that Failed*, 1890 (n); *Barrack-Room Ballads*, 1892 (p); *The Jungle Book*, 1894 (s); *The Second Jungle Book*, 1895 (s); *The Seven Seas*, 1896 (p); *Recessional*, 1897 (p); *The Slaves of the Lamp*, 1897 (n); *Captains Courageous*, 1897 (n); *Ballad of East and West*, 1899 (p); *The White Man's Burden*, 1899 (p); *Stalky & Company*, 1899 (s); *Kim*, 1901 (n); *Just So Stories for Little Children*, 1902 (s); *Puck of Pook's Hill*, 1906 (s); *Collected Verse*, 1907; *Rewards and Fairies*, 1910 (s); *The Female of the Species*, 1912 (p); *For All We Have and Are*, 1914 (p); *Rudyard Kipling's Verse, Inclusive Edition, 1885-1918*, 1919; *A Choice of the Songs from the Verse of Rudyard Kipling*, 1925; *Sea and Sussex from Rudyard Kipling's Verse*, 1926; *The Art of Fiction*, 1926 (c); *Rudyard Kipling's Verse, 1885-1926*, 1927; *A Book of Words, Selections from Speeches and Addresses Delivered Between 1906 and 1927*, 1928; *The One Volume Kipling, Authorized*, 1928 (misc.); *Poems, 1886-1929*, 1930; *The Complete Stalky & Company*, 1930 (s); *Rudyard Kipling's Verse, 1885-1932*, 1933; *All the Mowgli Stories*, 1933 (s); *Something of Myself*, 1937 (a); *Collected Works*, Bombay ed., 31 vols., 1913-38; *Rudyard Kipling's Verse*, definitive ed., 1940; *A Choice of Kipling's Verse*, ed. T. S. Eliot, 1941

Charles Carrington, *Kipling: His Life and Work*, 1955

ARTHUR KOESTLER
1905-

Spanish Testament, [Eng. adaptation], 1937 (n); *The Gladiators*, tr. Edith Simon, 1939 (n); *Darkness at Noon*, tr. Daphne Hardy, 1941 (n); *Scum of the Earth* [author's experiences in France, Aug. 1939-June 1940], 1941 (r); *Dialogue with Death*, tr. Trevor and Phyllis Blewitt [extracted from *Spanish Testament*], 1942; *Arrival and Departure*, 1943 (n); *The Yogi and the Commisar*, 1945 (e); *Twilight Bar*, 1945 (d); *Thieves in the Night*, 1946 (n); *Insight and Outlook*, 1949 (e); *The Age of Longing*, 1951 (n); *Arrow in the Blue*, 1942 (a); *Promise and Fulfillment, Palestine, 1917-1949*, 1952 (h); *The Invisible Writing* [sec. vol. of *Arrow in the Blue*], 1954 (a); *The Trail of the Dinosaur*, 1955 (e); *Reflections on Hanging*, 1956 (e); *The Sleepwalkers*, 1959 (e); *The Lotus and the Robot*, 1960 (e); *The Act of Creation*, 1964 (e)

ANDREW LANG
1844-1912

Ballads and Lyrics of Old France, 1872 (p, some tr); (with S. H. Butcher) *The Odyssey of Homer*, 1879 (many repr.) (prose tr); *Theocritus, Bion and Moschus*, 1880 (repr. 1922) (tr); *Ballades in Blue China*, 1880 (p); *Helen of Troy*, 1882 (p); (with Walter Leaf and Ernest Myers) *The Iliad of Homer*, 1883 (many repr.) (prose tr); *Custom and Myth*, 1884 (repr. to 1904) (e); *Ballades and Verses Vain*, sel. Austin Dobson, 1884 (p); *Rhymes à la Mode*, 1885 (p); *Books and Bookmen*, 1886 (repr. to 1912) (c); *In the Wrong Paradise* 1886 (s); *Letters to Dead Authors*, 1886 (rev. enlgd. as *New and Old Letters to Old Authors*, 1907); *The Mark of Cain*, 1886 (n); *Myth, Ritual and Religion*, 1887 (e); *Aucassin and Nicolete*, 1887 (tr); *Grass of Parnassus*, 1888 (p); *Lost Leaders*, 1889 (e); *Letters on Literature*, 1889 (c); *Life, Letters and Diaries of Sir Stafford Northcot*, 2 vols., 1890 (b); *Old Friends, Essays and Epistolary Parody*, 1890 (e); (with H. Rider Haggard) *The World's Desire*, 1890 (n); *Essays in Little*, 1891 (e); *Picadilly*, 1892 (t); *Homer and the Epic*, 1893 (c); *Ballades and Verses*, 1894 (p); *Ban and Arrière Ban*, 1894 (p); *Cock Lane and Common Sense*, 1896 (e); *The Book of Dreams and Ghosts*, 1897 (s,e); *Modern Mythology*, 1897 (e); *The Life and Letters of John Gibson Lockhart*, 1897 (b); *The Making of Religion*, 1898 (e); *Alfred Tennyson*, 1899 (c,b); *The Homeric Hymns*, 1899 (tr); *A History of Scotland from the Roman Occupation*, 4 vols., 1900-1907 (h); *Prince Charles Edward*, 1900 (b); *Magic and Religion*, 1901 (e); *The Disentanglers*, 1902 (s); *The Valet's Tragedy*, 1903 (s,e); *Historical Mysteries*, 1904; *The Clyde Mystery: A Study in Forgeries and Folklore*, 1905 (e); *New Collected Rhymes*, 1905 (p); *Adventures Among Books*, 1905 (c); *John Knox and the Reformation*, 1905 (h); *Sir Walter Scott*, 1906 (b); *Homer and His Age*, 1906, (e); *Ballades and Rhymes* (from *Ballades in Blue China* and *Rhymes à la Mode*), 1907 (p); *Tales of Troy and Greece*, 1907 (s); *The Maid of France*, 1908 (b); *Sir Walter Scott and the Border Minstrelsy*, 1910 (e); *The World of Homer*, 1910 (e); *A Short History of Scotland*, 1911 (h); *Shakespeare, Bacon and the Great Unknown*, 1912 (e); *A History of English Literature from Beowulf to Swinburne*, 1912 (h); *Oxford*, 1916 (t); *The Poetical Works*, ed. Mrs. Lang, 4 vols., 1923; *Andrew Lang*, 1926 (p); *The Lang Fairy Books*, 1929ff; *Fifty Favourite Fairy Tales Chosen from the Colour Fairy Books by Kathleen Lines*, 1963; also collections of fairy tales entitled *Blue, Red, Brown, Green, Crimson, Pink, Yellow, Grey, Lilac, Violet, Olive* and *Orange*

Roger Lancelyn Green, *Andrew Lang*, 1962

PHILIP LARKIN
1922-

The North Ship, 1945 (p); *Jill*, 1946 (repr. 1964) (n); *A Girl in Winter*, 1947 (n); *XX Poems*, 1951 (p); *Poems*, 1954 (p); *The Less Deceived*, 1955 (p); *The Whitsun Weddings*, 1964 (p)

MARGHANITA LASKI
1915-

Love on the Super Tax, 1944 (n); *To Bed with Grand Music*, 1946 (n); *Tory Heaven*, 1948 (Am. ed. *Toasted English*) (n); *Little Boy Lost*, 1949 (n); *Mrs. Ewing, Mrs. Molesworth, and Mrs. Hodgson Burnett*, 1950 (b); *The Village*, 1952 (n); *The Victorian Chaise-Longue*, 1952 (n); *Apologies*, 1955 (e); *The Offshore Island*, 1959 (d); *Ecstasy: a Study of Some Secular and Religious Experiences*, 1961 (e)

JAMES LAVER
1899-

(Selective Bibliography)

Note: Of Laver's writings on art only a sample is included.

Cervantes, 1921 (p); *His Last Sebastian*, 1922 (p); *Portraits in Oil and Vinegar*, 1925 (c); *The Young Man Dances*, 1925 (p); (with George Sheringham and others) *Design in the Theatre*, 1927 (e); *A Stitch in Time, or Pride Prevents a Fall*, 1927 (p); *The Theatre and Jean Cocteau*, 1928 (c); *Love's Progress, or The Education of Araminta*, 1929 (p); *English Costume of the Nineteenth Century*, 1929 (e); *A History of British and American Etching*, 1929 (h); *Whistler*, 1930 (b); *English Costume of the Eighteenth Century*, 1931 (h); *Nymph Errant*, 1932 (n); *Wesley*, 1932 (b); *Ladies' Mistakes: Cupid's Changeling, A Stitch in Time, Love's Progress*, 1933 (p); *Winter Wedding*, 1934 (p); *Background for Venus*, 1934 (n); *The Laburnum Tree*, 1935 (s); *Panic Among Puritans*, 1936 (n); *Nostradamus, or The Future Foretold*, 1942 (e); *Homage to Venus*, 1948 (art criticism illustrated); *The First Decadent, Being the Strange Life of J. K. Huysmans*, 1954 (b); *Oscar Wilde*, 1954 (b,c); *Edwardian Promenade*, 1958 (e); *Costume*, 1963 (e); *Women's Dress in the Jazz Age*, 1964 (e)

D. H. LAWRENCE
1885-1930

The White Peacock, 1911 (n); *The Trespasser*, 1912 (n); *Love Poems*, 1913 (p); *Sons and Lovers*, 1913 (n); *The Widowing of Mrs. Holroyd*, 1914 (d); *The Prussian Officer*, 1914 (s); *The Rainbow*, 1915 (n); *Twilight in Italy*, 1916 (t); *Amores*, 1916 (p); *Look! We Have Come Through*, 1917 (p); *New Poems*, 1918 (p); *Bay*, 1919 (p); (with S. S. Koteliansky) Leo Shestov, *All Things Are Possible*, 1920 (tr); *Touch and Go*, 1920 (d); *Women in Love*, 1920 (n); *The Lost Girl*, 1920 (n); (pseud. Lawrence H. Davison) *Movements in European History*, 1921 (h); *Psychoanalysis and the Unconscious*, 1921 (e); *Tortoises*, 1921 (p); *Sea and*

Sardinia, 1921 (t); *Aaron's Rod*, 1922 (n); *Fantasia of the Unconscious*, 1922 (e); *England, My England*, 1922 (s); *The Ladybird*, 1923 (Am. ed. *The Captain's Doll: Three Novelettes*) (3s); *Studies in Classic American Literature*, 1923 (c); *Kangaroo*, 1923 (n); *Birds, Beasts and Flowers*, 1923 (p); Giovanni Verga, *Mastro-Don Gesualdo*, 1923 (tr); (with M. L. Skinner) *The Boy in the Bush*, 1924 (n); Giovanni Verga, *Little Novels of Sicily*, 1925 (tr); *St. Mawr*, 1925 [together with "The Princess"] (1n,1s); *Reflections on the Death of a Porcupine*, 1925 (e); *The Plumed Serpent*, 1926 (n); *David*, 1926 (d); *Sun*, 1926 (s); *Glad Ghosts*, 1926 (s); *Mornings in Mexico*, 1927 (t); *Selected Poems*, 1928 (p); G. Verga, *Cavalleria Rusticana*, 1928 (tr); *Rawdon's Roof*, 1928 (s); *The Woman Who Rode Away*, 1928 (n); *Lady Chatterley's Lover*, 1928 (first authorized expurgated ed. 1932; first authorized unexpurgated ed. 1961) (n); *Collected Poems*, 1928; *Sex Locked Out*, 1928 (e); A. F. Grazzini, *The Story of Doctor Manente*, 1929 (tr); **The Paintings of D. H. Lawrence*, 1929 [D.H.L.'s paintings reproduced]; *Pansies*, 1929 (p); *My Skirmish with Jolly Roger*, 1929 (e); *Pornography and Obscenity*, 1929 (e); *The Life of J.Middleton Murry*, 1930(b); *Nettles*, 1930 (p) *Assorted Articles*, 1930 (e); *The Virgin and the Gypsy*, 1930 (n); *Love among the Haystacks*, 1930 (s); *Apocalypse*, 1930 (s); ***The Man Who Died*, 1931 (repr. 1950) (n); *Etruscan Places*, 1932 (t); *The Letters*, ed. Aldous Huxley, 1932; *Last Poems*, ed. Richard Aldington and Giuseppe Orioli, 1932 (p); *The Lovely Lady*, 1933 (s); *The Plays*, 1934 (3d); *The Ship of Death* [from *Last Poems*], 1933 (p); *The Tales*, 1934 (s); *Selected Poems*, 1934 (p); *A Collier's Friday Night*, 1934 (d); *A Modern Lover*, 1934 (6s and unfinished novel); *The Spirit of Place*, ed. Richard Aldington, 1935 (prose anthology); *Foreword to Women in Love*, 1936 (e); *Pornography and So On*, 1936 (e); *Phoenix, Posthumous Papers*, ed. Edward D. McDonald, 1936 (misc.); *Poems*, 2 vols., coll. ed., 1939; *Stories, Essays and Poems*, coll. ed., 1940; *Fire*, 1940 (p); *Full Score*, 1943 (s); *The First Lady Chatterley*, 1944 (n); *Selected Poems*, 1947 (p); *Letters to Bertrand Russell*, ed. Harry T. Moore,

1948; *A Prelude* [his first, previously unrecorded work], 1949 (s); *Selected Essays*, 1950 (e); *Selected Letters*, sel. Richard Aldington, 1950; *Selected Poems*, sel. W. E. Williams, 1950 (p); *Selected Poems*, ed. James Reeves, 1951 (p); *Complete Short Stories*, 3 vols., 1955; *Selected Literary Criticism*, ed. Anthony Beal, 1955 (c); *The Short Novels*, 2 vols. (n); *Complete Poems*, 3 vols., 1957; *Selected Poetry and Prose*, ed. T. R. Barnes, 1957; *Selected Letters*, ed. Diana Trilling, 1958; *The Collected Letters*, ed. Harry T. Moore, 2 vols., 1962; *The Symbolic Meaning: The Uncollected Versions of Studies in Classic American Literature*, ed. Armin Arnold, 1962 (c); *The Complete Poems*, ed. Vivian de Sola Pinto and Warren Roberts, 1964; **Paintings of D. H. Lawrence*, ed. Mervyn Levy, 1964 [collected edition of reproduction of paintings by D.H.L.]. ***first printed as *The Escaped Cock*, 1929, limited ed.

Warren Roberts, *A Bibliography of D. H. Lawrence*, 1963

T. E. LAWRENCE
1888-1935

(with C. L. Woolley) *Carchemish, Reports on the Excavations at Djerabis*, 1914; (with C. L. Woolley) *The Wilderness of Zin (Archaeological Reports)*, 1915; *Seven Pillars of Wisdom: A Triumph*, 1926 (e,r); *Revolt in the Desert*, 1926 (r,t) [Abridgement of *Seven Pillars*]; *The Odyssey of Homer*, 1932 (t); *Letters from T. E. Shaw to Bruce Rogers*, 1933; *More Letters from T. E. Shaw to Bruce Rogers*, 1936; *Crusader Castles*, 1936 (e); *The Diary of T. E. Lawrence, 1911* [Syria], 1937; *Letters*, ed. David Garnett, 1938; *T. E. Lawrence to his Biographer, Liddell Hart*, 1939 (a); *T. E. Lawrence to his Biographer, Robert Graves*, 1939 (a); *Oriental Assembly*, ed. A. W. Lawrence, 1939 (misc.); *Secret Dispatches from Arabia*, 1939 (a); *T. E. Lawrence's Letters H. S. Ede, 1927-1935*, 1942; *Selected Letters*, ed. David Garnett, 1952; *The Home Letters of T. E. Lawrence and his Brothers*, ed. M. R. Lawrence, 1954; *The Mint*, 1955 (r)

Elizabeth W. Duval, *T. E. Lawrence: a Bibliography*, 1938

F. R. LEAVIS
1895-

D. H. Lawrence, 1930 (c); *Mass Civilization and Minority Culture*, 1930 (e); *How To Teach Reading: A Primer for Ezra Pound*, 1932 (c); Ed. *Scrutiny*, 1932-1953; *New Bearings in English Poetry*, 1932 (c); (with Denys Thompson) *Culture and Environment*, 1933 (e); *For Continuity*, 1933 (c); *Revaluation: Tradition and Development in English Poetry*, 1936 (c); *Education and the University*, 1943 (e); *The Great Tradition*, 1948 (c); *The Common Pursuit*, 1952 (c); *D. H. Lawrence: Novelist*, 1955 (c); *Two Cultures: The Significance of C. P. Snow*, 1962 (Richmond lecture, Downing College, Cambridge Univ.)

LAURIE LEE
1914-

Viktor Fischl, *The Dead Village*, 1943 (tr); *The Sun My Monument*, 1944 (repr. 1961) (p); *The Bloom of Candles*, 1947 (p); *The Voyage of Magellan*, 1948 (rd); *Peasants' Priest*, 1952 (d); *My Many-Coated Man*, 1955 (p); *A Rose for Winter*, 1955 (t); *Cider with Rosie* (Am. ed. *The Edge of Day*), 1959 (n,a); *Selected Poems*, 1960 (p); *The Firstborn*, 1964 (e)

VERNON LEE
1856-1935

Tuscan Fairy Tales, 1880 (s); *Studies of the Eighteenth Century in Italy*, 1880 (e); *Belcaro, Being Essays on Sundry Aesthetical Questions*, 1881 (e); *The Prince of the Hundred Soups*, 1882 (also pub. as *Story of a Puppet Show*, 1889) (s); *Ottilie*, 1883 (s); *The Countess of Albany*, 1883 (b); *Miss Brown*, 1884 (n); *Euphorion, Being Studies of the Antique and the Medieval in the Renaissance*, 1884 (e); *A Phantom Lover*, 1886 (s); *Baldwin: Being Dialogues on Views and Aspirations*, 1886 (e); *Juvenilia: . . . Essays on Sundry Aesthetical Questions*, 1887 (e); *Hauntings, Fantastic Stories*, 1890 (s); *Vanitas, Polite Stories*, 1892 (rev. enlgd. 1911) (s); *Althea, a Second Book of Dialogues on Aspirations and Duties*, 1894 (e); *Au*

Pays de Vénus, 1894 (s); *Renaissance Fancies and Studies*, 1895 (e); *Limbo*, 1897 (e); *Genius Loci, Notes on Places*, 1899 (t); *Penelope Brandling, a Tale of the Welsh Coast*, 1903 (n); *Hortus Vitae*, 1904 (repr. 1928) (e); *Ariadne in Mantua*, 1903 (d); *The Enchanted Wood, and Other Essays on the Genius of Places*, 1905 (e); *Pope Jacynth*, 1904 (repr. Am. ed. as *Virgin of the Seven Daggers*, 1963) (n); *The Enchanted Wood, and Other Essays on the Genius of Places*, 1905 (e); *The Spirit of Rome: Leaves from a Diary*, 1905 (t); *Sister Benvenuta and the Christ Child*, 1906 (s); *The Sentimental Traveller*, 1907 (t); *Gospels of Anarchy*, 1908 (e); *Laurus Nobilis, Chapters on Art and Life*, 1909 (e); *The Beautiful*, 1910 (e); (with C. Anstruther-Thomson) *Beauty and Ugliness*, 1912 (e); *Vital Lies*, 1912 (e); *Louis Norbert*, 1914 (n); *The Tower of Mirrors*, 1914 (t); *The Ballet of the Nations, a Present-Day Morality*, 1915 (s); *Peace with Honour*, 1915 (e); *Satan the Waster: a Philosophic War Trilogy*, 1920 (d); *The Handling of Words and Other Studies in Literary Psychology*, 1923 (e); *Proteus, or The Future of Intelligence*, 1925 (e); *The Golden Keys and Other Essays on the Genius Loci*, 1925 (t); *The Poet's Eye*, 1926 (e); *For Maurice, Five Unlikely Stories*, 1927 (s); *A Vernon Lee Anthology*, sel. Irene Cooper Willis, 1929; *Music and Its Lovers*, 1932 (e); *The Snake Lady*, 1954 (s); *Supernatural Tales*, 1955 (s)

Peter Gunn, *Vernon Lee*, 1964

JOHN LEHMANN
1907-

A Garden Revisited, 1931 (p); *The Noise of History*, 1934 (p); *Prometheus and the Bolsheviks*, 1937 (e); *Evil Was Abroad*, 1938 (n); *Down River, a Danubian Study*, 1939 (t); *New Writing in Europe*, 1940 (c); *Forty Poems*, 1942 (p); *The Sphere of Glass*, 1944 (p); *The Age of the Dragon: Poems 1931-1951*, 1951; *The Open Night*, 1952 (e); *Edith Sitwell*, 1952 (c); Ed. *London Magazine*, 1954-1961; *The Whispering Gallery*, 1955 (a); *I Am My Brother*, 1960 (a); *Ancestors and Friends*, 1962 (b); *Collected Poems, 1930-1963*, 1963

ROSAMOND LEHMANN
1903-

Dusty Answer, 1927 (n); A Note in Music, 1930 (n); A Letter to a Sister, 1931 (e); Invitation to the Waltz, 1932 (n); The Weather in the Streets, 1936 (n); No More Music, 1939 (d); The Ballad and the Source, 1944 (n); The Gypsy's Baby, 1946 (s); The Echoing Grove, 1953 (n); Jean Cocteau, Les Enfants Terribles, as Children of the Game, 1955 (tr)

SHANE LESLIE
1885-

The Landlords of Ireland at the Cross-roads, 1908 (e); Songs of Oriel, 1908 (p); Lough Derg in Ulster, The Story of St. Patrick's Purgatory, 1909 (repr. 1917) (h); A Study of the Oxford Movement, 1909 (e); (with Padriac Colum and others) Eyes of Youth, 1910 (p); The Isle of Columbcille, 1910 (t); Verses in Peace and War, 1916 (p); The End of a Chapter, 1916 (rev. 1929) (n); The Celt and the World, 1917 (e); The Irish Issue in its American Aspect, 1918 (e); Henry Edward Manning, His Life and Labours, 1921 (b); The Oppidan, 1922 (n); Mark Sykes, His Life and Letters, 1923 (b); Doomsland, 1923 (n); Masquerades: Studies in the Morbid, 1924 (n); (with Francis Birrell) Plato's Symposium, 1925 (tr); The Cantab, 1926 (n); George the Fourth, 1926 (b); The Skull of Swift, An Extempore Exhumation, 1928 (b); The Delightful, Diverting and Devotional Play of Mrs. Fitzherbert, 1928 (d); The Poems of Shane Leslie, 1928 (p); The Greek Anthology, sel., 1929 (tr); A Ghost in the Isle of Wight, 1929 (e); The Anglo-Catholic, 1929 (seq. to The Cantab) (n); Memoir of John Edward Courtenay Bodley, 1930 (m); The Hyde Park Pageant, a Broadside, 1930 (p); Jutland, A Fragment of an Epic, 1930 (p); Studies in Sublime Failure [Cardinal Newman, Charles Stuart Parnell, Coventry Patmore, Lord Curzon, Moreton Frewen], 1932 (b); Poems and Ballads, 1933 (p); The Oxford Movement, 1833 to 1933, 1933 (h); The Passing Chapter, 1934 (e); Fifteen Odd Stories, 1935 (s); The Script of Jonathan Swift, 1935 (e); American Wonderland, 1936 (r); Men Were Different [Randolph Churchill, Augustus Hare, Arthur Dunn, George Wyndham, Wilfrid Blunt], 1937 (b); Sir Evelyn Ruggles-Brise, 1938 (m); The Film of Memory, 1938 (a); Mrs. Fitzherbert, 1939 (b); Poems from the North, 1945 (p); The Irish Tangle for English Readers, 1946 (Am. ed. The Irish Question); The Rubaiyat of the Mystics, 1950 (p); Salutation to Five, 1951 (b); Cardinal Gosquet, 1953 (b); Lord Mulroy's Ghost, 1954 (d); Ghost Book, 1955 (e)

DORIS LESSING
1919-

The Grass Is Singing, 1950 (n); This Was the Old Chief's Country, 1951 (s); Martha Quest (Vol. I of Children of Violence), 1952 (n); Five, 1953 (5n); A Proper Marriage (Vol. II of Children of Violence), 1954 (n); Retreat to Innocence, 1956 (n); The Habit of Loving, 1957 (s); Going Home, 1957 (a); A Ripple from the Storm (Vol. III of Children of Violence), 1958 (n); Each His Own Wilderness, 1959 (d); Fourteen Poems, 1959 (p); The Habit of Loving, 1960 (s); In Pursuit of the English, 1960 (a); The Golden Notebook, 1962 (n); Play With a Tiger, 1962 (d); A Man and Two Women, 1963 (s); African Stories, 1964 (s); (Am. ed.) Children of Violence, 1964 (this contains Vol. I, Martha Quest, and Vol. II, A Proper Marriage)

DENISE LEVERTOV
1923-

Overland to the Islands, 1958 (p); With Eyes at the Back of Our Heads, 1960 (p); The Jacob's Ladder, 1961 (p); Here and Now, 1962 (p); O Taste and See, 1964 (p)

BENN WOLF LEVY
1900-

This Woman Business, 1925 (d); Mud and Treacle, or, The Course of True Love, 1928 (d); A Man with Red Hair [from Hugh Walpole's novel], 1928 (d); Mrs. Moonlight, 1929 (d); Art and Mrs Bottle, or, The Return of the Puritan, 1929 (d); The Devil, 1930 (Am. ed. The Devil Passes) (d); (with J. Van Druten) Hollywood Holiday, 1931 (d); Springtime for Henry, 1932 (d); The

Poet's Heart: A Life of Don Juan, 1937 (d); *The Jealous God,* 1939 (d); *Clutterbuck,* 1947 (d); *Return to Tyassi,* 1951 (d); *Cupid and Psyche,* 1952 (d); *The Great Healer,* 1954 (d); *The Island of Cipango,* 1954 (d); *The Rape of the Belt,* 1957 (d); *The Truth about Truth,* 1957 (d)

ALUN LEWIS
1915-1944

Raider's Dawn, 1942 (p); *The Last Inspection,* 1943 (s); *Ha! Ha! Among the Trumpets,* 1945 (p); *Letters from India,* 1946; *In the Green Tree: Letters and Six Short Stories,* 1949

C. DAY LEWIS
1904-

Beechen Vigil, 1925 (p); *Country Comets,* 1928 (p); *Transitional Poem,* 1929 (p); *From Feathers to Iron,* 1931 (p); *The Magnetic Mountain,* 1933 (p); *A Hope for Poetry,* 1934 (c); *A Time to Dance,* 1935 (p); *Revolution in Writing,* 1935 (e); *Collected Poems 1929-1933,* 1935; *We're Not Going to Do Nothing,* 1936 (e); *The Friendly Tree,* 1936 (n); (with L. Susan Stebbing) *Imagination and Thinking,* 1936 (two addresses); *Starting Point,* 1937 (n); *Overtures to Death,* 1938 (p); *Child of Misfortune,* 1939 (n); *Poems in Wartime,* 1940 (p); *Selected Poems,* 1940 (p); *The Georgics of Virgil,* 1941 (tr); *Word Over All* (incl. *Poems in Wartime*), 1943 (p); *Selected Poems,* 1943 (p); *Paul Valéry, Le Cimetière Marin,* 1946 (tr); *The Colloquial Element in English Poetry,* 1947 (e); *Enjoying Poetry, A Reader's Guide,* 1947 (e); *The Poetic Image,* 1947 (Clark lectures, Univ. of Cambridge); *Collected Poems, 1929-1936,* 1948; *The Otterbury Incident,* 1948 (n); *Poems 1943-1947,* 1948 (p); *The Poet's Task,* 1951 (Oxford Univ., inaugural lecture); *Selected Poems,* 1951 (p); *The Grand Manner,* 1952 (Byron Foundation lecture); *The Aeneid of Virgil,* 1952 (tr); *The Lyrical Poetry of Thomas Hardy,* 1953 (Warton lecture); *An Italian Visit, 1953* (p); *Collected Poems,* 1954; *Notable Images of Virtue* [Emily Bronte, George Meredith, W. B. Yeats], 1954 (lectures, Queens Univ., Kingston, Ont.);

Christmas Eve, 1954 (p); *Pegasus,* 1957 (p); *The Poet's Way of Knowledge,* 1957 (c); *The Buried Day,* 1960 (a); *The Gate,* 1962 (p); *Virgil, The Eclogues,* 1963 (tr). Also, under pseud. Nicholas Blake, these detective stories: *A Question of Proof,* 1935; *Thou Shell of Death,* 1936; *There's Trouble Brewing,* 1937; *The Beast Must Die,* 1938; *The Smiler with the Knife,* 1939; *Malice in Wonderland,* 1940; *The Case of the Abominable Snowman,* 1941; *Minute for Murder,* 1947; *Head of a Traveller,* 1949; *Dreadful Hollow,* 1953; *The Whisper in the Gloom,* 1954; *A Tangled Web,* 1956; *End of a Chapter,* 1957; *Penknife in My Heart,* 1958; *The Widow's Cruise,* 1959

Clifford Dyment, *C. Day Lewis,* 1955

C. S. LEWIS
1898-1963

[Clive Hamilton, pseud.] *Spirits in Bondage: a Cycle of Lyrics,* 1919 (p); [Clive Hamilton, pseud.] *Dymer,* 1926 (repr. 1950) (p); *The Pilgrim's Regress,* 1933 (e); *The Allegory of Love,* 1936 (c); *Out of The Silent Planet* (Part I of trilogy), 1938 (n); *Rehabilitations,* 1939 (c); (with E. M. W. Tillyard) *The Personal Heresy,* 1939 (e); *The Problem of Pain,* 1940 (e); *Broadcast Talks,* 1942 (Am. ed. *The Case for Christianity*) (e); *A Preface to Paradise Lost,* 1942 (c); *The Screwtape Letters,* 1942 (e); *Christian Behaviour,* 1943 (e); *Perelandra* (Part II of trilogy), 1943 (n); *The Abolition of Man,* 1943 (e); *Beyond Personality: The Christian Idea of God,* 1944 (e); *That Hideous Strength* (Part III of trilogy), 1945 (n); *The Great Divorce, a Dream,* 1945 (e); *Miracles, a Preliminary Study,* 1947 (e); *Vivisection,* 1948 (e); *Transposition and Other Addresses,* 1949 (Am. ed. *The Weight of Glory*) (e); *The Literary Impact of the Authorized Version,* 1950 (lecture, Univ. of London); *Mere Christianity,* 1952 (rev. ed. of *Broadcast Talks, Christian Behaviour, Beyond Personality*) (e); *The Silver Chair,* 1953 (child's bk.); *English Literature in the Sixteenth Century, Excluding Drama* (Vol. III of *Oxford History of English Literature*), 1954 (h); *The Magician's Nephew,* 1955 (child's bk.); *Surprised by Joy,* 1955 (a); *Till*

We Have Faces, a Myth Retold, 1956 (n); *The Last Battle,* 1956 (child's bk.); *Reflections on the Psalms,* 1958 (e); *The Four Loves,* 1960 (e); *Miracles,* 1960 (e); *Studies in Words,* 1960 (e); *An Experiment in Criticism,* 1961 (c); *Screwtape Proposes a Toast,* 1961 (bound with *The Screwtape Letters*) (e); *They Asked for a Paper,* 1962 (c); *The Discarded Image, an Introduction to Medieval and Renaissance Literature,* 1964 (c); *Poems,* ed. Walter Hooper, 1964 (p); *The Chronicles of Narnia,* 1950-56, 7 books for children of which the above three are among the best known

Roger Lancelyn Green, *C. S. Lewis,* 1963

D. B. WYNDHAM LEWIS
1894-

A London Farrago, 1922 (e); *At the Green Goose,* 1923 (n); *At the Sign of the Blue Moon,* 1924 (n); *At the Blue Moon Again,* 1925 (n); *On Straw and Other Conceits,* 1927 (e); *François Villon,* 1928 (b); *King Spider: Some Aspects of Louis XI of France and his Companions,* 1929 (b); *Mr. Thake, His Life and Letters,* 1929 (b); *Emperor of the West, a Study of Charles V,* 1932 (b); *Take it to Bed,* 1944 (anecdotes); *Ronsard,* 1944 (b); *The Hooded Hawk; or, The Case of Mr. Boswell,* 1946 (c); *Four Favourites,* 1948 (b); *The Soul of Marshal Gilles de Raiz,* 1952 (b); *James Boswell: a Short Life,* 1952 (b); (with Ronald Searle) *The Terror of St. Trinian's,* 1952 (s); *Doctor Rabelais* 1957 (b); *A Florentine Portrait* [Saint Philip Benizi (1233-1285)], 1959 (b); *Molière, the Comic Mask,* 1959 (b); *The Shadow of Cervantes,* 1962 (b)

[PERCY] WYNDHAM LEWIS
1886-1957

Ed. *Blast: Review of the Great English Vortex,* 1914, and *Blast: No. 2,* 1915; *The Ideal Giant: The Code of a Herdsman; Cantleman's Springmate,* 1947 (c,s); *Tarr,* 1918 (rev. 1928, repr. 1951) (n); *The Caliph's Design: Architects! Where is Your Vortex?,* 1919 (e); (with Louis F. Fergusson) *Harold Gilman: an Appreciation,* 1919 (c); *The Tyro, Nos. 1, 2,* 1924 (e); *The Art of*

Being Ruled, 1926 (e); *The Enemy, Nos. 1, 2,* 1927 (c); *The Lion and the Fox: The Rôle of the Hero in Shakespeare,* 1927 (repr. 1955) (c); *Time and Western Man,* 1927 (e); *The Wild Body,* 1927 (s); *The Childermass, Vol. 1,* 1928 (n); *The Enemy, No. 3,* 1929 (e); *Paleface: The Philosophy of the Melting Pot,* 1929 (e); *The Apes of God,* 1930 (n); *Satire and Fiction,* 1930 (c); *The Diabolical Principle and the Dithyrambic Spectator,* 1931 (c); *Hitler,* 1931 (b); *The Wild Body,* 1932 (e); *The Enemy of the Stars,* 1932 (e); *Filibusters in Barbary,* 1932 (e); *Snooty Baronet,* 1932 (n); *The Old Gang and the New,* 1933 (e); *One-Way Song,* 1933 (also pub. as *Engine Fight-Talk*) (repr. 1960) (p); *Men Without Art,* 1934 (c); *Left Wings Over Europe,* 1936 (e); *Count Your Dead: They Are Alive!,* 1937 (e); *Blasting and Bombardiering,* 1937 (e); *The Revenge for Love,* 1937 (repr. 1951) (n); *The Mysterious Mr. Bull,* 1938 (e); *The Jews, Are They Human?,* 1939 (e); *The Hitler Cult,* 1939 (e); *America, I Presume,* 1940 (e); *The Vulgar Streak,* 1941 (n); *Anglosaxony,* 1942 (e); *America and Cosmic Man,* 1948 (e); *Rude Assignment,* 1950 (a); *Rotting Hill,* 1951 (n); *The Writer and The Absolute,* 1952 (e); *The Demon of Progress in the Arts,* 1954 (e); *Self Condemned,* 1954 (n); *The Human Age: Childermass* (rev.), *Monstre Gai and Malign Fiesta,* 1955 (3n); *The Red Priest,* 1956 (n); (Italian ed.) *Ezra Pound,* 1958 (c); *The Letters of Wyndham Lewis,* ed. W. K. Rose, 1964

Geoffrey Wagner, *Wyndham Lewis,* 1957

ROBERT LIDDELL
1908-

The Almond Tree, 1938 (n); *Kind Relations,* 1939 (n); *The Gantillons,* 1940 (n); *Watering Place,* 1945 (n); *A Treatise on the Novel,* 1947 (c); *The Last Enchantments,* 1948 (n); *Unreal City,* 1952 (n); *Some Principles of Fiction,* 1953 (c); *Aegean Greece,* 1954 (t); *The Novels of I. Compton-Burnett,* 1955 (c); *Byzantium and Istanbul,* 1956 (t); *The Morea,* 1958 (t); *The Rivers of Babylon,* 1959 (n); Demetrios Sicilianos, *Old and New Athens,* 1960 (tr); *The Novels of Jane Austen,* 1963 (c)

ERIC LINKLATER
1899-

Poobie, 1925 (p); Poet's Pub, 1929 (n); White-Maa's Saga, 1929 (repr. 1963); A Dragon Laughed, 1930 (p); Ben Jonson and King James, 1931 (b); Juan in America, 1931 (repr. 1956) (n); The Men of Ness, 1932 (n); Mary, Queen of Scots, 1933 (repr. 1952) (b); The Crusader's Key, 1933 (n); Magnus Merriman, 1934 (repr. 1959) (n); The Devil's in the News, 1934 (d); Robert the Bruce, 1934 (b); The Revolution, 1934 (s); The Lion and the Unicorn or What England has Meant to Scotland, 1935 (e); God Likes Them Plain, 1935 (s); Ripeness is All, 1935 (n); Juan in China, 1936 (repr. 1959) (n); The Sailor's Holiday, 1936 (n); The Impregnable Women, 1938 (repr. 1959) (n); Judas, 1939 (repr. 1956) (n); The Northern Garrisons, 1941 (h); The Cornerstones, 1941 (n); The Man on my Back, 1941 (a); The Highland Division, 1942 (h); The Raft and Socrates Asks Why, 1942 (e); The Great Ship and Rabelais Replies, 1944 (e); Crisis in Heaven, 1944 (d); Private Angelo, 1946 (n); Sealskin Trousers, 1947 (s); Art of Adventure, 1947 (e); A Spell for Old Bones, 1949 (s); Mr. Byculla, 1950 (s); Two Comedies: Love in Albania and To Meet the Macgregors, 1950 (2d); Laxdale Hall, 1951 (n); The Campaign in Italy, 1951 (h); The Mortimer Touch, 1952 (d); The House of Gair, 1953 (s); A Year of Space, 1953 (a); The Sultan and the Lady, 1954 (n); The Faithful Ally, 1954 (n); The Ultimate Viking, 1955 (e); The Dark of Summer, 1956 (n); A Sociable Plover, 1957 (s); Breakspear in Gascony, 1958 (d); Position at Noon (Am. ed. My Father and I), 1958 (n); The Merry Muse, 1959 (n); Edinburgh, 1960 (t); Roll of Honour, 1961 (n); Husband of Delilah, 1962 (n); A Man Over Forty, 1963 (n)

CHRISTOPHER LOGUE
1926-

Wand and Quadrant, 1953 (p); Devil, Maggot and Son, 1956 (p); The Man Who Told His Love [Pablo Neruda, 20 Poemas de Amor], 1958 (tr); A Song for Kathleen, 1958 (p); Songs, 1959 (p); Songs from "The Lily-White Boys",

1960 (p); Homer, Patrocleia [Iliad], 1962 (tr); The Arrival of the Poet in the City, 1964 (p)

FREDERICK LONSDALE
1881-1954

Aren't We All, 1924 (d); The Last of Mrs. Cheyney, 1925 (d); Spring Cleaning, 1925 (d); The Fake, 1927 (d); The High Road, 1927 (d); On Approval, 1927 (d); Canaries Sometimes Sing, 1929 (d); The Street Singer, 1929 (d); The Devil To Pay, 1930 (film story); Once is Enough, 1938 (Am. ed. Let Them Eat Cake) (d); Foreigners, 1939 (d); But for the Grace of God, 1946 (d); Another Love Story, 1948 (d); The Way Things Go, 1950 (d)

Frances Donaldson, Freddy Lonsdale, 1957

MALCOLM LOWRY
1909-1957

Ultramarine, 1933 (rev. 1963) (n); Under the Volcano, 1947 (n); Hear Us O Lord from Heaven Thy Dwelling Place, 1961 (s); Selected Poems, ed. Earle Birney and Margerie Lowry, 1962 (p)

PERCY LUBBOCK
1879-

Samuel Pepys, 1904 (repr. 1923) (b); Elizabeth Barrett Browning in Her Letters, 1906 (b); George Calderon: A Sketch from Memory, 1921 (m); The Craft of Fiction, 1921 (c); Earlham, 1922 (r); Roman Pictures, 1923 (e); The Region Cloud, 1925 (n); Mary Cholmondeley, 1928 (m); Shades of Eton, 1929 (r); Portrait of Edith Wharton, 1947 (b)

E. V. LUCAS
1868-1938

Bernard Barton and His Friends, 1895 (b); All the World Over, 1898 (p); The Book of Shops, 1899 (p); Domesticities, 1900 (e); Four and Twenty Toilers, 1900 (p); The Visit to London, 1902 (p); England Day by Day, 1903 (e); Highways and Byways in Sussex, 1904 (repr. 1934) (t); The Life of Charles Lamb, 2 vols., 1905 (5th ed. rev. 1910, repr. 1921) (b); A Wanderer in Holland,

1905 (20th ed. rev. 1931) (t); *A Wanderer in London*, 1906 (28th ed. rev. 1931) (t); *Fireside and Sunshine*, 1906 (e); *Listener's Lure*, 1906 (n); *A Swan and Her Friends* [Anna Seward], 1907 (b,h); *Character and Comedy*, 1907 (e); *Over Bemerton's*, 1908 (n); *One Day and Another*, 1909 (e); *A Wanderer in Paris*, 1909 (24th ed. rev. Audrey Lucas, 1952) (t); *Mr. Ingleside*, 1910 (n); *Old Lamps for New*, 1911 (e); (E.V.L. and G.M. [G. Morrow]), *What a Life!*, 1911 (a); *London Lavender*, 1912 (n); *A Little of Everything*, 1912 (sel.); *A Wanderer in Florence*, 1912 (14th ed. rev. 1928) (t); *Harvest Home*, 1913 (sel.); *The British School: an Anecdotal Guide to the British Painters and Paintings in the National Gallery*, 1913 (c); *Loiterer's Harvest*, 1913 (e); *Landmarks*, 1914 (n); *A Wanderer in Venice*, 1914 (5th ed. rev. 1923, repr. 1930) (t); *London Revisited*, 1916 (6th ed. rev. 1926) (t); *Cloud and Silver*, 1916 (e); *The Vermilion Box*, 1916 (n); *Variety Lane*, 1916 (e); *A Boswell of Baghdad, with Diversions*, 1917 (e); *Twixt Eagle and Dove*, 1918 (e); *The Phantom Journal*, 1919 (e); *Mixed Vintages, a Blend of Essays Old and New*, 1919 (e); *Adventures and Enthusiasms*, 1920 (e); *Specially Selected: a Choice of Essays*, 1920 (e); *David Williams, Founder of the Royal Literary Fund*, 1920 (b); *Verena in the Midst*, 1920 (n); *Roving East and West*, 1921 (t); *Rose and Rose*, 1921 (n); *Urbanities: Essays New and Old*, 1921 (e); *Edwin Austin Abbey*, 1921 (b); *Vermeer of Delft*, 1922 (b); *Genevra's Money*, 1922 (n); *Giving and Receiving*, 1922 (e); *You Know What People Are*, 1922 (sk); *Advisory Ben*, 1923 (s); *Luck of the Year*, 1923 (m,s); *A Wanderer among Pictures: a Companion to the Galleries of Europe*, 1924 (c); *Encounters and Diversions*, 1924 (e); *The Same Star*, 1924 (d); *John Constable, the Painter*, 1924 (c); *Michael Angelo*, 1924 (c); *Chardin and Vigée Le Brun*, 1924 (c); *Rembrandt*, 1924 (c); *Little Books on Great Masters* [of painting], 1924-26 (b,c); *Zigzags in France and and Various Essays*, 1925 (Am. ed. *Wanderings and Diversions*) (t); *Introducing London*, 1925 (t); *Events and Embroideries*, 1926 (e); *Selected Essays*, ed. E. A. Wodehouse, 1926 (e); *Three Hundreds and Sixty-Five Days and One*

More: being selections for every mornin of the year from the writings of E. V. Lucas, 1926 (sel.); *Franz Hals*, 1926 (c); *Giorgione*, 1926 (c); *Velasquez*, 1926 (c); *Van Dyck*, 1926 (c); *Leonardo da Vinci*, 1926 (c); *A Wanderer in Rome*, 1926 (5th ed. rev. 1951) (t); *London* (*A Wanderer in London, London Revisited*), 1926 (t); The Minerva Edition of *The Works*, 1926-; *A Fronded Isle*, 1927 (e); *The More I see of Men . . . Stray Essays on Dogs*, 1927 (sel.); *Vermeer the Magical*, 1928 (b,c); *A Rover I Would Be: Essays and Fantasies*, 1928 (e); *Introducing Paris*, 1928 (t); *The Colvins and their Friends*, 1928 (b,h); *Out of a Clear Sky: Essays and Fantasies about Birds*, 1928 (sel.); *Turning Things Over*, 1929 (e); *Windfall's Eve*, 1929 (n); *If Dogs Could Write*, 1929 (misc.); *Traveller's Luck: Essays and Fantasies*, 1930 (e); *"And Such Small Deer,"* 1930 (sel.); *Down the Sky*, 1930 (n); *No-Nose at the Show*, 1931 (p); *French Leaves*, 1931 (e); *The Barber's Clock*, 1931 (s); *Visibility Good*, 1931 (e); *At the Sign of the Dove*, 1932 (e); *Lemon Verbena*, 1932 (e); *Reading, Writing and Remembering*, 1932 (r); *English Leaves*, 1933 (e); *Saunterer's Rewards*, 1933 (t); *Animals All* (*"And Such Small Deer"* and *Out of a Clear Sky*), 1934 (e); *E. V. Lucas*, 1934 (anthology of his humorous work); *At the Shrine of Saint Charles: Stray Papers on Lamb for the Centenary of his Death*, 1934 (e); *The Old Contemporaries*, 1935 (r); *Pleasure Trove*, 1935 (e); *Only the Other Day*, 1936 (e); *All of a Piece: New Essays*, 1937 (e); *As the Bee Sucks*, chosen Ernest H. Shepard, 1937 (e); *Adventures and Misgivings*, 1938 (e); *Cricket All his Life: Cricket Writings in Prose and Verse*, chosen Rupert Hart-Davis, 1950; *Selected Essays*, chosen H. N. Wethered, 1954; Also a number of humorous books, many as E.V.L. with C.L.G. [Charles Larcom Graves], e.g. *Wisdom While You Wait*, 1903

Audrey Lucas, *E. V. Lucas: a Portrait* [list of bks.]

F. L. LUCAS
1894-

Seneca and Elizabethan Tragedy, 1922 (c); *Euripides and his Influence*, 1924 (c); *Authors Dead and Living*, 1926 (c); *The River Flows*, 1926 (n); *Tragedy in Relation to Aristotle's Poetics*, 1927 (repr. 1957) (c); *Time and Memory*, 1929 (p); *Eight Victorian Poets*, 1930 (2nd ed. *Ten Victorian Poets*, 1940) (c); *Marionettes*, 1930 (p); *Cécile*, 1930 (n); *The Wild Tulip*, 1932 (n); *Ariadne*, 1932 (p); *The Criticism of Poetry*, 1933 (c); *The Bear Dances*, 1933 (d); *Studies, French and English*, 1934 (repr. 1950) (c); (with P. D. Lucas) *From Olympus to the Styx*, 1934 (t); *Four Plays*, 1935 (d); *Poems, 1935*, 1935 (p); *The Decline and Fall of the Romantic Ideal*, 1936 (c); *The Woman Clothed with the Sun*, 1937 (s); *Doctor Dido*, 1938 (n); *A Greek Garland*, 1939 (tr); *Journal Under the Terror, 1938*, 1939 (h); *Vigil of Venus*, 1939 (tr); *Messene Redeemed*, 1940 (d); *Critical Thoughts in Critical Days*, 1942 (e); *Aphrodite*, 1948 (tr); *Greek Poetry for Everyman*, 1951 (tr); *Literature and Psychology*, 1951 (e); *From Many Times and Lands*, 1953 (p); *Greek Drama for Everyman*, 1954 (tr); *Style*, 1955 (c); *The Search for Good Sense* [Johnson, Chesterfield, Boswell, Goldsmith], 1958 (b); *The Art of Living* [Hume, Horace Walpole, Benjamin Franklin, Burke], 1958 (b); *The Greatest Problem and Other Essays*, 1960 (e); *The Drama of Ibsen and Strindberg*, 1962 (c)

ROB LYLE
1920-

Guitar, 1951 (p); (with Francisco Xavier Lizarza India) *The Destiny of Spain*, 1952 (e); *Halcyon: Poems 1943-53*, 1953 (p); *Mistral*, 1953 (e); *Heroic Elegies*, 1957 (p); *Poems from Limbo*, 1960 (p)

ROBERT LYND
1879-1949

Irish and English, Portraits and Impressions, 1908 (e); *Home Life in Ireland*, 1909 (e); *Rambles in Ireland*, 1912 (t); *The Book of This and That*, 1915 (e); *Ireland a Nation*, 1919 (h); *Old and New Masters*, 1919 (c); *The Art of Letters*, 1920 (c); *The Passion of Labor*, 1920 (e); *The Pleasures of Ignorance*, 1921 (e); *Books and Authors*, 1922 (c); *The Sporting Life*, 1922 (e); *Solomon in all his Glory*, 1922 (e); *The Blue Lion*, 1923 (e);

Selected Essays, 1923; *The Peal of Bells*, 1924 (e); *The Money Box*, 1925 (e); *The Little Angel*, 1926 (e); *The Orange Tree*, 1926 (e); *Dr. Johnson and Company*, 1927 (b); *The Goldfish*, 1927 (e); *The Green Man*, 1928 (e); *Old Friends in Fiction*, 1929 (c); *It's a Fine World*, 1930 (e); *Rain, Rain, Go to Spain*, 1931 (e); *The Cockleshell*, 1933 (e); *"Y.Y." An Anthology of Essays*, sel. Eileen Squire 1933 (e); *Both Sides of the Road*, 1934 (e); *I Tremble to Think*, 1936 (e); *In Defence of Pink*, 1937 (e); *Searchlights and Nightingales*, 1939 (e); *Life's Little Oddities*, 1941 (e); *Things One Hears*, 1945 (e); *Modern Poetry*, 1950 (c); *Essays on Life and Literature*, 1951 (e); *Books and Writers*, 1952 (c)

LILIAN BOWES-LYON
1895-1949

The Buried Stream, 1929 (n); *The White Hare*, 1934 (p); *Bright Feather Fading*, 1936 (p); *Tomorrow is a Revealing*, 1941 (p); *Evening in Stepney*, 1943 (p); *A Rough Walk Home*, 1946 (p); *Collected Poems*, 1948

ROSE MACAULAY
1881-1958

Abbots Verney, 1906 (n); *The Furnace*, 1907 (n); *The Secret River*, 1909 (n); *The Valley Captives*, 1911 (n); *Views and Vagabonds*, 1912 (n); *The Lee Shore*, 1912 (n); *The Two Blind Countries*, 1914 (p); *The Making of a Bigot*, 1914 (n); *Non-Combatants and Others*, 1916 (s); *What Not: A Prophetic Comedy*, 1919 (n); *Three Days*, 1919 (p); *Potterism*, 1920 (n); *Dangerous Ages*, 1921 (n); *Mystery at Geneva*, 1922 (n); *Told by an Idiot*, 1923 (n); *Orphan Island*, 1924 (n); *A Casual Commentary*, 1925 (e); *Catchwords and Claptrap*, 1926 (e); *Crewe Train*, 1926 (n); *Twenty-Two Poems*, 1927 (p); *Keeping Up Appearances*, 1928 (Am. ed. *Daisy and Daphne*) (n); *Staying with Relations*, 1930 (n); *Some Religious Elements in English Literature*, 1931 (e); *They Were Defeated*, 1932 (Am. ed. *The Shadow Flies*) (n); *Going Abroad*, 1934 (n); *Milton*, 1934 (b); *Personal Pleasures*, 1935 (e); *I Would Be Private*, 1937 (n); *The Writings of*

E. M. Forster, 1938 (c); *And No Man's Wit*, 1940 (n); *Life Among the English*, 1942 (e); *They Went to Portugal*, 1946 (e); *Fabled Shore: From the Pyrenees to Portugal*, 1949 (t); *The World My Wilderness*, 1950 (n); *Pleasure of Ruins*, 1953 (t); *The Disguises of Love*, 1953 (n); *The Towers of Trebizond*, 1956 (n); *The End of Pity*, 1958 (s); *Letters to a Friend*, ed. Constance B. Smith, 1961; *Last Letters to a Friend*, ed. Constance B. Smith, 1962

NORMAN MACCAIG
1910-

Far Cry, 1943 (p); *The Inward Eye*, 1946 (p); *Riding Lights*, 1955 (p); *The Sinai Sort*, 1957 (p); *A Common Grace*, 1960, (p); *A Round of Applause*, 1963 (p)

DESMOND MACCARTHY
1878-1952

The Court Theatre: 1904-1907, 1907 (h); *Lady John Russell: A Memoir with Selections from Her Diaries*, 1910 (m); (with S. Waterlow) [Jules Romains] *The Death of a Nobody*, 1914 (tr); *Remnants*, 1918 (e); Ed. *Life and Letters*, 1928-50; *Portraits*, 1931 (repr. 1954) (b); *Criticism*, 1932 (c); *William Somerset Maugham*, 1934 (c); *Experience*, 1935 (e); *Leslie Stephen*, 1937 (lecture); *Drama*, 1940 (c); *Shaw*, 1951 (c); *Humanities*, 1953 (e); *Memories*, 1953 (e); (with B. Guinness, etc.) E. T. W. Hoffman, *The Story of a Nutcracker*, 1953 (free tr); *Theatre*, 1954 (c)

E. M. Forster, *Desmond MacCarthy*, 1952 [no bibliog.]

HUGH MACDIARMID
1892-

Sangschaw, 1925 (p in Scots); *Penny Wheep*, 1926 (p); *A Drunk Man Looks at the Thistle*, 1926 (p); *Contemporary Scottish Studies*, 1926 (c); *The Lucky Bag*, 1927 (p); *Albyn, or, Scotland and the Future*, 1927 (e); *Scotland in 1980*, 1930 (e); *The Handmaid of the Lord*, 1930 (t); *To Circumjack Cencrastus, or, The Curly Snake*, 1930 (p); *Annals of the Five Senses*, 1930 (p,e); *First Hymn to Lenin*, 1931 (p); *Warning Democracy*, 1931 (e); *Tarras*, 1932 (p); *Second Hymn to Lenin*, 1932 (p); *Scots Unbound*,

1932 (p); *Five Bits of Miller*, 1934 (p); *Scottish Scene, or, The Intelligent Man's Guide to Albyn*, 1934 (e); *Stony Limits*, 1934 (repr. with *Scots Unbound*, 1956) (p); *At the Sign of the Thistle*, 1934 (e); *Selected Poems*, 1934 (p); *Scottish Eccentrics*, 1936 (b); *Direadh*, 1938 (p); *The Islands of Scotland*, 1939 (t); *Cornish Heroic Song for Valda*, 1943 (p); *Lucky Poet*, 1943 (a); *Selected Poems*, ed. R. Crombie Saunders, 1944 (p); *Speaking for Scotland: Selected Poems* (Am. ed.), 1946; *A Kist of Whistles*, 1947 (p); *Cunninghame Graham: a Centenary Study*, 1952 (c); *Selected Poems of Hugh MacDiarmid*, ed. Oliver Brown, 1954 (p); *Francis George Scott*, 1955 (e); *In Memoriam James Joyce*, 1955 (e); *Three Hymns to Lenin*, 1957 (p); *The Battle Continues*, 1957 (p); *Burns Today and Tomorrow*, 1959 (c); *The Kind of Poetry I Want*, 1961 (p); *Collected Poems*, 1962; *The Ugly Birds Without Wings*, 1962 (e); *The Man of (Almost) Independent Mind* [David Hume], 1962 (c); *Poems to Paintings by William Johnstone, 1933*, 1963 (p); *Poetry Like the Hawthorn*, 1963 (p); *The Terrible Crystal: A Vision of Scotland*, 1964 (p)

Kenneth Buthlay, *Hugh MacDiarmid*, 1964

ROGER MACDOUGALL
1910-

The Man in the White Suit, 1949 (d); *The Gentle Gunman*, 1950 (d); *To Dorothy, A Son*, 1952 (d); *Macadam and Eve*, 1952 (d); *Escapade*, 1953 (d); *The Facts of Life*, 1955 (d); *Double Image*, 1957 (d)

ARTHUR MACHEN
1863-1947

[Leolinus Siluriensis, pseud.] *The Anatomy of Tobacco*, 1884 (repr. 1926) (e); *The Heptameron, or, Tales and Novels of Marguerite, Queen of Navarre*, 1886 (tr); *The Grande Trouvaille*, 1887 (s); *The Chronicle of Clemendy . . . the Amorous Inventions and Facetious Tales of Master Gervase Perrot*, 1888 (n); *Thesaurus Incantatus*, 1888 (n); [Rabelais] *Fantastic Tales*, 1890 (tr); *The Great God Pan and The Inmost Light*, 1894 (repr. 1913) (s); *The*

Memoirs of Jacques Casanova, 1894 (repr. 1960) (tr); The Three Imposters, 1895 (n); Hieroglyphics, 1902 (e); Dr. Stiggins, His Views and Principles, 1906 (e); The House of Souls, 1906 (n); The Hill of Dreams, 1907 (repr. 1954) (n); The Angels of Mons, 1915 (s); The Great Return, 1915 (s); The Terror, 1917 (n); Far Off Things, 1922 (a); The Secret Glory, 1922 (n); Strange Roads, 1923 (e); The Caerleon Edition of the Works, 9 vols., 1923; Things Near and Far, 1923 (a); Dog and Duck, A London Calendar, 1924 (e); The Glorious Mystery, ed. Vincent Starrett [periodical contributions], 1924 (e); The London Adventure, 1924 (t); Ornaments in Jade, 1924 (e); The Canning Wonder [the Case of Elizabeth Canning], 1925 (e); Dreads and Drolls, 1926 (e); Notes and Queries, 1926 (e); Tom o' Bedlam and his Song, 1930 (e); The Green Round, 1933 (n); The Children of the Pool, 1936 (s); The Cosy Room, 1936 (s); Holy Terrors, 1946 (s); Tales of Horror and the Supernatural, 1948 (s); The Gray's Inn Coffee House, 1949 (e); Bridles and Spurs, 1951 (e)

Aidan Reynolds and William Charlton, Arthur Machen: A Short Account of His Life and Work, introd. D. B. Wyndham Lewis, 1963

COLIN MACINNES
1914-

To the Victors the Spoils, 1950 (r); June In Her Spring, 1952 (n); City of Spades, 1957 (n); Absolute Beginners, 1959 (n); Mr. Love and Justice, 1960 (n); England, Half English, 1961 (e); (with Kenneth Clarke and B. Robertson) Sidney Nolan, 1961 (c)

J. W. MACKAIL
1859-1945

(with others) Mensae Secundae, Verses Written in Balliol College, 1879 (p); Thermopylae, 1881 (Newdigate prize verse); (with H. C. Beaching and J. B. B. Nichols) Love in Idleness, 1883 (p); The Aeneid of Virgil, 1885 (tr); The Eclogues and Georgics of Virgil, 1889 (tr.); Select Epigrams from the Greek Anthology, 1890 (tr); (with H .C. Beaching) Love's Looking Glass, 1891 (p); Latin Literature, 1895 (h); Homer, Odysseus in Phaeacia [Bk. VI of Odyssey], 1896 (tr); The Life of William Morris, 1899 (repr. to 1950) (b); Homer, The Odyssey, 1903 (repr. 1932) (tr); Virgil in English Verse, 1903 (e); The Progress of Poesy, 1906 (inaugural lecture [Sheldonian Theatre]); The Springs of Helicon, a Study in the Progress of English Poetry from Chaucer to Milton, 1909 (h); Milton, 1909 (c); Swinburne, 1909 (Oxford Univ. lecture); Lectures on Poetry, 1911 (c); Lectures on Greek Poetry, 1911 (repr. 1926) (c); Pervigilium Veneris, 1912 (tr); The Study of Poetry, 1915 (e); Russia's Gift to the World, 1915 (e); Shakespeare after Three Hundred Years, 1916 (first annual Shakespeare lecture [Brit. Academy]); W. J. Courthope, 1842-1917, 1919 (e); Pope, 1919 (Leslie Stephen lecture); The Case for Latin in Secondary Schools, 1922 (e); Virgil and his Meaning to the World of Today (Vol. 15 of Our Debt to Greece and Rome), 1923 (e); The Classics, 1923 (Presid. Address, Classical Assoc.); The Alliance of Latin and English Studies, 1923 (e); Bentley's Milton, 1924 (Thomas Warton lecture); The Pilgrim's Progress, 1924 (e); What Is the Good of Greek?, 1924 (lecture); Classical Studies, 1925 (e); James Leigh Strachan-Davidson, Master of Balliol, 1925 (m); Studies of English Poets, 1926 (c); The Lesson of Imperial Rome, 1929 (lecture, Queen's Univ., Belfast); The Approach to Shakespeare, 1930 (Lord Northcliffe lectures); Largeness in Literature, 1930 (e); Virgil, 1931 (Annual lecture, Brit. Academy); Presidential Addresses, Brit. Academy, 1933, 1934, 1936; Studies in Humanism, 1938 (e)

Cyril Bailey, John William Mackail, 1947

COMPTON MACKENZIE
1883-

The Gentleman in Grey, 1906 (d); Poems, 1907 (p); The Passionate Elopement, 1911 (n); Carnival, 1912 (n); Kensington Rhymes, 1912 (p); Sinister Street, Vol. I, 1913 (n); Sinister Street, Vol. II, 1914 (Am. ed. Vol. I, Youth's Encounter, 1913; Vol. II, Sinister Street, 1914) (n); Guy and Pauline (Am. ed. Plashers Mead), 1915 (n); The Early Life and Adventures of Sylvia Scarlett (continues Sinister Street), 1918 (n); Sylvia and Michael (continues Sinister Street), 1919 (n); Poor Relations, 1919 (n); *The Vanity Girl*, 1920 (n); *Colum-bine*, 1920 (d); *Rich Relatives*, 1921 (n); *The Altar Steps*, 1922 (n); *The Seven Ages of Woman*, 1923 (s); (with Archibald Marshall) *Gramophone Nights*, 1923 (s); *The Parson's Progress* (seq. to *The Altar Steps*), 1923 (n); *The Heavenly Ladder* (seq. to *The Parson's Progress*), 1924 (n); *Santa Claus in Summer*, 1924 (n); *The Old Men of the Sea*, 1924 (n); *Coral* (seq. to *Carnival*), 1925 (n); *Fairy Gold*, 1926 (n); *Rogues and Vagabonds*, 1927 n); *The Life and Adventures of Sylvia Scarlett* (complete ed.), 1927 (n); *Vestal Fire*, 1927 (n); *Extremes Meet*, 1928 (n); *Extraordinary Women*, 1928 (n); *The Three Couriers*, 1929 (n); *Gallipoli Memories*, 1929 (r); *April Fools*, 1930 (n); *Told*, 1930 (n); *First Athenian Memories*, 1931 (a); *Buttercups and Daisies* (Am. ed. *For Sale*), 1931 (n); *Our Street*, 1931 (n); *The Lost Cause*, 1931 (d); *Unconsidered Trifles*, 1932 (e); *Greek Memories*, 1932 (withdrawn from publication, reissued 1940 (r); *Prince Charlie*, 1932 (b); *Water on the Brain*, 1933 (n); *Literature in My Time*, 1933 (c); *Reaped and Bound*, 1933 (e); *The Darkening Green*, 1934 (n); *Marathon and Salamis*, 1934 (e); *Prince Charlie and His Ladies*, 1934 (b); *Catholicism and Scotland*, 1936 (e); *Figure of Eight*, 1936 (n); *Pericles*, 1937 (b); *Four Winds of Love*, 1937-1945 [*The East Wind*, 1937; *The South Wind*, 1937; *The West Wind*, 1940; *West to North*, 1940; *The North Wind*, Vol. I, 1944; *The North Wind*, Vol. II, 1945] (n); *The Windsor Tapestry*, 1938 (b); *A Musical Chair*, 1939 (e); *Aegean Memories*, 1940 (r); *The Red Tapeworm*, 1941 (n); *The Monarch of the Glen*, 1941 (n); *Calvary*, 1942 (e); *Wind of Freedom*, 1943 (e); *Keep the Home Guard Turning*, 1943 (n); *Mr. Roosevelt*, 1943 (b); *Brockhouse*, 1944 (e); *Dr. Benes*, 1945 (b); *The Vital Flame*, 1945 (e); *Whisky Galore*, 1947 (n); *All Over the Place*, 1949 (e); *Hunting the Fairies*, 1949 (n); *Coalport*, 1951 (e); *Eastern Epic*, Vol. I, 1951 (e); *I Took a Journey*, 1951 (e); *The Rival Monster*, 1952 (n); *The Queen's House*, 1953 (e); *Echoes*, 1953 (e); *Realms of Silver*, 1953 (e); *Ben Nevis Goes East*, 1954 (n); *Eastern Epic*, Vol. II, 1954 (e); *My Record of Music*, 1955 (a); *Thin Ice*, 1956 (n); *Rockets Galore*, 1957 (n); *Sublime*

Tobacco, 1957 (e); *Tatting*, 1957 (n); *The Lunatic Republic*, 1959 (n); *Tight Little Island*, 1959 (n); *Greece in My Life*, 1960 (a); *Cat's Company*, 1960 (e); *Catmint*, 1961 (e); *Mezzotint*, 1961 (n); *On Moral Courage*, 1962 (e); *My Life and Times, Octave 1: 1883-1891*, 1963 (a); *My Life and Times, Octave 2: 1891-1900*, 1963 (a); *My Life and Times, 1900-1907, Octave 3: Vintage Oxford Years and Debut as a Writer*, 1964 (a)

Leo Robertson, *Compton Mackenzie*, 1954

LOUIS MACNEICE
1907-1963

Blind Fireworks, 1929 (p); [Louis Malone, pseud.] *Roundabout Way*, 1932 (n); *Poems*, 1935 (p); *The Agamemnon of Aeschylus*, 1936 (tr); (with W. H. Auden) *Letters from Iceland*, 1937 (t); *Out of the Picture*, 1937 (d); *The Earth Compels*, 1938 (p); *I Crossed the Minch* [Outer Hebrides], 1938 (t); *Modern Poetry*, 1938 (c); *Zoo*, 1938 (e); *Autumn Journal*, 1939 (p); *The Last Ditch*, 1940 (p); *Selected Poems*, 1940 (p); *Poems, 1925-1940*, 1940 (p); *Plant and Phantom*, 1941 (p); *The Poetry of W. B. Yeats*, 1941 (c); *Meet the U.S. Army*, 1943 (e); *Christopher Columbus*, 1944 (rd); *Springboard: Poems 1941-1944*, 1944 (p); *The Dark Tower*, 1947 (rd); *Holes in the Sky: Poems 1944-1947*, 1948 (p); *Collected Poems, 1925-1948*, 1949; *Goethe's Faust* (abridged), 1951 (tr); *Ten Burnt Offerings*, 1952 (p); *Autumn Sequel*, 1954 (p); *The Other Wing*, 1954 (p); *Visitations*, 1957 (p); *Eighty-Five Poems*, 1959 (p); *Solstices*, 1961 (p); *The Burning Perch*, 1963 (p); *The Mad Islands, and The Administrator*, 1964 (2rd)

CHARLES MADGE
1912-

The Disappearing Castle, 1937 (p); *The Father Found*, 1941 (p); *Society in the Mind*, 1964 (e)

OLIVIA MANNING
? -

The Wind Changes, 1937 (n); *The Remarkable Expedition*, 1947 (Am. ed. *The Reluctant Rescue: the Story of Stanley's*

Rescue of Emir Pasha from Equatorial Africa) (b); Growing Up, 1948 (s); Artist Among the Missing, 1949 (n); The Dreaming Shore [West Coast of Ireland], 1950 (t); School for Love, 1951 (n); A Different Face, 1953 (n); The Doves of Venus, 1955 (n); My Husband Cartwright, 1956 (n); The Great Fortune, 1960 (n); The Spoilt City, 1962 (n)

KATHERINE MANSFIELD
1885-1923

In a German Pension, 1911 (s); Prelude, 1918 (s); Je Ne Parle Pas Français, 1918 (s); Bliss, 1920 (s); The Garden Party, 1922 (s); The Dove's Nest, 1923 (s); Poems, 1923 (p); Something Childish, 1924 (Am. ed. The Little Girl) (s); Journal of Katherine Mansfield, ed. J. Middleton Murry, 1927 (enlgd. 1954); The Letters of Katherine Mansfield, ed. J. Middleton Murry, 1928; The Aloe, 1930 (s); Novels and Novelists, [reviews for Athenaeum, 1919-20], ed. J. Middleton Murry, 1930 (c); Stories: a Selection, ed. J. Middleton Murry, 1930; The Scrapbook of Katherine Mansfield, ed. J. Middleton Murry, 1938; Collected Stories, 1945; Letters to J. Middleton Murry, 1913-22, ed. J. Middleton Murry, 1951

Anthony Alpers, Katherine Mansfield, 1954

CHARLES MARRIOTT
1869-1957

The Column, 1901 (n); Love With Honour, 1902 (n); The House on the Sands, 1903 (n); Genevra, 1904 (n); Mrs. Alemere's Elopement, 1905 (n); The Lapse of Vivien Eady, 1906 (n); Women and the West, 1906 (s); The Remnant, 1907 (n); The Wondrous Wife, 1907 (n); The Happy Medium, 1908 (s); The Kiss of Helen, 1908 (n); A Spanish Holiday, 1908 (t); The Intruding Angel, 1909 (n); When a Woman Woos, 1909 (n); "Now!", 1910 (n); The Romance of the Rhine, 1911 (e); The Dewpond, 1912 (n); The Catfish, 1913 (n); Subsoil, 1913 (n); What a Man Wants, 1913 (n); The Unpetitioned Heavens, 1914 (n); Davenport, 1915 (n); Modern Art, 1918 (c); Modern Movements in Painting, 1920 (c); The Grave Impertinence, 1921 (n);

An Order to View, 1922 (n); Masterpieces of Modern Art, 1922 (c); Pencil Drawing, 1922 (e); Modern English Architecture, 1924 (c); Eric Gill as Carver, 1929 (c); A Key to Modern Painting, 1938 (c); British Handicrafts, 1943 (e)

EDWARD MARSH
1872-1953

Rupert Brooke, 1918 (m); Forty-Two Fables of La Fontaine, 1924 (tr); More Fables of La Fontaine, 1925 (tr); The Fables of La Fontaine, 1931 (tr); A Number of People, 1939 (r); The Odes of Horace, 1941 (tr); Minima, 1947 (p,tr); Fromentin, Dominique, 1948 (tr); M. L. Bibescu, The Sphinx of Bagatelle (tr); M. L. Bibescu, Proust's Oriane, 1952 (tr)

Christopher Hassall, Edward Marsh, 1959

JOHN MASEFIELD
1878-

Salt-Water Ballads, 1902 (p); Ballads, 1903 (rev. enlgd. 1910) (p); A Mainsail Haul, 1905 (rev. enlgd. 1913, 1954) (e); Sea Life in Nelson's Time, 1905 (p); On the Spanish Main, 1906 (e); A Tarpaulin Muster, 1907 (s); Captain Margaret, 1908 (n); Multitude and Solitude, 1909 (n); The Tragedy of Nan, 1909 (repr. 1926) (d); The Tragedy of Pompey the Great, 1910 (d); Ballads and Poems, 1910 (p); Martin Hyde: the Duke's Messenger, 1910 (repr. 1931) (n); A Book of Discoveries, 1910 (e); Lost Endeavour, 1910 (repr. 1923) (e); The Everlasting Mercy, 1911 (p); William Shakespeare, 1911 (rev. 1954) (c); The Street of Today, 1911 (n); Jim Davis, 1911 (repr. 1947) (n); The Story of a Roadhouse, 1912 (p); The Widow in the Bye Street, 1912 (Am. ed. The Everlasting Mercy and The Widow in the Bye Street) (p); Dauber, 1913 (p); The Daffodil Fields, 1913 (p); Philip the King, 1914 (p); The Faithful: a Tragedy in Three Acts, 1915 (d); The Locked Chest; The Sweeps of Ninety-Eight, 1916 (2d); John M. Synge, 1915 (r); Sonnets and Poems, 1916 (p); Good Friday, 1916 (repr. 1955) (pd); Lollingdon Downs, 1917 (p); Poems, 1917; A Poem and Two Plays, 1918;

Collected Poems and Plays, 1919; *Reynard the Fox, or The Ghost Heath Run*, 1919 (p); *Enslaved*, 1920 (p); *Right Royal*, 1920 (p); *King Cole*, 1921 (p); Jean Racine, *Berenice*, 1922 (Am. ed. *Esther and Berenice*) (2d,tr); *Melloney Hotspur*, 1922 (d); *Selected Poems*, 1922 (p); *Leather Pocket Edition of Masefield's Work*, 8 vols., 1922; *The Dream*, 1922 (p); *A King's Daughter: a Tragedy in Verse*, 1923 (pd); *The Taking of Helen*, 1923 (s); *Collected Poems*, 1923 (rev. enlgd. 1932, 1938, 1946); *Recent Prose*, 1924 (rev. 1932); *Sard Harker*, 1924 (n); *Shakespeare and Spiritual Life*, 1924 (Romanes Lecture); *The Trial of Jesus*, 1925 (d); *Collected Works*, 4 vols., 1925; *Odtaa*, 1926 (n); *Tristan and Isolt*, 1927 (pd); *The Midnight Folk*, 1927 (n); *The Coming of Christ*, 1928 (d); *Midsummer Night*, 1928 (p); *Poems*, 1929 (p); *The Hawbucks*, 1929 (n); *Easter*, 1929 (pd); *The Wanderer of Liverpool*, 1930 (misc.); *Chaucer*, 1931 (Leslie Stephen lecture); *Minnie Maylow's Story*, 1931 (s); *A Tale of Troy*, 1932 (p); *The Conway from Her Foundation to the Present Day*, 1933 (h); *End and Beginning*, 1933 (p); *The Bird of Dawning*, 1933 (n); *The Taking of the Gry*, 1934 (n); *The Box of Delights*, 1935 (n); *Victorious Troy, or The Hurrying Angel*, 1935 (n); *The Collected Works*, 5 vols., 1935, 1937; *Eggs and Baker*, 1936 (n); *A Letter from Pontus*, 1936 (p); *The Square Peg, or The Gun Fella*, 1937 (n); *The Country Scene*, 1937 (p); *Dead Ned*, 1938 (n); (with Edward Seago, ill.) *Tribute to Ballet*, 1938 (p); *Live and Kicking Ned* [seq. to *Dead Ned*], 1939 (n); *Basilissa: A Tale of The Empress Theodora*, 1940 (n); *Some Memories of W. B. Yeats*, 1940 (r); *Gautama, the Enlightened*, 1941 (p); *In the Mill*, 1941 (a); *Conquer: A Tale of the Nika Rebellion in Byzantium*, 1941 (n); *A Generation Risen*, 1942 (p); *Land Workers*, 1942 (p); *Wanderings Between One and Six Years*, 1943 (p); *New Chum*, 1944 (a); *A Macbeth Production*, 1945 (e); *Thanks Before Going*, 1946 (e); *A Book of Both Sorts*, 1947 (p,e); *Badon Parchments*, 1947 (n); *A Play of St. George*, 1948 (d); *On the Hill*, 1949 (p); *In Praise of Nurses*, 1950 (p); *St. Katherine of Ledbury and Other Ledbury Papers*, 1951 (e); *So Long to Learn*, 1952 (a);

Poems: Complete Edition, 1953; *The Bluebells*, 1961 (p); *Old Raiger*, 1964 (p)

Geoffrey Handley-Taylor, *John Masefield, O.M.: the Queen's Poet Laureate*, 1960; L. A. G. Strong, *John Masefield*, 1952

A. E. W. MASON
1865-1948

Blanche de Malétroit (founded on story by R. L. Stevenson), 1894 (d); *A Romance of Wastdale*, 1895 (n); *The Courtship of Morrice Buckler*, 1896 (repr. 1938) (n); *The Philanderers*, 1897 (repr. 1938) (n); *Lawrence Clavering*, 1897 (n); *Miranda of the Balcony*, 1899 (repr. 1938) (n); *The Watchers*, 1899 (repr. 1940) (n); *Parson Kelly*, 1900 (n); *Engsign Knightley*, 1901 (s); *Clementina*, 1901 (n); *The Four Feathers*, 1902 (repr. 1960) (n); *The Truants*, 1904 (n); *Running Water*, 1907 (n); *The Broken Road*, 1907 (n); *Colonel Smith*, 1909 (d); *At the Villa Rose*, 1910 (repr. 1949) (n) (dramatized by Mason, 1928); *Green Stockings*, 1910 (d); *The Witness for the Defence*, 1911 (n; also dramatized); *The Turnstile*, 1912 (n); *The Four Corners of the World*, 1917 (s); *The Royal Exchange*, 1920 (e); *The Summons*, 1920 (n); *The Winding Stair*, 1923 (repr. 1949) (n); *The House of the Arrow*, 1924 (n); *No Other Tiger* 1927 (repr. 1948) (n); *The Prisoner in the Opal*, 1928 (n); *The Dean's Elbow*, 1930 (n); *The A. E. W. Mason Omnibus*, 1931 (3s); *The Three Gentlemen*, 1932 (n); *The Sapphire*, 1933 (n); *A Present for Margate*, 1934 (d); *Dilemmas*, 1934 (s); *They Wouldn't Be Chessmen*, 1935 (n); *Sir George Alexander and the St. James's Theatre*, 1935 (b); *Fire Over England*, 1936 (n); *The Drum*, 1937 (s); *Königsmark*, 1938 (n); *The Life of Francis Drake*, 1941 (b); *Musk and Amber*, 1942 (n); *The House in Lordship Lane*, 1946 (n)

Roger Lancelyn Green, *A. E. W. Mason*, 1952

JOHN MASTERS
1914-

Nightrunners of Bengal, 1951 (n); *The Deceivers*, 1952 (n); *The Lotus and the Wind*, 1953 (n); *Bhowani Junction*, 1954 (n); *Coromandel!*, 1955 (n); *Bugles and a Tiger*, 1956 (a); *Far, Far the Mountain Peak*, 1956 (n); *Fandango Rock*, 1959 (n); *The Venus of Konpara*, 1960 (n); *The Road Past Mandalay*, 1961 (a); *To the Coral Strand*, 1962 (n); *Trial at Monomoy*, 1964 (n)

W. S. MAUGHAM
1874-

Liza of Lambeth, 1897 (n); *The Making of a Saint*, 1898 (n); *Orientations*, 1899 (n); *The Hero*, 1901 (n); *Mrs. Craddock*, 1902 (rev. 1955) (n); *A Man of Honour*, 1903 (d); *The Merry-go-round*, 1904 (n); *The Land of the Blessed Virgin* (pub. as *Andalusia*, 1920), 1905 (t); *The Bishop's Apron: A Study in the Origins of a Great Family*, 1906 (n); *The Explorer*, 1907 (n); *The Magician*, 1908 (repr. 1956 with *Fragment of an Autobiography*) (n); *Lady Frederick*, 1912 (d); *Jack Straw*, 1912 (d); dramatization of *The Explorer*, 1912; *Mrs. Dot*, 1912 (d); *Penelope*, 1912 (p); *The Tenth Man*, 1913 (d); *Landed Gentry*, 1913 (d); *Smith*, 1913 (d); *The Land of Promise*, 1913 (d); *Of Human Bondage*, 1915 (many reprs.) (n); *The Moon and Sixpence*, 1919 (repr. 1941) (n); *The Unknown*, 1920 (d); *The Circle*, 1921 (d); *The Trembling of a Leaf* (contains "Rain" pub. as *Sadie Thompson*, 1928) 1921 (s); *Caesar's Wife*, 1922 (d); *East of Suez*, 1922 (d); *On a Chinese Screen*, 1922 (t); *Our Betters*, 1923 (d); *Home and Beauty*, 1923 (d); *The Unattainable*, 1923 (d); *Loaves and Fishes*, 1924 (d); *The Painted Veil*, 1925 (n); *The Casuarina Tree*, 1926 (6s); *The Constant Wife*, 1927 (d); *The Letter*, 1927 (d); *Ashenden, or The British Agent*, 1928 (s); *The Sacred Flame*, 1928 (d); *The Gentleman in the Parlour* [Rangoon to Haiphong], 1930 (t); *Cakes and Ale, or The Skeleton in the Cupboard*, 1930 (n); *The Breadwinner*, 1930 (d); *Dramatic Works*, Vol. I-VI, 1931-1934; *Six Stories Written in the First Person Singular*, 1931 (s); *The Book Bag*, 1932 (c); *The Narrow Corner*, 1932 (n); *For Services Rendered*, 1932 (d); *Ah King*, 1933 (s); *Sheppey*, 1933 (d); *Altogether* (coll. short stories), 1934 (Am. ed. *East and West*)(s); *Non-Dramatic Works*, 1934-51; *Don Fernando, or Variations on Some Spanish Themes*, 1935 (rev. 1950)(n); *The Collected Works*, 1936-1938; *Cosmopolitans*, 1936 (s); *My South Sea Island*, 1936 (t); *The Favourite Short Stories*, 1937 (s); *Theatre*, 1937 (n); *The Summing Up*, 1938 (a); *The Round Dozen*, 1939 (s); *Christmas Holiday*, 1939 (n); *Princess September and The Nightingale*, 1939 (s); *Books and You*, 1940 (c); *The Mixture As Before*, 1940 (s); *Up at the Villa*, 1941 (n); *Strictly Personal*, 1941 (r); *The Hour Before the Dawn*, 1942 (n); *The Unconquered*, 1944 (s); *The Razor's Edge*, 1944 (n); *Then and Now*, 1946 (n); *Creatures of Circumstance*, 1947 (s); *Catalina*, 1948 (n); *Quartet*, 1948 (4s); *Great Novelists and Their Novels*, 1948 [Eng. ed. 1954, *Ten Novels and Their Authors*] (rev. enlgd. 1955 as *The Art of Fiction*)(c); *A Writer's Notebook*, 1949 (a); *Trio*, 1950 (3s); *The Complete Short Stories*, 1951; *The Writer's Point of View*, 1951 (e,r); *Encore*, 1952 (s); *The Collected Plays*, 1952; *The Vagrant Mood*, 1952 (e); *The Noble Spaniard*, 1953 [written and produced in London, 1909] (d); *The Selected Novels*, 1953; *Ten Novels and Their Authors*, 1954 (rev. 1955) (Am. ed *Great Novelists and Their Novels*, 1948) (c); *The Partial View* [contains *The Summing Up* and *A Writer's Notebook* with new preface], 1954; *The Travel Books of William Somerset Maugham*, 1955 (t); *Points of View*, 1958 (e); *Purely for My Pleasure*, 1962 [exhibition of his painting collection]

Raymond Toole Stott, *The Writings of William Somerset Maugham: A Bibliography*, 1956

AUBREY MENEN
1912-

The Prevalence of Witches, 1947 (n); *The Stumbling Stone*, 1949 (n); *The Backward Bride*, 1950 (n); *The Duke of Gallodoro*, 1952 (n); *Dead Men in the Silver Market*, 1953 (a,e); *Rama Retold*, 1954 (n); *The Abode of Love*, 1957 (n); *The Fig Tree*, 1959 (n); *Rome Revealed*, 1960 (t); *SheLa: a Satire*, 1962 (n); *Speaking the Language Like a Native* [on Italy], 1963 (t)

CHARLOTTE MEW
1870-1928

The Farmer's Bride, 1916, new ed. with 11 new poems, 1921 (Am. ed. *Saturday Market*, 1921) (p); *The Rambling Sailor*, 1929 (p); *Collected Poems*, ed. with biog. memoir A. Monro, 1953

E. H. W. MEYERSTEIN
1889-1952

The Door, 1911 (p); *Three Odes*, 1914 (p); *Ode to Truth*, 1915 (p); *Symphonies*, 1915 (p); *The Witches' Sabbath*, 1917 (p); (with Wilfrid Blair) *Black and White Magic*, 1917 (p); *Symphonies: Second Series*, 1919 (p); *Heddon*, 1921 (d); *Mysteria Mundi*, 1921 (p); *Wade's Boat*, 1921 (p); *The Trireme*, 1921 (n); *In Merlin's Wood*, 1922 (p); *Voyage of Ass*, 1922 (p); *The Monument*, 1923 (d); *Odes on Several Contemplative and Metaphysical Subjects*, 1923 (p); *Ratscastle: a Kentish Interlude*, 1924 (pd); *The Pleasure Lover*, 1925 (n); *Grobo*, 1925 (n); *The Boy: a Modern Poem*, 1928 (p); *Terence in Love*, 1928 (n); *The First Christmas*, 1930 (p); *A Life of Thomas Chatterton*, 1930 (b); *New Symphonies*, 1933 (p); *The Pageant*, 1934 (s); *Goemagog and Corineus*, 1934 (p); *A Letter to a Naturalist*, 1935 (p); *Selected Poems*, 1935 (p); *Terence Duke (The Pleasure Lover, In Love, The Windfall)*, 1935 (3n); *The Elegies of Propertius*, 1935 (tr); *New Odes*, 1936 (p); *Séraphine*, 1936 (n); *A Boy of Clare*, 1937 (p); *Briancourt*, 1937 (p); *Joshua Slade*, 1938 (n); *Sonnets. In Exitu Israel. Peace: an Ode*, 1939 (p); *Four People*, 1939 (n); *Eclogues*, 1940 (p); *The Visionary*, 1941 (p); *In Time of War*, 1943 (p); *Azure*, 1944 (p); *Kathleen: a Sonnet Sequence*, 1945 (p); *Division*, 1946 (p); *A Bristol Friendship: Thomas Chatterton and John Baker*, 1947 (Wedmore Memorial lecture); *Redcliff Hill*, 1948 (d); *Three Sonnets*, 1948 (p); *Quartets for Four Voices*, 1949 (p); *The Delphic Charioteer*, 1951 (p); *Robin Wastraw*, 1951 (n); *Tom Tallion*, 1952 (n); *The Unseen Beloved*, 1953 (p); *Phoebe Thirsk*, 1953 (n); *Verse Letters to Five Friends*, 1954 (p); *Of My Early Life*, ed. Rowland Watson, 1957 (a); *Bollond*, 1958 (s); *Some Letters of E. H. W. Meyerstein*, ed. Rowland Watson, 1959; *Some Poems*, ed. M. Wollman, 1960 (p)

[Bristol Public Libraries] *Edward H. W. Meyerstein, Poet and Novelist. A Bibliography*, 1938

ALICE MEYNELL
1847-1922

(A. C. Thompson) *Preludes*, 1875 (p); *The Poor Sisters of Nazareth*, 1889 (e); *The Rhythm of Life*, 1893 (e); (with W. Farrar) *William Holman Hunt, His Life and Works*, 1893 (b); *Poems*, 1893 (p); *The Colour of Life*, 1896 (e); *The Children*, 1896 (e); *Other Poems*, 1896 (p); *London Impressions* (with etchings and photogravure pictures by William Hyde), 1898 (e); *The Spirit of Place*, 1899 (e); *John Ruskin*, 1900 (e); *Venture: The Madonna*, 1901 (e); *Later Poems*, 1902 (repr. as *The Shepherdess*, 1914) (p); *Children of the Old Masters* (Italian School), 1903 (e); René Bazin, *The Nun*, 1908 (tr); *Ceres' Runaway*, 1909 (e); *Mary, the Mother of Jesus*, 1912 (e); *Poems*, 1913 (p); *Childhood*, 1913 (e); *Essays*, 1914 (e); *Ten Poems*, 1915 (p); *Poems on the War*, 1916 (p); *A Father of Women*, 1917 (p); *Hearts of Controversy*, 1917 (e); *The Second Person Singular*, 1921 (e); *The Last Poems*, 1923 (p); *Selected Poems and Prose*, ed. Albert A. Cock, 1928; *Wayfaring*, 1929 (e); *Selected Poems*, 1930 (p); *The Poems of Alice Meynell*, Complete Ed., ed. Frederick Page, 1940 (p); *The Poems of Alice Meynell*, Centenary Ed., ed. Sir Francis Meynell, 1947 (p); *Alice Meynell, 1847-1922: Catalogue of the Centenary Exhibit of Books, Mss., Letters and Portraits*, 1947; *Prose and Poetry*, Centenary Vol., ed. F.P. etc. [Frederick Page etc.], with biog. and crit. introd. V. Sackville-West, 1947

Terence L. Connolly, *Alice Meynell: Centenary Tribute*, 1948 (list of bks.)

VIOLA MEYNELL
1886-1956

Martha Vine, 1910 (n); *Cross-in-Hand Farm*, 1911 (n); *Lot Barrow*, 1913 (n); *Modern Lovers*, 1914 (n); *Columbine*, 1915 (n); *Narcissus*, 1916 (n); *Julian Grenfell*, 1918 (e); *Second Marriage*, 1918 (repr. 1935) (n); *Verses*, 1919 (p); *Antonia*, 1921 (n); *Young Mrs. Cruse*, 1924 (s); *A Girl Adoring*, 1927 (n); *Alice Meynell: A Memoir*, 1929 (m); *The Frozen Ocean*, 1930 (p); *Follow Thy Fair Sun*, 1935 (n); *Kissing the Rod*, 1937 (s); *First Love*, 1947 (s); *Ophelia*, 1951 (n); *Louise*, 1954 (s); *Francis Thompson and Wilfrid Meynell: A Memoir*, 1952 (m); *Collected Stories*, 1957

A. A. MILNE
1882-1956

Lovers in London, 1905 (e); *The Day's Play*, 1910 (e); *The Holiday Round*, 1912 (e); *Once a Week*, 1914 (e); *Happy Days*, 1915 (e); *Once on a Time*, 1917 (n); *Make-Believe*, 1918 (d); *Not That It Matters*, 1919 (e); *First Plays*, 1919 (5d); *If I May*, 1920 (e); *Mr. Pim*, 1921 (n); *Mr. Pim Passes By*, 1921 (d); *Second Plays*, 1921 (5d); *The Sunny Side*, 1921 (e); *The Stepmother*, 1921 (d); *Red House Mystery*, 1922 (n); *The Artist,* 1923 (d); *Three Plays*, 1923 (3d); *The Man in the Bowler Hat*, 1923 (d); *The Truth About Blayds*, 1923 (d); *The Dover Road*, 1923 (d); *Success* 1923 (d); *Vespers*, 1924 (p); *When We Were Very Young*, 1924 (child's bk.); *For the Luncheon Interval*, 1925 (p); *Ariadne*, 1925 (d); *A Gallery of Children*, 1925 (child's bk.); *To Have the Honour*, 1925 (d); *Four Plays*, 1926 (4d); *Winnie-the-Pooh*, 1926 (child's bk.); *The Boy Comes Home*, 1926 (d); *Portrait of a Gentleman in Slippers*, 1926 (child's bk.); *Now We Are Six*, 1927 (child's bk.); *The House at Pooh Corner*, 1928 (child's bk.); *The Ascent of Man*, 1928 (e); *The Ivory Door*, 1928 (d); *The Fourth Wall* (Am. ed. *The Perfect Alibi*), 1929 (d); (from Kenneth Grahame's *The Wind in the Willows*) *Toad of Toad Hall*, 1929 (child's bk.); *The Secret*, 1929 (s); *By Way of Introduction*, 1929 (e); *The Christopher Robin Story Book*, 1929 (child's bk.); *Michael and Mary*, 1930 (d); *Two People*, 1931 (n); *The Christopher Robin Verses*, 1932 (child's bk.); *Four Day's Wonder*, 1933 (n); *Other People's Lives*, 1935 (d); *Miss Elizabeth Bennett*, 1936 (d); *It's Too Late Now*, 1939 (a); *Sarah Simple*, 1939 (d); *Behind the Lines*, 1940 (p); *The Ugly Duckling*, 1941 (d); *Chloe Marr*, 1946 (n); *Birthday Party*, 1948 (s); *The Norman Church*, 1948 (p); *A Table Near the Band*, 1950 (s); *Before the Flood*, 1951 (d); *Year In, Year Out*, 1952 (a)

NAOMI MITCHISON
1897-

The Conquered, 1923 (n); *When the Bough Breaks*, 1924 (s); *Cloud Cuckoo Land*, 1925 (n); *The Laburnum Branch*, 1926 (p); *Black Sparta*, 1928 (s); *Anna Comnena*, 1928 (b); *Barbarian Stories*, 1929 (s); *The Hostages*, 1930 (s); *The Corn King and the Spring Queen*, 1931 (n); (with L. E. Gielgud) *The Price of Freedom*, 1931 (d); *The Powers of Light*, 1932 (s); *The Delicate Fire*, 1933 (s,p); *Naomi Mitchison's Vienna Diary*, 1934 (t); *Beyond this Limit*, 1935 (s); *We Have Been Warned*, 1935 (n); *The Fourth Pig*, 1936 (s,p); *An End and a Beginning*, 1937 (d); (with R. H. Crossman) *Socrates*, 1937 (b); *The Moral Basis of Politics*, 1938 (e); *The Blood of the Martyrs*, 1939 (n); *The Kingdom of Heaven*, 1939 (e); (with L. E. Gielgud) *As It Was in the Beginning*, 1939 (d); *The Bull Calves*, 1947 (n); *The Big House*, 1950 (n); (with Denis Macintosh) *Spindrift*, 1951 (d); *Lobsters on the Agenda*, 1952 (n); *Travel Light*, 1952 (n); *Graeme and the Dragon*, 1954 (s); *The Swan's Road*, 1954 (h); *To the Chapel Perilous*, 1955 (n); *The Land the Ravens Found*, 1955 (s); *Little Boxes*, 1956 (s); *Behold Your King*, 1957 (n); *The Far Harbour*, 1957 (s); *Five Men and a Swan*, 1957 (s,p); *Judy and Lakshmi*, 1959 (s); *The Rib of Green Umbrella*, 1960 (s); *The Young Alexander the Great*, 1960 (b); *Memoirs of a Spacewoman*, 1962 (n); *When We Become Men*, 1964 (n)

NANCY MITFORD
1904-

Highland Fling, 1931 (n); *Christmas Pudding*, 1932 (n); *Wigs on the Green*, 1933 (n); *Pigeon Pie*, 1940 (n); *The Pursuit of Love*, 1945 (n); *Love in a Cold Climate*, 1949 (n); A. Roussin, *La Petite Hutte*, 1951 (tr); Madame de Lafayette, *The Princess de Clèves*, 1950 (tr); *Madame de Pompadour*, 1954 (b); *Omnibus*, 1956 (s); *Noblesse Oblige*, 1956 (e); *The Blessing*, 1957 (s); *Voltaire in Love*, 1957 (b); *Don't Tell Alfred*, 1960 (n); *The Water Beetle*, 1962 (e)

ALLAN MONKHOUSE
1858-1936

Books and Plays, 1894 (e); A Deliverance, 1898 (n); Love in a Life, 1903 (n); The Words and the Play, 1910 (e); Dying Fires, 1912 (n); Mary Broome, 1912 (d); The Education of Mr. Surrege, 1913 (d); Four Tragedies, 1913 (d); War Plays, 1916 (d); Men and Ghosts, 1918 (n); True Love, 1919 (n); My Daughter Helen, 1922 (n); The Conquering Hero, 1923 (d); First Blood, 1924 (d); The Grand Cham's Diamond, 1924 (d); Marmaduke, 1924 (d); Sons and Fathers, 1925 (d); Suburb, 1925 (n); O Death, Where is thy Sting?, 1926 (d); Selected Essays, 1926 (e); Alfred the Great, 1927 (n); The King of Barvender, 1927 (d); The Rag, 1928 (d); Nothing Like Leather, 1930 (d); Paul Felice, 1930 (d); Farewell Manchester, 1931 (n); Cecilia, 1932 (d)

HAROLD MONRO
1879-1932

Poems, 1906 (p); Judas, 1907 (p); The Evolution of the Soul [of Christ], 1907 (e); Before Dawn: Poems and Impressions, 1911 (p); The Chronicle of a Pilgrimage: Paris to Rome on Foot, 1912 (t); Children of Love, 1914 (p); Trees, 1916 (p); Strange Meetings, 1917 (p); Some Contemporary Poets, 1920 (c); Real Property, 1922 (p); One Day Awake: a Morality, 1922 (d); Seventeen Poems, 1927 (p); The Earth for Sale, 1928 (p); The Winter Solstice, 1928 (p); Elm Angel, 1930 (p); Collected Poems, ed. Alida Monro, 1933; Recent Poetry, 1923-1933, ed. Alida Monro, 1933 (p); The Silent Pool, chosen by A. Monro, 1942 (p)

NICHOLAS MONSARRAT
1910-

Think of Tomorrow, 1934 (n); At First Sight, 1935 (n); The Whipping Boy, 1937 (n); This Is the Schoolroom, 1939 (n); H.M. Corvette, 1942 (s); East Coast Corvette, 1943 (s); Corvette Command, 1944 (s); Three Corvettes, 1945 (3s); H.M. Frigate, 1946 (r); Depends What You Mean By Love, 1947 (3s); My Brother Denys, 1948 (r); The Cruel Sea, 1951 (n); "H.M.S. Marlborough Will Enter Harbour," 1952 (s); The Story of Esther Costello, 1953 (n); The Tribe That Lost Its Head, 1956 (n); The Ship That Died of Shame, 1959 (s); The Nylon Pirates, 1960 (n); The White Rajah, 1961 (n); Smith and Jones, 1963 (n); A Fair Day's Work, 1964 (n)

GEORGE MOORE
1852-1933

Worldliness, 1874 (d); Flowers of Passion, 1878 (p); (with B. Lopez) Martin Luther, 1879 (d); Pagan Poems, 1881; A Modern Lover, 1883 (rev. as Lewis Seymour and Some Women, 1917) (n); A Mummer's Wife, 1885 (n); Literature at Nurse, or, Circulating Morals, 1885 (e); A Drama in Muslin, 1886 (rev. as Muslin, 1915) (n); A Mere Accident, 1887 (n); Parnell and His Island, 1887 (e); Spring Days, 1888 (n); Confessions of a Young Man, 1888 (r); Mike Fletcher, 1889 (n); Vain Fortune, 1890 (n); Impressions and Opinions, 1891 (c); Modern Painting, 1893 (c); The Strike at Arlingford, 1893 (d); Esther Waters, 1894 (n); The Royal Academy, 1895, 1895 (c); Celibates, 1895 (s); Evelyn Innes, 1898 (n); The Bending of the Bough, 1900 (d); Sister Theresa, 1901 (sec. ed. rewritten, 1909) (n); The Untilled Field, 1903 (s); The Lake, 1905 (n); Memoirs of My Dead Life, 1906 (r); Reminiscences of the Impressionist Painters, 1906 (r); The Apostle, 1911 (rev. 1923) (d); Hail and Farewell, Trilogy: Ave, 1911, Salve, 1912 (a); Esther Waters, 1913 (d); Elizabeth Cooper, 1913 (d); Vale, 1914 [last vol. of trilogy] (a); The Brook Kerith, 1916 (n); A Story-Teller's Holiday, 1918 (e); Avowals, 1919 (r,c); The Coming of Gabrielle, 1920 (d); Héloïse and Abélard, 1921 (n); In Single Strictness, 1922 (rev. as Celibate Lives, 1927) (s); Conversations in Ebury Street, 1924 (r); Longus, The Pastoral Loves of Daphnis and Chloe, 1924 (tr); Moore versus Harris, an Intimate Correspondence, 1925; Ulick and Soracha, 1926 (n); Peronnik the Fool, 1926 (s); The Making of an Immortal, 1927 (d); Letters from George Moore to Edward Dujardin, 1886-1922, tr. by John Eglinton, 1929; Aphrodite in Aulis, 1930 (rev. 1931) (n); A Flood, 1930 (s); The Passing of the Essenes, 1930 (d); George Moore in Quest of Locale, 1931 (e); The Talking Pine, 1932 (c); A Com-

munication to my Friends, 1933 (m); (with W. B. Yeats) *Diarmuid and Grania*, 1951 (d); *Letters to Lady Cunard 1895-1933*, ed. Rupert Hart-Davis, 1957

Joseph Hone, *The Life of George Moore*, 1936

NICHOLAS MOORE
1918-

A Book for Priscilla, 1941 (p); *A Wish in Season*, 1941 (p); *The Island and the Cattle*, 1941 (p); *The Carbaret, The Dancer, The Gentlemen*, 1942 (p); *Three Poems*, 1944 (p); *The Glass Tower*, 1944 (p); *Buzzing Around With a Bee*, 1948 (p); *Recollections of the Gala: Selected Poems, 1943-48*, 1950 (p); *Henry Miller*, 1953 (c); *The Bearded Iris*, 1956 (p)

T. STURGE MOORE
1870-1944

Maurice de Guérin, *The Centaur, The Bacchante*, 1899 (tr); *The Vinedresser*, 1899 (p); *Altdorfer*, 1900 (e); *Aphrodite Against Artemis*, 1901 (d); *The Centaur's Booty*, 1903 (p); *Danaë*, 1903 (p); *The Rout of the Amazons*, 1903 (p); *Absalom*, 1903 (d); *The Gazelles*, 1904 (p); *Pan's Prophecy*, 1904 (p); *Poems, Collected in One Volume*, 1904 (p); *Theseus, Medea, and Lyrics*, 1904 (p); *To Leda*, 1904 (p); *The Little School, a Posy of Rhymes*, 1905 (p); *Albert Dürer*, 1905 (b); *Corregio*, 1906 (b); *Art and Life*, 1910 (e); *Mariamne*, 1911 (p); *A Sicilian Idyll and Judith, a Conflict*, 1911 (p); *The Sea is Kind*, 1914 (p); *Hark to These Three Talk About Style*, 1915 (e); *Some Soldier Poets*, 1919 (c); *The Powers of the Air*, 1920 (d); *Danaë, Aforetime, Blind Thamyris*, 1920 (p); *Tragic Mothers*, 1920 (d); *Judas*, 1923 (p); *Roderigo of Bivar*, 1925 (d); *Armour for Aphrodite*, 1929 (c); *Mystery and Tragedy*, 1930 (2pd); *Nine Poems*, 1930; *The Poems of T. S. Moore, 1931-33*, 1933 (p); *Selected Poems of T. Sturge Moore*, 1934 (p); *The Unknown Known*, 1939 (p); *William Butler Yeats and T. Sturge Moore: Their Correspondence, 1901-1937*, 1953

Frederick L. Gywnn, *Sturge Moore and the Life of Art*, 1952

CHARLES MORGAN
1894-1958

The Gunroom, 1919 (n); *My Name Is Legion*, 1925 (n); *Portrait In a Mirror*, 1929 (also pub. as *First Love*), (n); *The Fountain*, 1932 (n); *Epitaph on George Moore*, 1935 (c); *Sparkenbroke*, 1936 (n); *The Simple Things in Life*, 1937 (e); *The Flashing Stream*, 1938 (rev. 1945 (d); *The Voyage*, 1940 (n); *The Empty Room*, 1941 (n); *Ode to France*, 1942 (p); *The House of Macmillan, 1843-1943*, 1943 (h); *Reflections in a Mirror*, 1944 (e); *The Artist in the Community*, 1945 (e); *Reflections in a Mirror*, second series, 1946 (e); *The Judge's Story*, 1947 (n); *The Liberty of Thought and the Separation of Powers* [Zaharoff lecture], 1948 (e); *The River Line*, 1949 (n); *A Breeze of Morning*, 1951 (n); *Liberties of the Mind*, 1951 (e); *The River Line*, 1949 (d); *The Burning Glass*, 1954 (d); *Dialogue in Novels and Plays*, 1954 (c); *On Learning to Write*, 1954 (Presid. address, Eng. Assoc.); *Challenge to Venus*, 1957 (n); *The Writer and his World*, 1960 (e)

Gilbert H. Fabes, *The First Editions of A. E. Coppard, A. P. Herbert and Charles Morgan*, 1933

R. H. MOTTRAM
1883-

(J. Marjoram, pseud.) *Repose*, 1907 (p); *New Poems*, 1909 (p); *The Spanish Farm*, 1924 (n); *Sixty-four, Ninety-four!*, 1925 (n); *The Crime at Vanderlynden's*, 1926 (n); *Our Mr. Dormer*, 1927 (n); *The Spanish Farm Trilogy, 1914-1919*, 1927 (n); *The English Miss*, 1928 (n); *The Apple Disdained*, 1928 (s); *Boroughmonger*, 1929 (n); *The New Providence*, 1930 (e); (with others) *Three Personal Records of the War* (Am. ed. *Three Men's War*), 1930 (r); *Poems Old and New*, 1930 (p); H. Daniel-Rops, *The Misted Mirror*, 1930 (tr); *Europa's Beast* (Am. ed. *A Rich Man's Daughter*), 1930 (n); *The Headless Hound*, 1931 (s); *The Lost Christmas Present*, 1931 (s); *Caste Island*, 1931 (n); *John Crome of Norwich*, 1931 (b); *Dazzle*, 1932 (n); *Through the Menin Gate*, 1932 (r); *Home for the Holidays*, 1932 (n); *The Lame Dog* (Am. ed. *At the Sign of the Lame Dog*), 1933 (n);

A Good Old-Fashioned Christmas, 1933 (n); *East Anglia*, 1933 (t); *The Banquet*, 1934 (s); *Strawberry Time*, 1934 (s); *Bumphrey's*, 1934 (n); *Early Morning*, 1935 (n); *Portrait of an Unknown Victorian*, 1936 (b); *Noah*, 1937 (e); *Time to be Going*, 1937 (n); *Autobiography With a Difference*, 1938 (a); *There Was a Jolly Miller*, 1938 (n); *Miss Lavington*, 1939 (n); *Trader's Dream*, 1939 (e); *You Can't Have it Back*, 1939 (n); *The Ghost and the Maiden*, 1940 (n); *The World Turns Slowly Round*, 1942 (n); *The Corbells at War*, 1943 (n); *Buxton the Liberator*, 1946 (n); *Visit to the Princess*, 1946 (n); *The Gentleman of Leisure*, 1948 (n); *Come to the Bower*, 1949 (n); *One Hundred and Twenty-eight Witnesses*, 1951 (n); *The Part that is Missing*, 1952 (n); *The Broads*, 1952 (t); *If Stones Could Speak*, 1953 (t); *John Galsworthy*, 1953 (c); *The Window Seat*, 1954 (a); *Over the Wall*, 1955 (n); *For Some We Loved*, 1956 (b); *Scenes that are Brightest*, 1956 (n); *Another Window Seat*, 1957 (a); *Vanities and Verities*, 1958 (r); *No One Will Ever Know*, 1958 (n); *Young Man's Fancies*, 1959, (n); *Musetta*, 1960 (n); *Time's Increase*, 1961 (n); *To Hell, with Crabb Robinson*, 1962 (n); *Happy Birds*, 1963 (n)

EDWIN MUIR
1887-1959

[E. Moore, pseud.] *Enigmas and Guesses*, 1918 (c); *Latitudes*, 1924 (c); *First Poems*, 1925 (p); *Chorus of the Newly Dead*, 1926 (p); *Transition, Essays on Contemporary Literature*, 1926 (c); *The Marionette*, 1928 (n); *The Structure of the Novel*, 1928 (e); *John Knox*, 1929 (b); *The Three Brothers*, 1931 (n); *Variations on a Time Theme*, 1934 (p); *Scottish Journey*, 1935 (t); *Scott and Scotland*, 1936 (e); *Journeys and Places*, 1937 (p); *The Present Age from 1914*, 1939 (c); *The Story and the Fable*, 1940 (rev. and enlgd. as *An Autobiography*, 1954) (a); *The Narrow Place*, 1943 (p); *The Voyage*, 1946 (p); *The Scots and their Country*, 1946 (e); *Essays on Literature and Society*, 1949 (e); *The Labyrinth*, 1949 (p); *Prometheus*, 1954 (p); *One Foot in Eden*, 1956 (p); *Collected Poems, 1921-1951*, 1952; *Collected Poems, 1921-1958*, 1960;

(with Willa Muir) tr. Franz Kafka as follows: *The Castle*, 1930; *The Great Wall of China*, 1933; *The Trial*, 1937; *America*, 1949; *In the Penal Settlement*, 1949; also, with Willa Muir, tr. Gerhart Hauptmann, C. Heuser, L. Feuchtwanger, Sholem Asch, etc.

Elgin W. Mellown, *Bibliography of the Writings of Edwin Muir*, 1964

C. K. MUNRO
1889-

At Mrs. Beam's, 1923 (d); *The Rumour*, 1923 (d); *Storm, or The Battle of Tinderley Down*, 1924 (d); *Progress*, 1924 (d); *The Mountain, or The Story of Captain Yevan*, 1926 (d); *Bluestone Quarry*, 1931 (d); *Three Plays*, 1932 (3d); *The True Woman, a Handbook for Husbands and Others*, 1932 (e); *Watching a Play*, 1933 (e); *The Fountains in Trafalgar Square*, 1952 (e)

IRIS MURDOCH
1919-

Sartre, 1953 (c); *Under the Net*, 1954 (n); *The Flight from the Enchanter*, 1956 (n); *The Sandcastle*, 1957 (n); *The Bell*, 1958 (n); *A Severed Head*, 1961 (n); *An Unofficial Rose*, 1962 (n); *The Unicorn*, 1963 (n); (with J. B. Priestley) dramatization of *A Severed Head*, 1964 (d); *The Italian Girl*, 1964 (n)

GILBERT MURRAY
1866-1957

Greek Comic Verse, 1886 (tr); *The Place of Greek in Education*, 1889 (inaugural lecture, Univ. of Glasgow); *A History of Ancient Greek Literature*, 1897 (Am. ed. *Literature of Ancient Greece*,1956) (h); *Andromache*, 1900 (d); *Carlyon Sahib*, 1900 (d); *The Hippolytus and The Bacchae of Euripides, with The Frogs of Aristophanes*, 1902 (tr); *The Electra of Euripides*, 1905 (tr); *The Trojan Women of Euripides*, 1905 (tr); *The Medea of Euripides*, 1906 (tr); *The Rise of the Greek Epic*, 1907 (repr. 1924) (h); *The Early Greek Epic*, 1908 (h); *The Interpretation of Greek Literature*, 1909 (c); *The Iphigenia in Taurus of Euripides*, 1910 (tr); Sophocles, *Oedipus, King of Thebes*, 1911 (tr); *The Story of Nefrekepta*, 1911 (p); *Four Stages of Greek Religion*, 1912 (second ed. *Five Stages of Greek Religion*, 1925) (h); *The Rhesus of Euripides*, 1913 (tr); *Euripides and His Age*, 1913 (h); *Hamlet and Orestes, a Study in Traditional Types*, 1914 (c); *The Alcestis of Euripides*, 1915 (tr); *Religio Grammatici*, 1918 (Pres. Address, Classical Assoc.); *Aristophanes and the War Party*, 1919 (Am. ed. *Our Great War and the Great War of "The Ancient Greeks"*) (e); *Satanism and the World Order*, 1920 (e); *The Agamemnon of Aeschylus*, 1920 (tr); *The Choëphoroe of Aeschylus*, 1920 (tr); *Essays and Addresses*, 1921 (Am. ed. *Tradition and Progress*) (e); *The Eumenides of Aeschylus*, 1925 (tr); *The Classical Tradition in Poetry*, 1927 (e); *The Oresteia* [of Aeschylus], 1928 (tr); *The Suppliant Women* [of Aeschylus], 1930 (tr); *Prometheus Bound* [of Aeschylus], 1931 (tr); *Aristophanes, a Study*, 1933 (c); *Then and Now*, 1935 (e); *Liberality and Civilization*, 1938 (e); *Stoic, Christian and Humanist*, 1940 (e); *Aeschylus, the Creator of Tragedy*, 1940 (c); *David Samuel Margoliouth*, 1942 (b); *A Conversation with Bryce*, 1944 (c); *Myths and Ethics*, 1944 (e); *Greek Studies*, 1946 (c); *The World of Learning*, 1947 (e); *Andrew Lang: The Poet*, 1948 (c); *Hellenism and the Modern World*, 1953 (e); *Collected Plays of Euripides*, 1955 (tr); *The Meaning of Freedom*, 1957 (e); *An Unfinished Autobiography*, ed. J. Smith, 1960 (a)

See: *Essays in Honour of Gilbert Murray*, eds. J.A.K.T. [J. A. K. Thomson] and A.J.T. [A. J. Toynbee], 1936; *Greek Poetry, Essays to be Presented to Professor Gilbert Murray*, 1936

JOHN MIDDLETON MURRY
1889-1957

Fyodor Dostoevsky, 1916 (c); (with S. S. Koteliansky) *Pages from the Journal of an Author, Fyodor Dostoevsky*, 1916 (tr); *Still Life*, 1916 (n); *The Evolution of an Intellectual*, 1916 (a); *The Critic in Judgment, or Belshazzar of Barons Court*, 1919 (c); *Aspects of Literature*, 1920 (c); *Cinnamon and Angelica*, 1920 (d); *Poems, 1916-1920*, 1921 (p); *Countries of the Mind*, 1922 (c); *The

Problem of Style, 1922 (c); *The Things We Are*, 1922 (n); *Pencillings*, 1923 (e); (with S. S. Koteliansky) *Dostoevsky, Letters and Reminiscences*, 1923 (tr); *The Voyage*, 1924 (n); *Discoveries*, 1924 (c); *To the Unknown God*, 1924 (e); *Wrap Me Up in My Aubusson Carpet*, 1924 (e); *Keats and Shakespeare*, 1925 (c); *The Life of Jesus*, 1926 (Am. ed. *Jesus, Man of Genius*) (b); *Things to Come* (seq. to *The Unknown God*), 1928 (e); *God*, 1929 (e); *D. H. Lawrence*, 1930 (c); *Studies in Keats*, 1930 (c); *Son of Woman, The Story of D. H. Lawrence*, 1931 (b); *Countries of the Mind*, Sec. Series, 1931 (c); *The Fallacy of Economics*, 1932 (e); *The Necessity of Communism*, 1932 (e); (with Ruth E. Mantz) *The Life of Katherine Mansfield*, 1935 (b); *Reminiscences of D. H. Lawrence*, 1933 (r,c); *William Blake*, 1933 (b); *Between Two Worlds*, 1935 (a); *Shakespeare*, 1936 (c); *The Necessity of Pacifism*, 1937 (e); *The Pledge of Peace*, 1938 (e); *Heaven and Earth*, 1938 (e); *The Defence of Democracy*, 1939 (e); *The Price of Leadership*, 1939 (e); *Studies in Keats, New and Old*, 1939 (c); *The Betrayal of Christ by the Churches*, 1940 (e); *Adam and Eve*, 1944 (e); *The Challenge of Schweitzer*, 1948 (e); *Looking Before and After*, 1948 (e); *The Free Society*, 1948 (e); *Katherine Mansfield and Other Literary Portraits*, 1949 (r,c); *The Mystery of Keats*, 1949 (c); *John Clare and Other Studies*, 1950 (c); *The Conquest of Death* [Benjamin Constant's *Adolphe*, with commentary], 1951 (tr); *Community Farm*, 1952 (a); *Jonathan Swift*, 1954 (b,c); *Swift*, 1955 (c); *Keats*, 1955 (c); *Unprofessional Essays*, 1956 (c); *Love, Freedom and Society* [on D. H. Lawrence, Schweitzer, etc.], 1957 (e); *Select Criticism, 1916-1957*, chosen Richard Rees, 1960 (c)

Philip Mairet, *John Middleton Murry*, 1956

L. H. MYERS
1881-1944

Arvat, A Dramatic Poem, 1908 (pd); *The Orissers*, 1922 (n); *The Clio*, 1925 (n); *The Near and the Far*, 1929 (n); *Prince Jali* (seq. to preceding), 1931 (n); *The Root and the Flower* [the two preceding novels and *Rajah Amar*], 1935 (n); *Strange Glory*, 1936 (n); *The Pool *of Vishnu*, 1940 (n); *The Near and the Far* [preceding title with *The Root and the Flower*], 1943 (n)

G. H. Bantock, *L. H. Myers: A Critical Study*, 1956

HENRY NEWBOLT
1862-1938

Taken from the Enemy, 1892 (n); *Mordred*, 1895 (pd); *Admirals All*, 1897 (p); *The Island Race*, 1898 (p); *The Sailing of the Long-Ships*, 1902 (p); *The Year of Trafalgar*, 1905 (h); *The Old Country*, 1906 (n); *Clifton Chapel*, 1908 (p); *Songs of Memory and Hope*, 1909 (p); *The New June*, 1909 (n); *Collected Poems, 1897-1907*, 1910; *The Twymans*, 1911 (n); *Poems: New and Old*, 1912 (p); *Drake's Drum*, 1914 (p); *Aladore*, 1914 (n); *The King's Highway*, 1915 (p); *A New Study of English Poetry*, 1917 (c); *St. George's Day*, 1918 (p); *The Book of the Long Trail*, 1919 (e); *Poetry and Time*, 1919 (c); *A Naval History of the War, 1914-18*, 1920 (h); *The Book of Good Hunting*, 1920 (e); *Studies Green and Gray*, 1926 (e); *A Child is Born*, 1931 (p); *My World As In My Time, 1862-1932*, 1932 (a); *Selected Poems*, 1940 (p); *The Later Life and Letters of Sir Henry Newbolt*, ed. Margaret Newbolt, 1942 (b)

P. H. NEWBY
1918-

A Journey to the Interior, 1945 (n); *Agents and Witnesses*, 1947 (n); *Mariner Dances*, 1948 (n); *The Snow Pasture*, 1949 (n); *The Loot Runners*, 1949 (s); *Maria Edgeworth*, 1950 (c); *The Young May Moon*, 1950 (n); *The Novel, 1945-50*, 1951 (c); *A Season in England*, 1951 (n); *A Step to Silence*, 1952 (n); *The Retreat*, 1953 (n); *The Picnic at Sakkara*, 1955 (n); *Revolution and Roses*, 1957 (n); *Ten Miles from Anywhere*, 1958 (s); *The Guest and His Going*, 1959 (n); *The Barbary Light*, 1962 (n)

BEVERLEY NICHOLS
1899-

Prelude, 1920 (n); *Patchwork*, 1921 (n); *Self*, 1922 (n); *Twenty-Five*, 1926 (a); *Crazy Pavements*, 1927 (n); *Are They the Same at Home?*, 1927 (e); *The Star-Spangled Manner*, 1928 (a); *Women and Children Last*, 1931 (e); *For Adults Only*, 1932 (e); *Down the Garden Path*, 1932 (e); *Evensong*, 1932 (n); (with Edward Knoblock) *Evensong*, 1933 (d); *A Thatched Roof*, 1933 (e); *Cry Havoc!*, 1933 (e); *Failures*, 1933 (d); *A Village in a Valley*, 1934 (e); *Mesmer*, 1935 (d); *The Fool Hath Said*, 1936 (e); *No Place Like Home*, 1936 (e); *News of England*, 1938 (e); *Green Grows the City*, 1939 (e); *Revue*, 1939 (n); *Men do Not Weep*, 1941 (e); *Poems*, ed. J. W. Mackail, 1943; *Verdict on India*, 1944 (e); *All I Could Never Be*, 1949 (m); *Shadow of the Vine*, 1949 (d); *Uncle Samson*, 1950 (e); *Merry Hall*, 1951 (e); *A Pilgrim's Progress*, 1952 (e); *Laughter on the Stairs*, 1953 (e); *No Man's Street*, 1954 (n); *The Moonflower*, 1955 (Am. ed. *The Moonflower Murder*) (n); *Death to Slow Music*, 1956 (n); *The Rich Die Hard*, 1957 (n); *The Sweet and Twenties*, 1958 (h); *Murder by Request*, 1960 (n)

ROBERT NICHOLS
1893-1944

Invocation, War Poems and Others, 1915 (p); *Ardours and Endurances*, 1917 (p); *The Budded Branch*, 1918 (p); *Aurelia*, 1920 (p); *The Smile of the Sphinx*, 1920 (s); *A Year's Grain*, 1921 (p); *Guilty Souls*, 1921 (d); *Fantastica*, 1923 (s); (with Norah Nichols) *Winter Berries*, 1924 (p); (with A. Mujamori) *Masterpieces of Chikamatsu*, 1926 (tr); (with Jim Tully) *Twenty Below*, 1927 (d); *Under the Yew, or, The Gambler Transformed*, 1928 (n); *Epic Wind*, 1928 (p); (with Maurice Browne) *Wings Over Europe*, 1929 (d); I. S. Turgenev, *Hamlet and Don Quixote*, 1930 (tr); *Fisbo, or, The Looking-Glass Loaned*, 1934 (p)

See John Gawsworth, *Ten Contemporaries*, 1932

NORMAN NICHOLSON
1914-

Men and Literature, 1943 (e); *The Fire of the Lord*, 1944 (n); *Five Rivers*, 1944 (p); *The Old Men of the Mountains*, 1946 (pd); *The Green Shore*, 1947 (n); *Rock Face*, 1948 (p); *Cumberland and Westmorland*, 1949 (t); *H. G. Wells*,

1950 (rev. enlgd. 1957) (b); *William Cowper*, 1951 (b); *The Pot Geranium*, 1954 (p); *The Lakers*, 1955 (e); *A Match for the Devil*, 1955 (pd); *Provincial Pleasures*, 1959 (e); *Birth by Drowning*, 1960 (pd)

HAROLD NICOLSON
1886-

Sweet Waters, 1921 (n); *Paul Verlaine*, 1921 (b); *Tennyson*, 1923 (repr. 1962) (b); *Byron, The Last Journey*, 1924 (b); *Swinburne*, 1926 (b); *The Development of English Biography*, 1927 (e); *Some People*, 1927 (repr. 1951) (b); *Sir Arthur Nicolson, Bart.* (Am. ed. *Portrait of a Diplomatist*), 1930 (b); *Swinburne and Baudelaire*, 1930 (c); *People and Things*, 1931 (e); *The New Spirit in Literature*, 1931 (c); *Public Faces*, 1932 (n); *Peacemaking, 1919*, 1933 (e); *Curzon, The Last Phase, 1919-1925*, 1934 (b); *Dwight Morrow*, 1935 (b); *Politics in the Train*, 1936 (e); *Helen's Tower*, 1937 (b); *The Meaning of Prestige*, 1937 (e); *The Painted Bed*, 1937 (n); *Small Talk*, 1938 (e); *Diplomacy*, 1939 (repr. 1950) (e); *Marginal Comment*, 1939 (e); *The Poetry of Byron*, 1943 (c); *Sweden and the New Europe*, 1943 (e); *The Desire to Please*, 1943 (b); *Friday Mornings, 1941-1944*, 1944 (e); *The Congress of Vienna*, 1946 (repr. 1961) (h); *The English Sense of Humour*, 1946 (e); *Tennyson's Two Brothers*, 1947 (b); *Voyage to Wonderland*, 1947 (e); *Benjamin Constant*, 1949 (b); *Comments 1944-1948*, 1949 (e); *King George V*, 1952 (b); *Good Behaviour*, 1955 (e); *Sainte-Beuve*, 1957 (b); *Journey to Java*, 1957 (t); *The Age of Reason, 1700-1789*, 1960 (h); *Kings, Courts and Monarchy*, 1962 (h)

ALFRED NOYES
1880-1958

The Loom of Years, 1902 (p); *The Flower of Old Japan*, 1903 (enlgd. 1907) (p); *Poems*, 1904; *The Forest of Wild Thyme*, 1905 (p); *Drake, An English Epic* (Books I-IXII), 1906-08 (repr. 1938) (p); *Forty Singing Seamen*, 1907 (p); *The Golden Hynde*, 1908 (p); *William Morris*, 1908 (b); *The Enchanted Island*, 1909, (p); *Collected Poems*, Vol. I-II 1910 (repr. 1950); *The Prayer for Peace*, 1911 (p); (Am. ed.) *Sherwood, or Robin Hood and the Three Kings*, 1911 (Eng. ed. *Robin Hood*, 1926) (d); *The Carol of the Fir Tree*, 1912 (p); *Tales of the Mermaid Tavern*, 1913 (p); *The Wine-Press, a Tale of War*, 1913 (p); *The Searchligts*, 1914 (p); *A Tale of Old Japan*, 1914 (p); *Rada, a Drama of War*, 1914 (also pub. as *A Belgian Christmas Eve*) (d); *The Lord of Misrule*, 1915 (p); *A Salute from the Fleet*, 1915 (p); *Walking Shadows*, 1918 (s); *The New Morning*, 1918 (p); *Collected Poems*, Vol. III, 1920; *The Strong City*, 1920 (p); *The Elfin Artist*, 1920 (p); *Beyond the Desert*, 1920 (s); *Selected Verse*, 1921 (p); *The Torch-Bearers*, 1922-30 (3 vols; 1-vol. ed. 1937) (p); *Songs of Shadow-of-a-Leaf*, 1924 (p); *Some Aspects of Modern Poetry*, 1924 (c); *The Hidden Player*, 1924 (s); *Dick Turpin's Ride*, 1927 (p); *Collected Poems*, 4 vols., 1927; *New Essays and American Impressions*, 1927 (e); *Ballads and Poems*, 1928 (p); *The Return of the Scare-Crow*, 1929 (Am. ed. *The Sun Cure*) (n); *The Opalescent Parrot*, 1929 (e); *Alfred Noyes: Twelve Poems*, 1931 (p); *Tennyson*, 1932 (c); *The Unknown God*, 1934 (e); *The Poems of Alfred Noyes* (author's selection for schools), 1935 (p); *Voltaire*, 1936 (b); *The Cormorant*, 1936 (p); *Orchard's Bay*, 1939 (reissued as *The Incompleat Gardener*. 1955) (e); *The Last Man*, 1940 (Am. ed. *No Other Man*) (n); *Pageant of Letters*, 1940 (c); *If Judgment Comes*, 1941 (p); *Poems of the New World*, 1942 (p); *The Edge of the Abyss*, 1944 (e); *Shadows on the Down*, 1945 (p); *Portrait of Horace*, 1947 (Am. ed. *Horace: A Portrait*) (b); *Collected Poems*, 1 vol. ed., 1950; *Two Worlds for Memory*, 1953 (a); *The Devil Takes a Holiday*, 1955 (s); *A Letter to Lucian*, 1956 (p); *The Accusing Ghost, or Justice for Casement*, 1958 (b)

Walter C. Jerrold, *Alfred Noyes*, 1930

SEAN O'CASEY
1884-1964

[P. O'Cathasaigh] *The Story of the Irish Citizen Army*, 1919; *Two Plays: Juno and the Paycock, The Shadow of a Gunman*, 1925 (2d); *The Plough and the Stars*, 1926 (d); *The Silver Tassie*, 1928 (d); *Within the*

Gates, 1933 (d); *Windfalls: Stories, Poems and Plays,* 1934; *Five Irish Plays,* 1935 (5d); *The Flying Wasp,* 1937 (c); *I Knock At the Door,* 1939 (a); *The Star Turns Red,* 1940 (d); *Purple Dust,* 1940 (d); *Red Roses for Me,* 1942 (d); *Pictures in the Hallway,* 1942 (a); *Drums Under the Windows,* 1945 (a); *Oak Leaves and Lavender,* 1946 (d); *Inishfallen, Fare Thee Well,* 1949 (a); *Cock-a-doodle Dandy,* 1949 (d); *Collected Plays,* 4 vols., 1950-51; *Rose and Crown,* 1952 (a); *Sunset and Evening Star,* 1954 (a); *The Bishop's Bonfire,* 1955 (d); *The Green Crow,* 1956 (e,c); *Five One-Act Plays,* 1958 (5d); *Mirror In My House,* 1958 (a); *The Drums of Father Ned,* 1960 (d); *Behind the Green Curtains* (with *Figuro in the Night* and *The Moon Shines on Kylenamoe*), 1961 (Am. ed. *Three Plays*) (3d); *Feathers From the Green Crow, Sean O'Casey 1905-1925,* ed. Robert Hogan, 1962 (e); *Under a Coloured Cap,* 1963 (misc.)

Saros Cowasjee, *Sean O'Casey: the Man behind the Plays,* 1964

FRANK O'CONNOR
1903-

Guests of the Nation, 1931 (s); *The Saint and Mary Kate,* 1932 (s); *The Wild Bird's Nest, Poems from the Irish,* 1932 (tr); *Bones of Contention,* 1936 (s); *Three Old Brothers,* 1936 (p); *In the Train,* 1937 (d); *The Big Fellow: A Life of Michael Collins,* 1937 (Am. ed. *Death in Dublin*) (b); *The Invincibles,* 1937 (d); *Lords and Commons* (from the Irish), 1938 (tr); *Moses' Rock,* 1938 (d); *The Fountain of Magic* (from the Irish), 1938 (tr); *Dutch Interior,* 1940 (n); *Three Tales,* 1941 (s); *A Picture Book,* 1943 (t); *Crab Apple Jelly,* 1944 (s); *The Midnight Court* (from Irish of Brian Merriman, *The Merry Man*), 1945 (tr); *Towards an Appreciation of Literature,* 1945 (c); *Selected Stories,* 1946; *The Art of the Theatre,* 1947 (e); *Irish Miles,* 1947 (t); *The Common Chord,* 1947 (s); *The Road to Stratford,* 1948 (t); *Leinster, Munster and Connaught,* 1950 (t); *Traveller's Samples,* 1951 (s); *The Stories of Frank O'Connor,* 1952 (s); *Domestic Relations,* 1957 (s); *The Mirror in the Roadway: A Study of the Modern Novel,* 1957

(c); *Kings, Lords and Commons* (anthology from Irish), 1959 (tr); *Shakespeare's Progress,* 1960 (c); *An Only Child,* 1961 (a); *The Lonely Voice: A Study of the Short Story,* 1963 (c); *The Little Monasteries* (Irish poems), 1963 (tr); *My Oedipus Complex* (sel. stories), 1963 (s); *Collection Two,* 1964 (s)

SEAN O'FAOLAIN
1900-

The Life Story of Eamon De Valera, 1928 (b); *Midsummer Night Madness,* 1932 (s); *A Nest of Simple Folk,* 1933 (n); *Constance Markievicz,* 1934 (b); *There's a Birdie in the Cage,* 1935 (s); *Bird Alone,* 1936 (n); *King of the Beggars,* 1938 (b); *She Had to do Something,* 1938 (d); *A Purse of Coppers,* 1938 (s); *De Valera,* 1939 (b); *An Irish Journey,* 1940 (t); *Come Back to Erin,* 1940 (n); *The Great O'Neill,* 1942 (b); *The Story of Ireland,* 1943 (e); *The Irish,* 1947 (h); *Teresa,* 1947 (s); *The Short Story,* 1948 (c); *A Summer in Italy,* 1949 (t); *Newman's Way,* 1952 (b); *South to Sicily,* 1953 (t); *The Vanishing Hero,* 1956 (c); *The Stories of Sean O'Faolain,* 1958 (s); *I Remember! I Remember!,* 1962 (s); *Vive Moi!,* 1964 (a)

LIAM O'FLAHERTY
1896-

Thy Neighbour's Wife, 1923 (n); *Spring Sowing,* 1924 (s); *The Black Soul,* 1924 (n); *The Informer,* 1925 (repr. 1949) (n); *Mr. Gilhooley,* 1926 (n); *Darkness,* 1926 (d); *The Tent,* 1926 (s); *The Assassin,* 1927 (n); *The Fairy Goose,* 1927 (s); *The Life of Tim Healy,* 1927 (b); *Red Barbara,* 1928 (s); *The House of Gold,* 1929 (n); *The Mountain Tavern,* 1929 (s); *Return of the Brute,* 1929 (s); *A Tourist's Guide to Ireland,* 1929 (t); *Two Years,* 1930 (r); *Joseph Conrad,* 1930 (c); *I Went to Russia,* 1931 (t,r); *The Ecstasy of Angus,* 1931 (s); *The Puritan,* 1931 (n); *Skerrett,* 1932 (n); *The Wild Swan,* 1932 (s); *The Martyr,* 1933 (n); *Shame the Devil,* 1934 (r); *Hollywood Cemetery,* 1935 (n); *Famine,* 1937 (n); *The Short Stories,* 1937 (repr. 1948) (s); *Land,* 1946 (n); *Two Lovely Beasts,* 1948 (s); *Insurrection,* 1950 (n); *Dúil,* 1953 (s)

See John Gawsworth, *Ten Contemporaries*, Sec. Series, 1933 [autobiog. note and bibliog.]

OLIVER ONIONS
1873-

The Compleat Bachelor, 1900 (n); *Tales from a Far Riding*, 1902 (s); *The Odd-Job Man*, 1903 (n); *The Drakestone*, 1906 (n); *Back o' the Moon*, 1906 (s); *Admiral Eddy*, 1907 (s); *Pedlar's Pack*, 1908 (n); *Draw In Your Stool*, 1909 (n); *Litle Devil Doubt*, 1909 (n); *The Exception*, 1910 (n); *The Work of Henry Ospovat*, 1911 (c); *Widdershins*, 1911 (s); *Good Boy Seldom*, 1911 (n); *In Accordance with the Evidence* (Vol. I of trilogy), 1912 (n); *The Debit Account* (Vol. II of trilogy), 1913 (n); *The Story of Louie* (Vol. III of trilogy), 1913 (n); *The Two Kisses*, 1913 (n); *A Crooked Mile*, 1914 (n) (Am. ed. *Gray Youth*, includes *The Two Kisses*); *Mushroom Town*, 1914 (n); *The New Moon*, 1918 (n); *A Case in Camera*, 1920 (n); *The Tower of Oblivion*, 1921 (n); *Peace in Our Time*, 1923 (n); *Ghosts in Daylight*, 1924 (s); *The Spite of Heaven*, 1925 (n); *Whom God Hath Sundered* (trilogy: *In Accordance with the Evidence, The Debit Account, The Story of Louie*), 1925 (n); *Cut Flowers*, 1927 (n); *The Painted Face*, 1929 (s); *The Open Secret*, 1930 (n); *A Certain Man*, 1931 (n); *Catalan Circus*, 1934 (n); *The Collected Ghost Stories of Oliver Onions*, 1935; *The Hand of Kornelius Voyt*, 1939 (n); *The Italian Chest*, 1939 (s); *Cockcrow, or Anybody's England*, 1940 (n); *The Story of Ragged Robyn*, 1945 (n); *Poor Man's Tapestry*, 1946 (n); *Arras of Youth*, 1949 (n); *A Penny for the Harp*, 1952 (n); *Bells Rung Backwards* (5 stories from *Collected Ghost Stories*), 1953 (s)
See John Gawsworth, *Ten Contemporaries*, Sec. Series, 1933

GEORGE ORWELL
1903-1950

Down and Out in Paris and London, 1933 (many repr.) (a); *Burmese Days*, 1934 (n); *A Clergyman's Daughter*, 1935 (n); *Keep the Aspidistra Flying*, 1936 (repr. 1954) (n); *The Road to Wigan Pier*, 1937 (e); *Homage to Catalonia*, 1938 (e); *Coming Up for Air*, 1939 (n); *Inside the Whale*, 1940 (c); *The Lion and the Unicorn: Socialism and the English Genius*, 1941 (e); *Animal Farm. A Fairy Story*, 1945 (many repr.) (n); *Critical Essays* (Am. ed. *Dickens, Dali and Others*), 1946 (c); *The English People*, 1947 (e); *Nineteen Eighty-Four*, 1949 (many repr.) (n); *Shooting an Elephant*, 1950 (e); *England, Your England* (Am. ed. *Such, Such Were the Joys*), 1953 (e); *Selected Essays, 1957* (e); *Collected Essays*, 1961

Sir Richard Rees, *George Orwell: Fugitive from the Camp of Victory*, 1961

JOHN OSBORNE
1929-

Look Back In Anger, 1957 (d); *The Entertainer*, 1957 (d); (with Anthony Creighton) *Epitaph for George Dillon*, 1958 (d); *The World of Paul Slickey*, 1959 (musical comedy); *Luther*, 1961 (d); *A Subject of Scandal and Concern*, 1961 (e); *Plays for England: The Blood of the Bambergs and Under Plain Cover*, 1963 (2d); *Inadmissible Evidence*, 1964 (d)

See John Russell Taylor, *Anger and After* (Am. ed. *The Angry Theatre*), 1962

WILFRED OWEN
1893-1918

Poems, 1920 (p); *The Poems of Wilfred Owen*, with notices of his life and work by Edmund Blunden, 1931; *The Collected Poems*, ed. C. Day Lewis, 1963

Note: Only four poems were published during his lifetime, and these were in periodicals; seven were included in *Wheels: Fourth Cycle*, 1919, ed. Edith Sitwell.

Dennis S. R. Welland, *Wilfred Owen, A Critical Study*, 1960; Harold Owen, *Journey from Obscurity: Wilfred Owen 1893-1918* (Memoirs of the Owen family, I, Childhood)

STEPHEN PHILLIPS
1868-1915

Orestes, 1884 (p); (with others) *Primavera. Poems by Four Authors*, 1890 (p); *Eremus*, 1894 (p); *Christ in Hades*, 1896 (repr. 1917) (p); *Poems*, 1898 (p); *Paolo and Francesca*, 1900 (repr. 1952) (pd); *Marpessa*, 1900 (p); *Herod*, 1901 (pd); *Ulysses*, 1902 (pd); *The Sin of David*, 1904 (pd); *Nero*, 1906 (pd); *Faust*, freely adapted from Goethe by S. P. and J. C. Carr, 1908; *New Poems*, 1908 (p); *Pietro of Siena*, 1910 (pd); *The New Inferno*, 1910 (p); *The King*, 1912 (pd); *Lyrics and Dramas*, 1913; *Armageddon*, 1915 (d); *Panama*, 1915 (p); *Harold*, 1927 (d)

EDEN PHILLPOTTS
1862-1960

Selective Bibliography

The entries for Phillpotts occupy eight double-column pages in the British Museum Catalogue of printed books. His first novel was published in 1891, and when he hit his stride, from 1938 to 1958, he published from two to five novels a year. Some of the novels may be classified as industrial novels (e.g. *The Spinners*, 1918); some, among the best known, as Dartmoor novels. Besides these, he published plays, fairy stories, mystery stories (e.g., *Bred in the Bones*, 1932 [Book of Avis. I]), "human boy" stories (e.g., *The Human Boy*, 1899, *The Human Boy Again*, 1908, *The Complete Human Boy*, 1930), poems, short stories, and essays. Included in the following list are samples of Phillpotts' enormous production, with emphasis on the regional (Dartmoor) writings.

My Adventure in the Flying Scotsman, 1888 (s); *The End of a Life*, 1891 (n); *In Sugar-Cane Land*, 1893 (e); *Down Dartmoor Way*, 1895 (s); *My Laughing Philosopher*, 1896 (e); *Children of the Mist*, 1898 (n); *Sons of the Morning*, 1900 (n); *The River*, 1902 (n); *My Devon Year*, 1903 (e); *The Secret Woman*, 1905 (n; dramatized 1912, rev. ed. of play 1935); (with Arnold Bennett) *Sinews of War*, 1906 (Am. ed. *Doubloons*) (n); *My Garden*, 1906 (e); *The Portreeve*, 1906 (n); *The Virgin in Judgement*, 1907 (n); *The Whirlwind*, 1907 (n); (with Arnold Bennett) *The Statue*, 1908 (n); *The Mother*, 1908 (Am. ed. *The Mother of the Man*) (n; dramatized 1913); *The Three Brothers*, 1909 (n); *The Thief of Virtue*, 1910 (n); *Dance of the Months*,

1911 (e); *The Beacon*, 1911 (n); *Demeter's Daughter*, 1911 (n); *The Forest on the Hill*, 1912 (n); *Widecombe Fair*, 1913 (repr. 1947) (n); *My Shrubs*, 1915 (e); *Brunel's Tower*, 1915 (n); *The Farmer's Wife*, 1916 (d); *A Shadow Passes*, 1918 (e,p); *Miser's Money*, 1920 (n); *Orphan Dinah*, 1920 (n); *A West Country Pilgrimage*, 1920 (t); *The Bronze Venus*, 1921 (n); *Cherrystones*, 1923 (p); *Children of Men*, 1923 (n); *Thoughts in Prose and Verse*, 1924; *A Harvesting*, 1924 (p); *Brother Man*, 1926 (p); (with Adelaide Eden Phillpotts) *Yellow Sands*, 1926 (d); *Selected Poems*, 1926 (p); *The Jury*, 1927 (n); *The Widecombe Edition of the Dartmoor Novels*, 20 vols., 1927-28; *Brother Beast*, 1928 (p); *Brother Man*, 1928 (s); *Fun of the Fair*, 1928 (s); *A West Country Sketch Book*, 1928 (sk); *Eden Phillpotts: Selected Tales*, 1929 (s); *Essays in Little*, 1931 (e); *West Country Plays* (*Buy a Broom*, *A Cup of Happiness*, (with Adelaide Eden Phillpotts) *The Good Old Days*), 1933 (3d); *Dartmoor Omnibus* (*Orphan Dinah*, *The Three Brothers*, *Children of Men*, *The Whirlwind*), 1933 (n); *A Year with Bisshe-Bantam*, 1934 (e); *A Dartmoor Village*, 1937 (p); *Fall of the House of Heron*, 1948 (n); *The Enchanted Wood*, 1948 (p); *There Was An Old Man*, 1958 (n)

Percival Hinton, *Eden Phillpotts: A Bibliography of First Editions*, 1931; Waveney Girvan, ed., *Eden Phillpotts, An Assessment and a Tribute*, 1953 [no bibliog.]

ARTHUR WING PINERO
1855-1934

Mayfair, 1885 (an adaptation of Sardou's *Maison neuve*) (d); *The Profligate*, 1887 (d); *The Cabinet Minister*, 1889 (d); *Hester's Mystery*, 1890 (d); *Lady Bountiful*, 1891 (d); *The Times*, 1891 (d); *The Hobby-Horse*, 1892 (d); *The Magistrate*, 1892 (d); *Dandy Dick*, 1893 (d); *Sweet Lavender*, 1893 (d); *The Schoolmistress*, 1894 (d); *The Second Mrs. Tanqueray*, 1894 (d); *The Weaker Sex*, 1894 (d); *The Amazons*, 1895 (d); *The Benefit of the Doubt*, 1895 (d); *The Notorious Mrs. Ebbsmith*, 1895 (d); *The Princess and the Butterfly*, 1896 (d); (with others)

The Beauty Stone, 1898 (d); Trelawny of the "Wells", 1898 (d); The Gay Lord Quex, 1899 (d); The Money Spinner, 1900 (d); Iris, 1901 (d); Letty, 1903 (d); Robert Louis Stevenson, the Dramatist, a Lecture, 1903 (repub. 1914); A Wife Without a Smile, 1904 (d); His House in Order, 1905 (d); In Chancery, 1905 (d); The Rocket, 1905 (d); The Squire, 1905 (d); The Thunderbolt, 1907-8 (d); Mid-Channel, 1908-9 (d); Preserving Mr. Panmure, 1910 (d); The "Mind the Paint" Girl, 1912 (d); The Widow of Wasdale Head, 1912 (d); Playgoers, 1913 (d); The Big Drum, 1915 (d); Mr. Livermore's Dream, 1916 (d); The Freaks, 1917 (d); The Social Plays of Arthur Wing Pinero, ed. Clayton Hamilton, 1917-1919; Quick Work, 1918 (d); The Enchanted Cottage, 1921 (d); A Seat in the Park, 1922 (d); Dr. Harmer's Holidays, 1924 (d); A Private Room, 1926 (d); Child Man, 1928 (d)

HAROLD PINTER
1930-

The Dumbwaiter, 1960 (d); The Room, 1960 (d); The Birthday Party, 1960 (d); The Caretaker, 1960 (d); A Slight Ache, 1961 (d); Three Plays, 1962; The Collection and The Lover, 1963 (2d); A Night Out, 1963 (d)

RUTH PITTER
1897-

First Poems, 1920 (p); First and Second Poems, 1927 (p); Persephone in Hades, 1931 (p); A Mad Lady's Garland, 1934 (p); A Trophy of Arms, 1936 (p); The Spirit Watches, 1939 (p); The Rude Potato, 1941 (p); The Bridge, 1945 (p); On Cats, 1947 (p); Urania [Poems from earlier vols.], 1950 (p); The Ermine, 1953 (p)

WILLIAM PLOMER
1903-

Turbott Wolfe, 1925 (n); Notes for Poems, 1927 (p); I Speak of Africa, 1927 (7s, 3n, 2 plays for puppets); The Family Tree, 1929 (p); Paper Houses, 1929 (n); Sado, 1931 (Am. ed. They Never Come Back) (n); The Case is Altered, 1932 (n); The Fivefold Screen, 1932 (p); The Child of Queen Victoria, 1933 (s); Cecil

Rhodes, 1933 (b); The Invaders, 1934 (n); Ali, the Lion [Ali of Tebeleni, pasha of Jannina, 1741-1822], 1936 (b); Visiting the Caves, 1936 (p); Selected Poems, 1940 (p); Double Lives, 1943 (a); The Dorking Thigh, 1945 (p); [William D'Arfey, pseud.] Curious Relations, 1945 (s); Four Countries, 1949 (s); Museum Pieces, 1952 (n); Gloriana, 1953 (opera libretto); A Shot in the Park, 1955 (p); Borderline Ballads, 1955 (p); At Home, 1958 (r); Collected Poems, 1960

STEPHEN POTTER
1900-

The Young Man, 1929 (n); D. H. Lawrence, a First Study, 1930 (c); Coleridge and S.T.C., 1935 (c); The Muse in Chains: a Study in Education, 1937 (e); The Theory and Practice of Gamesmanship, 1947 (e); Some Notes on Lifemanship, 1950 (e); One-upmanship, 1952 (e); Potter on America, 1956 (e); The Magic Number: The Story of "57", 1959 (h); Steps to Immaturity, 1959 (r); Supermanship, 1959 (e)

ANTHONY POWELL
1905-

Afternoon Men, 1931 (n); Venusberg, 1932 (n); From a View to a Death, 1933 (n); Agents and Patients, 1936 (n); What's Become of Waring, 1939 (n); John Aubrey and His Friends, 1948 (b); A Dance to the Music of Time, consisting of the following novels: A Question of Up-Bringing, 1951; A Buyer's Market, 1952; The Acceptance World, 1955; At Lady Molly's; Casanova's Chinese Restaurant, 1960; The Kindly Ones, 1962; The Valley of Bones [first vol. of second half of The Music of Time], 1964 (n)

Bernard Bergonzi, Anthony Powell (in Paul Bloomfield, L. P. Hartley and Anthony Powell), 1962

JOHN COWPER POWYS
1872-1963

Odes, 1896 (p); Poems, 1899; Twelve Lectures on Carlyle, Ruskin, Tennyson, 1900; Six Lectures on Selected Plays of Shakespeare, 1901; Visions and Revisions, a Book of Literary Devotions, 1915 (rev. 1955) (c); Wood and Stone, 1915 (n); Rodmoor, 1916 (n); Confessions of Two Brothers, John Cowper Powys, Llewellyn Powys, 1916 (r); One Hundred Best Books, with commentary, 1916 (c); Suspended Judgments, 1916 (e); Wolf's-bane; Rhymes, 1916 (p); Mandragon, 1917 (p); The Complex Vision, 1920 (a,e); Samphire, 1922 (p); Psychoanalysis and Morality, 1923 (c); The Religion of a Sceptic, 1925 (a); Ducdame, 1925 (n); The Meaning of Culture, 1929 (e); Wolf Solent, 1929 (n); The Owl, the Duck, and—Miss Rowe! Miss Rowe!, 1930 (s); (with Bertrand Russell) Debate! Is Modern Marriage a Failure?, 1930; In Defence of Sensuality, 1930 (e); Dorothy M. Richardson, 1931 (c); A Glastonbury Romance, 1932 (repr. 1955) (n); A Philosophy of Solitude, 1933 (e); Weymouth Sands, 1934 (Am. ed.; Eng. ed. Jobber Skald, 1935; rev. 1963) (n); Autobiography, 1934 (a); The Art of Happiness, 1935 (e) [text of Am. ed. differs]; Maiden Castle, 1936 (n); Morwyn, or The Vengeance of God, 1937 (n); The Enjoyment of Literature (also pub. as The Pleasures of Literature), 1938 (e); Owen Glendower, 1940 (n); Mortal Strife, 1941 (e); The Art of Growing Old, 1944 (e); Pair Dadeni, or, "The Cauldron of Rebirth," 1946 (e); Obstinate Cymric: Essays 1935-1947, 1947 (e); Dostoievsky, 1947 (c); Rabelais: His Life, The Story Told by Him, Selections Therefrom Newly Translated, and an Interpretation of His Genius and His Religion, 1948; Porius: A Romance of the Dark Ages, 1951 (n); The Inmates, 1952 (n); In Spite Of: A Philosophy for Everyman, 1953 (e); Atlantis, 1954 (n); The Brazen Head, 1956 (n); Lucifer, 1956 (p); Still the Joy of It, 1956 (r); Up and Out, 1957 (s); The Letters of J. C. Powys to Louis Wilkinson, 1935-56, ed. L. Wilkinson, 1958; Homer and the Aether (paraphrase of The Iliad), 1959; All or Nothing, 1960 (n); Selected Poems, ed. Kenneth Hopkins, 1964 (p)

I. E. Siberell, A Bibliography of the First Editions of John Cowper Powys, 1934; Reginald C. Churchill, The Powys Brothers, 1962

T. F. POWYS
1875-1953

An Interpretation of Genesis, 1908 (repr. 1929) (e); The Soliloquy of a Hermit, 1916 (Eng. ed. as Soliloquies of a Hermit, 1918) (e); Black Byrony, 1923 (n); The Left Leg, 1923 (s); Mark Only, 1924 (n); Mr. Tasker's Gods, 1925 (n); Mockery Gap, 1925 (n); Innocent Birds, 1926 (n); Feed My Swine, 1926 (s); A Strong Girl and The Bride, 1926 (2s); A Stubborn Tree, 1926 (s); What Lack I Yet?, 1926 (s); The Rival Pastors, 1926 (s); Mr. Weston's Good Wine, 1927 (n); The Dewpond, 1928 (s); The House with the Echo, 1928 (s); Fables, 1929 (repr. as No Painted Plumage, 1934) (s); Christ in the Cupboard, 1930 (s); The Key of the Field, 1930 (s); Uncle Dottery, 1930 (s); Uriah on the Hill, 1930 (s); The White Paternoster, 1930 (s); Kindness in a Corner, 1930 (n); Unclay, 1931 (n); The Only Penitent, 1931 (s); When Thou Wast Naked, 1931 (s); The Tithe Barn and The Dove and the Eagle, 1932 (2s); The Two Thieves, 1932 (3s); Captain Patch, 1935 (s); Coat Green, or The Better Gift, 1937 (s); Bottle's Path, 1946 (s); God's Eyes A-Twinkle, sel. C. Prentice, 1947 (s)

Henry Coombes, T. F. Powys, 1960; Reginald C. Churchill, The Powys Brothers, 1962

J. B. PRIESTLEY
1894-

[N.B. Most of Priestley's works have been kept in print so reprints are not noted here.]

The Chapman of Rhymes, 1918 (p); Brief Diversions, Being Tales, Travesties and Epigrams, 1922; Papers from Lilliput, 1922 (e,p); I For One, 1923 (e); Figures in Modern Literature, 1924 (c); The English Comic Characters, 1925 (c); George Meredith, 1926 (b); Talking, 1926 (e); The English Novel, 1927 (c); Open House, 1927 (e); Adam in Moonshine, 1927 (n); Benighted, 1927 (Am. ed. The Old Dark House) (n); Thomas Love Peacock, 1927 (b); Apes and Angels, 1928 (e); Too Many People, 1928 (e); (with Hugh Walpole) Farthing Hall, 1929 (n); The Good Companions, 1929 (n); English

Humour, 1929 (e); *The Balconinny*, 1929 (e); *The Town Major of Mirau-court*, 1930 (e); *Angel Pavement*, 1930 (n); *The Works of J. B. Priestley*, 1931; *Dangerous Corner*, 1932 (d); *Faraway*, 1932 (n); *Self-Selected Essays*, 1932 (e); *I'll Tell You Everything, A Frolic*, 1933 (n); *Albert Goes Through*, 1933 (n); *Wonder Hero*, 1933 (n); *The Round-about*, 1933 (d); (with Gerald Bullett) *English Journey, Autumn, 1933*, 1934 (t); *Eden End*, 1934 (d); *Laburnum Grove*, 1934 (d); *Four-in-Hand*, 1934 (misc.); *Cornelius*, 1935 (d); *Duet in Floodlight*, 1935 (d); (with Knoblauch) *The Good Companions*, 1935 (d from novel); *Three Plays and a Preface*, 1935 (3d); (with George Billam) *Spring Tide*, 1936 (d); *Bees on the Boat Deck*, 1936 (d); *They Walk in the City*, 1936 (n); *Time and the Conways*, 1937 (d); *I Have Been Here Before*, 1937 (d); *Two Time Plays* (the two preceding plays), 1937 (2d); *Midnight on the Desert: A Chapter of Autobiography*, 1937 (a); *People at Sea*, 1937 (d); *The Doomsday Men*, 1938 (n); *When We Are Married*, 1938 (d); *Mystery at Greenfingers*, 1938 (d); *Rain upon Godshill: A Further Chapter of Autobiography*, 1939 (a); *Johnson Over Jordan . . . And All About It*, 1939 (d,e); *Let the People Sing*, 1939 (n); *Postscripts*, 1940 (e); *Out of the People*, 1941 (p); *Three Plays*, 1943 (3d); *Daylight on Saturday*, 1943 (n); *They Came to a City*, 1944 (d); *Four Plays*, 1944 (4d); *Three Men in New Suits*, 1945 (n); *Three Comedies*, 1945 (3d); *How Are They at Home*, 1945 (d); *The Secret Dream: an Essay on Britain, America, and Russia*, 1946 (e); *Bright Day*, 1946 (d); *Russian Journey*, 1946 (t); *An Inspector Calls*, 1947 (d); *Jenny Villers*, 1947 (n); *The Long Mirror*, 1947 (d); *The Plays of J. B. Priestley*, 3 vols., 1948; *The Linden Tree*, 1948 (d); *The Golden Fleece*, 1948 (d); *The High Toby: A Play for the Toy Theatre*, 1948 (d); *Ever Since Paradise*, 1949 (d); *Home is Tomorrow*, 1949 (d); *Delight*, 1949 (a,e); *Bright Shadow*, 1950 (d); *Going Up*, 1950 (s); *Summer Day's Dream*, 1950 (d); *The Priestley Companion: A Selection*, 1951 (misc.); *Festival at Farbridge*, 1951 (n); *Private Rooms*, 1953 (d); *Mother's Day*, 1953 (d); *The Other Place*, 1953 (e); *Try It Again*, 1953 (d); *A Glass of Bitter*, 1954

(d); *Low Notes on a High Level*, 1954 (n); *The Magicians*, 1954 (n); *Treasure on Pelican*, 1954 (d); (with Jacquetta Hawkes) *Journey Down a Rainbow* [New Mexico and Texas], 1955 (t); *The Scandalous Affair of Mr. Kettle and Mrs. Moon*, 1956 (d); *All About Ourselves*, ed. Eric Gillet, 1956 (e); *The Writer in a Changing Society*, 1956 (e); *The Art of the Dramatist*, 1957 (e); *Thoughts in the Wilderness*, 1957 (e); *Topside, or, The Future of England*, 1958 (e); *The Glass Cage*, 1958 (d); *The Story of Theatre*, 1959 (h); *William Hazlitt*, 1960 (b,c); *Literature and Western Man*, 1960 (e); *Saturn Over the Water*, 1961 (n); *Charles Dickens*, 1961 (c); *The Thirty-First of June, a Tale of True Love, Enterprise, and Progress in the Arthurian and Ad-Atomic Ages*, 1961 (s); *The Shapes of Sleep*, 1962 (n); *Margin Released*, 1962 (r); *Sir Michael and Sir George*, 1964 (n); *Man and Time*, 1964 (e); (with Iris Murdoch) *A Severed Head*, 1964 (dramatization of Murdoch's novel)
David Hughes, *J. B. Priestley, an Informal Study of His Work*, 1958

F. T. PRINCE
1912-

Poems, 1938 (p); *The Italian Element in Milton's Verse*, 1954 (e); *Soldiers Bathing*, 1954 (p); *The Doors of Stone*, 1963 (p)

V. S. PRITCHETT
1900-

Marching Spain, 1928 (repr. 1933) (r); *Clare Drummer*, 1929 (n); *The Spanish Virgin*, 1930 (s); *Shirley Sanz*, 1932 (n); *Nothing Like Leather*, 1935 (n); *Dead Man Leading*, 1937 (n); *You Make Your Own Life*, 1938 (s); *In My Good Books*, 1942 (c); *It May Never Happen*, 1945 (s); *The Living Novel*, 1946 (rev. enlgd. 1964) (c); *Mr. Beluncle*, 1951 (n); *Books In General*, 1953 (c); *The Spanish Temper*, 1954 (t); *The Sailor; Sense of Humour*, 1956 (s); *Collected Stories*, 1956; *When My Girl Comes Home*, 1961 (s); *London Perceived*, 1962 (t); *The Key to My Heart*, 1963 (n); *Foreign Faces* (Am. ed. *The Offensive Traveller*), 1964 (t)

JOHN PUDNEY
1909-

Spring Encounter, 1933 (p); *Open the Sky,* 1935 (p); *And Lastly the Fireworks,* 1935 (s); *Jacobson's Ladder,* 1938 (n); *Uncle Arthur,* 1939 (s); *Dispersal Point and Other Air Poems,* 1942 (p); *The Green Grass Grew All Around,* 1942 (s); *South of Forty,* 1943 (p); *Beyond this Disregard,* 1943 (p); *Who Only England Know: Log of a War-Time Journey of Unintentional Discovery of Fellow-Countrymen,* 1943 (a); *Ten Summers: Poems 1933-1943,* 1944 (p); *Almanack of Hope: Sonnets,* 1944 (p); *Flight Above Cloud,* 1944 (p); *World Still There* [Impressions of various parts of the world in wartime], 1945 (sk); *Selected Poems,* 1946 (p); *It Breathed Down My Neck,* 1946 (s); *Low Life,* 1947 (p); *Estuary,* 1947 (n); *Commemo-rations,* 1948 (p); *The Europeans, Fourteen Tales of a Continent,* 1948 (s); *Shuffley Wanderers,* 1948 (n); *The Accomplice,* 1950 (n); *Hero of a Summer's Day,* 1951 (n); *Music on the South Bank: An Appreciation of the Royal Festival Hall,* 1951 (e); *His Majesty King George VI, A Study,* 1952 (e); *The Net,* 1952 (n); *A Ring for Luck,* 1953 (n); *Sixpenny Songs,* 1953 (p); *The Thomas Cook Story,* 1953 (h); *The Smallest Room* [a history of lavatories], 1953 (h); *Six Great Aviators* (incl. Lindbergh, Saint-Exupéry), 1955 (b); *Collected Poems* (incl. bibliog.), 1957; *Trespass in the Sun,* 1957 (n); *The Seven Skies: a Study of the BOAC and its Forerunners since 1919,* 1959 (h); *The Trampoline,* 1959 (p); *A Pride of Unicorns: Richard and David Atcherley of the RAF,* 1960 (b); *Thin Air,* 1961 (n); *The Camel Fighter,* 1964 (e)

Except in a few cases, each specified in a headnote, the editors have attempted to list all the separate publications of the authors, excluding only (1) privately printed works and those issued in very small limited editions; (2) ephemeral works such as wartime propaganda. Date of publication given is the earliest, whether of English or American edition. Title of an American edition is noted when it differs markedly from the English title. Reprints are noted only when, occurring twenty years or more after the original publication, they indicate continuing popularity or suggest (though, of course, they do not guarantee) availability. Wherever possible, a bibliography or, if none has been published in book form, a recent biographical study, usually including bibliography, has been added for each author.

For further information about the Bibliography, see Introduction in Volume I.